On Perl
Perl for Students and Professionals

Jugal K. Kalita

On Perl:
Perl for Students and Professionals

Universal Publishers/uPUBLISH.com
USA • 2004

ISBN: 1-58112-550-X

www.upublish.com/books/kalita.htm

In Memory of Loving Mother Nirala Kalita

Preface

During our life time, computers have been responsible for ushering in an unprecedented age of swift technological changes that have permeated every sphere of life. For more than three decades, the speed at which computers perform computations has been doubling every eighteen months following an informal "law" formulated in 1965 by Gordon Moore, a co-founder of the chip-making powerhouse, the Intel Corporation. Along with the phenomenal increase in power, speed and storage capacity of computers, the cost of CPU, memory chips, and peripherals such as printers, monitors and scanners have also been falling rapidly. These trends will continue if not accelerate in the years to come.

Experts agree that for a long time, progress in computer software had lagged behind the enormous strides made in hardware. However, during the past decade, the revolutionary software product called the World Wide Web (WWW) came into our lives and quickly changed the world. The WWW, conceived by the European physicist Tim Berners-Lee in Switzerland in 1989, caught the world by storm. It has accelerated the rate at which the world is becoming a global village. Although many historians and economists believe that the current pace of technological change pales in comparison with the developments that took place in the last five decades of the nineteenth century,[1] it is true that in a few years, the WWW has been able to penetrate into millions of homes and corporations around the world. Information on any conceivable topic is at our finger tips with a few key strokes and mouse clicks. People of all ages are spending countless hours chatting on the WWW, making friends and developing relationships. WWW-based commerce is already worth tens of billions of dollars and is growing by leaps and bounds every day. In a few years, the Web is probably destined to become the dominant medium for conducting business and personal communications.

From its early days, Perl has been one of the dominant programming languages of choice in the context of the World Wide Web. Perl has been used extensively for CGI programming for providing dynamic Web pages. The extensive use of CGI programming encourages a lot of programmers to learn Perl. Perl also provides powerful tools for writing programs that communicate across the World Wide Web and that access network databases. One of Perl's strengths is its extra-ordinarily powerful pattern matching ability that can be used in looking for patterns in text including Web pages, thus making it suitable for data mining in many different areas such as business intelligence gathering and genomic studies.

Origin of Perl

Perl stands for *Practical Extraction and Reporting Language*. The name reflects its origin. It is an interpreted language with primarily dynamic typing created by Larry Wall for generating textual reports. He was once rifling through a hierarchy of files with the goal of extracting relevant information by scanning for textual patterns. He was working on a Unix machine and the premier pattern searching and processing tool for Unix machines called *awk* was not up to the task. So, Mr. Wall, the avid programmer, wrote a tool for achieving his immediate goal and other tasks he had in mind. This was the first version of Perl.

---

[1] *The Future Came Faster in the Old Days* by Steve Lohr, *The New York Times*, October 5, 1997

From its humble beginnings, Perl has gone through a large number of revisions and extensions. Perl 1 was released in January 1988, Perl 2 in June 1988, Perl 3 in October 1989, and Perl 4 in March 1991. The currently available major version, Perl 5, was released in October 1994. Perl 6 is in the works as of late 2003. No longer it is a language for pattern matching, but it has developed into a full-fledged language that has excellent facilities for many diverse tasks. Sophisticated handling of regular expressions still remains one of its strong points and it is one reason why Perl is very popular with programmers who create dynamic pages for the World Wide Web (WWW) using the technique called Common Gateway Interface (CGI).

Major Features of Perl

Perl is a multifaceted language with many strengths that make it an ideal practical language for many diverse tasks. Perl is an excellent tool for many tasks such as rapid prototype development, systems administration, and networking in addition to text processing and WWW programming.

Rapid Prototype Development

Perl programs are easy to write and they are portable to many different platforms. One does not have to know a lot of Perl's syntax to start programming. Thousands of programmers around the world have found that Perl is one of the best languages currently available for developing complex application programs quickly. It is a very high-level language and even a small Perl program can do tasks that can take hundreds of line of code in other languages. Programs developed in Perl can be tested and modified quickly. In an age where software packages are becoming bigger day by day and new versions of every software package are released every few months, it is of great advantage to developers if they are able to create a prototype for a sophisticated piece of software quickly.

Systems Administration

Although Perl was initially developed for processing textual files, it has been used by systems administrators in the Unix environment from its early days. The Unix operating system has no standards. With the release of OS X based on BSD Unix for Macintosh computers, Unix is likely to gain substantial additional followers and users as well. Different versions of Unix are produced and sold by various corporations. To fulfill Unix systems administration tasks, such as creating logins for new users, allocating resources and maintaining a secure environment for all users, and installing and uninstalling software packages, systems administrators primarily use programming languages called *shells*. There are many different shells and they work differently on different versions of Unix. The shell programs or scripts as they are called, are not always portable from one version of Unix to another. This is where Perl comes as a blessing. Because Perl has been ported to all versions of Unix and Perl has many capabilities that systems administrators desire and use, Perl scripts have started taking the place of shell scripts for many systems administrators. Perl has also been ported to various flavors of the Windows operating system. As a result, Perl is finding widespread use in systems administration tasks in non-Unix environments also.

Networking

For the Internet and the WWW to work successfully, computers around the world have to be able to communicate with one another with ease. Not only for the Internet, but also for the seamless functioning of telephone and other communications systems, computer networks must work flawlessly and reliably without interruption. Networking software and hardware keep the channels of communication among computers around the world working the way they are expected. Perl has built-in facilities for developing and maintaining networking software. Since programs can be developed easily and quickly in Perl, a large amount of networking software is being written in Perl.

Modules and Libraries

Perl is a large language. It attempts to do many things. Larry Wall, the creator and maintainer of Perl, and many others who have developed software for Perl have created a large set of reusable modules for Perl. There are hundreds of useful and reusable Perl modules that can do any conceivable task. This availability of a large number of reusable software modules is yet another reason for Perl's continued and increasing popularity.

Free Availability

Perl is a language whose interpreter can be obtained for free. This is because Perl's author, Larry Wall, wanted Perl to be free from the beginning. Perl's core modules and documentation have been written by volunteers. It has been ported to many platforms by volunteer programmers. Using the WWW is the simplest way to obtain Perl source code and executables.

Perl's large number of modules and libraries are also available for free. More modules and libraries are being written all the time. The best way to look for any information on Perl is to visit either of the URLs, `http://www.perl.com` or `http://www.perl.org` and start navigating through the linked documents. Another useful site, particularly for Windows systems is `http://www.activestate.com` where a version of Perl called *ActivePerl* is available for downloading along with many modules. The Comprehensive Perl Archive Network (CPAN, `http://www.cpan.org`) is a large archive containing source code, ports, documentation, scripts, modules and extensions. The modules available at CPAN are a superset of those available at `activestate.com`. `www.perl.org` and `www.perl.com` have links to CPAN which is mirrored in many machines around the world. There are also several USENET newsgroups on Perl. They are *comp.lang.perl.misc, comp.lang.perl.modules, comp.lang.perl.tk, comp.lang.perl.announce*, and *comp.infosystems.www.authoring.cgi*, etc.

Purpose of the Book

The purpose of this book is to introduce the student to the rich features of Perl. The text includes a large number of examples of working Perl programs in each chapter. I feel that well-motivated examples with accompanying brief explanations present the best pedagogical style in describing a programming language. A student who reads the chapters of the book, types in the example programs provided and develops his or her own code in parallel, should become an expert in Perl in a short period of time.

The material covered in this book has been used in several classes in the Computer Science Department at the University of Colorado at Colorado Springs. These are **CS 301**: Web Programming, **CS 509**: Bioinformatics, **CS 582**: Artificial Intelligence, **CS 583**: Advanced Artificial Intelligence, and **CS 592**: Applied Cryptography. In CS 301, the material is used for about 6 to 8 weeks, and then referred to throughout the rest of the class. In CS 301, the emphasis is on getting familiar with Perl and write CGI programs. In CS 509, students use Perl to search genome and protein databases, perform pair-wise and multiple alignments in genomic and protein databases. CS 583 focusses on intelligent Internet Systems and the students start programming on the Internet right away. Perl is useful to building systems that fetch materials from the Internet for analysis. Students working on projects such as building search engines of various levels of sophistication, categorizing and classifying material on the Web, personalizing Web pages, learning programs that distill information from the Web, have used the material in this book. In CS 592, network programming and cryptographic programming are discussed.

The material in the book also has been used by professional programmers who are either new to Perl or have used it before, but not for a long period of time. The book is ideal for a professional programmer who wants to get started with Perl without any delay whatsoever. Some of the examples in the book are smaller versions of the programs the author himself has written while consulting with several companies during summers away from academia. For example, the author has used Perl, while working for a company, to write programs that detect spam in incoming email using Bayesian probabilities as well as evolutionary programming. The author used Perl to write code that crawls the Web and creates personalized newspapers. The author has also used Perl to interact with large databases.

In summary, the author recommends this book to college and university students who want to use Perl for programming for class assignments and projects, but do not have access to a class that teaches Perl in depth. It is also for students who want to use Perl for their thesis or dissertation programming in diverse areas such as Web programming, databases, artificial intelligence, networking, bioinformatics, etc. I also recommend the book to those in industry or those who are self-employed and want to use Perl in of these areas, and have to learn it on their own.

This is my first effort at writing a book. Please send any comments or error reports to the author at the address given below.

Jugal Kalita
Associate Professor
Department of Computer Science
University of Colorado
1420 Austin Bluffs Parkway
Colorado Springs CO 80918
Email: kalita@pikespeak.uccs.edu
URL: http://www.cs.uccs.edu/~kalita

December 20, 2003

Contents

Chapter 1

On The First Steps

In This Chapter

Perl is a massive language. It provides the basic data structures and syntactic constructs most high level programming languages have. In addition, it provides many extras such as a sophisticated pattern matching facility, many operators for handling files and directories, for network programming, and for interacting with the underlying operating system. On top of the large array of facilities the language itself provides, there are many packages and modules that are freely available for doing any task imaginable. It is both the built-in capabilities of Perl and the availability of a large number of well-written modules that have made Perl a popular language.

Perl is a glue language. The many capabilities that Perl provides may seem to be disconnected at first. However, Perl does an excellent job of putting the seemingly disparate parts into a coherent whole. Mastering Perl takes many years of programming experience. However, it is a language that is surprisingly easy to learn. It is not necessary to know all of its syntax to get started or to even write fairly sophisticated programs.

This chapter promptly immerses us in the immensity of Perl. We get introduced to syntactic features of Perl using simple examples. We illustrate the essential elements of the language in real programs, without getting bogged down in details and fine print. In this chapter, we are not trying to be complete or even precise, except that the examples we provide are correct and functional. We want the reader to get as quickly as possible to the point where the learner can write useful programs, and some fairly complex ones. As a consequence, we get into a few complex topics toward the end of the chapter. We feel that familiarity with some complex features in the beginning will excite a learner by increasing his or her level of curiosity. One does not have to be nervous if one does not understand all of the programs and discussions since we present the same issues at length later in the book. Since we do not use the full power of the language, the examples may not be as concise and elegant as they should be. In addition, later chapters necessarily repeat the ideas discussed in this chapter. We hope that the repetition helps one learn better.

A careful reading of this chapter will give the student a sense of accomplishment in a short period of time. Programmers experienced in one or more high level programming languages should be able to extrapolate from the material to their own programming needs. Beginners should supplement it by writing small, similar programs of their own. The best way to learn any programming language is to understand the motivation behind example programs, read them, understand them, sit at a computer, type in the sample examples, and finally code on one's own. That is why the chapters in this book have many example programs.

In this book, when we talk about Unix or Unix-like systems, we not only mean varieties of Unix available, but also include Unix-like systems such as Linux or Macintosh OS X, or simulation of Unix in Windows systems such as `cygwin`. When we talk about non-Unix systems, we mean varieties of Windows operating systems from Microsoft, Inc., and pre-OS X versions of Macintosh OS from Apple Computer, Inc.

1.1 The First Perl Program

We start by learning to write a very simple Perl program. It is a program that we see used as a first example in most programming language texts. Let us assume we want our program to simply write "Hello, world!" onto the terminal. It is as if we come from an alien planet and start the first step in communicating with the human world using a computer. The complete text of the program is given below.

Program 1.1

```
#!/usr/bin/perl
#file hello.pl

print "Hello, world! \n";
```

Technically, this program has only one line or statement of code. The first two lines are comments. # starts a comment in Perl. When Perl finds # on a line of input, it ignores the line starting at the next character till the end of the line.

The first line is needed *only* on a Unix system to indicate where the Perl interpreter is situated in the system. Although, it is not necessary for a comment line to start in the first column, this particular first line must start in the first column. In the particular Unix system where we run the program, the Perl interpreter is /usr/bin/perl. The #! is used as a convention in many interpreted languages to tell the underlying Unix system where to find the interpreter. If you are using a Unix system and the Perl interpreter is located somewhere else, you will have to find out the full name from your systems administrator and put it in place of the pathname given here.

On non-Unix systems, the first line of comment is unnecessary. However, having the first line of comment doesn't hurt on non-Unix systems. In fact, it is a good idea, especially if you want your program to be portable across platforms.

The second line is also a comment. Of course, this line is not required on any system. This comment line does not have to start in the first column as shown in the sample code above. It says that the program is stored in the file hello.pl, and is useful for a human reader.

The only real line of code in this program is the print statement. The print command, as used here, takes a string as its only argument. The string is started and ended, i.e., delimited by double quotes. The last character in the string is \n. If used inside a string enclosed in double quotes, as we do here, \n, literally a sequence of two separate characters, means the newline character. In other words, it ends a line of string and starts a new one. Such a two-sequence character with \ in the front is considered a single unit and is called a *backslashed escape sequence* or simply an *escape character*. Perl allows strings to be enclosed within single quotes also. If a string is single quoted, a backslashed escape character like \n, stands for two individual characters and does not make special sense as a two-character sequence with \ in the front. A statement is terminated by ; in Perl.

Let us assume that the program is stored, as stated in the comment line, in the file hello.pl. Note that Perl doesn't require program files to have any specific extension at the end of the file's name although we have used the .pl. extension here. On a Windows system, the extension .pl can be associated with the Perl interpreter. We can create the file in any editor with which we are comfortable.

On any system, whether Unix or non-Unix, we can run the program in a terminal by giving the file name as an argument to the perl command as given below.

```
perl hello.pl
```

Here, we assume that % is the system prompt. There is no need to compile the program since Perl is an interpreted language.

On a Windows system, one can also run the Perl program by by making a choice on a pop-up menu that says something like Execute Perl script and then select the name of the file containing the code to run.

To run the program on a Unix machine, one can also do the following. First, we need to make the file executable, i.e., give it execute permission for the user. Then, we run the program by typing its name at the system prompt. On a terminal, we type the following.

```
%chmod u+x hello.pl
%hello.pl
```

Note that changing the file's permission to allow execution needs to be done only once, even if we edit the program file later. In a Unix system, the chmod command changes the modes or permissions associated with files. The first argument u+x asks the system to add the execute permission for the user. u stands for user, and x stands for execute permission. The plus sign (+) adds the permission. The last argument to the chmod command is the file name hello. We are assuming that % is the Unix prompt. We don't have to type the % sign.

The output of the Perl program is simply

```
Hello, world!
```

as expected.

1.2   Using Scalar Variables

A *scalar variable* is a placeholder or a name whose value has a single component, unlike a more complex variable such as an array variable or a hash variable which can contain many parts or components. We will see arrays and hashes later in the chapter. Perl allows two types of scalar variables commonly used— numbers and strings. A number is either an integer (such as 10) or a float (such as 2.35, -1.414e-10 or 1.414E10). As mentioned earlier, a string can be enclosed either within single quotes or double quotes.

The next program shows us how to use scalar variables in Perl. We use numbers as well as strings.

Program 1.2

```
#!/usr/bin/perl
#file scalars.pl

$day = "Wednesday";
$date = 28;
$month = 'May';
$year = "2003";
$space = " ";

$you = "justin";
$me = 'jugal';

$high = 65.2; $low = 40.3;

print "Dear \u$you,\n\n";
print $space x 5;
print "How are you doing? ";
print "Today is $day, $month $date, $year.\n";
print "Today's high and low temperature were $high and $low degrees F. ";
$tomorrow = $date + 1;
print "Tomorrow is $month $tomorrow, $year.\n";
print "\n\u$me\n";
```

First, we assign values to a number of scalar variables. It is not necessary to declare the variables and their types before we use them. Declaring a variable means telling the system that we intend to use a variable before we actually use it. A variable is usually of a certain type, such as scalar, array and such. We can assign a value to a variable wherever in the program we find it convenient. All scalar variables in Perl must have names that start with the dollar sign: $.

The program assigns values to a number of string variables. The scalar variables $day, $year, $space and $you have been assigned double-quoted string values. The scalar variables $month and $me have been assigned single-quoted string values. Double quoted strings must be used if we want the string to contain backslashed escape characters such as \n. In this example, the string assignments do not have any such backslashed two-character sequences although the string arguments to some of the print commands have them.

We have also used numeric variables. In Perl, although we can use integers and floats, internally all numbers are stored as double-precision floating point values. Here, $date, $high and $low are scalar variables that have been assigned numeric values. Later in the program, we see a scalar variable $tomorrow that has been assigned the value obtained by adding 1 to $date.

In this simple program, we see some interesting operations that Perl allows on strings. The first print statement.

```
print "Dear\u$you,\n\n";
```

The string argument is a double-quoted string. As a result, it can contain backslashed escape characters such as \u and \n. \u requires Perl to uppercase the next letter it prints. In this case, the next word to print is obtained by *variable interpolation* or by substituting a variable by its value. Since we have the \u escape character in front of $you, the first letter in the value of $you is be uppercased before printing. That is Perl prints Justin instead of justin.

The second print statement is

```
print $space x 5;
```

The x is the string repetition operation. Here the value of the variable $space is repeated 5 times before printing. Since the value of $space is a single blank space, Perl prints five blank spaces.

The rest of the program is straight-forward.

We can create the text of the program using any text editor. Let the file where the program is stored be called scalars.pl. The output of this program is given below.

```
Dear Justin,

     How are you doing? Today is Wednesday, May 28, 2003.
Today's high and low temperature were 65.2 and 40.3
degrees F. Tomorrow is May 29, 2003.

Jugal
```

1.3 Declaring Variables: Pragmas

Unlike many other programming languages, it is not necessary to declare variables before use in Perl. Declaring a variable with a certain name simply means stating to the Perl interpreter that the program needs a variable with the given name. It enables the programming system to perform housekeeping such as allocating the appropriate amount of space for the variable. A variable is declared before we actually use the variable for the first time. In Perl, if a variable is not declared before its use, it just springs into existence as soon as it is used in the program in a statement that provides it with a value. If an undeclared and unassigned variable is used for the first time, it assumes a default value such as 0, the empty string, or the empty list, depending on its type and the context of usage.

Declaration of variables helps the Perl allocate space and makes Perl run a bit faster. It also helps write programs that are easier to debug. Perl can be instructed to complain if we use a variable name that has not been declared before its use. This means that if we make an error in spelling the name of a variable inside the program, Perl catches the error and lets us know. It is considered a good programming practice to declare any variable used in the program. Perl does not enforce pre-declaration of variables. It leaves the choice to the programmer. If a programmer wants the benefits that accrue from declaration of variables, he or she may choose to enforce this discipline on himself or herself. This is consistent with a fundamental belief of Perl's creator that as few rules as possible should be enforced when writing software to stifle creativity. However, many academics and practitioners disagree with such a position arguing that program maintainability is a casualty.

Perl has several ways for declaring variables. The most common way is by using the my declaration. It is sufficient for most simple programs. A variable declared with my is a so-called *lexically scoped* variable in that it is available only within the block in which it is declared. For simple programs such as the ones we have seen so far, the whole file is assumed to belong to one block. In the following program which is a rewrite of the immediately preceding program, the scope of each variable is the whole program. A block is usually contained inside curly brackets, { and }. We will see examples of such blocks in the next section.

Even when declaration for variable names is enforced, unlike many languages, Perl does not require that all declarations be made at the top of the block, although it is a good practice. In such situations, Perl is happy as long as the variable is declared anywhere inside the block, but before its first use.

Program 1.3

```perl
#!/usr/bin/perl
#file scalars-strict.pl

use strict vars;

my $day;
my $date;

#Several 'my' declared variables can be put in a list also.
my ($month, $year, $space, $you, $me);
my ($high, $low,  $tomorrow);

$day = "Wednesday";
$date = 28;
$month = 'May';
$year = "1997";
$space = " ";

$you = "justin";
$me = 'jugal';

$high = 65.2; $low = 40.3;
print "Dear \u$you,\n\n";
print $space x 5;
print "How are you doing? ";
print "Today is $day, $month $date, $year.\n";
print "Today's high and low temperature were $high and $low degrees F. ";
$tomorrow = $date + 1;
print "Tomorrow is $month $tomorrow, $year.\n";
print "\n\u$me\n";
```

In this program, each variable has been declared before usage by using my. We can declare each variable in a statement by itself. We can also declare several variables in one statement. If we declare several variables in one statement, the list of variables must be included inside parentheses.

In the program given above, we have made it mandatory that every variable used be pre-declared using my. We have ensured this by using a *pragma* or Perl directive at the top of the program or the block in question:

```
use strict;
```

A directive requires Perl to look out for things as asked. If we use any variable in this program that is not declared a priori using my, Perl will give an error. The pragma could have been written also as:

```
use strict vars;
```

This is because use strict; looks for several things, only one of which is ensuring declaration of variable names. The word vars can be quoted also.

1.4   Flow of Control

In the programs we have seen so far, the statements in the program have been run sequentially, one after the other. This is the default behavior. The flow of execution of a program can also be controlled by a programmer. One simple way to change a program's flow of control is to organize a sequence of one or more steps into a group or *block* that works a single unit. The block of statements is executed several times, each time performing slightly different computation. We see examples of such control of program flow in this section.

We want to write a program that converts temperatures given in Fahrenheit to Celsius using the standard formula $C = \frac{5}{9} \times (F - 32)$. Here, F is a temperature specified in the Fahrenheit scale, and C is the equivalent temperature in the Celsius scale. The program starts with $0°$ Fahrenheit and goes up to $300°$ Fahrenheit with a step size of $20°$. For each Fahrenheit temperature, it prints the corresponding Celsius temperature. Each temperature pair is printed in a line. The output of the program is given below.

```
  0   -17.8
 20    -6.7
 40     4.4
 60    15.6
 80    26.7
100    37.8
120    48.9
140    60.0
160    71.1
180    82.2
200    93.3
220   104.4
240   115.6
260   126.7
280   137.8
300   148.9
```

Here, the first column represents a Fahrenheit temperature, and the second column represents the Celsius equivalent.

1.4.1   The `while` construct

In a programming language, usually there are several ways to achieve the same task just like as humans, we can say the same thing in many ways. In this section, we look at two different ways of performing *iteration*, i.e., performing the same computation several times with possibly different inputs in every iteration.

A program that produces the desired output follows.

Program 1.4

```perl
#!/usr/bin/perl
#file farenheit.pl
use strict vars;
my ($lower, $upper, $step, $fahrenheit, $celsius);

#print Fahrenheit-Celsius table for 0, 20, ..., 300 degrees Fahrenheit

$lower = 0;    #lower limit of temperature table
$upper = 300; #upper limit
$step = 20;    #step size

$fahrenheit = $lower;
              #loop through the Fahrenheit values
while ($fahrenheit <= $upper){
    $celsius = 5/9 * ($fahrenheit - 32);
    printf "%4.0f %6.1f\n", $fahrenheit, $celsius;
    $fahrenheit = $fahrenheit + $step;
}
```

The program initializes the lower and upper Fahrenheit limits of the table we want to print. Next, it initializes the value by which a Fahrenheit degree is increased in each iteration of the loop to be 20 degrees.

We use a `while` loop in the program. The expression inside parentheses following the `while` keyword gives the condition that must be satisfied for the statements inside the loop to be executed. The condition simply states that the value of `$fahrenheit` must be less than or equal to the value of `$upper` for the body of the `while` loop to be executed. The *body* of the `while` loop contains all the statements enclosed within { and }. The body is an example of a block. Since the entry condition is satisfied, the loop is executed at least once.

In the body of the loop, there are three statements. The first statement computes the Celsius temperature for the Fahrenheit temperature given as the value of the scalar variable `$fahrenheit` using the formula we discussed earlier. The value of the scalar `$celsius` is set to the value computed.

The next statement allows us to print formatted output. That is why it is called `printf`.

```perl
    printf "%4.0f %6.1f\n", $fahrenheit, $celsius;
```

The first argument to `printf` is a doubly-quoted string that tells Perl what to print and how. It contains formatting directives that start with %. There can be any number of arguments following the first argument. Here we have two such arguments: `$fahrenheit` and `$celsius`. The first formatting directive inside the first argument is `%4.0f`. The f at the end tells us that we are printing a floating point number using a decimal point. There are 4 digits before the decimal point and none after the decimal point. The value of `$fahrenheit`—the second argument to the `printf` command— is printed according to the first formatting directive. The value of the third argument to `printf` is printed according the `%6.1f` directive.

That is, $celsius is printed in a floating point format using a decimal point. There are up to six digits before the decimal point, and one digit after the decimal point.

The last statement in the loop increments the value of $fahrenheit by the value of $step. Control of the program is then sent back to the top of the while loop. The entry condition for the loop is evaluated once again. If the entry condition is satisfied, the loop is entered again and its body statements are performed. If the entry condition is not satisfied, the loop is not entered another time and the program execution ends.

1.4.2 The for Loop

Another program that produces the output given in the beginning of the section is given below. Here, we use a for loop instead of a while loop to achieve the same purpose.

Program 1.5

```perl
#!/usr/bin/perl
#file fahrenheit1.pl

#print Fahrenheit-Celsius table for 0, 20, ..., 300 degrees Fahrenheit

use strict 'vars';
my $fahrenheit;
my $celsius;

            #loop through the Fahrenheit values
for ($fahrenheit = 0; $fahrenheit <= 300; $fahrenheit = $fahrenheit+20){
    $celsius = 5/9 * ($fahrenheit - 32);
    printf "%4.0f %6.1f\n", $fahrenheit, $celsius;
}
```

Here, we do not have the variable initializations that we had in the previous program prior to getting inside the loop.

The for statement has two parts to it. The first part is enclosed inside (and). The first part has three expressions in it, each expression separated from the following using the semicolon: ;. An expression is usually not a complete statement, but is a component of a statement. A statement is like a sentence in a natural language like English, and an expression is like a phrase. The first expression gives us the initial value for a variable that is used for controlling the number of iterations of the loop. The second expression gives us the condition that must be satisfied for the block of expressions inside the loop to be executed. Here, the loop is entered only if the value of $fahrenheit is less than or equal to 300. The last expression inside the parentheses tells Perl how the control variable $fahrenheit is modified after every iteration through the loop. The value of $fahrenheit is incremented by 20 in each iteration. Since the value of $fahrenheit starts at 0 in the first iteration and is incremented by 20 in each iteration, eventually the value of $fahrenheit crosses the upper limit of 300 and the execution of the program halts.

The second part of the for statement is included inside { and } and is a block. It contains one or more statements to be executed in each iteration through the for loop.

As a final note, it is not possible to claim that a while loop is better than or worse than a for loop. The choice depends on the programmer and the context of usage. Usually if there is only one initialization and one update expression, for is more convenient and compact than while.

1.5   Reading From the Terminal

Now, we now learn how to read user input from the terminal. In Perl, the terminal is designated as the standard input or STDIN. In computer terminology, the terminal is called a *stream* because that is where a stream of characters or lines are input or output by the computer. Perl calls such things *filehandles*. Perl encloses a filehandle or stream inside angle brackets (i.e., < and >) when it is used for reading purposes. <STDIN> reads the next line of input from the terminal when used in a situation where a scalar is expected.

1.5.1   Reading a Single Value From the Terminal

The following program prints a prompt on the terminal asking the user to enter a Fahrenheit temperature. It converts the temperature to Celsius and prints the answer.

Program 1.6

```
#!/usr/bin/perl
#file fahrenheit2.pl
use strict;
my ($fahrenheit,$celsius);

print "Please enter a Fahrenheit temperature >> ";
$fahrenheit = <STDIN>;
chomp ($fahrenheit);

$celsius = 5/9 * ($fahrenheit - 32);
printf "%4.0f degrees Fahrenheit is equal to %6.1f degrees Celsius.\n",
    $fahrenheit, $celsius;
```

The line of code after variable declaration in the program is a `print` statement. Here printing is done on the user's terminal. The terminal is called STDIN for reading and STDOUT for writing. STDOUT stands for the standard output stream or filehandle. These are two names for the same thing for two purposes. The `print` statement can be rewritten with STDOUT as follows:

```
    print STDOUT "Please enter a Fahrenheit temperature\n";
```

In general, the first "argument" to `print` is a filehandle and if the filehandle is not provided, STDOUT is taken as the default. We use double quotes to indicate that it is not a real argument in the traditional sense because it is not followed by a comma.

The next statement in the program reads a line of input from the default filehandle.

```
    $fahrenheit = <STDIN>;
```

The left hand side of the assignment statement has a scalar variable. The right hand side reads from the STDIN filehandle. Because the left side is scalar, such a reading is said to take place in a *scalar context*. In a scalar context, <STDIN> reads the next input line and assigns it to the $fahrenheit variable.

When Perl reads, it reads the whole line of input, *i.e.*, up to and including the first \n character. Thus, a line of input contains what is seen on the terminal followed by the newline character \n at the very end. This newline character is removed from the end of the input line by using the chomp operation. chomp is a built-in function that takes a string as its argument and removes the last character only if the last character is \n. If the last character is not \n, it is not removed. chomp is particularly useful for reading lines from the terminal. There is a related function called chop that takes a string argument and removes the last character no matter what it is.

1.5.2   Reading Many Values Sequentially From the Terminal

Now, we are going to put the statement that reads the STDIN filehandle inside a loop and read one Fahrenheit temperature after another till end-of-file is indicated by the user by typing in Control-D in a Unix system, or Control-Z on Windows systems. As we read a Fahrenheit temperature, we convert it to Celsius and print both values. The program is given below.

Program 1.7

```
#!/usr/bin/perl
#file fahrenheit3.pl
use strict vars;
my ($fahrenheit,$celsius);

print "Please enter a Fahrenheit temperature >> ";
while ($fahrenheit = <STDIN>){
    chomp ($fahrenheit);
    #print "\$fahrenheit = $fahrenheit\n";
    $celsius = 5/9 * ($fahrenheit - 32);
    printf "%4.0f degrees Fahrenheit is equal to %6.1f degrees Celsius.\n",
            $fahrenheit, $celsius;
    print "Please enter a Fahrenheit temperature >> ";
}
```

The conditional of the while loop,

```
    ($fahrenheit = <STDIN>)
```

is an assignment statement. As usual, <STDIN> reads the current line from the standard input and assigns the line read to be the value of the scalar $fahrenheit. After the assignment, the current value of $fahrenheit is taken as the condition to be tested for entering the while loop. This is because an assignment statement returns the value of the expression on the right hand side as its value. So, if we enter a temperature value at the terminal, it is converted to Celsius. When we enter the end-of-file indicator (Control-D in Unix, and Control-Z in Windows systems) at the prompt, it is also taken as the value of $fahrenheit. The end-of-file indicator actually evaluates to undef which is again taken as the empty string by Perl. In Perl, the empty string or the number 0 (zero) evaluates to *false*. So, entering the end-of-file indicator will cause the conditional for the while loop to evaluate to false and the loop will be exited. undef is a special value that is produced by several built-in functions when there is nothing to return.

The following gives a sample session when we run the program. At the last prompt, the user had entered Control-D on a Unix machine.

```
    %fahrenheit3.pl
    Please enter a Fahrenheit temperature >> 100
     100 degrees Fahrenheit is equal to   37.8 degrees Celsius.
    Please enter a Fahrenheit temperature >> 230
     230 degrees Fahrenheit is equal to  110.0 degrees Celsius.
```

```
Please enter a Fahrenheit temperature >> 3000
3000 degrees Fahrenheit is equal to 1648.9 degrees Celsius.
Please enter a Fahrenheit temperature >>
```

The program can be written in a slightly cryptic manner. The only difference between the previous program and the next one is in the conditional of the `while` loop, and its effects within the body of the loop.

Program 1.8

```perl
#!/usr/bin/perl
#file fahrenheit4.pl

use strict;
my $celsius;

print "Please enter a Fahrenheit temperature >> ";
while (<STDIN>){
    chomp;
    $celsius = 5/9 * ($_ - 32);
    printf "%4.0f degrees Fahrenheit is equal to %6.1f degrees Celsius.\n",
            $_, $celsius;
    print "Please enter a Fahrenheit temperature >> ";
}
```

Here, inside the conditional of the `while` loop, we are not performing an assignment like we did before. In such a case, Perl does an assignment any way. If and only if the input operator is the only thing inside the conditional of a `while` loop, Perl assigns the value of the funny-looking scalar variable `$_` to the line read from STDIN. This is a special case situation that may look unorthodox, but Perl does it as a short cut because such a situation arises in many Perl programs. Perl has a large number of built-in variables called *special variables*. `$_` is one of them. It is a default argument to many of Perl's commands. It is also the default input variable when (`<STDIN>`) is used as the conditional of a `while` or `for` loop. The value of `$_` can be used in computations later in the program. The `$_` variable must not be declared with `my`, and `use strict` does not give us compiler error.

In the first statement inside the `while` loop, we call `chomp` without any argument. In such a case, `$_` is taken as the default argument passed to it. The use of `$_` as a default argument makes a lot of Perl statements shorter.

1.6   Simple File Operations

In this section, we learn to read from a file and write to a file. Reading and writing are performed using filehandles.

1.6.1   Reading from a file

The program given below prompts for the name of a file. When the user types in the name of a file, the program prints out the contents of the file with the lines numbered one by one.

Program 1.9

```perl
#!/usr/bin/perl
#file name: read-file.pl
use strict;
my ($filename, $linecount);

print "Please give me a file name >> ";
$filename = <STDIN>;
chomp ($filename);

$linecount = 1;
print "Printing file $filename\n\n";

open (INFILE, $filename);
while (<INFILE>){
    print "$linecount\t$_";
    $linecount++;
    }
```

To read from a file, Perl opens a filehandle. Here the filehandle is called INFILE. Opening the filehandle INFILE associates the filehandle with the file whose name is the value of the $filename variable. In this case, the value of the variable $filename is obtained by reading the user's input at the terminal. This value is a string.

The conditional of the while loop ensures that every line of the file is read and printed on the terminal. Each line is preceded by the line number. The line number is incremented every time a line is read and printed. ++ is the increment operation; it has two plus signs with no intervening space. The operator is used here in the postfix format. In other words, the operator follows the argument. Incrementing is done by 1.

An interaction with this program is given below. Here, we read the file containing the above program itself.

```
% perl file-read.pl
Please give me a file name >> file-read.pl
Printing file file-read.pl

1          #!/usr/bin/perl
2          #file name: read-file.pl
3          use strict;
4          my ($filename, $linecount);
5
6          print "Please give me a file name >> ";
7          $filename = <STDIN>;
8          chomp ($filename);
9
10         $linecount = 1;
11         print "Printing file $filename\n\n";
12
13         open (INFILE, $filename);
14         while (<INFILE>){
15             print "$linecount\t$_";
16             $linecount++;
17             }
```

1.6.2   Copying a File

Now, we write a program that copies contents of one text file into another. Copying a file involves reading from a file and writing to another file. So, we need two filehandles, one for the file from which the program reads and another for the file into which the program writes.

Program 1.10

```perl
#!/usr/bin/perl
#file copy1.pl
#copying everything from one file to another

use strict;
my ($oldfilename, $newfilename);

print "Please give me a file name >> ";
$oldfilename = <STDIN>;
chomp ($oldfilename);
$newfilename = $oldfilename . ".new";

open (IN, $oldfilename);
open (OUT, ">$newfilename");

while (<IN>){
    print OUT $_;
}

close (IN);
close (OUT);

print "File '$newfilename' is an exact copy of file '$oldfilename'\n";
```

The program prompts the user for the name of the file to copy. The name of the file to copy is stored in the variable $oldfilename. The name of the file is a string. Next, the program creates a name for the file into which the copying will be done. The name of the new file is obtained by concatenating .new to the name of the file entered by the user. In Perl, string concatenation is done by using the dot (.) operator.

The program opens a filehandle called IN for reading the contents of the file whose name is entered by the user. The program also creates another filehandle OUT for writing purposes. To open a filehandle for writing, the second argument to open must have the name of the file preceded by >. When a file is opened for writing, the file is created if the file does not exist and the user has permission to create/write files. If the file already exists and the user has permission to write into the file, the file is overwritten. Note permissions are usually an issue only in Unix systems.

The while loop simply reads a line of text from the IN filehandle and prints it out to the OUT filehandle. Printing the line to the OUT filehandle causes the line to be written into the new file.

1.7   Lists and Arrays

A *list* is a Perl data structure where the position of an item matters. A list can grow or shrink during program execution. Elements of a list are accessed by using numeric index. In a list, the first element is considered to be in position 0.

The following program declares five lists using my. It then assigns values to these lists. It changes the values of a few list elements. Finally, it prints corresponding elements of the list row by row.

Program 1.11

```perl
#!/usr/bin/perl
#file arrays.pl

use strict;
my (@friends, @hometowns, @heights, @weights, @ages, $i);

@friends = qw(Tommy Chad Jeff Aaron Rick Sean Todd);
@hometowns = ('Washington', 'San Francisco', 'Boulder', 'Golden', 'Montreal',
              'Montreal', 'Colo Springs');
@heights = (66, 73, 70, 68, 67, 67, 73);
@weights = (140, 180, 145, 155, 135, 140, 190);
@ages = (18, 23, 21, 23, 21, 21);

$weights [3] = 157;
$ages [6] = 22;
$hometowns [0] = 'Washington DC';

print "Name \t Hometown \t Height \t Weight \t Age \n";
print "-" x 65, "\n";

for ($i = 0; $i <= 6; $i++){
 print
  "$friends[$i] \t $hometowns[$i] \t $heights[$i] \t\t $weights[$i] \t\t $ages[$i]\n";
}
```

The five lists used by the program are @friends, @hometowns, @heights, @weights and @ages. In Perl, the name of every variable that stores list data must begin with the "at" sign (@). This is another of the unusual syntactic features of Perl. The lists @friends and @hometowns have string elements. The lists @heights, @weights and @ages have numbers.

One way to write a list is by writing out all of its elements separated by commas. For the time being, let us assume that a list's component elements are either all numbers or all strings. However, it is possible to have a list where some elements are numbers and some are strings.

Each list used in this program has several elements. For example, @hometowns has a list of single-quoted strings as its elements. Its 0th element is 'Washington' and its 6th element is 'Colo Springs'. In Perl, list elements are numbered starting 0. The 0th element of the list @hometowns is obtained by writing $hometowns[0]. When one accesses an element of a list, one must replace the @ in the name of the list by $. This is because the dollar sign ($) states that we are looking at a scalar, and a specific element of a list is always a scalar.

Let us now look at the first list @friends. It has seven strings as elements. We could have written the line that assigns a value to @friends in the regular manner.

```perl
@friends = ('Tommy', 'Chad', 'Jeff', 'Aaron', 'Rick', 'Sean', 'Todd');
```

Here, we have seven single-quoted strings as elements of the list. When such a situation arises, we can leave out the quotes and the commas, and write the list as we have done in the program.

```perl
@friends = qw(Tommy Chad Jeff Aaron Rick Sean Todd);
```

qw stands for *quoted words*. We can use qw only when the constituent elements are singly quoted strings. As discussed earlier, strings can be single- or double-quoted. Single-quoted strings do not allow us to use backslashed escape characters. Single-quoted strings also do not allow variable names to be used inside for interpolation or expansion. Double-quoted strings allow both of these.

Specific elements of a list can be assigned values during program execution.

```
$weights [3] = 157;
$ages [6] = 22;
$hometowns [0] = 'Washington DC';
```

Here, we change the value of $weights[3] and $hometown[0]. The array @ages initially is 6 elements long. It is made seven elements long by performing an assignment to $ages[6].

Perl allows assignment to the nth element of a list that is smaller than n elements long. Let the list be m elements long where $m < n$. In such a case, all the elements between index m and $n - 1$ are assumed to have undef as the value. undef simply means that the value is undefined. For example, in the program above, @friends is 7 elements long. Its last index is 6. If we now make an assignment to the 19th element by writing

```
$friends [19] = 'Johnny';
```

elements $friends[7] through $friends[18] have undef as their value.

In the for loop at the bottom of the program, we access the $ith element of each of the lists and print the values separated by a tab. The output of the program is given below.

```
Name        Hometown         Height       Weight          Age
- - - - - - - - - - - - - - - - - - - - - - - - - - - - - - - - - - - - - - - - - -
Tommy       Washington DC    66           140             18
Chad        San Francisco    73           180             23
Jeff        Boulder          70           145             21
Aaron       Golden           68           157             23
Rick        Montreal         67           135             21
Sean        Montreal         67           140             21
Todd        Colo Springs     73           190             22
```

In a computer science curriculum, it is customary to have a class in the beginning of the curriculum that deals with data structures of various kinds and their implementations. In such a class, arrays and lists are discussed as two different multi-component of collection data structures. A data structure is an abstraction for an entity that can store data and has operations that can be performed on the data. The array data structure and the list data structures have different operations defined on them although it is possible to implement a list using an array.

The data structure we have discussed in this section is a list. A list is a collection of items accessible one after another, i.e., sequentially. At a minimum, a list can be accessed at the very beginning, and then can be traversed forwards (sometimes, backwards as well), one step at a time. Thus, the operations required on a list data structure at a minimum are obtaining the first element, and obtaining the next element given one element (and, obtaining the previous element given an element). A list data structure is not of fixed length, and can grow and shrink during the execution of the program.

An array is a data structure that also represents a collection of objects. All objects in an array have to be of the same type. An array can be thought of as a collection of items which are randomly accessible using numeric index. Thus, in the case of an array, an operation that is crucially needed is to obtain an element given its numeric index in the array. An array data structure is conceptually simpler than a list. An array is usually of fixed length. That is, there is a limit to the number of items that can be stored within an array, although this limit can be large. If an array is sufficiently large, it can be used to mimic a list which grows and shrinks within the limit imposed by the array's size.

A list can be implemented in more than one way. Perl implements the list data structure using an array. Hence, in Perl, we use the two terms, list and array, interchangeably, although in a strict sense it is not correct to do so. Thus, conceptually although we have two data structures, in practice, we have just one.

1.8 Command Line Arguments

Now that we have learnt about lists, we can write Perl programs that accept and manipulate command line arguments. A command line argument is one that is typed after the name of the Perl program or command on the same line.

We have seen the special scalar variable $_ that Perl provides as the default input argument inside loops. $_ is also used as the default argument for many commands such as print and chomp. In addition, Perl provides a set of special list variables. One such variable is @ARGV. Perl also provides a special filehandle called ARGV. These two special variables, which have similar names, are used for writing Perl programs that can take command line arguments.

1.8.1 @ARGV: The Special List Variable

Suppose we want to write a program called myargv.pl that takes any number of command line arguments and writes them out to the standard output filehandle STDOUT with some comments. A call to the program in an Unix environment looks like:

```
%myargv.pl x y z abc uvw
```

Here x, y, and z are command line arguments to the program myargv.pl. When we specify a list of command line arguments, the list is not included in parentheses like a regular function call. Also, the arguments are not comma-separated. They are separated simply by one or more spaces.

The program writes out the arguments with some additional comments. The output looks like:

```
Command line argument #0 = x
Command line argument #1 = y
Command line argument #2 = z
Command line argument #3 = abc
Command line argument #4 = uvw
All command line arguments printed.
```

This program can take any number of arguments. A program is given below.

Program 1.12

```
#!/usr/bin/perl
#file myargv.pl

#Prints the arguments given in command line, one per line with
#some additional comments

use strict;
my $i;
```

```
for ($i=0; $i <= $#ARGV; $i++){
    print "Command line argument #$i = $ARGV[$i]\n";
    if ($i == $#ARGV) {
        print "All command line arguments printed.\n";
    }
```

This program uses a variable called $i that acts as an index to the @ARGV special list variable that is au-tomatically defined inside the program. The special list variable @ARGV contains all the arguments with which the program has been called. Since @ARGV is a special variable, it must not be declared with my.

The body of the program has a for loop. This loop has an index variable that starts with a count of zero and goes up to $#ARGV. If we have a list variable whose name starts with @, we can obtain the index of the last element in it by writing $# in front of it instead of @. The $ sign tells us that it is a scalar. So, the for loop is executed for every element in the @ARGV list. In other words, the body of the for loop is executed once for every command line argument to the myargv.pl command.

The body of the loop prints the element of @ARGV corresponding to the current value of the loop index. If it is the last element of the argument list, it prints a newline, otherwise, it prints an empty space character.

1.8.2   Treating Command Line Arguments as Files

Quite frequently, it is useful to write a program that takes a list of files as command line argument and performs the same action(s) on each of the files. Let us write a program that takes a list of files and prints out every line of every file to the user's terminal. If the program given below is stored as printfile.pl, the following call

```
%printfile.pl file1 file2 file3 file4
```

prints the contents of the four files on the terminal one file after the other.

Perl provides us with a simple mechanism to perform tasks repeated over two or more files that are given as command-line arguments. This is done by using the special input filehandle <ARGV>. When we write <ARGV> inside the conditional of a loop, it is taken by Perl to act as an input filehandle for each of the files mentioned in the command line. The files mentioned as command line arguments are considered for input sequentially.

Actually, something more happens if we use a variable like the special variable $_ (any other variable will work the same way) as the input variable along with the <ARGV> input filehandle. The first line of the first program is read into the $_ variable and printed. Next, the second line of the first file is printed and so on till the last line of the first file is printed to the terminal. At this time, the first line of the second file becomes available as the value of the $_ and is printed. The process is repeated and as a result every line of the second file is printed. Similarly, every line of every file mentioned as a command line argument is also printed. When the last line of the last file is read, the <ARGV> filehandle returns false and the reading and printing cycle finishes.

Program 1.13

```
#!/usr/bin/perl
#file printfile.pl

#This prints every line of every file give as args
#A possible call is: printfile.pl file1 file2 file3
```

```
while ($_ = <ARGV>){
        print $_;
        }
```

The <ARGV> filehandle is very useful in some circumstances. It is so useful that Perl provides us with a way to make it even shorter. If we leave out the filehandle and simply write < > in the conditional of a while or for loop, it is taken as <ARGV>. The program given above can also be written as the program given below.

Program 1.14

```
#!/usr/bin/perl
#file printfile1.pl

while (<>){
        print;
        }
```

Here, <> stands for an input handle that considers every file provided in the command line for input one after the other. In this program, we have also taken out the assignment to $_ inside the conditional of the loop since $_ is taken as the default input variable if no assignment is done inside such a conditional. In addition, we have not given an argument to the print command which takes $_ as the default argument.

1.9   Hashes or Associative Arrays

A *hash* or an *associative array* is a special kind of list where pairs of consecutive elements are related or associated with one another. For example, we may want to associate the name of a person to his hometown, his height, or his weight. The following program uses four hashes.

Program 1.15

```
#!/usr/bin/perl
#file hashes.pl

use strict;
my (%hometowns, %heights, %weights, %ages, $friend);

%hometowns = ('Tommy' => 'Washington', 'Chad' =>'San Francisco',
              'Jeff' => 'Boulder',
              'Aaron' => 'Golden', 'Rick' => 'Montreal', 'Sean' => 'Montreal',
              'Todd' => 'Colo Springs');
%heights = ('Tommy', 66, 'Aaron', 68, 'Rick', 67, "Chad", 73, 'Jeff', 70,
            'Sean', 67, "Todd", 73);
%weights = ("Tommy" => 140, "Sean" => 140, "Todd" => 190, "Chad" => 180,
            "Jeff" => 145,
            "Aaron" => 155, "Rick" => 135 );
%ages = ('Aaron', 23, "Rick", 21, 'Tommy', 18, "Sean", 21, 'Chad', 23,
         'Jeff', 21);
```

```
$weights {Aaron} = 157;
$ages {"Todd"} = 22;
$hometowns {'Tommy'} = 'Washington DC';

printf "%5s %15s %5s %5s %3s\n", "Name", "Hometown",
    "Height", "Weight", "Age";
print "-" x 45, "\n";

foreach $friend (keys %hometowns){
  printf "%5s %15s   %3d    %3d     %2d\n", $friend, $hometowns{$friend},
        $heights{$friend}, $weights{$friend},  $ages{$friend};
}
```

In Perl, the name of a hash variable must be preceded by the percentage sign (%). The first hash used in the program is %hometowns.

```
%hometowns = ('Tommy' => 'Washington', 'Chad' =>'San Francisco',
              'Jeff' => 'Boulder', Aaron' => 'Golden', 'Rick' => 'Montreal',
              'Sean' => 'Montreal', 'Todd' => 'Colo Springs');
```

It associates a person's name with a place. So, 'Tommy' is associated with 'Washington', and 'Chad' is associated with 'San Francisco'. In the first pair, 'Tommy' is the *key* and 'Washington' is the *value*. %hometown has seven keys associated with seven values. The usual syntax in Perl is to write an associated pair with the key first, followed by =>, and the value. Key-value pairs are separated by commas. Each key or each value is scalar. The key is a string that can be single or double quoted. If the string is double-quoted, any variables inside are interpolated as usual. If we use => to separate a key from its corresponding value, it is not necessary to quote the key string. Perl automatically puts quotes around the key string in such a case. The key-value pairs can be specified in any order as long as the key and the corresponding value are together.

It is also possible to write a hash without using the => to separate a key from the associated value. A hash can be written just like a regular list where every element is separated from the next by a comma.

```
%ages = ('Aaron', 23, "Rick", 21, 'Tommy', 18, "Sean", 21, 'Chad', 23, 'Jeff', 21);
```

In such a case, the hash variable name must still start with % and the key strings must be quoted. Consecutive elements of the list are paired up as key and value.

Unlike a list, elements of a hash are not accessed using integer indices corresponding to positions. Elements of a hash are accessed using string-valued keys. For example, to access Tommy's hometown, we write

```
$hometowns {'Tommy'}
```

The key is enclosed within braces ({ and }) instead of square brackets used with lists. The key may or may not be quoted. If it is not quoted, Perl automatically quotes it. Also note that the % sign in the name of the hash must be changed to $ when we access an individual element of the hash. Once again, this is because in Perl, the $ prefix corresponds to a scalar and any value in a hash is scalar. In this case, the value of $hometowns {'Tommy'} happens to be 'Washington' after the initial assignment to the hash @hometowns.

We can change the value corresponding to a specific key in the hash. For example, in our program, the assignment

```
$hometowns {'Tommy'} = 'Washington DC';
```

changes the value associated with the key 'Tommy' in the hash @hometowns to 'Washington DC' from the initial value of 'Washington'. We can also insert new key-value pairs into a hash table. In the program we are discussing, the initial assignment to the hash %ages does not have the key 'Todd'. But, we can add a pair by doing an assignment as we have done in the program.

```
$ages {"Todd"} = 22;
```

At the very end of the program there is a foreach loop.

```
foreach  $friend (keys (%hometowns)){
  printf "%5s %15s    %3d    %3d    %2d\n", $friend,  $hometowns{$friend},
          $heights{$friend},  $weights{$friend},   $ages{$friend};
}
```

We have not seen foreach in our discussion so far. foreach takes a list and loops over a block of expressions included inside curly brackets. In each iteration, the value of an iteration or index variable is set to the next element in the list. In the program fragment given above, the index variable is called $friend and the list over whose elements iterations take place is obtained as the result of a call to the keys function.

keys is a function that takes a hash as its only argument and returns the list of all the keys in the hash. For example, the following call to keys

```
keys (%hometowns)
```

returns the list

```
('Tommy', 'Chad', 'Jeff', 'Aaron', 'Rick', 'Sean', 'Todd');
```

as its result. It must be noted that when Perl returns the list of keys, the values need not come out in the order given above. They may come out in any order based on the internal hash function that Perl uses to store the hash.

So, in the program fragment given above, iteration takes place over this list of names. A name is taken and is assigned as the value of $friend and the printf statement inside the loop is performed. Here, Perl prints a name of a friend, and follows it by printing his hometown, height, weight and age.

The output of the program is given below.

```
Name          Hometown Height Weight Age
------------------------------------------------
Chad    San Francisco    73    180    23
Rick          Montreal    67    135    21
Aaron           Golden    68    157    23
Todd     Colo Springs    73    190    22
Jeff           Boulder    70    145    21
Tommy    Washington DC    66    140    18
Sean          Montreal    67    140    21
```

1.10 Subroutines

When we have a block of statements that performs a clearly designated task, we can give the block a life and identity of its own. One way to do this is by organizing the statements of the block into a subroutine. A subroutine has a name. The statements inside the subroutine can be executed as a single group by invoking the name of the subroutine. Thus, if a block of statements is executed several times in a program, we can avoid rewriting the statements, again and again, reducing the length of the program.

A subroutine can be written so that it takes one or more arguments. A subroutine with arguments can be called with different argument values at different times. Thus, the same block of statements can be executed repeatedly such that one execution is slightly different from the next.

1.10.1   A Subroutine with no Parameters

The following is a simple subroutine in Perl that has no parameters.

Program 1.16

```
#file subhello.pl
use strict;

my $name;
$name = "Brian";

hello ();

#########################
#Main program ends
#A subroutine that says hello.
sub hello{
        #note that $name is variable that is global in the whole program
        print "Hello! How are you doing $name?\n";
        }
```

A subroutine can be defined anywhere in the program. Some prefer to have all subroutine definitions at the top of the program, others at the very bottom. Here, we define subroutines at the bottom of the program.

The program has two distinct parts. Informally, we call the upper part of the program above the subroutine definition, the *main program*. The second part follows, and in this part, we have defined the subroutine. If we had several subroutines, we can define them one after the other. The order of the main program and subroutine(s) can be reversed. It is usually not a good idea to intersperse subroutine definitions and statements of the main program.

The main program declares a variable called $name available everywhere within the program. The variable is assigned a value Brian. The next statement is hello (). This statement *calls* or invokes the subroutine.

The main program is separated from the subroutine using comment lines. A subroutine definition starts with the special word or *keyword* sub. It is followed by its block of statements included inside curly braces. The name of the subroutine becomes associated with its block of statements. The statements can be executed in the main program or inside another (or, even the same) subroutine by using the name of the subroutine. This is referred to as *calling* or *invoking* the subroutine.

The subroutine hello is called in the main program, and it has access to the value of the variable $name within it.

If the program is stored in the file subhello.pl, it can be run by typing its names on the command-line argument.

```
%subhello.pl
```

The output of the program is given below.

```
Hello! How are you doing Brian?
```

The execution of the last statement in the main program calls the subroutine `hello`.

Note that a subroutine is not executed if it is not called. Thus, it is possible that there is a subroutine definition in the body of a program, and the subroutine is useless in the sense that it is not called. Having such subroutines is not a good practice, but in large programs, it can happen as the program evolves.

The subroutine `hello` given above does not have any parameters. This is clear because the parentheses pair next to the subroutine's name in the call does not enclose anything. Use of a parameter allows us to make slightly different calls to the same subroutine. We see this in the next section.

1.10.2   A Subroutine with Parameters

We now write a subroutine that takes parameters. The fact that the same subroutine can be called with different values of parameters is powerful. It allows us to indentify a subroutine with a task that can be invoked differently, as appropriate for the context. We explain with an example.

Program 1.17

```
#!/usr/bin/perl
#file subhello1.pl

#####################
#main program starts
use strict;
my $name;

#some invocations or calls
$name = "Reeves";
hello1 ($name);

#Second call
$name = "Dulu";
hello1 ($name);

#Third call
$name = "Nicole";
hello1 ($name);


################################
#Main program ends; subroutine section below
#Another subroutine that says hello.
#This one takes arguments. Arguments are put in the @_ variable

sub hello1 {
    my ($friend);
    $friend = $_[0];
```

```
        print "How are you doing $friend?...\n";
}
```

Let us first look at subroutine invocations. There are three calls and each one is the same although the value assigned to the variable used in the calls is different every time. Every time, the subroutine is invoked with one parameter only: $name. Actually, the subroutine is called with a list that contains one element. The list is ($name) containing only one element. When a subroutine is executed, this list of parameters from the call is available inside the subroutine in a special list variable @_. Use of @_ is the mechanism by which parameters are passed to a subroutine.

In the beginning of the hello1 subroutine, we declare a variable $friend with my. The $friend variable is available only inside the subroutine and not outside. We then set the scalar variable $friend to the 0th element of the parameter list @_. The zeroth element of @_ is obtained by writing $_[0]. Thus, the statements

```
        my ($friend);
        $friend = $_[0];
```

declare the variable $friend to be available within the subroutine and then assigns it the only value contained in the list @_. The variable $friend can be manipulated inside the subroutine without affecting anything outside.

The output of the program is given below.

```
How are you doing Reeves?...
How are you doing Dulu?...
How are you doing Nicole?...
```

1.11   Pattern Matching

One of the strongest points of the Perl programming language is its powerful and efficient pattern matching capability. We will get a flavor for pattern matching capabilities of Perl in this section. Pattern matching allows one to look for specific textual patterns inside a string. The patterns themselves are expressed in terms of what are called *regular expressions*.

The following program prompts the user for a text file name and then prints those lines that have the five vowels in order. The vowels can be separated by zero or more intervening characters.

Program 1.18

```
#!/usr/bin/perl
#file scanvowels1.pl

#Prompts for a file name and prints all those lines in
#that file that contain the vowels in order.

print "Please give a file name >> ";
$filename = <STDIN>;
chomp $filename;
open (IN, $filename);
```

```
while (<IN>){
    if ($_ =~ m/a.*e.*i.*o.*u/){
        print $_;
    }
}
```

The `while` loop reads every line of the text file. In any iteration, the current line is read as a string and is assigned to the special variable $_. The conditional of the `if` statement is a pattern matching operation. The syntax of a pattern matching operation is the following.

> *string-variable* =~ m/*regular-expression*/[*qualifier*]

The pattern matching is performed on *string-variable*. In the example, pattern matching is performed on the value of $_ or the current line of input from the text file. *regular-expression* is the pattern that the program searches for in *string-variable*. The regular expression or the pattern is enclosed between m/ and /. Optionally there can be one or more qualifiers after the second /. In this example, there is no qualifier.

There is an elaborate syntax regarding how a pattern is stated. We have a whole chapter devoted to this topic later in the book, namely, Chapter 4. We get just a glimpse in this section. The *regular-expression* may have certain characters that must literally occur in the target *string-variable*. An example of a literal character is the first letter of the alphabet a. The regular expression may also have some unusual characters such as . that do not stand for any specific literal character. In particular, . is a wild card character that stands for almost any character we can type. Then, there are other characters such as * that do not stand for any character at all, but specify the count or the number of times a preceding character should occur. The regular expression in this example contains all three types of characters.

The pattern a.*e.*i.*o.*u that is being matched in this program is somewhat complex, but if we understand the parts, it turns out to be really simple. The first character in the pattern: a simply specifies that we are looking for one occurrence of the character a anywhere in *string-variable*. The next two characters in the pattern .* need to be considered together to make sense. This pair specifies that we are looking for zero or more occurrences of any character other than the newline character \n. The period (.) is a shorthand notation for any character other than \n. The quantity is specified by the asterisk (*). The asterisk means *zero or more*. So, the first three characters in the pattern: a.* instruct Perl to look for one a followed by zero or more non-newline characters.

The next nine characters in the pattern: e.*i.*o.* tell Perl to look for one e followed by zero or more intervening non-newline characters followed by one i followed by zero or more non-newline characters followed by one o followed finally by zero or more non-newline characters.

The final character in the pattern is u which instructs Perl to look for one occurrence of the character u. The pattern doesn't care what follows after this first u.

Now, we see that the whole pattern taken together specifies that we are looking for the five vowels occurring in order.

An example run with a specific file is given below. Only the first few of the many lines printed by the program are shown.

```
%vowels1.pl
Please give a file name >> pattern-matching.tex
looking for patterns in textual documents. We can write
in each of these files where one word or pattern is substituted
there are several thousand files in this directory structure. Suppose
```

In the first line, the vowels captured are the ones that are in bold face:

> looking for p**a**tt**e**rns **i**n textual d**o**c**u**ments. We can write

Why these specific occurrences of the vowels are selected are discussed in Chapter 4. It is clear that the five vowels occur in sequence. In this specific run, we counted the number of lines in the file `pattern-matching.tex` and the number of lines that satisfy the regular expression. There are 3964 lines in the file and 338 of these have the five vowels in sequence. Of course, there may be zero or more intervening characters including vowels between two consecutive vowels of interest.

1.11.1   A Few Shortcuts in Pattern Matching

The program given below shows a few shortcuts we can use in pattern matching. First, if we are pattern matching against the special variable $_, it is not necessary to specify it to the left of the =~ operator. If we do not mention the variable on the left, we do not need to specify the =~ operator too. Next, we do not have to specify the operation as m signifying it is a match operation. We can simply start with the left delimiter /.

Program 1.19

```perl
#!/usr/bin/perl
#file scanvowels2.pl

use strict;
my $filename;

print "Please give a file name >> ";
$filename = <STDIN>;
chomp $filename;
open (IN, $filename);

while (<IN>){
    if (/a.*e.*i.*o.*u/i){
        print;
    }
}
```

Finally, in the pattern specification above, we have used a qualifier i after the right-delimiting /. It commands Perl to `ignore` the case of the matching characters in the pattern. So, the vowels for which we are looking can be upper case or lower case.

We end this section by writing a program that is a generalization of the program given above. The program takes a list of files as command line argument and prints every line that contains the five vowels in order, in every file that is given as a command line argument.

Program 1.20

```perl
#!/usr/bin/perl

#Takes a list of files and prints all those lines in
#the files that contain the vowels in order.

while (<>){
        if (/a.*e.*i.*o.*u/i){
```

```
        print;
    }
}
```

Here, we have used the empty diamond (<>) inside the conditional of a while loop. As discussed earlier, in such a case, Perl considers every command line argument as a file for input. Each file is considered in the sequence it is given. So, the following call to the program in a Unix environment, assuming it is stored in the file scanvowels.pl,

```
    %scanvowels.pl file1 file2 file3 file4
```

will scan the four files for lines that contain the five vowels in sequence and print such lines if found. If we are in a Unix environment, we can use some shortcuts in specifying the names of files. For example, if in a Unix environment, we type

```
    %scanvowels.pl *
```

the program will look for the pattern in every file in the current directory. In Unix, the asterisk (*) is used to refer to all files in a certain directory.

In general, pattern matching in Perl can be quite complex. We will discuss pattern matching in detail in Chapter 4.

1.12   Packages, Modules, and Objects

A *package* allows us to put a boundary around a portion of our code. The concept of a package enables us to organize our code into small partitions that we can use to achieve a larger task. If the program that we want to write is large and several people work on parts of it, the concept of a package will allow us to break up the code into parts that can be developed by independent groups or individuals as long as the interfaces are stated well. The concept of *modules* is very similar to that of packages. Finally, using the concept of packages and the concept of references (to be discussed later), we can do object-oriented programming in Perl. We will not discuss these three topics in this chapter. These are complex topics and details are left for Chapter 5.

1.13   Working With File Information

There are many ways in which Perl programs can communicate with the environment. We have already seen how we can read from and write to the terminal. We have also seen how we can read from and write to one or more files. We will see some other examples that will illustrate additional capabilities that are built into Perl for finding various useful information about a file.

In addition to reading and writing files, we can check to see the type of files that we have on our system. Perl provides us with several built-in predicates (functions that return true or false) to test file type or the access permissions associated with files. For example, there is a predicate -r that takes a filename as its argument and tells us if the file is readable. So,

```
    (-r file_name )
```

when used as a condition in an if statement, will return true if *file_name* is a readable file. The name of the predicate is somewhat unusual in the sense that it starts with a minus (-) sign. Here are some other examples of such predicates that test file access permissions.

Predicate	The Test Performed
-B	The argument is a binary file
-d	The argument is a directory
-e	The argument is a file or directory that exists
-o	The argument is a file or directory owned by the user
-r	The argument is a file or directory that is readable by the Perl program
-T	The argument is a text file
-w	The argument is a file or directory that is writable by the Perl program
-x	The argument is a file or directory that is executable by the Perl program

The program given below takes a list of file names as command line arguments and prints, on the terminal, the contents of those files that are readable and textual.

Program 1.21

```perl
#!/usr/bin/perl
#Checks to see which files given as command line argument are text files and
#readable. If a file is a text file and readable, it prints its
#contents with each line numbered. Otherwise, it prints a message
#saying the file is unreadable and/or not textual.
#A possible command-line argument is *.

for ($i=0; $i <= $#ARGV; $i++){
    $filename = $ARGV[$i];
    print "File #$i: The current file is $filename\n";

    #if the file is a text file and is readable, then continue
    if ((-T $filename) && (-r $filename)){
        print "File #$i: $filename is a readable text file";
        print "\n" x 5;
        $linecount = 0;

        open (READ, $filename);  #Print every line of the file to STDOUT
        while ($_ = <READ>){
            print "$linecount\t$_";
            $linecount++;
        }
        print "\n" x 5;
        sleep (5);
    }

    else{ #if the file doesn't satisfy the text and readability condition
        print "File #$i: $filename is  unreadable and/or not a text file";
        print "\n" x 5;
        sleep (1);
    }
}
```

The program loops through the special variable @ARGV that contains all the command line arguments. In each iteration, it prints the file name. It then checks to see if the current file is a text file and is readable. This test is accomplished using

```
((-T $filename) && (-r $filename))
```

as the condition in the `if` statement. The conjoining operator is written by writing two ampersands together (`&&`). Note that the total conjoined or anded condition must be included inside parentheses although the individual conditions do not have to be. So, the following condition would have been acceptable.

```
(-T $filename && -r $filename)
```

Inside the `if` block of statements, the program prints a statement saying the file satisfies the test conditions and initializes a line counter. Then, it opens the current file for reading. It enters a `while` loop and prints every line of the file preceded by a line count. Once the whole file is printed, it waits for five seconds. This is done by the `sleep` command.

```
sleep (5);
```

`sleep` takes one argument that is interpreted as time in seconds

If the file is not textual and/or not readable, the program prints a message saying so.

We can call this program with * as the only command line argument if we want to look at all the readable text files in our current directory.

1.14 Perl Switches

The first line of each of our Perl programs so far has been the line

```
#!/usr/bin/perl
```

This line is actually a comment, but it tells the underlying Unix system where the Perl interpreter is located. This line can be used in non-Unix systems as well without any problems although the line is treated in such systems as simply comment. However, it provides for easier portability across systems. Of course, we should specify where the Perl interpreter is located on the system. In this first line of comment, it is possible to specify arguments to modify the behavior of the Perl interpreter. These arguments are single letters and are preceded by the minus (-) sign. Such arguments are called *switches*. Perl has many command-line switches. We will look at just a few of them here.

The `-h` switch does not run the Perl program, but prints all the switches that are available. Similarly, the `-v` option, instead of running the program, tells us what version of Perl we are running. If we do not want to execute the program, but just check if it is syntactically correct, we use the `-c` switch. In such a case, the first line of the program should be

```
#!/usr/bin/perl -c
```

Another useful switch is the `-w` option. If we put

```
#!/usr/bin/perl -w
```

as the first comment of our Perl code, the Perl compiler gives us a lot more warning than usual. For example, it will complain about scalar variables that are used before initialization. It will complain about subroutines that are redefined, and about filehandles that are used improperly, e.g., a read filehandle being used for writing. There many other errors that Perl may otherwise ignore, but will check for us if we use the `-w` option.

If we are having logical problems running our code that is syntactically correct, we can use the `-d` switch to run the Perl code under the *debugger*.

```
#!/usr/bin/perl -d
```

The debugger will enable us to do many useful things to isolate our problem. We can single step through the program if we like. In single stepping, we run one instruction at a time. We can look for the presence of a certain pattern or regular expression in the code, both forwards and backwards from the current line of code. If we are inside a subroutine, we can force to return from the subroutine. We can set *breakpoints* anywhere in the code. A breakpoint is a point in the code where the program execution stops, waiting for us to restart. We can perform various exploratory actions at a breakpoint before proceeding again. We can examine the value of a variable at a certain point in execution. We can do a lot of other things in our attempt to find the problem or problems why our code is not giving the expected results.

A very interesting switch is the -n switch. It is there for the convenience of a programmer who wants to write a program that takes a number of files as command line argument and runs the program on all the files. We have seen how to do this in the section of pattern matching. We can include the program's code inside a while loop that has (<ARGV>) or equivalently (<>) as the conditional. Since this seems to happen quite frequently, Perl provides us with the -n switch. When this switch is used, Perl automatically wraps the code provided within a while loop with <ARGV> as the conditional.

So, when we run the following program with a command line argument * in Unix representing all files in the current directory, the program is run on all files.

Program 1.22

```
#!/usr/bin/perl -n

#Takes a list of files and prints all those lines in
#the files that contain the vowels in order.

if (/a.*e.*i.*o.*u/i){
    print;
}
```

The program is run as if the actual code is

```
    while (<>){
        if (/a.*e.*i.*o.*u/i){
            print;
        }
    }
```

We can use more than one switch at the same time. For example, if we want to use the -w, -n and -d switches at the same time, we can write

```
    #!/usr/bin/perl -w -n -d
```

where the three switches can be written in any order. Equivalently we can put two or more switches together and precede them by just one minus (-) sign. If we want to state all three switches together, we can write

```
    #!/usr/bin/perl -wnd
```

1.15   POD Documentation

Plain Old Documentation or POD is a way to document Perl programs. POD documentation allows multi-line comments to be inserted in Perl programs. In addition, POD documentation allows comments to be inserted that can be extracted to produce standalone documentation for Perl programs and modules. In fact, all documentation at the CPAN site, *www.cpan.org* is produced from POD documentation. Documentation on installed modules on a system can be obtained using the `perldoc` command. Such documentation is also produced using POD. The discussion in this section is with respect to the programs given in Section 6.12. Documentation can be obtained in HTML from a POD-documented script file by running the command `pod2html` with the script file name as argument. There are several Perl modules to process POD documentation as well. POD documents can be easily converted to text, PDF, LaTeX, and Unix man page formats.

Multiple line comments can be introduced in a Perl program by including them within =pod and =cut markers or tags. Each marker must start in the first column and must be followed by a blank line. To produce documentation in HTML form, we can use POD tags such as =head1, and =over. =head1 produces a first level HTML header, i.e., a header included within HTML tags `<H1>` and `</H1>` when pod2html is run on the program file. =over starts a list. =over takes an argument that indicates indentation of list items. =item is used to produce list items in HTML. =back is used to signal the end of a list started by =over. =cut is used to indicate the end of POD documentation. Every POD marker or tag must be followed by a blank line. POD documentation can occur anywhere in a program file. There are several other POD tags that we have not discussed here.

The first script given in Section 6.12 is called `archive.pl`. It is a regular Perl script with POD directives inside the code. To obtain HTML documentation for `archive.pl`, we run the following command.

```
%pod2html archive.pl > archive.html
```

Here, we redirect the HTML output of the pod2html command to the file `archive.html`. When viewed using a Web browser, the documentation looks like that in Figure 1.1.

1.16   Conclusions

This has been a long chapter inundating the reader with a large number of details. The intention has been to introduce to the reader as much of Perl's capabilities as possible. Once the reader has read this chapter, the reader should have a very good understanding of what Perl can do and is well on his or her way to mastering Perl. In fact, Perl can do a lot more, and the rest of the book will discuss many of these new topics. Note that some of the examples in this chapter were modeled after examples [KR98].

1.17   Exercises

1. *(Easy: System Exploration, Software Installation)*
   Check if you have Perl on your system. Learn to download Perl from the Internet if you do not have it. Perl comes pre-loaded on most Unix systems. If you do not have Perl, go to *www.cpan.org* and find Perl for your system. If you are on a Windows system, *www.activestate.com*'s *ActivePerl* is the best bet. If you are using a pre-OS X Macintosh, download and install MacPerl from *www.macperl.com*. Write down the exact location where Perl is loaded on your system. Also, write down where all the Perl modules are saved.

2. *(Easy: Web Surfing, Documentation Reading)*
   Learn to navigate *www.cpan.org*, The Comprehensive Perl Archive Network. Learn how to search for

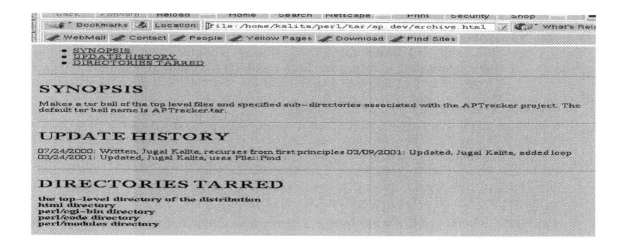

Figure 1.1: POD Documentation Generated by `pod2html`

documentation on core Perl to know more about built-in variables and functions, and other information about so-called core Perl, i.e., the language itself without any modules. Also, learn to search module documentation.

3. *(Easy: System Exploration, Documentation Reading)*
Learn to use `perldoc` to find documentation on Perl. `perldoc` should work if the Perl system has been installed properly. Examples of usage are given below.

```
%perldoc -f my
%perldoc -q quote
%perldoc CGI
```

The first uses the `-f` option to obtain information on a Perl function. The second uses the `-q` option to obtain information on a keyword. The third obtains information on Perl module.

4. *(Easy: System Exploration; Module Installation)*
Learn to install a Perl module. On a Unix system, learn to use

```
%perl -MCPAN -e shell
```

to search for installed modules, and modules available at *www.cpan.org* or many of its mirrors. On a Windows machine, if you installed ActivePerl from *www.activestate.com*, you should be able to use the command called ppm to do the same. ppm stands for Perl Package Manager.

5. *(Easy: Drill)*
Type in each of the programs in this chapter on your computer and see if it works. The programs as given in this chapter work on a Unix machine. If you have a PC or a Macintosh, find out what modifications, if any you need to make to make the programs work.

6. *(Easy: File Access)*
   Write two Perl scripts that do the following:

   (a) Write a program that keeps an integer in a file that you name. Every time you call the script, the counter is incremented by 1. This is a counter. The counter does not have a name.

   (b) Now, write a script that keeps track of as many counters as needed. The values are all kept in the same file. Each one is incremented by one when you call the script with the appropriate counter name as a command-line argument. Each counter has a name. A line of the file has the counter name followed by two colons and then the count. Assume the counter name has no space in it.

7. *(Medium: Regular Expressions, Pattern Matching)*
   Write a program that removes all comments from a Perl program. Given a program file, it creates a new file where the comments have been removed. It checks to see if the first line has a comment starting at column 1. It does not remove this comment. A comment starts with #. In general, a comment can start at any column. A comment starting with # continues till the end of the current line. The program name is given as a command-line argument. The modified program has the same name as the original, but is written to a different directory.

   Extend the program so that it removes comments from every Perl script file in a directory. Assume the name of a Perl script file ends in .pl or .pm. The program looks only at Perl scripts. The modified program have the same name as the original, and are written to a different directory that has been created earlier.

8. *(Medium: Regular Expressions, File Handling)*
   Write a program that takes a command-line argument that is a file name. It asks for the location of the Perl interpreter on your computer. It then looks at the file name, and if the name ends in .pl, checks to see if the first line is a comment specifying the location of the Perl interpreter. If not, it adds the comment as seen in programs in this book. The first comment line is not needed on PCs and older Macintosh operating systems. However, it is not a bad idea to place them if we want the programs to be portable across systems. Remember paths on PCs and older Macintoshes are written differently than on a Unix machine.

   Extend the program so that the comment line specifying the location of the interpreter is added to every file in a directory, if necessary.

9. *(Easy: Arithmetic)*
   Write a program that asks for someone's height in feet and inches, and converts it into meters. It writes the result in the form x.xxx where x before the decimal point is the meter value and the three xs after the decimal point are centimeters.

10. *(Easy: Arithmetic)*
    Write a program that takes four numbers as command-line arguments. The first two give a distance in feet and inches to start from. The last two give a distance value to end. The program converts distances in increments of one inch from feet and inches to meters and centimeters. It prints the results in a nice-looking tabular format to the screen, and to a file.

    Write versions of the program using `for` and `while`.

11. *(Easy: Subroutine, Arithmetic)*
    Write a subroutine that converts a length given in feet and inches into centimeter. Use this subroutine to write a modification of the previous program.

12. *(Medium to Hard: File Handling, Statistics, Graphics)*
    Write a program that prints the number of lines in a file whose name is given as command-line argument.

Extend the program so that it prints the name of every file in a directory and the number of lines in it. It prints the result to a file.

Extend the program further so that the results are are printed in the form a horizontal histogram. Scale the numbers so that the histogram lines fit the screen. Usee repetition of an alphabetic character, say x, to draw the lines.

13. *(Medium: File Handling, Statistics, Arrays)*
    Write a program that obtains the names of all files in a directory. It stores the names in an array. The program also has a second array. In the second array, it stores the number of lines in each of the files. The two arrays have 1-1 mapping. Finally, the program prints, in a nice tabular form, the name of the file and the number of lines in it. Print the result to a file.

14. *(Medium: File Handling, Statistics, Hashes)*
    Write a program that obtains the names of all files in a directory. This time, the program contains a hash. The keys in the hash are names of files in the directory. The values are the line counts. The program fills up this hash, and then prints the names of files and corresponding line counts in a nice tabular format to a file. It also summarizes with the total number of files in the directory, and the total space taken by all the files.

15. *(Easy: Command-line Arguments)*
    Write a program that takes a few command-line arguments. Some of the command-line arguments have the non-alphanumeric character @ in them. It prints out all command-line arguments that contain @ and ignores the others. It prints the output one per line.

16. *(Easy: File Test)*
    Write a program that prints out the names of all text files in a directory. The directory name is given as command-line argument.

17. *(Easy: File Test, Loop)*
    Write a program that looks at all files in the current directory. First, it prints a list of all the text files. Next, it prints a list of all the binary files. It prints a nice heading to each of the two sets of files. If there are no files in a certain set, it does not print the corresponding heading. Do not obtain the names of all files in a directory twice.

18. *(Easy: Debugger, System Exploration, Documentation Reading)*
    Learn how to use the debugger in Perl. Run all the programs given above through the debugger.

Chapter 2

On Expressions, Statements and Functions

In This Chapter

Writing a program is like writing a recipe for a dish or directions to a destination. A program is a sequence of well-thought out and precise steps to achieve a goal. When we write a recipe for an interesting dish or directions to a chosen location in English, there are two significant aspects to the writing: syntax and semantics. What we write must be syntactically correct, and also make sense at the same time. The syntax may be proper English or an abbreviated version or a dialect of it. The words are the basic components of the text we compose syntactically as well semantically. A sequence of words makes a phrase, and phrases make a sentence. If we have several sentences, they may be structured in the form a coherent paragraph. We may have several paragraphs even in a simple recipe or set of directions. Thus, words, phrases, sentences and paragraphs constitute increasingly more complex components of the text. At each stage, we choose the components carefully so that are syntactically well-formed and that they make sense, and that they are useful to expressing the objective at hand. Quite similarly, a program is composed of its constituents. The lowest level constituent that corresponds to words of English are the literals, the variables, and the operators. They are used to build expressions. One or more expressions make a statement. One or more expressions and statements make a compound statement.

A programming language's syntax and semantics are complex topics. In particular, among the many issues we need to understand when learning any programming language are the following.

- The *data types* the language supports and the values the data types can take. Examples of data types are numbers, characters, strings of characters, lists, etc. Depending on the data type, there are restrictions on the values. For example, a number can usually have digits and at most one decimal point in it. It is not usually correct to write a number to contain an alphabetic character such as a or u.

- The *variables*, how the names of variables are constructed, and where their values can be seen and used. Variables are like place holders. They are names of data elements. A variable may have been given a value by using an assignment statement or by other means, or may be unassigned at a certain point in time. Variables of different types have restrictions on how the names are spelled. For example, the name of a list variable in Perl always starts with the @ symbol. A variable can be global—seen and usable all through a program, or may be confined to a region of the program.

- The *operators* and *expressions* the language supports. An operator specifies a simple and common computation performed on one or more parameters or arguments. For example, + is the addition operator that takes two arguments that it adds. An expression is an operator with its arguments. For example, 2 + 2 is an expression.

- The *statements* that the programming language allows, and how control flows among the statements comprising a program as its is executed. A statement corresponds to either a simple or a complex sentence in English. A simple statement is composed of expressions and operators. A complex or compound statement corresponds to a full paragraph or even several contiguous paragraphs. Flow of control signifies in what order the statements of a program are executed.

- The type of *subroutines* the programming language allows, how parameters are passed to subroutines and how values are returned. A subroutine is a group of statements that are usually given a name so that they can be talked about by using the name. A subroutine is an abstraction that can stand for a simple or complex task.

- The subroutines, the variables and constants the language has been endowed with from start to provide basic vocabulary. Any self-respecting language provides some variable names, and possibly named constants that have been set aside by its designers. A modern programming language has a stash of pre-defined subroutines; these are called *built-in* functions.

- The *modules* or *packages* that are available to a programmer. A language such as Perl has hundreds of useful modules that have been contributed by developers from around the world. Perl is language that is freely available. Its developers give the language away. There are many benefactors who have written many extremely useful and complex subroutines and packaged them such that they are available as a group. These are called packages or modules. One of Perl's spectacular characteristics is the large number of valuable modules available for free downloading from the Internet.

Perl supports three primary data types: *scalars*, *lists* and *hashes*. More complex data types such as list of lists, hash of hashes, or list of list of hashes, can be created fairly easily. In this chapter, we mostly deal with scalars although lists and hashes are also gently introduced. The scalar data type in Perl refers to a data type that has only one component. This is in contrast to a multi-component data structure such as a list. The two primary scalar data types are *numbers* and *strings*. In Perl, the name of a variable indicates whether it refers to a scalar, a list or a hash. The name of a scalar variable starts with a $ symbol. The name of a list variable starts with an @ symbol. A hash is also called an associative array since it associates one or more keywords with corresponding values. The name of a hash variable in Perl starts with the % symbol. Thus, $a is the name of a scalar, @a is the name of a list variable, and %a is the name of a hash variable. These are three distinct variable names.

In Perl, we do not have to state the name of a variable before we use it. Stating the name of a variable before use is called *declaring a variable*. This is an absolute necessity in many programming languages including Java and C. This laxity in Perl is like Lisp. However, we can force a discipline on ourselves if we so desire, asking Perl to make certain that all variable names are declared before first usage. This is a good habit to inculcate because it assists in writing programs that can be easily debugged, maintained and reused. In Perl, a variable name that has not been declared is usually global and is available in the whole program. An explicitly declared variable can be made available only within a specific area of the program. Where a variable is visible and thus, usable is called the *scope* of a variable.

Perl has a large number of *operators* defined for its data types. An expression is usually composed of one or two parameters along with an operator. The parameters are called *operands*. An operator produces a result. Based on the kinds of operands an operator takes, and the value it returns, we have two important types of expressions, among others: *arithmetic expressions* and *logical expressions*. A statement is an expression with a side effect. A side effect may alter the value of one or more variables, or produce an output, or read an input value, among other possibilities. In this chapter, we discuss expressions and statements in Perl in great detail.

Let us consider a very simple program in Perl and illustrate the components.

Program 2.1

```
#!/usr/bin/perl
#file simplest.pl

use strict;
my ($a, $b, @c);
$a = 20;
$b = "Hello!";
@c = (1, 2, 3, 4);
print '$a = ', $a, "\n";
print "\$b = ", "$b\n";
print "\@c = @c\n";
```

Here, each line of the program is a statement. Each statement is simple. There are no compound statements in this program. The first statement is required in a Unix system, and specifies where the Perl interpreter is located. It must start on the first column. It does not really do anything since it starts with # and thus, is a comment. The second statement is also a comment. Unlike the first comment, it is not required. The statement starting with use is called a *pragma*. It asks Perl to use definitions from a pre-defined module called strict.pm that the system knows where to find. This module ensures that variables are declared before first use. There are two scalar variables: $a and $b, and list variable @c that are used in the program. my declares them to be available within the current program's file. The statement

```
$a = 20;
```

is an assignment statement. `$a`, the scalar variable name, and `20`, a numeric literal are simple expressions. `=` is the assignment operator. `$a = 20` is an expression that has the side effect of giving a value to `$a`. The use of `;` at the end makes it a statement. The second assignment statement uses the string literal `"Hello!"` that is doubly-quoted. The assignment statement

```
@c = (1, 2, 3, 4);
```

has the list variable `@c` on the left-hand side of the assignment operator, and a list literal on the right-hand side. The list literal is `(1, 2, 3, 4)` and is composed of a sequence of numeric literals separated from each other by the punctuation symbol `,`. The parentheses group them together into a whole. The `print` statement takes one or more arguments. Each argument is a string. If it is not, it is converted or coerced into one. For example, in the first `print` statement, `$a` is a number with the value `20`. It is coerced into the string `"20"` before printing. In the second `print` statement, there is a string argument `"$b\n"`. Here, `\n` is the escaped newline character. `$b` is a scalar variable written inside a doubly-quoted string, and hence its value is put in its place before printing. In other words, `$b`'s value is interpolated. The last `print` statement has one argument string: `"\@c = @c\n"`. This string contains `@c`, a list variable whose value is interpolated. The individual elements are printed separated by the default list element separator, an empty space. The whole program is an implicit block delimited by the boundaries of the physical file `simple.pl` in which it resides. The output of the program is given below.

```
$a = 20
$b = Hello!
@c = 1 2 3 4
```

2.1   Operators and Expressions in Perl

An expression is a program phrase that is evaluated to obtain a value [Wat90]. There are many kinds of expressions composed in various ways. The ones we discuss in this chapter are given below.

- Literals

- Variables

- Arithmetic Expressions

- Conditional or Logical Expressions

2.1.1   Literals

The simplest kind of expression is a *literal*. It is a fixed and manifest or explicit value of some kind. In other words, it is an instance of a data value that appears in a program. Since Perl has scalars, lists and hashes as primitive data types, literals can be of any of these types. We start with scalar data types because they are simple. Perl allows numbers, and strings as scalars. Perl does not distinguish between a number and a string and uses them interchangeably, coercing one into the other as need arises. Lists and hashes are discussed in Chapter 3.

A numeric literal in Perl can be an integer, a floating point number in decimal or scientific notation, a number in hexadecimal or octal notation. Examples of numeric literals are given in Table 2.1. The table shows that numeric literals can have a sign in front of them. Also, an underscore can be inserted to improve readability. Perl also accepts numeric values in binary, octal and hexadecimal bases. A binary literal must have `0b` in front. The `b` indicates it is binary. A binary number can have only 0s and 1s in it. An octal literal starts with `0` and contains digits between 0 and 7. A hexadecimal number has `0x` in front of it and contains digits in the range 0 through $9, a, b, c, d, e$ and f.

Literal	Description
1234	an integer
1.234	a floating point number
-1.234	a negative floating point number
1_000_005	One can use _ to improve readability
1.234E45	a floating point number in scientific notation
0x77b	a number in hexadecimal notation
01745	a number in octal notation
0b0011	a number in binary notation

Table 2.1: Numeric Literals in Perl

String literals can be singly-quoted or doubly-quoted. A string can have characters that are printable but that cannot be transcribed in a straight-forward manner. Such a character cannot be written as one single viewable character. A sequence of two or more characters is sometimes used to represent just one printable character like a linebreak or a tab space. The linebreak is represented as \n and a tab space as \t. These are called *escape sequences*. Singly-quoted string literals allow the use of only one back-slashed character or so-called escape sequence. It is \n. Thus,

```
'It is bright and sunny.\nMuch better than yesterday!'
```

is a singly-quoted string literal in Perl that contains a linebreak after the first sentence. Doubly quoted strings allow the use of \n as well as other escape sequences such as \t for a tab space. An example of a doubly-quoted string literal is the following.

```
"Name\tRank\nJ. Kalita\tAssociate Professor\n"
```

This doubly-quoted string contains two newline characters and two tab space characters. There is another major difference between a singly-quoted string and a doubly-quoted string. A singly-quoted string does not interpolate variables whereas a doubly-quoted string does. This means that if we have a scalar variable name or string variable name inside a doubly quoted string, the name is replaced by the value of the variable.

Assume that we have a scalar variable $friend with the value "Justin O'Malley", and have the following two strings—one singly-quoted and the other doubly-quoted.

```
'$friend lives in Colorado Springs\n'
"$friend lives in Colorado Springs\n"
```

If we now print the two string using Perl's print built-in function, we see the following, respectively.

```
$friend lives in Colorado Springs
Justin O'Malley lives in Colorado Springs
```

When the singly-quoted string is printed, $friend is printed literally. However, when we print the doubly-quoted string, $friend is replaced by its value Justin O'Malley. This is called *variable interpolation* inside a string. List variable names are interpolated as well inside a doubly-quoted string. However, hash variable names are not interpolated.

2.1.2 Assigning A Variable

A very useful operator is the assignment operator. It requires a variable name to the left and a value to the right. In Perl, a scalar variable's name starts with a $ in front. Thus, $temperature is a scalar variable name in Perl. So, is $friend. We can assign values to scalar variables using the *assignment operator* =.

```
$temperature = 30;
$friend = "Justin O'Malley"
```

The assignment operator associates a value with a variable. Thus, after these assignments, whenever we use $temperature in an expression or statement, its value is taken to be 30. Similarly, the value of $friend is taken to the string "Justin O'Malley". Perl makes no distinction whether a scalar is a string or a number. Thus, if we want, we can make the following assignments as well.

```
$temperature = "30 degrees Fahrenheit";
$temperature = '30F';
```

Here, $temperature is given a string value as opposed to the earlier assignment to a numeric value. Perl does not care whether the value given to a scalar is numeric or string. However, we should be careful whether a scalar is a string or a number. This is because the operators that we see a little later works differently with strings and integers. Perl coerces or converts a string to a number if needed and vice versa. Here x is the string repetition operator we see later.   Thus, when we write

```
01 x 20
```

Perl converts 01 into the string "01" and repeats it 20 times to form

```
0101010101010101010101010101010101010101
```

because x expects a string operand on the left. Here x is the string repetition operator we see in Section 2.1.3.2. Since it does not get a string, it converts the number to a string by putting quotes around it. Similarly, if we write

```
2 + "a23b4"
```

Perl converts the string "a23b4" to a number by trying to salvage something out of the string. It scans the string from left to right and picks out the first substring of contiguous digits and converts the substring to a number. Here, from the string "a23b4", it picks the substring "23" and uses it as the number 23. Thus, the result of the addition is 25.

2.1.3   Operators

An *operator* is usually thought of as denoting a function that takes one or two arguments. Operators can be *unary* or *binary*. An example of a unary operator is the - sign when it stands for negative. For example, -9 is negative 9. Another unary operators is not that stands for logical negation. Binary operators are written using the *infix notation* in Perl. In other words, the operator is written in between the two operands. For example, in 2 + 3, + is the binary addition operator written between two operands 2 and 3. There are many binary operators. A lot of them are from arithmetic that we know from school.

2.1.3.1   Arithmetic Operators and Expressions

An arithmetic expression consists of operators, operands, parentheses and function calls. We will discuss function calls in Chapter 12. An arithmetic operator takes one or two operands. The list of arithmetic operators provided by Perl is given Table 2.2.

Of the operators shown in Table 2.2, + and - can be unary as well as binary. When used as unary, they signify the sign of a number. The auto-increment and auto-decrement operators are unary as well. Every other operator listed in Table 2.2 is binary. The ++ and -- operators are discussed in Section 2.7. The range operator produces the list of numbers from a start point to an end point incremented by 1. Thus, 1..10 when used in a list context produces the following list.

Operators	Description
+	Unary positive
-	Unary negative
+	Addition
-	Subtraction
*	Multiplication
**	Exponentiation
/	Division
%	Modulus operation or remainder
++	Auto-increment
--	Auto-decrement
..	Range

Table 2.2: Arithmetic Operators

(1, 2, 3, 4, 5, 6, 7, 8, 9, 10)

The following program shows the use of several numeric operators.

Program 2.2
———————————————

```perl
#!/usr/bin/perl
#file simpleArith.pl

use strict;
my ($a, $b, @c);
$a = 20;
$b = 30.5;

print '$a + $b = ',    $a + $b, "\n";
print '$a - $b = ',    $a - $b, "\n";
print '$a * $b = ',    $a * $b, "\n";
print '$b / $a = ',    $b / $a, "\n";
print '$b ** $a = ',    $b ** $a, "\n";
print '$b % $a = ',    $b % $a, "\n";
@c = $a .. $b;
print '$a .. $b = ',    "@c", "\n";
```
———————————————

The program simply prints the obvious result of applying the arithmetic operators.   The output of this program is given below.

```
$a + $b = 50.5
$a - $b = -10.5
$a * $b = 610
$b / $a = 1.525
$b ** $a = 4.85284909839324e+29
$b % $a = 10
$a .. $b = 20 21 22 23 24 25 26 27 28 29 30
```

Operators	Description
.	Concatenation of two strings
x	Repetition of a string
. .	Range operator

Table 2.3: String Operators

The remainder operator prints its result in integer form after truncating any digits after the decimal point. The range operator produces a list @c that is printed later. When a list is input or typed, the elements are enclosed within parentheses. The parentheses are not printed when a list is output using the print state-ment. By default, when a list is interpolated inside a doubly-quoted string, any two contiguous elements are separated by a blank space. Otherwise, the output is self-explanatory.

2.1.3.2   String Operators

The string scalars have several operators. Three useful operators are listed in Table 2.3. All three operators shown in Table 2.3 are binary. Thus,

```
"Justin O'Malley,\t" . "Christopher Paul\n"
```

produces the single string

```
"Justin O'Malley,\tChristopher Paul\n"
```

by putting them together or concatenating them. The x operator takes a string operand on the left and causes the string to be repeated the number of times indicated by the second operand to produce a longer string. Thus,

```
"_" x 50
```

produces

----

by repeating the underscore 50 times. This is sometimes useful when we want to print nice-looking tables or lines indicating boundaries among parts of a large printed output. The range operator, used in the list context, produces a list of the intervening elements. Thus,

```
'a'..'f'
```

produces the list given below.

```
('a', 'b', 'c', 'd', 'e', 'f')
```

The following program shows the use of a few string operators.

Program 2.3

```perl
#!/usr/bin/perl
#file simpleString.pl

my ($justin, $chris, @list);
```

```
$justin = "Justin O'Malley, and ";
$chris = "Christopher Paul";

print '$justin . $chris = ', $justin . $chris, "\n";
print '$justin x 2 . $chris  = ', $justin x 2 . $chris, "\n";
@list = aa .. au;
print 'aa .. au = ', "@list\n";
```

The output of this program is very easy to understand and is given below. A long line of output has been broken into to two for printing purposes.

```
$justin . $chris = Justin O'Malley, and Christopher Paul
$justin x 2 . $chris  = Justin O'Malley, and Justin O'Malley, and
                                    Christopher Paul
aa .. au = aa ab ac ad ae af ag ah ai aj ak al am an ao ap aq ar as at au
```

The range operator produces all the intervening two-character strings between aa and au.

2.1.3.3   When is a scalar true or false?

A scalar can be a string, a number or a reference. A string scalar is considered false if it is the empty string or the string containing just a zero, i.e., the single character string "0". Thus, there are only two string values that are considered false. The empty string is written as "" or ''. Any other string is considered true. Thus, the string "000" or "0.00" are considered true because neither is exactly the string "0". To evaluate a numeric scalar for truth or falsehood, it is first coerced to a string. The numeric value 0 is always coerced into the single character "0", even if the numeric zero is written with more that one digits, with a decimal point, or as the result of an expression. Thus, the number 0.00 is converted to the string "0". Thus, 0 or 000 or 10-10 are considered false because when coerced into a string, they all become the single character string "0". Anything that is not considered false is considered true. Any undefined value is considered false. The rules are explicitly the following [WCS96]:

1. Any string is true except for "" and ''.

2. Any number is true except 0.

3. Any reference is true. We have not seen references yet. A reference refers to the address of a variable, data or a subroutine.

4. An undefined value is false. There are situations in which the value of a variable can be undefined.

Whether a scalar is evaluated true or false has important implications when writing statements that are executed conditionally, or that are executed iteratively based on whether a conditional expression is true or false.

2.1.3.4   Comparison or Relational Operators

An operator that compares two parameters is a relational operator. There are arithmetic relational operators and string relational operators. Perl's relational operators are listed in Table 2.4. The operators are obvious except the three-way comparison operators <=> and cmp. <=> takes two numeric operands and returns -1, 0 or 1, depending upon whether the first operand is less than, or equal to, or greater than the second operand. <=> is called the *ship operator* by some. cmp is similar except that it treats the two arguments given to it as string and compares them alphabetically and not as numbers.

The following program shows the use of a few numeric relational operators.

Description	Numeric	String
is equal to	==	eq
is not equal to	!=	ne
is less than	<	lt
is greater than	>	gt
is less than or equal to	<=	le
is greater than or equal to	>=	ge
three way comparison	<=>	cmp

Table 2.4: Numeric and String Comparison Operators

Program 2.4

```
#!/usr/bin/perl
#file arithCondition.pl

my ($a, $b, $result);
$a = 20;
$b = 30;
$result = $a > $b;
print "result = $result\n";
$result = $a < $b;
print "result = $result\n";
$result = $a == $b;
print "result = $result\n";
$result = $a <=> $b;
print "result = $result\n";
```

Relational operators are not usually used like the way they are in this program where we assign scalar variables with the result returned by them. Normally, relational expressions formed by using relational operators are used in conditional statements and loops to control the number of iterations. Here, we assign scalar variables to the result of applying relational operators in order to simply illustrate how they work. Consider the statement given below.

```
$result = $a > $b;
```

The value of $a is 20 and $b is 30. Therefore, $a > $b is false. The relational operator returns the empty string as the value of $a > $b. Thus, $result gets the value empty string. However, in the statement

```
$result = $a < $b;
```

$a < $b is true, and the < operator returns "1" in this case. Any non-zero string or any string that is not empty is considered true, but Perl decides to return "1" for simplicity. The <=> or the ship operator returns -1 because the first argument $a is less than the second argument $b.

The output of this program is given below.

```
result =
result = 1
result =
result = -1
```

Description	Operator
Logical negation	!
Logical negation (low precedence)	not
Logical conjunction	&&
Logical conjunction (low precedence)	and
Logical disjunction	||
Logical disjunction (low precedence)	or

Table 2.5: Logical Operators

The first result is printed as nothing because the value of $result is the empty string in this case. The following program shows the use of a few string relational operators: eq, lt and cmp.

Program 2.5

```perl
#!/usr/bin/perl
#file stringCond.pl
use strict;

my ($justin1, $justin2, $result);
$justin1 = "Justin O'Malley";
$justin2 = "Justin Paul";
$result = $justin1 eq $justin2;
print "result = $result\n";
$result = $justin1 lt $justin2;
print "result = $result\n";
$result = $justin1 cmp $justin2;
print "result = $result\n";
```

The output of running this program is given below.

```
result =
result = 1
result = -1
```

Once again, false is returned by an operator as an empty string and true as the string "1". cmp returns -1 since Justin O'Malley is alphabetically before Justin Paul.

2.1.3.5   Logical Operators

Logical operators allow one to combine results of several true or false results. The logical operators available in Perl are given in Table 2.5.

There are two versions to each operator. The difference between the two is that one version is of much lower precedence. The lower precedence operators are there so that individual complex expressions that are put together using the operators need not be parenthesized much. The following program shows the use of these logical operators.

Program 2.6

```perl
#!/usr/bin/perl
#file logical.pl

use strict;
my ($a, $b, $c, $d, $result);
$a = 20;
$b = 30;
$c = 40;
$d = 50;

$result = not ($a > $b);
print "result = $result\n";
$result = ! ($a > $b);
print "result = $result\n";
$result = ($a > $b) or ($b > $c) or ($c > $d);
print "result = $result\n";
$result = ($a > $b) || ($b > $c) || ($c > $d);
print "result = $result\n";
$result = ($b > $a) or ($c > $b) || ($d > $c);
print "result = $result\n";
$result = ($b > $a) and ($c > $b) and ($d > $c);
print "result = $result\n";
$result = ($b > $a) && ($c > $b) && ($d > $c);
print "result = $result\n";
$result = (($b > $a) or ($c > $b)) && ($d > $c);
print "result = $result\n";
```

The output of the program is given below.

```
result = 1
result = 1
result =
result =
result = 1
result = 1
result = 1
result = 1
```

Obviously or and || can be used interchangeably in many situations. So can and and &&. Also, not and ! can be used interchangeably. Once again, false is returned as an empty string while true is returned as the string "1". Obviously, the empty string is printed as nothing.

2.1.3.6 Operator Precedence

When we have have an expression with more than one operator, its semantics may not be easily understood unless we know the order of computation. For example, in the expression

```perl
$a + $b + $c + $d
```

we may like to know the order in which the computation is performed, whether from left to right, or right to left, or in some other order. In this case, we have the same operator + repeated several times. The +

---

operator is *left associative*.   This means that the leftmost + operator is evaluated first before the second + which is evaluated before the third +, etc. Therefore, the expression given is equivalent to the following fully parenthesized expression.

```
(($a + $b) + $c) + $d
```

Of course, we have assumed that all four variables are numeric scalars. There are some operators that are *right associative*, e.g., the exponentiation operator: **. So,

```
$a ** $b ** $c ** $d
```

actually means

```
$a ** ($b ** ($c ** $d))
```

where pairs of operators are parenthesized from the right end. Thus,

```
2 ** 3 ** 4
```

means $2^{(3^4)} = 2^{81} = 2417851639229258349412352$ and not $(2^3)^4 = 8^4 = 4096$. For every operator in Perl, the designers of the language specify its associative nature. The arithmetic operators follow normal rules of arithmetic, but with the others, the designers are more free to choose.

Associativity rules apply when we have the same operator repeated several times in an expression. We may have several distinct but contiguous operators as well, but these operators must have the same *precedence* for associative rules to apply. Each operator has a precedence number associated with it although it is not necessary to know what it is. Normally, it suffices to know how the operators are ranked considering precedence. When several operators appear in an expression, the highest precedence operator is performed first, next the operator with the second highest precedence, and so on. For example,

```
$a + $b ** $c
```

is evaluated as if it were parenthesized as

```
$a + ($b ** $c)
```

and not

```
($a + $b) ** $c
```

because * has higher priority than + and thus, * is evaluated first. All precedence and associative rules can be dispensed with if we explicitly and completely parenthesize an expression. The associativity and precedence of some common Perl operators are given in Table 2.6. One is advised to use parentheses liberally even if there is the slightest doubt in writing an expression. Operators within the same horizontal grouping in Table 2.6 have the same precedence. When several such operators are used in succession in an expression, associativity rules apply. Several operators are specified as non-associative. For such operators, exclusive parenthesization is necessary if used several times in an expression in succession. An example of a list operator or function is the command for opening files: open because it takes a list of two arguments: a filehandle name and a file name.

2.2   The Statement

The text of any program can be printed on a piece of paper. The text of the program can be read, studied, and analyzed. When we write a program or understand a program's text, we usually do so by imagining

Operator	Description	Associativity
++	auto-increment	non-associative
--	auto-decrement	non-associative
**	exponentiation	right
!	logical not	right
+	unary plus	right
-	unary minus	right
=~	matches	left
!~	does not match	left
*	multiplication	left
/	division	left
%	remainder	left
x	string repetition	left
+	addition	left
-	subtraction	left
.	string concatenation	left
&&	logical and	left
||	logical or	left
..	range	non-associative
=	assignment	right
+=	plus assignment	right
-=	minus assignment	right
*=	multiply assignment	right
.=	concatenate assignment	right
	list operators or functions	non-associative
not	logical not	right
and	logical and	left
or	logical or	left
xor	logical xor	left

Table 2.6: Associativity and Precedence of Operators

in our head the way the the program is executed. A program consists of a set of precisely written steps for the implementation of an objective. The steps are executed in a certain order. The execution order does not need to be the same as the textual order, i.e., the order in which the program is written or printed on paper. Only in an extremely simple program, the execution order of statements is sequential. In such a simple program, the steps in the program are executed one after the other. In most programs, the sequential and default execution order of statements is altered using what are called control structures.

Statements are of two types: *simple* and *compound*. The statements can be organized into related groups or compound statements, and the statements—simple or compound—can be executed in an order that is different from the print order. A block of statements is simply a sequence of statements separated by ; and enclosed within braces. A block is a compound statement. Blocks of statements can be repeatedly executed, or sometimes skipped based on the evaluation of conditional statements. Subroutines, which are an essential part of any realistic program, are usually placed at the end or the beginning of the program, but called or executed from almost anywhere in the program, including from the same or other subroutines.

An individual executable component or building block of a program is called a *statement*. A statement must be independently executable. Thus,

```
$temperature = 10;
```

or

```
$temperature = <STDIN>;
```

is a statement. In particular, each one of the above is an *assignment statement*. In each case, the statement can be executed independently. In Perl, each statement is ended by ;. The ; is like the period (.) in a declarative English sentence. A ; is necessary unless the statement is the last statement of a block, discussed later in this chapter. We emphasize the need for statements to be independently executable as opposed to expressions. An expression is executable as well, but is usually a part of statement. For example, in the statement

```
$celsius = 5/9 * ($fahrenheit - 32);
```

what we have to the right of the = sign, viz.,

```
5/9 * ($fahrenheit - 32)
```

is an expression and not a statement. It normally does not make sense to write it as an independent statement as given below.

```
5/9 * ($fahrenheit - 32);
```

Of course, if we write a statement as the one given immediately above, the computation is performed, but the result is wasted without the assignment. In particular, 5/9 * ($fahrenheit- 32) is an arithmetic expression.

2.2.1   Simple Statement

Statements are of two types: simple and compound, just like simple and compound sentences in a natural language such as English. The statement

```
$celsius = 5/9 * ($fahrenheit - 32);
```

is a simple statement. A simple statement can be considered an expression that has one or more side effects. In this case, the side effect is assigning a value to the variable $temperature.

A simple statement is like a simple sentence in English. A simple statement is independently executable. It is a minimal piece of independently executable code ended by a ;. Assignment statements are simple statements. Other examples of simple statements are subroutine calls, and returns from subroutines. We see them in Chapter 12 on functional programming. There is a class of simple statements that allow one to exit a program or a part of a program such as a loop, either normally or abnormally. These include statements such as die, warn, next, redo, and last. We see some of them later in this chapter.

2.2.2   Compound Statement

A compound statement is usually constructed by using special words called *keywords,* conditional or logical expressions and blocks. We see what blocks are shortly. Depending on the programming language under consideration, what is true and what is false may be interpreted differently. For example, the following is a compound statement called the if statement in Perl.

```
if ($temperature >= 100){
    print "It is scorching hot!\n";
}
```

It has the keyword if, a parenthesized logical expression, and a block delimited by { and } containing only one statement. if is a reserved keyword signaling a specific type of compound statement. There are many types of compound statements that Perl allows. Examples of compound statements are blocks, conditional statements, and loop or iterative statements.

2.3   A Block of Statements

A block of statements is simply a sequence of statements that are related in some fashion. There are two types of blocks: *implicit blocks* and *explicit blocks.* Usually implicit blocks are not really thought of as blocks although they are. In normal parlance, a block is usually an explicit block. An explicit block can be a compound statement itself. Usually though, an explicit block is used to construct compound statements with one or more keywords and expressions.

2.3.1   Implicit Block of Statements

Let us look at a very simple program that converts a temperature from Fahrenheit to Celsius.

 Program 2.7

```
#!/usr/bin/perl
#file temp1.pl

use strict vars;
my ($fahrenheit, $celsius);

$fahrenheit = 50;
$celsius = 5/9 * ($fahrenheit - 32);
printf "%4.0fF = %6.1fC\n", $fahrenheit, $celsius;
```

The program is simple. It has very few lines of code. A program is an implicit block. The statements in an implicit block are executed in sequence unless dictated otherwise by the code. An implicit block is usually delimited by the extent of a file. In this example, the whole program is in a file called `temp1.pl`, and everything contained in this file is an implicit block. Variables declared with my are available in the current block only, in this case, the extent of the file. The output of the program is given below.

```
50F =    10.0C
```

2.3.2   Explicit Block of Statements

A group of sequential statements can be explicitly structured to belong to a block. A block of statements is a sequence of statements enclosed inside braces. The { and } are the front-side and back-side fences delimiting the boundary of a block. We can modify the program given above to contain an explicit block. The modified program is given below.

Program 2.8

```
#!/usr/bin/perl
#file temp2.pl

use strict vars;
my ($fahrenheit, $celsius);

{
$fahrenheit = 50;
$celsius = 5/9 * ($fahrenheit - 32);
printf "%4.0fF = %6.1fC\n", $fahrenheit, $celsius;
}
```

Here, we see an explicit block of statements surrounded by { and }. From the point of usefulness, this block is not really necessary. It does not change the behavior of the program. The output is the same as that of the program in Section 2.3.1. The statements in the explicit block are executed one by one in sequential order, just like in an implicit block. Although we see only one explicit block in this program, the whole program itself is an implicit block although it is not delimited by { and } at the top and the bottom, respectively. Therefore, there are two blocks in this program, the outer implicit block containing the inner explicit one. The variables declared with my in the outer implicit block are available throughout the outer block or the file, including any contained blocks.

A block such as the one above is called a *bare block*. A bare block is considered a simple variant of more complex loop statements (a type of compound statement) that executes only once. Perl allows one to place names or labels before a loop statement. Thus, a bare block can be labeled. We discuss loop statements and labels later in the chapter. Bare blocks are usually not used unless they have a label and used as a variant of a loop statement using loop jump operators such as redo. We see jump operators later in the chapter.

2.4   The Conditional Statement

A conditional statement contains some reserved keywords, one or more conditional expressions, and one or more blocks of statements. Depending on which conditional expression evaluates to true, a block of statements is executed. If there are multiple blocks, all other blocks of statements are ignored. There are two types of conditional statements in Perl: the if statement and the unless statement.

2.4.1   The `if` statement

The `if` statement is a compound statement that has several forms. A simple `if` statement has the syntax given below.

`if` (*conditional*) *block*

Here, `if` is a reserved keyword and must be written literally. The *conditional* is an expression that evaluates to true or false. *block* is an explicit block enclosed within { and }. The block of statements is executed if the conditional evaluates to true, i.e., a non-false value. If the conditional evaluates to false, the block is not executed. In such a case, an `if` statement does nothing. Usually, an `if` statement is written with the `if` and the conditional in one line and the block of statements indented a little more to the right than the `if`. Each statement in the block is indented to the same level.

Below, we write a few programs that convert temperatures from one scale to another. They illustrate the use of variants of the `if` statement. In the first program, we assume that we are given the temperature as a string that contains a number followed by a letter. The letter is an F signifying that the temperature is in Fahrenheit and needs to be converted to Celsius. For example, an acceptable input is the string 30F whereas the string 30 or 30C is unacceptable. The program reads the temperature from the command line. The program is given below.

Program 2.9

```perl
#!/usr/bin/perl
#file temp3.pl

use strict vars;
my ($temperature, $fahrenheit, $celsius);

print "Please enter a temperature to convert >> ";
$temperature = <STDIN>;
chomp ($temperature);

if ($temperature =~ /F$/){
        $celsius = 5/9 * ($temperature - 32);
        printf "%4.0fF = %6.1fC\n", $temperature, $celsius;
}
```

The program prompts the user to enter a temperature. It removes the newline character that comes with the input by using `chomp`. The program checks if the temperature value given ends with an F by using a pattern matching expression inside the conditional of the the `if` statement. We discuss regular expressions and pattern matching in detail in Chapter 4. The conditional is repeated below.

`$temperature =~ /F$/`

The conditional is satisfied if at the very end of the value of `$temperature`, the character F occurs. The pattern is delimited by / at the two ends. Therefore, the actual pattern is F$. The character F in the pattern requires the character to be literally present in the string `$temperature`, the target of the comparison operator =~. The $ sign following F indicates that the target string must terminate after F matches. In other words, the value of `$temperature` must be a string that ends with F. What occurs in the string before the end does not matter.

An interaction with the program is given below.

```
Please enter a temperature to convert >> 20F
  20F =    -6.7C
```

The user enters 20F and the program prints the converted temperature as shown above. Two other interactions are given below.

```
%temp3.pl
Please enter a temperature to convert >> 20C
```

```
%temp3.pl
Please enter a temperature to convert >> 20
```

If the temperature does not have F at the end, the program does not do anything at all.

Now, we look at the second variant of the if statement.

if   (*conditional*) *block*
else *else-block*

Usually, when one writes such a statement, the if and the else are indented to the same level. Each statement in the if block and the else block are usually indented a little more to the right. Just like if, else is also a reserved keyword. In other words, programmers cannot use else as a variable name, for example. The syntax requires the if keyword to be followed by a block of statements as we have seen already. Immediately following the block, the else keyword appears followed by a second block of statements. The first block of statements is executed if the conditional of the if is satisfied. If the if's conditional is satisfied, the *else-block* is completely ignored. The second block of statements is executed if the conditional of the if is not satisfied. We have a version of the program given above that uses the if and else combination.

Program 2.10

```perl
#!/usr/bin/perl
#file temp4.pl

use strict vars;
my ($temperature, $fahrenheit, $celsius);

print "Please enter a temperature to convert >> ";
$temperature = <STDIN>;
chomp ($temperature);

if ($temperature =~ /F$/){
        $celsius = 5/9 * ($temperature - 32);
        printf "%4.0fF = %6.1fC\n", $temperature, $celsius;
}
else{
        print "The temperature must end with an F\n";
}
```

Four runs of this program are given below.

```
% temp4.pl
```

```
Please enter a temperature to convert >> 30F
  30F =    -1.1C

%temp4.pl
Please enter a temperature to convert >> 30
The temperature must end with an F

%temp4.pl
Please enter a temperature to convert >> 30C
The temperature must end with an F

%temp4.pl
Please enter a temperature to convert >>
The temperature must end with an F
```

The first run converts 30F to centigrade and prints the result of the conversion. In the second run, the input given is 30 without a trailing F and the program does not do temperature conversion, but following the code in the else block tells us what is wrong. The same holds for the third input. Here there is a trailing C and not a trailing F as required. In the fourth run, the user did not give any input number at all. Even then, the program comes back with the same response.

The behavior of the program given immediately above can be improved if we can distinguish the three cases regarding the input: when it is not provided, when it has a value that ends in F, when it has a value that does not end in F. The following program is able to distinguish between the situation when an input is provided by the user and when the user does not give an input. It uses the third incarnation of the if statement.

```
if      (conditional0)  block
elsif   (conditional1)  elsif-block-1

        .

        .

        .

elsif   (conditionaln)  elsif-block-n
else    else-block
```

There can be more than one elsif with associated statement blocks. The if's conditional is always tested first. If it is satisfied, the corresponding block is executed. The rest of the elsifs and the else are ignored. If the conditional of the if is false, the conditional of the first elsif is evaluated. If it is satisfied, the corresponding block is executed. Everything else that follows is ignored. In general, the block following the first elsif whose conditional is satisfied is executed. The following elsifs and the else is ignored. If the conditional of neither the if nor any of the elsifs is satisfied, the block corresponding to the else is executed.

Program 2.11

```
#!/usr/bin/perl
#file temp5.pl

use strict vars;
my ($temperature, $fahrenheit, $celsius);

print "Please enter a temperature to convert >> ";
$temperature = <STDIN>;
```

```
chomp ($temperature);

if ($temperature =~ /^$/){
      print "You must provide some input\n";
      }
elsif ($temperature =~ /^(.+)F$/){
      $temperature = $1;
      $celsius = 5/9 * ($temperature - 32);
      printf "%4.0fF = %6.1fC\n", $temperature, $celsius;
      }
else {
      print "The input must end in F\n";
}
```

In particular, the structure of this program is given below. The program has only one `elsif` keyword and its corresponding block.

```
if    (conditional1) { block1 }
elsif (conditional2) { block2 }
else  { block1 }
```

The conditional of the `if` is given as the following.

```
($temperature =~ /^$/)
```

It is a pattern match expression. The target of the pattern match expression is the current value of the variable `$temperature`. The pattern or regular expression being looked for in the target string is `/^$/`. The actual regular expression is `^$`. `^` is a so-called regular expression *anchor* that indicates that the target string must start at this point in the match. The `$` is also an anchor indicating that the target string must end at this point. There is nothing in the regular expression between the two anchors indicating that the target string is empty. Thus, the conditional of the `if` is satisfied if the string input at the keyboard by the user is empty. In such a case, the corresponding block is executed. This block contains only one statement that reminds the user that he or she should have provide some input.

The conditional of the `elsif` is given below.

```
($temperature =~ /^(.+)F$/)
```

The regular expression being looked for is `/^(.+)F$/`. The `^` indicates that what follows in the regular expression occurs at the beginning of the target string. What follows is `(.+)`. The parentheses group parts of a regular expression. Here, the dot indicates that any character, except for the newline character (`\n`) can match. The `+` following the `.` indicates that the dot pattern is repeated one or more times. Thus, `+` is the *multiplier* for the dot pattern. In other words, `(.+)` requires Perl to match a sequence of one or more non-`\n` characters at the beginning of the target string `$temperature`. The `F$` at the end of the regular expression requires the target string to end in the literal character `F`. Thus, the whole regular expression `^(.+)F$` requires the presence of one or more non-`\n` characters in the target string followed by `F`. This is what we want the input string typed by the user to look like. Therefore, if the user types in `30F`, the `30` matches `(.+)`, and the `F` in `30F` matches the `F` in `^(.+)F$`. Thus, the conditional of the `elsif` is satisfied if the user types something like `30F` or `30.2F`.

However, there is one additional aspect of parenthesization in a regular expression we should know. There is a significant and useful side-effect to parenthesization. We may or may not avail ourselves of this side-effect in a program. The presence of one or more parenthesized sub-expressions triggers Perl to remember what characters in the target string matches the parenthesized sub-expressions in the regular expression. Here, we have only one parenthesized sub-expression, viz., (.+). This sub-expression matches 30 if the input string is 30F. The substring 30 that matches is remembered by Perl as the value of the special variable $1. It is called $1 because it corresponds to the first parenthesized sub-expression in the regular expression. If there were several such parenthesized sub-expressions, the corresponding remembered values will be in terms of special variables $1, $2, $3, etc. Inside the block corresponding to the elsif, we have the following assignment.

```
$temperature = $1;
```

This assignment sets the new value of $temperature to the value extracted from the beginning part of the old value of $temperature.

No conditional is specified with the keyword else. It is followed by a block of statements that are executed when the conditional of the if and the conditional of the elsif are not satisfied. Thus, the block specified with elsif is the fallback block to be executed.

The output of this program for four possible inputs is given below. Only the last one provides the input as required.

```
%temp5.pl
Please enter a temperature to convert >>
You must provide some input
%temp5.pl
Please enter a temperature to convert >> 30
The input must end in F
%temp5.pl
Please enter a temperature to convert >> 30c
The input must end in F
%temp5.pl
Please enter a temperature to convert >> 30F
   30F =    -1.1C
```

2.4.2   The unless Statement

Perl also has an unless statement which is akin to the if statement. However, the conditional of the unless statement is evaluated as negated. For example, we can write a small program that prints if an input temperature is above the boiling point of water using an if statement.

Program 2.12

```perl
#!/usr/bin/perl
#file if10.pl

use strict;

print "Please enter a temperature in Fahrenheit>> ";
my $temperature = <STDIN>;
chomp $temperature;

if ($temperature > 212){
    print "$temperature F is above the boiling point of water\n";
}
```

The exact same program can be written using the `unless` statement. To do so, we have to logically invert the conditional of the `if` statement. The program is given below.

Program 2.13

```perl
#!/usr/bin/perl
#file unless1.pl

use strict;

print "Please enter a temperature in Fahrenheit>> ";
my $temperature = <STDIN>;
chomp $temperature;

unless ($temperature <= 212){
    print "$temperature F is above the boiling point of water\n";
  }
```

A couple of interactions with this program are given below.

```
%unless1.pl
Please enter a temperature in Fahrenheit>> 300
300 F is above the boiling point of water

%unless1.pl
Please enter a temperature in Fahrenheit>> 20
```

The program does not do anything at all if the value entered by the user in response to the program's prompt is not above 212 degrees F. It comes back empty-handed in such a situation.

The `unless` statement has a second version with an `else`. It works similarly to the `if-else` combination we have seen earlier. It does not have a third version with `elsif`s. A program that illustrates the second version is given below.

Program 2.14

```perl
#!/usr/bin/perl
#file unless2.pl

use strict;

print "Please enter a temperature in Fahrenheit>> ";
my $temperature = <STDIN>;
chomp $temperature;

unless ($temperature <= 212){
    print "$temperature F is above the boiling point of water\n";
  }
  else{
    print "$temperature F is below the boiling point of water\n";
  }
```

Two interactions with this program are given below.

```
% unless2.pl
Please enter a temperature in Fahrenheit>> 300
300 F is above the boiling point of water

%unless2.pl
Please enter a temperature in Fahrenheit>> 0
0 F is below the boiling point of water
```

2.4.3   The `defined` and `undef` Functions: Uninitialized Scalars

Before we proceed any further, we look at the function that helps us determine if a scalar variable has been assigned a value either by assignment statement or by other means such as Perl itself during some computation it is asked to do. The function is `defined`. As we know, scalar variables in Perl can be of three different subtypes: numbers, strings and references. A scalar variable that has not been initialized has an undefined value. This undefined value translates to zero when used in a numeric context and to a string of length zero when used in a string context.

We can test to see if a scalar has a value using `defined`. In the program below, we have declared two scalar variables using `my`. `$aScalar` is uninitialized whereas `$bScalar` has been initialized to the empty string. The two `if` statements test to see if the scalar has been defined, and print appropriate diagnostics.

Program 2.15

```perl
#!/usr/bin/perl

use strict;
my ($aScalar, $bScalar);
$bScalar = "";

if (defined ($aScalar)){
    print "\$aScalar is defined with an empty string as its value\n";
}
else{
    print "\$aScalar has no defined value\n";
}

if (defined ($bScalar)){
    print "\$bScalar is defined with an empty string as its value\n";
}
else{
    print "\$bScalar has no defined value\n";
}
```

In this case, the program prints the following.

```
$aScalar has no defined value
$bScalar is defined with an empty string as its value
```

Some operations return the undefined value under exceptional conditions such as end of file, system error, when assigning an uninitialized variable and such, and it may be important in some situations to test whether a scalar has an initialized value. In particular, `defined` allows us to distinguish between two cases in the case of strings: a string variable that has undefined null value, and a string variable that has defined null value. This is what we tested in the simple script given above.

An existing value can be undefined using the built-in function `undef`. `undef` optionally takes a scalar variable (starting with $), a list variable (starting with @), or a hash variable (starting with %), and makes its value undefined. It returns the undefined value. `undef` is a unary operator.

2.5 Iterative Statements or Loop Statements

The concept of looping has been essential to programming starting at the time when all programming was done at the machine language level. All higher-level languages have one or more loop statements. Some programming language experts distinguish between two types of iterative statements:

- definite iteration, and

- indefinite iteration.

In the case of indefinite iteration statements, the number of iterations is not known in advance, but is determined dynamically based on evaluation of a conditional expression either before or after every iteration. The `while` statement is an example of indefinite iteration. In the case of definite iteration, the number of iterations is not known explicitly by the programmer in advance. Examples of definite iterative statements in Perl are the `for` and `foreach` statements.

2.5.1 Indefinite Iteration

There are two indefinite iteration statements in Perl. They are `while` and `until`.

2.5.1.1 The `while` Statement

The general syntax of the `while` statement is given below.

while (*conditional*) *block*

`while` is a reserved keyword that a programmer is not allowed to use. The conditional evaluates to true or false. The following program is repeated from Section 1.4.1 where it is first presented.

Program 2.16

```perl
#!/usr/bin/perl
#file fahrenheit.pl

use strict vars;
my ($lower, $upper, $step, $fahrenheit, $celsius);

#print Fahrenheit-Celsius table for 0, 20, ..., 300 degrees Fahrenheit

$lower = 0;    #lower limit of temperature table
$upper = 300; #upper limit
```

```
$step = 20;     #step size

$fahrenheit = $lower;
                #loop through the Fahrenheit values
while ($fahrenheit <= $upper){
    $celsius = 5/9 * ($fahrenheit - 32);
    printf "%4.0f %6.1f\n", $fahrenheit, $celsius;
    $fahrenheit = $fahrenheit + $step;
}
```

In this program, three variables, $lower, $upper and $step, are given numeric values. Then, a variable $fahrenheit is assigned the initial value of $lower. $fahrenheit is the variable that determines the number of iterations of the loop. Its value changes during the iteration of the loop and the current value determines if the loop's body or the block of statements is executed another time. In this particular case, the conditional is given as follows.

```
($fahrenheit <= $upper)
```

$upper has a fixed value of 300 during the course of the program. The initial value of $fahrenheit is 0 before the while statement is executed.

There is a block of statements associated with the while keyword. This block of statements is executed as long as the conditional is satisfied. In the first iteration, the conditional is evaluated as 0 <= 300. This conditional returns true. Therefore, the body of the while is executed at least once. Note that if the conditional is not satisfied initially, the body of the while loop is not executed even once. In such a case, the program control flows to the statement, if any, after the while loop. Otherwise, the program terminates. Inside the block that is the body of the loop, the value of $fahrenheit is converted to Celsius degrees and the two temperatures printed. The last statement inside the block changes the current value of the determining variable $fahrenheit by adding $step to it.

```
    $fahrenheit = $fahrenheit + $step;
```

Thus, at the end of the block at the end of the first iteration, the value of $fahrenheit is updated and becomes 20.

In a while loop, the program control always moves to the top of the loop after the block of statements is executed once. The conditional of the while loop is evaluated again with the updated values of the variable. In this particular case, the conditional is evaluated as 20 <= 300. This still returns true. Thus, the block is executed a second time. In this fashion, repeated evaluation of the loop continues with the responsible loop variable updated at the end of each iteration. Note that there may be several variables whose values are updated in each iteration. The values do not need to be necessarily updated at the end of each iteration, but anywhere inside the block is acceptable. In this specific case, the iteration continues till the value of $fahrenheit becomes 300. This is the last iteration of the loop. At the end of this iteration, the value of $fahrenheit becomes 320 and the conditional is evaluated as 320 <= 300. This returns false and the control of the program moves to the statement, if any, below the while loop. If there is no such statement, the program ends.

A very important point must be noted when we write while loops. We must usually choose one or more variables as loop control variables. These variables must be given initial values. The conditional of the while loop must be written carefully noting that the loop may not be executed even once if the conditional is not satisfied at the outset. Inside the loop's body, the values of the loop control variables must be updated. If the values are not updated, it is quite likely that the execution of the loop will continue for ever. This is usually an error condition that is called the *infinite loop* error. The problem occurs frequently not only with beginning programmers, but with experienced programmers as well. Everyone writes an infinite loop once in a while! Thus, when writing a loop, whether it is a `while` loop or anything else, utmost caution should be exercised to ensure that the loop's execution actually terminates.

Sometimes it is necessary to write a `while` loop that has a conditional that always evaluates to true. In such situations, usually the conditional is given simply as the number 1. The following program is a variation of the previous program that uses this second way of writing a `while` loop.

Program 2.17

```
#!/usr/bin/perl
#file while1-1.pl

use strict vars;
my ($lower, $upper, $step, $fahrenheit, $celsius);

#print Fahrenheit-Celsius table for 0, 20, ..., 300 degrees Fahrenheit
$lower = 0;    #lower limit of temperature table
$upper = 300; #upper limit
$step = 20;    #step size

$fahrenheit = $lower;
                #loop through the Fahrenheit values
while (1){
    $celsius = 5/9 * ($fahrenheit - 32);
    printf "%4.0f %6.1f\n", $fahrenheit, $celsius;
    $fahrenheit = $fahrenheit + $step;
    if ($fahrenheit > $upper){last;}
}
```

In this case, it is not really necessary and it may not be a good idea to write the program in this fashion. We do it to illustrate that the two versions of the program are semantically the same. A `while` loop written in this fashion **must be explicitly exited**. The exiting in this program is done by the following statement.

```
    if ($fahrenheit > $upper){last;}
```

The `last` statement used inside the loop's body moves the control to *after* the last statement in the block. The control is not sent up to the top of the loop for another evaluation of the conditional and possible repetition of the loop body's execution. This effectively means that the execution of the loop terminates. Thus, `last` is an operator used to alter the normal flow of control in a loop. The normal flow of control in the current loop dictates the program control to move to the top of the block after it is executed once, and do this for ever. `last` changes the location where flow of control moves if the conditional is satisfied. `last` works with loop statements such as `while`. Here, the loop does not have a name or a label. In such a case, `last` takes control to the statement immediately following the } that closes the block's statements. If there are several blocks enclosed one within the other, `last` exits the innermost block in which it occurs if none of the blocks is labeled. If any of the blocks has an explicit name or label, `last` can be given the label of the block to exit. If `last` is given a block's label, it can exit blocks which are not necessarily the innermost. Thus, to exit out of a non-innermost enclosing block, labels on loops are essential. Some looping blocks have what is called a `continue` block. The `last` statement prohibits the program from executing the `continue` block associated with the looping block being exited or broken out of.

The following is another simple program that prints the current time on the screen. It does so continuously till the program is killed by typing an interrupt signal such as Control-C in Unix, or the window in which the program is running is killed.

Program 2.18

```perl
#!/usr/bin/perl
#while1.pl
use strict;
my $time;

while (1){
  $time = localtime ();
  print "$time\n";
  sleep 1;
}
```

Once again, one needs to be careful in that a program such as this one is in an infinite loop and thus, may eat up system resources that can be used elsewhere. In this program, we make the program sleep for one second before printing the time again. localtime is a built-in Perl function that gives the current local time. The output of this program looks like the following, but continues for ever.

```
Thu Jun   7 03:50:28 2001
Thu Jun   7 03:50:29 2001
Thu Jun   7 03:50:30 2001
Thu Jun   7 03:50:31 2001
Thu Jun   7 03:50:32 2001
Thu Jun   7 03:50:33 2001
Thu Jun   7 03:50:34 2001
Thu Jun   7 03:50:35 2001
Thu Jun   7 03:50:36 2001
Thu Jun   7 03:50:37 2001
Thu Jun   7 03:50:38 2001
Thu Jun   7 03:50:39 2001
Thu Jun   7 03:50:40 2001
```

Notice that the time printed by the program may not move ahead by an exact second from one iteration to another. This may be for various reasons such as the amount of time taken by the rest of the program, and what else is running on the machine, and whether it is a machine with one user or multiple users.

Before we finish our discussion of while, we discuss a common use of the while loop which is to read lines from a file or a set of files. The following program repeated from Section 1.6.1 show such use.

Program 2.19

```perl
#!/usr/bin/perl
#file name: read-file.pl
use strict;
my ($filename, $linecount);

print "Please give me a file name >> ";
$filename = <STDIN>;
chomp ($filename);

$linecount = 1;
```

```
print "Printing file $filename\n\n";

open (INFILE, $filename);
while (<INFILE>){
    print "$linecount\t$_";
    $linecount++;
    }
```

The program asks for a file name from the user. It then opens the file using the filehandle INFILE. The conditional of the while loop that follows is given as

```
(<INFILE>)
```

that uses the angle operator < > to read a line from a file. The special variable $_ is assigned the line read. $_ is the variable implicitly used in this and many other situations in Perl. Inside the body of the while loop, the line just read is printed. A line number is printed in the front of the line. An interaction with this program is given in Section 1.6.1.

The crucial point to note in this case is that when the file is finished reading, the < > operator returns undef as the value. undef evaluates to false in a scalar context. Thus, the while loop is exited after a file is read completely.

2.5.1.2   The until Statement

The until statement is similar to the while statement except that the meaning of the conditional is reversed. The conditional is still evaluated before the loop is executed. The following is a rewrite of the temperature conversion program given earlier in Section 2.5.1.1. It uses an until statement instead of while.

Program 2.20

```
#!/usr/bin/perl
#file until1.pl

use strict vars;
my ($lower, $upper, $step, $fahrenheit, $celsius);

#print Fahrenheit-Celsius table for 0, 20, ..., 300 degrees Fahrenheit

$lower = 0;    #lower limit of temperature table
$upper = 300; #upper limit
$step = 20;    #step size

$fahrenheit = $lower;
              #loop through the Fahrenheit values
until ($fahrenheit > $upper){
    $celsius = 5/9 * ($fahrenheit - 32);
    printf "%4.0f %6.1f\n", $fahrenheit, $celsius;
    $fahrenheit = $fahrenheit + $step;
}
```

Notice that the conditional of the `while` loop in Section 2.5.1.1 is

```
($fahrenheit <=upper)
```

whereas the conditional of the `until` is

```
($fahrenheit > $upper).
```

Although the conditional specifies a termination condition, it is evaluated before the loop is executed. Thus, if the conditional evaluates to false to begin with, the loop is not executed even once.

2.5.1.3   Simulating A `while` Loop with a Bare Block

We can simulate how a `while` loop works with a bare block if we know how to alter the control flows in a loop. In a loop such as `while` or `until`, the conditional is evaluated and based on its value, the loop is either executed or control falls to the statement following the loop. However, this normal course of flow of control can be altered using the so-called loop control or jump operators: `last`, `next` and `redo`. We have seen how `last` works already. We see the use of `redo` in addition to `last` in the example that follows. The block used here also has a label although it is not necessary. In Perl, a bare block is considered a loop that is executed just once, and thus, can be labeled. Although a bare block is normally executed only once, we execute it like a `while` loop below.

In this program, the bare block is given a label or name called CONVERT. A label must be followed by a colon. The first statement inside the block tests to see if the loop should be executed one more time or exited. If $fahrenheit, the loop control variable, crosses the upper limit given by $upper, the loop is exited.

```
last CONVERT;
```

takes control to just after the closing brace of the loop, thus killing the loop's activities. Following this loop control statement, the program converts the current Fahrenheit temperature to Celsius, prints the results and updates it by adding $step to it. The last statement of the loop tests the updated value of $fahrenheit to see if the loop needs to be executed again. In this case, if $fahrenheit is less than or equal to $upper, the program is instructed to execute the loop named CONVERT again. The `redo` statement takes control to the top of the loop and re-executes it without evaluating the conditional of the loop, if any. In this case, there is no conditional, and thus `redo` causes another iteration of the loop. This continues till the iterations are stopped by the exit from the loop, caused by `last`. The `redo` command prohibits the program from executing the corresponding `continue` block if any.

The last loop control command is `next`. `next` stops executing the current iteration of the loop wherever it is, executes the corresponding `continue` block if any. It then evaluates the conditional to decide if the loop should be executed again or not.

Program 2.21

```
#!/usr/bin/perl
#file while10.pl

use strict vars;
my ($lower, $upper, $step, $fahrenheit, $celsius);

#print Fahrenheit-Celsius table for 0, 20, ..., 300 degrees Fahrenheit
```

```
$lower = 0;    #lower limit of temperature table
$upper = 300;  #upper limit
$step = 20;    #step size

$fahrenheit = $lower;
            #loop through the Fahrenheit values

CONVERT:
{    if ($fahrenheit >  $upper){last CONVERT;}
     $celsius = 5/9 * ($fahrenheit - 32);
     printf "%4.0f %6.1f\n", $fahrenheit, $celsius;
     $fahrenheit = $fahrenheit + $step;
     if ($fahrenheit <=  $upper){redo  CONVERT;}
}
```

2.5.2 Definite Iteration

In definite iteration, the number of iterations is determined in advance. We may not always have the number of iterations on our finger tips, but if we want to compute the exact number, we can easily do so. Definite iteration also uses of a *loop control variable* which is connected to the loop in a fashion much more tightly than indefinite iteration. The loop body is executed with the control variable taking each of a pre-determined sequence of values. The values may be arithmetic values that are incremented or decremented in each step. They may also be the individual values from a pre-determined sequence such as a list, or a set such as all the keys of a hash. The sequence of values that the loop control variable takes is sometimes called the *control sequence*. Perl has two such constructs: for and foreach.

2.5.2.1 The for Statement

The for loop or a cousin of it appears in all high level programming languages. The for loop is controlled by a loop control variable. The variable is given an initial value. How the value of this variable is updated after every iteration is explicitly given. In addition, a conditional expression is provided to determine if the iterations should go on or halt. Perl does not require us to specify any of these three, but they normally are given explicitly. If any one of them is not specified, the programmer must assume complete responsibility to ensure that the loop does not continue indefinitely unless there an explicit and rare need for infinite loop execution.

The general syntax of the for loop is given below.

for (*initialization* ; *termination-condition* ; *update*) *block*

The for keyword is necessary. The initialization of the loop control variable, the termination condition, and the manner in which it is updated after every iteration is provided within parentheses following the keyword for. The block of statements is executed as many times as dictated by the loop control variable's changing value through the life of the loop. The termination condition must essentially test the value of the loop control variable in some fashion. It does not have to be a simple equality or inequality test, but may be fairly complicated involving more complex expressions and function calls. The loop control variable does not have to an arithmetic scalar.

The following program is repeated here from Section 1.4.2

Program 2.22

```
#!/usr/bin/perl
#file farenheit1.pl

#print Fahrenheit-Celsius table for 0, 20, ..., 300 degrees Fahrenheit

use strict 'vars';
my $fahrenheit;
my $celsius;

            #loop through the Fahrenheit values
for ($fahrenheit = 0; $fahrenheit <= 300; $fahrenheit = $fahrenheit+20){
    $celsius = 5/9 * ($fahrenheit - 32);
    printf "%4.0f %6.1f\n", $fahrenheit, $celsius;
}
```

In this program, the loop control variable is $fahrenheit. Its initial value is 0 and is updated by adding 20 after each iteration. The loop continues as long as $fahrenheit's value is 300 or less. The output of the program can be seen in Section 1.4.

Different programming languages treat the loop control variable in different manners as to its status. In Perl, it is an ordinary variable that must be declared a-priori if we specify use strict or a variation of it in the current block. In a language like Ada, the use of the for statement itself constitutes a declaration of the loop control variable. Thus, in Perl, the program given above could have been written in the following slightly different manner.

Program 2.23

```
#!/usr/bin/perl
#file farenheit1-1.pl

#print Fahrenheit-Celsius table for 0, 20, ..., 300 degrees Fahrenheit

use strict 'vars';
my $celsius;

            #loop through the Fahrenheit values
for (my $fahrenheit = 0; $fahrenheit <= 300; $fahrenheit = $fahrenheit+20){
    $celsius = 5/9 * ($fahrenheit - 32);
    printf "%4.0f %6.1f\n", $fahrenheit, $celsius;
}
```

If we look at the expression after the for keyword, we see that the $fahrenheit variable is declared in the expression with my and given an initial value.

A loop written using for can be easily converted to a loop using while whereas the reverse many not that easy. In fact, the programs given in Section 2.5.1 and this section are versions of the same program, one written using while and the other written using the for loop although we did not use the continue keyword earlier. The following program shows that the continue block, if used, should be used to specify the updates to the loop control variables. A continue block is not found in most other programming languages. Its semantics is such that it is executed after the loop's body is evaluated, before the conditional is tested again. With the continue keyword and its associated block, we can rewrite the program given immediately above as the following.

Program 2.24

```perl
#!/usr/bin/perl
#file while11.pl

use strict vars;
my ($lower, $upper, $step, $fahrenheit, $celsius);

#print Fahrenheit-Celsius table for 0, 20, ..., 300 degrees Fahrenheit
$lower = 0;   #lower limit of temperature table
$upper = 300; #upper limit
$step = 20;   #step size

$fahrenheit = $lower;
                #loop through the Fahrenheit values
while ($fahrenheit <= $upper){
    $celsius = 5/9 * ($fahrenheit - 32);
    printf "%4.0f %6.1f\n", $fahrenheit, $celsius;
}
continue{
    $fahrenheit = $fahrenheit + $step;
}
```

The continue block updates the value of the loop control variable $fahrenheit. It is executed after the body of the block is executed and before control moves to the top of the block for possible another iteration. The use of a continue block allows one to write an exact equivalent of a for loop in terms of while without being kludgy.

The initialization and update expressions, and the conditional expression inside the parentheses in a for loop are optional. In such a case, we must provide the appropriate loop exit statement to finish the loop. The following program shows a use of for without anything inside the parentheses that immediately follow the keyword for.

Program 2.25

```perl
#!/usr/bin/perl
#file forEmpty.pl
#print Fahrenheit-Celsius table for 0, 20, ..., 300 degrees Fahrenheit

use strict 'vars';
my $fahrenheit;
my $celsius;

                #loop through the Fahrenheit values
#for ($fahrenheit = 0; $fahrenheit <= 300; $fahrenheit = $fahrenheit+20){
$fahrenheit = 0;
for (;;){
```

```
    $celsius = 5/9 * ($fahrenheit - 32);
    printf "%4.0f %6.1f\n", $fahrenheit, $celsius;
    $fahrenheit = $fahrenheit + 20;
    if ($fahrenheit > 300){last;}
}
```

Here, the for loop is exited explicitly using last when the termination condition is satisfied. This is like the while loop when 1 is used as a conditional.

2.5.2.2   The foreach Statement

The foreach statement goes over each element of a list of elements and executes the body of the loop once for every element. The program given above can be rewritten using a foreach loop assuming that the increments in temperature are in steps of one.

Program 2.26

```
#!/usr/bin/perl
#file foreach1.pl
#print Fahrenheit-Celsius table for 0, 20, ..., 300 degrees Fahrenheit

use strict 'vars';
my $fahrenheit;
my $celsius;

            #loop through the Fahrenheit values
$fahrenheit = 0;
foreach $fahrenheit(1..10){
    $celsius = 5/9 * ($fahrenheit - 32);
    printf "%4.0f %6.1f\n", $fahrenheit, $celsius;
}
```

Here, we use the range operator 1..10 to list the values that the for loop iterates over. 1..10 actually creates the list (1, 2, 3, 4, 5, 6, 7, 8, 9, 10). We see lists in detail in Chapter 3. The foreach loop goes over this list's items sequentially one by one and executes the body of the loop. A foreach loop can also have a continue block although it is difficult to envision much use for it.

If the increments are not in steps of one, but in steps of an arbitrary value, as in the previous programs, we will have to pre-compute the list of values to iterate over. This may not be the best use of the foreach statement. We are better off using for or a while loop in such a situation. We show how it can be done using map in Section 2.8. Note that the list from which individual elements are used to iterate over can be any list such as the following.

```
(1, 10, 11, 25, "abc")
```

It can be even a mix of numbers, strings, references as long as we know how to handle each entry inside the body of the loop. The output of the program is given below.

```
   1   -17.2
   2   -16.7
```

```
 3   -16.1
 4   -15.6
 5   -15.0
 6   -14.4
 7   -13.9
 8   -13.3
 9   -12.8
10   -12.2
```

The `foreach` statement is used quite frequently with hashes to go over all elements. The following example has been discussed earlier in Section 1.9. Here, we illustrate how `foreach` can be used with a hash. Hashes are discussed in detail in Chapter 3. A hash is multi-component data structure like a list, but where elements are addressed or indexed using not positional integers such as 0 or 10, but using strings.

Program 2.27

```perl
#!/usr/bin/perl
#file hashes.pl

use strict;
my (%hometowns, %heights, %weights, %ages, $friend);

%hometowns = ('Tommy' => 'Washington', 'Chad' =>'San Francisco',
              'Jeff' => 'Boulder',
              'Aaron' => 'Golden', 'Rick' => 'Montreal', 'Sean' => 'Montreal',
              'Todd' => 'Colo Springs');
%heights = ('Tommy', 66, 'Aaron', 68, 'Rick', 67, "Chad", 73, 'Jeff', 70,
              'Sean', 67, "Todd", 73);
%weights = ("Tommy" => 140, "Sean" => 140, "Todd" => 190, "Chad" => 180,
              "Jeff" => 145, 'Aaron' => 155, "Rick" => 135, );
%ages = ('Aaron', 23, "Rick", 21, 'Tommy', 18, "Sean", 21, 'Chad', 23,
                'Jeff', 21);

$weights {Aaron} = 157;
$ages {"Todd"} = 22;
$hometowns {'Tommy'} = 'Washington DC';

printf  "%5s %15s %5s %5s %3s\n", "Name", "Hometown", "Height",
          "Weight", "Age";
print "-" x 45, "\n";

foreach  $friend (keys (%hometowns)){
 printf "%5s %15s    %3d    %3d    %2d\n", $friend,  $hometowns{$friend},
      $heights{$friend}, $weights{$friend},  $ages{$friend};
}
```

Here, there are four hashes, %hometowns, %heights, %weights and %ages. Values can be assigned to a hash by giving a list of pairs. The index and the value of a pair can be separated either by => or just a comma. Thus, as we see in the assignment to %hometowns, that we use => to separate the index and key of a pair, and comma to separate individual pairs from one another. In the assignment to %ages and

%heights, the elements are all separated by , and thus look like a regular list although the elements are paired up as key and value. Individual elements of a hash can also be assigned. In

```
$weights {Aaron} = 157;
```

we are assigning a value to the element that corresponds to the key Aaron in the hash %weights.
The foreach statement occurs at the end of the program. Its structure is

```
foreach  $friend (keys (%hometowns)){...}
```

where the dots are replaced by the block's content. This foreach statement loops over every element of the list given below.

```
keys (%hometowns)
```

keys is a built-in function that gives all the keys of a hash. In this case, the list of keys is the following.

```
('Tommy', 'Chad', 'Jeff'', 'Aaron', 'Rick', 'Sean', 'Todd');
```

The keys function can return the keys in an arbitrary order. The foreach loop goes over each element of this list of keys. When it picks an element from this list, it temporarily calls it $friend. Inside the loop, the value stored in the various hashes corresponding to the keyword $friend are printed. The output of this program is given in Section 1.9.

2.6   Block Labels and continue Blocks

We have seen the use of labels on loops already in this chapter. In general, a label can be placed before any loop statement. This means that a label can be placed before while, until, for and foreach statements. A label can also be placed before a bare block. Thus, the following are acceptable.

> *LABEL:* while (*expression*) *block*
> *LABEL:* while (*expression*) *block* continue *block*
> *LABEL:* until (*expression*) *block*
> *LABEL:* until (*expression*) *block* continue *block*
> *LABEL:* for (*initialization* ; *termination-condition* ; *update* ;) *block*
> *LABEL:* foreach *variable* (*list*) *block*
> *LABEL:* foreach *variable* (*list*) *block* continue *block*
> *LABEL:* *block*
> *LABEL:* *block* continue *block*

This list is taken from [WCS96]. Labels are not allowed with if or unless statements. A label is a string of alphanumeric characters. A label needs to be followed by a colon. It is customary, but not required to write the label in all upper case letters so that it stands out from among the rest of the code. A label is usually used to allow ways to control how the block associated with a loop statement is executed. Loop control statements: next, last and redo can use loop labels. A label names the loop as a whole and not just the top of the loop. Thus, a loop control command referring to a loop's label works with respect to the loop as a whole.

We see that only some of the loop statements allow one to use the continue block. The continue block if used, provides the bridge to continue from one iteration to the next unless skipped explicitly. The continue block is not executed the last time. The block is optional. last makes a program skip the continue block. The redo command skips the continue block. The redo command skips condition testing for the next iteration as well. The next command causes the continue block to be executed. The next command requires the conditional to be tested before the next iteration.

2.7   Statement Modifiers

Any simple statement can have one of four possible modifiers attached to them at the end. The modifiers cannot be appended to blocks, only to individual simple statements. The modifiers are given below.

> if *expression*
> unless *expression*
> while *expression*
> until *expression*

The keywords have the obvious meaning. We have an example of in Section 2.10. One example from this section is given below.

```
die $errorStmt if (($n < 0) or ($n =~ /[.]/));
```

We can write this statement also as the following if we want.

```
die $errorStmt unless (($n >=  0) or ($n !~ /[.]/));
```

Section 2.10 has several other usage of die. Two more are repeated below.

```
open (IN, $oldfilename) or die "Cannot open $oldfilename for reading: $!";
open (OUT, ">$newfilename") ||  die "Cannot open $newfilename for writing: $!";
```

These two can alternatively be written as the following.

```
die "Cannot open $oldfilename for reading: $!"
                    unless (not open (IN, $oldfilename));
die "Cannot open $newfilename for writing: $!"
     unless (not open (OUT, ">$newfilename"));
```

The following program shows additional use of statement modifiers. The use of while and until modifiers is not really useful, but made up to illustrate the point.

Program 2.28

```
#!/usr/bin/perl
#whilemod.pl

$b = $a++ while ($a <= 100);
print "a = $a\tb=$b\n";

$b = ++$a while ($a <= 200);
print "a = $a\tb=$b\n";

$b = $a-- until ($a <= 50);
print "a = $a\tb=$b\n";

$b = --$a until ($a <= 0);
print "a = $a\tb=$b\n";
```

The modifiers used are while and until. The initial value of $a is 0. It is incremented to 101 and then printed. It is then incremented again to 201 and printed. Next, it is decremented using two statements with the until modifier. In every increment and decrement statement, $b is assigned. The output of the program is given below.

```
a = 101 b=100
a = 201 b=201
a = 50 b=51
a = 0 b=0
```

The first assignment statement with the while modifier increments $a after performing the assignment. Therefore, after the last iteration of the first statement, the value of $b is 100, the value of $a before the first increment. The second assignment statement with the while modifier assigns a value to $b before incrementing $a. $a-- returns the value for the assignment to $b and then decrements. --$a decrements the value of $a and then returns the value for assignment. Thus, placing ++ or -- before the name of the scalar variable causes incrementing or decrementing to happen first, then the value returned for use. The opposite happens if ++ or -- is placed after the variable.

2.8   Mapping

The map function is discussed in more detail in Chapter 12. However, it is introduced here because it is definitely a very useful and powerful program control structure.

We often execute a block of statements for every element of a list. This is exactly what foreach is meant to do. foreach is a loop statement. There is a built-in function called map that performs the exact same objective in a slightly different manner. Mapping is very commonly used in a functional programming language such as Lisp. In Perl, map is not so commonly used although sometimes it can be used to produce elegant pieces of code. Thus, map is a functional equivalent of foreach. map receives its name from its origin in a purely functional programming language where it is used to map a function onto every element of a list. Perl is a hybrid language that provides strong functional programming abilities. Functional programming is discussed at length in Chapter 12.

The following program, once again, converts Fahrenheit temperatures to Centigrade. It does so by mapping a function onto the pre-computed list of Fahrenheit temperature values. Because of this need for prior computation of the list of values, it may not always be convenient.

Program 2.29

```
#!/usr/bin/perl
#file fahrenheitmap.pl
use strict;
my ($lower, $upper, $step, @values);

#print Fahrenheit-Celsius table for 0, 20, ..., 300 degrees Fahrenheit
$lower = 0;    #lower limit of temperature table
$upper = 300;  #upper limit
$step = 20;    #step size

#obtain the list of Fahrenheit temperatures to convert; may potentially be big
@values = map {$_ * $step} (0..$upper/$step);
map {convertM ($_)} @values;
```

```
#perform the conversion on the list of Fahrenheit values

####################################
####subroutine to convert a list of Fahrenheit temperatures
sub convertM{
    my ($fahrenheit) = @_;
    my $celsius = 5/9 * ($fahrenheit - 32);
    printf "%4.0f %6.1f\n", $fahrenheit, $celsius;
}
```

The program computes the list of Fahrenheit temperatures and stores them in the list @values. @values is computed in the following manner.

```
@values = map {$_ * $step} (0..$upper/$step);
```

This statement shows the essential characteristics of map. In Perl, map takes a block of statements that is executed for every element of a list. In this case, this list is obtained using the expression

```
0..$upper/$step
```

that uses the range operator. The range operator, as used here, produces a list of values in incremental sequence where the increment is 1. It produces the integer sequence given below.

```
1, 2, 3, 4, 5, 6, 7, 8, 9, 10, 11, 12, 13, 14, 15
```

The map function iterates over every element of the list given to it. It takes an element one by one, calls it the special variable $_ and executes the block of statements on it. The block is

```
{$_ * $step}
```

and therefore, map produces the list with the following elements.

```
0, 20, 40, 60, 80, 100, 120, 140, 160, 180, 200, 220, 240, 260, 280, 300
```

Next, there is another call to map.

```
map {convertM ($_)} @values;
```

This map statement calls the convertM function or subroutine on every element of the list of Fahrenheit temperatures. This concludes the main program although the subroutine is still to be discussed.

Subroutines are a very important part of any programming language. A special type of subroutine is called a function. Subroutines are discussed at great length in Chapter 12. A subroutine has a name and an associated block called the body. A subroutine in Perl gets a list of arguments. This list of arguments is always known by the special variable @_. In the subroutine convertM, the argument list has only one value, a Fahrenheit temperature. The statement

```
    my ($fahrenheit) = @_;
```

takes the only element in the list of arguments and calls it $fahrenheit. The my declaration ensures that this variable $fahrenheit is local to the body of the subroutine and not available outside the subroutine. The subroutine converts the Fahrenheit temperature to Centigrade and prints it. This is the subroutine that is mapped onto the list of Fahrenheit temperatures in the main program.

2.9   Recursion

Recursion means calling oneself. A recursive program calls itself. When we talk about a recursive program, we actually are talking about a program that has one or more recursive subroutines. A recursive subroutine is one in whose body it calls itself. Recursion is the primary means of flow of control in a functional programming language such as Lisp, or a logical programming language such as Prolog. In the following program, we have a recursive subroutine that converts a sequence of Fahrenheit temperatures to Centigrade. This example is not the best exemplar of a recursive subroutine. It is presented here to illustrate that recursion is an alternative to iteration. Whether recursion is viable as an efficient alternative to iteration in general, depends on how well recursion is implemented in the language and how much emphasis is placed on recursion by the designers of the programming language. Recursion requires significant overhead for implementation. In languages like Lisp and Prolog, recursion is of utmost importance for flow of control and therefore, implemented in a very optimized fashion, and even preferred over iteration. In Perl, recursion is not as well implemented and should be used if the potential number of recursive calls is not excessively large. However, there are problems for which recursion is the best way to think of a solution. The following program has a recursive subroutine.

Program 2.30

```perl
#!/usr/bin/perl
#file fahrenheitr.pl

use strict;
my ($lower, $upper, $step);

#print Fahrenheit-Celsius table for 0, 20, ..., 300 degrees Fahrenheit
$lower = 0;    #lower limit of temperature table
$upper = 300;  #upper limit
$step = 20;    #step size
convertR ($lower, $upper, $step);

#############################
#subroutine: recursively go through the Fahrenheit values;
#quit when upper limit crossed
sub convertR{
   my ($fahrenheit, $upLimit, $increment) = @_;
   my ($celsius);
   if ($fahrenheit > $upLimit){return;}
   $celsius = 5/9 * ($fahrenheit - 32);
   printf "%4.0f %6.1f\n", $fahrenheit, $celsius;
   convertR ($fahrenheit + $increment, $upLimit, $increment);
}
```

The recursive subroutine takes an argument list containing three elements: a Fahrenheit temperature to convert, an upper limit, and an increment. There is one call to this function in the main program.

```perl
convertR ($lower, $upper, $step);
```

The subroutine's first statement as given below.

```perl
   my ($fahrenheit, $upLimit, $increment) = @_;
```

As indicated earlier, a Perl subroutine gets only one argument, a list `@_` where the elements are undifferentiated as regards to their identity and purpose. Inside the subroutine, the programmer is advised to give the individual elements of `@_` names to make it more readable and maintainable. The three elements in the argument list that the subroutine `convertR` gets are called `$fahrenheit`, `$upLimit` and `$increment`. These names are declared with `my` and thus, are available for use only within the block that is the subroutine's body. A recursive subroutine must have a way to finish or exit. Otherwise, it will recurse for ever eating up all system resources. Like an infinite loop in an iterative statement, an infinite case of recursion must be avoided in writing recursive subroutines by writing one or more judicious termination situations. The subroutine `convertR` finishes its recursion because of the following statement.

```
if ($fahrenheit > $upLimit){return;}
```

If there is a recursive call such that the value of the temperature to convert `$fahrenheit` is more than the value of `$upLimit`, the subroutine call ends or `returns` without doing anything. This ensures that the recursive subroutine does not go on for ever. The subroutine converts the Fahrenheit temperature to Centigrade and prints it. It then recursively calls `convertR`.

```
convertR ($fahrenheit + $increment, $upLimit, $increment);
```

This crucial call to itself makes the subroutine recursive. The second and the third arguments to the recursive call are the same as the original call in the main program. The first argument to the recursive call is the original Fahrenheit temperature incremented by adding `$increment`. Thus, we have a sequence of recursive calls to `convertR`.

```
convertR (0, 300, 20)
convertR (20, 300, 20)
convertR (04, 300, 20)
  .
  .
  .
convertR (300, 300, 20)
convertR (320, 300, 20)
```

The last call `returns` or exits because the termination condition is satisfied. The `return` from the last call causes `returns` from the previous calls in the backward order. When the first call

```
convertR (0, 300, 20)
```

`returns` the call to

```
convertR ($lower, $upper, $step);
```

in the main program finishes. As a result, the whole program's execution is finished at this time.

2.10   The `warn` and `die` Statements

Perl provides two statements `die` and `warn` to enable the system to return a brief description of an error when an unusual situation arises during the course of execution. If the unusual situation is such that the program cannot continue any more, the `die` statement can be used to kill the program as well as inform the reason why the program cannot execute any more. The `warn` function is used when an unusual or error situation arises, but the error is forgivable and the program can continue running in spite of the problem.

The following program computes $n!$, the factorial of n. We know that $n!$ is not computable for negative integers or rational numbers. The following program prompts the user to enter a non-negative integer n and computes $n!$. However, if the user enters something inappropriate, the program automatically dies.

Program 2.31

```perl
#!/usr/bin/perl
#file factorial1.pl

my ($n, $errorStmt);
print "Please enter a non-negative integer>> ";
$n = <STDIN>;
chomp $n;
$errorStmt =
    "n! cannot be computed for a negative integer or a non-integer!\n";
die $errorStmt if (($n < 0) or ($n =~ /[.]/));
print &factorial($n) . "\n";

#subroutine to compute factorial
sub factorial{
    my ($no) = @_;
    if (($no == 0) or ($no == 1)){
        return 1;
    }
    else{
        return ($no * &factorial ($no -1));
    }
}
```

The program asks the user to enter a non-negative integer, and reads the user's input. However, it is quite possible that the user does not enter a non-negative integer although the program explicitly asks for one. A user can do so absent-mindedly, or if the user does not understand the program's instruction. In this case, the instruction is clear and simple, but in the case of more complex instructions, there is room to be misunderstood. Here, the die statement is used in conjunction with validation of the input.

```perl
die $errorStmt if (($n < 0) or ($n =~ /[.]/));
```

Any single or simple statement in Perl can have a modifier such as an if clause. There are several modifiers that are allowed. This is *not* an if statement; the statement is die with an if clause as *modifier*.

die is called with one argument. It is the string to be printed when die is invoked. In this case, the string to be printed is $errorStmt. The conditional associated with the if modifier is

```perl
(($n < 0) or ($n =~ /[.]/));
```

The die statement is invoked if the value read, $n, is less than 0 of if it contains a period inside. We are making the simplistic assumption that the presence of a period indicates it is an number with a decimal point in it. Of course, one can enter a string that has non-digits, several decimal points, etc., but we are not worried about an exhaustive validation of the input here.

The main program calls the factorial subroutine with $n as the sole argument and prints the returned value. The call to the subroutine has an ampersand (&) in front. The & is not essential when invoking functions, but some programmers use it to indicate explicitly that it is a call to a subroutine.

The factorial subroutine is recursive since there is a call to itself embedded in its body. The incoming argument list @_ contains only one element. It is fished out and is called $no locally inside the body of the subroutine. As mentioned earlier, writing proper termination conditions is of utmost importance in writing a recursive function. Otherwise, the subroutine will continue for ever. Here, if $no is 0 or 1, the value returned by the factorial subroutine is 1. This corresponds to the mathematical facts

$$0! = 1! = 1.$$

If the value of $no is larger than 1, the value returned is computed by the following expression.

```
$no * &factorial ($no -1)
```

The call to the function we are writing, viz., factorial in this expression makes this subroutine recursive. It must be emphasized that the argument given to the recursive call to factorial is $no -1. This argument is one less than the value of $no, the argument passed to the original call to factorial. This ensures that as factorial is called again and again recursively, the value of the argument comes down by 1 each time. Since the argument becomes smaller every time and starts with a non-negative integer, after a finite number of recursive calls to factorial, the argument becomes 1. At this point, the call to factorial immediately quits, returning 1 due to the termination condition. This call is our savior ensuring proper termination of the recursive process. When the last call returns 1, the call just prior to it performs the multiplication to produce 2!. This call returns the value, and the call prior to it computes 3!. Similarly, 4!, 5!, $\cdots$, etc., are computed. Finally, the first call to factorial performs the multiplication that computes $n!$ and returns it to the main program. This is the value printed by the print statement in the bottom of the main program.

The die statement is frequently used with file open or socket opening, among other situations. If we are trying to open a file to read, write or append to, and the file cannot be opened for the purpose at hand, quite frequently the program should not proceed any more. The following program is a modified version of the file copying program first discussed in Section 1.6.2. To copy a file, we need to open a file for reading and open another file for writing at the same time. We read a line from the first file and write it to the second. This continues till all lines have been copied.

Program 2.32

```
#!/usr/bin/perl
#file copyDie.pl
#copying everything from one file to another

use strict;
my ($oldfilename, $newfilename);

print "Please give me a file name >> ";
$oldfilename = <STDIN>;
chomp ($oldfilename);
$newfilename = $oldfilename . ".new";

open (IN, $oldfilename) or die "Cannot open $oldfilename for reading: $!";
open (OUT, ">$newfilename") ||
    die "Cannot open $newfilename for writing: $!";;

while (<IN>){
    print OUT $_;
}

close (IN) or die "Cannot close $oldfilename: $!";;
close (OUT) or die "Cannot close $newfilename: $!";;
```

```
print "File `$newfilename' is an exact copy of file `$oldfilename'\n";
```

The program prompts for a file name, chomps the \n that follows to obtain the string containing the file name only. The opening of the two filehandles is done by the following statements.

```
open (IN, $oldfilename) or die "Cannot open $oldfilename for reading: $!";
open (OUT, ">$newfilename") ||  die "Cannot open $newfilename for writing: $!";;
```

These statements show the use of die as well as the use of orand || as a means of controlling the flow of execution. Let us look at the first of these two statements. The or operator connects two full-fledged statements

```
open (IN, $oldfilename)
```

and

```
die "Cannot open $oldfilename for reading: $!"
```

each one of which can be written as independent statements terminated by ;. The first statement is an open statement that returns a non-false or true value if successful. If unsuccessful in opening a file for reading for whatever reasons, it returns false. If the first statement is successful, or is happy and skips looking at the second statement. Thus, the die statement is skipped if the file can be opened for reading. However, if the file cannot be opened, the die statement is executed. The die statement takes a string as its argument. The string contains a programmer written error message. It also uses the system generated error string $!. This special variable contains the description of the error as Perl sees it. The second statement uses the || version of logical disjunction. The program contains two additional such die statements that work with the closeing of filehandles.

In this program, we see two versions of the logical disjunction operation: or and ||. Both are essentially the same except that or has much lower precedence than ||. or is also a more readable version of the logical disjunction. Similarly, and is a more readable version of the logical conjunction. open is considered a list operator because it takes a list of two elements as an argument. The precedence of the logical operators written in words is much lower than most operators. As a result, when the logical operators written as word are used, there is less need to parenthesize the operands.

The $! when used in a string context, prints an error message. In a non-string context it prints an error number. A problematic run of the program is given below along with an error message.

```
%copyDie.pl
Please give me a file name >> abc.pl
Cannot open abc.pl for reading:
    No such file or directory at copyDie.pl line 13, <STDIN> line 1.
```

The printout of the program has been broken into two lines so that it does not print outside the margin.

Sometimes when an error occurs and the error is not so serious in that the program can continue although something happened that was not quite expected. In such a case, it makes sense to type a warning instead of fieing. For example, we can rewrite the factorial program given above so that we allow a user to enter a non-negative relational number, i.e., a number with decimal digits in it. We truncate it off to make an integer out of it and proceed with factorial computation. However, if the number entered is negative the program dies. The program is given below.

Program 2.33

```
#!/usr/bin/perl
#file factorial3.pl

my ($n, $errorStmt1, $errorStmt2);
print "Please enter a non-negative integer>> ";
$n = <STDIN>;
chomp $n;
$errorStmt = "ERROR: n! cannot be computed for a negative integer: $!\n";
$warnStmt =
  "Warning: n! cannot be computed for a rational, but will truncate: $!\n";
die  $errorStmt if  ($n < 0);
if ($n =~ /^\d+[.]\d+$/){
    warn $warnStmt;
    $n = int ($n);
}
print "Computing $n!\n";
print &factorial($n) . "\n";


#subroutine to compute factorial
sub factorial{
    my ($no) = @_;
    if (($no == 0) or ($no == 1)){
        return 1;
    }
    else{
        return ($no * &factorial ($no -1));
    }
}
```

The die statement checks to see if $n < 0 and kills the program if so. The warn statement is inside the if block. It is invoked if the conditional given below is satisfied.

$n =~ /^\d+[.]\d+$/

This requires the value of $n to be a string that contains one or more digits, followed by the decimal point, followed by one or more digits. If the condition is satisfied, the warning message is printed. It is followed by truncating the $n by keeping its integer part using the built-in function int. The factorial subroutine is called with the value of $n, whether the original or modified.

2.11 Conclusions

In this chapter, we have discussed Perl's scalars, operators, and statements. We also have briefly discussed mapping and recursion, two other significant means of exercising control over the execution of a program's code. The variety of statements available endows a programming language with expressive versatility. Perl is blessed with a wide repertoire of statement types. Not many languages are this fortunate. The options for verbalizing a programming goal in Perl in terms of its constituent statements are many and varied. Thus, the programmer is able to exercise his or her own control, and develop a style or behavior best suited to his or her personality, likes and dislikes, and needs. However, one must be cautioned to keep programming statements clears, concise and efficient. These are conflicting goals, but clarity must receive primacy if programs are to be understood by individuals other than the programmer, easily maintainable, and hence cost-efficient in the long run.

If one wants to know the formal syntax of expressions and statement in various languages, one is encouraged to read books that survey programming languages. Some such good books are [Seb99], [Wat90], [AV97] and [Hor84]. As of now, most books do not discuss Perl though.

2.12   Exercises

1. *(Easy: Internet Exploration, Documentation Reading)*
   Either visit www.cpan.org on the World Wide Web, or use perldoc on your system to read documentation on Perl operators and basic syntax. Use

   ```
   %perldoc perldoc
   ```

   to learn more about perldoc. Detailed documentation on Perl operators is available by running

   ```
   %perldoc perlop
   ```

   Use perlnumber as the argument to find documentation on Perl numbers and numeric operators. Use perlsyn as the argument to find documentation on basic Perl syntax.

2. *(Easy: Indefinite Iteration)*
   Write a while loop that prints a table of angle measures along with their sine and cosine values. The initial degree, the final degree and the step size are given as command-line arguments. The Perl built-in functions to compute sine and cosine are sin and cos, respectively. Each takes a radian argument.

3. *(Easy: Iteration)*
   Write a program that takes a command-line input n and computes

   $$n + (n-1) + (n-2) + \cdots + 2 + 1$$

   using iteration. Rewrite the program so that it uses recursion. n is a positive integer. Check for errors and print error messages when needed.

4. *(Easy: Recursion)*
   Write a program that prints the nth Fibonacci number $fibonacci(n)$. n is given as a command-line argument. A Fibonacci number is defined in the following way.

   $$
   \begin{aligned}
   fibonacci(0) &= 1 \\
   fibonacci(1) &= 1 \\
   fibonacci(n) &= fibonacci(n-1) + fibonacci(n-2) \qquad\qquad n >= 2
   \end{aligned}
   $$

   First write the program recursively. Then, write it iteratively. What are some of the salient differences between the two versions? Which version is better and why? Check for errors and print error messages when needed.

5. *(Easy: Recursion, Iteration)*
   Write a program that computes $n!$ recursively. It takes n as a command-line argument. Write a version where it is computed non-recursively. Which version is more efficient? In what way? Check for errors and print error messages when needed.

6. *(Easy: Arithmetic)*
   Write a program that determines the day number (1 to 366) in year for a date that is provided as input data. As an example, January 1, 2000 is day 1. December 31, 1999 is day 365. December 31, 2004 is day 366 because 2004 is a leap year. A leap year is divisible by 4, and any year divisible by 100 is a leap year if it is divisible by 400. The program takes month, day and year as integers and on the command-line. Perform error checks as needed.

7. *(Medium: Arithmetic, Formatting(*
   Write a program to generate a calendar for a year. The program takes the year and the day of the week for January 1 of that year. Assume 1 is Sunday, 2 is Monday, etc. Remember February has 29 days if it is a leap year.

8. *(Medium: Binary Arithmetic, Hexadecimal Arithmetic)*
   Write a program `itob` that takes an argument: n. n is an unsigned binary integer. It returns a binary character representation of n. `itob` takes the integer as command-line argument.

   Write `itoh` that converts an integer into hexadecimal representation.

9. *(Easy: Infinite Loop, Temperature Conversion)*
   Write a program that has a `while` loop that runs for ever. Inside the loop, it prompts the user for a Fahrenheit temperature to convert to Celsius. If the user does not enter a valid number at the prompt, the program `warns` the user. It `warns` up to three times and then `dies`. Otherwise, it continues with the loop.

10. *(Easy: Loop, File Copying)*
    Write a program that repeatedly asks for a file name in each iteration of the loop. If the user enters the name of a file that does not exist, it `warns` the user. If the user enters a valid file name, it copies the original file to a new file which has the same name except the string `.copy` at the end. Therefore, the file `a.pl` is copied into `a.pl.copy`. The program also `warns` if the file is not readable by the user or it is a directory.

11. *(Easy: Arithmetic, Loops)*
    Write a program that takes n as a command-line argument and computes the following sum.

    $$\sum_{i=1}^{n}\sum_{j=1}^{i}j^2$$

    Use two labeled loops. Use `last`, `next` and any other loop control operators to make the loops work. Do not use straight-forward looping statements.

12. *(Easy: Loops, Arithmetic)*
    Write `while`, `until`, or `for` loops to computer the following. Try to write `foreach` loops also if you can.

    (a) $1 + 3 + 7 + \cdots + (2^{20} - 1)$
    (b) $1 \times 2 \times 4 \times 8 \times \cdots 2^{20}$
    (c) $e^x = 1 + x + \frac{x}{2!} + \cdots$
        e is an important constant in mathematics. The formula given above is also very important in mathematics. Stop the iteration in the program when adding the next term changes the sum by less than 10^{-n}. Here x and n are command-line arguments.
    (d) $1 + (1 + 4) + (1 + 4 + 7) + (1 + 4 + 7 + 10) + \cdots$
        Add this sequence to n terms where n is a command-line argument. Note that each term of the sequence is a sequence itself.
    (e) $1 - \frac{1}{2} + \frac{1}{3} - \frac{1}{4} + \cdots$
        Stop the iteration when the result is correct up to five decimal digits.

(f) $sin\ x = x - \frac{x^3}{3!} + \frac{x^5}{5!} + \cdots$

Stop iteration after n decimal digit precision after the decimal point. x and n are command-line arguments.

13. *(Easy to Hard: Prime Numbers, Arithmetic)*

A *prime number* is an integer greater than one and divisible by one and itself. Write a Perl program that returns 1 if its command-line argument is a prime number.

Write another program that prints out all prime numbers below n where n is a command-line argument. Check for errors and print error messages when needed.

14. *(Medium to Hard: Arithmetic)*

A *perfect number* is a positive integer that is equal to the sum of its proper divisors. A proper divisor is a positive integer other than the number itself that divides the number without a remainder. For example, six is a perfect number because the sum of its proper divisors 1,2, and 3 equal 6. Eight is not a perfect number. Write a Perl program that takes a positive integer as command-line argument and determines whether it is perfect. Check for errors and print error messages when needed.

Chapter 3

On Data Types

In This Chapter

Like all programming languages, Perl provides several built-in basic data types:

1. Scalars: numbers, strings and references

2. Arrays or lists

3. Hashes

We have already been exposed to all of them in Chapter 1 and Chapter 2. Scalars are discussed at length in Chapter 2, and are hence, not re-discussed here, except for references that we present in Section 3.3.

A scalar is a single-component data structure whereas lists and hashes are multi-component. A multi-component data structure provides representational efficiency since related data can be stored, accessed, and processed compactly and efficiently, without resorting to a plethora of similar-sounding variable names. This increases a program's comprehensibility as well as its maintainability. Lists and hashes differ in the manner in which individual components of the data structure are accessed and stored. Accessing a multi-component data structure's individual parts requires being able to specify an address or *index* such that the elements can be distinguished from one another and accessed immediately in constant time or more or less constant time. Whether it is the first element, or an element buried way back in the data structure should not cause a major difference in accessing time. Both lists and hashes are flat data structures, allowing only one level of inclusion. In the case of a list, the addressing or indexing is done using numeric addresses for the elements. A list is a sequential data structure and the addressing scheme uses non-negative integers starting from zero. A hash's indexes are arbitrary scalars. Hashes require complex mathematical computation so that elements are stored without fear of loss, and accessed efficiently. An interested reader can consult a book such as *Introduction to Algorithms* [CLR97] to understand how hashes are implemented.

3.1 Arrays or Lists

A *list* is a multi-component data structure where the position of an element in the structure matters. That is, the idea of what is before a certain element and what is after a certain element is paramount. A list is a variable length data structure. An array is usually a fixed length data structure which is simpler than a list, and where elements can be accessed using numeric indices. Perl implements the list data structure using an array. The distinction between the two data structures is briefly discussed in Section 1.7. For a more detailed discussion, the reader is referred to a text book on data structures such as [TC03].

We will use the two terms, array and list, interchangeably although it is not strictly correct. An element in a list or an array must be a scalar and is identified by its position. The name of an array variable in Perl starts with the symbol @. Therefore, @friends, @aList, @myArray100, and @name_array are valid names of arrays. _friends, friends, or %friends are not valid array names in Perl.

In Perl, an array can be only single dimensional although multi-dimensional structures can be simulated. Since an array, strictly speaking, is single-dimensional, the term *array* is actually somewhat of a misnomer. What we have here is a vector although we will continue using the term array due to tradition.

3.1.1 Uninitialized Array or List

We know that it is not necessary in Perl to declare a variable name before we use it unless we force ourselves to do so using the use strict 'vars' construct in the beginning of a block. In such a case, all variables in the block must be declared before they are used. Whether or not we declare a variable before its first use, it is possible that a variable is uninitialized before it is used. An array variable that has not been initialized has the empty array or list as its value. When we print the empty list, nothing is printed.

3.1.2   Assigning Value to an Array

One can make an assignment to an array variable by specifying the values of the elements.

```
my @friends98 = ('John Hart', 'Jeff Ellis', 'Brett Walters', 'Blake Escort');
```

The values are given as a comma-separated list enclosed in parentheses. We can also assign an array to another array. When we write

```
@myFriends = @friends;
```

the value of @friends is assigned to @myFriends.

Elements of an array are scalars, but they need not be all strings or all numbers or all references. Mixing is allowed.

```
@numbers = (1, 2, "3", "four", 'five', 6);
```

When we write an array using parentheses and give all its values, we call it the *literal representation* of the array. In the assignment given above, (1, 2, "3", "four", 'five', 6) is the literal representation. When we assign value to an array using parentheses, we can have scalar variables inside the parentheses. Therefore, the following is correct assuming we have assigned values to $firstFriend, $secondFriend and $lastFriend already.

```
@friends = ($firstFriend, $secondFriend, 'Brett Walters',
     'Justin OMalley', $lastFriend);
```

We can, in fact, intersperse scalar variables, literal scalars and array variables when we perform assignment. The following program fragment shows this.

```
my (@friends, $friend);
my @friends98 = ('John Hart', 'Jeff Ellis', 'Brett Walters', 'Blake Escort');
my $friend97 = "Tom Toybee";
my @oldFriends = ('Chad Blonding', "Jeff Perich");
my @friends = ("Hakan Kvarnstrom", @friends98, $friend97, @oldFriends);
```

Here the last assignment has a constant scalar string, a scalar variable, and two array variables in the literal array representation used on the right hand side of the assignment. The value of @friends at the end of the last assignment statement is given below.

```
("Hakan Kvarnstrom", 'John Hart', 'Jeff Ellis', 'Brett Walters', 'Blake Escort'
            "Tom Toybee", 'Chad Blonding', "Jeff Perich");
```

An array variable such as @friends98, when used inside a list is opened up and its elements are placed where the variable name was. This is simply an example of variable flattening. In Perl, a list or an array is always only one level deep. That is, there are no embedded lists. In other words, an array is always one-dimensional. Also, it is not necessary to write the parentheses around a list unless needed. However, we need to know that the comma (,) is just a list element separator inside a list given inside parentheses. Outside a list in parentheses, it means something different. It then is the so-called *comma operator* that evaluates the left operand, ignores the result, evaluates the right operand, and returns its result.

3.1.3   Elements of an Array or a List

We can access an individual element of an array by using its index. Elements are indexed in Perl starting with the number 0. Therefore, if we have an array @friends, its first element is actually its zeroth element. To access the zeroth element of @friends, we write $friends [0]. The @ sign in front of the name of the array changes to a $ to signal that we are focusing on one element of the array and each element of an array is a scalar. The index 0 is included in square brackets.

If @friends has 20 elements in it, the index of the last element in it is 19. The last element is obtained by writing $friends [19].

An element of an array is a scalar, and hence, assigning a value to an element of an array is the usual scalar assignment operation. We individuate the element of the array using an index and place it to the left of the assignment operator. For example, to assign a value to the $ith element of the array @friends, we write the following.

```
$i = 6;
$friends [$i] = "Chad Blonding";
```

Here, $i has been given the value 6 prior to the assignment. It is not an error to have an array literal when when we obtain an element of an array using an index. Therefore the following is correct.

```
$friend = ("John",  "Jeff",  "Brett",  "Justin",  "Tom") [2];
```

3.1.4   The Index of the Last Element of an Array

The index of the last element of the array @friends can be obtained by writing $#friends. Therefore, if @friends has 20 elements in it, the value of $#friends is 19. So, one way to iterate over all elements of an array and perform an operation on each element is using a for loop and changing the loop index variable from an initial value of 0 and going up to the last index in steps of 1. In obtaining the index of the last element of an array, the $ prefix is used to indicate that number of elements is a scalar. All scalars in Perl have $ as the first character in their names. The following program takes an array and simply prints every element in it.

Program 3.1

```
#!/usr/bin/perl
use strict;
my (@friends, $i);
@friends = ('John Hart', 'Jeff Ellis', 'Brett Walters', 'Justin OMalley',
    'Tom Toybee');
for ($i=0; $i <= $#friends; $i++){
    print (uc $friends[$i], "\n");
}
```

The program uppercases every element before printing it, one per line. uc is a function that takes one argument, and if the argument evaluates to a string, uppercases it.

Perl allows us to assign a value to the last index of an array. If @friends is an array and it has 5 elements, setting $#friends to a value less than 4, say 3, will cause Perl to discard the last element from the array. Assigning $#friends to a value more than 4, say 20, will cause Perl to allocate space for elements with index 5 through 20. The values of these elements will be undef to begin with. Perl expands or shrinks an array as elements are added or deleted. Hence, it is not necessary to assign a value to the last index in most situations.

If we want to make a list empty, we can assign the value of -1 to the corresponding $# variable. For example,

```
$#friends = -1;
```

is the same as

```
@friends = ();
```

3.1.5   Accessing Elements Beyond the Last Element

Perl is very forgiving about many errors that other high level programming languages do not tolerate. When we use an array in Perl for the first time, we do not have to specify its maximum size. Even if we use

```
use strict;
strict vars;
```

or write use strict vars, we simply have to declare the name of the array and not its size. For example, the following is a declaration of an array using my.

```
my @friends;
```

In this declaration, there is no size specification.

In Perl, it is possible to access an element in an array beyond the last index. Thus, even if @friends has 5 elements, we can access its 56th element or 1010th element by writing $friends [55] or $friends [1009]. Perl will not complain because it does not perform array bounds checking. It will simply return undef as the value of any element beyond the last index. As a result of this lax attitude on the part of Perl, it may be sometimes difficult to debug programs that may misbehave due to array index crossing the array bound.

One can check if a certain element of an array has a defined value by using the defined function on an element with a specific index. Suppose we are working with an array @friends and it has 5 elements to begin with. We can assign a value to its 21st element, for instance. This causes the last index to increase to 20. Perl allocates space for all elements with index 5 through 20 although the elements with index 5 through 19 remain undefined. When Perl prints an undefined scalar, it prints nothing. The following program shows this. It is a modification of the previous program that now prints 6 values instead of 5.

Program 3.2

```
#!/usr/bin/perl
use strict;
my (@friends, $i);
@friends = ('John Hart', 'Jeff Ellis', 'Brett Walters', 'Blake Escort',
    'Tom Toybee');
$friends [20] = 'Jeff Perich';
for ($i=0; $i <= $#friends; $i++){
    if (defined $friends[$i]){
        print "$i\t", (lc $friends[$i], "\n");
    }
}
```

3.1.6   Elements Prior to Index 0

Perl allows a programmer to use negative integer indices to access elements of an array. The index -1 indexes the last element, -2 obtains the element before the last, etc. Thus, if n is the total number of elements in an array, the index $-n$ gives the first element of the array. Negative indices can be used down to $-n$. Use of the index $-(n+1)$ or smaller gives an error. In addition, setting the $# variable that gives the index of the last element of the array, to -1, empties the list. The following program illustrates the discussion in this paragraph very clearly.

```perl
#!/usr/bin/perl

#file arrayindex.pl

use strict;
my (@array);
@array = (1, 2, 3, 4, 5);
print "array = ", join (" ", @array), "\n";

#print the last element, the element before last, the element before that, etc.
print "\$array [-1] = ", $array [-1], "\n";
print "\$array [-2] = ", $array [-2], "\n";
print "\$array [-3] = ", $array [-3], "\n";
print "\$array [-4] = ", $array [-4], "\n";
print "\$array [-5] = ", $array [-5], "\n";
print "\$array [-6] = ", $array [-6], "\n";


#Changes the last element of an array
$array [-1] = 2;
print "array = ", join (" ", @array), "\n";

$array [-3] = 33;
$array [-4] = 44;
#The following if used is an error; it is commented here
#$array [-7] = 77;};


print "array = ", join (" ", @array), "\n";

#Empty an array
$#array = -1;
print "array = ", join (" ", @array), "\n";
```

The output of this program is given below. Please clearly understand the output to know how negative indices work.

```
array = 1 2 3 4 5
$array [-1] = 5
$array [-2] = 4
$array [-3] = 3
```

```
$array [-4] = 2
$array [-5] = 1
$array [-6] =
array = 1 2 3 4 2
array = 1 44 33 4 2
array =
```

When nothing is printed, it means the value is undefined or does not exist.

3.1.7 Accessing a Slice of Elements from an Array

In addition to accessing a single element from an array, it is possible to access several elements in one shot. Such a sequence of elements is called a slice. If @friends has elements with index 4 and 20 defined, and we want to extract these elements, we can write

```
@selectFriends = @friends [4,20];
```

A slice produces a sequence of elements and hence is a list or a vector by itself. Therefore, when we use a slice on the right hand side of an assignment, the target of the assignment must be a list or a vector itself. In obtaining the slice, the indices of the selected elements are separated by comma.

In obtaining a slice from a list or a vector, we can use the double dot operator between integers to specify a range of indices. To obtain the slice containing elements with indices $0, 2, 3, 4$, and 20 we can write

```
@selectFriends = @friends [0, 2..4, 20];
```

2..4 expands to a list containing $2, 3$ and 4.

We can access an element or a slice from an array literal also. A literal is one in which the values are specified explicitly.

```
$firstFriend = ('Jeff Luvellis', 'Brett Walters', 'Justin OMalley',
               'Aaron Sturtevent') [0];
@selectFriends =  ('Jeff Luvellis', 'Brett Walters', 'Justin OMalley',
               'Aaron Sturtevent') [1,3];
```

3.1.8 Assigning Values to a Slice of an Array

It is permissible to perform an assignment to a slice of an array. For example, we can rewrite the previous program as follows.

Program 3.3

```
#!/usr/bin/perl
#file friends4.pl
use strict;
my (@friends, $i);
@friends = ('John Hart', 'Jeff Ellis', 'Brett Walters',
    'Blake Escort', 'Tom Toybee');
$friends [20] = 'Jeff Perich';

#Setting  a slice
@friends [5..7] = ("Ramen Talukdar", "Sekhar Ojha", "Amar Kalita");
```

```
for ($i=0; $i <= $#friends; $i++){
    if (defined $friends[$i]){
        print "$i\t", lc ($friends[$i]), "\n";
    }
}
```

Here `@friends[5..7]` gives values to previously undefined values. The output of this program is given below.

```
0        john hart
1        jeff ellis
2        brett walters
3        blake escort
4        tom toybee
5        ramen talukdar
6        sekhar ojha
7        amar kalita
20       jeff perich
```

If the slice `@friends[5..7]` had values from before, the values will be overwritten.

3.1.9 An Array in a Scalar Context

When an array is used in a scalar context, the number of elements in the array is returned by Perl, as the value of the array. For example, if we write

```
$friendCount = @friends;
```

the value of `$friendCount` is set to the number of elements in `@friends`. A scalar context is one in which a scalar value is required. Here, to the left of the assignment statement, we have a scalar `$friendCount`. This makes the context a scalar one. If `@friends` has 5 elements, `$friendCount` will have the value 5.

The fact that, in a scalar context, an array variable gives the number of elements (not the last index) in an array is quite frequently used in loops as a condition. This can be used in a situation in which, inside the loop, elements of the array are consumed one by one, and the iteration ends when all elements are consumed. We will see an example of such a loop when we discuss the `push` and `pop` functions later in this section.

Perl also has a built-in function called `scalar` that transforms a list into a scalar. That is, it returns the length of a list. Thus,

```
$friendCount = scalar(@friends);
```

gives the number of elements in an array. If there are `undef` elements in an array, they are counted as well. The following program illustrates this discussion.

```
#!/usr/bin/perl
#file array-scalar.pl

use strict;
my (@friends);
```

```
@friends = ('Matthew Gustafson', 'Brian Freeman', 'Justin OMalley');
print "I have ", scalar (@friends), " new friends\n";
print "Once again, I have ", $#friends + 1 , " new friends\n";

$friends [10] = 'Adam Lawler';
$friends [14] = "Nathan Ekenberg";
$friends [20] = "Luke Warner";
print "I have ", scalar (@friends), " new friends\n";
print "Once again, I have ", $#friends + 1 , " new friends\n";
```

The output of this program is given below.

```
I have 3 new friends
Once again, I have 3 new friends
I have 21 new friends
Once again, I have 21 new friends
```

3.1.10   Coercion Between an Array and a Scalar

We have seen that when we write

```
$var = @list;
```

the scalar variable $var gets the length of the array. This is because the presence of a scalar on the left hand side of the assignment statement causes Perl to expect a scalar on the right hand side also. In such a scalar context, Perl returns a scalar, the number of elements in the array. However, there is a word of caution. Perl behaves differently if we do not have a single array variable such as @list on the right hand side. For example, if we write

```
$count = @friends98, @friends99;
```

the comma is not considered a list element separator, but the so-called comma operator. The comma operator causes Perl to evaluate the left operand @friends98, ignore the result of the evaluation, then evaluate the right hand operator @friends99, and return the result of the second evaluation as the value of the comma operation. @friends99 is evaluated in scalar context. Therefore, $count contains the length of the second list after the statement is executed. However, after executing

```
$count = (@friends98, @friends99);
```

$count has the length of the combined list.

On the other hand, it is also possible to write something like the following. Perl does not complain.

```
@list = $var;
```

In this case, on the left hand side of the assignment, we have an array. So, Perl expects an array on the right hand side also, but finds a scalar. Perl makes a list with $var as its only element and assigns this value to the list.

Such assignments, as the ones discussed above, work silently, without complaining, but it is not good programming practice. Unless one knows what one is doing, such assignments make the program difficult to debug and difficult to understand by others.

3.1.11   Using an Array Literal on the Left Hand Side of an Assignment

It is possible to use an array literal on the left hand side of an assignment. In such a case, the array literal must be composed of all variables, whether scalars or arrays. Using undef is acceptable in place of a scalar variable.

Assuming @friends has been assigned a value (it is alright even if it is unassigned and is empty), we can write the following.

```
($firstFriend, $secondFriend, @restFriends) = @friends;
```

The assignment statement will cause the two scalars $firstFriend, $secondFriend and the array @restFriends to be assigned. If @friends has the value

```
('Justin OMalley', 'Jeff Ellis', 'Brett Walters', 'Blake Escort')
```

$firstFriend will have the value 'Justin OMalley', $secondFriend will have the value 'Jeff Ellis' and @restFriends will have the value ('Brett Walters', 'Blake Escort'). The value of @friends does not change.

If @friends was empty to begin with, the two scalar variables will have undef value and the array will be empty after the assignment. If @friends had only one element, only $firstFriend will be assigned. $secondFriend will have undef value and the array @restFriends will remain empty. An array used on the left hand side of the assignment is all-consuming in the sense that it will hog all remaining elements of the array given on the right hand side. So, although it is syntactically correct to write more than one array variable on the left hand side, anything following the first array variable will remain unassigned. For example, if we write

```
($firstFriend, $secondFriend, @someFriends, $middleFriend, @restFriends)
    = @friends;
```

the value of $middleFriend will always be undef. In addition, @restFriends will always be empty. This is because the array @someFriends will consume all elements that are left after @friends assigning values to the two scalars.

If we want to ignore the first element of the list when performing the assignment, we can write

```
(undef, $secondFriend, @someFriends, $middleFriend, @restFriends) = @friends;
```

The idea of using array literals can be used for swapping values of scalar variables. For example, if we write

```
($firstFriend, $secondFriend) = ($secondFriend, $firstFriend);
```

the values of the two variables are swapped.

The technique of extracting elements from an array is used quite frequently inside subroutines to extract specific arguments and give them specific names.

3.1.12   Printing Elements of a List or an Array

Of course, we can print elements of a list or an array by looping through the elements of the array using a for loop. The following program loops through every element of the list @friends and prints the elements one by one, one per line.

Program 3.4

```
#!/usr/bin/perl
use strict;
my @friends;
@friends = ('John Hart', 'Jeff Ellis', 'Brett Walters',
    'Blake Escort', 'Tom Toybee');

for ($i=0; $i <= $#friends; $i++){
        print "$friends[$i]\n";
}
```

In this program, the expression `$friends[$i]` inside the double quotes is interpolated to obtain the element with index `$i` in the array `@friends`.

A simpler way to print every element of an array is to simply use the `print` function on the whole array.

Program 3.5

```
#!/usr/bin/perl
use strict;
my @friends;
@friends = ('John Hart', 'Jeff Ellis', 'Brett Walters', 'Blake Escort',
    'Tom Toybee');

print @friends;
print "\n";
```

This program prints all elements of the list `@friends` in one single line without any space between two consecutive elements. However, if we write the array variable inside double quotes, *i.e.*, write

```
print "@friends";
print "\n";
```

the elements of the array are written out in a single line, but this time, two consecutive elements of the array are separated from each other by an empty space, the default list element separator. That is, an array variable is interpolated inside a string using the default element separator.

We can change the value of the list item separator by assigning a value to the special variable `$"`. We can set `$"` to a sequence of one or more characters. The list items will be printed separated by the sequence of characters specified. The list separator is not printed after the last element of the list. It can be assigned several times inside a program. We should note that setting the list element separator does not have any effect unless a list is printed inside double quotes. Also, the list separator in effect at a certain time in the program will affect every list printed.

Program 3.6

```
#!/usr/bin/perl
#file friends8.pl

use strict;
my @friends;
@friends = ('John Hart', 'Jeff Ellis', 'Brett Walters',
```

```
                'Blake Escort', 'Tom Toybee');
#print the list elements separated by a comma and a space
$" = ", ";
print "@friends";
print "\n";

#print the list elements in the form of an HTML list
$" = "</li>\n<li>";
print "<ul>\n<li>";
print "@friends";
print "</li>\n</ul>\n";
```

First we set $" to print the list elements separated by a comma and a space character. Next, we set the value of $" to </li>\n<li>. This will cause the list items to be printed separated by a newline character and the sequence <li>, the HTML list item tag. Since the list element separator is not printed before the first element, we print <li> before the first element. Also, we print the tag <ul> to start an HTML unordered list, and the tag </ul> at the end to end the unordered list. A program fragment like this can be used to produce an HTML list inside a Perl program. The output of the program is given below.

```
John Hart, Jeff Ellis, Brett Walters, Blake Escort, Tom Toybee
<ul>
<li>John Hart</li>
<li>Jeff Ellis</li>
<li>Brett Walters</li>
<li>Blake Escort</li>
<li>Tom Toybee</li>
</ul>
```

Perl also has a special variable $, that can be used to set the value of the separator string printed between two array elements for an array variable that is not interpolated. That is, the separator string is used when an array variable is printed directly without any double quotes. The following program has the exact same HTML output as the immediately previous one.

```
#!/usr/bin/perl
#file friends11.pl

use strict;
my @friends;
@friends = ('John Hart', 'Jeff Ellis', 'Brett Walters',
            'Blake Escort', 'Tom Toybee');
#print the list elements separated by a comma and a space
$" = ", ";
print "@friends";
print "\n";

#print the list elements in the form of an HTML list
$, = "</li>\n<li>";
print "<ul>\n<li>";
```

```
print @friends;
print "</li>\n</ul>\n";
```

3.1.13   Looping Through Every Element of a List or an Array

There are several ways we can loop through every element of a array. We have already seen how we can use the `for` loop along with a numeric index that steps from 0 to the last index in the array. We will see another way to iterate over every element of an array.

We can use the `foreach` construct to loop through every element of a loop. The `foreach` construct has the structure

```
foreach $variable (@list){...}
```

`$variable` is the *loop control* variable. It is bound to an individual element of the array at a time. To start, `$variable` is bound to the first element of the list or the array; the body of the loop is performed for this bound value. Then, the variable is bound to the second element of the array and the body of the loop is executed for this value. This way it continues till the whole list is traversed.

Once again, the following program prints every element of an array in HTML format.

Program 3.7

```
#!/usr/bin/perl
#file friends9.pl

use strict;

my (@friends, $friend);
@friends =   ('Michael Saden', 'Brent Hays', 'John Hart', 'Jeff Ellis',
              'Brett Walters', 'Blake Escort', 'Tom Toybee');

print "<ul>\n";

foreach $friend (@friends){
    print "<li>$friend</li>\n";
}

print "</ul>\n";
```

If the loop control variable is not specified, it is implicitly taken to be the special variable `$_`. We have another version of the preceding program below.

Program 3.8

```
#!/usr/bin/perl
#file friends10.pl

use strict vars;
```

```perl
my @friends;
@friends =  ('Michael Saden', 'Brent Hays', 'John Hart', 'Jeff Ellis',
             'Brett Walters', 'Blake Escort', 'Tom Toybee');

print "<ul>\n";

foreach (@friends){
    print "<li>$_</li>\n";
}

print "</ul>\n";
```

The only difference between this program and the previous one is in the string argument to print inside the foreach loop. The use of $_ makes the second program a bit tighter, but cryptic at the same time.

3.1.14   pushing onto and popping off an Array

We can add an element to the end of an array by pushing it onto the array. The first argument push takes is the original list. The first argument can be followed by either a single scalar, or a list of items. If we have a scalar following the first argument, it is added to the end of the original list. If we have a list following the first argument, the elements of the second list are tacked onto the end of the first list, one by one. Thus, push makes the first argument behave like a stack data structure. The following program shows several examples of the use of push.

Program 3.9

```perl
#!/usr/bin/perl
#file push1.pl
use strict vars;
$" = ", ";

my (@friends, $friend);
my @friends99 = ('Justin OMalley', 'Timothy Valley', 'Brent Hays',
                                   'Michael Saden');
my @friends98 = ('John Hart', 'Jeff Ellis', 'Brett Walters', 'Blake Escort');
my $friend97 = 'Tom Toybee';
my @oldFriends = ('Chad Blonding', 'Jeff Perich');
@friends = ("Hakan Kvarnstrom");

push @friends, 'Tommi Eriksson', 'Jonas Olsson';
push @friends, (@friends99, @friends98);
push @friends, $friend97, @oldFriends;
print "@friends\n";
```

This function prints the names of the friends in the order given below.

```
Hakan Kvarnstrom, Tommi Eriksson, Jonas Olsson, Justin O'Malley,
Timothy Valley, Brent Hays, Michael Saden, John Hart, Jeff Ellis,
Brett Walters, Blake Escort, Tom Toybee, Chad Blonding, Jeff Perich
```

Although we have broken up the list into several lines, it is actually printed on one line.

The push function returns the length of the resulting list. In the following program, the value returned by push is used to assign a variable $newLength.

Program 3.10

```perl
#!/usr/bin/perl
use strict vars;
$" = ", ";
my (@list1, @list2);

@list1 = ('Jeff Perich', 'Justin OMalley', 'Aaron Sturtevent');
@list2 = ('Michael Saden', 'Brett Walters', 'John Hart', 'Matt Van Zandt');
my $newLength = push @list1, @list2;

print "newLength = $newLength\n";
```

The value of $newLength at the end is 7. At the end of the program, $list1 has 7 items and $list2 has the original 4 items.

In Perl, most functions return a value. This is a characteristic of functional programming that Perl supports. The thing to note here is that push does not return the new list, but its length. This is unlike some other programming languages that support functional programming, such as LISP. Therefore, it would be wrong to write

```perl
my @list1 = push @list1, @list2;
```

if we want @list1 to contain the new list. It happens automatically without an assignment. In the following program, we perform such a wrong assignment.

Program 3.11

```perl
#!/usr/bin/perl
use strict vars;
$" = ", ";
my (@list1, @list2);

@list1 = ('Jeff Perich', 'Justin OMalley', 'Aaron Sturtevent');
@list2 = ('Michael Saden', 'Brett Walters', 'John Hart',
          'Matt Van Zandt');
@list1  = push @list1, @list2;   #WRONG! WRONG! WRONG!

print "list1 = @list1\n";
```

At the end of the program, @list1 does not contain the seven names, but it becomes an one-element list containing the number 7—the length of the the resulting list after the push. It is because

```perl
push @list1, @list2; #WRONG! WRONG! WRONG!
```

returns the number 7. On the left hand side of the assignment

```
@list1   = push @list1, @list2;
```

we have the list @list1 and on the right hand side, the scalar 7. Perl coerces 7 into a list containing one element 7.

The function pop takes a list as an argument and removes the last element of the list. The value returned by pop is the element removed from the end of the list. The side effect of the pop operation is that the original list is reduced by one element.

In the following program, we pop items one by one from a list. The popping of individual elements is done inside a while loop.

Program 3.12

```
#!/usr/bin/perl
use strict vars;

my $friend;
my @friends =   ('Justin OMalley', 'Timothy Valley', 'Brent Hays',
                  'Michael Saden',
                  'Matt Van Zandt', 'Reeves Smith', 'Matt Bolton');

#An array in a scalar context such as the condition of a while loop
while (@friends){
        $friend = pop (@friends);
        print "$friend\n";
}
```

At the end of the program, the list @friends has nothing in it. It is because all elements in it have been popped. We use @friends as the condition of the while loop. The conditional of a while loop expects a scalar value which it treats as a boolean. In a scalar context, a list is evaluated as the number of elements in it. Inside the while loop, we pop an element off the right of the loop. In every iteration, the list is reduced by one element. Therefore, when the last element has been popped, the conditional returns a value of 0. 0 is considered *false* in Perl and the while loop gets finished. Following our discussions earlier, the while loop can also be written as the following.

```
while (scalar (@friends)){
        $friend = pop (@friends);
        print "$friend\n";
        }
```

An alternative way to push an element is the following.

```
@friends = (@friends, $newFriend);
```

Here, $newFriend is tacked onto the end of the list @friends and the resulting list is called @friends. This is the same as doing push except that the number of elements in the resulting list is not returned.

3.1.15   shift **and** unshift

unshift takes two arguments: a list and a scalar (actually, it can take a list as the second argument) and inserts the second argument in the front of the list. Therefore, it is just like push except that push inserts element(s) at the end of the list whereas `unshift` inserts the new element(s) in the front. `unshift` returns the number of elements inserted.

`shift` is the counterpart of `pop`. `shift` moves the whole list to the left by one element, thus removing the first or the leftmost element. `shift` returns the element removed. The reduction of the list happens as a side effect.

Consider the following program that builds a list by unshifting elements onto it. These elements are put in the front of the array one by one by `unshift`ing. If a list is `unshift`ed, the elements of the second list are put in the front of the original list.

Program 3.13

```
#!/usr/bin/perl
use strict;
$" = "\n";
my (@friends, $friend);
my @friends99 = ('Michael Richter', 'Justin O\'Mallory', 'Rene Myers');
my @oldFriends = ('Brett Walters', 'Jeff Perich');

unshift @friends, "Hakan Kvarnstrom";
unshift @friends, @friends99;
unshift @friends, @oldFriends;
unshift @friends, "Matt Dawson";
while (@friends) {
        $friend = shift (@friends);
        print "$friend\n";
}
```

The list `@friends` becomes empty at the end of the `while` loop. Before emptying, the list is printed in the following order.

```
Matt Dawson
Brett Walters
Jeff Perich
Michael Richter
Justin O'Malley
Rene Myers
Hakan Kvarnstrom
```

It must be pointed out that when the second argument to `unshift` is a list, the elements of this last are added to the front of the first argument list in the unreversed order.

3.1.16 `splice`ing a List into Another List

We can take a sub-sequence of elements in a list and replace them by elements from another list using the `splice` function. Consider the following program.

Program 3.14

```
#!/usr/bin/perl
use strict;
```

```
$" = ", ";
my @friends = ("Shonna Dyer", "Rich Rogers", "Nicole Nugent", "John Warner",
               "Reeves P. Smith", "Jeff Perich", "Susan Worley");
my @newFriends = ("Michael Richter", "Abhijit Bezbarua", "Jugma Bora");

my @noMoreFriends = splice (@friends, 4, 2, @newFriends);
print "My friends are: @friends\n";
print "Some of my friends from years ago are: @noMoreFriends\n";
```

We use the built-in function `splice` in this program. It takes four arguments. `@friends` is the original list. `@newFriends` is the list whose elements are `splice`d into `@friends`. `splice`ing starts with the element obtained by counting 4 elements over from the beginning of the list to the 5th element. It then removes 2 elements from the list and replaces them with the contents of the list `@newFriends`. A list containing the removed elements are returned as the value of the `splice` function. The output of the program is given below. This list of returned values used to set the variable `@noMoreFriends`. The output of the program is given below.

```
My friends are: Shonna Dyer, Rich Rogers, Nicole Nugent, John Warner,
Michael Richter, Abhijit Bezbarua, Jugma Bora, Susan Worley
Some of my friends from years ago are: Reeves P. Smith, Jeff Perich
```

The first line of output has been broken into two lines for presentation.

It is not necessary to give the fourth argument in a call to `splice`. It is also possible to make a call without the third argument as well. If the fourth argument which provides the replacement list, is not given, no replacement is done for the removed elements. For example, if in the previous program, we replace the call to `splice` by the following call

```
my @noMoreFriends = splice (@friends, 4, 2);
```

then, the output will change to the following. We have broken the output when necessary to fit the printed page.

```
My friends are: Shonna Dyer, Rich Rogers, Nicole Nugent, John Warner,
                Susan Worley
Some of my friends from years ago are: Reeves P. Smith, Jeff Perich
```

If we do not provide the last argument, all elements in the original list after the 4th lement are removed. In this case, the output will be the following.

```
My friends are: Shonna Dyer, Rich Rogers, Nicole Nugent, John Warner
Some of my friends from years ago are: Reeves P. Smith, Jeff Perich
```

3.1.17 Sorting Elements of an Array

Elements of a list can be sorted using the built-in `sort` function. Consider the following simple program.

Program 3.15

```
#!/usr/bin/perl
#file sort2.pl
```

```
use strict vars;
$" = ", ";

my @friends  = ('Reeves P. Smith III', 'Matthew Van Zandt',
                'Kristofer Todd', 'Ryan Slaughter');
@friends = sort  @friends;

print "@friends\n";
```

The program prints

```
Kristofer Todd, Matthew Van Zandt, Reeves P. Smith III, Ryan Slaughter
```

as the sorted list with the comma as the item separator.

Sorting takes place using the default ascending order for strings. Undefined values go to the front, defined null values are next, and then strings with values in the proper alphabetical order. In the following program, one of the values to be sorted is undefined, being an uninitialized element of an array.

Program 3.16

```
#!/usr/bin/perl
#file sort3.pl
use strict vars;
$" = ", ";

my @friends99;

my @friends  = ($friends99[12], 'Reeves P. Smith III', 'Matthew Van Zandt',
                'Kristofer Todd', 'Ryan Slaughter');
@friends = sort  @friends;

print "@friends\n";
```

The output of this program is

```
, Kristofer Todd, Matthew Van Zandt, Reeves P. Smith III, Ryan Slaughter
```

The undef value comes in the front, but we know that undef is printed as the empty string.

Now, if we sort a list of numbers, say (53, 29, 11, 32, 7, 112, 291), Perl returns (11, 112, 29, 291, 32, 53, 7). Perl does not care that we have all numbers in the list. It sorts them as if they were all strings. Once again, if we sort the list (1, "2", "three", 4, 'five'), Perl returns (1, 2, 4, five, three). Perl does so because it assumes every element in the list to be sorted is a string, and as a results sorts them as characters although some of the elements may be numbers.

sort can optionally take a first argument that is a subroutine. If such an argument is given, the subroutine must be one that takes two arguments. The subroutine must compare these two arguments and return either a negative number, 0, or a positive number. If a negative number is returned, the first argument given to the subroutine comes before the second argument in the final sort order. If 0 is returned, the two arguments are equal and they can occur in any order in the sorted list. If a positive number is returned, the first element appears after the second element in the final sorted order.

Thus, to sort a list of numbers, we write a subroutine that compares two numbers at a time, and returns a negative value, zero, or a positive number, depending on if the first number is smaller than, equal to, or greater than the second number.

Program 3.17

```
#!/usr/bin/perl
use strict vars;
$" = ", ";

#Subroutine for comparing two numbers
sub inAscendingOrder{
    if ($a < $b)      {return -1.1;}
    elsif ($a == $b) {return 0;}
    else             {return 1.2}
}

my @numbers = (1, 2, 11, 12, 121);
@numbers = sort  inAscendingOrder @numbers;
print "@numbers\n";
```

The output of the program is a printout of the sorted list.

```
1, 2, 11, 12, 121
```

There are several things to note about the subroutine used for sorting. It takes two arguments. However, the arguments are implicit. The first argument must be referred to by the name $a inside the subroutine, and the second argument by the name $b. This is kludgy, but this how Perl works. The authors of Perl say that "in the interest of efficiency, the normal calling code for subroutines is bypassed" in this situation.

The subroutine must not be recursive; that is it must not make a call to itself. This is also for the sake of efficiency. In addition, the normal convention that arguments passed to a subroutine are available as the value of the special array @_ inside the subroutine, does not hold if the subroutine is used for sorting. If the subroutine is used for sorting, there are only two scalar arguments, and they must be called $a and $b, in order. $a and $b must not be declared using my inside the subroutine.

The subroutine also must not perform any assignments to $a and $b. This is because the arguments $a and $b are passed to the subroutine from the calling program, by using so-called *reference*. That is, references to their addresses are passed; the literal values are not passed to the subroutine by the calling program. If assignments are done to $a or $b inside the subroutine, the original two elements of the array being compared will undergo change. In other words, sort will destroy the original array.

Finally, the array is supposed to return a negative number if the first number is less than the second number, and a positive number if the first number is larger than the second number. Therefore, although we have returned −1.1 and 1.2, respectively, in these two situations, any other values will also work.

The subroutine we have written for sorting numbers in ascending order is so commonly used that Perl provides a built-in operator <=> for a comparison of two numbers that returns −1, 0 and 1 respectively, in the three situations discussed. Therefore, the previous program can be written in the following manner also.

Program 3.18

```
#!/usr/bin/perl
```

```
use strict vars;
$" = ", ";

sub inAscendingOrder{
    $a <=> $b;
}

my @numbers = (1, 2, 11, 12, 121);
@numbers = sort  inAscendingOrder @numbers;
print "@numbers\n";
```

Perl, actually, allows us to write the body of the sorting subroutine as a block of statements instead of a subroutine. Therefore, the following also works.

Program 3.19

```
#!/usr/bin/perl
use strict vars;
$" = ", ";

my @numbers = (1, 2, 11, 12, 121);
@numbers = sort  {$a <=> $b;}  @numbers;
print "@numbers\n";
```

It makes sense to write the subroutine "in-line" as a block of code only if it is short. If it is big, stylistically, it is better if we write it as a separate subroutine.

If we want sort the numbers in descending order, we simply need to change the subroutine such that the order of usage of $a and $b is reversed in the comparisons. One of the following subroutines will work.

```
sub inDescendingOrder{
    if ($a > $b)      {return -1;}
    elsif ($a == $b) {return 0;}
    else             {return 1}
}

sub inDescendingOrder{
    $b <=> $a;
}
```

We can also write the subroutine "in-line" if we want.

If we are trying to sort a list of strings, we know that the string ascending order is used automatically. In other words, no subroutine argument needs to be passed to sort. However, if we want to write a subroutine, we can do so to mimic the default comparison function.

Program 3.20

```
#!/usr/bin/perl
use strict vars;
$" = ", ";
```

```
#Subroutine for comparing two strings
sub inAscendingOrder{
    $a cmp $b;
}

my @friends = ('Rene Myers', 'Brooke Peterson', 'Sharon Heatherington');
@friends = sort  inAscendingOrder @friends;
print "@friends\n";
```

cmp is a built-in function that is used to compare two strings. It is similar to <=> in what it returns. Instead of using cmp, we can spell out the details of the comparison as the following subroutine.

```
sub inAscendingOrder{
    if    ($a lt $b) {return -1;}
    elsif ($a eq $b) {return 0;}
    else             {return 1;}
}
```

If we have a list that has a mix of numbers and strings, we can write a comparison subroutine that uses both cmp and <=>. Let us look at the following program and discuss what happens.

Program 3.21

```
#!/usr/bin/perl
use strict vars;
$" = ", ";

#Subroutine for comparing two strings
sub inAscendingOrder{
    ($a <=> $b) || ($a cmp $b);
}

my @list = (1, 'Rene Myers', 11, 'Brooke Peterson', 21,
               'Sharon Heatherington', 111);
@list = sort  inAscendingOrder @list;
print "@list\n";
```

The result printed by this program is the following.

```
Brooke Peterson, Rene Myers, Sharon Heatherington, 1, 11, 21, 111
```

Let us try to understand why this happens.

When the comparison subroutine inAscendingOrder compares two numbers, say 1 and 121, it returns −1 because 1 is less than 121. Therefore, 1 appears before 121 in the sorted list. Since −1 is considered *true* in Perl, $a cmp $b is not executed. || is the so-called short-circuit *or* operator which stops evaluating the boolean conditions as soon as it gets a true value. If the two numbers compared are equal, 0 is returned by <=>; in such a case, $a cmp $b is called. Two equal numbers when compared as string are also equal. Therefore, 0 is returned by the subroutine. Two equal numbers can occur in any order in the resulting list.

If we are comparing two strings, say 'a' and 'abc', the first comparison $a <=> $b compares them as numbers. Perl tries to salvage a number from both the strings, but because they do not contain any embedded digits, the salvaged numbers are both 0. As a result the number comparison returns 0. In such a case, $a cmp $b is used to compare and the proper order results in the sorted list.

If one argument to the comparison subroutine is a number, and the other is a string, say 121 and 'abc', the first comparison using <=> actually compares 121 and 0 (the number salvaged from 'abc') and returns 1. This causes the numbers to float to the end of the sorted list.

If in the program given above, we write the comparison function as

```
sub inAscendingOrder{
    ($a cmp $b) || ($a <=> $b);
}
```

the sorted list will be printed as

```
1, 11, 111, 21, Brooke Peterson, Rene Myers, Sharon Heatherington
```

because the cmp comparison will be done first. The cmp comparison will treat numbers also as strings. Therefore, the <=> comparison will never be done.

3.1.18 Mapping A Function Onto a List

We discuss mapping functions briefly here, for the sake of completion of our discussion on arrays or lists.

Suppose we have a function called square that multiplies a number by itself. If we want to square all the numbers in a list, we can apply the square function to every element of a list. Applying a block of code to every element of a list is called mapping.

Program 3.22

```
#!/usr/bin/perl
#file map4.pl

use strict 'vars';
use strict 'subs';
$" = ", ";

#a subroutine that multiplies a number by itself
sub square{
    my ($n) = @_;
    return $n * $n;
}

my @nList = (1, 2, 3, 11);
my @squares = map {square ($_);} @nList;
print "List of squares = @squares\n";
```

The output printed by this function is given below.

```
List of squares = 1, 4, 9, 121
```

The map function, as used here, takes two arguments: a block of statements to execute and a list. Here the block simply contains a call to the square function. This function is called with $_ as the argument. map iterates over every element of a list, and as it iterates over an element of the list, the element is available to it as $_. The result returned by the block of statements for a particular value of $_ is remembered. map collects all the results of such computation and returns them in a list. Thus, map performs an implicit iteration over the elements of a list and also returns an additional result list.

We use the

```
use strict 'subs';
```

declaration or pragma to tell Perl that a subroutine name cannot be used before it has been declared.

We do not really have to write a function if the mapped block of statements is simple. We can do the mapping directly. The following program is a rewrite of the program given above.

Program 3.23

```
#!/usr/bin/perl
use strict 'vars';
$" = ", ";

my @nList = (1, 2, 3, 11);
my @squares = map {$_ * $_;} @nList;
print "List of squares = @squares\n";
```

If we do not want the results returned by map, but simply want map to have a side effect such as printing something in each iteration, we do not have to assign the result returned by map. The following program prints each squared number on a line by itself.

Program 3.24

```
#!/usr/bin/perl
use strict 'vars';
my @nList = (1, 2, 3, 11);
map {print $_ * $_, "\n";} @nList;
```

If we want to have a side-effect such as printing, and also obtain a result list, the mapped block of statements must return a certain value at the end for each element of the list. This can be done by simply evaluating an expression at the end of the block. The value returned by a block of statements is the value returned by the last statement in it.

The following program maps a block of statements onto a list of numbers. The mapped block computes the square and the cube of each number. In addition, it prints the square and the cube for the numbers, one pair per line. The final statement of the block simply evaluates to a list containing two elements: the square and the cube. The last statement of the program prints the returned list.

Program 3.25

```
#!/usr/bin/perl
use strict 'vars';
$" = ", ";
```

```
my @nList = (1, 2, 3, 11);
my @squaresAndCubes = map {my $square =  $_ * $_;
                           my $cube = $square * $_;
                           print "$square\t$cube\n";
                           ($square, $cube);
                          }
                     @nList;
print "List of squares and cubes = @squaresAndCubes\n";
```

The output of the program is given below.

```
1 1
4 8
9 27
121 1331
List of squares and cubes = 1, 1, 4, 8, 9, 27, 121, 1331
```

If the last statement inside the block was removed, the last line of the output printed by the program will be the following.

```
List of squares and cubes = 1, 1, 1, 1
```

This is because the `print` function returns an 1 every time it succeeds in printing something.

If the block of statements that is mapped becomes somewhat large, it makes sense to write it out as a separate function. This function must take one scalar value as argument and return something to construct the resulting list. We can call this function with $_ as the argument inside the mapped block. We had given an example like this in the beginning of this section.

3.1.19   `split`ting a String, `join`ing a List, `grep`ping from a List

Perl provides us with a straight-forward way to take a string and extract sub-strings that are separated from each other in a consistent way. For example, if want to extract all the individual words from a line of text, we can do so very easily. We know that each word is separated from the word in front and the word behind by one or more blank spaces, except, of course, the first word and the last word.

Program 3.26

```
#!/usr/bin/perl
use strict 'vars';
$" = "\n";

open(IN, "input.txt");
my $line = <IN>;
my @words = split /\s+/, $line;
print "@words\n";
```

This program reads the first line of text from the file `input.txt` and breaks it apart into a list of smaller strings based on the pattern `\s+`. When a line is read from a file, it is read as a single continuous string from beginning to the end. `split` takes two arguments: a pattern based on which splitting is performed, and the string being split. We will learn more about patterns and regular expressions later in the book, but for the time being, we should know that the predefined escape sequence \s when used inside a pattern stands for a space character—i.e., either a blank space, a tab space, a new line character, a return character, and a form feed character. \s+ means one or more \s characters. Now, $line does not have any new line character \n in it. Therefore, @words will contain all the words in the line read. The output of this program looks like the following.

```
Perl
provides
us
with
a
straight-forward
way
to
take
a
string
and
extract
```

These are all the words that occur in that line. They have been separated out. If we know for sure that the words are separated from each other by one or blank spaces only, we could have written the line that does the splitting as follows.

```
my @words = split / +/, $line;
```

Here, the pattern specification / +/ has a blank space character. In Perl, patterns are most usually specified by delimiting them within / in the front and at the end.

We can see that the program given above can be easily extended to read a whole file (or, even all the files in a given directory, possibly recursively) and to count and enumerate all the distinct words that occur.

The built-in function join simply takes a list of strings and puts them together sequentially into a large string. join takes two arguments: the first—a string that is used as the glue, and the second—a list of strings. For example, if we want to write out all the words that occur in the first line of the file, sorted in ascending order and one per line, in the form of an HTML list, we can write the following.

Program 3.27

```
#!/usr/bin/perl
use strict 'vars';
$" = "\n";

open(IN, "input.txt");
my $line = <IN>;
my @words = sort (split /\s+/, $line);
my $printedWords = join "</li>\n<li>", @words;
print "<ul>\n<li>$printedWords</li>\n</ul>\n";
```

The output of this program is given below.

```
<ul>
```

```
<li>Perl</li>
<li>a</li>
<li>a</li>
<li>and</li>
<li>extract</li>
<li>provides</li>
<li>straight-forward</li>
<li>string</li>
<li>take</li>
<li>to</li>
<li>us</li>
<li>way</li>
<li>with</li>
</ul>
```

grep is a built-in function that takes a pattern as the first argument and a list as the second argument and picks out the elements from the list that satisfy the pattern. The following program prints out the names of those friends that have the pattern sson in them.

Program 3.28

```perl
#!/usr/bin/perl
use strict 'vars';
my @friends = ("Hakan Kvarnstrom", "Dawson Leary", "Jonas Olsson",
               "Tommi Jokinen",
               "Magnus Eriksson", "Brooke Peterson");
my @specialFriends = grep /sson/, @friends;
print join ("\n", sort @specialFriends), "\n";
```

The output printed by this program is given below.

```
Jonas Olsson
Magnus Eriksson
```

3.1.20   Reading a File in One Swoop

We know by now that a file handle can be used to read a line at a time form a file. For example, if we write

```perl
open IN, "input.txt";
$line = <IN>;
```

$line has the first line of the file input.txt. We can easily write a while loop that reads every line of the file and performs some task. Here $line is a scalar. Therefore, the reading of the file takes place in scalar context. In scalar context, the angle bracket operator (i.e., <>) operator reads the next line from the file specified in the filehandle. However, there may be situations where we may want to read the whole file in one read operation. This happens if <> is used in array or list context. For example, if we write

```perl
@lines = <IN>;
```

all the lines in the file specified by the handle IN will be read. Each line read will be an element of the array @lines. The lines are available in the same sequence as they occur in the file. We are assuming that we have a text or ASCII file. The following program simply prints the number of lines in a text file.

Program 3.29

```
#!/usr/bin/perl
use strict 'vars';
open (IN, "input.txt");

my @lines = <IN>;
my $lineCount = $#lines + 1;
print "Number of lines in the file = $lineCount\n";
```

The output of this program is something like the following.

```
Number of lines in the file = 131
```

3.2   Associative Arrays or Hashes

Perl provides a specialized type of array called associative arrays or hashes. The main difference between a regular array and a hash is that in an array the elements are indexed by integers whereas in a hash, the entries are indexed by arbitrary strings.

A hash is an important data structure used frequently in programming. A hash has a chunk of memory allocated to it by the system. Usually, the memory allocated to a hash table is quite a bit higher than the amount of space needed at the current time. A hash can grow and shrink during the course of a program. Additional space is allocated to a hash when it gets filled to a certain capacity, say 50% or 60%. In Perl, this threshold is set by the system whereas in programming languages like Lisp, the default can be overridden easily by a programmer.

The idea behind using a hash is that sometimes numeric indices do not make much sense in associating two or more sets of data values. For example, if we want to associate the names of friends with the colleges they go to, we can use the two arrays given below. The following program builds an HTML table from the contents of two arrays.

Program 3.30

```
#!/usr/bin/perl
use strict "vars";
my @friends = ("Jeff Perich", "Michael Richter", "Alex Dunn", "Reeves Smith",
          "Karen Carter");
my @schools = ("University of Colorado-Boulder", "Otero Junior College",
          "University of Pennsylvania", "Fort Lewis College",
          "University of Pennsylvania");

open OUT, ">friends.html";

print OUT  "<html>\n<title>Friends and Colleges</title>\n";
print OUT
   "<body bgcolor = bisque text=darkblue><h2>Friends and Colleges</h2>\n";
print OUT  "<table bgcolor=lightyellow  border=1>\n";
print OUT  "<tr><th>Name</th><th>College</th></tr>\n";
```

```perl
for (my $i=0; $i <= $#friends; $i++){
    my $oneRow = "<tr><td>$friends[$i]</td>\t";
    $oneRow .= "<td>$schools[$i]</td></tr>\n";
    print OUT $oneRow;
}


print OUT "</table>\n</body>\n</html>\n";
```

This program creates a nice-looking HTML table. It writes out the table to a file called `friends.html`. It sets up background colors for the HTML page and the table. We need to make sure that the two arrays `@friends` and `@schools` have the same number of elements. We need to make sure that we store a person's name and his or her school in the same position in the two arrays, respectively. `$i`, the index of the loop helps us navigate through the two arrays synchronously. The statement

```perl
$oneRow .= "<td>$schools[$i]</td></tr>\n";
```

is used to concatenate the string on the right hand side of `.=` to the variable `$oneRow` on the left hand side.

There are problems that can arise in working with arrays that are related. It is possible that in typing, we may get the order of elements mixed up. It is also possible that the numbers of entries in the two arrays is not the same. We may also make mistake in updating the two arrays if they get somewhat large.

A better idea is to write a program that uses hashes or associative arrays. Note that this program uses a function called `keys` that gives the list of all keys in a hash in a random order. This function is discussed later in Section 3.2.2.

Program 3.31

```perl
#!/usr/bin/perl
use strict "vars";
my %friends = ("Jeff Perich" => "University of Colorado-Boulder",
               "Michael Richter" => "Otero Junior College",
               "Alex Dunn" => "University of Pennsylvania",
               "Reeves Smith" => "Fort Lewis College",
               "Karen Carter" => "University of Pennsylvania");

open OUT, ">newFriends.html";

print OUT "<html>\n<title>Friends and Colleges</title>\n";
print OUT
   "<body bgcolor = bisque text=darkblue><h2>Friends and Colleges</h2>\n";
print OUT  "<table bgcolor=lightyellow  border=1>\n",
   "<tr><th>Name</th><th>College</th></tr>\n";

foreach my $friend  (sort (keys %friends)){
    my $oneRow = "<tr><td>" . $friend . "</td>\t";
    $oneRow .= "<td>" . $friends {$friend} . "</td></tr>\n";
    print OUT $oneRow;
}

print OUT "</table>\n</body>\n</html>\n";
```

Writing the information in the form of a hash makes the association explicit. For example, the part of the hash declaration,

```
"Reeves Smith" => "Fort Lewis College"
```

makes it clear that `"Reeves Smith"` is associated with `"Fort Lewis College"`. Here `"Reeves Smith"` is called the *key* and `"Fort Lewis College"` is the corresponding *value*. In addition, the possibility of making errors is reduced.

A hash is usually written with the key and the value pairs separated by the `=>` operator. The pairs of key-value pairs are separated by the comma. It is possible to specify a hash without the `=>` operator because it is nothing but syntactic sugar. Instead of `=>`, we can write a comma. Therefore, the following is acceptable in specifying the hash table.

```
my %friends = ("Jeff Perich", "University of Colorado-Boulder",
               "Michael Richter", "Otero Junior College",
               "Alex Dunn", "University of Pennsylvania",
               "Reeves Smith", "Fort Lewis College",
               "Kathleen Turner", "University of Pennsylvania");
```

Whether we specify a hash using `=>` or not, the key-value pairs are stored internally using a hashing function. Therefore, the key-value pairs can be stored in any order, not the order given. Given a key value, Perl computes position in the hash array to find out where the value corresponding to the key should be stored. It saves the value in the computed position. A good hashing function "guarantees" that the position for a specific key value is unique. The hash function always transforms the key to the same position.

3.2.1   Assigning a Hash and Its Elements

We can assign one hash to another. So, an assignment such as the following works.

```
%newFriends = %friends;
```

It is possible to assign a literal list to a hash variable. Therefore, the following assignment is correct.

```
my %friendsHash = ("Jeff Perich", "University of Colorado-Boulder",
               "Michael Richter", "Otero Junior College",
               "Alex Dunn", "University of Pennsylvania",
               "Reeves Smith", "Fort Lewis College",
               "Karen Carter", "University of Pennsylvania");
```

The elements of the hash table are paired up automatically. So, `"Jeff Perich"` is associated with `"University of Colorado-Boulder"`, and so on and so forth.

If the number of elements in the hash `%friendsHash` were odd, the elements would still be paired up as key and value. The last element will become a key with no corresponding value.

It is possible to assign a list variable to a hash. We see that in the following code fragment.

```
my @friendsList = ("Jeff Perich", "University of Colorado-Boulder",
               "Michael Richter", "Otero Junior College",
               "Alex Dunn", "University of Pennsylvania",
               "Reeves Smith", "Fort Lewis College",
               "Karen Carter", "University of Pennsylvania");

my %friendsHash = @friendsList;
```

Once again, the values are paired up. If the list has an odd number of elements, the last element becomes a key in the hash with no associated value.

If we assign a hash to a list, the key-value pairs become elements of the list. A key and a value of the hash occur next to each other in the list, but beyond that the order of the pairs is arbitrary, based on the hashing function used. In the following program, the hash has an odd number of elements.

Program 3.32

```perl
#!/usr/bin/perl
use strict "vars";
$" = ", ";

my %friendsHash = ("Jeff Perich", "University of Colorado-Boulder",
              "Michael Richter", "Otero Junior College",
              "Alex Dunn", "University of Pennsylvania",
              "Reeves Smith", "Fort Lewis College",
              "Karen Carter");


foreach my $friend  (sort keys (%friendsHash)){
    my $oneRow = "$friend\t" . $friendsHash{$friend} . "\n";
    print  $oneRow;
}
```

As a result, the last value `"Karen Carter"` becomes a key with no associated value. When we coerce the hash to a list, the list now has a pair of elements, one of which is `"Karen Carter"` and the one following it is empty. In total, the list has an even number of elements. The order in which the pairs occur in the resultant list is arbitrary. They are no longer considered pairs although they occur next to each other.

To access an element of a hash, we use the syntax `$hash {$key}` where `%hash` is a hash variable and `$key` a key variable or value. For example, to say that `"Rich Rogers"` is associated with `"Iowa State University"`, we can write the following.

```perl
$friends {"Rich Rogers"} = "Iowa State University";
```

We use a `$` sign in front of `friends` to indicate that a value in a hash is a scalar. A key is also a scalar. Curly braces are used to enclose the key or the string index. If the key `"Rich Rogers"` does not exist in the hash, the key-value pair is added to the hash. If there is already such a key, the value associated with it is replaced by the new value. Thus, the hash can grow and shrink automatically. When we specify the key for a hash entry, using either the curly brackets, or to the left of `=>`, it is not necessary to put quotes around if it is a bare word, i.e., a string with no blank spaces in between. So, writing the following is

```perl
$friends {Rich} = "Iowa State University";
```

is syntactically correct whereas the following is not.

```perl
$friends {Rich Rogers} = "Iowa State University";
```

3.2.2   Looping on Key-Value Pairs: Printing a Hash

Hash variables are not automatically interpolated when used inside a string. This is unlike a scalar or a list variable. For example, if we write the following

```
print "%friend\n";
```

Perl would literally print %friend without any interpolation.

To print, we must iterate over all key value pairs ourselves. We can use the keys built-in function for this purpose. It takes a hash variable as an argument and returns the keys in the hash in an arbitrary order. The following program prints the keys and the corresponding values, one pair per line.

Program 3.33

```
#!/usr/bin/perl
use strict "vars";
my %friends = ("Jeff Perich" => "University of Colorado-Boulder",
               "Michael Richter" => "Otero Junior College",
               "Alex Dunn" => "University of Pennsylvania",
               "Reeves Smith" => "Fort Lewis College",
               "Karen Carter" => "University of Pennsylvania");
$friends {"Rich Rogers"} = "Iowa State University";

print "Friends and Colleges\n";
print "-" x 60, "\n";

foreach my $friend  (keys %friends){
    print "$friend\t\t\t" .  $friends {$friend} . "\n";
}
```

The output of the program is given below.

```
Friends and Colleges
------------------------------------------------------------
Rich Rogers                     Iowa State University
Karen Carter                    University of Pennsylvania
Michael Richter                 Otero Junior College
Jeff Perich                     University of Colorado-Boulder
Reeves Smith                    Fort Lewis College
Alex Dunn                       University of Pennsylvania
```

In this program, we obtain the keys in the %friends hash. We then iterate over every key by using the foreach construct. Inside the loop, for each key, we print it and the corresponding value. The value is obtained by writing

```
$friends {$friend}
```

because $friend is the key and $friends {$friend} obtains the value corresponding to the key from the hash %friends.

3.2.3   Slices of a Hash

Just like we can access and assign a slice of an array, we can access a slice from a hash and assign value to a slice of a hash. However, when we obtain a slice from a hash, we obtain the values only. The keys are not a part of the slice obtained. In the following program, we obtain a slice of the hash corresponding to the Smith family. Later, we assign a slice corresponding to the Kalita family.

Program 3.34

```perl
#!/usr/bin/perl
use strict "vars";

my %friends = ("Jeff Perich" => "University of Colorado-Boulder",
               "Michael Perich" => "Pikes Peak Community College",
               "Jennifer Perich" => "Colorado State University",
               "Reeves Smith" => "Fort Lewis College",
               "Sarah Smith" => "University of Buffalo",
               "Rich Rogers" =>  "Iowa State University");

#Obtain all Smiths
my @SmithFamily = ("Reeves Smith", "Sarah Smith");
my @SmithFamilyColleges  = @friends {@SmithFamily};
print "Smith Family  and Colleges\n";
print "-" x 60, "\n";
for (my $i=0; $i <= $#SmithFamily; $i++){
    print $SmithFamily [$i] . "\t\t\t" .  $SmithFamilyColleges [$i] . "\n";
}


#Introduce the Kalitas
@friends {"Jugal Kalita", "Jukti Kalita"} = ("University of Pennsylvania",
                                             "Columbia University");
print "\nAll Friends  and Colleges\n";
print "-" x 60, "\n";
foreach my $friend (sort (keys %friends)){
    print "$friend\t\t\t" .  $friends {$friend} . "\n";
}
```

Let us look at the following lines where we obtain a slice.

```perl
my @SmithFamily = ("Reeves Smith", "Sarah Smith");
my @SmithFamilyColleges  = @friends {@SmithFamily};
```

Here, we define an array `@SmithFamily` and obtain a slice of values using the elements of `@SmithFamily` as keys to the hash `%friends`. Therefore, `@SmithFamilyColleges` has the names of the colleges for the Smiths. In obtaining a slice of values, the syntax used must be followed. That is, we need to know that we are obtaining an array or list of values. Here, the resulting slice is written as

```perl
@friends {@SmithFamily}
```

indicating that we are obtaining an array. That is why the prefix used in `@`. We have to specify the keys inside curly brackets. Instead of defining a list for the keys, we could have written them directly as given below.

```perl
my @SmithFamilyColleges  = @friends {"Reeves Smith", "Sarah Smith"};
```

The following line of code in the program assigns a slice.

```perl
@friends {"Jugal Kalita", "Jukti Kalita"} = ("University of Pennsylvania",
                                             "Columbia University");
```

Here, on the right hand side, we have a list of values. On the left hand side of the assignment, we specify that the values corresponding to the list of keys need to be assigned. Once again, we need to be careful about the syntax used. The slice of hash values, once again, needs to be indicated as a list, using the @ prefix.

3.2.4   Printing the Elements of a Hash in Sorted Order

The `keys` function returns the keys in a list in an arbitrary order. So, if we want to print the keys in sorted order (with their corresponding values), we have to sort the list of keys using the built-in `sort` function. So, we can modify the `for` loop of the previous program in the following manner.

```
foreach my $friend  (sort (keys %friends)){
    print "$friend\t" .  $friends {$friend} . "\n";
}
```

This prints the keys (with their values) in the default sorted order for strings. The keys are printed in default ascending sort order.

If we want to change the order of sorting, we have to write a subroutine or a block of statements that decides on the sorting order. The following is a segment of code that uses a block of statements to guide the sorting process.

```
my @sortedKeys = sort {$b cmp $a;}   keys (%friends);

foreach my $friend  (@sortedKeys){
    print "$friend\t\t\t" .   $friends {$friend} . "\n";
}
```

If we use this fragment to replace the `foreach` loop in the previous program, the output will have the names of friends sorted in descending order.

```
Friends and Colleges
-------------------------------------------------------------
Rich Rogers                      Iowa State University
Reeves Smith                     Fort Lewis College
Michael Richter                  Otero Junior College
Karen Carter                     University of Pennsylvania
Jeff Perich                      University of Colorado-Boulder
Alex Dunn                        University of Pennsylvania
```

Instead of writing a block of statement and give it as argument to the `sort` function, we could have written a separate subroutine and passed the subroutine name to the `sort` function. The following shows this alternative approach.

```
foreach my $friend  (sort inDescendingOrder (keys %friends)){
    print "$friend\t" .   $friends {$friend} . "\n";
}

sub inDescendingOrder {
    $b cmp $a;
}
```

We can make the block of statements or the sorting subroutine as complex as possible depending on our sorting needs. The following program `splits` the name of a friend into two parts: first name and last name, and then sorts first by last name and then by first name.

Program 3.35

```perl
#!/usr/bin/perl
use strict "vars";

my %friends = ("Jeff Perich" => "University of Colorado-Boulder",
                "Michael Perich" => "Pikes Peak Community College",
                "Jennifer Perich" => "Colorado State University",
                "Reeves Smith" => "Fort Lewis College",
                "Sarah Smith" => "University of Buffalo");
$friends {"Rich Rogers"} = "Iowa State University";

print "Friends and Colleges\n";
print "-" x 60, "\n";

my @sortedKeys = sort {
    my ($firstName1, $lastName1) = split /\s+/, $a;
    my ($firstName2, $lastName2) = split /\s+/, $b;
    ($lastName1 cmp $lastName2) || ($firstName1 cmp $firstName2);
    }
    keys (%friends);

foreach my $friend  (@sortedKeys){
    print "$friend\t\t\t" .  $friends {$friend} . "\n";
}
```

The output of the program is given below.

```
Friends and Colleges
------------------------------------------------------------
Jeff Perich                 University of Colorado-Boulder
Jennifer Perich             Colorado State University
Michael Perich              Pikes Peak Community College
Rich Rogers                 Iowa State University
Reeves Smith                Fort Lewis College
Sarah Smith                 University of Buffalo
```

3.2.5   Deleting an Element from a Hash

A key-value pair can be deleted from a hash using the `delete` function. Given a the key, it deletes the corresponding value from the specified hash. For example,

```perl
delete $friends {"Rich Rogers"};
```

deletes the key `"Rich Rogers"` as well as the value associated with it. Below, we give a program that deletes all friends whose names have the word `Smith` in them. It removed the key as well as the value for each. It then prints the resulting hash.

Program 3.36

```perl
#!/usr/bin/perl
use strict "vars";

my %friends = ("Jeff Perich" => "University of Colorado-Boulder",
               "Michael Perich" => "Pikes Peak Community College",
               "Jennifer Perich" => "Colorado State University",
               "Reeves Smith" => "Fort Lewis College",
               "Sarah Smith" => "University of Buffalo",
               "Rich Rogers" =>  "Iowa State University");

#Remove all Smiths
foreach my $friend  (grep /Smith/, keys (%friends)){
    delete $friends {$friend};
}

print "Friends and Colleges\n";
print "-" x 60, "\n";

foreach my $friend  (sort (keys %friends)){
    print "$friend\t\t\t" .  $friends {$friend} . "\n";
}
```

The output of this program is given below.

```
Friends and Colleges
------------------------------------------------------------
Jeff Perich                        University of Colorado-Boulder
Jennifer Perich                    Colorado State University
Michael Perich                     Pikes Peak Community College
Rich Rogers                        Iowa State University
```

The delete function takes an expression as its only argument. In this example, the argument is an expression that specifies a hash element. The delete function can take an expression that specifies an array element or an array slice or a hash slice, and delete the specified element(s). For example,

```perl
delete ($friends [5]);
```

replaces the element at position 6 of the array @friends by undef.

```perl
delete (@friends [2..4]);
```

replaces every element in the array slice specified by undef. Similarly, delete works with a hash slice as well. To delete every element of an array or a hash, one can use assignment statements like the ones given below.

```perl
@friends = ();
%friends = ();
```

for efficiency.

```perl
undef @friend;
```

or

```
undef %friend;
```

removes any trace of the array @friend or the hash %hash from the program being executed.

3.2.6 The `values` function

We have used the `keys` function to obtain the keys in a hash in an arbitrary order returned by Perl's hash function. There is a similar function called `values` that returns the values stored in the hash. The order in which the values are returned is the same as the order in which the keys are returned. Of course, both are returned in the form of list or array. Below, we have a program that obtains the keys and the values of a hash separately and prints them. The printing is done by looping through the key array and the value array at the same time.

Program 3.37

```perl
#!/usr/bin/perl
use strict "vars";

my %friends = ("Jeff Perich" => "University of Colorado-Boulder",
               "Michael Perich" => "Pikes Peak Community College",
               "Jennifer Perich" => "Colorado State University",
               "Reeves Smith" => "Fort Lewis College",
               "Sarah Smith" => "University of Buffalo",
               "Rich Rogers" =>  "Iowa State University");

my @friendNames = keys %friends;
my @friendColleges = values %friends;
print "Friends  and Colleges\n";
print "-" x 60, "\n";
for (my $i=0; $i <= $#friendNames; $i++){
    print $friendNames [$i] . "\t\t\t" .  $friendColleges [$i] . "\n";
}
```

We can use the `keys` and `values` to merge two hashes. It is done in the following program.

Program 3.38

```perl
#!/usr/bin/perl
use strict "vars";

my %friends = ("Jeff Perich" => "University of Colorado-Boulder",
               "Michael Perich" => "Pikes Peak Community College",
               "Jennifer Perich" => "Colorado State University",
               "Reeves Smith" => "Fort Lewis College",
               "Sarah Smith" => "University of Buffalo",
               "Rich Rogers" =>  "Iowa State University");

my %Kalitas =  ("Jugal Kalita" => "University of Pennsylvania",
               "Jukti Kalita" => "Columbia University");
```

```
#Insert the key-value pairs in %Kalitas in %friends.
#That is, merge the two hashes.
@friends {keys %Kalitas} = values %Kalitas;

print "\nAll Friends  and Colleges\n";
print "-" x 60, "\n";
foreach my $friend (sort (keys %friends)){
    print "$friend\t\t\t" .  $friends {$friend} . "\n";
}
```

Here, the line of code that does the merging is repeated below.

```
@friends {keys %Kalitas} = values %Kalitas;
```

On the right hand side of the assignment, we have all the values from the %Kalitas hash. On the left hand side, inside the curly brackets, we have all the keys from the %Kalitas hash in the same order. Thus, we perform an assignment to a slice in the hash %friends such that the keys are the keys from the %Kalitas hash and the values are the values from the same %Kalitas hash. This could have been done also as

```
%friends = (%friends, %Kalitas);
```

The second option is not preferred because it is slower according to the authors of the Perl language. But, it does not matter for small hashes.

In both of the assignments, the second hash takes precedence in the sense that if there are duplicate keys, the values from the second hash override the values for the first hash.

3.2.7   Another Way to Loop Over a Hash: The each function

Perl provides us with a function called each that takes a hash as an argument. It returns a key-value pair from the hash in the form of a two-element list. When we use the each function on a hash, Perl remembers where it stops in the hash. The next time when each is used again on the same hash, Perl returns the next pair of key and value. Perl keeps on doing this till it has traversed the whole hash. After this point, each returns an empty list. Thus, each can be used inside a while loop to iterate over every element of a list. The following while loop does this.

```
while (my @pair = each %friends){
    print $pair [0] . "\t\t\t" . $pair [1] . "\n";
}
```

Here, @pair is a two-element list. We can rewrite the loop as follows if we want to be a little clearer.

```
while (my ($friend, $college)  = each %friends){
    print $friend . "\t\t\t" . $college  . "\n";
}
```

Here, we assign two scalar variables to the two elements of the two-element list that is returned by each call to each.

3.3   References

A *reference* is a pointer to a piece of data structure stored in the computer in an appropriate internal representation. Perl allows two ways of referencing a piece of data—*soft reference*s and *hard reference*s. In this section, we will talk about hard reference only since hard reference is similar to the concept of pointers we have in most other high level programming languages. There are several ways to create hard references in Perl. We will look at several such ways in this section.

3.3.1   The Backslash Operator for Reference Creation

We can create a reference to any variable by using the unary backslash (\) operator in front of it. The following are some examples of reference creation.

```
$number =1;
@names = ("Kevin", 'Aaron', 'Tommy');
%uadmin = ( chairman => 'Sebesta', dean => 'Sega', chancellor => 'Shade');

#Now we create the references
$numberref = \$number;
$namesref = \@names;
$uadminref = \%uadmin;
```

Now, $numberref stores a reference to the scalar $number, $namesref holds a reference to the list @names, and $udaminref stores a reference to the hash %uadmin. The reference variables are scalar.

3.3.2   Dereferencing

To *dereference* a scalar reference variable means to access the data structure that is pointed to by the reference variable. For example, dereferencing the scalar reference variable $uadminref means getting access to the pointed hash variable %uadmin. There are several ways to dereference. The ones we discuss are the following:

1. Dereferencing Using the Reference Variable Name,

2. Dereferencing Using the Reference Variable Name in a Block Structure, and

3. Dereferencing Using the Arrow Operator.

3.3.2.1   Dereferencing Using the Reference Variable Name

The first way to dereference a reference is to precede the reference variable by either $, @, or % depending on the type of variable pointed to by the reference variable. In particular, to dereference the scalar variable $number, we write

```
$$numberref
```

and to dereference the list and the hash variables we write the following.

```
@$namesref
%$uadminref
```

The value of $$numberref is exactly the same as the scalar $number, the value of @$namesref is the list @names, and %$uadminref is the same as the hash %uadmin.

3.3.2.2   Dereferencing Using the Reference Variable Name in a Block Structure

This is quite similar to the previous method for dereferencing. We enclose the reference variable name in braces that are usually used for delimiting the statements inside a block. We precede the left brace by either $, @, or % depending on the type of variable pointed to by the reference variable.

The three reference variables used above are dereferenced as the following.

```
${$numberref}
@{ $namesref}
%{ $uadminref }
```

It is acceptable to have one or more spaces between the left brace and the reference variable name.

3.3.2.3   Accessing Elements Using a Referenced List or Hash: The Arrow Operator

To access elements using a variable name that references a list or a hash, we can dereference the list or the hash and follow it by the subscript or index. As usual, in the case of a list, the index is enclosed within square brackets, and in the case of a hash, the index is enclosed within curly brackets or braces. Any one of the following dereferences is acceptable.

```
${ $namesref}[1]
$$namesref[2]
${$namesref} [0]
${ $uadminref }{chairman}
${$uadminref}{chairman}
$$uadminref {dean}
```

The first $ sign in each of the dereferences above indicates that we are accessing one element of a list or a hash and that such an element is always scalar. The second $ sign in each expression is due to the fact that a reference variable is also always scalar.

Perl provides another syntactic mechanism to access the elements of a dereferenced list or hash. This is by using the arrow operator (->). The arrow operator is placed between the reference variable name and the numeric or string index. The following are syntactically correct dereferences.

```
$namesref -> [1]
$uadminref -> {chancellor}
```

The first one gives us the element with index 1 (i.e., the second element) in the list referenced by the variable $namesref. The second gives us the value corresponding to the key 'chancellor' in the hash referenced by $uadminref. When we use the -> syntax, there is no need to precede the name of the reference variable by an additional $ as we did earlier because when we use the arrow, Perl implicitly assumes the result of the -> operator to be a scalar.

The following program illustrates the use of referencing and dereferencing using the techniques we have discussed.

Program 3.39

```
#!/usr/bin/perl

#These are the basic data structures
$number =1;
@names = ("Kevin", 'Aaron', 'Tommy');
```

```
%uadmin = (chairman => 'Sebesta', dean => 'Sega', chancellor => 'Shade');

#Now we create the references
$numberref = \$number;
$namesref = \@names;
$uadminref = \%uadmin;

#Printing the scalar
#The statement below prints 1
print "The number = $$numberref\n\n";

#Printing the list as a whole
#The  statement below prints the elements of the list
print "list = @$namesref\n\n";

#Accessing individual elements of the list separated by semicolon
for ($i=0; $i <= 2; $i++){
    print "${$namesref}[$i]; ";
}
print "\n\n";

#prints the elements of the hash %uadmin in a tabular format
printf "%-10s\t%-10s\n", "Title", "Name";
print "-" x 25; print "\n";
foreach $title (keys (%$uadminref)){
    printf "%-10s\t%-10s\n",  $title, $uadminref -> {$title};
}
```

In the `printf` statement, the minus sign tells Perl to print the corresponding string value in a left-justified fashion.

3.3.3 Creating Anonymous Lists and Hashes

In the previous program, we have created a reference to a list in the manner given below.

```
@names = ("Kevin", 'Aaron', 'Tommy');
$namesref = \@names;
```

We have two statements. The first creates the list and the second creates the reference. It is possible to put these two together into one statement.

```
$namesref = ["Kevin", 'Aaron', 'Tommy'];
```

Here, we no longer have a name for the list any more, a name that starts with @. The list is created and referenced using the reference variable $namesref. The list created thus is appropriately called an *anonymous list*. Perl requires us to use square brackets instead of parentheses when we create a reference to a list. We can access the list and its elements using the syntactic constructs we have discussed above. Examples of accesses that work are given below.

```
@$namesref
$$namesref[0]
```

```
${$namesref}[0]
$namesref -> [0]
```

The first one gives us the whole list, and each of the rest gives us the 0th element of the list referenced by `$namesref`.

As a two-step process, we can create a reference to a hash by defining the hash first and then the reference.

```
%uadmin = (chairman => 'Sebesta', dean => 'Sega', chancellor => 'Shade');
$uadminref = \%uadmin;
```

Instead of doing the above, we can create an *anonymous hash* by writing the following.

```
$udaminref = {chairman => 'Sebesta', dean => 'Sega',
        chancellor => 'Shade'};
```

Now, the hash does not have a name on its own. We have to access the hash or its elements using the reference variable. Examples of references that work are given below.

```
%$udaminref
$$udaminref{dean}
${$udaminref}{dean}
$udaminref -> {dean}
```

The first gives us the whole hash whereas each of the rest gives us the value corresponding to the key 'dean' in the hash referenced by `$uadminref`.

3.3.4   A Complex Data Structure: An Array of Arrays

In Perl, individual elements of a list or a hash must be scalars. There are three kinds of scalars that we have seen so far: numbers, strings and references. Since elements of a list or a hash can be references, it is possible to construct complex data structures such as a list of hashes, a hash of lists, a hash of hashes, a list of hashes of lists, and so on.

Let us revisit one of the programming examples we saw during the discussion of lists and hashes. We have information about a set of individuals. Let us assume that the information about each individual is in a list where the elements are in a specific order: name, hometown, height, weight and age. We can construct a complex data structure that is a list of lists that contains information about all the individuals. Such a data structure is used in the following program.

Program 3.40

```
#!/usr/bin/perl
use strict;
my $friends,  my $i;

$friends = [ ['Tommy', 'Washington', 66, 140, 18],
             ['Chad', 'San Francisco', 73, 180, 23],
             ["Jeff", 'Boulder', 70, 145, 21],
             ['Aaron', 'Golden', 68, 157, 23],
             ['Rick', 'Montreal', 67, 135, 21],
             ['Sean', 'Montreal', 67, 140, 21],
             ['Todd', 'Colo Springs', 73, 190, 22]
    ];
```

```perl
printf "%-5s %-15s %5s %5s   %3s\n",
         "Name", "Hometown", "Height", "Weight", "Age";
print "-" x 45, "\n";

for ($i = 0; $i <= 6; $i++){
         printf "%-5s %-15s   %3d     %3d     %2d \n",
            $friends -> [$i]->[0], $friends -> [$i] -> [1],
            $friends->[$i]->[2], $friends->[$i]->[3], $friends->[$i]->[4];
}
```

In this program, we create an anonymous reference to a list called $friends. This upper level list contains seven elements each of which is an anonymous reference to a list itself. Inside the for loop, we print the values of the elements in the lists referenced by these top level elements. For example, the 0th element of the 0th top level element of the list referenced by $friends is accessed by writing

```perl
$friends->[0]->[0];
```

Here, we first obtain the first element of the top level list as

```perl
$friends->[0];
```

This element happens to be a reference to a list itself. This anonymously referenced list is

```perl
['Tommy', 'Washington', 66, 140, 18]
```

We then obtain the 0th element of this embedded list. The value comes out as 'Tommy'.

3.3.5   A Complex Data Structure: An Array of Hashes

In this section, we discuss a program which is a slight variation of the program in the previous section. Here, we use an array of hashes. The array is anonymous. It contains scalars that are references to hashes.

Program 3.41

```perl
#!/usr/bin/perl
use strict;
my ($friends,  $name, $friendNames);


$friendNames = ['Tommy', 'Chad', 'Jeff', 'Aaron', 'Sean', 'Rick', 'Todd'];

#anonymous array of anonymous hashes
$friends = [{Tommy => 'Washington',
            Chad => "San Francisco",
            Jeff => 'Boulder',
            Aaron => 'Golden',                #Hometowns
            Rick => 'Montreal',
            Sean => 'Montreal',
            Todd => "Colorado Springs"},
       {Tommy => 66, Chad => 73, Aaron => 68,
```

```
                    Jeff => 70, Rick => 67, Sean => 67,
                    Todd => 73 },                        #height
      {Tommy => 140, Chad => 180, Aaron => 157,
                Jeff => 145, Sean => 140, Todd => 190,
                Rick => 135},                        #weight
      ];

#assignment to a whole row with anonymous hashes
$friends -> [3] = {Tommy => 18, Chad => 23, Aaron => 23,
                   Jeff => 21, Todd => 22, Sean => 21};        #age

#assignment to individual components of included anonymous hashes
$friends -> [0] -> {Tommy} = "Washington DC";
$friends -> [3] -> {Rick} = 21;

#print headers
printf "%-5s %-15s %5s %5s  %3s\n",
        "Name", "Hometown", "Height", "Weight", "Age";
print "-" x 45, "\n";

#Print details
foreach $name (sort @$friendNames){
        printf "%-5s %-16s  %3d    %3d  %3d\n",
            $name, $friends -> [0] -> {$name},
            $friends -> [1] -> {$name},
            $friends -> [2] -> {$name},
                $friends -> [3] -> {$name};
}
```

In this program we have a variable $friendNames that is a reference to an anonymous array containing names of friends. Then, we assign a value to the reference scalar $friends. $friends is a reference to an anonymous array. The individual elements of this anonymous array are anonymous hashes themselves.

As we have seen in the earlier example, when we write an anonymous array, the values inside the array are written inside square brackets (viz., [and]). The individual elements are written separated by commas. When we write an anonymous hash, the values are written, as usual, enclosed inside curly braces (viz., { and }).

The anonymous array referred to by $friends has three elements in it. Each is a reference to a hash. These can be accessed using the syntax discussed earlier. For example, the first of these references can be obtained by writing $friends -> [0]. The program performs an assignment to the element with index 3 in the array referenced by $friends by using the following statement.

```
$friends -> [3] = {Tommy => 18, Chad => 23, Aaron => 23,
                   Jeff => 21, Todd => 22, Sean => 21};        #age
```

The anonymous array pointed to by $friends did not have an element corresponding to index 3 earlier, but it now has one.

In the following two statements, the program assigns values to individual components of the hashes. The statements are given below.

```
$friends -> [0] -> {Tommy} = "Washington DC";
$friends -> [3] -> {Rick} = 21;
```

The first one of these statements updates the value corresponding to the key Tommy in the 0th element of the array pointed to by $friends. The initial value was Washington, and after the update, the value is Washington DC. The second of these statements inserts a new value to one of the anonymous hashes. There was no value corresponding to the key Rick in the anonymous array that referenced by the 3rd element of the array pointed to by $friends. Now, there is a value 21.

The last part of the program is a foreach loop that prints the details that are in the array of hashes. It obtains the values corresponding to various keys in the individual hashes and prints them out. The key is $name. For example, corresponding to this key, it obtains the value stored in the 0th hash using the expression given below.

```
$friends -> [0] -> {$name}
```

The first arrow obtains the reference to the 0th hash in the array pointed to by $friends. The second arrow obtains the value corresponding the key $name from this hash.

The output of the program is given below.

```
Name   Hometown          Height Weight  Age
-------------------------------------------
Aaron  Golden              68    157    23
Chad   San Francisco       73    180    23
Jeff   Boulder             70    145    21
Rick   Montreal            67    135    21
Sean   Montreal            67    140    21
Todd   Colorado Springs    73    190    22
Tommy  Washington DC       66    140    18
```

3.4   Conclusions

This chapter has discussed lists, hashes and references at length. Scalars are discussed in Chapter 2. The manner in which Perl implements lists is in the spirit of a true list processing language such as Common LISP. Perl is unique among major non-specialized programming languages of the day in its treatment of lists. Because of Perl's felicitous treatment of lists, and its regular expression capabilities (discussed in Chapter 4), Perl has become widely valued and used by programmers and researchers interested in artificial intelligence who want a mainstream language to program, with possibly strong networking, database handling and other capabilities. Hashes make programming more natural and fun for many problem-solving situations. Hashes have an implementation overhead in terms of the mathematics needed for the underlying address calculation that is transparent to the programmer. But, this is a minor price to pay for the naturalness in expressive ability that hashes afford a programmer.

The infra-structure Perl provides in terms of its building blocks for data storage is strong whereas the number of operators and statement types it provides (see Chapter 2) is exceptionally abundant. These are two salient aspects of a programming language and Perl shines in both, compared to languages such as C, C++, Java, and Pascal. However, one can present a muted criticism that the repertory of data structures can be improved further. This faint criticism can be immediately answered with ease because Perl provides a large number of contributed modules that provide a wide array of data type handling functionality. Some of these modules facilitate mundane and popularly useful tasks, whereas others are exotic and highly specialized. Perl has contributed modules for handling arrays, sets, trees of various complexity, heap data structures, graphs, finite state automatons, bit vectors, matrices, mathematical structures of an exceptionally wide variety, date and time in many formats, etc. Perl has contributed modules to enable recursive copying of nested data structures. Perl has several contributed modules to store complex data structures in data files after serialization so that the structures can be re-constructed after reading from the file. Perl allows one to tie the standard core data structures—scalars, lists and hashes—to files so that they are persistent from one invocation of a program to the next. Tying data structures to files also allows the data structures to grow very large, if the need arises.

An exemplar of a contributed module that shatters the myth of Perl's unsuitability to complex mathematical computation is PDL.pm. It stands out in that it provides fast storage and efficient computation for large matrices. If one wants to deal with a matrix that represents the pixels of a 1024x1024 graphical image, or the units of a much larger audio or video data file, the computation can be performed blazingly fast. Unless extreme efficiency is the need of the hour, Perl is more than sufficient for such tasks.

In conclusion, Perl does not lack any at all in the data structure department. In fact, it is the richest programming language known at this time in making all modules, including those that support data structures, easily downloadable from one single repository on the Internet, and making them easy to use. This repository is the Comprehensive Perl Archive Network (CPAN) available at *www.cpan.org*.

3.5   Exercises

1. *(Easy: Documentation Reading, Internet Exploration)*
   Either visit www.cpan.org on the World Wide Web, or use perldoc on your system to read documentation on Perl operators and basic syntax. Use

   ```
   %perldoc perldoc
   ```

   to learn more about perldoc. Detailed documentation on Perl data structures is available by running

   ```
   %perldoc perldata
   ```

   Use perldsc as the argument to find documentation on the so-called Perl Data Structures Cookbook. Use perlref to find documentation on Perl references and complex data structures. perllol is the section in the on-line documentation that talks about how to build and manipulate list of lists.

2. *(Easy: Arrays)*
   Write a program that computes the dot product of two vectors. Represent the vectors as lists. Read the vectors from two files whose names are given as command-line argument. Write the result into a file whose name is also given as command-line argument. Suppose the two vectors are $\mathbf{P_1}$ and $\mathbf{P_2}$ with components given below.

   $$\mathbf{P_1} = (p_{11}, p_{12}, \cdots, p_{1n})$$
   $$\mathbf{P_2} = (p_{21}, p_{22}, \cdots, p_{2n})$$

   They have the same dimension n. Give n as a command-line argument. The dot product is given as the following.

   $$\mathbf{P_1} \circ \mathbf{P_2} = (p_{11} \times p_{21}, p_{12} \times p_{22}, \cdots p_{1n} \times p_{2n})$$

3. *(Easy: Arrays)*
   Write the following functions that rotate a list's elements.

   (a) Define the function rotateLeft that takes a list as its argument and returns a new list in which the former first element becomes the last.

   (b) Define rotateRight like rotateLeft except that it rotates the list in the other direction:

(c) Now define rotate, as a function of two arguments, reference to a list L and an integer N. It returns reference to a new list formed by rotating the list L N times to the right if $N > 0$ and to the left if $N < 0$. You should use the two previous functions to do the work, of course.

4. *(Medium: Text Processing, Hashes, Research)*
Write a program that counts the frequency of words in English (irrespective of case). Ignore all non-alphabetic characters or "words" with non-alphabetic characters. Process as much text as you can obtain, from any source. For example, process all the text files that you have under a certain large directory. As you encounter a word, you will have to increment the number of times it has occurred so far. Use a hash to store frequency of occurrence. A word is a key and its frequency of occurrence is its value.

Study what are called Huffman codes that can be used to represent letters. Generate Huffman codes for the letters based on their frequency count.

5. *(Easy: Sorting, File Operations)*
Write a program that sorts a list of numbers using *bubble* sort. Read about bubble sort on your own. Bubble sort is one of the simplest sorting techniques. There are many other sorting algorithms studied by computer scientists. What are some of these techniques? *Quicksort* is an efficient and popular technique. Implement quicksort in addition to bubble sort.

Modify your program so that you can read a long list of numbers from a file, sort the list, and write back the sorted list to another file. Name the new file the same as the original, but add the suffix .sorted to it.

6. *(Medium: Sorting, Command-line Arguments)*
Modify the sort program so that it takes the following options. It already takes a command-line argument that gives the input list of elements to sort.

-c Checks to see if the file is already sorted. If so, it does not sort.

-o FILE Writes the result to the output file specified.

-n The file contains only numbers. Ignore an entry in the file if it is not a number, i.e., contains non-numeric characters.

-s Consider the entries in the file as string. Therefore, perform character comparison, i.e., do not use numeric comparison.

7. *(Medium to Hard: Sorting, Order Computation, Research)*
Write a program to find the next to the smallest element of an array. Assume that there are no duplicate entries in the array. Return -1 if the array has only one item. There are several such techniques to find such an element. The most obvious one is to sort the numbers in ascending order and pick the second element in the sorted list. However, this need not be the most efficient way. Implement two ways to find the second smallest element of a list. Consult a book on computer algorithms if necessary. Read the list of numbers from a file.

8. *(Easy: Matrix Operations)*
Write a program that represents a 2-D matrix of numbers. It is an $n \times n$ matrix. Now, extend the program so that it can add two matrices. Read the input matrices from two files whose names are given as command-line argument. Write the output matrices to files as well. Make up the names of the output files from the names of the input files by adding a suffix you think of.

9. *(Easy: Matrix Operations)*
Write a program that obtains the product of two matrices whose dimensions are $m \times n$ and $n \times p$. Read the two input matrices from two files given as command-line argument. Specify m, n and p as command-line argument as well.

10. *(Easy: Arrays, Merging)*
    Given two sorted lists, write an algorithm to merge them so that the resulting list is also sorted in the same sorting order. Read the two sorted lists from files. If one or more of the input lists is not sorted, write an error statement to the screen and kill the program. Do not use Perl's `sort` function.

11. *(Medium: Arrays, Merging)*
    Extend the previous program so that it can merge *n* sorted lists. Read each list from a file. The value of *n* and the names of files containing the lists are in a file by themselves. Provide this file's name as a command-line argument.

12. *(Medium: Arrays, Permutations)*
    Given a short list, say less than 10 elements long, write an algorithm to obtain all permutations of the elements. Read the elements from a file and write all permutations to another file.

13. *(Medium: Arrays, Hashes, Set Operations)*
    Assume a list is used to represent a *set*. A set is a collection of things in which there are no duplicates. Write the following Perl functions.

    (a) `isSet` is a function that takes one argument x and returns 1 if its single argument is a set.

    (b) `setUnion` is a function that takes two arguments *set1* and *set2*, and returns their union.

    (c) `setIntersection` is a function that takes two arguments *set1* and *set2*, and returns their intersection.

    (d) `setDifference` is a function that takes two arguments *set1* and *set2*, and returns their difference.

    (e) `setAdd` takes an arbitrary element X and a set S, and returns a set that has X as a member or element.

    (f) `setEqual` takes two arguments *set1* and *set2*, and returns 1 if the two contain the same elements.

    (g) `setify` takes one argument *lst* and transforms it into a set, i.e., a list with no duplicates.

14. *(Medium: Natural Language Processing, Grammar)*
    Write a function `generate` which takes a representation of a *context-free grammar* and returns *random* sentences generated according to the grammar. A context-free grammar is given as a hash of grammar rules specifying the ways in which each *non-terminal element* of the grammar can be converted into a sequence of *non-terminal* and *terminal* elements. A *sentence* is a sequence of terminal elements. A simple grammar is shown below.

```perl
my $grammar = {s => ["np", "vp"],
               np => [["det", "adj", "n"], ["det, n"]],
               vp => ["iv", ["tv", "np"]],
               det => ["a", "the"],
               n => ["duckling", "piano"],
               adj => ["purple", "mean"],
               iv => ["skis", "studies"],
               tv => ["plays", "breaks"]
};
```

The ideas is to start from the root non-terminal symbol s, randomly selecting a way to expand each of the non-terminal elements in its expansion until there is a sequence consisting of terminal symbols only. Each time `generate` is called, it should return another random sentence. For example, the call

```perl
generate (%$grammar)
```

may produce

`"the purple ducking plays a mean piano"`

A second call to generate may produce

`"the purple piano skis"`

A third call may produce

`"the purple duckling breaks the mean duckling"`

Notice the structure used to represent a grammar. A grammar is a hash of rules. Each non-terminal is a key of this hash. The value corresponding to a key is the list of possible expansions for the non-terminal. An expansion is either a single string or a list of strings. A string represents a non-terminal symbol if there is a rule in the grammar describing how it can be expanded. A string represents a terminal symbol if there is no rule in the grammar for expanding it.

Chapter 4

On Pattern Matching and Text Processing

In This Chapter

One of Perl's main strengths is its elaborate facilities for looking for patterns in textual documents. We can write a short program that can scan through many hundreds of files and look for simple or complex textual patterns. The program can also perform a global substitution in each of these files where one word or pattern is substituted by another. For example, a person managing a World Wide Web site for an organization or company may have a hierarchy of directories and files where he or she stores all relevant files. Assume there are several thousand files in this directory structure. Suppose the name of the company is **Assam-Soft**. Now suppose the company buys another company called **Maoi Technologies** and changes its name to **AssamMaoi Technologies**. The person who manages the Web pages has the daunting task of scanning thousands of files and changing every reference of **AssamSoft** to the new name **AssamMaoi Technologies**. Of course it will take a long time to go through all the directories and all the files. It is possible that certain directories and files will be missed. It is also possible that certain occurrences of **AssamSoft** will be missed even in files that are scanned manually. This becomes an arduous task taking many days or weeks. It becomes an expensive and error-prone task.

However, a language such as Perl can come to rescue in a situation such as this. It is possible to write a Perl script that is quite short and performs this task without leaving out any files or directories or any occurrences of **AssamSoft** in the files that it scans. In addition, the program does so a lot faster than any human being can.

Situations such as this arise frequently in big organizations. This can happen in many situations. It is possible that a person in charge of Web pages for an organization wants to see how many links to other Web pages there are in his or her site. It is possible he or she wants to check if people are inserting huge graphic or audio or video files in their Web pages. He or she wants to find out if there are links in the thousands of Web pages in his site that are dead in that they lead to pages that do not exist any more or were wrongly typed in the first place.

Among the high level languages that are widely available and popular, Perl has the most sophisticated pattern matching capabilities. We look at Perl's pattern matching capabilities in depth in this chapter.

4.1 Searching for a Pattern in Files

We will start by writing a simple program that takes as its first argument a pattern. It takes one or more additional arguments to specify one or more files where it looks for the pattern. If it finds a pattern, it prints the line where the pattern is found, preceded by the name of the file.

Program 4.1

```perl
#!/usr/bin/perl
$pattern = shift(@ARGV);

while (<>){
    if (/$pattern/){
        print "\nFile $ARGV:";
        print "\t$_";       #prints the line
    }
}
```

Assuming the program is stored in the file `grepfile.pl`, an example call is the following.

```
%grepfile.pl theoretical *.tex
```

Here, the first argument given to the script is `theoretical`. `theoretical` is considered a pattern. The second argument given to the script is `*.tex`. It expands to a list that contains the names of all files in the current directory that end with `.tex`. So, the script looks for the pattern `theoretical` in all such files. It is a very simple pattern that happens to be a sequence of alphabetic characters.

The script is given the pattern and the names of all the files as one single list called `@ARGV`. The script removes the first element of this list and calls it `$pattern`. The names of the files remain in `@ARGV`. It then uses the angle bracket input construct inside a `while` loop to read each line from each of the files whose names are in `@ARGV`. It looks for `$pattern` in each line it scans and if it succeeds, it prints the name of the file followed by the line containing `$pattern`. The special variable `$ARGV` contains the name of the current file from `@ARGV` that is being processed. In this specific call, `$pattern` has the value `theoretical` and therefore, the script prints all lines containing `theoretical` of all files in the current directory whose names end with `tex`. The output looks like the following:

```
File nature.tex:        theoretically satisfying, will be
File nature.tex:        operators to compose actions which are more complex. In
                                        theoretical
File whole.tex:         discuss theoretical and practical details of the components in
File whole.tex:         Indeed, many (though not all) theoretical
                                        discussions of semantic
File whole.tex:         place this on a solid theoretical foundation, and we
                                        expect it to offer
File whole.tex:         from a theoretical perspective, we claim that the
                                        animations produced
File whole.tex:         more rigorous theoretical foundation.
```

In the output single lines have been broken into two to fit the printed page.

We should note here that when we specify a pattern inside forward slashes, we can use variables inside the pattern. In the example given above, the pattern is specified solely in terms of the scalar variable `$pattern`. The variable `$pattern` as in `/$pattern/` is first interpolated for its value before pattern matching starts. In this respect, the delimiting forward slashes (/) behave like double quotes (" ").

4.2 Match Delimiters

The regular expression match operator is `=˜`. On the left hand side, we have the target of the match. On the right hand side we have the regular expression along with any modifiers, if any. An example is

```
$string =˜ m/theoretical/
```

Here, we are looking for the pattern `theoretical` in `$string`.

If on the left hand side, the variable over which we are doing the pattern matching is the special variable `$_`, we need not write the variable as well as the operator `=˜`. Therefore,

```
$_ =˜ m/theoretical/
```

and

```
m/theoretical/
```

mean exactly the same. In addition, if / is used as the delimiter, the use of m is not necessary. Therefore, we can write the previous expression as

```
/theoretical/
```

also.

Actually, Perl allows us to use any non-alphanumeric, non-whitespace character as the delimiter if we use m to indicate the match operation. In the specific example, we have shown earlier, any of the following will work instead of m/$pattern/.

```
m@$pattern@
m#$pattern#
m=$pattern=
m!$pattern!
m~$pattern~
m%$pattern%
m^$pattern^
m*$pattern*
m-$pattern-
m+$pattern+
m:$pattern:
m;$pattern;
m"$pattern"
m|$pattern|
m\$pattern\
m,$pattern,
```

However, there are some exceptions. For a complete discussion, one should look at the book *Mastering Regular Expressions* [Fri97]. Here are some of the exceptions. Although we said any non-alphanumeric character will work as the delimiter, the four "natural" delimiters need to be used in complementary pairs. In other words, the following do not work:

```
m{$pattern{
m[$pattern[
m($pattern(
m<$pattern<
```

but they work in natural pairs as in the following.

```
m{$pattern}
m[$pattern]
m($pattern)
m<$pattern>
```

If we use ? as the delimiter, the pattern matches only once. For example, if the previous example were changed to

Program 4.2

```
#!/usr/bin/perl
$pattern = shift(@ARGV);
```

```
while (<>){
    if (m?$pattern?){
        print "File $ARGV:";
        print "\t$_";       #prints the line
    }
}
```

the result will be

```
File nature.tex: theoretically satisfying, will be
```

That is, only the first match will take place.

Finally, if we use the single quote as the delimiter, the pattern behaves like a string delimited with a single quote. That is, variables inside the string are not be interpolated. Specifically, in this example, if we change the pattern matching to

```
m'$pattern'
```

Perl looks for the literal presence of the string $pattern in the files.

4.3   Simple Regular Expressions

Patterns are also called regular expressions. Perl gives us an elaborate syntax for writing regular expressions. We start with the simplest and then slowly build up to complex expressions.

4.3.1   A Single Character

The simplest regular expression is a single character expression. For example, when we write /z/, we are looking for the character z.

There are certain characters that are treated as special in Perl. Such characters are preceded by the backslash inside a Perl string. Inside a regular expression, we can use the same backslashed characters, such as \n or \t.

Inside a simple pattern like the ones we have seen so far, we can use the dot character (.) to represent any one character. By default, . does not match \n, but it can be forced to match \n also if needed. Therefore,

```
/ab.c/
```

matches the line

```
The Chinese used abacus to perform simple arithmetic computations.
```

because abacus contains an a, followed by a b, followed by any single non-newline characters, which happens to be an a here, and then a c. When a regular expression such as ab.c matches a string, such as the line given above, the match does not have to happen in the beginning. As long as the whole regular expression matches starting at any position before the end of the string, it suffices.

4.3.2 Character Classes

It is possible to specify that a single character in a string must be a member of a certain set or class. For example, if we write

```
/[abcdefghijklmnopqrstuvwxyz]/
```

we are saying that this pattern matches a single alphabetic character. So, if we match this pattern against the string

```
123456 xyz
```

it matches at x. Some other examples of classes that we can state are given below.

```
/[0123456789]/
/[a-h]/
/[a-zA-Z0-9_]/
```

Here, the first class matches a single digit. The second class matches any lower case character between a and h. We can specify a contiguous range of characters using the dash as in the second example. Several singly specified characters or ranges can be used to specify a single class as in the third example. This example represents a single alphanumeric character where an alphanumeric character is either a lower case or upper case alphabetic character, or a decimal digit between 0 and 9, or the underscore character _. If the dash (-) is specified in a character class, it must be backslashed. However, a - can occur at the beginning or the end of the class without being backslashed as in [-+] or [+-].

It is possible to define the so-called negative character classes also. This is done by putting a caret (^) at the beginning of the character class. For example,

```
/[^0123456789]/
```

or

```
/[^0-9]/
```

is a pattern that matches with a single character that is not a decimal digit. Similarly,

```
/[^a-zA-Z0-9_]/
```

represents a single non-alphanumeric character.

To make matters a little simple in specifying character classes, Perl provides a few built-in character classes and negative character classes as well. They are the following.

\d is the same as [0-9]
\w is the same as [0-9a-zA-Z_]
\s is the same as [\f\n\r\t]

The last one represents the white space character class and includes the space character, the form feed character \f, the newline character \n, the return character \r, and the tab character \t.

Perl also provides the following negative classes.

\D is the same as [^0-9]
\W is the same as [^0-9a-zA-Z_]
\S is the same as [^ \f\n\r\t]

4.3.3 Sequencing

One can write a sequence of characters one after another to specify a pattern that has several characters in it in order. We have seen the

```
/ab.c/
```

pattern already. As explained earlier, here we are looking at a pattern that has an a followed by a b, followed by any non-newline character, followed by a c.

4.3.3.1 Finding citations: First try

Here is a simple pattern matching program that looks at a text file that contains an academic paper written in a certain format. In this format, any papers or books cited are written using a syntax called the *bibtex* syntax. When one cites a reference in this paper, one does so by using a citation index. Let us assume that the citation index is something like \cite{AuthorYY} where Author is the last name of an author and YY is the last two digits of the year in which the paper was published.

Note that there can be several citations in one \cite usage. If there are more than one citation in one use of \cite, there are no spaces in between. Each citation is referred to by some index made up by the author of the paper. Here, the indices used by the author of the paper has the last name of the first author followed by the last two digits of the year. Another author can decide to use any other style of indexing. Here are a few sample lines of text from the file that contains the academic paper in TeX/LaTeX form.

```
There has been considerable work on the semantics of  action verbs by
Talmy \cite{Talmy83,Talmy85}, Jackendoff \cite{Jackendoff91}, Palmer
\cite{Palmer85}
and others. The work by Herskovits \cite{Herskovits86} on spatial
prepositions is also  relevant to the work reported here.  The
```

If we want to find all the references cited in the paper, we can start by writing the following program.

Program 4.3

```
#!/usr/bin/perl

while (<>){
    if (/\\cite/){
        print $_;
    }
}
```

Here, we are looking for the pattern \cite. Let us now write an alternate program to do the same. This second program, which is presented simply to illustrate the use of pre-defined character classes, is not as good as the previous one considering the fact that we want to find citations. However, it is done simply as an example.

Program 4.4

```
#!/usr/bin/perl
```

```
while (<>){
    if (/\D\D\d\d}/){
        print $_;
    }
}
```

The program looks at each line of a set of files specified as command line argument for a pattern where we have two non-digits, followed by two digits, followed by }, and then followed by the right curly bracket, }. This is not very smart, but it shows the use of character classes. A possible result of running this program on a file may be the following.

```
\cite{Palmer85}
Webster's dictionary \cite{Webster81}
according to Webster's dictionary \cite{Webster81}
Webster's dictionary \cite{Webster81} defines {\em slide} as {\em to
\cite{Random73} defines {\em slide} as {\em to move along in
A handbook of prepositions by Funk and Wagnalls \cite{Funk53}
Fahlman \cite{Fahlman74} devised  complex heuristic and mathematical
Funk and Wagnalls \cite{Funk53}
orientation, is due to Herskovits \cite{Herskovits86} who
Douglas {\it et al.} \cite{Douglas87}
\cite{Frawley92} and by us in this paper,  a preposition such as {\em
```

Since we take a simplistic approach in the second program, it is possible that we print lines that are not intended. The program's search accuracy can be improved as we learn more about regular expressions. Our eventual goal is to gather all the citation indices in one place, sort them, remove duplicates and then obtain the descriptions of these citations from another bibliographic database that is stored in ASCII format.

4.3.3.2 Finding who has sent mail: First try

The next program we write looks at a file where mail messages are stored. On Unix machines, usually all incoming mail for a certain individual is stored in one single file. The program that reads mail looks at this file and prints the mail messages in a user-friendly manner. This may involve just presenting the sender, the time of arrival, and the subject line for each pending e-mail message. The e-mail reader program allows the user to see the actual message, reply to a message, and forward a message. Right now, our goal is to look at the repository file and print some selected lines out of it. On the Unix machine I am working on, all pending mail for me is stored in the file /var/spool/mail/kalita. Suppose I want to write a program that prints the sender of each message and its subject and the time of arrival.

In the repository file, each message is stored in the following manner. Here, we see a complete message.

```
From mrpedri@WebAccess.net  Thu Oct  2 16:05:17 1997
Delivery-Date: Thu, 02 Oct 97 16:05:20 -0600
Return-Path: mrpedri@WebAccess.net
Received: from ns4.webaccess.net by pikespeak.uccs.edu;
        (5.65/1.1.8.2/24Jul96-8.2MAM)
        id AA11775; Thu, 2 Oct 1997 16:05:17 -0600
Received: from 204.163.168.72 - 204.163.168.72 by webaccess.net
                with Microsoft SMTPSVC;
```

```
            Thu, 2 Oct 1997 16:09:13 -0600
Message-Id: <343429B9.7367@WebAccess.net>
Date: Thu, 02 Oct 1997 16:09:46 -0700
From: Mark Pedri <mrpedri@WebAccess.net>
X-Mailer: Mozilla 3.0Gold (Macintosh; I; PPC)
Mime-Version: 1.0
To: kalita@pikespeak.uccs.edu
Subject: Machttp
Content-Type: text/plain; charset=us-ascii
Content-Transfer-Encoding: 7bit
Return-Path: mrpedri@WebAccess.net
Status: RO
X-Status:

Good Afternoon,
     Here is where you can get the setup information for machttp (upper
levels) and the setup information at this level.
    <http://www.starnine.com/support/qa/webstar/preinstall.html>
Also check out this link for more information.
    <http://arpp.carleton.ca/mac/question/network.html.>
Also, Matthias Ulrich Neeracher <neeri@iis.ee.ethz.ch> is the lady that
wrote MacPerl.  She is very nice and very helpful.


                Mark Pedri
```

Each message has a set of lines on top that gives a field and its value. These are called header lines. For example, there are header lines corresponding to `From`, `To`, `Content-Type`, etc. Each header line has a field name followed by a colon, followed by a space character and then the value of the field. There can be many such header lines. The header lines are called Simple Mail Transfer Protocol (SMTP) headers. The last header line is followed by a blank line. After this blank line, the text of the message follows. After the first message is finished, there are several blank lines and the next message starts.

We can start by writing a very simple program that looks at each line of this file and prints out the lines that have the strings `From:`, `Date:` and `Subject:` in them. The program that does this is given below.

Program 4.5

```
#!/usr/bin/perl

while (<>){
    if (/From:/ or /Subject:/ or /Date:/){
        print $_;
    }
}
```

If this program is stored in a file called `grepfrom.pl`, and we make the call

```
%grepfrom.pl /usr/spool/mail/kalita
```

we will get an output on the terminal that looks like the following.

```
From: "Mike Millner" <mike@bewellnet.com>
```

```
Subject: Re: vedanti.com and shillong.com
Date: Fri, 24 Jul 1998 14:32:22 -0600
> From: J. Kalita <kalita@pikespeak.uccs.edu>
> Subject: vedanti.com and shillong.com
> Date: Friday, July 24, 1998 1:34 PM
Delivery-Date: Fri, 24 Jul 98 15:02:48 -0600
From: hostmaster@internic.net
Date: Fri, 24 Jul 1998 13:27:59 -0400 (EDT)
Subject: Re: [NIC-980724.18471] NEW DOMAIN indiashipping.com (fwd)
Delivery-Date: Fri, 24 Jul 98 16:16:12 -0600
From: "Brahma, Malavika (Exchange)" <MBrahma@Bear.COM>
Subject: RE: FW: Exe. Comm
Date: Fri, 7 Aug 1998 14:08:50 -0400
> From: J. Kalita [SMTP:kalita@pikespeak.uccs.edu]
> Subject:      Re: FW: Exe. Comm
> > > From:      Chatterjee, Rajeeb [SMTP:rajeeb.chatterjee@intel.com]
> > > Subject:  RE: Exe. Comm
> > > > From:       KBhuyan@aol.com [SMTP:KBhuyan@aol.com]
> > > > Subject:     Exe. Comm
Delivery-Date: Fri, 07 Aug 98 12:22:36 -0600
```

Obviously, this is not the best looking output we can get. A professional mail reader program presents the output in a much more user-friendly manner. However, it gives us the information we want. There is a little surprise though. We intended to print three lines per pending e-mail message. But, our e-mail file has a field called `Delivery-Date` in addition to `Date`. As a result, both fields are printed. So, we have four fields printed per message. In addition, if a message has any of the three words mentioned in any lines in its body, such lines are printed also. This has happened in the printed output when messages are forwarded or included in other messages.

4.3.4 Multipliers

Multipliers are used to specify how many times a pattern or a subpattern is repeated. There are several multipliers in Perl.

4.3.4.1 *: Zero or more

The simplest multipliers are `*`, `+` and `?`. The multiplier `*` means zero or more of a certain character or subpattern. For example, if we write `\D*\d*`,

Program 4.6

```
#!/usr/bin/perl

while (<>){
    if (/\D*\d*/){
        print $_;
    }
}
```

we are looking for a pattern of zero or more non-digits followed by zero or more digits. Note that this pattern matches an empty string. If we call this program with a file, it prints every line including empty lines because the pattern matches in the beginning of every line without even looking at the rest of the line.

4.3.4.2   +: One or more

We can write another version of the program that actually works a little better in finding citations.

Program 4.7

```
#!/usr/bin/perl

while (<>){
    if (/\\cite{[^}]+}/){
        print $_;
    }
}
```

In the program given above, the pattern we look for is the sequence \cite followed by a starting brace. Then we look for one or more characters from the negative character class [^}]. In other words, we are looking for one or more non-} characters. This is because the closing brace finishes our citation entry. We specify that we are looking for one or more characters from the negated class by surrounding the class description by a set of parentheses and putting the multiplier + after the closing parentheses. Here, the parentheses are used for grouping a subpattern. In this case, this example works with or without the parentheses. Specifically, we do not use a parenthesis pair here.

This program seems to find citations, but it is not strict enough in the sense that it does not look for the syntax of the string we are using as citation index. The index, as used by the author of the paper, consists of an uppercase letter, followed by zero or more other letters, followed by two digits giving the year of publication. We work toward more strict parsing in the following sections.

4.3.4.3   ?: Zero or one

The multiplier ? is used to indicate zero or one occurrence of a character or a subpattern. For example, if we write

```
/ab.?o/
```

we are looking for an a followed by a b, followed by zero or one non-\n character, followed by a c. So, this line matches the line

```
It is difficult to do an absolute determination of
```

as well as the following line.

```
It was reported that about three quarters
```

The second line matches because we have an a followed by a b, followed by nothing, followed by o.

The question mark ? can be used as a multiplier after a subpattern grouped using parentheses.

Let us now change our program a bit more and try to look for citation indices that satisfy a certain syntax that we have imposed on ourselves. Note that this syntax is not enforced by the word processing program

TeX or LaTeX. It is simply a convention to which we want to adhere. We require a citation index to start with an uppercase letter, then follow it by one or more letters of either case, and then follow it by two digits giving the year of publication. The next program we write is the following.

Program 4.8

```
#!/usr/bin/perl

while (<>){
    if (/\\cite{[A-Z][a-zA-Z]*\d\d}/){
        print $_;
    }
}
```

This program looks for the string \cite followed by a {, followed by an uppercase letter, followed by zero or more uppercase or lowercase letters, followed by two digits and finally a }. This program prints all those lines from the text file where we have citations with one author in each citation.

Let us now change the syntax of a citation index a little more by making the specification of the year of publication slightly more complex. We want to allow two digits for the year as we have already done. But, in addition, we want to allow four digits for the year also. However, in such a case, we want to make sure that the first two digits are 19 referring to the twentieth century. Therefore, in this new syntax, either one of the following is acceptable: Kalita93 or Kalita1993. However Kalita2001 is not acceptable. The following program accomplishes this specification.

Program 4.9

```
#!/usr/bin/perl

while (<>){
    if (/\\cite{[A-Z][a-zA-Z]*(19)?\d\d}/){
        print $_;
    }
}
```

In this program, the subpattern

```
(19)?\d\d}
```

allows us to parse the number specification properly. Here, we group 19 into a subpattern by putting it inside parentheses. Then we put a ? after the closing parenthesis. This makes the subpattern 19 optional.

4.3.4.4 Counting Occurrences

We have seen that ? counts zero or one occurrence of a character or a parenthesized subpattern. * and + do not count, but simply say zero or more, and one or more, respectively. It is possible to do an exact count when we perform pattern matching. For example, when we write

```
/Bob{2}/
```

we are looking for exactly two lower-case b's at the end of the pattern. Therefore, this pattern matches a string containing Bobby and Bobbit, but does not match Bolivar or Bobster.

We can change the last program we presented so that we use a count of two when we are looking for the last two digits of a citation index. In the last program we wrote \d\d toward the end of the pattern. This time, we write \d{2} instead. That is the only difference between the last program and the current one.

Program 4.10

```
#!/usr/bin/perl

while (<>){
    if (/\\cite{[A-Z][a-zA-Z]*(19)?\d{2}}/){
        print $_;
    }
}
```

Instead of specifying an exact count, we can specify a range as seen below.

```
/b{2,4}/
/b{2,}/
/b{0,5}/
```

In the first case, we are looking for between two and four b's, in the second case two or more b's, and in the third case between zero and five b's. We must put 0 as the lower limit if we want to say zero or more. Therefore,

```
/b*/
/b+/
/b?/
```

are exactly the same as

```
/b{0,}/
/b{1,}/
/b{0,1}/
```

respectively. However, for these three special cases, most people prefer to use *, + and ? as multipliers because of tradition as well as brevity.

4.3.4.5 Another Version of the Citation Program

We have seen that sometimes we may have two or more citation indices used in one use of \cite. In such cases, the indices are separated from each other by a comma. In the programs we have presented so far, one set of programs look for non-} characters inside the braces that follow \cite. These programs do not look to see if the citation indices follow the syntax we need them to have. The other set of programs look for only one citation index inside the braces following the use of \cite. Therefore, in essence, both sets of programs are not strictly correct to achieve the goal we have set for ourselves. The program that we present next attempts to solve both of these problems. It looks for multiple citation indices that follow the syntax specified.

Program 4.11

```
#!/usr/bin/perl

while (<>) {
    if (/\\cite{([A-Z][a-zA-Z]*(19)?\d{2},)*[A-Z][a-zA-Z]*(19)?\d{2}}/) {
        print $_;
    }
}
```

Here, each index is checked for the presence of an uppercase letter, followed by zero or more lowercase letters followed by two digits. The subpattern [A-Z][a-zA-Z]*(19)?\d{2} picks out one such index. However, we are looking for two or more such indices. Therefore, we break up the problem into two parts. In the first part, we look for zero or more occurrences of a subpattern where we have one citation index followed by a comma. In the second part, we then look for the occurrence of the last citation index. To look for the first part, we put the subpattern for a citation index followed by a comma into a group. We form a group by using parentheses around the subpattern. In this case, this group is indicated by ([A-Z][a-zA-Z]*(19)?\d{2},). We then put an asterisk after this group to indicate that we are looking for zero or more occurrences of the subgroup. This is specified as ([A-Z][a-zA-Z]*(19)?\d{2},)*. Finally, we specify the second part of the problem by writing out once again the subpattern for an index.

4.4 Alternation

We can specify alternations in a subpattern using |. So, when we write

/a|b/

we are looking for either an a or a b. We can have more than one character in alternations. Therefore, if we write

/ab|ac|ad/

we are looking for either ab or ac or ad. We could have written this pattern more compactly as

/a(b|c|d)/

as well. Suppose now we want to modify our citation program a little more. Let us assume that the specification of year in the citation index can be either two digits or four digits. In addition, we assume that if it is four digits long, we must have either 19 or 20 as the first two optional digits. We can now rewrite the last program as given below.

Program 4.12

```
#!/usr/bin/perl

while (<>) {
    if (/\\cite{([A-Z][a-zA-Z]*(19|20)?\d{2},)*[A-Z][a-zA-Z]*(19|20)?\d{2}}/) {
        print $_;
    }
}
```

The program given above repeats a big subpattern twice. This is not a very good idea because it duplicates effort in writing the sub-patterns. We can easily make mistakes in typing it. In addition, the pattern has become very large. A more compact regular expression that does more or less the same is given below.

Program 4.13

```perl
#!/usr/bin/perl

while (<>){
    if (/\\cite{(([A-Z][a-zA-Z]*(19)?\d{2},?)+}/){
        print $_;
    }
}
```

But, this is not perfect either because it accepts citations such as \cite{Badler96,Kalita99,} where there is an extraneous , at the end.

A third version of the program is given below.

Program 4.14

```perl
#!/usr/bin/perl
#file findcite351.pl
$pattern = "[A-Z][a-zA-Z]*(19|20)?[0-9]{2}";
#$pattern = "[A-Z][a-zA-Z]*(19|20)?\\d{2}";

while (<>){
    if (/\\cite{($pattern,)*$pattern}/){
        print $_;
    }
}
```

In this version of the program, we have defined a scalar variable $pattern that stores part of the regular expression for which we are looking. It stores the part of the regular expression that contains the specification of an author's name and the prefix of the year (either 19 or 20, this prefix being optional), and the two-digit year. Inside the while loop where we perform pattern matching in the conditional of the if, we use the variable $pattern a couple of times. The part of the regular expression, given as

```perl
($pattern,)*
```

matches zero or more occurrences of one reference string. Each reference string is separated from the next using a comma. Next, the pattern consists of $pattern} matching the last reference string followed by } and no comma. Note that there are two versions of the assignment to $pattern variable in the program, one of which is commented. Both work. The commented version shows that when a \ is used inside a pattern variable, it must be escaped. when a \ is used inside a pattern variable, it must be escaped. Therefore, we have \\d{2} instead of \d{2}.

4.5 Anchoring

In the mail examples in Section 4.3.3.2 when we looked at a pattern such as /From:/, /Date:/ or /Subject:/, we essentially said that the pattern can occur anywhere in the target string, not at a specific location. For example, if we search for the pattern /From:/ in the /usr/spool/mail/kalita file we talked about earlier, it matches each one of the following four lines because each one contains the substring From:.

```
From: "Brahma, Malavika (Exchange)" <MBrahma@Bear.COM>
> From: J. Kalita [SMTP:kalita@pikespeak.uccs.edu]
> > > From:      Chatterjee, Rajeeb [SMTP:rajeeb.chatterjee@intel.com]
> > > > From:      KBhuyan@aol.com [SMTP:KBhuyan@aol.com]
```

Now, if we are dealing with a mail file in Unix, the first corresponds to a complete message from MBrahma@Bear.COM in the mailbox file whereas the second corresponds to a message included or forwarded from kalita@pikespeak.uccs.edu. This forwarded message in turn contains two recursively forwarded or included messages. Most mailer programs indent included or forwarded messages and precede each line or an included message with a certain character such as > for each level of inclusion or forwarding.

4.5.1   The Caret Anchor

If we need to specify a specific location inside the string for the pattern to occur, we need to use what are called *anchors*. In this specific case, if we want to capture only the SMTP headers for complete messages and not for enclosed or forwarded messages, we want the string From: to start in the beginning of the string or the line with no preceding spaces. We can make Perl look for this condition if we *anchor* the pattern at the beginning of the string. In Perl, we do so by putting a caret (^) in the beginning of the pattern. Therefore, the following is an update to the previous program on finding who has sent mail.

Program 4.15

```perl
#!/usr/bin/perl

while (<>){
    if (/^From:/ or /^Subject:/ or /^Date:/){
        print $_;
    }
}
```

The output of this program looks like the following.

```
From: "Mike Millner" <mike@bewellnet.com>
Subject: Re: vedanti.com and shillong.com
Date: Fri, 24 Jul 1998 14:32:22 -0600
From: hostmaster@internic.net
Subject: Re: [NIC-980724.18471] NEW DOMAIN indiashipping.com (fwd)
Date: Fri, 24 Jul 1998 13:27:59 -0400 (EDT)
From: "Brahma, Malavika (Exchange)" <MBrahma@Bear.COM>
Subject: RE: FW: Exe. Comm
Date: Fri, 7 Aug 1998 14:08:50 -0400
```

Note that no MIME headers from forwarded or enclosed messages are included. This is because we have included the caret in each of the three patterns that we have in the program. We also note that the Delivery-Date: MIME header is not included any more. This is because such a MIME header does not have Date starting at column zero.

The caret (^) is only one of several anchors that Perl provides. Another anchor is $ that anchors a pattern to the very end of a string. Two other useful anchors are \b that stands for a word boundary and \B that stands for "not a word boundary." We will see uses of these in some examples below.

4.5.2   Checking for Scalar Types: Using Both the Caret and $ Anchors

Perl does not provide any built-in type checking for its variables and constants. Suppose we have a scalar variable and want to determine what kind of a variable it is. The following program is a first attempt at such type checking for scalar variables.

Program 4.16
_____

```perl
#!/usr/bin/perl
use strict;

sub findScalarType{
    my ($item) = @_;

    if ($item =~ /^\d+$/)
        {print "whole number\n";}
    elsif ($item =~ /^[-+]?\d+$/)
        {print "signed integer\n";}
    elsif ($item =~ /^[-+]?\d+(\.\d*)?$/)
        {print "non-integral decimal number\n";} #case 1
    elsif ($item =~ /^[-+]?\.\d+$/)
        {print "non-integral decimal number\n";} #case 2
    elsif ($item =~ /^\D+$/)
        {print "string\n";}
    elsif ($item =~ /\D/)
        {print "possibly string\n";}
}
```
_____

Subroutines in Perl start with the keyword sub. It is followed by the name of the subroutine. The body of the subroutine is enclosed inside braces. The subroutine findScalarType takes one argument that is a scalar. In Perl, inside a subroutine, all its arguments are available in terms of a special array variable called @_. Here, we have only one argument to the subroutine. We extract this argument from @_ and call it $item. The subroutine, simplistic as it is, prints one message for an input given to it.

The first if statement contains the pattern expression

```perl
$item =~ /^\d+$/
```

as the conditional. The pattern is simply \d+, but it is anchored at the front of the target string $item as well as at the end. This essentially means that the whole string must be covered from the beginning to the end by the pattern. In other words, the string or scalar we are looking at must have only *digits* in it. That is, it a *whole number* or an unsigned integer.

The next if statement contains the pattern for a signed integer, one that has a + or - in the front.

The next two if statements look for decimal numbers (i.e., numbers with base 10) that are not yet covered. In other words, they look for decimal numbers that are not integers. The first one of these has the following conditional.

```
$item =~ /^[-+]?\d+(\.\d*)?$/
```

It looks for an optional sign followed by one or more digits. After this first set of digits, there may be a decimal number followed by zero or more digits. This first alternative matches a string or a scalar such as +123, -123.45, 123, "123.0", or "123.45". The second alternative matches strings like "+0.56" or "-0.56". Note that this may not be the best definition of decimal numbers, but it is a good start.

Here are some calls to the subroutine. The calls

```
findScalarType ("abc");
findScalarType ("123");
findScalarType (123);
```

print string, whole number and whole number respectively.

Each of the calls

```
findScalarType (123.45);
findScalarType (-0.25);
findScalarType (123e-5);
findScalarType (-.25);
```

prints non-integral decimal number (case 1). The first two are obvious. However, the third and the fourth cases are not so obvious. In the third case, Perl converts 123e-5 to 0.00123 first before sending it to the function. As a result it falls under the first case of non-integral decimal numbers. In the fourth case, Perl converts -.25 to -0.25 before sending it to the function. Therefore, even in this case, the first alternative for non-integral decimal numbers holds.

The call

```
findScalarType (".25");
```

prints the second alternative for non-integral decimal number. It is because Perl considers the argument to be a string and does not do any numeric conversion of any kind before sending it to the function.

Finally, the following two calls

```
findScalarType ("abc2d");
findScalarType ("123e-5");
```

print possibly string.

4.6 Grouping and Remembering a Sub-Pattern

We have seen the use of parentheses to group a subpattern inside a pattern. For example, in the pattern

```
/\\cite{([^}])+}/
```

there is one group [^}]. Here, this subpattern is required to be repeated one or more times. In the pattern

```
/\\cite{([A-Z][a-zA-Z]*(19|20)?\d{2},)*[A-Z][a-zA-Z]*(19|20)?\d{2}}/
```

there are two parenthesized sub-patterns or groups. These are given below.

```
([A-Z][a-zA-Z]*(19|20)?\d{2},)
(19|20)
```

The first can be repeated zero or more times. It is indicated by putting a * behind the closing parentheses. The second is contained in the first and occurs in another place also. In each of the two occurrences of the subpattern, the occurrence is optional. This is achieved by putting a ? after the subpattern.

In these examples, parentheses have been used to group a subpattern so that we treat the subpattern like a single entity and then use a multiplier such as *, +, ?, or {2,5} after it. We have also seen that one subpattern can be inside another.

Using parentheses to group a subpattern does have an additional effect. Perl remembers what part of the target string matches a grouped subpattern. Let us look at some examples to clarify the point.

4.6.1 Extracting Components From A URL

Assume we are looking at the source of an HTML file displayed by a Web browser. Suppose we have the following lines in the HTML file.

```
<a href="http://www.assam.org:80/orgs/asa/index.html"> Assam Society</a> was founded in 1973.
<a href="http://www.assam.org:80/orgs/asa/index.xml"> Assam Society</a> was founded in 1973.
<a href="http://www.assam.org/orgs/asa/index.html"> Assam Society </a>was founded in 1973.
<a href="http://www.assam.org/orgs/asa/"> Assam Society </a> was founded in 1973.
<a href="http://www.assam.org/orgs/asa"> Assam Society </a> was founded in 1973.
<a href="http://www.assam.org"> Assam Society </a> was founded in 1973.
```

The file shows the various manners in which URLs can be written. We assume that there is only one URL per line. Our goal is to read such a file, extract the URL if any, from a line read, and then extract parts of the URL such as the server name, the HTTP port number, the path, and the name of the file, if any, and the type of the file. We will write several programs to achieve our goal.

The first program simply reads lines from an HTML file and extracts URLs.

Program 4.17

```perl
#!/usr/bin/perl
#file extractURL0.pl
while (<>){
    if ($_ =~ m@http://([^"]+)"@){
        $url = $1;
        print "URL = ", $url, "\n";
    }
}
```

The while loop reads lines from the file one by one. The only programming construct inside the while loop is an if statement. The conditional of the if statement does pattern matching against the line that was read into $_. In the conditional, there is one set of matched parentheses enclosing a subpattern. If the conditional is not satisfied, the line is ignored. If the conditional is satisfied by a particular line read, the part of the target string $_ that matches the subpattern inside the parentheses (i.e., ([^"]+)) is remembered by Perl. Since there is only one instance of remembering in the regular expression under consideration, the remembered substring is stored in the special variable with the name $1. Later we assign to the variable $url the value of $1. Therefore, the program prints the following.

```
URL = www.assam.org:80/orgs/asa/index.html
URL = www.assam.org:80/orgs/asa/index.xml
URL = www.assam.org/orgs/asa/index.html
URL = www.assam.org/orgs/asa/
URL = www.assam.org/orgs/asa
URL = www.assam.org
```

Any time we use parentheses to group a subpattern, the remembering effect is triggered. If we have several parenthesized subpatterns or subexpressions in a regular expression, the number of special variables created for the purpose of remembering is equal to the number of parenthesized pairs. The variables are numbered $1, $2, $3, etc. $1 stores the substring of the target string that matches the first parenthesized subexpression, $2 stores the substring that matches the second parenthesized subexpression, etc.

After we have extracted the URL, we now want to extract two substrings out of it, the path and the file name. The program given below accomplishes this goal.

Program 4.18

```perl
#!/usr/bin/perl
#file extractURL111.pl
while (<>){
    $url = $fileName = $serverPath = "";
    if ($_ =~ m@http://([^"]+)"@){
        $url = $1;

        $url = $url . "/"
            if (($url !~ m@/$@) and  ($url !~ m@[.](html|xml)$@));
        print "URL = ", $url, "\n";

        $url =~ m@^(.+)/([^/]+\.(html|xml))?$@;

        $fileName = $2;
        $serverPath = $1;
    }
    print "Server and path = $serverPath\nFile = $fileName\n\n";

}
```

In this program, like before, we have a `while` loop that reads lines one by one from one or more input files. In the loop, we start by setting each of the variables $url, $fileName and $serverPath to the empty string to ensure that there are no residual values from a previous iteration of the loop. Next, we have an if block, the conditional of which captures, in the special numbered variable $1, the URL if any, in the current line. The URL is then stored in the variable $url, just like the previous program. The statement that follows is repeated below.

```perl
$url = $url . "/" if (($url !~ m@/$@) and  ($url !~ m@[.](html|xml)$@));
```

This statement checks to see if the URL does not end with a / and in addition, does not end with either one of the two file extensions: .html or .xml. If it does not, it concludes that it is a directory name without a trailing /, and it appends the URL with a /. In our example, this happens in the case of the last two URLs in the data file being parsed. This preparatory step of pre-processing the URL makes it easier to extract the components we need. The extraction is done in the following statement.

```perl
$url =~ m@^(.+)/([^/]+\.(html|xml))?$@;
```

The regular expression that appears on the right hand side is anchored with the ^ anchor to start matching with the target string $url from the beginning. The regular expression is also constrained to match till the end of the target string because it is also anchored to the end of the string by the anchor specifier $. Thus, the regular expression must match $url starting in the beginning, and must match $url till the end. This simply means that the regular expression must match $url completely.

There are three parenthesized subexpressions in the full regular expression. The first parenthesized subexpression is (.+), the second parenthesized subexpression is ([^]+\.(html|xml)), and the third parenthesized subexpression is a part of the second and is (html|xml). Since there are three parenthesized subexpressions, three special variables, $1, $2 and $3 are assigned values by the pattern match operator =~. The value of $3 is ignored in this program after the pattern matching is done.

The first parenthesized subexpression uses the multiplier +. The second parenthesized subexpression, ([^]+\.(html|xml)), also has the multiplier + inside it. The second parenthesized subexpression is optional because it is followed by the multiplier ?. Thus, it is possible that pattern match against $url satisfies without the URL having a file name such as index.html or index.xml seen in some of the example URLs. In our data file, the URLs that do not need to match this optional second parenthesized subexpression even once are the following.

```
URL = www.assam.org/orgs/asa/
URL = www.assam.org/orgs/asa
URL = www.assam.org
```

Note that in the case of the last two URLs above, a trailing / is appended by the program step discussed earlier. In the case of all three URLs, the second parenthesized subexpression does not match any substring in the URL. Thus, the value of $2 is the empty string after the match. The third parenthesized subexpression, (html|xml), which is included inside the second, cannot also match any part of the target string, and hence $3's value is also the empty string. In these cases, the + multiplier in the first parenthesized subexpression consumes all characters in the modified URL except the trailing /.

Now, consider the first three URLs of the data file, repeated below.

```
URL = www.assam.org:80/orgs/asa/index.html
URL = www.assam.org:80/orgs/asa/index.xml
URL = www.assam.org/orgs/asa/index.html
```

Each one of these has a file name at the end, it being index.html, index.xml and index.html, respectively. In matching against these targets, all three subexpressions match substrings in the URLs. Thus, $2 and $3, in addition to $1, are assigned non-empty values after the pattern match is performed. But what values do $1, $2, and $3 get in these cases?

As we know, the first parenthesized subexpression has a multiplier +, and so does the second parenthesized subexpression. The first multiplier consumes as much of the target string $url as possible. The first subexpression (.+) theoretically can consume the whole string because . matches every character except \n and there is no \n in the $url string. After matching the first parenthesized subexpression, we must find a / in the target string. Then, matching the second parenthesized subexpression begins. The second parenthesized subexpression starts by looking for a sequence of one or more characters, each one of which is not /, followed by the period and a file extension: html or xml. This means that the first parenthesized subexpression matches the target URL all the way up to the last /, of course, excluding the /. Thus, $1 gets the value

```
www.assam.org:80/orgs/asa
www.assam.org/orgs/asa
www.assam.org/orgs/asa
```

respectively, in the three cases under discussion. Next, in each case, the / is matched. The second parenthesized subexpression matches

```
index.html
```

```
index.xml
index.html
```

respectively, for the three URLs.

In general, Perl's pattern-matching multipliers such as * and + are *left greedy*. If there are several multipliers in a regular expression, the ones on the left consume as much as possible of the target string. However, their greed is limited by the requirement that the ones that follow must be able to consume at least some of the input, if they are to match as specified. So, after the first multiplier has consumed all it can, the regular expression engine tries to match other parts of the expression that follow. If there is a failure in matching what follows, Perl backtracks and tries to match the first multiplier again by consuming a little less that it did the first time. In the case of the three URLs under consideration, the first subexpression (.+) cannot consume everything because there are other multipliers and other non-parenthesized and non-multiplied parts of the regular expression that follow. We do not go into the details of how it all works except that the left-most multipliers consume as much as they can, but they are willing to consume a little less if the other multipliers that follow do not have anything to consume for satisfaction.

The result of running this code on the data file shown earlier is the following.

```
URL = www.assam.org:80/orgs/asa/index.html
Server and path = www.assam.org:80/orgs/asa
File = index.html

URL = www.assam.org:80/orgs/asa/index.xml
Server and path = www.assam.org:80/orgs/asa
File = index.xml

URL = www.assam.org/orgs/asa/index.html
Server and path = www.assam.org/orgs/asa
File = index.html

URL = www.assam.org/orgs/asa/
Server and path = www.assam.org/orgs/asa
File =

URL = www.assam.org/orgs/asa/
Server and path = www.assam.org/orgs/asa
File =

URL = www.assam.org/
Server and path = www.assam.org
File =
```

Suppose extracting the two parts that the previous program does not satisfy our ultimate objective. Now, we want to extract the name of the server (which is www.assam.org), the HTTP port number (80, in the first two cases), the path and the file name separately. The following code does this for us.

Program 4.19

```
#!/usr/bin/perl
#file extractURL2.pl
while (<>){
    $url =  $machine = $port = $file = "";
```

```perl
    if ($_ =~ m@http://([^"]+)"@) {
        $url = $1;
        print "URL = ", $url, "\n";
        $url = $url . "/" if (($url !~ m@/$@) and ($url !~ m@[.](html|xml)$@));

        $url =~ m@^([^:/]+)(:(\d+))?/(.+?)([^/]+[.](html|xml))?$@;
        $machine = $1;
        $port = $3;
        $path = $4;
        $file = $5;
        print "Machine = $machine\nPort = $port\nPath = $path\nFile = $file\n\n";
    }
}
```

This program is quite similar to the previous one. The first few lines of code are just like what we had earlier. The difference comes when we extract components from the variable $url. The pattern matching statement is given below.

```perl
$url =~ m@^([^:/]+)(:(\d+))?/(.+?)([^/]+[.](html|xml))?$@;
```

Here, there are six parenthesized subexpressions. The part in the URL before the first / is the machine or server name followed optionally by a colon and a port number, e.g., :80. The extraction till the first / is done using the following part of the regular expression.

```perl
([^:/]+)(:(\d+))?
```

The matching starts at the beginning of the URL, and continues till a /, the first /. First, it looks for one or more characters belonging to the negative character class [^:/], i.e., one or more characters that are not : or /. This means that the first parenthesized subexpression, ([^:/]+) matches the server name, and this value is remembered in the variable $1.

Next, we look for the optional port number in the URL. The second parenthesized subexpression, (:(\d+))? tells us that the specification of the port number is optional. If a port number is provided (say, 80), the first set of parentheses matches :80. However, : is not a part of the port number, it is a separator required by syntax. That is why we have the second set of parentheses (the inside set) in (:(\d+))?. The second set matches the port number (i.e., 80). The port number does not have to be just two digits, it can be longer. This approach to capturing the port number means that the substring that matches the first set of parentheses in (:(\d+))? is not really useful. Useful or not, :80 is the value of $2. Since it is not useful, in the assignment statements that follow we do not use $2 anywhere.

There is another point that needs to be discussed. A multiplier such as + or * is a *maximal multiplier* in that the multiplier causes Perl to consume as much of the text as possible. This maximal or all-consuming behavior of a multiplier can be changed by placing a ? after the multiplier. In such a case, the multiplier is forced to consume the least amount of characters possible such that it still satisfies. Such usage is called a *minimal multiplier*. We see such a use in the parenthesized subpattern (.+?). This subpattern matches the path part of the URL in this case.

When we run this program on the same file as before, the output is the following.

```
URL = www.assam.org:80/orgs/asa/index.html
Machine = www.assam.org
Port = 80
Path = orgs/asa/
File = index.html
```

```
URL = www.assam.org:80/orgs/asa/index.xml
Machine = www.assam.org
Port = 80
Path = orgs/asa/
File = index.xml

URL = www.assam.org/orgs/asa/index.html
Machine = www.assam.org
Port =
Path = orgs/asa/
File = index.html

URL = www.assam.org/orgs/asa/
Machine = www.assam.org
Port =
Path = orgs/asa/
File =

URL = www.assam.org/orgs/asa
Machine = www.assam.org
Port =
Path = orgs/asa/
File =

URL = www.assam.org
Machine = www.assam.org
Port =
Path =
File =
```

In summary, the special variables created by Perl are numbered $1, $2, ... This is one case when Perl starts numbering from 1 instead of 0. The numbering depends on the occurrence of the left parentheses. As usual, parentheses are allowed inside parentheses. In such a case, the first left parentheses corresponds to a lower numbered special variable.

When Perl remembers matched substrings in terms of special numbered scalars, Perl's =~ operator also returns a list containing all the remembered substrings in sequence if it is used in a list or array context. In the following program, the array context is triggered because what is returned by =~ is used to set the value of an array.

Program 4.20

```perl
#!/usr/bin/perl
#extractURL31.pl

while (<>) {
    my $url;
    if ($_ =~ m@([\w]+://[^"]+)@i) {
        $url = $1;
        print "url  = $url\n";

        $url = $url . "/"
```

```
                        if (($url !~ m@/$@) and  ($url !~ m@[.](html|xml)$@));

        @allParts =
           ($url =~
              m@(\w+)://([^:/]+)(:(\d+))?((/[^/]+)*)/([^/]+[.](html|xml))?@);

        print "Protocol = $allParts[0]\n";
        print "Machine = $allParts[1]\n";
        print "Port = $allParts[3]\n";
        print "Path = $allParts[4]\n";
        print "File = $allParts[6]\n";
        print "File type = $allParts[7]\n\n";
    }
}
```

The parentheses around the two operands of =~ in the following lines is optional. The =~ operators binds its two arguments or operands more tightly than the assignment operator =. Here, there are eight pairs of parentheses. Therefore, eight substrings are remembered by Perl in terms of the special variables $1, $2, $3, $4, $5 and $6. In such a case, Perl's match operation =~ returns a list which contains the values of the six substrings in order. We have put parentheses around the two arguments to the =~ operator to make things clear.

This program prints the following.

```
url  = http://www.assam.org:80/orgs/asa/index.html
Protocol = http
Machine = www.assam.org
Port = 80
Path = /orgs/asa
File = index.html
File type = html

url  = http://www.assam.org:80/orgs/asa/index.xml
Protocol = http
Machine = www.assam.org
Port = 80
Path = /orgs/asa
File = index.xml
File type = xml

url  = http://www.assam.org/orgs/asa/index.html
Protocol = http
Machine = www.assam.org
Port =
Path = /orgs/asa
File = index.html
File type = html

url  = http://www.assam.org/orgs/asa/
Protocol = http
Machine = www.assam.org
```

```
Port  =
Path  =  /orgs/asa
File  =
File type  =

url   = http://www.assam.org/orgs/asa
Protocol = http
Machine = www.assam.org
Port  =
Path  =  /orgs/asa
File  =
File type  =

url   = http://www.assam.org
Protocol = http
Machine = www.assam.org
Port  =
Path  =
File  =
File type  =
```

If we change the code slightly so that we have scalar literals in a list on the left side of the pattern-matching operation, it still works exactly the same way. Since we have a list with scalar literals on the left of an assignment statement, the scalars get assigned appropriately.

Program 4.21

```
#!/usr/bin/perl
#extractURL41.pl

while (<>){
    my $url;
    if ($_ =~ m@([\w]+://[^"]+)@i){
        $url = $1;
        print "url   = $url\n";

        $url = $url . "/"
            if (($url !~ m@/$@) and  ($url !~ m@[.](html|xml)$@));

        my ($protocol, $machine, undef, $port,
            $path, undef, $file, $fileType) =
        ($url
            =~  m@(\w+)://([^:/]+)(:(\d+))?((/[^/]+)*)/([^/]+[.](html|xml))?@);

        print "Protocol = $protocol\n";
        print "Machine = $machine\nPort = $port\n";
        print "Path = $path\nFile = $file\n";
        print "File type = $fileType\n\n";
    }
}
```

We put `undef` in the index position two of the list since we do not want to do any assignment with the third element of the list returned by `=~`. This third element happens to be `:80`.

4.6.2 Extracting Components from a Unix-Style Date

Now, we present another example that illustrates remembering results of pattern matching. Here, we assume we are on a Unix machine. Using backticks, we call the Unix `date` command which returns something like the following.

```
Mon Aug 17 19:17:00 MDT 1998
```

In this program, we match over a string that contains such a date string. The pattern expression has ten starting parentheses and ten closing parentheses. Therefore, ten variables, $1 through $10 are set. The matched substrings are remembered and stored in the array `@fields`. In the assignment statements that follow, sometimes we assign from a numbered variable and sometimes from an element of `@fields`.

Program 4.22

```perl
#!/usr/bin/perl

$date = `date`;
@fields =
   ($date =~ /^(\w+) ((\w+) (\d+)) ((..):(..):(..)) (\w+) (\d+)/);
$day = $1;
$monthdate = $2; $month = $3; $date = $4;
$time = $5; $hour = $fields[5];
$minutes = $fields[6]; $seconds = $fields[7];
$timeZone = $9;
$year = $10;

print "Day = $day\nMonth and  Day = $monthdate\n";
print "Month = $month\nDate = $date\n";
print "Time = $time\nHour = $hour\n";
print "Minutes = $minutes\nSeconds = $seconds\n";
print "Time Zone = $timeZone\nYear = $year\n";
```

4.7 Three Useful Functions: `split`, `join` and `grep`

There are three very useful functions that Perl provides for us. `split` and `grep` each takes a pattern as an argument. `join` does not take a pattern as an argument, but simply a string.

4.7.1 Translating Path Name Formats

`split` takes two arguments: a pattern and a string. It breaks up the string into one or more substrings based on the pattern. The call to `split` returns all the substrings in the original sequence.

Suppose we have a file name with path in the Unix style. Assume we want to convert it into the Microsoft Windows style. In the Unix style, directory and file names are separated by /. Therefore, a valid name is something like the following.

```
/users/server/faculty/kalita/public_html/index.html
```

The same name in the Microsoft Windows style looks like

```
\users\server\faculty\kalita\public_html\index.html
```

There are many ways to do this conversion. One way is given below. Note that this is not the most efficient way to do so.

Program 4.23

```perl
#!/usr/bin/perl

print join ("\\", split (m@/@, $ARGV[0])), "\n";
```

Assuming the script is stored in the file `convert.pl`, a call to this script is something like

```
%convert.pl /users/server/faculty/kalita/public_html/index.html
```

It prints the name in the Microsoft Windows style.

```
\users\server\faculty\kalita\public_html\index.html
```

First, `split` takes the argument given to it and produces a list whose elements are

```
"users" "server" "faculty" "kalita" "public_html" "index.html"
```

Next, the `join` operator takes a string of length zero or more (*not* a pattern) and uses this string as the glue to put the list (the second argument) together. In this case, putting the list back together with \ as the glue or the separator gives us the file name in the Microsoft style. The backslash needs to be escaped using another backslash inside a string.

4.7.2   Counting Frequencies of Letters

We now write two more scripts that use `split` and pattern matching. The first one counts the frequency of alphabetic letters in a set of files. The second counts the frequency of words in a set of files. The first program follows.

Program 4.24

```perl
#!/usr/local/bin/perl
while (<ARGV>){
  @letters = split(//, $_);
  foreach $letter (@letters){
    if ($letter =~ /[a-zA-Z]/){
      $frequency{$letter} += 1;
    }
  }
}
@indexes = keys (%frequency);
foreach (sort (@indexes)){
    print $_, ": ",$frequency{$_},"\n";
}
```

The program looks at every line of every file given to it as an argument. As it reads a line, it splits that line into a list @letters. The splitting is done with an empty pattern argument. This means that each character is split out separately from the input line. Once this is done, the program goes through each of the characters and if the character is an alphabetic character, lowercase or uppercase, the program keeps a count of the number of occurrences in an associative array called %frequency.

Following the while loop, the program sorts the keys in %frequency. This sorting is done because the keys in an associative array can come out in any order if not sorted. Finally, the letters and their frequencies are printed. The output of a call of this program with one document file as argument is given below.

```
A:  1314
B:  1143
C:  1372
D:  807
E:  361
F:  382
G:  1423
H:  338
I:  740
J:  125
K:  213
L:  666
M:  611
N:  982
O:  391
P:  1019
Q:  11
R:  660
S:  855
T:  837
U:  769
V:  122
W:  357
X:  169
Y:  495
Z:  65
a:  17008
b:  3835
c:  6048
d:  6756
e:  25020
f:  4260
g:  2857
h:  7671
i:  15893
j:  436
k:  1531
l:  8222
m:  6464
n:  14394
o:  15621
```

```
p: 4828
q: 285
r: 14581
s: 13817
t: 18359
u: 6354
v: 1864
w: 2140
x: 1062
y: 2932
z: 272
```

4.7.3 Counting Word Frequency

The next program counts the frequencies of all words in a set of files. It looks for words with alphabetic characters only. First we give the program and then we explain it and show a sample output.

Program 4.25

```
#!/usr/bin/perl
if ($ARGV[0] =~ m/^-tex$/){
    shift @ARGV;
    @ARGV = grep (/\.tex$/, @ARGV);
}

while ($text = <ARGV>){
    @words = split (/\W*\s+\W*/, $text);
    @words = grep (/^[a-zA-Z\-]+$/, @words);
    foreach $word (@words){
        $wordCount{$word}++;
    }
}

#printing the words in alphabetical order
print "*" x 60, "\n";
print "Printing the words alphabetically\n";
print "*" x 60, "\n";

foreach $word (sort keys (%wordCount)){
        printf "%-20s %d\n", $word, $wordCount{$word};
}
```

In this program also, we distinguish between cases of letters. Therefore, It and it are treated as different words.

First, we look at the arguments given to the call. If the first argument is given as -tex, we consider it to be a Unix-style *switch*. If the first argument is given as -tex, we look at files that are written in the TeX/LaTeX format only. Such files have the .tex extension in their names. If the first argument happens to be this switch, we cull the file names that have the requisite extension using the grep command.

Next, inside the while loop, we look at each line of each file one by one. A line of input is read into the scalar variable $text. Next, we take the string $text and break it apart using one or more space characters surrounded by zero or more non-word characters as the separator. This separates out every word in the current line of text from the current file. A word separator is a contiguous substring of one or more non-space and non-word characters. Then, we use the grep function to keep only those words that have alphabetic characters and hyphens in them. Then, we go through each word and increment the frequency count for each occurrence. All this is done for every chosen element of @ARGV, i.e., every qualified file name culled from those used as a command line argument. Finally, in the last foreach loop, we sort the words and print them out sequentially with frequency.

Let us store this script in a file called wordcountTeX.pl. Now, if we make a call such as

```
%wordcountTeX.pl -tex *
```

we get an output that is like the following. We show only part of the output.

```
A                      24
AI                     5
ASAM                   2
Above                  1
Abstracts              1
According              2
Achieving              1
Across                 3
Action                 9
Action-n               2
Actions                1
Additional             1
Additionally           2
Adverbs                1
After                  1
Ag                     20
Aleksander             1
Align                  4
Aligned                1
All                    2
Allen                  1
Almost                 1
Also                   3
Alspector              1
Although               7
Altogether             1
Among                  5
An                     5
Analysis               1
Analyzing              2
And                    11
Another                2
Approximate            2
As                     7
Asam                   5
Aspect                 1
Assuming               3
At                     4
```

4.8   Match Modifiers

Perl allows a programmer to modify how the pattern match operator works by specifying *modifiers*. The modifiers are also called *options* or *qualifiers*. We will discuss Perl's pattern match modifiers in the rest of the section.

4.8.1   The m//i Modifier

When pattern matching is performed over alphabetic characters, whether a letter is in upper case or lower case usually matters. Of course, the case of a letter is important in many situations such as in the beginning letters in proper names. However, there are situations where the case of a letter does not matter. This frequently happens in an interactive program. For example, we may ask the user a question whose answer can be either yes, no or quit. Let us assume that the user can respond by either typing in the first letter of a response or the whole word. So, y, Y, yes, Yes, YES or even YeS are valid responses when the user wants to answer in the affirmative. In other words, whether the response is in upper case or lower case, does not matter. We can make these pattern matches using the following regular expressions.

```
/^y$/i  or  /^yes$/i
/^n$/i  or  /no$/i
/^q$/i  or  /^quit$/i
```

The ^ and $ anchors make sure that the response is what we want. So, n, N, or NO are acceptable, but nowhere, not or nomad is not.

4.8.1.1   Counting Frequencies of Letters: Again

We now write two more versions of the letter frequency counting program that we discussed in an earlier section. The first version we present is almost identical to the previous program except that the conditional using pattern match has changed a little.

Program 4.26
_____

```perl
#!/usr/local/bin/perl

while (<ARGV>){
  @letters = split(//,$_);
  foreach $letter (@letters){
    if ($letter =~ /[a-z]/i){
      $frequency{$letter} += 1;
    }
  }
}

@indexes = keys(%frequency);

foreach(sort(@indexes)){
    print $_,": ",$frequency{$_},"\n";
}
```

_____

The conditional of the if block inside the while loop is now written as

```
$letter =~ /[a-z]/i
```

instead of

```
$letter =~ /[a-zA-Z]/
```

that we had earlier. In the newer version, we use the modifier i after the regular expression /[a-z]/. It is the *ignore case* option or modifier. It instructs Perl to ignore the case of the matched alphabetic character or characters. In this case, both match operations perform exactly the same because

```
/[a-z]/i
```

matches both lower case and upper case letters. The frequencies printed by the new version of the program is exactly the same as those printed by the previous version. In both cases, frequencies for lower case and upper case letters are computed and printed separately.

Now, suppose we want to print frequencies of letters in a set of files without regard to the cases of the letters. That is, frequencies for a lower case letter and the corresponding upper case letter are lumped together. The following is a modification of our program that does so.

Program 4.27

```
while (<ARGV>){
  @letters = split(//,$_);
  foreach $letter (@letters){
    if ($letter =~ /[a-z]/i){
      $frequency{lc ($letter)} += 1;
    }
  }
}

@indexes = keys(%frequency);

foreach(sort(@indexes)){
    print $_,": ",$frequency{$_},"\n";
}
```

Here, the line of code that has changed from the previous version is the one that increments frequency. It is now

```
$frequency{lc ($letter)} += 1;
```

instead of

```
$frequency{$letter} += 1;
```

that we had in the previous two versions of the program. lc is a built-in function that takes a string argument and converts it into lower case. The output printed by the program for a sample call is given below.

```
a: 18322
b: 4978
c: 7420
```

```
d: 7563
e: 25381
f: 4642
g: 4280
h: 8009
i: 16633
j: 561
k: 1744
l: 8888
m: 7075
n: 15376
o: 16012
p: 5847
q: 296
r: 15241
s: 14672
t: 19196
u: 7123
v: 1986
w: 2497
x: 1231
y: 3427
z: 337
```

4.8.2   The m//x Modifier

Quite frequently, regular expressions become quite complex and hence, difficult to read. An example of a complex regular expression that we have seen earlier in this chapter is repeated below.

```
/\\cite{([A-Z][a-zA-Z]*(19|20)?\d{2},)*[A-Z][a-zA-Z]*(19|20)?\d{2}/
```

In such a situation, readability may be improved by allowing whitespaces (space characters, tabs, return characters, etc.) to separate out characters or groups of characters inside a regular expression.

The m//x modifier allows us to use such needed spaces inside the specification of a regular expression. If we need to specify a space character inside a regular expression, it must be escaped except inside a character class. Space characters inside a character class are not ignored. That is, elements in a character class still need to be written compactly, without intervening space. Finally, the x modifier allows us to use # in a line of code inside the specification of the regular expression to indicate the beginning of a comment.

Here is a rewrite of the program that uses the complex regular expression given above using the x modifier.

Program 4.28

```perl
#!/usr/bin/perl

while (<>){
    if (/
        \\                      #backslashed \
        cite                    #the string
        {                       #the brace
        (                       #BEGIN SUB-PATTERN
          [A-Z]                 #citation index starts with an uppercase letter
```

```
            [a-zA-Z]*         #follow by zero or more letters
            (19|20)?          #first two digits of  year are 19 or 20 if given
            \d{2},            #last two year digits
          )*                  #END SUB-PATTERN, repeat subpattern 0 or more times

        [A-Z][a-zA-Z]*(19|20)?\d{2} #the same subpattern


      /x)
    {
    print $_;
    }
}
```

4.8.3   The `m//g` Modifier

Usually, when Perl performs a match operation, the pattern matches only once on the target string. The regular expression matches in the position in the target string where the expression is satisfied the first time. It is possible that the regular expression matches in several positions in the target string. In such situations, all but the first occurrence are ignored. However, it is possible to force Perl to match all occurrences of a regular expression in the target string. This modification of Perl's pattern matching behavior can be effected using the `g` modifier.

4.8.3.1   Counting Word Frequencies: Again

Let us now try to write another version of the program to count word frequencies in a set of files. We do not want to use the `split` function as we did before. We want to try it another way. Be warned that the first update of the program we present next does not work correctly.

Program 4.29

```perl
#!/usr/bin/perl
if ($ARGV[0] =~ m/^-tex$/){
    shift @ARGV;
    @ARGV = grep (/\.tex$/, @ARGV);
}

while ($text = <ARGV>){
    @words =  ($text =~ /([a-zA-Z\-]+)/);
    foreach $word (@words){
        $wordCount{$word}++;
    }
}

#printing the words in alphabetical order
print "*" x 60, "\n";
print "Printing the words alphabetically\n";
print "*" x 60, "\n";

foreach $word (sort keys (%wordCount)){
```

```
        printf "%-20s %d\n", $word, $wordCount{$word};
}
```

This program changes the code inside the `while` loop from the previous version. In the previous version, the `while` loop looked like the following.

```
while ($text = <ARGV>) {
    @words = split (/\W*\s+\W*/, $text);
    @words = grep (/^[a-zA-Z\-]+$/, @words);
    foreach $word (@words) {
        $wordCount{$word}++;
    }
}
```

Now, the code inside the `while` loop has changed to the following.

```
while ($text = <ARGV>) {
    @words =  ($text =~ /([a-zA-Z\-]+)/);
    foreach $word (@words) {
        $wordCount{$word}++;
    }
}
```

Otherwise, everything else in the program is the same as what we had earlier. In the new program, we read in a line of text into the scalar called `$text` and then perform a pattern match operation on it. The pattern match operation remembers the substring that matches and puts the matched substring in the array called `@words`.

When we run this program, we find that the word frequencies obtained are much smaller than the frequencies printed by the previous version of the program. If we look carefully in the text of the `while` loop, we find out why this is the case. When we perform pattern match over `$text`, since we do not use any options or modifiers, only the first word of each line of text is captured in the array `@words`. In other words, only the first word of each line is considered when we compute the frequencies of words in the file. This is definitely wrong and results in gross undercounting. The first few frequencies printed by the program on the same files as before are given below.

```
A                    10
AFF                  2
Across               1
Additionally         2
AdvP                 1
After                1
All                  2
Almost               1
Also                 1
Among                2
An                   2
Analyzing            2
And                  7
Another              1
As                   5
```

We see that many words that occurred earlier are missing and for other words, the frequencies are undercounted.

Our objective is to extract all words from each line of text and not just the first word. We can accomplish this with a very little change in our program. We need to specify g or the *global match* option or modifier in the pattern match operator. It instructs Perl to match the pattern globally. In other words, it tells Perl to modify its usual behavior of matching only once for a target string, but match as many times as possible. If we have ten words per line of text, Perl matches all of these words. Moreover, Perl's =~ operator returns a list containing all the matched words when we use it in a context where a list is expected. This is such a situation because the value returned by =~ is used to set an array variable. As a result, @words contains all the words in line of text from the input file and not just the first word. Hence, the program counts the frequencies of all words in the files that are given as arguments. The text of the program is given below.

Program 4.30

```
#!/usr/bin/perl
if ($ARGV[0] =~ m/^-tex$/){
    shift @ARGV;
    @ARGV = grep (/\.tex$/, @ARGV);
}

while ($text = <ARGV>){
    @words =  ($text =~ /([a-zA-Z\-]+)/g);
    foreach $word (@words){
        $wordCount{$word}++;
    }
}

#printing the words in alphabetical order
print "*" x 60, "\n";
print "Printing the words alphabetically\n";
print "*" x 60, "\n";

foreach $word (sort keys (%wordCount)){
        printf "%-20s %d\n", $word, $wordCount{$word};
}
```

The line of code that extracts the words from a line of text is given below.

```
@words =  ($text =~ /([a-zA-Z\-]+)/g);
```

This line has the g modifier appended to the specification of the regular expression. This modifier does the trick for us. The target string is $text. The pattern match operation

```
$text =~ /([a-zA-Z\-]+)/g
```

succeeds every time the pattern specified is found in the target string. Not only that, every time the pattern matches, the substring that matches is remembered by Perl because the pattern is enclosed in parentheses. So, if there are ten words in the target string, all of these words are captured by Perl. The list of these words is returned by the =~ operator. @words is assigned this list of words from the target string.

4.8.3.2 m//g Works With Multi-Line Strings or Paragraphs

So far, when we have done pattern matching, we have done so over a line of text or a string that does not contain the \n character or contains \n at the very end. However, it is possible that a string has multiple lines. That is, it has one or more embedded \n characters. An example of such a string is given below.

```
$friends = "Tommy\tWashington\nChad\tSanFrancisco\nJeffP";
$friends .= "\tBoulder\nJeffC\tColoradoSprings\n";
```

The string $friends has several embedded newline characters. As a result, if printed, it comes out as several lines on the terminal or on paper. Such a string can either be typed the way we have just done or can be read from a file although we have not yet seen how we can read multiple lines or a paragraph from a file in one read operation.

4.8.3.2.1   Pattern Matching Over Multi-Line Strings With No Modifiers   Things can become complicated when we talk about pattern matching over multiple lines of text. We get to the complications later. Let us look at the simplest case of multi-line strings first.

It is possible to match over multi-line strings without using any modifiers at all. Unless we want to change the behavior of the anchors ^ and $, or want the dot (.) character to match \n (which it normally does not), pattern matching over multiple lines of text can be done the normal way. Here is an example program. We want to find out the first instance of two integers in sequence and add them and print the result.

Program 4.31

```
#!/usr/bin/perl

$textAndNumbers = "\t\n A \t B \n\n\n12\t\n\t\t13 \t \nC\t20\n\t31\t40\nD";
($first, $second) =
    $textAndNumbers =~ m/(\d+)\s+(\d+)/;
print $first + $second, "\n";
```

Here, the fact that there are embedded \n's in the target string does not matter at all. The \s+ subpattern inside the regular expression matches one or more \n's and other white-space characters. The program prints 25 as the result of adding the first two consecutive numbers it finds.

4.8.3.2.2   Capturing Pairs of Words From a Multi-Line String   When we want the pattern matching operation to work in a little more complex manner over multi-line strings, we need to use modifiers. Each one of three match modifiers: m, g or s can be used to match over multiple lines, but each one modifies the behavior of the m// operator differently. We start with the use of the g modifier in multi-line matching.

Given a string with embedded newlines, suppose we want to pick out each of the words from all the lines of text. It can be done simply by using one line of pattern-matching code.

Program 4.32

```
#!/usr/bin/perl
$" = "\t";
$friends = "Tommy\tWashington\nChad\tSanFrancisco\nJeffP";
$friends .= "\tBoulder\nJeffC\tColoradoSprings\n";

@allWords = ($friends =~ /(\w+)/g);
print "All words = @allWords\n\n";
```

We use the pattern match operator with the g modifier. The target string $friends has multiple lines. The regular expression or pattern used (\w+) usually captures the first substring that it matches in the target string. However, since we use the g modifier, all substrings that match are captured by Perl. The fact that the target string has multiple lines is immaterial when we use the g modifier. As a result, this program prints out the following.

```
All words = Tommy        Washington     Chad    SanFrancisco      JeffP
                      BoulderJeffC    ColoradoSprings
```

The output has been broken into two lines by hand.

We use a special variable $" in this program. It holds what is called the list item separator. When a list is printed by specifying it inside double quotes, the elements of the list are printed with the separator that is the current value of $". It defaults to a single space if not provided.

Suppose now we want to start with the same multi-line string and construct an associative array or hash that has the name of a friend as the key and his hometown as the value. The following program achieves this for us.

Program 4.33

```perl
#!/usr/bin/perl

$friends = "Tommy\tWashington\nChad\tSanFrancisco\nJeffP";
$friends .= "\tBoulder\nJeffC\tColoradoSprings\n";

@allFriends = ($friends =~ /(\w+\s*\w+)/g);

foreach $friend (@allFriends){
    ($name, $hometown) =
        $friend =~ /(\w+)\s*(\w+)/;
    $friends {$name} = $hometown;
}

print "Friend\tHometown\n".("-" x 20)."\n";
foreach (keys %friends){
    print $_, "\t", $friends{$_}, "\n";
}
```

The first pattern match operation

```perl
@allFriends = ($friends =~ /(\w+\s*\w+)/g);
```

picks out each one of the lines from the string $friends. @allFriends contains these lines as individual elements. Later, we construct a hash or associative array whose keys are the names and whose values are hometowns.

Now, suppose we change the target string $friends so that there can be embedded \n's between a name and a hometown. That is, a hometown still follows a name, but there can be any number of intervening newlines and other space characters anywhere in the string. For example, assume $friends is assigned the value given below.

```perl
$friends = "\nTommy\n\tWashington\t\n\n\nChad\nSanFrancisco\nJeffP\n\t";
$friends .= "\n\nBoulder\nJeffC\tColoradoSprings\n";
```

Does the program given above for extracting name-hometown pairs still work? Actually, it does. The fact that there are intervening newlines between the two elements of a pair does not matter. In situations like this, it is not necessary to use any of the so-called multi-line modifiers such as s or m. This is because we are not trying to change the behavior of the anchors ^ or $, or the dot character.

Once again, as we have mentioned earlier, it is not syntactically or semantically wrong to have a target string for the match operation that is a multi-line string and use none of the modifiers. Therefore, we can write the following.

```perl
@allFriends = ($friends =~ /(\w+\s*\w+)/);
```

in the program given above. But, in such a situation, @allFriends will contain only the first line containing the pair Tommy and Washington.

4.8.3.2.3 Capturing All URLs From A Web Page We now write a program that takes a Web page, i.e., an HTML file and extracts all the URLs from it. In a Web page, a URL is specified inside an *anchor* tag. An anchor tag is written with an <a> in the beginning and with an </a> at the end. The tag or an attribute of the tag such as href can be written either in lower case or upper case. Here is an example of the use of the anchor tag.

```
<a href="http://www.assam.org:80/orgs/asa/index.html">Assam Society </a>
    was established in 1973.
```

Note that the output has been broken into two lines by hand. The URL is specified following the href =. The URL is enclosed inside double quotes. The following program extracts all URLs from an HTML file using the <a> tag.

Program 4.34

```perl
#!/usr/bin/perl
use strict;

my @HTMLText = <ARGV>;
chomp @HTMLText;

my $text = join " ", @HTMLText;
my @lines  = ($text =~ /<A\s+href\s*=\s*"([^"]+)"/ig);
print join ("\n", sort @lines), "\n";
```

An HTML file has free-form syntax. There can be any number of blank spaces or newlines between any two words. For example, in the case of the <a> tag, there can be any amount of space or any number of newlines between <a and href. To avoid complications that arise due to the free form nature, we use the diamond (<>) read operation in an array or list context. When we read from a filehandle in the list context, all lines of the corresponding file are read at once. For example, when we write

```perl
@fileContents = <FILEHANDLE>;
```

@fileContents will contain all lines read from FILEHANDLE, each as an element. We can then manipulate the list containing the lines of the file and extract the URLs.

The program given above can be called with a list of HTML files. Suppose our call is the following.

```
%findURLs.pl index.html index1.html
```

% is the Unix prompt, `index.html` and `index1.html` are two HTML files. The statement

```
my @HTMLText = <ARGV>;
```

in the program reads both files and makes their lines available in the list `@HTMLText`. Next, the line of code

```
chomp @HTMLText;
```

takes away the newline character from the end of each element of `@HTMLText`. Then, we take all these chopped lines and put them together into a big string called `$text`. Depending on how many files are given as command line arguments and the sizes of these files, the string `$text` can become large. So, this may not be the best way to program in a real environment. To make the program better in such situations, we should modify the program to read one file at a time instead of all the files together. There may be other better solutions.

Finally, the line of code

```
my @lines  = ($text =~ /<A\s+href\s*=\s*"([^"]+)"/ig);
```

searches through the string `$text` and picks out all URLs. A URL occurs following `href` and the = sign. Around the equal sign there may be empty spaces. After these empty spaces we have the double quote. Anything following the double quote till the next double quote is the URL string. Here, we use the `i` modifier to indicate that case of letters does not matter in the specification of HTML tags and the attributes of HTML tags. We have the `g` modifier because we want to pluck out all substrings that match the regular expression for a URL. The output of the program looks like the following.

```
aboutus.htm
contact.htm
cultural.html
feedback.htm
http://www.cs.uccs.edu/cgi-bin/kalita/hello.pl
http://www.cs.uccs.edu/~kalita/accesswatch/accesswatch-1.32/index.html
http://www.rahul.net/kgpnet/iit/iit.html
http://www.uccs.edu
http://www.upenn.edu/index.html
http://www.usask.ca
images/ascol.gif
links.htm
mailto:webmaster@assamcompany.com
research.html
schedule.html
search.htm
whosting.htm
```

4.8.4 The `m//m` Modifier

Now, we look at another modifier that can be used when we pattern match over multi-line strings. The `m` in the specification of the modifier stands for *multiple lines*. It instructs the Perl pattern parser to consider a multi-line string to be composed of multiple lines. This sounds like restating the obvious, but the modification of behavior that the `m` modifier imposes on the `=~` operator is not that straight-forward and needs explanation.

To understand the `m` modifier, we should revisit two of the anchors that can be used inside regular expressions. These are `^` and `$`. `^` enforces the match to the beginning of the target string. `$` ensures that the match occurs at the end of the target string if the string has no newline characters in it. If the string has one or more newline characters in it, the match occurs just before the first newline character.

The m modifier modifies where the anchors ^ and $ match in multi-line strings. If we use the m modifier, ^ matches at the beginning of every line in the string. That is, ^ matches at the very beginning of the multi-line string. In addition, ^ matches after every embedded \n signaling the beginning of a new line of text. Of course, if \n happens to be the last character in the multi-line string, ^ does *not* match immediately after it.

Similarly, if we use the m modifier, the $ anchor forces the match to occur just before every embedded newline character. If the multi-line string ends with \n, $ matches just before it. If the multi-line string does not end with \n, $ anchors the match to the end of the string.

Beyond modifying the behavior of the two anchors, the m modifier does not change anything else in the pattern matching operation.

We now give an example program to illustrate the use of the m modifier. Let us use a multi-line string similar to the one that we used in the discussion of the g modifier in the previous section. We give the new assignments to the scalar $friends below.

```
$friends = "Tommy\tWashington\nChad\tSanFrancisco\nJeffP";
$friends .= "\tBoulder\nJeffC\tColoradoSprings\n";
```

Suppose, once again we are interested in picking out each of the friend-hometown pairs from this string. Each friend-hometown pair occurs in a separate line of text in the string. Each line inside the string starts with the name of a friend and each line ends with the name of the friend's hometown. If we extract the first word in each line, we get the names of the friends. If we pluck out the last (out of only two) word in each line, we get the names of the hometowns. We assume that each line has only two words in it.

The following program does what we did using the g modifier earlier, but uses both the m and g modifiers. It also uses the ^ and $ anchors.

Program 4.35

```
#!/usr/bin/perl
$" = "\t";

$friends = "Tommy\tWashington\nChad\tSanFrancisco\nJeffP";
$friends .= "\tBoulder\nJeffC\tColoradoSprings\n";

@allFriends =
    $friends =~ /(^\w+)/gm;
@allHometowns =
    $friends =~ /(\w+$)/gm;

for ($i=0; $i <= $#allFriends; $i++){
    $friends {$allFriends[$i]} = $allHometowns[$i];
}

print "Friend\tHometown\n".("-" x 20)."\n";
foreach (keys %friends){
    print $_, "\t", $friends{$_}, "\n";
}
```

We first extract the names of all our friends from the multi-line string $friends. This is done using the following line of code.

```
@allFriends =
    $friends =~ /(^\w+)/gm;
```

We perform a pattern match operation on the string $friends. We look for each word that occurs at the beginning of a line in the string. This is enforced by the g modifier. However, if we had used the g modifier alone, it would have caused the line of code to pick out only the first word of the multi-line string. This is because we have anchored the pattern match using ^. It would have meant that we are looking for the word located at the beginning of the whole string. If we have used the g modifier alone, the ^ anchor would have behaved as it behaves usually. That is, if we had used just the g modifier, the ^ anchor would have matched only once, at the very beginning of the string $friends. The fact that the string is multi-line would be immaterial if we had used only the g modifier.

To make the program work correctly, we need to make the g modifier make the ^ anchor match many times; at the beginning of every line of text in the multi-line string. We enforce this by using the m modifier in addition to g. The use of the m modifier changes the behavior of =~ operator so that ^ matches right after each \n in the multi-line string. ^ does not match after a \n if it happens to be the last character of a multi-line string. ^ also matches at the beginning of the string.

Similar to the line of code that extracts the names of friends, we have a line of code that extracts the names of hometowns.

```
@allHometowns =
    $friends =~ /(\w+$)/gm;
```

Once again, we use the g and m modifiers. We also use the $ anchor to force the match operation to look at the end of each embedded line. In this case, the last word in each line is a hometown and the list of all hometowns is returned by the =~ operator.

Before we end the discussion of the m modifier, let us look at a few what-if situations. If in our program, we had used the line

```
@allFriends = $friends =~ /(\w+)/m;
```

@allFriends would have picked the first friend's name (i.e., Tommy) only. This is because although m modifies the meaning of the anchors ^ and $, Perl still executes the pattern match operation given above only once, not multiple times or *globally* as enforced by the g modifier. The use of the m modifier in this case is useless because we do not use either of the two anchors ^ or $ in the regular expression.

Suppose in our program, we had used the following two lines.

```
@allFriends = ($friends =~ /(^\w+)/g);
@allHometowns = ($friends =~ /(\w+$)/g);
```

This would have been also wrong because @allFriends still would have the first friend's name only. Also, @allHometowns now would contain the name of the hometown from the last line of text in the multi-line string, namely ColoradoSprings.

4.8.4.1 Two More Anchors for Beginning and End of String

Perl provides us with a pair of additional anchors \A and \Z that are similar to ^ and $. For single-line strings, ^ and \A behave exactly the same way. Similarly, for single-line strings, $ and \Z are exactly the same. However, for multi-line strings, the anchoring properties differ. \A always matches the beginning of the string—single line or multi-line. However, as we have seen already, although usually ^ matches at the beginning of a string, if we use the m modifier, ^ matches at the beginning of every line in a multi-line string. Similarly, \Z always forces matching at the end of a string; whether is is a single line string or multi-line string does not matter. $ usually forces matching at the end of a string. But, if the m match modifier is used, $ forces pattern matching at the end of each embedded line in a multi-line string.

Each of the following picks out only the first friend's name (i.e., Tommy).

```
@allFriends = ($friends =~ /(\A\w+)/);
@allFriends = ($friends =~ /(\A\w+)/g);
@allFriends = ($friends =~ /(\A\w+)/m);
@allFriends = ($friends =~ /(\A\w+)/gm);
```

Using various modifier combinations does not change where \A anchors, namely the beginning of the string. Similarly, each of the following extracts only the hometown of the last friend.

```
@allHometowns = ($friends =~ /(\w+\Z)/);
@allHometowns = ($friends =~ /(\w+\Z)/g);
@allHometowns = ($friends =~ /(\w+\Z)/m);
@allHometowns = ($friends =~ /(\w+\Z)/gm);
```

4.8.5   The m//s Modifier

There is another modifier that is used in pattern matching when the target is a string that contains embedded newline characters. Just as the effect of the m modifier is limited to changing the meaning of the anchors ^ and $, the effect of using the s modifier is also limited. It is limited to what the dot (.) matches inside the string.

Usually, inside a regular expression, the dot matches any character but \n. This can be a drawback when the target string has embedded \n's. For example, we may be looking for typos where one types the same word right next to each other. In such a case, we may want to write a program that removes one of the two instances. Sometimes the two instances are on the same line of text, but sometimes, it can so happen that the first occurrence is at the end of one line and the second occurrence is in the next line with intervening newlines and other space characters.

To address a situation like this, it is sometimes necessary that the dot (.) be forced to match \n in multi-line strings. Of course, one can force . to match \n in single-line strings also, but it is useless. In pattern matching, we can force the dot character to match \n if we use the s modifier. Here is a program that shows the use of this modifier. This program finds the first word in a multi-line string that is repeated later in the string. It also finds out the number of intervening words between the two occurrences.

Program 4.36

```
#!/usr/bin/perl
#file repeatedWords2.pl

$textString = "We have revised the entire paper to reduce the background knowledge that a\n";
$textString .= "reader would require.   We now  describe  the basic aspects of the MP with\n";
$textString .= "minimal background assumed.  There are many linguistic papers, but none\n";
$textString .= "in computational linguistics as far as we know,  that deal with the\n";
$textString .= "MP. Of course, pure linguistic papers such as\n";
$textString .= '\cite{Chomsky95,Merlo95,Zwart94} assume quite ';
$textString .= "extensive GB background, but we have\n";
$textString .= "spent a large amount of time  making  the paper accessible to a reader\n";
$textString .= "who is somewhat familiar with modern linguistics. We also\n";
$textString .= "have included\n";
$textString .= "extensive references with page numbers to assist the  reader\n";
$textString .= "interested in more details.\n";

#print $textString;
```

```
($repeatedWord, $separatingString) = $textString =~ m/\b(\w+?)\b(.*?\b)?\1\b/s;

@separatingWords = split (/\s+/, $separatingString);
print 'Separating Words =' . "@separatingWords\n";

print "Repeated Word = $repeatedWord\n";
print "Number of intervening words = $#separatingWords\n";
```

The output of the program is given below. The first line of output has been broken up into two lines for printing.

```
Separating Words = have revised the entire paper to reduce the background knowledge
                   that a reader would require.
Repeated Word = We
Number of intervening words = 15
```

We see the word We as the first character of $textString. There is no other instance of We in the first line of text. However, the second line of text has another occurrence of We. \1 captures this second occurrence of We. \1 is a way to refer to the value of the special variable $1 inside a regular expression. The distance between the two occurrences in fifteen words. The intervening substring between the two occurrences is captured by (.+?) in the regular expression. By using the s modifier, we force the dot character to match the intervening \n also. The ? after the multiplier + asks Perl to perform minimal modifier. Without ?, Perl will print the following output.

```
Repeated Word = We
Number of intervening words = 84
```

This is the distance between the first occurrence of We and the last occurrence of We in the string. This is because without ? after the multiplier +, Perl performs maximal match and consumes as much as possible for the multiplier. With the ?, it consumes as little as possible for the multiplier.

4.9   Reading Multiple Lines From A File In One Read Operation

In previous sections, we have discussed multi-line strings that contain embedded newline characters. We conveniently built such strings using assignment and string concatenation. We have not seen yet how multiple lines can be read from a file in one read operation.

Perl provides a special variable called $/ that can be used to read multiple lines or paragraphs from a file. $/ is the so-called *input record separator*. The default value of the input record separator is \n. That is why when Perl reads from a file using a filehandle, it usually reads one line at a time. The newline character separates what Perl reads in one read operation from what it reads in the next.

By changing the value of the input record separator, Perl can be made to read several lines at a time. The value of $/ can be set to a single character or a string with multiple characters.

4.9.1   Reading A Paragraph At A Time

Before we get into assigning values to $/, let us look at a special case. If $/ is assigned the empty string as the value, Perl considers itself to be in a paragraph read mode. That is, in a single read operation, instead of reading one single line from a filehandle, Perl reads a full paragraph. This happens with STDIN also. Perl assumes that one or more blank lines delimit a paragraph. In other words, a sequence of at least two \n's can be considered the input record separator in the paragraph read mode. Therefore, the assignment

```
$/ ="";
```

is somewhat equivalent to the assignment

```
$/ = "\n\n";
```

but it is not quite so because one can have more than two newline characters between a paragraph and the next. One can also have other kinds of white space such as \t or the blank space interspersed with the \n character.

Below, we write a program that reads a file paragraph by paragraph. It assumes it is a simple text file. It reports the length of the longest paragraph, in terms of number of words. We do not check if the "words" contain non-alphabetic characters as we have done in some of our earlier programs.

Program 4.37

```
#!/usr/bin/perl

$/ = "";
$file = $ARGV[0];
open (IN, $file);
$maxWordCount = 0;

while ($paragraph = <IN>){
    @paraWords = split /\W*\s+\W*/, $paragraph;
    if ($#paraWords > $maxWordCount){
        $maxWordCount = $#paraWords+1;;
    }
}

print "The maximum number of words in a paragraph = $maxWordCount\n";
```

We know that for an array, the last index in the array can be found by replacing the @ in front by $#. Since Perl counts index from zero and not one, we add one to the last index to obtain the number of elements in the array.

The output of the program when called with a file looks like the following.

```
The maximum number of words in a paragraph = 316
```

4.9.2   Reading A Whole File In One Read Operation

If $/ does not have a defined value, there is no input record separator and the whole file is read in one shot even in scalar context. In the following program, we find the file with the maximum and minimum number of words from among the list of files given as command line argument.

Program 4.38

```
#!/usr/bin/perl

undef $/;
$maxWordCount = 0;
$maxFileName = "";
$minWordCount = 10000000;
```

```
$minFileName = "";

for ($i = 0; $i <= $#ARGV; $i++){
    open (IN, $ARGV[$i]);
    $file = <IN>;
    @fileWords = split /\W*\s+\W*/, $file;
    if ($#fileWords  > $maxWordCount){
        $maxWordCount = $#fileWords;
        $maxFileName = $ARGV[$i];
    }
    if ($#fileWords < $minWordCount){
        $minWordCount = $#fileWords;
        $minFileName = $ARGV[$i];
    }
}

print "The maximum number of words in a file = $maxWordCount\n";
print "The file with maximum number of words = $maxFileName\n";
print "The minimum number of words in a file = $minWordCount\n";
print "The file with minimum number of words = $minFileName\n";
```

In the program we undefine the value of $/ by using the built-in function undef. We initialize the maximum word count to 0 and the minimum word count to a large number assuming no file has more words than this number. We also initialize the identity of the files with maximum and minimum number of words to the empty string.

Next, we loop through every file given as command line argument. We open each file for reading, and read the whole file at once. We split the file into its individual words. We compare with the maximum and minimum word counts so far and reset them if necessary. If we reassign a value to the maximum or the minimum count, we remember the name of the file. Finally, outside the loop, we print which file has the maximum number of words and which file has the minimum number of words. We also print the maximum number of words and the minimum number of words.

A call to this program looks like the following.

```
%fileWords.pl paper*
```

The output of the program looks like the following.

```
The maximum number of words in a file = 17587
The file with maximum number of words = paper1.tex
The minimum number of words in a file = 2345
The file with minimum number of words = paper2.txt
```

We note that the number of words we see printed above is different from the number of words returned by the Unix command wc because the word splitting pattern we use is different from what Unix uses.

4.9.3   Reading A "Record" At A Time

Let us now assign a value to $/ other than the empty string or the undefined value. To illustrate such use of $/, we go back to the bibliographic example we have discussed off and on in this chapter. Assume we have a special bibliographic file or database to hold all our bibliographic entries. In the case of TeX/LaTeX bibliographic entries, we follow a pre-specified syntax that we have adopted for ourselves to indicate individual entries. Two example entries in the database file are given below. The bibliographic file is stored in ASCII format.

```
@InBook{Abney92,
    author =        "Steven P. Abney",
    title =         "Principle-Based Parsing: Computation and Psycholinguistics",
    chapter =       "Parsing by Chunks",
    publisher =     "Kluwer Academic Publishers",
    year =          "1992",
    editor =        "Robert C. Berwick and Steven P. Abney and Carol Tenny",
    pages =         "257-278",
    address =       "Dordrecht, Netherlands"
}

@Book{Aoun93,
    author =   "J. Aoun and A. Li",
    title =    "The Syntax of Scope",
    publisher =   "MIT Press",
    year =    "1993",
    address =   "Cambridge, MA"
}
```

The bibliographic entry indicates the nature of the entry. In this case, the second is a book and the first is a chapter of a book. There are several other possibilities such as a paper in conference proceedings, a Ph.D. thesis and an unpublished manuscript, We assume there are no double quotes inside the value of an attribute such as `title` or `author`. We also assume that the attributes can occur in any order.

Our goal in this program is to go through a bibliographic database like this and for each entry, print the name of the author, the publisher, the year of publication and the address of the publisher. The program is given below.

Program 4.39

```perl
#!/usr/bin/perl

$/ = "}";
$file = $ARGV[0];
open (IN, $file);

while ($record = <IN>) {
    if ($record =~ /@\w+{\w+,(.+)/s) {
        $attrValPair = $1;
        ($author) = ($attrValPair =~ /author\s*=\s*"([^"]+)/);
        ($title) = ($attrValPair =~ /title\s*=\s*"([^"]+)/);
        ($publisher) = ($attrValPair =~ /publisher\s*=\s*"([^"]+)/);
        ($year) = ($attrValPair =~ /year\s*=\s*"([^"]+)/);
        ($address) = ($attrValPair =~ /address\s*=\s*"([^"]+)/);
         print "$author, $title, $publisher, $year, $address.\n"
    }
}
close IN;
```

The program sets the value of the input record separator to }. This is done with the assumption that the closing brace does not occur anywhere inside an entry. As a result, every time we read from the file, we read a whole record. After Perl has read a record, we extract the attribute-value pairs as one string. From this string, we extract the values of the various attributes that we want and then print them. The output of this program looks like the following. For each record, the program prints one line although in the output printed below the lines may be broken up into two or more.

```
Steven P. Abney, Principle-Based Parsing: Computation and Psycholinguistics, Kluwer
      Academic Publishers, 1992, Dordrecht, Netherlands.
J. Aoun and A. Li, The Syntax of Scope, MIT Press, 1993, Cambridge, MA.
Adriana Balletti, Generalized Verb Movement, Rosenburg and Sellier, 1990, Turin, Italy.
Joseph Bayer, Directionality and Logical Form, Kluwer Academic Publishers, 1996, Dordrecht,
      Netherlands.
Joseph Bayer, Final Complementizers in Hybrid Languages, , November, 1995, Katholieke
      Universiteit Brabant, Tilber.
Chris Collins, Local Economy, MIT Press, 1997, Cambridge, Massachusetts.
Nelson Correa, Principle-Based Parsing: Computation and Psycholinguistics, Kluwer Academic
      Publishers, 1992, Dordrecht, Netherlands.
Peter W. Culicover, Principles and Parameters: An Introduction to
                    Syntactic Theory, Oxford University Press, 1997, Oxford, England.
M. Diesing, Indefinites, MIT Press, 1992, Cambridge, MA.
Samuel Epstein, Principle-Based Parsing: Computation and Psycholinguistics, Kluwer Academic
      Publishers, 1992, Dordrecht, Netherlands.
M. V. Liliane Haegeman, Introduction to Government and Binding Theory, Oxford University
      Press,  1994, Cambridge, MA.
Norbert Hornstein, Logical Form, From GB to Minimalism, Blackwell Publishers, 1995,
      Cambridge, MA.
Mark Johnson, Principle-Based Parsing: Computation and Psycholinguistics, Kluwer Academic
      Publishers, 1992, Dordrecht, Netherlands.
```

Some lines have been broken into two for printing.

4.10   Substituting A Pattern: The s/// Operator

Quite frequently, we need to make substitutions in a piece of text. We may perform substitutions on one string, a whole file, all files in a directory, or all files spread out over many directories. A substitution can possibly correct a spelling error, reflect changes in names of individuals or organizations, or perform pre-processing to facilitate more complex tex processing, among others. When a person gets married, a person's name may change. When a company is bought or merged with another company, its name may change. When a person gets promoted, his or her designation may change. If such changes need to be reflected over one page, or many pages, it is not advisable to do so manually. A program can do such tasks better than a human, without making any mistakes or without missing any occurrence.

The substitution operation is performed using s. s takes two arguments—a pattern and a substitution string as shown below.

> s/*pattern*/*substitutionString*/

It looks for the presence of *pattern* in a string and replaces *pattern* by the *substitutionString*.

The following program takes a string and replaces the words Assam Company by Assam Company of America, Inc.. This is because is because the company is formally incorporated, and the change reflects the same.

Program 4.40

```
#!/usr/bin/perl
#assam1.pl

use strict;
my $string = "Assam Company was established in 1997.\n";
$string =~ s/Assam\s+Company/Assam Company of America, Inc.,/;
print $string;
```

The output of the program is given below.

```
Assam Company of America, Inc., was established in 1997.
```

Now, suppose we want to make this change in a file. We want to change every occurrence of the words Assam Company by Assam Company of America, Inc.. In the original file, the name Assam Company is used in several places. The modified or substituted text file is given below. It is called *index.html*.

```
<!DOCTYPE HTML PUBLIC "-//W3C//DTD HTML 4.01 Transitional//EN">
<html>
  <head>
    <title>Assam Company of America, Inc.,</title>
  </head>

  <body>
    <h1>Assam Company of America, Inc.,</h1>
    Assam Company of America, Inc., was established in 1997. It has been operational
    without a name for more than a year at that time. Assam Company of America, Inc.,
    specializes in intelligent information processing and
    Internet security.
    <hr>
    <address><a href="mailto:kalita@pikespeak.uccs.edu">J Kalita</a></address>
<!-- Created: Sat Jul 21 10:11:47 MDT 2001 -->
<!-- hhmts start -->
Last modified: Sat Jul 21 10:17:07 MDT 2001
<!-- hhmts end -->
  </body>
</html>
```

The program that performs the replacement everywhere is given below.

Program 4.41

```
#!/usr/bin/perl
#assam2.pl

use strict;
undef $/;
my $file = $ARGV[0];
open (IN, "$file");
open OUT, ">$file.new";
my $fileContents = <IN>;
$fileContents =~ s/Assam\s+Company/Assam Company of America, Inc.,/g;
```

```
print  OUT $fileContents;
unlink $file;
rename $file.".new", $file;
chmod 0644, $file;
```

The program reads the whole file in one read operation because we are looking for the string Assam Company that contains two words that may appear broken in the middle in two sentences. Here, we have used the global modifier g with the s operation. Before doing that, we read the whole file into one string called $fileContents. This is read in one read operation because we set $/ to undef. This has been discussed earlier in the chapter.

Once the file has been read to a string, we perform substitution globally. We write out the changed contents to a file that has the same name as the original, but with a suffix .new. So, if the program assam2.pl is called with the command-line argument index.html, a file index.html.new is created. We then delete the old file index.html, and rename the file index.html.new to index.html. Since HTML files must be readable by everyone to be viewable on the Web, we make it so using the chmod command. Changing accessibility mode is necessary only on a Unix machine.

Note that the need to write a new file, delete the old file, and rename the new file, etc., can be obviated by editing the file *in-place*. Perl allows editing in-place if we give a value to the special variable $^I. Perl automatically does the necessary work to keep an old version of the file by appending the value of $^I to the file being changed. The updated file or new file is stored in the original file name. Using $^I works only if we use the diamond operator <> when used with nothing inside or the special filehandle ARGV. Of course, when there is no filehandle inside, it means ARGV. So, even if there is one file, we need to use <> or <ARGV>. The ARGV filehandle iterates through every file in the special variable @ARGV. Therefore, we can assign @ARGV to get in-place editing effect if we want. The program is given below.

Program 4.42

```
#!/usr/bin/perl
#assam3.pl

use strict;
$^I = ".old";
undef $/;
while (<>) {
        $_ =~ s/Assam\s+Company/Assam Company of America, Inc.,/g;
        print $_;
}
```

We must use the <> or <ARGV> filehandle, and read lines into the default variable $_ for in-place editing to work. If we make the following call

```
%assam3.pl index.html
```

the old file is stored as index.html.old and the new, modified file is stored as index.html. If the value of $^I is set to the empty string or is undefed, no copy of the old file is kept. However, this is not advised because if something is wrong during input-output, the original file as well as the new file may be lost.

The program given immediately above does the substitution in all files whose names are given as command-line argument. Suppose that while typing the files, we had mixed cases because we were not careful typing. That is, in some places, we wrote ASSAM COMPANY or Assam COMPANY or ASSAm COmpany, etc. We want these cases also to be substituted. We can simply do so by using the i option with the s operation in addition to the g option. The modified program is given below.

Program 4.43

```
#!/usr/bin/perl
#assam4.pl

use strict;
$^I = ".old";
undef $/;
while (<>){
        $_ =~ s/Assam\s+Company/Assam Company of America, Inc.,/gi;
        print $_;
}
```

Although the use of $^I makes a program tight and small, it is tricky to use correctly. The restrictions are the following.

1. One has to use it with <> or <ARGV>.
2. One has to use the $_ variable that is set by <>. Using another variable does not work. It will destroy the original file. For example, ($myVar = <>) does not work.
3. It has to be used with a while loop.
4. One has to print $_ without a filehandle.

If all of these are not followed exactly, it is almost guaranteed that the original file's contents will be lost. If there are are many files to be read and processed, all of them will be reduced to empty files. This could be disastrous. If there are several filehandles, or a while loop cannot be used, or using $_ is not convenient or transparent, etc., performing in-place editing may be difficult. In fact, it is quite common that a lot of programmers lose contents of files in this manner. This has caused grief to a lot of programmers who have lost whole directories in this manner. Thus, the use of $^I is not recommended by the author of this book. The use of $^I makes a program short and endows it with some elegance, but the potential dangers associated cause its usage to be perilous. If one insists on using it, one should copy all relevant files to a temporary directory, write the program and experiment with it several times to make sure no data is lost, before using it on the actual data. In other words, one should back up the files before making sure everything works.

A program that performs substitution can be used to make an HTML file look consistent. For example, we may want all our HTML tags to be written in uppercase so that they stand out. It is possible that they are not so to begin with because various individuals produced the pages using raw HTML or by using various tools. The following program makes an initial attempt at doing so. We do not use the $^I variable here.

Program 4.44

```
#!/usr/bin/perl
#file htmlTags2.pl
use strict ;
my $backExt = ".old";

my (@HTMLTags, $HTMLTag, $uppedHTMLTag, $textLine, $file, $outFile);
```

```
@HTMLTags  = qw (html head title br h1 h2 h3 p a img table);
print "\@ARGV = @ARGV\n";

foreach $file (@ARGV){
  open IN, $file;
  $outFile = $file . $backExt;
  open OUT, ">$outFile" or die "Cannot open $outFile: $!";
  while ($textLine = <IN>){
      foreach $HTMLTag (@HTMLTags){
            $textLine =~ s/<($HTMLTag)>/"<" . uc($1) . ">"/gie;
            $textLine =~ s/<($HTMLTag)\s+/"<" . uc($1)  . " "/gei;
            $textLine =~ s#</($HTMLTag)># "</"  . uc($1) . ">"#gei;
      }
    print OUT $textLine;
    }
  close OUT;
  unlink $file;
  rename $outFile, $file;
  chmod 0644, $file
}
```

Here we list some HTML tags we are interested in. We use the function uc to get the upper-cased version of the tag. The call to the uc function can be made in the call to the s operator itself. We use the s///e modifier to evaluate the substitution string. That is, instead of using the substitution string literally, we can consider it as an expression to be evaluated.

Consider one of the uses of the substitution operator.

```
$textLine =~ s/<($HTMLTag)>/"<" . uc($1) . ">"/gie;
```

Here, the pattern is given between the first two delimiters: /. The substitution string is given between the second and the third delimiters. It is possible to use other delimiters, just like with the pattern match operator: =~. Just like in regular expression matching, when we have a parenthesized sub-expression, the part of the string that matches, is stored temporarily in the special variable $1. This variable can be used in the substitution expression. Here, the substitution expression is

```
"<" . uc($1) . ">"
```

This expression performs string concatenation twice. The built-in function uc takes $1 as an argument. e is given as a modifier or option to the s operator causing Perl to evaluate the expression to obtain the actual substitution string. The s operation causes the HTML tag to be upper-cased. Sometimes HTML tags are followed immediately by >, and at other times are not, particularly when a tag accepts attribute values. The third use of the s operator in this program substitutes the closing HTML tags. Because the e modifier causes the substitution string to be evaluated, it is possible for the the programmer to write a subroutine that is invoked if necessary, performing complex processing.

The s operator accepts s and m modifiers as well with the meanings discussed in the context of the match operator =~. s changes the meaning of the . character in a pattern match, allowing it to match \n as well as any other character. The m changes the meaning of the ^ and $ anchors allowing them to match at the beginning and end, respectively, of every line in a multi-line string. The reader is referred to Section 4.8 for detailed discussions on these two modifiers.

The following program contains a sequence of unrelated uses of the s operator below. The uses of the s operator, in each case, is explained in terms of comments.

Program 4.45

```perl
#!/usr/bin/perl
#simplePatterns1.pl

#-------------------
$string = "Mr. Clinton goes to Washington.\nMr. Gore goes\nwith him.\n";

# /g automatically works with multi-line strings
$string =~ s/Mr\./Mister/g;
#Mister Clinton goes to Washington.
#Mister Gore goes
#with him.
print "$string";

$count = ($string =~ s/Mister/Mr\./g);
#Changed 2 times
print "Changed $count times\n";

$string  =~ s/(.)/\1\1/g;
#MMrr..  CClliinnttoonn  ggooeess  ttoo  WWaasshhiinnggttoonn..
#MMrr..  GGoorree  ggooeess
#wwiitthh  hhiimm..
#Note: \n is not duplicated
print "$string";

$string = "Mr. Clinton goes to Washington.\nMr. Gore goes\nwith him.\n";
$string  =~ s/(.)/\1\1/gs;
#MMrr..  CClliinnttoonn  ggooeess  ttoo  WWaasshhiinnggttoonn..
#
#MMrr..  GGoorree  ggooeess
#
#wwiitthh  hhiimm..
#
#Note: \n is also duplicated because we have used /s modifier
print "$string";

$string = "Mr. Clinton goes to Washington.\nMr. Gore goes\nwith him.\n";
$string  =~ s/(.)/\1\1/gm;
#Because we don't use /s modifier, . doesn't match \n
#MMrr..  CClliinnttoonn  ggooeess  ttoo  WWaasshhiinnggttoonn..
#MMrr..  GGoorree  ggooeess
#wwiitthh  hhiimm..
print "$string";

$_ = "I will pay \$10000 for the car.\n";
s/(\d+)/$1 * 2/e;
#I will pay $20000 for the car.
print;
#I will pay $40000 for the carcar.
s/(\w+)/if ($1 eq "car") {$1 x 2} else {$1}/ge;
print;

$_ = "I will pay ten thousand dollars for the car\n";
s/\w+/sprintf ("%-9s", $&)/ge;
#I         will       pay         ten        thousand   dollars    for         the        car
```

```
sub repeat{
    my ($string) = @_;
    return ($string x 2);
}

$_ = "I love Dawson Creek\n";
s/\w+/&repeat ($&)/eg;
#II lovelove DawsonDawson CreekCreek
print;

#------------
s/(\w+)\1/$1 $1/g;
#I I love love Dawson Dawson Creek Creek
print;

#-------
#trim white space
$_ = "It   is   very  nice and    sunny   day.\n";

s/(\w+)\s+/$1 /g;
#It is very nice and sunny day.
print;
```

The g modifier automatically works with multi-line strings. The substitution operation returns the number of substitutions performed in a scalar context. When parts of the pattern are parenthesized, the substrings in the target string that match are remembered. We can use special variables that are numeric, such as $1, $2, etc., to refer to them. We can also use \1, \2, etc., to refer to the values of $1, $2, etc. . For the period (.) to match \n, we need to use the s modifier. The program shows several uses of the e modifier. In pattern matching as well as substitution, the part of the target string that matches successfully with a pattern is stored in another special variable called $&. We use this variable in some of the examples given in the program.

4.11 Finding Citations: Another try

We now write a program that makes the discussions regarding finding citations in a TeX/LaTeX file more complete. Unlike files that are created for word processors such as Microsoft Word or Adobe FrameMaker, the files created for processing by the word processor called TeX and a more user-friendly version of it called LaTeX, are text files. Therefore, it is easy for a user to manipulate such files on his or her own. In this program, we will focus on the initial processing of citations only.

We assume that the format of the bibliographic database is similar to what we have discussed in a previous section. To simplify our program, let us assume that we have only books in the bibliographic text database.

The bibliographic database may have a large number of entries. Many of these entries may not be referenced in the text of our article or paper. When we refer to a book or a paper in an article, we do so by using the \cite command. In the simplest use of \cite, we specify the index of only one book or paper. For example, to cite Allen's book, we write in the text of the article, \cite{Allen95} since Allen95 is the citation index of the book. There can be one or more spaces surrounding the left and the right braces.

There are some complications that can arise when we specify citations in an article. Some of the complications are given below.

- We make an assumption that each reference index has an uppercase letter, followed by zero or more lower/uppercase letters followed by either two or four digits. If there are two digits, the year of publication is assumed to be the twentieth century. If there are four digits, the first two digits must be 19 or 20. According to this self-imposed syntax, `Allen95`, `Allen1995` or `Allen2005` are all acceptable. We check for this syntax in our program. This is not a syntax imposed by TeX or LaTeX. It is a syntax we have decided to impose on ourselves to enforce a uniformity over the creation of index terms.

- It is possible that we can have more than one use of \cite in one line of text.

- In one single use of \cite, we may have more than one citation referenced, for example, we can have a line in the paper which looks like the following:

```
Natural language parsing techniques are discussed in \cite{Allen95,Fong92}.
```

  In such cases, the entries need to be separated by a comma. In addition, there cannot be any space between the entries although spaces are allowed surrounding the braces.

- When we specify a citation, it is possible to have an optional field included inside square brackets as in \cite[p. 200]{Kalita91}. In such a case, there can be blank spaces between \cite and the optional entry. Also, there can be spaces between the right square bracket and the left curly brace. There can be spaces inside the optional entry although no space is allowed inside the actual citation index.

- It is quite possible that the use of \cite is followed by a punctuation mark such as a period, a comma, a question mark, etc.

- There may be a single lowercase letter after the year as in \cite{Kalita91a} if there are several citations attributed to the same author in the same year.

TeX/LaTeX processes the citations, removes duplicates, sorts the citations in some user-specified order and then prints them out at the end of the article following some user-specified format. Depending on the publication or the publisher, there are many standard formats for writing bibliographies and references.

In the program given below, we want to perform some of the tasks that TeX or LaTeX performs on its own.

Program 4.46

```perl
#!/usr/bin/perl
use strict;
my (@refs, $refString, @tempRefs, $tempRefString, $tempRef);

while (<>){
    my @words = split (/\s+/, $_);
    my @citations = grep (/\\cite *{ *[^}]+ *}/, @words);
    map {if (/[,.?!]$/) {chop}} @citations;

    foreach $refString (@citations){
        ($tempRefString) = $refString =~ /\\cite *{ *([^}]+) *}/;
        if ($tempRefString =~ /,/){
            @tempRefs = split /,/, $tempRefString;
            push @refs, @tempRefs;
        }
        else{
            push @refs, $tempRefString;
        }
    }
}
```

```
}

@refs = grep /^[A-Z][a-zA-Z]*(19|20)?\d{2}[a-z]?$/, @refs;
@refs = removeDuplicates (@refs);
@refs = sort (@refs);
print (join ("\n", @refs), "\n\n");

sub removeDuplicates{
    my @list = @_;
    my (%tempList, $element);

    foreach $element (@list){
        $tempList {$element}++;
    }
    @list = ();
    foreach $element (keys %tempList){
        push @list, $element;
    }
    return  @list;
}
```

The program is actually quite simple. We repeatedly use split and grep. split takes a pattern and a string as its two arguments and returns an array or list where the original string has been broken up into several parts using the pattern as the separator. grep takes a pattern and a list as its two arguments. It returns a list containing those elements of the list that satisfy the pattern.

If we call the file that contains the program findTeXcites.pl, a call to the program will be something like

```
%findTeXcites.pl paper.tex
```

where paper.tex is the TeX-formatted file containing the paper.

The program reads the lines of the file one by one and processes it. Below we see some lines from the file.

```
\cite{Winograd72}, Herskovits \cite{Herskovits86}, and many others
deficiencies and drawbacks of CDGs \cite{Wilks75,Levin87,Palmer85}. Unlike
unification-based grammar formalisms \cite[p. 185]{Carpenter92},
```

The first line of the program inside the while loop takes a line of text from the file and breaks in apart using one or more space characters as the separator. The separated substrings are returned in the list or array @words. So, after the first line is processed, the array @words contains the following elements.

```
\cite{Winograd72},   Herskovits   \cite{Herskovits86},  and many others
```

There are six substrings and two of the substrings contain the comma inside them. Next, the program looks at this list of strings and picks out or greps those elements that contain the pattern

```
/\\cite *{ *[^}]+ *}/
```

Here, the / is used as the pattern delimiter. In this pattern, we are looking for the string \cite first. The first backslash needs to be escaped. After \cite, there can be zero or more blank spaces followed by the left brace {. After the opening brace, there can be zero or more blank spaces. After the blank spaces, if any,

---

we are looking for one or more characters that are not the closing brace }. Before the closing brace, we can have one or more blank spaces also.

Once this `grep` command works on @words, the resulting @citations list contains all the citations in the line. In this specific case, the @citations list contains the following strings.

```
\cite{Winograd72},   \cite{Herskovits86},
```

For the second and third lines given above, at this point the @citations list will contain the following substrings at this point in time.

```
\cite{Wilks75,Levin87,Palmer85}.
\cite[p. 185]{Carpenter92},
```

So, for the second and third lines, @words or @citations contains only one element in each case.

Next, the program has a `foreach` loop that goes over every element of the current value of @citations. For the first line, this list contains two elements and for the other two lines, it contains one element each. Inside the loop, the program has the following line.

```
($tempRefString) = $refString =~ /\\cite *{ *([^}]+) *}/;
```

The program is looking for the pattern

```
/\\cite *{ *([^}]+) *}/;
```

The pattern matching operation is being done on the the variable $refString that contains the element of the array @citations that is being looked at. If the pattern match succeeds, the program remembers the citation index or indices inside the braces. It removes spaces from the front and the end of the index or indices. So, for the first citation of the first line, it picks out and remembers Winograd72 for the second citation of the first line it remembers Herskovits86. For the second line, there is only one citation and the remembered string is the following.

```
Wilks75,Levin87,Palmer85
```

For the third line, the remembered string is

```
Carpenter92
```

If the remembered string has several indices as in the case of the second line, the program breaks up the string using the comma as the separator. The program stores each individual citation index from such a separated list in the list @refs. If the remembered substring has no comma inside it, it has only one index and this index is also `pushed` into the @refs array.

So, once the `foreach` loop has been executed for all lines of the paper, we have all the citation indices stored in the @refs array. Next, the program checks to make sure that each index satisfies the syntax that we have required it to have. Once again, note that this syntax is self-imposed and is not required by TeX/LaTeX. The line that does this parsing uses the `grep` command.

```
@refs = grep /^[A-Z][a-z]*(19|20)?\d{2}[a-z]?$/, @refs;
```

It keeps those substring entries from @refs that contain the pattern specified above. This pattern requires that the index starts with an uppercase letter and is then followed by zero or more lower case letters, followed by two digits. Finally, there is optionally a single lower-case letter. Then the index must end. We use the anchors ^ and $ to make sure that the index contains nothing else in it.

After picking out the citation indices that conform to our syntax, we remove duplicates and sort them and then print them out. In a real program, we should at this point consult the bibliographic database file and then print details corresponding to each entry that has been cited in the paper.

To remove duplicates, we use the subroutine `removeDuplicates`. This subroutine looks at every element of the list, makes the element a key of an associative array and stores a count for the element in the associative array. Once all elements of the list are processed, the associative array contains every citation index as a key and the number of times the citation index is used in the paper as the value. The program simply goes through every key of this associative array and puts it in a list. The subroutine then returns the list. Since an associative array can return the elements in any order, the list that is returned needs to be sorted in the main program.

Output of the program is a set of indices that are sorted.

```
Beckwith1991
Borigault1992
Chen1994
Church1988
CoreLex98
Deerwester1990
Harman1995
Jesse1997
Kalita1986
Kalita1989
Laham1997
Lancaster1969
Lehnert1986
Levi1978
Mahesh1995
Mahesh1997
Paice1993
Rus1997
Salton1990
Salton1994
Swanson1989
Voutilainen1993
```

This program can be expanded a little to obtain the details from the bibliographic text file for the cited references. In an earlier section, we saw how we can obtain such details from the bibliographic file. However, that program needs to be modified so that bibliographic details are printed only for the cited entries and not for all records in the bibliographic text database.

4.12   `eval`, Pattern Matching and Rule-Based Programming

Perl provides us a function called `eval` that can be used to evaluate or execute a Perl expression. This is a powerful function that is similar to a similarly named function in the functional programming language called Lisp. Lisp is the language of choice for many programmers in the field of Artificial Intelligence.

`eval` takes one argument that is either a Perl expression or a Perl block enclosed inside braces. `eval` executes its argument as if it were a short Perl program. This in-line program is executed in the context of the current Perl program. Therefore, any variables that were assigned before executing the argument to `eval`, are available inside the code argument to `eval`. The argument given to `eval` is treated like a Perl block. So, variables declared inside this code using `my` or `local` are available only inside the block.

`eval` returns the value of the last expression inside the code given to it as argument. One can use the `return` operator to return a value from the code given to `eval`. If there is a syntax error or a run-time error in the code given to `eval`, Perl returns the undefined value `undef`. In such a case, an error message is put in the special variable $@. If there is no error and the code given to eval executes correctly, $@ is set to the null string. Because of this reason, eval is regularly used as a means for evaluating an expression with the intent that if an error arises, the error is captured and handled in some manner. This is called exceptions handling, although we do not discuss it any further.

4.12.1 Evaluating Terminal Input

Let us write a program that works like a simple calculator. We type in an arithmetic expression and it returns the result after evaluating the expression. In fact, this program can do more. If we type in any Perl expression in a single line, it executes the expression and prints the result.

The program is surprisingly simple and is given below.

Program 4.47

```perl
#!/usr/bin/perl

while (<STDIN>){
        print eval $_, "\n";
    }
```

The program reads a line from the terminal and evaluates it and prints the result. A simple interaction with this program is given below.

```
1+2*3;
7
2 * log (10)
4.60517018598809
$a = 0;
0
$a=10; $a = $a + 100;
110
for (1..10){print $_ x 3, " "}
111 222 333 444 555 666 777 888 999 101010
```

The user types in an expression and the program prints out a result. The first line of a pair in the transcript is user input and the second line is the computer's output. This continues till the user finishes the interaction by typing in control-D (in a Unix environment).

4.12.2 An ELIZA-like Conversation Program

ELIZA is a conversational program written in the 1960s. It is a program that dazzled the scientific community of the 1960s by showing that it is possible to write computer programs that can converse in a natural human language such as English. However, we soon see that the techniques used were very simple and the claims computer scientist made on the basis of ELIZA's performance were hyperbolic to a great extent.

ELIZA is a program that behaves like a psychiatrist. The program chats with a psychiatric "patient." The "patient" types in a sentence in natural language and the program responds to it appropriately. Here is an actual sample of conversation with the original ELIZA program written at MIT by Weizenbaum [Bod87].

```
input>  Men are all alike
        IN WHAT WAY
```

```
input>  They're are always bugging us about something or other
        CAN YOU THINK OF A SPECIFIC EXAMPLE
input>  Well my boyfriend made me come here
        YOUR BOYFRIEND MADE YOU COME HERE
input>  He says I am depressed most of the time.
        I AM SORRY TO HEAR YOU ARE DEPRESSED
input>  It's true. I'm unhappy.
        DOES THAT HAVE ANYTHING TO DO WITH THE FACT THAT
        YOUR BOYFRIEND MADE YOU COME HERE
input>  I need some help that much seems certain.
        WHAT WOULD IT MEAN TO YOU IF YOU
        GOT SOME HELP THAT MUCH SEEMS CERTAIN.
input>  Perhaps I could learn to get along with my mother.
        WHY DO YOU SAY YOUR MOTHER.
```

Our goal now is to write a program that illustrates how ELIZA was written. Our version of ELIZA is not as sophisticated as the original ELIZA in conversational ability. ELIZA is written based on the concept of *rules*. A rule is simply a data structure or list that has two parts to it—the left hand side (LHS) and the right hand side (RHS). The LHS and RHS can be anything including strings. A rule-based program has a set of rules called a *rule base*. The program examines the rule base starting from the top. It compares the LHS of a rule to the current state or context of the program and takes an action if the comparison gives a positive response. This state can be complex, but is usually as simple as a string of words. Let us assume it is a string of words for the purpose of our discussion.

The rule-based program compares or pattern matches the context string with the LHSs of the rules in the rule base one by one. The first rule whose LHS matches in some way with the context string is *fired* by the program. This simply means that the program takes an action based on the content of the RHS of the fired or triggered rule. This action can be as simple as doing variable interpolation in the RHS string and then printing it.

In fact, the original ELIZA program and the ELIZA program we present here work in this manner. We have a set of rules or a rule base for ELIZA. For the illustration program, the rule base has only three rules. The program can be made more sophisticated by adding more rules and by adding simple morphological processing to it. Let us call the file that contains the rule `ElizaRules.dat`. The file's contents are show below.

```
/I\b(.+)\byou\./ && $1     => /If you  $1 me, I $1 you too\./
/I\b(.+)\byou\b(.+)\./ && $1 && $2 => /We $1 you $2 too\./
/I\s+love\s+your\b(.+)\./ && $1 => /Your $1 is beautiful too. You are simply wonderful!/
```

Each line of this file is a rule. We impose a syntax on each rule. The rule's LHS and RHS are separated by `=>`. Each LHS has a pattern expression followed by one or more numbered scalar variables separated by two ampersands (`&&`). Let us take the first rule. The LHS is

```
/I\b(.+)\byou\./ && $1
```

and the RHS is

```
/If you  $1 me, I $1 you too\./
```

The first part of the LHS

```
/I\b(.+)\byou\./
```

matches with an input sentence typed on the terminal such as

```
I love you.
```

or

```
I do love you.
```

\b stands for the word-boundary anchor. The group inside the parentheses can match any number of words. The part of the input sentence that matches the group is remembered as the value of the variable $1. The second part of the LHS is $1 separated from the regular expression by &&. && is used in Perl as the *and*ing operator in addition to and. This LHS is used to test to see if the pattern

```
/I\b(.+)\byou\./
```

matches with the input sentence such that $1 is assigned a non-null value.
Let us suppose the input sentence is

```
I do love you.
```

So, there is a match between the input sentence and the pattern and the value of $1 is do love. Now, let us look at the RHS of this rule.

```
/If you  $1 me, I $1 you too\./
```

If the value of $1 is substituted into the RHS expression, we get

```
If you do love me, I do love you too.
```

ELIZA produces this sentence as the output for the input sentence

```
I do love you.
```

That is, when ELIZA's patient says

```
I do love you.
```

ELIZA, the psychiatrist program responds by printing

```
If you do love me, I do love you too.
```

Similarly, each of the other two rules in our rule base is designed to produce an output corresponding to a certain sentence type. The ELIZA program compares the input sentence with each rule one by one. The first rule that matches with the assignment of values to the appropriate number of special number variables is used to produce ELIZA's output.

Now that we have discussed how ELIZA behaves, we look at the actual code.

Program 4.48

```
#!/usr/bin/perl

print "I am Eliza, a psychiatrist.\n";
print "Please say something to me.\n";
print "Say 'Bye' to finish.\n\n";

NEXT_INPUT:
    while ($userInput = <STDIN>){
```

```
            chomp ($userInput);

            if ($userInput =~ /^Bye/i){ #IF-1
                print "Thanks!\nSee you again soon!\n";
                last NEXT_INPUT;
            } #IF-1 ends
            else{ #ELSE-1
                open (RULES, "ElizaRules.dat");
                while ($rule = <RULES>){   #WHILE-2
                    chomp ($rule);
                    ($lhs, $rhs) = split ('\s*=>\s*', $rule);
                    $patternMatchCode = '($userInput =~ ' . $lhs . ')';

                    if (eval $patternMatchCode){ #IF-2
                        ($substitutionLeft) = ( $lhs =~ m#(/.+)/# );
                        $substitutionCode =
                                '$userInput =~ ' . 's' . $substitutionLeft . $rhs;
                        eval $substitutionCode;
                        $systemOutput = trimSpace ($userInput);
                        print "$systemOutput\n";
                        next NEXT_INPUT;
                    }  #IF-2 ends
                }     #WHILE-2 ends
                #No more rules in rulebase
                print "Please go on!\n";
                close (RULES);
            } #ELSE-1 ends
}

close (RULES);

#If there are more than one blank spaces between the words in
#a string, remove them so that there is only one blank space
#between two words
sub trimSpace
{
    my $input = $_[0];
    $input =~ s/\s+(\w+)\s+/ $1 /g;
    return $input;
}
```

The program prints some preliminary statements and goes into a while loop where it reads an input from the user and responds to it till the user types in bye or a variation of it.

The processing of the user input happens in the else block of the if-else statement on the top of the main while loop. The program opens the file ElizaRules.dat that contains the rule base. It reads each rule one by one inside the embedded while loop. It reads a rule and immediately splits it up using Perl's split function, using => as the splitting boundary. This gives us the LHS and the RHS of the rule, called $lhs and $rhs, respectively, inside the program.

The user's input sentence is stored in the variable $userInput. The program constructs a string called $patternMatchCode that it executes later. This code is constructed using string concatenation.

```
$patternMatchCode = '($userInput =~ ' . $lhs . ')';
```

The string that is constructed has the LHS of the rule in it. So, $patternMatchCode looks something like

```
$userInput =~ /I\b(.+)\byou\./ && $1
```

assuming the first rule is being processed. Next, we have an `if` block with the condition

```
eval $patternMatchCode
```

that evaluates a conditional that was constructed a little earlier.

```
$userInput =~ /I\b(.+)\byou\./ && $1
```

It is as if the `if` block looks like

```
if ($userInput =~ /I\b(.+)\byou\./ && $1){...}
```

instead of the way it is written.

If this condition is satisfied, we go into the body of the `if` block. Inside this `if` block, we construct a string that is actually a piece of code that has the substitution operator `s///` in it followed by an LHS and a RHS. That is, we build a string that looks like the following.

```
$userInput =~ s/PATTERN/SUBSTITUTION/
```

The construction is done in parts. First, we obtain the value of the string called `$substitutionLeft`. The value of `$substitutionLeft` comes from the pattern matching operation given below.

```
($substitutionLeft) = ( $lhs =~ m#(/.+)/# );
```

As a result of this, the actual pattern match portion is extracted from the variable `$lhs`. Therefore, if the first rule is the relevant rule, the value of `$lhs` is

```
/I\b(.+)\byou\./ && $1
```

and the value of `$substitutionLeft` is

```
 /I\b(.+)\byou\./
```

and this value can be used in constructing an `s///` string. The `s///` string is constructed next using the following statement.

```
$substitutionCode =
      '$userInput =~ ' . 's' . $substitutionLeft . $rhs;
```

If we are dealing with the first rule, the value of `$substitutionCode` is a string that looks something like the following.

```
$userInput =~ s/I\b(.+)\byou\./If you  $1 me, I $1 you too\./
```

This string is evaluated by the Perl expression

```
eval $substitutionCode;
```

and this evaluation produces a new value for `$userInput` as

```
If you do love me, I do love you too.
```

assuming the original value of `$userInput` was

```
I do love you.
```

So, we see that the new value of $userInput is actually the output after stripping extra spaces among words, if any.

This process continues for every input that the user types on the terminal. The first rule that is satisfied by pattern matching with the use input is used to produce the system's output. If several rules can potentially match, only the first is used. So, the ordering of the rules is important. If no rule matches, ELIZA tries to fake by saying

```
Please go on!
```

and waiting for the next user input.

The patient-ELIZA interaction continues till the user or the patient types in Bye or a variation of it, at which time ELIZA responds by saying

```
Thanks!
See you again!
```

Here, is a complete, but very brief sample interaction with our version of ELIZA. You should increase the number of rules so that you can get more sophisticated conversational behavior.

```
I am Eliza, a psychiatrist.
Please say something to me.
Say 'Bye' to finish.

I love you.
If you love  me, I love you too.
I hate you.
If you hate  me, I hate you too.
I love you so much.
We love you so much too.
I love your hair.
Your hair is beautiful too. You are simply wonderful!

Please go on!
bye
Thanks!
See you again soon!
```

4.13   Conclusions

In this chapter, we have discussed at length Perl's pattern-matching capabilities. Although the chapter is long and has a large number of examples, we are able to discuss the topic only partially. One is advised to read *Programming Perl* [WCS96] to learn all about regular expressions and pattern-matching in Perl. In addition, to get a detailed understanding of regular expressions in Perl and other languages as well, one should read *Mastering Regular Expressions* [Fri97].

Perl's pattern-matching functionality has been inspired by the Unix-based programs *AWK* [AK88] and *sed* [DR97]. These are tools that were expressly developed for performing sophisticated pattern-matching tasks in text strings. They come pre-installed in most Unix and Unix-like machines. These are two individual tools that are independent of any programming language. None of the widely-used general purpose programming languages except for Perl provides pattern-matching and regular expression capabilities like Perl does.

String handling is one of the strongest and most unique characteristics of Perl. Of late, the language called JavaScript used for Web client-side programming has started providing some rudimentary regular expressions capabilities [Fla00, Lin99, NS98]. JavaScript programs are run on Web browsers and one of their main purposes is to validate data users enter in HTML-based forms. Java has started to provide a Perl-type regular expressions capability in recent years.

Quite often, the unparalleled string handling prowess of Perl attracts a programmer to venture into using Perl for the first time. Human communication in a modern society often takes place in terms of written words, and Perl provides a perfect general purpose programming language to parse and analyze such communication. The string handling capabilities often are used in artificial intelligence and information processing. The World Wide Web is an extremely large and ever-growing repository of human knowledge—good or bad, general or specialized, mundane or exotic. Perl is often used to mine hidden information from the vast expanse of the Web. Perl is also used in traditional data mining from databases. The growing and emerging field of bioinformatics uses Perl extensively to perform sophisticated string matching it its quest to map the genome of humans and related animals.

4.14   Exercises

1. *(Easy: Documentation Reading)*
   Read the Perl documentation on regular expressions and pattern matching by running the following.

   ```
   %perldoc perlre
   ```

2. *(Easy: String Processing, Tabs)*
   Write a program `tabbify` that replaces strings of blank spaces by the minimum number of tabs and blank spaces to achieve the same spacing. Assume a tab stop is n blank characters at most. The program takes n as a command-line argument.

3. *(Easy to Medium: String Processing, File Reading)*
   Assume that you have a file where each row contains a person's name followed by two tabs followed by his or her job title.

   ```
   Kalita          Associate Professor
   Sebesta         Associate Professor
   Badal           Professor
   Augusteijn      Professor
   Nystuen         Senior Instructor
   ```

   Write a program that reads this file in one read operation into a multi-line string. Next, the program takes this string that has tabs and newlines inside it and converts the tabs into the requisite number of spaces. The purpose of the tabs is to align the characters that immediately follow the tabs. So, in what we have above, the S from `Senior Instructor`, the A from `Associate Professor`, and the P from `Professor` must be aligned to be in the same column.

   Note that the maximum number of spaces a tab expands to is 8. So, \t\t can expand to a maximum of 16 spaces. Depending on the number of characters before the tab, the number of spaces may be fewer. Assume that the name before the tabs in each line are not more than 15 characters long.

4. *(Medium: Text Processing)*
   Write a program that reads a file and breaks long lines into smaller lines. It takes a command-line argument that is an integer n and checks to make sure that it is an integer. It breaks lines after the last non-blank character that occurs before the nth column of input.

   Extend the program to do the same for all text files in a directory.

5. *(Medium to Hard: Text Processing, Program Parsing)*
   Write a program to check a Perl program for unbalanced parentheses, braces and brackets. Also, look to see if single and double quotes are properly ended. Note that a quote cannot cross line boundary.

6. *(Medium: Text Processing)*
   Write a program to remove trailing blanks and tabs from each line of input. Also, delete more than one consecutive blank line.

7. *(Medium: E-mail Addresses, Data Mining)*
   Write a program that mines e-mail addresses from all files in a directory. For example, if you store e-mail messages you receive and send in a certain directory, the files in this directory are likely to contain many e-mail addresses. Print all collected e-mail addresses to a file. Do not print an e-mail address twice. Sort the e-mail addresses such that

   - they are sorted by the mail server name, i.e., the part of the e-mail address after @. If the portion after @ is not fully specified, fill it up correctly so that it is a complete e-mail address. For this purpose, provide a default complete ending. For example, an e-mail address with an incomplete server name may be `kalita@pikespeak`, or even `kalita`. If the default mail server is `pikespeak.uccs.edu`, the e-mail address can be completed as `kalita@pikespeak.uccs.edu` so that it is a fully qualified Internet address.
   - For each e-mail server name, sort the e-mail addresses alphabetically.

8. *(Medium: File Reading, Histograms, Statistics, Web Graphics)*
   Write a program to print a histogram of the number of words in the text files in a directory. First, draw the histogram horizontally using a character such as x. There is a row for each file. Repeat the character as many times as necessary. Scale the number of words so that the histogram is visible on the screen. Next, modify the program so that the results can be displayed on a Web page. In other words, create HTML and draw nice lines for the histogram. You should do better than a character-based histogram.

9. *(Medium: Web Log Analysis, HTML Tables)*
   All accesses to a Web or HTTP server are stored in the file `/var/httpd/logs/access_log` on a Red Hat Linx 7.1 system. Find out where this file is on your system. The file may be large. Please look at a line of this file given below. It is a single line although it has been broken it up into two lines here.

   ```
   aazoli.cstp.umkc.edu - - [27/Apr/2001:08:03:59 -0600]
   ''GET /~kalita/index.html HTTP/1.0'' 200 595
   ```

   It has the machine that has accessed a page, the date and time of access, and information about the HTTP protocol command that it received. It also stores the name of the file that is accessed.

   Process this file to find which machines have accessed a certain user's files how many times: today, this month, and this year. Specify the name of the user as a command-line argument. Now, create an HTML file that will contain a presentation of this information in tabular form. See how this page looks like in a Web browser.

10. *(Medium: Bibtex, Creating HTML, Research)*
    There are two related text processing packages called TeX and LaTeX that many in academia frequently use. These are markup languages that were invented by Donald Knuth in the late 70's and early 80's. Create a large bibliographic file for this word processor using the *Bibtex* format. One such example file is at `http://www.cs.uccs.edu/\~kalita/work/bibtex.html`.

    A bibliographic file has a large number of entries which follow a given format. Entries look like the following.

```
@InProceedings{Kalita91,
   author =          ``Jugal K. Kalita and Norman I. Badler'',
   title =           ``Interpreting prepositions
                     physically'',
   booktitle =       ``Proceedings of the Annual Conference of the American
                     Association for Artificial Intelligence '',
   year =            ``July, 1991'',
   address =         ``Anaheim, California'',
   pages =           ``105-110''
}
@Book{edward-gait-1906,
   author =          ``Gait~b1863, Edward Albert'',
   title =           ``A History of Assam'',
   publisher =       ``Thacker, Spink \& Co.'',
   year =            ``1906'',
   editor =          ``'',
   volume =          ``'',
   series =          ``'',
   address =         ``Calcutta'',
   edition =         ``'',
   month =           ``'',
   note =            ``PATG''
}
```

The first entry tells us that it is an entry from a conference proceedings. It has an internal index called `Kalita91`. Then, it gives us some details about the entry.

Please note that there are several kinds of records with different fields. In addition, some fields may not be specified.

Please look at the file provided. Find documentation on *Bibtex* format on the Web. let the user supply one or more keywords and search the " database". Get the entries that mention the keyword(s). Process the selected entries to produce a presentable HTML document that contains the bibliographic entries. Find out from a book of styles (e.g., *The Chicago Manual of Style*) how they can be presented. Once again, load this HTML file into a browser to display it.

11. *(Easy: Text Processing)*
    Write a program that reads a file a paragraph at a time. It reports the lengths of the longest and the smallest paragraphs in the document, in terms of numbers of words. It also reports the lengths of the shortest and the longest sentences, in numbers of words. Make any simple assumptions you need regarding when a sentence starts.

12. *(Easy: Text Processing)*
    In Perl you can include one file in another by writing either `require` *file* or `use` *file*. Write a program that takes a set of file names as command line arguments and prints which file includes which ones. The output should look something like the following:

```
Name     Includes
-----    --------
file1    file5, file6, file20
file2    file3, file4
```

13. You have a text file `customers` with a large number of records. A record looks like the following

```
#
name = ''Kalita, Jugal'';
e-mail = ''kalita@pikespeak.uccs.edu'';
phone = ''719-574-3656''

# next record begins
```

Note that the fields may be jumbled up. Also, there may be any number of spaces or newlines scattered in the file.

Treat this file as a mailing list. Generate a mail message with a body that looks like the following to every person listed in the "database."

```
Dear Jugal,
 How are you doing? Is 719-574-3656 still your phone number?
Sincerely,

Customer Service Representative
```

This mail message is sent to kalita@pikespeak.uccs.edu.

14. *(Medium: Text Processing, "Database" Processing)*

Let us make an initial effort at writing a grocery store program.

We make up a syntax for entering our grocery store items. This may not be the best syntax, but it gives us the flexibility that we need for our purposes.

Let us assume that we have grocery items belonging to the following categories Produce, Deli, Dairy, Meat, Beverages, Snack Foods, Paper Products, Books and Magazines, Spices and Condiment, and Frozen Foods.

Write up a file for the grocery items that we have in the store. Let this file have 15 items belonging to any five categories given above. Have 3 items per category.

An entry in this file looks like the following.

```
@Item{
  ID =                    ''20-130-5000'',
  name =                  ''Philadelphia Cream Cheese'',
  category =              ''Dairy'',
  manufacturer =          ''General Foods, Inc.'',
  price =                 ''0.99'',
  unit=                   ''ounce'',
  unitsPerItem =          ''16'',
  packaging =             ''plastic and paper'',
  inventory =             ''1000'',
  description =           ''Low calorie; No fat''
}
```

It tells us that it is a grocery item. It has an internal ID. Then, it gives us details about the entry. Note that some fields may not be specified. Also, a field may be specified over several lines.

Our goal now is to make up a Web page from the item file. By processing this file, we want to make an HTML page where the item categories are shown as clickable links. Show the items in a sorted manner. When a user clicks on a link for a certain category, show all the products in that category with detailed information that you deem important. You should sort the items.

15. *(Easy: Text Processing)*
    Suppose we have XML elements that look like the following.

```
<Photographs>
        <Photograph>
                <URL>http://www.cs.uccs.edu/~kalita/kalita1.jpg</URL>
                <Caption>Jugal Kalita on a summer afternoon</Caption>
                <Width>150</Width>
                <Height>150</Height>
        </Photograph>
        <Photograph>
                <URL>http://www.cs.uccs.edu/~kalita/jk1.jpg</URL>
                <Caption>Jugal Kalita on a boat on Lake Umtru</Caption>
                <Width>200</Width>
                <Height>200</Height>
        </Photograph>
</Photographs>
```

Parse this XML fragment to obtain the Photograph elements. For each Photograph element, obtain the sub-elements. Create a string for each Photograph element where the sub-elements are separated by the separator : :. Write the strings to a file, one string per line.

16. *(Easy to Hard: Text Processing)*
    Write a program that compares two files like the diff program in Unix. Implement as many options as you can.

17. *(Easy: Text Processing, Loops)*
    Write definitions for the following group of functions. In each case, the function takes two arguments. The first argument must evaluate to a list and the second is a regular expression. What each function returns is given below:

    (a) forall *lst pattern*: This function returns 1 if the *pattern* is satisfied for every item in the list *lst* and 0 otherwise. This function should always return 1 if the first argument is the empty list.

    (b) forsome *lst pattern*: This function returns 1 if the *pattern* is satisfied for some item in the list *lst* and 0 otherwise. This function should always return 0 if its first argument is the empty list.

    (c) formost *lst pattern*: This function returns 1 if the *pattern* is satisfied for most of the items in the list *lst* and 0 otherwise. Let *most* mean *half or more* of the items in the list. This function should always return 1 if the first argument is the empty list.

18. *(Medium to Hard: Calculus, Pattern Matching, Symbolic Differentiation)*
    This problem asks you to complete a symbolic differentiation function. The goal of the function is to take an arithmetic expression containing variables and to produce another representing its first derivative with respect to the variable X. Thus given the expressions:

```
((x ^ 2) + (3 * x)),
```

we want to produce the new expression

```
((2 * x) + 3)}.
```

We assume the expressions are fully parenthesized for simplicity.

The standard rules for differentiation are given below. Here, x stands for the variable x, c for any constant symbol, u and v for any arbitrary arithmetic expressions and du and dv for their derivatives. Note that the rules are recursive. The fourth rule, for example, states that the derivative of the sum of two expressions is the sum of their derivatives.

(a) *d/dx[c] = 0*, where c is a numeric constant.

(b) *d/dx[x] = 1*

(c) *d/dx[v] = 0*, where v is a variable other than x.

(d) *d/dx[u + v] = d/dx[u] + d/dx[v]*

(e) *d/dx[u - v] = d/dx[u] - d/dx[v]*

(f) *d/dx[-v] = - d/dx[v]*

(g) *d/dx[u * v] = u * d/dx[v] + v * d/dx[u]*

(h) *d/dx[u / v] = (v * d/dx[u] - u * d/dx[v]) / v^2*

Try to simplify the results of differentiation. Take the following approach. Use simplifying patterns such as the following.

pattern $x + 0$ $0 + x$ $x * 0$ $0 * x$ $x * 1$ $1 * x$ $x/1$ $0/x$
result x x 0 0 x x x 0

In the returned expression, look for any of the above pattern and additional patterns that you write, and if you find any replace it by the corresponding result. And, keep on doing this till no more simplifications can be done. Note that x need not be a symbol; it can be any complicated expression.

Chapter 5

On Modules and Objects

In This Chapter

A *package* enables a programmer or a group of co-ordinating programmers to demarcate fortified boundaries around portions of the code. The use of packages enables organization of code into small partitions that can be used to achieve a complex task. If the program under construction is large and a team of developers is involved, the use of packages allows the project manager to break up the code into parts that can be developed by independent groups or individuals. The interface among the constituent components must be agreed upon and stated with precision.

In general, there can be several packages in a file. When a file contains only one package, and some simple naming conventions are obeyed, we get a *module*. Modular programming enables portions of code developed for one project to be reused in other projects. Finally, using packages and references (discussed in Section 3.3), one can write object-oriented programs in Perl. We discuss each of these three topics in this chapter.

5.1   Packages

A package allows us to define what is called a *namespace*. A package defines a unit of code within which the variable and function names used are safe from being overridden by other units of code that may use the same variable and function names.

In Perl, like any programming language, names of variables and functions are stored in an internal table called the *symbol table*. When we do not declare packages on our own, all names are stored in the symbol table for a package called main. However, when we partition our code into packages, each package has its own symbol table. As a result, the same name can be used in two or more packages without any confusion if we qualify the name of the variables with its home package's name.

The program given below is very simple. We have broken it up into packages only for the purpose of illustration. Usually packages are not needed if the program is small in size.

Program 5.1

```perl
#!/usr/bin/perl
package Sean;

$firstname = "Sean"; $hometown = "Montreal";
$height = 67; $weight = 140;
$age = 21; $year_met = 1995;

#---------
package Tommy;

$firstname = "Tommy"; $hometown = "Washington DC";
$height = 66; $weight = 140;
$age = 18; $year_met = 1997;

#--------
package main;

$firstname = "Chad"; $hometown = "San Francisco";
$height = 73; $weight = 180;
$age = 23; $year_met = 1995;

printf "%s\t%s\t%s\t%s\t%s\t%s\n", $firstname, $main::hometown, $height,
        $weight,
        $age, $year_met;
printf "%s\t%s\t%s\t%s\t%s\t%s\n", $Tommy::firstname, $Tommy::hometown,
        $Tommy::height, $Tommy::weight, $Tommy::age,   $Tommy::year_met;
printf "%s\t%s\t%s\t%s\t%s\t%s\n", $Sean::firstname, $Sean::hometown,
        $Sean::height, $Sean::weight, $Sean::age,   $Sean::year_met;
```

The beginning of a package with the name *package_name* is signaled by the declaration

> package *package_name*

The scope of a package declaration starts immediately after the package statement and continues either till the end of the innermost block that contains the statement or till another package statement is encountered. In the program given above, there are three packages. The first package is called Sean, the second package is called Tommy and the last package is called main. The Sean package starts from the

> package Sean;

statement and continues till we encounter the

```
package Tommy;
```

statement. In package `Sean`, we assign values to a set of scalar variables.

The next package is called `Tommy` and in this package, we assign values to the same set of scalars as we did in the `Sean` package. But, the two sets of variables are in two packages and therefore the earlier values do not get overridden. The two sets of names are in two namespaces and therefore remain unviolated by one another.

Finally, we have a package called `main`. The `main` package is default and if there is no confusion regarding where it begins, the

```
package main;
```

declaration is not needed. However, in this case, without this statement, we would not know where the `Tommy` package ends and the `main` package begins. In the `main` package also, we have assigned values to exactly the same set of variables as we did in the previous two packages. But, once again, since the three sets of names are in three different namespaces or symbol tables, they do not disturb one another and coexist in harmony within their own fenced spaces.

The `main` package is the default package. So, to refer to variables which reside in the main package we can simply write the variable name as we have done earlier. However, it is also possible to qualify the name of a variable in the `main` package using the name of the package, i.e., the symbol `main`. So, `$main::hometown` and `$hometown` refer to the same variable in the `main` package. When we use the name of a package as a qualifier, the `$` sign that tells us that a variable is a scalar must be placed before the name of the package. In other words, we need to write the `$` sign, then the name of the package without any intervening space, then two colons `::`, and finally the name of the variable without the `$` sign.

In the `main` package, to refer to the name of a variable in a package that is not `main`, we must qualify the name of the variable by the package's name. Therefore, in `main`, we refer to the `$firstname` variable in the `Sean` package as `$Sean::firstname` and we refer to the `$firstname` variable in the `Tommy` package as `$Tommy::firstname`.

The program given above prints the values of the `$firstname`, `$hometown`, `$height`, `$weight`, `$age` and `$year_met` variables from the three packages: `main`, `Tommy` and `Chad`.

The output of the program is given below.

```
Chad    San Francisco   73      180     23      1995
Tommy   Washington DC   66      140     18      1997
Sean    Montreal        67      140     21      1995
```

In this example, a package contains only simple scalar variables. If a package contains list or hash variables or functions, their names must also be qualified outside the home package, i.e., outside the package in which they are defined. For a list variable, the `@` sign must precede the name of the package, and for a hash variable the `%` sign must precede the name of the package. Outside the home package, if we place the `&` symbol before the name of a subroutine, we must place it before the name of the home package. In addition, a filehandle in another namespace can be used in the currently extant package by using the package modifier in front.

This example shows that several packages can reside in the same physical file. Usually, it is a good habit to write one package in one file, but it is not necessary. When we have several packages in one file, it is possible to go back and forth among the packages. To enter a package we use the `package` declaration with the name of the package whose namespace we want to use. There is no explicit way to leave a package. We leave a package when another package starts or the program ends. The `package` declaration can be used inside explicit blocks created using braces. Once a package starts in a program, all unqualified names are in the designated namespace. Note that all our variables in the program being discussed are global in scope because we have not pre-declared them.

What we have seen in this section is an extremely simple example showing the use of packages. There are many other details that we need to know if we want to use packages effectively. For example, there is a mechanism to *export*, from the home package, variable and function names so that the names can be used without qualifiers in non-home packages.

5.2   Modules and `use`

Modules are nothing but packages. In the example of packages we see in the previous section, we use three packages, but all three are defined within the same file. In Perl, a file can have many packages or a package can span over many files. The language puts no strictures on how packages should be organized. However, if we restrict one package to one file, what we get are called *modules*. In Perl, the name of the file (i.e., the name of the module) in which the package is stored must be the same as the name of the package, but with a .pm extension. pm stands for Perl module. So, if the name of the package corresponding to a module is *a_package*, the name of the file where the package is stored must be called *a_package*.pm.

We now rework the example that we saw in the previous section and build modules out of the packages. We write three modules Sean, Tommy, and another one that has a slightly longer name Friends::Chad. We discuss the significance of the long name for the last module shortly. We also have the main program. So, there are a total of four files.

To create the first two modules, we create two files Sean.pm and Tommy.pm in the current directory. The files need not have execute permission. The file Sean.pm holds the definition of the Sean package. Its contents are what we have seen earlier, but repeated below.

Program 5.2

```
#!/usr/bin/perl
#file Sean.pm
package Sean;

$firstname = "Sean"; $hometown = "Montreal";
$height = 67; $weight = 140;
$age = 21; $year_met = 1995;


1;
```

This file declares that we are inside the Sean package, and assigns value to a few scalar variables. The definition of a package must return true. The use function returns the value of the last statement in the package in addition to making the package's definition available where it is used. Usually, the last statement of a package is

```
1;
```

which is the quitessential true statement. The contents of the file Tommy.pm are also repeated below. They are quite similar to the contents of the Sean.pm file.

Program 5.3

```
#!/usr/bin/perl
#file Tommy.pm
package Tommy;
```

```
$firstname = "Tommy"; $hometown = "Washington DC";
$height = 66; $weight = 140;
$age = 18; $year_met = 1997;


1;
```

To store the third module, we create a directory called Friends in the current directory. In this directory, we create a file called Chad.pm. The contents of the file Friends/Chad.pm are given below. This file also does not have to be executable.

Program 5.4

```
#!/usr/bin/perl
#file Friends/Chad.pm
package Friends::Chad;

$firstname = "Chad"; $hometown = "San Francisco";
$height = 73; $weight = 180;
$age = 23; $year_met = 1995;


1;
```

Note that the package has been declared with the name Friends::Chad and not simply Chad.

Now, let us look at the main program. In the main program, we want to have access to the contents of all the three modules and print the values the variables have been assigned in the three modules. Here is the main program.

Program 5.5

```
#!/usr/bin/perl
#file simple2package.pl

use Sean;
use Tommy;
use Friends::Chad;


printf "%s\t%s\t%s\t%s\t%s\t%s\n", $Friends::Chad::firstname,
        $Friends::Chad::hometown, $Friends::Chad::height, $Friends::Chad::weight
        $Friends::Chad::age, $Friends::Chad::year_met;
printf "%s\t%s\t%s\t%s\t%s\t%s\n", $Tommy::firstname, $Tommy::hometown,
        $Tommy::height, $Tommy::weight, $Tommy::age,  $Tommy::year_met;
printf "%s\t%s\t%s\t%s\t%s\t%s\n", $Sean::firstname, $Sean::hometown,
        $Sean::height, $Sean::weight, $Sean::age,  $Sean::year_met;
```

The first two modules that are in the same directory as the main program are accessed by writing the statements

```
use Sean;
use Tommy;
```

However, to access the contents of the module named `Friends::Chad` that is stored as `Chad.pm` in the subdirectory `Friends`, we need to write

```
use Friends::Chad;
```

Additional levels of subdirectories can be used if appropriate for the task at hand. To get the value of a variable such as `$hometown` in the `Friends::Chad` package, we need to write `$Friends::Chad::hometown`. Otherwise, nothing is much different from the program given in the previous subsection on packages. The output of executing the main program is the same as what we see in the previous section. If we use the `use` statement, the names can be used without qualifiers. However, in this case, without the package name qualifier, the names are ambiguous.

A package, in its definition, can have a list of exported variables. A package can export variables that are globally available. A variable that is available globally inside a package may be

1. global only within the package, or
2. global within the block in which the package lies.

As an example of the second type of global variable occurs when a variable is global in a file that contains several packages. There are several ways of creating global variables of various kinds.

1. A variable that is undeclared and just used in an expression or a statement is a global variable. An undeclared global variable inside a package need not be explicitly exported.
2. A variable declared with `my` is not considered global, and thus, cannot be exported and made available outside a package.
3. A variable declared with `our` is considered global within a block (which may contain one or more packages), and thus, can be exported and made available outside the home package.
4. A variable declared with the pragma `use vars` is considered global inside a package, and thus, can be exported and made available outside the home package.

The `use` function imports the named package's list of exported variables. Exported variables are ones that have been explicitly exported by the module within its definition. An exported identifier can be used without using the package qualifier although it is a good habit to use the package qualifier even when not needed so that the source package of a variable name, a filehandle, or a subroutine is always clear. This is especially so if there are many modules being used. In the current set of modules, we have not explicitly exported any identifiers from the `Sean`, `Tommy` and `Friends::Chad` modules. However, non-exported global variables such as the ones we see in these three modules are available anywhere else if we use fully qualified names. Thus, it is not possible to make variables in the three modules discussed here, invisible or private to a module even if we want to because of the way these modules are written at this time. Of course, an identifier or a name in a module can be made selectively available outside. We see how to do such selective exporting of variable names later.

When we write one or more modules, it is possible that we organize them tidily by placing them in a clearly named directory. For example, if in this case, we create a directory called `friendlib` with the full path `/home/kalita/perl/packages/friendlib`, we can make the modules available in Perl program by `use`ing the pragma called `lib` before we use the modules. So, if `Sean.pm` and `Tommy.pm` are situated in `/home/kalita/perl/packages/friendlib` and `Chad.pm` is situated in the directory `/home/kalita/perl/packages/friendlib/Friends`, the following sequence works.

```
use lib '/home/kalita/perl/packages/friendlib';
```

```
use Sean;
use Tommy;
use Friends::Chad;
```

A module installed by a system's administrator resides in one or more pre-designated directories for Perl libraries. For example, on a Linux machine, it usually is one or more sub-directories in the directory `/usr/lib/perl5` for Perl 5. Perl has a large number of libraries that come with the core distribution. They are normally placed below `/urs/lib/perl5` in one sub-directory whose name is the Perl version number, say `5.8.0` or `5.005`. Usually, all modules downloaded later are placed in a directory called `site_perl` under `/usr/lib/perl5`. If a user-written set of Perl modules are placed in a new sub-directory in `/usr/lib/perl5`, it is not necessary to specify the location of the modules using `use lib` as long as the module name clearly specifies the directory and file structure below the `/usr/lib/perl5` directory. Of course, the names of all the directories can vary from system to system. The module files and all directories above them must be accessible to everyone. This means, in Unix, the files must be readable by everyone. All directories must be readable and executable by everyone in Unix. In a non-Unix environment, accessibility permissions are usually not an issue.

Finally, we also see that a module is reusable code. It can be written by one person, then given to another who can use it as long as it is placed where Perl can find it.

5.3   Packages and Scope of Variables

A package is a namespace. A name such as a variable, function, or filehandle name belongs to a package. A package declaration affects only the so-called global names. Global names are those that are normally not explicitly declared before first use. In a file, a global name once used is available everywhere afterwards. An unassigned global variable has an undefined value. Variables declared with my are not considered global in Perl. They are statically scoped in that they are available within the current block—explicitly contained within braces, or an implicit block such as a whole file. When we have a variable declared with my on top of a file, it is available everywhere in the file unless we my-redeclare a variable with the same name in the same or a contained block.

A package declaration affects the scope of a variable name, i.e., where the variable name can be seen and accessed. Let us look at the program given below.

Program 5.6

```
#!/usr/bin/perl
#file global.pl

$hometown = "Colorado Springs";
print "hometown = $hometown\n";
print "hometown again = $main::hometown\n";

package Tommy;
print "Tommy's hometown = $hometown\n";
print "Tommy's hometown again = $main::hometown\n";
$state = "Colorado";
print "Tommy's state = $state\n";

package Sean;
print "Sean's hometown = $hometown\n";
print "Sean's state = $state\n";
```

```
package main;
print "Our hometown = $hometown\n";
print "Our state = $state\n";
```

There are three packages in this program file: main, Tommy and Sean. main is the package on top where no package name has been specified. main is the package in the bottom of the program where it is explicitly entered. $hometown as used on top is a global variable. As we know, only a global variable is affected by the package declaration. When we print $hometown on the top of the program in the default main package right after the declaration, it is printed as expected. In the main package, we can qualify the variable name with the package name main if we want.

In the package Tommy, the global variable $hometown is not available without qualification since $hometown is a name or identifier that resides in the main package. Similarly, $hometown is not available in the Sean package without qualification. It is available again at the bottom, with or without qualification in the package main. The $state variable is available without qualification only in package Tommy. The output of this program is given below.

```
hometown = Colorado Springs
hometown again = Colorado Springs
Tommy's hometown =
Tommy's hometown again = Colorado Springs
Tommy's state = Colorado
Sean's hometown =
Sean's state =
Our hometown = Colorado Springs
Our state =
```

The next program drives home the point.

Program 5.7

```
#!/usr/bin/perl
#file global1.pl

package Tommy;
$hometown = "Colorado Springs";
print "Tommy's hometown = $hometown\n";

package Sean;
print "Sean's hometown = $hometown\n";

package main;
print "hometown = $hometown\n";
```

Here, the variable $hometown is global because it is an undeclared variable. It resides in the Tommy package and hence not available in any other package without qualification. The output of the program is given below.

```
Tommy's hometown = Colorado Springs
Sean's hometown =
hometown =
```

Variables declared with my are statically scoped. Such variables are not considered global. That is, their scope or availability within the program is determined by the block in which they are declared. In Perl, only a global variable is limited by a package declaration to belong to a certain namespace. A package declaration does not place any such restriction on my-declared variables. A variable declared with my cannot be qualified by a package name. The following program illustrates these scoping concepts.

Program 5.8
_____

```perl
#!/usr/bin/perl
#file my.pl
use strict;

my $hometown = "Colorado Springs";
print "hometown = $hometown\n";
print "hometown again = $main::hometown\n";

package Tommy;
my $state = "Colorado";
print "Tommy's hometown = $hometown\n";
print "Tommy's state = $state\n";
print "Tommy's state again = $Tommy::state\n";

package  Sean;
print "Sean's hometown = $hometown\n";
print "Sean's state = $state\n";

package main;
print "Our hometown = $hometown\n";
print "Our state = $state\n";
```
_____

$hometown is declared with my on the top of the program. Hence, it is in the textual extent of the main package. However, it is not considered to belong to the main package. It is considered to be statically-scoped for availability in the complete textual extent of the file my.pl. Thus, there is a subtle distinction between what is considered global and what is statically-scoped. The two sets, as seen now, are disjoint. When we print $hometown, its value is printed, but when we print $main::hometown, Perl prints nothing since it does not print the value of the variable just assigned, but a global variable in the default package main. There is no such variable and therefore nothing is printed. A non-existent variable name qualified with a package name does not cause compilation error in Perl.

In package Tommy, a variable $state is declared with my and given a value. Since it is declared with my, it becomes statically available in the block where it is located. Here, there is only one implicit block, the whole file. Therefore, $state is available through the rest of the file. Since it is my-declared, its name cannot be pinned down to a specific package.

In package Sean, both variables printed get the values assigned earlier. The two variables have the values printed in the main package as well. The output of the program is given below.

```
hometown = Colorado Springs
```

```
hometown again =
Tommy's hometown = Colorado Springs
Tommy's state = Colorado
Tommy's state again =
Sean's hometown = Colorado Springs
Sean's state = Colorado
Our hometown = Colorado Springs
Our state = Colorado
```

In general, my-declared lexical variables are completely hidden from the outside world. That is, they are not seen from anywhere outside the block where they are declared, no matter what. In other words, they cannot be exported successfully.

Perl gives us a second way to declare a variable: our. The scope of a variable declared by our is exactly the same as that of a my-declared variable. That is, an our-declared variable is visible within the current block which may be the whole file. However, an our-declared variable becomes a global variable unlike a my-declared variable. Thus, an our-declared variable is a global variable visible within the lexical scope of a block. Without our, only undeclared variables are global. Thus, our achieves what my and non-declaration achieve separately. Earlier we have seen that my-declared variables cannot be seen outside a block, and that my-declared variables cannot be qualified with a package name. We have also seen that an undeclared variable can be seen outside its home package and can be qualified with a package. our-declared variables can also be seen outside the current block and can be qualified with a package name.

The following program is a modification of the immediately preceding program where the two my declarations have been changed to our.

Program 5.9

```
#!/usr/bin/perl
#file our.pl
use strict;

our $hometown = "Colorado Springs";
print "hometown = $hometown\n";
print "hometown again = $main::hometown\n";

package Tommy;
our    $state = "Colorado";
print "Tommy's hometown = $hometown\n";
print "Tommy's state = $state\n";
print "Tommy's state again = $Tommy::state\n";

package  Sean;
print "Sean's hometown = $hometown\n";
print "Sean's state = $state\n";

package main;
print "Our hometown = $hometown\n";
print "Our state = $state\n";
```

The output of the program is given below.

```
hometown = Colorado Springs
hometown again = Colorado Springs
Tommy's hometown = Colorado Springs
Tommy's state = Colorado
Tommy's state again = Colorado
Sean's hometown = Colorado Springs
Sean's state = Colorado
Our hometown = Colorado Springs
Our state = Colorado
```

We clearly see that an our-declared variable is

- available outside its home package without a package qualifier like an undeclared global variable, and
- can be qualified with a package name.

our makes a variable globally accessible in the current block. The current block may have several packages in terms of textual content. our does not make a variable globally accessible only inside the current package.

Now, we discuss a way to make a variable viewable globally inside a package. The package may be the only one in a file, or it may be one of several in a file. Of course, a real module may have many explicit blocks enclosed within braces. A package-global variable is accessible anywhere in the package unless a variable with the same name is declared elsewhere in the same package. A package-global variable is not available without qualification outside the home package. We make a variable package-global by declaring it with the pragma use vars. use vars takes a list of words and makes them globally available inside the current package. By global scope inside a package, we mean that the name is available inside all blocks that the package may contain. Also, if the package is available over several files (by using the package declaration), the name or identifier is available everywhere in the package. The following program illustrates the use of use vars.

Program 5.10

```
#!/usr/bin/perl
#file usevar.pl

use strict;

use vars qw($hometown);
$hometown = "Colorado Springs";
print "hometown = $hometown\n";
print "hometown again = $main::hometown\n";

package Tommy;
use vars qw($state);
$state = "Colorado";
print "Tommy's hometown = $main::hometown\n";
print "Tommy's state = $state\n";
print "Tommy's state again = $Tommy::state\n";

package Sean;
print "Sean's hometown = $main::hometown\n";
```

```
print "Sean's state = $Tommy::state\n";

package main;
print "Our hometown = $hometown\n";
print "Our state = $Tommy::state\n";
```

In this program, once again, we have the default package main, and two other packages Tommy and Sean. We start the program by declaring $hometown as a global variable within the confines of the implicit package main. use vars takes a list of quoted words. We can use qw to provide such a list if we want. Thus, $hometown can be seen in the package main only, without any qualification. It is not seen in any other package without the package name in front.

In the package Tommy, we declare $state as a package global variable. When we print $hometown declared in the package main in Tommy, it must be accessed as $main::hometown. Similarly, in the Sean package, both variables need to be qualified with the package name. The output of the program is given below.

```
hometown = Colorado Springs
hometown again = Colorado Springs
Tommy's hometown = Colorado Springs
Tommy's state = Colorado
Tommy's state again = Colorado
Sean's hometown = Colorado Springs
Sean's state = Colorado
Our hometown = Colorado Springs
Our state = Colorado
```

5.4   Packages and Subroutines

A subroutine declared in a package is available only within the package without qualification by the package name. We can always qualify with the package name although it is redundant to qualify a subroutine's name in the package in which it is defined. In another package, the subroutine cannot be called without the package name qualifier. The following program illustrates these findings.

Program 5.11

```
#!/usr/bin/perl
#file sub.pl

use strict;

sub hello{
    print "Hello: I am the main man!\n"
}

hello;
&main::hello;

package Tommy;
&hello;
&main::hello;
```

The output of the program is given below.

```
Hello: I am the main man!
Hello: I am the main man!
Undefined subroutine &Tommy::hello called at sub.pl line 14.
```

Here, there are four calls to the subroutine `hello` and the third call causes runtime error. Note that when a subroutine in another package is called, Perl does not check if it exists during compilation, but only during execution. When a program gives an error and exits, it is possible to capture the error in order to handle it in some fashion to take care of the situation, and not let Perl runtime environment exit automatically. We can use the `eval` function to do that. `eval` can take a sequence of statements enclosed in braces and execute them. The statements inside the `eval` are parsed at the same time as the rest of the code. The code inside the `eval` is executed when the rest of the code is executed, i.e., in the context of the current Perl program. The value returned by `eval` is the value of the last contained statement. If there is a syntax error that results within the `eval` after execution (it is possible for one to construct a statement on the fly inside the `eval`) or there is a runtime error, or a `die` statement is executed within the `eval`, an undefined value is returned by `eval`, and the special variable `$@` is set. `$@` contains the error message. If there is no error inside the eval, `$@` has the null or empty value. Any error string printed to STDERR (usually, the screen or the terminal) by the contained statements are still printed. Thus, `eval` can trap otherwise fatal errors. Actions can be taken by a program based on the error.

The following is a rewrite of the previous program where errors are *trapped* from two `eval`s.

Program 5.12

```
#!/usr/bin/perl
#file sub1.pl

use strict;
my $error;

sub hello{
    print "Hello: I am the main man!\n"
}

hello;
&main::hello;

package Tommy;
eval{&hello} or warn "$@";
if ($@){print "Error in the call to hello\n";}

eval{&main::hello} or warn "$@";
if ($@){print "Error in the call to main::hello\n";}
```

It shows that the calls to `hello` in the `main` package are good calls and executed. In the `Tommy` package, the first call is unacceptable because the name of the subroutine is not qualified by the package name. The error is captured and the handler simply prints a string though in practice, it may be more complex. However, as we see the program does not die, and continues to the next statement. The last call to `hello` is fully qualified with the name of the package.

```
Hello: I am the main man!
Hello: I am the main man!
Undefined subroutine &Tommy::hello called at sub1.pl line 15.
Error in the call to hello
Hello: I am the main man!
```

5.5   Exporting Identifiers from a Module

In this section, we discuss how variables and subroutines in a module can be made visible (or, invisible), and thus, usable (or, unusable) outside the module. In the modules we have seen in Sections 5.1, 5.2 and 5.6, all the variables are global, and hence visible from elsewhere. In other words, none of the variables in the packages or modules have been pre-declared. In these modules, all the variables are global, and hence visible from elsewhere when the names are fully qualified with the name of the package in front. In Section 5.3, we see how variable names can be made global inside a block, or global inside a package. In the example that follows in this section, we make all the variables local to the file by declaring them with my. Variables declared with my have static scope in the block in which they occur. In this case, the block is the whole file. A file has only one package or module in it. Thus, these variables are invisible outside the module unless explicit mechanisms are made to make them visible. This ensures privacy and allows selective exporting of names. This holds for subroutine or method names as well.

We have a module called Sean.pm that is given below.

Program 5.13

```perl
#!/usr/bin/perl
#file Sean.pm
use strict;

package Sean;
use Exporter;
use vars qw(@ISA @EXPORT);
@ISA = ('Exporter');
@EXPORT = qw($firstname  $hometown &height  &weight &age &year_met);
our($firstname);
my ($hometown, $height, $weight, $age, $year_met);
$firstname = "Sean"; $hometown = "Montreal";
$height = 67; $weight = 140;
$age = 21; $year_met = 1995;

sub height{
    return $height;
}

sub weight{
    return $weight;
}

sub age{
    return $age;
}
```

```
sub year_met{
   return $year_met;
}

1;
```

The package declaration is right on top. As a result, the module goes into a new package where its variables and functions are stored. It uses a module called `Exporter` to be able to make selected identifiers available outside the module's definition. Then, there is the following statement.

```
use vars qw(@ISA @EXPORT);
```

This statement declares variables that are to be used only inside one package. Here, we declare variables that are global inside a package. Since the file contains only one package, they are global inside the file as well.

```
@ISA = ('Exporter');
```

This makes the current package `Sean.pm` inherit from the `Exporter.pm` module. `Exporter.pm` has a method called `import` that is inherited by `Sean.pm`. Thus, when in another program, one says

```
use Sean;
```

Perl calls the method

```
Sean->import()
```

that is inherited from `Exporter.pm`. This makes the exported variables, functions and methods available in the `use`ing package.

The next statement assigns a value to `@EXPORT`. `@ISA` and `@EXPORT` are special Perl variables that are available inside each package. `@EXPORT`'s value specifies all variable, function and method names that are available outside. However, there is a catch that we see next.

The module has one variable `$hometown` declared with `my`. Variables declared with `my` are visible in the current file since the whole file is an implicit block. These variables' values are not available outside the current file even if exported. The current file contains only one package and as a result, the variables declared with `my` are not seen outside the package and are thus, private to the package.

This is why Perl provides another way to declare statically scoped variables in addition to `my`. It is `our`. `our` declaration makes a variable scoped inside a block (which can be a file), but allows it to be exported when used in a situation where `use strict` is enforced. This is because `our` makes a variable global inside the block in addition to making it statically scoped inside the block. Note that we use & before names of exported functions to explicitly indicate that they are functions. The use of & is not necessary before a function name in Perl.

In the rest of the program, there are some assignment statements and function definitions. Next, we have a program that uses the package `Sean.pm`. This program is called `friends1.pl`.

Program 5.14

```
#!/usr/bin/perl
#file friends1.pl
use strict;
use Sean;
```

```perl
print "Sean's firstname = ", $Sean::firstname, "\n";
print "Sean's hometown =  ", $Sean::hometown, "\n";
eval{print "Sean's hometown = ", Sean::hometown(), "\n";}
    or warn "$@";
eval{print "Sean's  height = ", height(), "\n";}
    or warn "$@";
print "Sean's weight = $Sean::weight\n";
eval{print "Sean's age = ", Sean::age(), "\n";}
    or warn "$@";
eval{print "Year I met Sean =", Sean::year_met(), "\n";}
    or warn "$@";
```

The file uses the package Sean.pm. It simply prints the values of a few variables and makes a few function calls. We see that the value of $firstname is printed correctly because it is declared with our in Sean.pm. However, the value of $hometown is not exported correctly from Sean.pm to friends1.pl in spite of the fact that $hometown is explicitly exported. That is because it is declared with my in Sean.pm and hence its value cannot be sent out even if its name is exported.

The other thing to note is that we make calls to the exported functions inside eval statements. This usage executes statements inside an eval. If there is an exception i.e., an error, eval catches it and makes it available in the variable $@. Without eval, any error is likely to cause the program to die. The output of the program is given below.

```
%friends1.pl
Sean's firstname = Sean
Sean's hometown =
Undefined subroutine &Sean::hometown called at friends1.pl line 8.
Sean's  height = 67
Sean's weight =
Sean's age = 21
Year I met Sean =1995
```

There is a way in which we can modify the Sean.pm so that variables can still be exported. It is by changing the our declaration to a declaration that uses use vars. We know that the use vars pragma makes the variables global inside the package. Let us change the Sean.pm to look like the following .

Program 5.15

```perl
#!/usr/bin/perl
#file Sean.pm
use strict;

package Sean;
use Exporter;
use vars qw(@ISA @EXPORT);
@ISA = ('Exporter');
@EXPORT = qw($firstname  $hometown &height  &weight &age &year_met);
use vars qw($firstname $hometown);
my ($height, $weight, $age, $year_met);
$firstname = "Sean"; $hometown = "Montreal";
```

```
$height = 67; $weight = 140;
$age = 21; $year_met = 1995;

sub height{
    return $height;
}

sub weight{
   return $weight;
}

sub age{
   return $age;
}

sub year_met{
   return $year_met;
}

1;
```

If we now run the `friends1.pl` program given earlier, the output is the following.

```
Sean's firstname = Sean
Sean's hometown =  Montreal
Undefined subroutine &Sean::hometown called at friends1.pl line 8.
Sean's  height = 67
Sean's weight =
Sean's age = 21
Year I met Sean =1995
```

5.6 Object-Oriented Programming

In order to write object-oriented programs in Perl, we need to use the concepts of references and packages. Unlike most other languages, Perl does not provide much additional syntax for creating and manipulating objects.

First, let us briefly discuss some basic concepts regarding object-oriented programming in general. To write object-oriented programs in a certain domain of interest, we need to identify *classes* of objects in the domain. Sometimes, we can represent the set of classes using a hierarchy. Sometimes, a hierarchy is not enough. A network is needed for representation if there are classes that have more than one ancestor class. In the example we discuss in this section, we have a simple hierarchy where each subclass has only one parent class. Therefore, the set of classes in our example can be organized as a tree.

A class that does not have any ancestor is called the *root* class. A class may have descendants. Direct descendants are called *subclasses* or *children* of the class; the original class then is also called the *parent class* or the *direct superclass*. An example of a class is one we can name `Person` that stores information about a person in general. We can create children classes of `Person` such as `Friend`, `Acquaintance` and `Enemy`. These three classes may have children classes of their own.

A class or subclass at any level may have *instances*. An instance is a specific example of an individual belonging to that class. For example, we can have instances named `$erin` and `$ron` of the class called

Person, and instances such as $tommy and $jeff of the subclass Friend.

The reason for organizing classes in a hierarchy is to be able to store information about a related set of classes and instances in an efficient manner. This efficiency is achieved due to the use of *inheritance*. A descendant class inherits information from its ancestor classes. A property that is associated with a class is inherited by all descendant classes. For example, if we assume that the class Person has a property called name, the children classes Friend, Acquaintance and Enemy all will have the same property name. Usually, object-oriented programming languages allow two types of inheritance:

- inheritance of simple properties or slots or fields; these may be scalars or more complex data structures, and

- inheritance of subroutines that perform useful tasks for the subclass as well as the ancestors.

Subroutines that are defined inside a class definition are usually called *methods* in object-oriented terminology. In Perl, inheritance is performed by using the @ISA list variable in each package where a class is defined. Below we see how this is done.

In the program given below, we first define two classes: Person and Friend. In Perl, we define a class by defining a package of the same name. All information regarding the class must be stated inside this package. Person is the root class, and Friend is its subclass. We do not define the classes Acquaintance and Enemy to keep the program short. The definition of the class Person is contained in the package Person and the definition of the class Friend is contained in the package named Friend. The class Friend is a direct child class of the class Person.

Finally, in the program, we have the package main. In this package, we define two instances of the class Person and two instances of the class Friend. Then, we print the information contained in these four instance objects. When we print the contents of the instances of the child class Friend, we note that it inherits two methods set_name and get_name from the parent class Person. We also note that Perl allows inheritance of methods only. It does not allow inheritance of simple fields like most other programming languages do. Inheritance of simple properties of a class must be simulated using inheritance of subroutine-based properties or methods. We see how this is done in the example program that follows.

Program 5.16

```
#!/usr/bin/perl

package Person;
#If we write 'use strict' here, we will have problems because the @ISA
#variable in a package cannot be declared with 'my'. We can write
#'use strict' in package Person if it was put in a module Person.pm by itself.

sub make{               #A method to create an instance of class Person
    my ($self, $class);
    $self ={};          #Initialize $self to reference an empty hash.
    $class = $_[0];     #This is the class of the instance to create
    $self -> {name} = undef;  #Set the 'name' field to an undefined value
    bless ($self, $class);  #$self is 'blessed' to become an instance of $class
    return $self;
}

sub set_name {          #A method to assign the name field
  my $self = $_[0];
  $self -> {name} = $_[1];
  }
```

```perl
sub get_name{            #A method to access the name field
  my $self = $_[0];
  my $name = $self -> {name};
  return $name;
}
#------------------------------
package Friend;
#We will have to write 'use Person' here if we had a module Person.pm where
#the definition for Person class was stored;

@ISA = ("Person");    #A 'Friend' is a subclass of class 'Person'

sub make {              #A constructor method for class 'Friend'
 my $self = {};         #Class 'Friend' has two fields and inherits one from
 my $class = $_[0];  #parent class 'Person'
 $self -> {hometown} = undef;  #Set the two fields to 'undef'
 $self -> {age} = undef;
 bless ($self, $class);  #Person has no parents
}

sub set_hometown {
  my $self = $_[0];
  $self -> {hometown} = $_[1];
 }

sub get_hometown{
  my $self =  $_[0];
  return $self -> {hometown};
}

sub set_age {
  my $self = $_[0];
  $self -> {age} = $_[1];
 }

sub get_age{
  my $self = $_[0];
  return $self -> {age};
}


#-----------------------------------
package main;
#We will have to write 'use Friend' here if we had a module Friend.pm where
#the definition for Person class was stored;

#Create two instances of Person, and two instances of Friend
my ($erin, $ron,  $jeff, $tommy);

$erin = Person -> make; $erin -> set_name ("Erin");
```

```
$ron = Person -> make; $ron -> set_name ("Ron");

$jeff = Friend -> make; $jeff -> set_name ("Jeff");
$jeff -> set_hometown ("Boulder");
$jeff -> set_age (21);

$tommy = Friend -> make; $tommy -> set_name ("Tommy");
$tommy -> set_hometown ("Washington DC");
$tommy -> set_age (18);

#Print information contained in the object instances
printf "%-7s\n", $ron -> get_name;
printf "%-7s\n", $erin -> get_name;
printf "%-7s%-15s%d\n", $jeff -> get_name,
       $jeff -> get_hometown, $jeff -> get_age;
printf "%-7s%-15s%d\n", $tommy -> get_name,
       $tommy -> get_hometown, $tommy -> get_age;
```

The output of running this program is given below.

```
Ron
Erin
Jeff    Boulder         21
Tommy   Washington DC   18
```

5.6.1   Deciding How an Object Instance is Stored

Before writing an object-oriented program in Perl, we must first decide how individual object instances are implemented. We can have any implementation we want, but most commonly an object instance is implemented in terms of an anonymous hash as we have done in the program given above. Some programmers may use anonymous arrays for implementing object instances.

In the program, the components of the hash used to define an object instance are assigned values by making calls to methods. The two classes we have defined, Person and Friend, each has a set of methods to assign values to and access values of components of the anonymous hashes that implement object instances.

5.6.2   Defining a Class

We have defined two classes: Person and its child class Friend. In any class we define, we should preferably have a *constructor* subroutine or method. The constructor method is used to create instance of the class. In our program, both methods have constructor classes. In each case, the constructor method is named make. Many programmers prefer to name the constructor methods new.

5.6.2.1   Defining a Constructor Method

Let us look at the constructor method make in the Person class. It has two lexically scoped scalars: $self and $class. $self is assigned a reference to the empty hash that is going to store the object instance being created. $class stores the name of the class whose instance is being created. The value of $class comes from the call to the make method. Instances of class Person contain only one field or slot or property: name. The value of the name slot is given the value undef at initialization. Next, the make method calls a pompously named built-in function `bless` that takes two arguments: a reference to an instance being created, and the class to which this instance belongs. `bless` anoints the reference variable as a reference to an instance of the named class. In creating an instance of a class, the `bless` function must always be used. The `bless`ed data structure which is an anonymous hash still remains a hash, but additionally becomes an instance of the class under consideration. Finally, the `make` method returns a reference to the instance that was created. As an example, in the program, we create an empty instance of the class `Person` called `$erin` in the `main` package by making the call

```
$erin = Person -> make;
```

Here, the method `make` of the class `Person` is being called with one argument which is the string `'Person'`. The syntax is a little unusual in that the argument `'Person'` is not written down explicitly. The same call could have been made as

```
$erin = Person::make ('Person');
```

with exactly the same meaning. The `->` operator provides a shortcut for writing calls to methods. `->` is an infix operator. It has the class name on the left side and the name of a method for the class on the right side. The first argument of the method is implicitly assumed to be the name of the class in string form. In this specific instance, when we use the `->` syntax call to `make` there is no explicit argument, but `'Person'` is assumed to be the implicit first argument anyway.

5.6.2.2   Defining Methods that Access and Manipulate Fields of an Instance

The `Person` class has only one field: `name`. In addition to the constructor named `make`, in the definition of the `Person` class we have two more subroutines or methods: `set_name` and `get_name`. Once an empty instance of class `Person` is created using the `make` method, the `set_name` method is used to set the name field in this instance. In our example, in the package `main`, we call the `set_name` method in the following manner.

```
$erin -> set_name ("Erin");
```

This call sets the `name` field of the instance of `Person` pointed to by the referencing scalar `$erin` to `"Erin"`. The `get_name` method takes a variable that points to an instance of the `Person` class and returns the value of the `name` field. For example, we can get the value of the `name` property or field of the `$erin` variable by writing

```
printf "%-7s\n", $erin -> get_name;
```

5.6.2.3   Defining a Child Class

Next, in our program, we define a class called `Friend`. This is a subclass of the `Person` class. This is indicated by setting a list variable called `@ISA` in the beginning of a class's definition. In our case, the statement that establishes this child-parent or *is-a* relationship is given as

```
@ISA = ("Person");
```

As a result of the fact that the class `Person` is a parent of the class `Friend`, all methods in the `Person` class are inherited by the `Friend` class unless expressly overridden. In this case, the methods `set_name` and `get_name` of the `Person` class are inherited by the `Friend` class. However, the constructor method `make` is not inherited by `Friend` from `Person` because `Friend` defines a `make` method of its own. When a subclass defines a method of the same name as that of a parent, the inheritance of the method is overridden.

So, we see that the child class Friend has its own make method for constructing its own instances. In the make method in the Friend class, two fields hometown and age are initialized to undef. These are two fields that an instance of Friend has in addition to the field name that is inherited from the Person class. In this example, we see that although Perl does not allow inheritance of a field or a slot, such inheritance of a field can be effectively implemented by inheriting methods that assign value and access the value of the field.

The Friend class has four other methods or subroutines: set_hometown, get_hometown, set_age and get_age. These are used for setting and accessing the values of the two fields. A sequence of statements that create and assign values to fields of an instance of the Friend class are given below.

```
$tommy = Friend -> make; $tommy -> set_name ("Tommy");
$tommy -> set_hometown ("Washington DC");
$tommy -> set_age (18);
```

$tommy is created as instance of the class Friend by calling the make method of the Friend class. Next, the name field of the instance pointed to by $tommy is set to "Tommy" by the call to the set_name method. We must note that the set_name method is not actually defined in the Friend class, but is inherited from the Person class. Following this statement, we have two calls to two methods defined in the Friend class, namely, set_hometown and set_age.

At the very end of the program, we print the information contained in the four object instances that the program creates. For example, the information referenced by the $tommy variable is an instance of Friend and this information is printed using

```
printf "%-7s%-15s%d\n", $tommy -> get_name,
        $tommy -> get_hometown, $tommy -> get_age;
```

The output of the program is given below.

```
Ron
Erin
Jeff    Boulder        21
Tommy   Washington DC  18
```

5.6.3   Each Class Definition in a File of Its Own

Of course, instead of having all the class definitions and the main program in just one file as in the previous program, we can write each class definition in a file of its own. Below, we rewrite the program given in the beginning of this section. Now, we have two module files: Person.pm and Friend.pm. We also have a "main" program in a file called allfriends.pl. First, we show the Person.pm file containing the Person module.

Program 5.17

```
#file Person.pm
use strict;

package Person;

#Since there are no variables to export, it is not necessary to use the Exporter
#module and the package-global variable @EXPORT
```

```
sub make{                 #A method to create an instance of class Person
   my ($self, $class);
   $self ={};             #Initialize $self to reference an empty hash.
   $class = $_[0];        #This is the class of the instance to create
   $self -> {name} = undef;  #Set the 'name' field to an undefined value
   bless ($self, $class);  #$self is 'blessed' to become an instance of $class
   return $self;
}

sub set_name {            #A method to assign the name field
  my $self = $_[0];
  $self -> {name} = $_[1];
 }

sub get_name{             #A method to access the name field
  my $self = $_[0];
  my $name = $self -> {name};
  return $name;
}

1;
```

As usual, this module defines a constructor method called make, and two additional methods set_name and get_name for the class Person. Note that we do not use the mechanism we discussed earlier for exporting any names or identifiers. Of course, there are no variables or fields in the module to export. Method names need not be exported. A method is called on an object instance of a specific class, and Perl knows where to find the definition.

Next, we show the Friend.pm file containing the Friend module.

Program 5.18

```
#file Friend.pm
use strict;
package Friend;
use Person;
use Exporter;

use vars ('@ISA', '@EXPORT');
@ISA = ("Person", "Exporter");   #A 'Friend' is a subclass of class 'Person'
#Since no variables are exported, it is not really necessary to use
#the Exporter class and the package-global @EXPORT variable.
#Subroutines are available outside a package without being exported
#when used with an object instance.
@EXPORT = ();             #Here, it's set to the empty list.

sub make {                #A constructor method for class 'Friend'
 my $self = {};           #Class 'Friend' has two fields and inherits one from
 my $class = $_[0];       #parent class 'Person'
 $self -> {hometown} = undef;  #Set the two fields to 'undef'
 $self -> {age} = undef;
```

```
  bless ($self, $class);   #Person has no parents
}

sub set_hometown {
  my $self = $_[0];
  $self -> {hometown} = $_[1];
  }

sub get_hometown{
  my $self =  $_[0];
  return $self -> {hometown};
}

sub set_age {
  my $self = $_[0];
  $self -> {age} = $_[1];
  }

sub get_age{
  my $self = $_[0];
  return $self -> {age};
}

1;
```

The `Friend` module defines the class `Friend`. `Friend` is a sub-class of the class `Person` defined as module `Person` in the file `Person.pm`. All files are in the same directory. This module defines a constructor method make, and four additional methods: `set_hometown`, `get_hometown`, `set_age` and `get_age`. A module needs to return a true value when used. That is why `1;` is the last statement of a module. It is always true.

The main program is called `allfriends.pl` and is given below.

Program 5.19

```
#!/usr/bin/perl
#allfriends.pl

use strict;
use Friend;

#Create two instances of Person, and two instances of Friend
my ($erin, $ron, $jeff, $tommy);

$erin = Person -> make; $erin -> set_name ("Erin");
$ron = Person -> make; $ron -> set_name ("Ron");

$jeff = Friend -> make; $jeff -> set_name ("Jeff");
$jeff -> set_hometown ("Boulder");
$jeff -> set_age (21);
```

```
$tommy = Friend -> make; $tommy -> set_name ("Tommy");
$tommy -> set_hometown ("Washington DC");
$tommy -> set_age (18);

#Print information contained in the object instances
printf "%-7s\n", $ron -> get_name;
printf "%-7s\n", $erin -> get_name;
printf "%-7s%-15s%d\n", $jeff -> get_name,
       $jeff -> get_hometown, $jeff -> get_age;
printf "%-7s%-15s%d\n", $tommy -> get_name,
       $tommy -> get_hometown, $tommy -> get_age;
```

Note that a module cannot be executed, only the program `allfriends.pl` can. The output of this program is the same as before, but is repeated below.

```
Ron
Erin
Jeff    Boulder        21
Tommy   Washington DC  18
```

5.7 Pre-Defined and Downloadable Modules

Perl has a large number of pre-defined modules. The modules are all downloadable from The Comprehensive Perl Archive Network (CPAN) at *www.cpan.org* or many of its mirror or copy sites. For Unix machines including Macintosh OS X, modules are easily downloadable and installable. For a Windows system, a large number of modules are available from *www.activestate.com* in addition to CPAN. The modules available at *www.activestate.com* are a subset of those found at CPAN. These are the best choice for downloading if the Perl running is ActivePerl. ActivePerl is easy to install on Windows systems. On a Unix machine, one should use

```
%perl -MCPAN -e shell
```

to manage modules including installation. ActivePerl contains a program called ppm (Perl Package Manager) to perform similar tasks. Perl is usually able to download and install modules from CPAN or one of its many mirrors on its own. But, sometimes it fails. In such a case, one should try the following steps. The steps are clearly spelled out at the CPAN Web site for many different kinds of machines. The details given below pertain to Unix or Unix-like systems only.

1. Find the module's source file and download it to one's system. One must have root or super-user permission to install modules in general. On Unix machines permissions are an issue, but not usually on Windows or Macintosh machines prior to OS X. It is possible to install Perl modules in one's own directory as a user. But, in such a case, they are unavailable to any other user unless the permissions are changed. The downloaded file comes with a `.tar.gz` extension. In particular, the example module we install for illustration purposes is FreezeThaw, version 0.41. Its compressed source archive file found at CPAN is `FreezeThaw-0.41.tar.gz`. This module is able to store complex data in a file in string form and later retrieve it from the file in its original form.

2. This file has been compressed using the GNU compression program gzip. Therefore, it has to be uncompressed.

```
%gunzip FreezeThaw-0.41.tar.gz
```

This produces a file `FreezeThaw-0.41.tar`. This a so-called *tar* archive and should be unarchived.

```
%tar -xvf FreezeThaw-0.41.tar
FreezeThaw-0.41/
FreezeThaw-0.41/Changes
FreezeThaw-0.41/FreezeThaw.pm
FreezeThaw-0.41/Makefile.PL
FreezeThaw-0.41/MANIFEST
FreezeThaw-0.41/README
FreezeThaw-0.41/t/
FreezeThaw-0.41/t/FreezeThaw.t
```

In the particular case under consideration, this produces a directory called `FreezeThaw-0.41` in the current directory. It usually has the following files among many others: MANIFEST, `Makefile.PL`, README., and `test.pl`. It may have sub-directories. Many Perl modules are not pure Perl modules, but have many files in C. Therefore, many C language files may be present. In addition, files with extensions `.xs`, `.xsi`, `.xst`, etc., may appear. These files allow a C language program to be linked to Perl programs. We do not discuss how this can be done here.

3. We go to the `FreezeThaw-0.41` directory by `cd`ing to it. The MANIFEST file usually lists the important files. This is what the file contains for the `FreezeThaw` module.

```
FreezeThaw.pm
t/FreezeThaw.t
MANIFEST
Makefile.PL
Changes
README
```

We can read the README file to see how the installation process should proceed next. The `Makefile.PL` file looks like the following.

```
use ExtUtils::MakeMaker;
# See lib/ExtUtils/MakeMaker.pm for details of how to influence
# the contents of the Makefile that is written.
WriteMakefile(
    NAME => 'FreezeThaw',
    VERSION_FROM => "FreezeThaw.pm",
    );
```

The `Makefile.PL` is a Perl program that uses a package called `ExtUtils::MakeMaker`. Without worrying about the details of what actually happens, in short, it probes the current computer system for the existence of various software tools and libraries that are essential for performing the installation process. Executing the `Makefile.PL` script creates a file called `Makefile`.

```
%perl Makefile.PL
Checking if your kit is complete...
Looks good
Writing Makefile for FreezeThaw
```

Usually, the output is a lot longer. It produces a file called Makefile suited to the current system. The Makefile file is usually quite long and contains instructions regarding how the source should be compiled, how tests should be performed, and how temporary directories and files created should be cleaned up after installation, etc.

4. We next run the following command.

```
%make
```

In this case, the printout is like the following.

```
mkdir blib
mkdir blib/lib
mkdir blib/arch
mkdir blib/arch/auto
mkdir blib/arch/auto/FreezeThaw
mkdir blib/lib/auto
mkdir blib/lib/auto/FreezeThaw
mkdir blib/man3
cp FreezeThaw.pm blib/lib/FreezeThaw.pm
Manifying blib/man3/FreezeThaw.3pm
```

It looks at the Makefile file and compiles with the right flags, i.e., with the appropriate compiler options. It usually uses a C compiler. The next command to run is the following.

```
%make test
PERL_DL_NONLAZY=1 /usr/bin/perl -Iblib/arch -Iblib/lib
    -I/usr/lib/perl5/5.6.0/i386-linux -I/usr/lib/perl5/5.6.0
    -e 'use Test::Harness qw(&runtests $verbose); $verbose=0;
    runtests @ARGV;' t/*.t
t/FreezeThaw.......ok
All tests successful.
Files=1, Tests=27,  0 wallclock secs ( 0.19 cusr +  0.01 csys =  0.20 CPU)
```

This runs one or more specified tests that come with the distribution. Some tests may fail. But, the installation can proceed even if some of the tests fail. Quite frequently, automatic installation of Perl modules using

```
%perl -MCPAN -e shell
```

fails because some tests do not succeed. But, using the manual process we are undertaking now, the installation can still be made, even though the module is not 100% functional.

5. Finally, if most tests are satisfied, we can go ahead and install by typing the following.

```
%make install
Installing /usr/lib/perl5/site_perl/5.6.0/FreezeThaw.pm
Installing /usr/share/man/man3/FreezeThaw.3pm
Writing /usr/lib/perl5/site_perl/5.6.0/i386-linux/auto/FreezeThaw/.packlist
Appending installation info to /usr/lib/perl5/5.6.0/i386-linux/perllocal.pod
```

This process, if successful, places the module's files in the appropriate places. It also places the documentation in the right place. Documentation for an installed module can be read by running the `perldoc` system command with the module name as the argument. On a Red Hat Linux machine, the usual location is in sub-directories below `/usr/lib/perl5/`. The files may be distributed into several directories.

The process discussed works only on Unix systems including Mac OS X. Similar steps exist for Windows systems when downloading a module from CPAN. If ActivePerl is the version of Perl, an easy-to-run program called `ppm` helps install modules very easily. Not all modules are available at the ActivePerl site. So, even on a Windows machine, once in a while we have to through an elaborate process.

5.8   An Example Downloadable Module: `GD.pm`

In this section, we briefly discuss a downloadable module called `GD.pm`. It an be downloaded from *www.cpan.org* using the steps given in Section 5.7. It is a module that allows a programmer to draw colored graphical objects with a large number of drawing primitives in formats such as JPEG or PNG.

Some downloadable modules provide an object-oriented interface, others a functional interface, and others both. `GD.pm` provides only an object-oriented interface. To understand how the module can be used to program one should run

```
%perldoc GD.pm
```

after the module has been installed and read the documentation. Usually, the documentation contains a wealth of information.

The `GD.pm` module has a large number of methods. They are classified in its accompanying documentation into the following categories.

- Creating and saving images
- Creating and controlling colors
- Creating special effects such as brushes and tiling
- Drawing commands
- Copying images
- Drawing characters and strings
- Drawing polygons
- Dealing with fonts

The program reads a number from the terminal, `chomps` it to remove the trailing newline, makes it into a string using the `sprintf` function. The program draws this string into a graphical object that is later saved in two formats: JPEG and PNG. The JPEG image can be seen on a Web browser without any plug-ins. The program is given below.

Program 5.20

```perl
#!/usr/bin/perl
#file counterGD.pl
use strict;
use GD;

my ($number, $counter, @digits, $length);
my ($im, $black, $white, $blue, $green, $i);
```

```
print "Please give me an integer to draw>>";
$counter = <STDIN>;
chomp $counter;

@digits = split(//, "$counter");
print "digits = @digits\n";
$length = length($counter);
print "length = $length\n";
$im = new GD::Image($length*14,20);
$black = $im->colorAllocate(0, 0, 0);
$white = $im->colorAllocate(255, 255, 255);
$blue = $im->colorAllocate(0,0,255);

for ($i=0; $i < $length; $i++)
{ $im->string(gdLargeFont, 2+$i*14, 0, $digits[$i], $white);
  if($i < $length-1)
  { $im->filledRectangle(12+$i*14, 0, 13+$i*14, 20, $blue);
  }
}

open PNG, ">$counter.png";
open JPEG, ">$counter.jpg";
print PNG $im->png;
print JPEG $im->jpeg;
close PNG;
close JPEG;
```

To understand the program well, one should read the documentation for GD.pm for the description of the methods available. To draw a graphic object, the new method is invoked.

```
$im = new GD::Image($length*14,20);
```

This creates an object of type GD::Image. The arguments are length and height of the image object in pixels. Then, a few colors are created or allocated. The colors are $black, $white, and $blue. colorAllocate takes three arguments: red, green and blue (RGB). Black has each of the three components 0, and white has each component the maximum value of 255.

Next, in the for loop, the image is drawn. string is a method that draws a string. The arguments are font description, x position, y position, the string to draw, and the color to draw with, respectively. Here, the current digit is drawn in white. A rectangle is drawn around the digits in blue. filledRectangle is a drawing method. Its arguments are x_1, y_1, x_2, y_2, and a color. It draws a rectangle whose lower left coordinates are (x_1, y_1), and upper right coordinates are (x_2, y_2), and fills it up with the specified color. Finally, two files are opened. A JPEG image is drawn in one and a PNG image is drawn in another. The png method creates a description of the current image in PNG format. Similarly, the jpeg method writes the image in JPEG format. The file names have the digit in front followed by .jpg or .png as extension. An interaction with the program is given below.

```
Please give me an integer to draw>>1234567890123
digits = 1 2 3 4 5 6 7 8 9 0 1 2 3
length = 13
```

Figure 5.1: A Counter Image Produced Using GD.pm

Two image files are produced: `1234567890123.jpg` and `1234567890123.png`. Both files contain the exact same image. The image produced viewed on a Linux machine with the *Electric Eyes* (`ee`) utility looks like the one in Figure 5.1.

5.9   Conclusions

Perl has a very large number of pre-written modules that can perform almost any conceivable task. All these modules are documented at the Comprehensive Perl Archive Network (CPAN) site with the URL `http://www.cpan.org`. Documentation on these modules is available for consultation to determine if it is suitable for the purpose desired. Once installed, documentation is available using the `perldoc` command with the name of the Perl module as an argument. The rest of the book introduces a large number of Perl modules suitable for a wide range of tasks. However, a book such as this can only touch the tip of the iceberg. There are a great many modules that are not mentioned in this book, let alone discussed. The reader is encouraged to venture into *www.cpan.org* to get a better glimpse of the types of modules and their capabilities.

5.10   Exercises

1. *(Easy: Documentation Reading)*
   Use `perldoc` to learn about modules and object-oriented programming in Perl. Read the sections given in Table 5.1 by providing the section name as an argument to `perldoc`.

Section Name	Description
perlmod	How Perl modules work
perlmodlib	How to write and use Perl modules
perlmodinstall	How to install Perl modules from CPAN
perlobj	Perl objects
perlboot	Perl object-oriented tutorial for beginners

   Table 5.1: Modules and Object-oriented Programming in Perl

   If you downloaded Perl from *www.cpan.org*, these should be automatically installed in your system. If you cannot find these on your system, visit *www.cpan.org* and read the documentation on these topics.

2. *(Easy: Documentation Reading)*
   There is a very large number of Perl modules contributed by individuals from around the world. Visit *www.cpan.org* on the Web and get an overall view of the modules available at the current time. They are classified according to the type of work they perform. Read detailed documentation on modules that interest you.

3. *(Easy: Module Installation)*

   Install two modules of your choice from *www.cpan.org*. Perform installation on your own, without using an installation tool. That is, go through the steps discussed in this Chapter. Document any problems, if any, you face during installation. Try to find solutions for your problems. Write simple application scripts to test that the modules you install work. Figure out where files corresponding to modules are helpt on your system. Read documentation on these modules on your system using `perldoc`.

4. *(Easy: Class Definition)*

   Define a class called `Circle` in a file of its own. It has three fields: `centerX`, `centerY` and `radius`. These are exported for others to access. Define two methods: `findCircumference` and `findArea` in the `Circle` class. The class has a constructor that takes no arguments and sets all the class fields or variables to undefined values.

   Now, in a separate file `circles.pl`, define an instance of `Circle` called `myCircle`. Specify values to `myCircle`'s fields: `centerX`, `centerY` and `radius`. Compute the area and circumference of `myCircle` and print them.

5. *(Easy: Class Definition, Several Constructors)*

   Define a class called `Circle` in a file of its own. The class has three fields or properties: `centerX`, `centerY` and `radius`. It also has three constructor methods: new, new1 and new2. new does not take any arguments and sets the values of the three fields to undefined values. new1 takes three arguments correspoding to `centerX`, `centerY` and `radius`. It sets the values of the fields to the values passed from the call. new2 takes a value corresponding to `radius` as argument. It sets the value of the field to the argument passed to it.

   It also has two non-constructor methods: `findCircumference` and `findArea` as in the previous problem.

   Write an application file `circles.pl`. Make calls to each one of the three constructor methods and the two non-constructor methods. Create three instances of circles. Provide values for the three fields of each circle. Use the `toString` method to print each circle's details in a readable manner.

6. *(Easy: Printing Values in Readable Format)*

   Extend the code you write for the previous problem by adding a `toString` method in the `Circle` class. It prints the values of the fields of an instance of `Circle` in a nice readable string format.

7. *(Easy: Class Definition, Several Constructors)*

   Define a class called `Person`. It has four fields: `name`, `age`, `homeTown` and `profession`. There are three constructor methods: make, make1, and make2. make takes four arguments corresponding to the four fields. make1 takes two arguments corresponding to `name` and `profession`. make2 takes an argument corresponding to `name`.

   Write an application script `person.pl` and make the following calls.

```
$jugal = Person->make1 ("Jugal", "professor");
$justin = Person->make ("Justin", 19, "model", "Colorado Springs");
$christopher = Person->make2 ("Christopher", "software engineer");
```

8. *(Easy: Class Definition)*

   Define a class `Name` in a file of its own. It has three fields: `firstName`, `lastName` and `title`. These are exported. It has one constructor function: new that takes two arguments, corresponding to `firstName` and `lastName`. It sets the values appropriately. The method `setTitle` gets one argument and uses it to set the value of the `title` field. `getInitails` returns the value of the `firstName` field. The method `getLastFirst` returns a string containing the last name, followed by a comma, followed by the first name. The method `getFirstLast` returns a string containing the first name followed by the last name.

Write a script `names.pl` that assigns values to the variables and then calls the methods.

9. *(Easy: Class Definition, Inheritance)*
   Write two class definitions: `Rectangle` and `Square`. A `Rectangle` has several exported fields: `height`, `width`, `perimeter` and `area`. The class has a constructor new that takes two number corresponding to `height` and `width` as argument. It has three other methods; `findPerimeter`, `findArea` and `toString`. The method `findPerimeter` computes the perimeter of a rectangle. The method `findArea` computes the area of a rectangle. `toString` returns a string containing the values of a rectangle's four fields in an easily readable format. The string returned can be printed to gather information about instances of rectangles.

   The class `Square` is a subclass of `Rectangle`. It has one method `toString`. It inherits from `Rectangle`. It has no other methods of its own. This `toString` method overrides the `toString` method of the parent class.

   Write a script `geometry.pl` that instantiates a rectangle and a circle and prints their areas, perimeters and string descriptions.

10. *(Easy: Class Definition, Random Numbers)*
    Define a class called `Dice` in a file of its own. It has six instance fields, one field for each face. For example, we may have an instance of a dice whose faces are labeled $1, 2, 3, 3, 4$ and 4 respectively. Write an instance method `throwDice()` that simulates a throw of a dice. When one throws a dice, one of the faces shows up on top at random. The method returns the integer etched on the face on top.

    Write a script called `dice.pl` that creates an instance of a `Dice`, and assigns labels to each of the faces of the dice. Make a few calls to `throwDice` to simulate a sequence of dice throws.

11. *(Easy: Class Definition, Time String Formats)*
    Define a class called `Time` with the following instance fields: `year`, `month`, `date`, and `hour`. Each one of these fields is an integer. The field `hour` stores the hour in a military style ranging from 0 to 23, 0 being midnight and 12 being noon. The `year` field is stored as an integer that has four digits in it, such as 2002. Make sure the constructor and other methods check for validity of the data provided as argument.

    Write a method `toString()` for this class that returns the time. Sample calls to `toString()` return the following.

```
4 PM on 4/5/02
6 AM on 4/5/02
noon on 4/5/02
midnight on 4/5/02
```

For the cases given above, the values of the fields (i.e., `year`, `month`, `date` and `hour`) for the instances of the `Time` class are

```
2002, 4, 5, 16
2002, 4, 5, 6
2002, 4, 5, 12
2002, 4, 5, 0
```

respectively.

12. *(Easy: Class Definition, Arithmetic, Geometry)*
    Define a class called `Rectangle`. It has four fields: `bottmLeftX, bottomLeftY, height` and `width`. The first two fields give the X and Y coordinates of the bottom left vertex in two-dimensional space. All fields are exported.

    (a) Write a method called `findPerimeter()` for the class that takes no argument and returns the area of a rectangle.

    (b) Write a second method by the name `findCircleRadius()` that returns the radius of the circle that has the same perimeter as that of a rectangle.

    (c) Write a third method called `printTopRight()` that takes no argument and returns nothing, but prints to screen the X and Y coordinates of the top right vertex of a rectangle.

    Assume that values of X increase toward the right of the screen. Also assume that values of Y increase toward the top of the screen.

    Write a script called `rectangles.pl` and make sample calls to all methods.

13. *(Easy: Class Definition, Arithmetic, Geometry)*
    Define a class called `Sphere`. A sphere is an object that has three-dimensional extent. A sphere has a center and a radius. It takes three coordinates to specify the center of an instance of `Sphere`. Declare the data fields for the `Sphere` class accordingly. In addition, allow each instance of a sphere to have fields for storing its surface area and volume.

    Now, we define four constructors for the `Sphere` class. Let the first constructor take three coordinates and a radius and create an instance of `Sphere`. The second constructor creates an instance of `Sphere` given a radius. It makes the center default to (`0.0, 0.0, 0.0`), the origin of the three dimensional space. The third constructor creates an instance of a sphere with the same radius and center as that of another. The fourth constructor creates an instance of `Sphere` and makes the center default to (`0.0, 0.0, 0.0`) and the radius default to `1.0`.

    Define a method `findArea` to compute the surface area of a sphere. Define a method `findVolume` to compute the volume of a sphere. Define a method called `toString()` that takes no argument and returns a string containing the details of an instance of `Sphere`. You will call this method several times to print the details of the spheres in an accompanying script called `spheres.pl`.

    In `spheres.pl` create four instances of `Sphere`. The first one has its center at (`2.0, 3.0, 4.0`) and radius `1.0`. The second one simply has a radius of `5.0` as is located at the default location of (`0.0, 0.0, 0.0`). The third one is located where the first one is located. Its radius is same as that of the first one. The fourth one has a default radius of `1.0` and the center is located at (`0.0, 0.0, 0.0, 0.0`).

    Make sure you call each of the constructors you define at least once.

    Compute the surface areas and the volumes of the four spheres. Store the surface areas and volumes for the spheres in the fields that you have defined for them when you defined the class `Sphere`. Print the results in a nicely formatted table. Use the `toString` method to print the details of a sphere instance.

14. *(Medium to Hard: Class Definition, Family Relatoinships, Inheritance)*

    In this problem, you enter information about individuals in the Kalita family and print information out about individuals in the family as asked. The information you see is fictitious.

    You define two classes that work together to solve this problem. The classes are `Person` and `Date`. You define each class in a separate file. Also, write a script called `kalitas.pl`.

Next, define a class called Date in a file called Date.pm. An instance of Date has three data fields: year, month, and date. Each one of this is an integer. The class has one constructor. It takes a year, a month, and a date as input.

There is a second method in the class called before() that takes an argument that is another instance of the class Date. It returns a boolean. In particular, if we have declared $d1 and $d2 as given below:

```
$d1 = Date->new (2002, 1, 12);
$d2 = Date->new (2002, 2, 28);
```

the call

```
$d1->before ($d2);
```

returns true.

There is a third method in the class called toString(). It returns a string corresponding to an instance of the Date class. For example, corresponding to $d1 above, it returns the string "1/12/2002".

You now define a class called Person in a separate file called Person.pm. The fields are firstName, middleName, yearlyIncome, birthDay, mother and father. Note that birthDay is of type Date. mother and father are of type Person. firstName and middleName are string. The class has several methods. You can write more methods than asked if you think it helps solve sub-problems for the methods that I ask. There is a constructor that takes a first name (a string) and a date of birth (a Date).

There are two methods setFather() and setMother(). Each one takes a Person as argument. They give values to the father and mother fields respectively.

Now, define a method called findFather() that finds the father of a certain person. It returns an object of type Person. Note that we may not have a father for each person. In such a case, return an undefined value.

Define a method called findFatherName() that returns the first name of the father of a certain person. If there is no father, it returns the string "Unknown". This method should call the findFather() method defined above.

Now, define a method called findMother() that finds the mother of a certain person. It returns an object of type Person. Note that we may not have a mother for each person. In such a case, return an undefined value.

Define a method called findMotherName() that returns the first name of the mother of a certain person. If there is no mother, it returns the string "Unknown".

Now, define a method called findPaternalGrandFather() that finds the paternal grand father of a certain person. It returns an object of type Person. Note that we may not have a paternal grandfather for each person. In such a case, return an undefined value.

Define a method called findPaternalGrandFatherName() that returns the first name of the paternal grand father of a certain person. If there is no paternal grandfather, it returns the string "Unknown".

Next, write a method setYearlyIncome() to set the yearly income of a certain person. Write a method findRicher() that finds the richer of two persons. The next method is called findOlderPersonName(). It finds the name of the older between two persons. Finally, write a toString() method to print details about an individual. It can help you print the family relationship table you need to print in the application file kalitas.pl.

The file kalitas.pl creates instances of individuals in the Kalita family performs computations using the methods defined for the two classes specified earlier. Create seven instances of Person with the following details.

First Name	Date of Birth
Joel	July 5, 1966
Jake	July 5, 1966
Mukul	December 14, 1960
Dole	September 11, 1967
Ben	March 10, 1933
Nirala	August 15, 1943
Ron	January 21, 1998

Use the setFather() method in the Person class to indicate the following.

First Name	Father
Joel	Ben
Jake	Ben
Mukul	Ben
Dole	Ben
Ron	Jake

Use the setMother() method in the Person class to indicate the following.

First Name	Mother
Joel	Nirala
Jake	Nirala
Mukul	Nirala
Dole	Nirala

Next print a table giving the family relationships in the Kalita family. That is, print everyone's mother and father in a table.

Next, using the setYearlyIncome() method in the Person class, indicate the following.

First Name	Yearly Income
Joel	59565.05
Jake	110020.29
Mukul	20005.12
Dole	5010.31
Ben	1100.42
Nirala	0
Ron	0

Next, print who is richer of Joel and Jake using the findRicher() method in the Person class. Also, print who is richer of Jake and Dole.

Now, print who is older of Mukul and Joel. Finally, print who is older of Joel and Jake. Use the findOlderPersonName() method in the Person class to do so.

15. *(Medium to Hard: Class Definition, Arithmetic, Amortization)*

There are three overall goals to the assignment. First, you will print a loan amortization table assuming the loan uses simple interest. Second, you will print a table that shows how many months it takes to pay back loans. You will do this varying the principal borrowed, the rate of interest and the monthly payment.

What classes do you need to define

This assignment asks you to define a class called `Loan` to solve a problem. You also write an application script called `loans.pl`. You can write any other classes and methods if you think it will help solve the problem.

Class `Loan`

Define a class called `Loan` in a file called `Loan.pm`. An instance of `Loan` has four data fields: `principal`, `rate`, and `principalRemaining` and `monthlyPayment`.

You need to write two methods for this class. You can write additional methods if it helps you.

There is a method in the class called `printPaymentTable()` that takes no argument. It prints an amortization table given a `Loan` object with a certain principal, a certain rate of interest and a certain monthly payment.

This is how we calculate the amortization or payment table. Suppose you take out a loan with principal p, rate of interest r, and monthly payment m. We assume that interest is calculated monthly and it is simple interest.

We assume that during the month we take out the loan, we do not pay anything. But, starting the next month, which we call the first month of the loan, we pay a fixed amount back to the lender. This amount is m. This amount is divided by the lender into two parts. The first part i goes to pay interest on the principal remaining at the beginning of the month. and the next part l goes to lower the principal. i is computed using the standard formula for simple interest which is

$$i = p * n * r / 100$$

where n is the duration in years for which the interest is computed. Here, we are talking about a month and hence $n = \frac{1}{12}$.

l is computed as $m - i$. So, every month the principal is reduced by an amount equal to l. Therefore, the next month when we calculate interest, it is calculated on the remaining principal, not the principal we borrowed to start with.

Every month subsequent to the first month, we pay to the lender the same monthly payment m, but progressively the share of it toward interest comes down because the principal keeps on getting smaller. Consequently, in every subsequent month, we pay more toward the principal.

As a result of our payments, the principal keeps on coming down, and finally one month, it becomes lower than the monthly payment. This is the last month of the loan's duration. During this month, we pay the principal remaining and get done with the loan.

The first required method `printPaymentTable()` for the `Loan` class computes what is called an amortization table that shows how for every month during the duration of the loan, how much of your monthly payment goes toward the principal, how much goes toward paying interest, and how much principal remains to be paid.

The second method called `monthsNeedeToPayBack()` is a modification of the first method. This second method tells us how many months are needed to pay back a loan with a certain principal at a certain rate of interest when we have a certain constant monthly payment to make.

Application script `loans.pl`

It creates instances of loans, changes various fields of loans and prints two tables: an amortization table for a specific loan, and a table showing the number of months to pay back a loan for various values of principal, rate of interest and monthly payment.

First, you print the amortization table for a loan for which the principal is $10,000.00$, the rate of interest is 18.00% and the monthly payment is 200.00. We call this instance of a loan: `visaLoan`.

Next, we print the table that shows the number of months needed to pay back a loan. We vary the amount of principal borrowed from $15,000$ to $18,000$ increasing with a step of 1000.00. For each loan amount, we vary the rate of interest from 8.00% to 18.00% with a step of 1.00%. For each combination of a principal and a rate of interest, we vary the monthly payment from $100.00 to $1000.00 incrementing with a step size of $100.00. For each combination of principal, rate of interest and monthly payment, we print the number of months needed to pay back the loan.

Just be aware that if the monthly payment is too low, a loan may never be repaid. In such a case, say that the number of months to pay back is `infinity`. Also, make sure that all your results are printed only up to two decimal places. Perform all your computations to only two places after the decimal. You can perform regular computation with more digits, but you must modify the results in every stage so that they are rounded to two places after the decimal point.

Chapter 6

On Files and Directories

In This Chapter

Perl has an extensive set of built-in functions that deal with files and directories. We discuss some of these functions in this chapter.

We have seen in earlier chapters how to read from a file and write to a file. We can copy a file by reading from it and then writing to another. In this chapter, we see that we can perform many operations on files and directories directly without having to read or write lines of content. What we discuss here works in the Unix environment including Macintosh OS X. They should mostly work in other environments such as IBM-compatible PCs and pre-OS X Macintoshes, but are not guaranteed to do so. This chapter also illustrates that recursive programming can be a natural tool in handling a graph such as a directory structure on a computer. There are many examples of recursive subroutines in this chapter. The chapter is primarily devoted to the study of directories and how to perform various operations on them.

6.1   File Test Operators

File test operators are discussed in Section 1.13. We discuss additional file test operators in this chapter. They are -s, -M, -A, and -C.

6.2   Directory Handles

In Perl, we can create a directory handle and read the list of files in a directory. A directory handle is just like a filehandle in many ways, but there are differences. To open a file, we use the open command with a filehandle argument. To open a directory, we use the opendir command with a directory handle. When we open a file with the open command, we can indicate whether we want to open the file for reading, writing, appending, and reading as well as writing, etc. However, with directory handles, we can only read the names of files in the directory, we cannot write or append to a directory. This sounds quite logical. Just opening a directory does not accomplish anything unless we read the contents of the directory. readdir gives the list of files in a directory. Once we have read a directory and obtained the file list, we can close the directory handle before we process the files. closedir is the command to close a directory handle. The following program prints the names of the files in the current directory in a sorted order.

Program 6.1

```
#!/usr/bin/perl

use strict;
opendir (THISDIR, ".");
my @files = readdir (THISDIR) or warn "Cannot open directory .; $!";
closedir THISDIR;

$" = "\n";
my @sortedFiles = sort @files;
print "@sortedFiles\n";
```

Unlike open used with filehandles, opendir requires a comma after the first argument. opendir is used only for opening a directory for reading the list of files. Opening a directory simply means that the program has access to the data structure stored by the operating system. Once we have read the list of files, we can close the directory handle if we are simply interested in getting the list of files. It is not necessary to keep the directory handle open unless we want to do further processing of the directory data structure or *node*, as it is called. It is customary to use all uppercase letters for the name of a directory handle although it not required. This is also the case with filehandles. In the Unix operating system, the current directory is known by the special name . and .. is the name of the parent directory. These two are printed as the contents of any directory. In the program given above, we open the current directory by using . to refer to it. Therefore, if we want to process the list of files obtained by reading a directory, we should remove these two files from the file list.

The output of the program given above looks like the following.

```
.
..
a
argv.pl
```

```
b
c
copy.pl
copy0.pl
copy1.pl
file-age.pl
file-read.pl
file-read1.pl
fileread.pl
include
junk
oldest.pl
printfile.pl
printfile1.pl
printfile2
printfile2.1
printfile2.2
read-file.pl
readdir.pl
readdir1.pl
readdirR.pl
readdirR0.pl
readdirR1.pl
readdirR2.pl
readdirR3.pl
readdirR4.pl
remove
size.pl
size1.pl
sizeR.pl
sizeR1.pl
tls
tls2
```

The following program also reads the names of files in a directory. It does so using a subroutine called readdirNR. The subroutine readdirR removes the two entries . and .. from the list of files it returns.

Program 6.2

```perl
#!/usr/bin/perl

use strict;

sub readdirNR{
    my ($dir) = @_;
    opendir DIR, $dir;
    my @files = readdir DIR;
    closedir DIR;
    @files = grep {$_ !~ /^(\.|\.\.)$/} @files;
    return @files;
}
```

```perl
my @files = readdirNR (".");

$" = "\n";
my @sortedFiles = reverse sort @files;
print "@sortedFiles\n";
```

The subroutine removes the two special file names using the line given below.

```perl
@files = grep {$_ !~ /^(\.|\.\.)$/} @files;
```

From the list of files @files, this statement greps or culls those lines that satisfy the condition given in the block of statements that grep takes as the first argument. The regular expression given inside the block checks to see if the file name does not literally match either . or .., and only if it does not match, it keeps the name of the file. Therefore, @files after the grep statement is executed has all but the two special files. The pattern given above could also have been written as the following.

```perl
/^[.]{1,2}$/
```

6.3   Reading Directories Recursively

We now write a program that reads a directory recursively and prints the list of files in the directory and in all subdirectories. We expand the subroutine used in the previous program and make it recursive for achieving our objective.

Many people find it difficult to write recursive programs. Recursive programs can be avoided in many situations, but in a context like the present one, they are the natural choice. A recursive subroutine calls itself one or more times. For a recursive subroutine to terminate, the subroutine must have one or more termination conditions that must be reached by the subroutine after a sequence of calls. Finding the termination conditions and specifying them in the program correctly is half the battle in writing recursive programs. Recursive subroutines are usually more expensive than subroutines that use loops, but if time efficiency is not of crucial concern, they are useful and natural in many situations.

The program that follows has a subroutine called readdirR that is called recursively.

Program 6.3

```perl
#!/usr/bin/perl
use strict;

sub readdirR{
    my @FDList = @_;

    my $first = shift @FDList;

    if (!$first){
        return ();
    }
    elsif (-f $first){
        return ($first, readdirR (@FDList));
    }
```

```
    elsif (-d $first){
        opendir DIR, $first || warn "Cannot open directory $first: $!";
        my @files = readdir DIR ;
        closedir DIR;
        @files = grep {$_ !~ /^[.]{1,2}$/} @files;
        @files = map {"$first/$_"} @files;
        return ($first, readdirR (@files), readdirR(@FDList));
    }
}

####main program###########
$" = "\n";
my @FDToRead = @ARGV;

if (!@FDToRead)
    {@FDToRead = ".";}

my @allFiles = readdirR (@FDToRead);
@allFiles = sort @allFiles;
print "@allFiles\n";
```

If the program is stored in file readdirR0.pl, the following are some example calls in Unix.

```
%readdirR0.pl *
%readdirR0.pl .
%readdirR0.pl ..
%readdirR0.pl a
```

In the first call, the program's command line arguments consist of the names of all the files in the current directory. In the second call, the program is given the current directory as the only command line argument. In the third call, the program is given the parent directory of the current directory as its argument. In the fourth call, the argument is a file or directory with the name a. Thus, the program takes a list of files and directories as argument. The program returns the names of all the files and directories included recursively in the arguments given. If the program is called with a list of files only, the same list is returned. But, if there are one or more directories in the command line arguments, these directories are opened recursively and the list of files in them returned. If there is no command line argument given, it lists the list of files in the current directory recursively.

Let us first look at the main part of the program. The program takes the command line arguments and calls the subroutine readdirR with the list of command line arguments. If no command line argument is given, readdirR is called with the directory named . which in the case of Unix stands for the current directory. readdirR reads the list of all files and directories recursively and returns the result list which is sorted and printed.

Let us now look at the subroutine readdirR. It is a recursive subroutine. In other words, there are one or more calls to itself inside its body. We see three recursive calls.

As mentioned earlier, a recursive subroutine must have one or more termination conditions. Otherwise, it runs for ever. Not providing a correct termination condition is one very common error that people make in writing recursive programs. The subroutine readdirR uses the local variable name @FDList for the list of files and directories sent to it. Here F stands for files and D stands for directories. The subroutine obtains the first element of @FDList by shifting it and calls it $first. Depending on what this first element is, it takes various actions in the code that follows. Now, it is possible that @_, the list of files and directories passed to the subroutine, is empty to begin with, i.e., before assigning @FDList and shift it. This condition is used as a termination condition in what follows.

When readdirR is called the first time, it always gets a non-empty list of files and directories. The subroutine makes one or more recursive calls depending on the arguments the initial call gets. These recursive calls may make other recursive calls in turn. The recursive calls can be visualized in the form of a recursion tree showing which call makes which other calls with what arguments. The recursion tree must end in leaves that correspond to the termination conditions. In other words, every leaf corresponds to a call to readdirR with an empty argument. This call returns immediately and returns nothing. When a recursive call returns, it passes the result back to the previous call which processes them to obtain its own results. Results are passed back until the initial call to the subroutine returns its results to the main program. This returned value is used to assign the variable @allFiles in the main program. This returned value contains all the files and directories with their relative path names starting from the current directory. This list is sorted and printed.

The subroutine readdirR has an if-elsif-elsif statement. The main action takes place here. Before anything is done by the subroutine, it tests to see if the termination condition corresponding to an empty input list @_ is satisfied. If the condition is satisfied, no recursive call is made and the subroutine does nothing. This ensures termination. The input list @_ is empty if the value of $first obtained by shifting @_ is empty.

Next, the subroutine proceeds by case. Depending on whether $first is a file or a directory, it takes appropriate actions discussed below.

If $first is a file, the subroutine performs the following return statement.

```
return ($first, readdirR (@FDList));
```

To compute the returned value, a recursive call is made to readdirR with the argument @FDList, that is, the list of all files and directories but the first. The argument passed to the recursive call of readdirR is smaller than the argument passed to the original call. Similarly, other recursive calls that this recursive call makes have still smaller arguments, ensuring eventual termination of the program. This recursive call makes as many recursive calls as necessary to readdirR. Once all recursive calls are finished and it has the list of all files and directories, it makes a list by placing $first in the beginning of the list returned by the recursive call. This new list contains all the files and directories that we are seeking and is returned to the main program.

If $file is a directory itself, the subroutine opens this directory, reads the list of files in it, and removes the two special files named . and .. referring to the current directory and the parent directory, respectively. It makes a call to map to prepend each file name with the name of the directory. The call is given below.

```
@files = map {"$first/$_"} @files;
```

This can be done with a loop also. This step is crucial because each Perl program has a home directory where it is situated and if it has to open and read files and directories that are not situated in the home directory, the names have to be qualified with directory information. Otherwise, the program will not be able to access the files or directories although it has their names. Finally, the subroutine makes two recursive calls and creates a list of files by placing $first in the front and returns the resulting list. This is the list of all files and directories requested. The return statement is given below.

```
return ($first, readdirR (@files), readdirR(@FDList));
```

The first recursive call recursively reads the list of all files and directories in the files and directories contained within the directory $first, except of course the . and .. directories. The second recursive call obtains the list of files and directories contained in the rest of the argument list passed to the original subroutine.

We now show the list printed by this program for several calls. Let the file where the program is stored be readdirR0.pl. The call

```
%readdir .
```

produces the output like what is given below. Here % is the Unix prompt.

```
.
./a
./a/a1
./a/a2
./a/a3
./a/ad1
./a/ad1/ad1a
./a/ad1/ad1b
./a/ad1/ad1c
./a/ad1/ad1d1
./a/ad2
./a/ad3
./argv.pl
./b
./c
./copy.pl
./copy0.pl
./copy1.pl
./file-age.pl
./file-read.pl
./file-read1.pl
./fileread.pl
./include
./junk
./oldest.pl
./printfile.pl
./printfile1.pl
./printfile2
./printfile2.1
./printfile2.2
./read-file.pl
./readdir.pl
./readdir1.pl
./readdirR.pl
./readdirR0.pl
./readdirR1.pl
./readdirR2.pl
./readdirR3.pl
./readdirR4.pl
./remove
./remove/rmTeXfiles.pl
./remove/rmTeXfiles1.pl
./remove/rmTeXfiles2.pl
./tls
./tls2
```

The output contains the list of all files in the current directory. The . is contained in this list because it is the name of the directory with which we call the program. If the call were

```
%readdirR0.pl *
```

the same list is produced, but it does not contain the . as an element. Also, the file and directory names are not prefixed with ./ as it is in the earlier call. Finally, if we make the call

```
%readdirR0.pl a
```

the output is the following.

```
a
a/a1
a/a2
a/a3
a/ad1
a/ad1/ad1a
a/ad1/ad1b
a/ad1/ad1c
a/ad1/ad1d1
a/ad2
a/ad3
```

We now present another recursive program that does exactly the same as the program given above, however, it does it a little differently.

Program 6.4

```perl
#!/usr/bin/perl
use strict;

sub readdirR{
    my ($dir) = @_;
    opendir DIR, $dir || warn "Cannot open directory $dir: $!";
    my @files = readdir DIR ;
    closedir DIR;
    @files = grep {$_ !~ /^(\.|\.\.)$/} @files;

    my @simpleFiles = grep -f, (map {"$dir/$_"} @files);
    my @directories = grep -d, (map {"$dir/$_"} @files);
    my @recursiveFileList = map {readdirR ($_)} @directories;

    return (@simpleFiles, @directories,  @recursiveFileList);
}

##main program###########
$" = "\n";
my @FDToRead = @ARGV;

if (!@FDToRead)
    {@FDToRead = ".";}

my @simpleFiles = grep -f, @FDToRead;
my @directories = grep -d, @FDToRead;
```

```perl
my @recursiveFiles = map {readdirR ($_);} @directories;

my @allFiles = sort (@FDToRead, @recursiveFiles);
print "@allFiles\n";
```

This program uses map liberally. In the main program, we separate out the command line arguments into two lists: @simpleFiles—a list of files and @directories—a list of directories. It then calls the subroutine readdirR once for each member of the list @directories. This is accomplished in the line given below.

```perl
my @recursiveFiles = map {readdirR ($_);} @directories;
```

The subroutine readdirR takes only one argument–a directory. The map function is used to call readdirR on each element of @directories. The names of the files and directories returned by this recursive call is stored in @recursiveFiles. The main program then creates the list @allFiles by concatenating two lists: @FDToRead—the list of files and directories given as command line argument; and @recursiveFiles—the list of files and directories obtained by recursively reading the directories from among the command line arguments.

The subroutine readdirR gets only one directory as argument. It reads the list of files in the directory and removes the special files . and .. from the list. From this list, like in the main program, it separates out the files and directories, and then recursively reads the directories. It returns the list of files and directories after all recursive calls terminate by executing the statement given below.

```perl
return (@simpleFiles, @directories,  @recursiveFileList);
```

6.4   Changing the Current Directory

Perl has a function called chdir that changes the current directory. Every program running has a current working directory. By default, it is the directory in which the program is located. Therefore, when a program accesses files and directories with just their names, it assumes that they are in the current working directory. Of course, it is possible to give absolute file names such as /home/kalita/classes/cs301/perlcode/read.pl. In Unix, an absolute file name starts with / indicating the root directory for the whole system. It is also possible to give relative path names such as ../../read.pl or files/remove/recursive.pl. In the first case, the file name takes two levels up in the file hierarchy and finds the file read.pl. In the second case, the file is located two levels below the current working directory.

We can change the current working directory in the program using the chdir command. This may obviate giving a qualified path name as we work on files and directories in the program. The first program in this section reads a directory by first changing the current working directory.

Program 6.5

```perl
#!/usr/bin/perl
$"= "\n";
my $path = "/home/kalita/classes/cs301/perlcode/";
chdir ($path) or die "Cannot chdir to $path: $!";
opendir (DIR, ".") or die "Cannot open $path: $!";
my @files = readdir DIR;
print "@files\n";
chdir ();
```

The program has a variable $path that stores the fully qualified name of a directory. The program's current working directory to begin with is wherever it is located. It then chdirs to the directory specified in $path. chdir changes the current working directory for the program. As a result, when it opendirs the current working directory . next, it opens the directory specified by $path. The program then reads the list of files in the current directory, and prints them out. Finally, it calls chdir once again with no argument. Such a call to chdir changes the current working directory to the home directory of the user. This may not necessarily be the directory in which the program is located. In Unix, every user has a home directory which can be reached with the shortened name ~*username*.

After changing the current working directory inside program, it is always a good habit to bring the working directory back to where it was before. Otherwise, it can become quite confusing to locate files and directories. For the program given above, we made the assumption that it is situated in the user's home directory.

6.5   Finding the Current Working Directory

In the previous section, we assumed the program is situated in the home directory of the user. This need not always be the case. The Perl language does not have a built-in function to find the current working directory. But, it provides a standard module called Cwd that has such a function. This package comes with the Perl language source distribution. The function is called cwd. It is called with no arguments to find the current working directory inside a program. Modules are discussed in Chapter 5.

Below we have a variation of the program given in the previous section.

Program 6.6

```perl
#!/usr/bin/perl
use Cwd;
use strict;

$"= "\n";
my $initDir = cwd ();
print "The current working directory is: ", $initDir, "\n";
my $path = "/home/kalita/classes/";

chdir ($path) or die "Cannot chdir to $path: $!";
print "The current working directory is: ", cwd (), "\n";
opendir (DIR, ".") or die "Cannot open $path: $!";
my @files = readdir DIR;
print "@files\n";

chdir ($initDir);
print "The current working directory is: ", cwd (), "\n";
```

The program first declares that it uses the Cwd package using the use statement. It finds and prints the current working directory by making a call cwd(). Next, it changes the current working directory to the one specified in the $path variable. It opens the current working directory, reads the list of files and prints the list. Having done that, it calls chdir with the name of the original directory to change the current working directory back to what it was before. The program prints the current working directory in several places to make sure that things happen as expected. The output of the program may look like what is given below.

```
The current working directory is: /home/kalita/classes/cs301/perlcode/files
The current working directory is: /home/kalita/classes
.
..
cs420-520
cs482-582
cs586
cs145
cs589
cs460-560
penn-classes
phd-exams
cs305
cs112
cs583
cs480-580
cs301
lfix.tex
tutoring-projects
decl.tex
penn-comp-ling-class
cs472-572
acm-prog-contest
cs401
The current working directory is: /home/kalita/classes/cs301/perlcode/files
```

Finally, we have a program that reads and prints the names of files recursively. It is a variation of the recursive programs we have seen earlier in the chapter. But, unlike the previous programs that use qualified relative names to access a directory as well as print names of files and directories, this program chdirs to a directory before reading its contents. It does so recursively. However, it also remembers which directory to go back to once it has finished reading a certain directory. The program is given below.

Program 6.7

```perl
#!/usr/bin/perl
use strict;
use Cwd;

sub printdirR{
    my ($recursionLevel, @FDList) = @_;
    my $first = shift @FDList;

    if (!$first){return ()}
    elsif (-f $first){
        print "  " x $recursionLevel, "$first\n";
        map {printdirR ($recursionLevel, $_);} @FDList;
    }
    elsif (-d $first){
        my $currdir = cwd ();
```

```
        chdir ($first) or warn "Cannot chdir to $first: $!";
        opendir DIR, "." or warn "Cannot opendir $first: $!";
        my @files = sort (readdir DIR);
        closedir DIR;
        @files = grep {$_ !~ /^[.]{1,2}$/} @files;
        print "  " x $recursionLevel, "$first/\n";

        printdirR ($recursionLevel + 1, @files);
        chdir ($currdir);
        map {printdirR ($recursionLevel, $_)}  @FDList;
    }
}

#main program
$" = ", ";
my @FDToPrint = @ARGV;
if (!@FDToPrint) {@FDToPrint = ".";}
map {printdirR (0, $_);} (sort @FDToPrint);
```

If the main program is not called with any command-line arguments, the program decides to print the files and directories contained within the current working directory. It calls the recursive subroutine printdirR for each element of the list @FDToPrint by mapping the function call on the list. The statement that maps the call is given below.

```
map {printdirR (0, $_);} (sort @FDToPrint);
```

printdirR is called with two arguments: a number that denotes the level of recursion and an element from the list obtained by sorting @FDToPrint. The first argument to printdirR is used to print the names of files and directories in a nicely indented manner.

The subroutine printdirR first separates out the two arguments passed to it. The list of files and directories is called @FDList. It obtains the first element of @FDList and calls it $first. Next, we have an if-elsif-elsif statement that recursively prints contained files and directories. If $first is null, i.e., if @FDList is empty, the subroutine does not do anything, but returns immediately.

If $first is a regular file, the subroutine prints the name of the file. It precedes the name of the file by a number of spaces based on the number of recursion levels the program is in at the time. Once the name of the file is printed with the correct level of indentation, it calls printdirR recursively on the remaining list of files and directories: @FDList. It passes the current level of recursion to the recursive calls.

If $first is a directory, we need to traverse this directory recursively and print the files and directories contained within it. For this purpose, the subroutine has to change the current working directory recursively if it goes down levels of directory. Once a recursive call is over, the subroutine has to remember which directory to go back to. Therefore, before making any recursive calls, it remembers where it is by executing the following statement.

```
my $currdir = cwd ();
```

The subroutine than goes down to the directory $first by doing a chdir. It reads the contents of the current working directory, and removes the two special files . and .. corresponding to the current directory and the parent directory, recursively. Before doing anything else, the subroutine prints the name of the directory $first, and appends a / to indicate that it is a directory and not a simple file. Next, it executes the following statements.

```
printdirR ($recursionLevel + 1, @files);
chdir ($currdir);
map {printdirR ($recursionLevel, $_)}  @FDList;
```

The first statement calls `printdirR` recursively on each of the files and directories contained within the original directory `$first`. Since, this makes the program move down one level deeper in the file hierarchy, the program increases the recursion level by 1 as it makes these recursive calls. This ensures that the contained files and directories are printed with the proper number of spaces in the front. These recursive calls may cause the program to change the current working directory many times. Once all the recursive calls are over, the subroutine comes back to the working directory `$currdir` which corresponds to the directory named in `$first`. This ensures that after all subtrees of the file hierarchy are read, the program is back where it started. If we do not make this call to the remembered directory, the subroutine would not know where it is supposed to be in the file hierarchy. After the subroutine reestablishes the current working directory, it again makes recursive calls to `printdirR` on the remaining list of files and directories stored in the list `@FDList`. This time, the recursion level is not increased because it is reading files and directories at the same level as `$first`.

Assuming the program is stored in the file `printddirR.pl` and there is a directory named a in the directory where the program is contained, we can making the following call.

```
%printdirR.pl a
```

The output of the call is something like what is given below.

```
a/
  a1
  a2
  a3
  ad1/
    ad1a
    ad1b
    ad1c
    ad1d1/
  ad2/
  ad3/
```

As we can see, the files and directories are printed nicely indented to show the inclusion structure or the file hierarchy. The program indicates directories by printing a / at the end.

Finally, we end this section with a comment on the recursive subroutine. In the `if-elsif-elsif` statement that we see in the program, it is not really necessary to have the following `if` statement.

```
if (!$first){return ()}
```

It is because the program does nothing for the case when `$first` is empty. We write this to keep the various recursive subroutines in this chapter maintain consistent structure. However, it is acceptable in this case to have a program that has just an `if-elsif` structure with the `if` testing whether the first element of the list is a file and `elsif` testing whether the first element is a directory.

6.6   Deleting a File

Assuming we have write permission to a directory, we can delete a file by using the `unlink` command. In Unix, we must have write access to a directory to delete a file although write access to the file is not necessary. File permissions are usually not an issue in Windows and the Macintosh operating system prior to OS X.

Below, we write a program that takes a command line argument that it considers to be a list of files. It removes those files that have ~ (the tilde) at the end. One frequently sees such files on Unix machines. In Unix, these are usually old copies of files that were created as backup by various text editors during the editing process.

Program 6.8

```perl
#!/usr/bin/perl
use strict;

my $file;
my @files = grep /~$/, @ARGV;
foreach $file (@files){
    unlink $file;
}
```

The `unlink` command reduces the number of links a file has by 1. For files that have not been linked from elsewhere, the number of links is just one. So, for such files, `unlink` deletes them.

Assume the program given above is stored in a file `cleand1.pl`. A possible call to the program is given below.

```
%cleand1.pl *
```

`unlink` returns the number of files that it has successfully unlinked. However, in this program, we are not using the returned value for any purpose.

As a second example, we consider an environment in which we use the text processor called *LaTeX* or *TeX*. These word processors create files with `.dvi`, `.log` and `.aux` endings. They may also create other temporary files depending on the task requested. These temporary files are normally not needed after processing and printing the files. The following program deletes all such files from a directory. We can run this program after word processing a document file with LaTeX.

Program 6.9

```perl
#!/usr/bin/perl

use strict;
my ($file, @extensions);
@extensions = qw(dvi log aux);

my @files = map {my $extension = $_;
                 grep /\.$extension/, @ARGV;
                 }
                 @extensions;
print "files = @files\n";

foreach $file (@files){
    unlink $file;
}
```

This program has a set of extensions for files it wants to remove. The extensions are stored in the list @extensions. In this case, the extensions are dvi, log, and aux. Next, the program has a block of code that is mapped over the list @extensions. This block of code obtains all files with the specified extensions from the list of files in @ARGV and places them in @files. The program, then, goes over all the found files and unlinks them.

If the program is stored in the file rmTeXfiles.pl, a sample call to the program is given below.

```
%rmTeXfiles.pl *
```

This call removes all files in the current directory with the given extensions.

We may want the program to report to us if it cannot delete or unlink any file from the list of files to remove. We can do that by using the warn function along with the call to unlink.

A version of the previous program that uses warn is given below.

Program 6.10

```
#!/usr/bin/perl

use strict;
my ($file, @extensions);
@extensions = qw(dvi log aux);

my @files = map {my $extension = $_;
                 grep /\.$extension/, @ARGV;
                 }
                 @extensions;
print "files = @files\n";

foreach $file (@files){
    if (!(unlink $file)){
        warn "Cannot delete file $file: $!";
    }
}
```

The unlink command returns true if it is able to remove the file. Otherwise, it returns false. When unlink returns false in the program given above, the program calls warn to print a warning message. The unlink command sets the special variable $! if there is an error. In string context, $! is a descriptive error message saying what the problem is.

In Unix systems, it is possible to remove files even if the user does not have read or write permission or both for the file. The ability to remove a file is determined by if the user has permission to write to the directory containing the file. Therefore, if the directory containing the files does not have write permission, the program will print an error message saying something like the following.

```
Cannot delete file a.aux: Permission denied at rmTeXfiles1.pl line 15.
```

Here, rmTeXfiles1.pl is the name of the program that we are running.

The warn function is more expressive than a print statement. The warn and the unlink functions can be used as show in either of the following statements.

```
unlink $file || warn "Cannot delete file $file:",    $!;
unlink $file or  warn "Cannot delete file $file:",    $!;
```

If unlink is able to delete the file, it returns true. In such a case, the warn command is not run. However, if unlink fails and returns false, || (or, or) allows the warn command to be executed. Both || and or are short-circuit operators. or is easier to read and has lower precedence than ||.

6.7   Deleting Files Recursively

We now write a program that deletes files with specified extensions recursively from a list of files and directories given to it as command-line argument. The reader should read carefully the recursive programs given earlier in the chapter to follow this program. The program we write removes only regular files. It does not remove directories. In other words, after the program executes, the directories still exist although the files are all removed recursively. One may write an extension of this program that deletes a directory if all the files and sub-directories in it have been deleted. It is left as an exercise.

Program 6.11

```perl
#!/usr/bin/perl

use strict;

my @extensions =  qw(dvi log aux);

#Return 1 if $file has an extension in the list @exts
#Otherwise, return 0
sub hasExtension{
    my ($file, @exts) = @_;
    my $ext;

    foreach $ext (@exts){
        if ($file =~ /\.$ext$/){
            return 1;
        }
    }
    return 0;
}

#delete files recursively
sub deleteR{
    my @FDList = @_;
    my $first = shift @FDList;

    if (!$first){
        return ();
    }
    elsif (-f $first and hasExtension($first, @extensions)){
        unlink $first;
    }
    elsif (-d $first){
```

```perl
        opendir DIR, $first or  warn "Cannot open directory $first: $!";
        my @files = readdir DIR;
        closedir DIR;

        @files = grep {$_ !~ /^[.]{1,2}$/} @files;
        my @simpleFiles = grep -f, (map {"$first/$_"} @files);
        my @directories = grep -d, (map {"$first/$_"} @files);

        map {if (hasExtension ($_, @extensions)){
                print "Deleting $_\n";
                unlink $_;
            }
  } @simpleFiles;

        map {deleteR ($_)} @directories;
    }
}

#######main program
my @FDToDelete = @ARGV;

if (!@FDToDelete){ @FDToDelete = ".";}
map {deleteR $_} @FDToDelete;
```

The main part of the program is quite simple. If the program is not called with command-line arguments, the program looks at the current directory or the . directory. The main program maps the deleteR subroutine on every file given to it as a command-line argument, or ., otherwise.

The program has two subroutines: hasExtension and deleteR. hasExtension is a helper subroutine that returns true if the name of a file given to it as argument has an extension specified in the variable @extensions that is global to the whole program.

The main work is done in the subroutine deleteR. The structure of the recursive subroutine is similar to that of one of the recursive routines we have seen earlier in the chapter.

The subroutine deleteR is called with a list of files and directories. This list is called @FDList inside the subroutine. The termination condition for this recursive subroutine occurs if @FDList is empty. Otherwise, the subroutine looks at the first element of @FDList and does different things based on whether it is a file or a directory. This first element is called $first. If $first is a file and has one of the extensions specified as undesirable, the program unlinks the file. If it is a file and does not have such an extension, we do not do anything.

If $first is a directory, we opendir it, and read the list of files in it. From this list of files we remove . and .. that correspond to the current and the parent directories, respectively. We then separate out the files and the directories in the current directory into the lists @simpleFiles and @directories, respectively. In applying the -f and -d tests to check if it is a file or a directory, we must provide the qualified name of the file with respect to the current directory. That is why we prepend the names with $first/ when we map the -f and -d tests on the list of files and directories.

Next, the subroutine looks at the list of files called @simpleFiles and maps a block of statements on this list. This block of statements deletes a file if it has one of the pre-specified extensions. Finally, the subroutine calls itself recursively on every directory. This is done by using map as given below.

```perl
map {deleteR ($_)} @directories;
```

The program prints the names of files it deletes to inform the user. It may be a good idea to modify this `deleteR` subroutine so that it asks the user for confirmation before deleting a file.

6.8   Deleting Directories Recursively

We can delete a directory using the `rmdir` function. It removes a directory if the program's owner has permission to write to the directory. `unlink`, the command used to remove a file should not be used to remove a directory.

Now, we discuss a program that is an extension of the immediately preceding program. Just like the previous program, it recursively removes files that have certain prespecified extensions. In addition, if a directory is already empty to begin with, or becomes empty after the files with the given extensions are removed, the directory is also removed. We modify `deleteR` subroutine in the previous program to do this. The modified subroutine is given below.

```perl
sub deleteR{
    my @FDList = @_;
    my $first = shift @FDList;

    if (!$first){
            return ();
    }
    elsif (-f $first and hasExtension($first, @extensions)){
        unlink $first;
    }
    elsif (-d $first){
        opendir DIR, $first or  warn "Cannot open directory $first: $!";
        my @files = readdir DIR;
        closedir DIR;

        @files = grep {$_ !~ /^[.]{1,2}$/} @files;
        @files = map {"$first/$_"} @files;
        my @simpleFiles = grep -f, @files;
        my @directories = grep -d, @files;
        my @filesToRemove = grep {hasExtension($_, @extensions)} @simpleFiles;
        my @filesToKeep = grep {!hasExtension($_, @extensions)} @simpleFiles;
        my $noOfFilesRemoved = unlink @filesToRemove;

        my $noOfDirectoriesRemoved = 0;
        my $directory;
        foreach $directory (@directories){
            if (deleteR ($directory)){
                $noOfDirectoriesRemoved++;
            }
        }

        if (!@filesToKeep and
            ($noOfFilesRemoved == $#filesToRemove + 1)  and
            ($noOfDirectoriesRemoved == $#directories + 1) ){
            rmdir ($first) or warn "Cannot remove directory $first: $!";
            return 1;
```

```
}
else{
            return 0;
        }
    }
}
```

As before, the subroutine returns nothing if the argument given to it is the empty list. Also like the previous version, deleteR removes the first element of the argument list if it is a file and has a prespecified extension in its name. The difference comes when the first element of the argument given to deleteR is a directory. As usual, it reads the list of contained files and directories, removes the . and .. entries, and then separates out the contents of the current directory into two lists: @simpleFiles and @directories. It then obtains the list of simple files to remove and stores them in @filesToRemove and the list of simple files to keep in @filesToKeep. Then, it executes the statement given below.

```
my $noOfFilesRemoved = unlink @filesToRemove;
```

unlink can take a list as argument. It removes as many files as possible from this list. It then returns the number of files it is able to remove. We note that if unlink is used in this manner, it is not possible to find which files are removed and which files remain afterward to issue warnings or perform other actions.

Next, the program performs the following statements.

```
foreach $directory (@directories){
    if (deleteR ($directory)){
            $noOfDirectoriesRemoved++;
    }
}
```

This is where we loop over the list of directories contained and make a recursive call to deleteR for each directory. This recursive call is made as the conditional of an if statement. deleteR returns 1 if it succeeds in deleting a directory. If the subroutine can delete a directory, it increments the number of directories removed. Keeping count of the number of directories removed is crucial if we want to remove directories recursively.

Then, the following group of statements is executed to determine what deleteR should return.

```
        if (!@filesToKeep and
            ($noOfFilesRemoved == $#filesToRemove + 1)   and
            ($noOfDirectoriesRemoved == $#directories + 1) ){
                if (rmdir ($first)){
                    return 1;
            }
            else {
                    warn "Cannot remove directory $first: $!";
                    return 0;}
}
else{
            return 0;
        }
```

We return 0 if we are unable to delete the directory $first. We can delete a directory only if three conditions are satisfied. First, it must be true that we determine that there are no simple files in it to keep. In other words, there are no simple files to begin with. The second condition to satisfy is that we are able to remove all simple files that we should remove. In other words, no unforeseen conditions occurred (such as lack of permission) allowing us to remove all the files that we want to remove. The third condition is that the subroutine is able to remove all the directories included during the recursive calls it makes. If all these conditions are satisfied, the subroutine deletes the directory $first and returns a value of 1. If the conditions are not satisfied, the subroutine returns a zero. This returned value is used to determine if all the directories are removed recursively.

6.9   Finding the Size of a File

The amount of memory occupied by a file can be obtained by using the -s command. It looks like a file test operator, but in addition to checking for the existence of a file, it returns the size of the file in bytes.

The following program takes a file name as command line argument and if the file exists, returns its size.

Program 6.12

```perl
#!/usr/bin/perl

use strict;

my ($file) = @ARGV;
if (-s $file){
    print "Size of file $file = " . (-s $file) . "\n";
}
else{
    print "File $file does not exist.\n";
}
```

If there is a file called copy.pl in the current directory, and the program given above is stored in a file called size.pl, the call

```
%size.pl copy.pl
```

produces the following output.

```
Size of file copy.pl = 192
```

If the file name given is actually a directory, it returns a certain size that the directory occupies. On the system the author is working with, the size of every directory is 1024 bytes. The program does not return the cumulative size of files contained inside the directory.

We now write a program that takes a list of files as command line argument and prints out the names of the files in sorted order from the largest to the smallest.

Program 6.13

```perl
#!/usr/bin/perl

use strict;

my (@files) = @ARGV;
```

```
my ($file, %size);

foreach $file (@files){
    $size{$file} = (-s $file);
}

foreach $file (sort bySize (keys %size)){
    printf "%-20s%10d\n", $file, $size{$file};
}

sub bySize{
    $size{$b} <=> $size{$a};
}
```

The program stores the sizes of files in bytes in a hash table %size. The key is the name of a file and the corresponding value is the size of the file. It prints the files sorted in descending order of size. It does so by sorting the keys in %size such that keys of files of larger size occur before keys of files of smaller size. The expression that does this sorting is given below.

```
sort bySize (keys %size)
```

Here bySize is a subroutine that takes two predefined arguments $a and $b and returns a value of -1, 0, or 1 depending on whether $a is before, equal, or after $b in sort order. The value returned by bySize is determined by the following statement.

```
$size{$b} <=> $size{$a};
```

Here, the ship operator <=> returns -1 if the value corresponding to $b in %size is less than the value corresponding to $a. In other words, the key (or, the name of a file) with smaller size is pushed to the back in the sort order. Similarly, a file name with bigger size is pushed to the front. If two files have the same size, their order is arbitrary.

Assuming the program is stored in the file size1.pl, the output of the program when called as

```
%size1.pl *
```

looks something like what is given below.

```
readdirR2.pl                1509
readdirR3.pl                1121
file-read1.pl               1066
a                           1024
b                           1024
c                           1024
remove                      1024
readdirR.pl                  882
file-age.pl                  861
readdirR1.pl                 776
include                      732
readdirR0.pl                 717
readdirR4.pl                 717
tls                          680
oldest.pl                    483
```

```
copy1.pl                         438
argv.pl                          403
readdir1.pl                      383
tls2                             362
read-file.pl                     314
file-read.pl                     313
size1.pl                         271
readdir.pl                       215
copy0.pl                         192
copy.pl                          192
size.pl                          171
printfile2                       162
fileread.pl                      160
printfile.pl                     152
printfile2.1                     127
printfile2.2                      51
printfile1.pl                     39
junk                               0
```

Note that all the directories, in the version of Linux operating system that the author uses, have size of 1024, as mentioned earlier.

Next, we extend the program to examine directories recursively. The program given below takes a list of files and directories, and returns the list of files and directories sorted by their size. Directories are opened recursively. The program given here is a modification of one of the recursive programs given earlier.

Program 6.14

```perl
#!/usr/bin/perl
use strict;
$" = "\n";
my %size;

sub sizeR{
    my @FDList = @_;
    my $first = shift @FDList;

    if (!$first){
        return ();
    }
    elsif (-f $first){
        $size{$first} = (-s $first);
        sizeR (@FDList);
    }
    elsif (-d $first){
        opendir DIR, $first || warn "Cannot open directory $first: $!";
        my @files = readdir DIR ;
        closedir DIR;
        @files = grep {$_ !~ /^[.]{1,2}$/} @files;
        @files = map {"$first/$_"} @files;
        $size{$first} = (-s $first);
        sizeR (@files);
```

```
        sizeR(@FDList);
    }
}

sub bySize{
    $size{$b} <=> $size{$a};
}

####main program###########
my @FDToRead = @ARGV;
if (!@FDToRead)
    {@FDToRead = ".";}

sizeR (@FDToRead);

my $file;
foreach $file (sort bySize keys %size){
    printf "%-30s%10d\n", $file, $size{$file};
}
```

This program opens directories recursively by using the subroutine `sizeR`. Whenever it looks at a file or a directory, it stores the size of the file in the hash `%size`.

The subroutine `sizeR` determines the action to take based on the first element of the argument list passed to it. If the argument list is empty, the subroutine terminates. If the first element is a file, it stores its size in the hash table `%size`. If the first argument is a directory, it stores its size in the hash as well. In addition, it calls the subroutine `sizeR` recursively twice: once with the list of files in the directory, and then with the list of all but the first element of the list with which `sizeR` is originally called. The effect of these two recursive calls is to find the size of all files and directories included recursively.

The program prints the contents of the hash in descending size order at the end. The output of this program for the call

```
%sizeR.pl *
```

is something like what is given below.

```
readdirR2.pl                          1509
readdirR3.pl                          1121
file-read1.pl                         1066
a/ad1/ad1d1                           1024
a/ad2                                 1024
c                                     1024
a/ad3                                 1024
remove                                1024
a                                     1024
a/ad1                                 1024
b                                     1024
readdirR.pl                            882
file-age.pl                            861
sizeR.pl                               843
readdirR1.pl                           776
include                                732
```

```
sizeR.pl~                                   717
readdirR0.pl                                717
readdirR4.pl                                717
tls                                         680
oldest.pl                                   483
copy1.pl                                     438
argv.pl                                      403
readdir1.pl                                  383
tls2                                         362
remove/rmTeXfiles1.pl                        326
remove/rmTeXfiles2.pl                        316
read-file.pl                                 314
file-read.pl                                 313
remove/rmTeXfiles.pl                         274
size1.pl                                     271
readdir.pl                                   215
copy.pl                                      192
copy0.pl                                     192
size.pl                                      171
printfile2                                   162
fileread.pl                                  160
printfile.pl                                 152
printfile2.1                                 127
printfile2.2                                  51
printfile1.pl                                 39
a/a2                                           0
a/a3                                           0
junk                                           0
a/ad1/ad1a                                     0
a/ad1/ad1c                                     0
a/ad1/ad1b                                     0
a/a1                                           0
```

6.10   Finding the Age of a File

Perl provides with several functions to find the age of a file or directory. They look like the file test operators because each has a - sign in front. The three age functions or operators are -M, -A and -C. In Unix, a node is maintained for each file or directory that exists in the system. Among other information, the information that a node contains three pieces of time information: the time the file was last modified, the time file was last accessed, and the time the node information for the file was last changed. The node information for a file can be changed even if the file's contents are not modified, e.g., when a file is accessed, or its ownership changed, etc. The first program in this section, simply takes a list of files as command-line arguments, and iterates over all the files passed as argument and print the three pieces of time information stored for it. Perl returns the time in number of fractional days.

Program 6.15

```perl
#!/usr/bin/perl

for ($i = 0; $i <= $#ARGV; $i++){
```

```
    $filename = $ARGV[$i];
    print "\n\nFile no $i: $filename\n";

    printf "\tFile last modified:  %4.4f days ago.\n", -M $filename;
    printf "\tFile last accessed: %4.4f days ago.\n", -A $filename;
    printf "\tFile information last changed: %4.4f days ago\n", -C $filename;

    sleep (1);
}
```

After processing a file, the program waits a second before presenting information on the next file or directory. The `sleep` function does this. The output of the program, when called with a command-line argument * meaning all files in the current directory, looks something like what is given below for one file.

```
File no 35: sizeR.pl
File last modified:  12.1289 days ago.
File last accessed: 4.1983 days ago.
File information last changed: 12.1289 days ago
```

Since file ages are provided in fractional days, in some circumstances it may have to be converted to minutes, seconds, etc., for presentation.

The next program takes a list of files and directories as command-line argument and prints the oldest file where age is counted in terms of modification. In other words, it prints the file that was modified the earliest.

Program 6.16

```
#!/usr/bin/perl
$oldest_age = 0;

while (@ARGV) {
    $file = shift @ARGV;
    $age = -M $file;

    if ($oldest_age < $age) {
        $oldest_name = $file;
        $oldest_age = $age;
    }
}
print "The oldest file is $oldest_name.\n";
print "It is  $oldest_age days old.\n";
```

When called with a command-line argument of *, meaning all files in the current directory, the output of the program looks something like the following.

```
The oldest file is printfile.pl.
It is 1168.4364 days old
```

6.11   Modules that Deal with Files and Directories

So far in this chapter, we have seen in detail how we can work with files and directories using only built-in functions provided by Perl. Perl also provides a large number of packages to make dealing with files and directories easier. We will discuss a few such modules in this section.

6.11.1   Copying Files: `File::Copy` Module

The `File::Copy` module makes copying and moving of files easy. Perl does not have a built-in function to copy files. We have a copying program in Section 1.6.2. In that program, we opened filehandles and read from one file and copied to the other. It is simple, but still a chore.

The following program uses the `copy` method of the `File::Copy` module to make a copy of a file.

Program 6.17

```perl
#!/usr/bin/perl
#file filecopy.pl
use File::Copy;
use strict;

my ($src, $dest) = @ARGV;
if (!$src or !$dest){
    print "Usage: filecopy sourcefile destfile\n";
    exit 1;
  }
File::Copy::copy ($src, $dest) or die "Cannot copy $src to $dest: $!";
```

This program takes two arguments: the file to be copied and the name of the copy. If two arguments are not provided, the program exits with an error. Otherwise, it simply copies the file corresponding to the source to the destination. We use the fully qualified name of the `copy` function to make explicit its source. The following is a call to `filecopy.pl`

```
%filecopy.pl mkdir.pl mkdir1.pl
```

If the directory where the program is running is such that the user has permission to write, the program simply copies the file `mkdir.pl` to new file `mkdir1.pl`.

The `File::Copy` module also provides a method called `move` to rename a file, i.e., move a file to a new location. Its usage is exactly the same as that of `copy`. Here we use a functional interface to call a method of the module.

The two file names specified in calls to `copy` or `move` can be in directories different from where the program is situated. Of course, the original file has to exist for us to be able to copy from it. In addition, the directory into which the file is being copied or moved also must exist. A program cannot copy into a non-existent directory. It does not create the directory if it does not exist. For example, the following call gives an error.

```
%filecopy.pl mkdir.pl a/b/mkdir.pl
Cannot copy mkdir.pl to a/b/mkdir.pl:
    No such file or directory at filecopy.pl line 11.
```

If we want to copy in such a case, we will have to parse the destination file name, obtain the path for the file, create the directories in the path, and then `copy` or `move` the file.

6.11.2   Copying Files Recursively: `File::NCopy` **Module**

Sometimes, it is necessary to copy files and directories recursively. It can be done with not much difficulty following the discussion earlier in the chapter, either recursively or non-recursively. There is a module called `File::NCopy` that makes recursive copying of files and directories really easy. The following program shows the use of `File::NCopy`.

Program 6.18

```perl
#!/usr/bin/perl
#file ncopy.pl

use File::NCopy;

#non-recursive copying
$f = File::NCopy->new();
$f->copy ("jk1.jpg", "jk3.jpg");
$f->copy("jk1.jpg", "aa");
$f->copy("jk1.jpg", "aa/jk4.jpg");
$f->copy("a", "aa");

#recursive copying
$f = File::NCopy->new('recursive' => 1);
$f->copy("a", "aa");
```

The module's functions or methods can be called using a functional interface as well as an object interface. We discuss the object interface here. To start copying, we create a new instance of a `File::NCopy` object. The first instance of the `File::NCopy` object can copy only non-recursively because no options were given to the new method.

The first `copy` method call copies the file `jk1.jpg` to `jk3.jpg`. The second call copies the file `jk1.jpg` into the directory aa. The third call copies the file `jk1.jpg` into the directory aa with the name `jk4.jpg`. The fourth call copies the directory a into the directory aa. A recursive listing of the a directory, at this time, shows the following.

```
a:
b/

a/b:
c/

a/b/c:
jk1.jpg   mkdir.pl*
```

So, there is a directory b under a, and a directory c under a/b and two files in the a/b/c directory. However, the fourth call to `copy` does not copy anything into the aa directory because the copy is not done recursively. To perform a recursive copying, we need to make the `File::NCopy` object recursive as shown in the following declaration.

```perl
$f = File::NCopy->new('recursive' => 1);
```

After this call to new, the following call to copy copies the directory a recursively into the director aa.

```
$f->copy("a", "aa");
```

Now, a recursive listing of the directory aa show the following.

```
aa:
a/  jk1.jpg  jk4.jpg

aa/a:
b/

aa/a/b:
c/

aa/a/b/c:
jk1.jpg  mkdir.pl*
```

6.11.3 Parsing File Names: `File::Basename` **Module**

The `File::Basename` module allows us to parse file names easily. Of course, we can write our own regular expression to parse a file name and get the components out of it. However, things become a little difficult if we want to do it correctly all the time and across platforms. The formats used are different in systems such as Unix, Windows and Macintosh OS 9, for specifying full path names. The `File::Basename` module comes to our help. The following program prompts for a file name and prints its base name and the directory path preceding the base name. The base name is the name of the actual file.

Program 6.19

```
#!/usr/bin/perl
#file basename.pl

use File::Basename;
use strict;

my ($file, $basename, $dirname);

while (1){
     print "Give me a file name: ";
     $file = <STDIN>;
     chomp $file;

     $basename = File::Basename::basename ($file);
     $dirname = File::Basename::dirname ($file);
     print "base name = $basename; path = $dirname\n";
   }
```

The basename function parses the file name and gives the actual name of the file. The `dirname` method gives the path up to the actual file name. Here is a small interaction with this program.

```
%basename.pl
Give me a file name: abc.html
```

```
base name = abc.html; path = .
Give me a file name: /a/b/abc.html
base name = abc.html; path = /a/b
Give me a file name: /usr/home/public_html/work/cs509.html
base name = cs509.html; path = /usr/home/public_html/work
Give me a file name: /usr/home/public_html/work/
base name = ; path = /usr/home/public_html
Give me a file name:
```

The program usually works, but messes up if the directory name separator which happens to be / in Unix, is the last character in the name. Thus, for it to work, we should pre-process the name given so that it works all the time. Here, an error occurs in the last example.

6.11.4   Creating and Removing Directories: `File::Path` **Module**

When dealing with file copying or moving, if the destination for the copy or move action has a path specification with a sequence of directories and one or more directories in the path do not exist, we have to create the destination directory. The built-in function mkdir can be used in this case. We have to extract the path using the function File::Basename::dirname and then split it using the directory separator, and then create the directories one by one from top to bottom. The following program shows how this can be done.

Program 6.20

```perl
#!/usr/bin/perl
#file myMkpath.pl

use strict;
use Cwd;

my ($dirName, $dirSeparator);
my ($rootDir, @dirs);
$dirSeparator = "/";
$rootDir = "/";
$permissions = "0777";

$dirName = $ARGV[0];
die "Usage: myMkpath.pl directoryName\n" unless $dirName;
@dirs = split ($dirSeparator, $dirName);

my $oldDir = Cwd::cwd ();
$dirs[0] = $rootDir if $dirs[0] =~ /^$/;

my $i;
for ($i = 0; $i <= $#dirs; $i++){
  unless (-e $dirs[$i]){
    print "Creating directory " . $dirs[$i] . "\n";
    mkdir ($dirs[$i], $permissions) or die "Cannot create $dirs[$i]: $!";
  }
  chdir ($dirs[$i]) or die "Cannot chdir to $dirs[$i]: $!";
  print "Just chdired to $dirs[$i]\n";
}
```

```
chdir ($oldDir);
```

The program `myMkpath.pl` works only in a Unix of Unix-like environment. For it to work on a Windows machine or a Macintosh (pre-OS X), the values `$dirSeparator` and `$rootDir` have to be given appropriate values for the operating system. We look at such issues in Section 6.11.6.

The program uses the `Cwd` module to use the function `cwd` to obtain the current working directory. The program obtains the name of the directory to create from the command line. The directory specified can be an absolute directory or a relative specification of path.

The program splits the name of the directory given around the directory separator which is / in Unix. If the directory given is relative, e.g., a/b/c/d/e/f/g/h, the path does not start with a /. However, if the directory given is absolute, e.g., /home/kalita/perl/file/a/b/c/d/e/f, the initial character of the path is /, which is the root directory in addition to being the directory separator. When such an absolute file address is split about the directory separator /, we get the empty string as the first element for the separated list of directories, @dirs in this case. Thus, in the case of an absolute directory address, we set the initial directory to $rootDir.

Following the initial pre-processing of the list of directories on the path, the program goes into a `for` loop where it traverses each element in the directory list from the beginning. For example, if the path is relative and is a/b/c/d/e/f/g/h, the loop first looks at the directory a. If this directory does not exist, it creates this directory if it can. The program then `chdir`s to a, whether it is newly created or existed from before. Next, from within this directory a, the program creates the directory b, and so on and so forth. If the path is absolute, e.g., /home/kalita/perl/file/a/b/c/d/e/f, the program first `chdir`s to / which always exists on a Unix machine. It next `chdir`s to /home which exists on some Unix or Unix-like machines such as Linux. If this directory does not exist, the program tries to create this directory if it is possible. Most users do not have the permission to create a directory at the top level. If /home exists, the program next `chdir`s to /home/kalita. Once again, it is a directory most users cannot create. Then, it creates /home/kalita/perl if it does not exist and has the permission to create. A few example interactions with this program are given below.

```
% myMkpath.pl /home/kalita/perl/file/a/b/c/d/e/f
Just chdired to /
Just chdired to home
Just chdired to kalita
Just chdired to perl
Just chdired to file
Just chdired to a
Just chdired to b
Just chdired to c
Just chdired to d
Just chdired to e
Just chdired to f
% myMkpath.pl /a/b/c/d/e/f
Just chdired to /
Creating directory a
Cannot create a: Permission denied at myMkpath.pl line 27.
% myMkpath.pl a/b/c/d/e/f/g/h
Just chdired to a
Just chdired to b
Just chdired to c
Just chdired to d
```

```
Just chdired to e
Just chdired to f
Creating directory g
Just chdired to g
Creating directory h
Just chdired to h
```

The directories in the path have to be created one by one because mkdir can create a directory only one level at a time. This step-wise creation of directories can be avoided if we use File::Path module that provides us with a function called mkpath that is like mkdir, but that can create intermediate directories if necessary, and if it is able to. Using the File::Path module, the previous program can be written much more simply as the one given below.

Program 6.21

```
!/usr/bin/perl
#file myMkpath1.pl

use strict;
use File::Path;

my ($dirName, $permissions);
$permissions = "0777";

$dirName = $ARGV[0];
die "Usage: myMkpath1.pl directoryName\n" unless $dirName;
if (-e $dirName){
    print "Directory $dirName exists\n";
    }
else{
    File::Path::mkpath ($dirName, $permissions)
        or die "Cannot create $dirName: $!";
    }
```

This program simply calls mkpath to create the directory hierarchy if needed. Here is a simple interaction with this program.

```
%myMkpath1.pl a/b/c/d/e/f/g/h
mkdir a
mkdir a/b
mkdir a/b/c
mkdir a/b/c/d
mkdir a/b/c/d/e
mkdir a/b/c/d/e/f
mkdir a/b/c/d/e/f/g
mkdir a/b/c/d/e/f/g/h
```

Here, the program had to create every directory in the path.

Now, we can write a more robust version of the filecopy.pl program discussed in Section 6.11.1. The program is given below.

Program 6.22

```perl
#!/usr/bin/perl
#file filecopy1.pl
use File::Copy;
use File::Basename;
use File::Path;
use strict;

my ($src, $dest) = @ARGV;
my $permissions = "0777";

if (!$src or !$dest){
    print "Usage: filecopy sourcefile destfile\n";
    exit 1;
  }

my $destDirname = File::Basename::dirname ($dest);
unless (-e $destDirname){
  File::Path::mkpath ($destDirname, $permissions) or
      die "Cannot mkpath $destDirname: $!";
}

File::Copy::copy ($src, $dest) or die "Cannot copy $src to $dest: $!";
```

This program parses the destination file name to find the path. If the destination directory does not exist, it creates it using `File::Path::mkpath`. Then, the program copies the source file to the destination file. Below, we see a couple of calls to to the program.

```
% filecopy1.pl mkdir.pl mkdir1.pl
% filecopy1.pl mkdir.pl a/b/c/d/mkdir1.pl
mkdir a
mkdir a/b
mkdir a/b/c
mkdir a/b/c/d
```

The module `File::Path` also provides a function called `rmtree` to remove a directory structure with all contained files and directories. The removal is recursive and is final. So, one should be cautious in using this function. The following program takes a directory name as a command line argument to remove recursively, asks for confirmation, and if confirmed calls `rmtree` on the directory.

Program 6.23

```perl
#!/usr/bin/perl
#file rmtree.pl
use File::Path;
use strict;

my $dir = $ARGV[0];
if (!$dir){
```

```
        print "Usage: rmtree.pl directoryName";
        exit 1;
    }

print "Are you sure you want to delete $dir recursively? (Y|N): ";
my $response = <STDIN>;
chomp $response;
if ($response =~ /^y$/i){
        File::Path::rmtree ($dir) or warn "Cannot rmtree $dir: $!";
    }
```

6.11.5   Recursively Traversing a File Hierarchy

We saw in great detail how we deal with a file hierarchy earlier in this chapter. We discussed how we can write recursive functions to deal with file hierarchies. Perl has a module called File::Find that provides the ability to traverse a file hierarchy recursively. This module makes it quite easy to write the programs that were written from first principles earlier. The module provides a function called find that traverses a file hierarchy and performs useful actions on each element of the file hierarchy. The module has another function finddepth that also traverses the nodes in a file hierarchy, but using depth-first search. For some applications, it is important that the traversal of the file hierarchy is depth-first to ensure that contained files and directories are traversed before the containing directory is traversed. find and finddepth take two arguments each: a reference to a function of no arguments and a top-level directory. Both find and finddepth call the first argument function on every element, i.e., file or directory, in the file hierarchy underneath the top-level directory given as the second argument.

Thus, find or finddepth does the traversal of the hierarchy, and the processing of the current node during traversal simply involves executing the function passed as the first argument to find or finddepth. We can call this function a *node-processing function*. We can do whatever we want, simple or complex, in this function. By changing the definition of this function, we can perform a recursive listing of the files and directories, find the cumulative size of all files and directories in the hierarchy, or find the oldest file. The functions for such tasks are fairly simple. Inside such a node-processing function, three variables are available. They are $File::Find::name, $File::Find::dir, and $_. $File::Find::name contains the fully qualified name of the current file being processed. $File::Find::dir contains the full name of the current (sub-)directory being processed. $_ is the name of the file within the current directory. Thus, this package assigns value to the commonly used special variable $_ and one should keep this in mind when programming. $File::Find::name is actually $File::Find::dir/$_. Our node-processing functions use one or more of these variables to achieve the goal at hand.

First, we write a module called FileR.pm that contains several functions that can be used to traverse file hierarchies in various manners. Next, we present a simple program that shows how the subroutines used defined in FileR.pm are used. The module definition follows.

Program 6.24

```
#file FileR.pm
package FileR;

use File::Find;
use File::Path;
use strict;
my (@ISA,  @EXPORT);
```

```perl
#Export subroutines
use Exporter;
@ISA = ('Exporter');
@EXPORT = qw (lsdirR lsdirTR lsdirBR sizeR rmdirR findOldest);

my (@ALL_FILES, @ALL_TEXT_FILES, @ALL_BINARY_FILES);
my $SIZE;
my ($OLDEST_FILE, $OLDEST_AGE);

#recursive listing
sub lsdirR{
    my ($topDir) = @_;
    @ALL_FILES = ();
    &File::Find::find (\&listAllFiles, $topDir);
    return @ALL_FILES;
  }
sub listAllFiles{
  @ALL_FILES = (@ALL_FILES, $File::Find::name);
}

#recursive listing of text files
sub lsdirTR{
    my ($topDir) = @_;
    @ALL_TEXT_FILES = ();
    &File::Find::find (\&listTextFiles, $topDir);
    return @ALL_TEXT_FILES;
  }
sub listTextFiles{
  my $file = $File::Find::name;
  @ALL_TEXT_FILES = (@ALL_TEXT_FILES, $file) if (-T $file);
}

#recursive listing of binary files
sub lsdirBR{
    my ($topDir) = @_;
    @ALL_BINARY_FILES = ();
    File::Find::find (\&listBinaryFiles, $topDir);
    return @ALL_BINARY_FILES;
  }
sub listBinaryFiles{
  my $file = $File::Find::name;
  @ALL_BINARY_FILES = (@ALL_BINARY_FILES, $file) if (-B $file);
}

#computing cumulative size
sub sizeR{
    my ($topDir) = @_;
    File::Find::find (\&calculateSize, $topDir);
    return $SIZE;
  }
```

```perl
sub calculateSize {
  my $file = $File::Find::name;
  $SIZE = (-s $file) + $SIZE;
}

#recursive removal of contents of a directory
sub rmdirR{
    my ($topDir) = @_;
    print "Are you sure you want to delete $topDir recursively? (Y|N) ";
    my $response = <STDIN>;
    exit unless ($response =~ /^y$/i);
    File::Find::finddepth (\&removeRecursively, $topDir);
  }

sub removeRecursively{
  my $file = $File::Find::name;
  print "Removing file $file\n";
  if (-d $file){
    rmdir $file or warn "Cannot delete directory $file: $!";
   }
   else{
    unlink $file or warn "Cannot delete file $file: $!";
   }
}

#finding the oldest file and its age
sub findOldest{
  print "In findOldest...\n";
  my ($topDir) = @_;
  $OLDEST_FILE = "";
  $OLDEST_AGE = 0;

  File::Find::find (\&findOldestFile, $topDir);
  return ($OLDEST_FILE, $OLDEST_AGE);
}
sub findOldestFile{
  my $file = $File::Find::name;
  my $age = -M $file;
  if ($OLDEST_AGE < $age){
      $OLDEST_AGE = $age;
      $OLDEST_FILE = $file;
    }
}

1;
```

The module starts by declaring its name FileR. It uses modules File::Find and File::Path. It also uses the strict module that makes sure that all variables are declared before first use. We declare two variables as globals.

```perl
my (@ISA,  @EXPORT);
```

These two variables are needed to be able to export names from the FileR package.

For the module FileR to make names of variables and subroutines visible and hence, usable by programs outside, we need to export them. Exporting is done by placing names or identifiers in the @EXPORT list. @EXPORT is a global variable specific to a package. We use the package called Exporter to help with exporting of names from the package. The Exporter package looks for global variables in the package being defined to determine what it exports and how. @ISA is also a per-package global variable that the Exporter module looks at. When a program says use FileR; to use variables and functions defined inside the FileR package, Perl automatically calls a method FileR->import(). In our module definition for FileR, we have not written such a method called import. However, there is such a method in the Exporter package that can be used generally, and that is why we are useing this package. The content of @ISA makes sure that we inherit the import method from the Exporter package. The statement

```
@ISA = ('Exporter');
```

says that the current package or class is a subclass of the Exporter.pm package or class. A subclass inherits from its superior classes. In Perl, to inherit from a package, we need to place the superior package's name in the global variable @ISA. Perl looks at the modules in the @ISA package to inherit any definitions that are not in the current package. The @EXPORT array in the package FileR specifies all the identifiers that can be imported by another package. When another package imports this module FileR, the variables and functions listed in the @EXPORT array become available in the importing package without qualification with package names. That is, the names in the @EXPORT are aliased into the importing package.

The package defines six functions that can be called from outside the package. They are lsdirR, lsdirTR, lsdirBR, sizeR, rmdirR and findOldest. These are all specified in the @EXPORT variable. The package has several global variables that are used by the subroutines in the package. The global variables used by the subroutines in the package are: @ALL_FILES, @ALL_TEXT_FILES, @ALL_BINARY_FILES, $SIZE, $OLDEST_FILE, and $OLDEST_AGE. These global variables are available only within this package and not from the outside.

Not all subroutines in the package can be accessed from the outside. Only the ones in the @EXPORT array are accessible from the outside. Let us look at all the subroutines one by one.

The first exported subroutine is lsdirR that takes a directory name as an argument and obtains a recursive listing of the files. First, it sets the global variable @ALL_FILES to the empty list although it is not necessary to do so. It does so to be doubly sure that there are no extraneous values in the variable from the previous runs. It then calls the function find in the File::Find module. The call is given below.

```
&File::Find::find (\&listAllFiles, $topDir);
```

We do not have to qualify the name of the function because it is automatically imported to the current program, but we do so just to make clear where it comes from. We also do not have to specify the & before the name of the qualified function name. find's first argument is a reference to another function that takes no arguments. The second argument is the name of a directory that is to be processed recursively. The function whose reference is passed is listAllFiles defined in this module, but not exported. $topDir specifies the top-level directory for recursive processing. The subroutine listAllFiles is automatically called on each file and directory in the file hierarchy starting from $topDir. Inside this subroutine, which is sometimes called the *wanted* subroutine, the fully qualified name of the current file is available in the scalar $File::Find::name. In the subroutine listAllFiles, the name of the current file is simply appended to the current list of files in @ALL_FILES. The calling subroutine lsdirR returns the value in the variable @ALL_FILES after the last call to listAllFiles is over. In other words, the names of all files and directories in the file hierarchy is returned.

The next subroutine exported is lsdirTR. This subroutine returns the list of all text files in the file hierarchy. It does so by using an auxiliary, non-exported function listTextFiles. The list becomes available in the global variable @FileR::ALL_TEXT_FILES after the last recursive call to the auxiliary node-processing function.

The third exported subroutine is `lsdirBR` that returns the names of all binary files in the file hierarchy. It uses the auxiliary subroutine called `listBinaryFiles` to obtain this list. The list is available in the global variable `@ALL_BINARY_FILES`.

The fourth subroutine is `sizeR` that returns the cumulative size of all directories and files in the file hierarchy. It does so by calling the internal function `calculateSize`. This non-exported subroutine is called automatically for every file and directory in the hierarchy. In each call, the size of the current file or directory is found by calling the file operator `-M`. In each call, it adds the size of the current file or directory to the current value of the global variable `$SIZE`.

The fifth exported subroutine is `rmdirR` that removes the contents of a file hierarchy recursively. It asks to make sure that the file hierarchy is to be removed recursively. Once confirmed, it calls the auxiliary subroutine `removeRecursively` to remove each file and directory in the file hierarchy. One has to be a little careful though in removing files and directories. A directory must be completely empty before it can be removed. Thus, all contained files and directories must be removed before any directory is removed. This is accomplished by not calling `File::Find::find`, but `File::Find::finddepth`. The `finddepth` function traverses the file hierarchy using *dept-first search*. In depth-first search, a tree's depth is searched or traversed first before its root is traversed. Here root is the directory itself and all contained files are nodes underneath the root. Thus, the deleting process removes all internal files and directories before removing the directory itself. This ensures that all directories are deleted recursively without any hitch. Simple files are removed using `unlink` whereas directories are removed using `rmdir`. It must be noted here that the `rmtree` function in the `File::Path` package also removes the contents of a directory structure recursively. What we have here is a possible implementation of `File::Path::rmtree`.

The sixth exported function is `findOldest` that finds the oldest file or directory in a file hierarchy. It returns the name of the oldest file and its age in days. The auxiliary subroutine called is `findOldestFile` that returns two scalars, the name of the oldest file and its age. These two subroutines use two global variables, `$OLDEST_FILE` and `$OLDEST_AGE`.

A program that calls all the exported functions is given below.

Program 6.25

```perl
#!/usr/bin/perl
#file fileFuns.pl

use FileR;
use Cwd;
use strict;

$" = "\n";

my ($dir, @fileListing, $oldestFile, $oldestAge);
$dir = $ARGV[0] or $dir = qq{.};

#Print a listing of all files under the directory; recursive
#There is a problem with permissions while listing files..
print "dir = $dir\n";
@fileListing = FileR::lsdirR ("$dir");
print "*" x 50, "\n";
print "File list: \n";
print "@fileListing\n";

#Print a listing of all rest files in the directory; recursive
@fileListing = FileR::lsdirTR ("$dir");
```

```
print "*" x 50, "\n";
print "Text file list: \n";
print "@fileListing\n";

#print a listing of all binary files in the directory; recursive
@fileListing = FileR::lsdirBR ("$dir");
print "*" x 50, "\n";
print "Binary File list: \n";
print "@fileListing\n";

#find the cumulative size of all files in the directory; recursive
my $size = FileR::sizeR ("$dir");
print "*" x 50, "\n";
print "Cumulative size of files = $size kilobytes\n";

#find the oldest file in the directory and its age; recursive
($oldestFile, $oldestAge) = &FileR::findOldest ("$dir");
print "oldest file = $oldestFile\n";
printf  "oldest age = %5.2f days\n", $oldestAge;

#Finally, ask for the name of a directory and delete it, recursively
print "*" x 50, "\n";
print "Name a directory to delete recursively: ";
my $delDir = <STDIN>;
chop $delDir;
#If the directory name is not absolute, absolutize it;
#    works in Unix, recursive
if ($delDir !~  m@^/@){
    $delDir = (Cwd::cwd()) . "/$delDir";
    print "delDir = $delDir\n";
  }
&FileR::rmdirR ("$delDir");
```

This function calls each one of the six exported functions one by one. It expects to get a directory name as a command-line argument, and if the command-line argument is missing, it uses the current directory. At the very end, it asks for the name of a directory, either absolute or relative, to remove recursively. It confirms the name entered by asking the user, and if confirmed removes the contents of the directory recursively. A sample interaction with this program is given below.

```
%fileFuns.pl /home/kalita/perl/file
dir = /home/kalita/perl/file
**************************************************
File list:
/home/kalita/perl/file
/home/kalita/perl/file/fileCopy.plx
/home/kalita/perl/file/filecopytest.pl
/home/kalita/perl/file/dircopytest.pl
/home/kalita/perl/file/mkdir1.pl
/home/kalita/perl/file/checkPath.plx
/home/kalita/perl/file/filecopy.pl
/home/kalita/perl/file/mkdir.pl
```

```
/home/kalita/perl/file/basename.pl
/home/kalita/perl/file/FileR.pm
/home/kalita/perl/file/fileparse.pl
/home/kalita/perl/file/FileR1.pm
/home/kalita/perl/file/myMakePath.pl
/home/kalita/perl/file/myMkpath.pl
/home/kalita/perl/file/myMkpath1.pl
/home/kalita/perl/file/fileFuns.pl
/home/kalita/perl/file/filecopy1.pl
/home/kalita/perl/file/rmtree.pl
/home/kalita/perl/file/jk1.jpg
/home/kalita/perl/file/a
/home/kalita/perl/file/a/b
/home/kalita/perl/file/a/b/c
/home/kalita/perl/file/a/b/c/mkdir1.pl
/home/kalita/perl/file/a/b/c/jk1.jpg
****************************************************
Text file list:
/home/kalita/perl/file/fileCopy.plx
/home/kalita/perl/file/filecopytest.pl
/home/kalita/perl/file/dircopytest.pl
/home/kalita/perl/file/mkdir1.pl
/home/kalita/perl/file/checkPath.plx
/home/kalita/perl/file/filecopy.pl
/home/kalita/perl/file/mkdir.pl
/home/kalita/perl/file/basename.pl
/home/kalita/perl/file/FileR.pm
/home/kalita/perl/file/fileparse.pl
/home/kalita/perl/file/FileR1.pm
/home/kalita/perl/file/myMakePath.pl
/home/kalita/perl/file/myMkpath.pl
/home/kalita/perl/file/myMkpath1.pl
/home/kalita/perl/file/fileFuns.pl
/home/kalita/perl/file/filecopy1.pl
/home/kalita/perl/file/rmtree.pl
/home/kalita/perl/file/a/b/c/mkdir1.pl
****************************************************
Binary File list:
/home/kalita/perl/file
/home/kalita/perl/file/jk1.jpg
/home/kalita/perl/file/a
/home/kalita/perl/file/a/b
/home/kalita/perl/file/a/b/c
/home/kalita/perl/file/a/b/c/jk1.jpg
****************************************************
Cumulative size of files = 229099 kilobytes
In findOldest...
oldest file = /home/kalita/perl/file/fileCopy.plx
oldest age = 240.06 days
****************************************************
Name a directory to delete recursively: a
```

```
delDir = /home/kalita/perl/file/a
Are you sure you want to delete /home/kalita/perl/file/a recursively? (Y|N) Y
Removing file /home/kalita/perl/file/a/b/c/mkdir1.pl
Removing file /home/kalita/perl/file/a/b/c/jk1.jpg
Removing file /home/kalita/perl/file/a/b/c
Removing file /home/kalita/perl/file/a/b
Removing file /home/kalita/perl/file/a
```

First, the program gives a complete recursive listing of the files in the hierarchy. Next, it prints the recursive list of text files and then the recursive list of binary files. Directories and graphic files are considered binary files. The program determines that the cumulative size of all files and directories in the hierarchy is 226554 kilobytes and that the oldest file is /home/kalita/perl/file/fileCopy.plx and that this file is 240 days old. It then prompts for the name of a directory, and the user responds with the name a. It deletes this sub-directory recursively. It prints the names of files being removed, in removal order.

Finally, a word of caution about using the File::Find package. Experience has showed that the find and finddepth functions can be quite slow especially when dealing with large directory structures, say ones containing many hundreds of files or more. For example, when run on a directory such as /, the top-level directory in Linux and Mac OS X Server with fairly fast machines, it took many hours for the listings to start printing on the screen. This is not acceptable. So, it may be better to use a subroutine especially a non-recursive implementation of depth-first or breadth-first search, for faster processing. In addition, when running in Unix, the find and finddepth functions seem to have permission problems with files and directories in unexpected places. The permission problems do not occur with the programs discussed earlier in the chapter.

6.11.6   Portability in File Names: Module File::Spec::Functions

File names are written in different ways in different operating systems. For example, in Unix and variations of it such as Linux and Mac OS X or Mac OS X Server, the root directory is named /, whereas in Windows the root directory starts with the name of a drive such as C:\. In Mac OS prior to OS X, a full pathname starts with the name of the volume or disk without any prefix. So, if there is a disk or volume called Macintosh HD, a fully qualified name starts with the name Macintosh HD:. The directory separator in Unix is /; it is \ in Windows and : in Mac OS 9 or lower. Therefore, if we want to write programs that deal with files and directories and want these programs to work without much modification across operating systems, we need to exercise care right from the beginning.

Perl provides a set of modules under the File::Spec class that deal with names of files and directories in a general way. The module called File::Spec is object-oriented and provides several methods to manipulate file and directory names. There are also several subclasses such as File::Spec::Unix, File::Spec::Mac, File::Spec::Win32 and File::Spec::OS2 that provide operating system specific functionalities. There is an additional module called File::Spec::Functions that allows one to use the methods defined in File::Spec as functions. We discuss the last module in this section.

The File::Spec module loads the appropriate module for the current operating system. The File::Spec::Functions module is a subclass of File::Spec and hence works with the current operating system. Among the functions available in the File::Spec::Functions module are functions for finding the name of the root directory appropriate for the operating system, concatenating names of directories, concatenating names of a sequence of directories with that of a file name, and to find out if the name of a file is absolute or not.

The following program uses a selection of functions in the File::Spec::Functions module.

Program 6.26

```perl
#!/usr/bin/perl
#fileSpec.pl

use strict;
use File::Spec::Functions qw(:ALL);
$" = "\n\t";

print "The Operating System is " . $^O . "\n";
print "The root directory is " . File::Spec::Functions::rootdir () . "\n";
my $curdir = File::Spec::Functions::curdir ();
print "The current directory is " . $curdir . "\n";
print "The current absolutized directory is " .absolutize ($curdir) ."\n";
print "The up directory is " . File::Spec::Functions::updir () . "\n";
my @path = File::Spec::Functions::path ();
print "The PATH environment variable contains\n\t@path\n";


my $dir1 = File::Spec::Functions::rootdir() .
           File::Spec::Functions::catdir ("home", "kalita", "perl");
print "The directory is $dir1\n";
my $dir2 = File::Spec::Functions::catdir ("kalita", "perl");
print "The directory is $dir2\n";
my $file1 = File::Spec::Functions::catfile (
                    File::Spec::Functions::catdir ("kalita", "perl"),
                 "mkdir.pl");
print "The file is $file1\n";

opendir (DIR, "$curdir") or
         die "Cannot open directory: $!";
my @files = readdir DIR or die "Cannot open directory: $!";
@files = File::Spec::Functions::no_upwards (@files);
printf "\n%-20s %-20s %-30s\n", "Original Name", "Absolute", "Relative";
print "-" x 55, "\n";
foreach (@files){
  printf "%-20s %-20s %-30s\n", "$_", &relativize($_),  &absolutize($_);
}

#absolutize a file name
sub absolutize{
  my ($file) = @_;
  return $file if (File::Spec::Functions::file_name_is_absolute ($file));
  return File::Spec::Functions::rel2abs ($file);
}
#relativize a file name
sub relativize{
   my ($file) = @_;
   return $file unless (File::Spec::Functions::file_name_is_absolute ($file));
   return File::Spec::Functions::abs2rel ($file);
}
```

When we use the File::Spec::Functions module a few of the subroutine names are imported automatically, but a few are not. That is why, we use the :ALL keyword in the use statement. What is imported automatically from a module and what needs to be explicitly imported is a choice the authors of the modules make. To import only a few of the optional ones, their names can be directly specified in the use statement. To find out what needs to be imported explicitly, one must read the documentation for the module.

The program first prints the name of the current operating system by looking at the special variable $^O. It then prints the representation used by the operating system for the current directory and the directory one level above the current directory. In Unix, these simply are the two dot files. The program next prints the PATH environment variable using the path function.

The module File::Spec::Functions provides a function called rootdir to obtain the root directory in the operating system. It has a function called catdir to concatenate a sequence of directory names, and a function called catfile to take one or more directory names and a file name and make a complete path.

The program next opens the current directory. It uses the no_upwards function to remove the two dotfiles. This is handy. Otherwise, we have to remove these dotfiles on our own, as we have done in most of our programs dealing with directories so far. The program goes through a loop and prints the name of each file in the current directory both as a relative and an absolute name.

There are two simple subroutines that absolutize and relativize a file or directory name. These two subroutines use the method file_name_is_absolute to do so. The absolutize function calls the function rel2abs to make a file or directory name absolute. The relativize function uses the abs2rel to make the file names relative. These two functions: abs2rel and rel2abs are not automatically exported by the File::Spec::Functions module. To import these two functions, we had used the :ALL keyword with the use statement. There are other functions, not discussed here that also need to be imported explicitly.

A output of running this program on a Linux machine is given below.

```
The Operating System is linux
The root directory is /
The current directory is .
The current absolutized directory is /home/kalita/perl/file
The up directory is ..
The PATH environment variable contains

        .
        /home/kalita/bin
        /bin
        /usr/bin
        /usr/local/bin
        /usr/sbin
        /usr/bin/X11
        /usr/bin/mh
The directory is /home/kalita/perl
The directory is kalita/perl
The file is kalita/perl/mkdir.pl
```

Original Name	Absolute	Relative
jk1.jpg	jk1.jpg	/home/kalita/perl/file/jk1.jpg
dircopytest.pl	dircopytest.pl	/home/kalita/perl/file/dircopytest.pl
mkdir1.pl	mkdir1.pl	/home/kalita/perl/file/mkdir1.pl
checkPath.plx	checkPath.plx	/home/kalita/perl/file/checkPath.plx
filecopy.pl	filecopy.pl	/home/kalita/perl/file/filecopy.pl
mkdir.pl	mkdir.pl	/home/kalita/perl/file/mkdir.pl
ncopy.pl	ncopy.pl	/home/kalita/perl/file/ncopy.pl
basename.pl	basename.pl	/home/kalita/perl/file/basename.pl
FileR.pm	FileR.pm	/home/kalita/perl/file/FileR.pm

```
fileparse.pl        fileparse.pl        /home/kalita/perl/file/fileparse.pl
a                   a                   /home/kalita/perl/file/a
myMakePath.pl       myMakePath.pl       /home/kalita/perl/file/myMakePath.pl
myMkpath.pl         myMkpath.pl         /home/kalita/perl/file/myMkpath.pl
aa                  aa                  /home/kalita/perl/file/aa
myMkpath1.pl        myMkpath1.pl        /home/kalita/perl/file/myMkpath1.pl
fileFuns.pl         fileFuns.pl         /home/kalita/perl/file/fileFuns.pl
rmtree.pl           rmtree.pl           /home/kalita/perl/file/rmtree.pl
fileSpec.pl         fileSpec.pl         /home/kalita/perl/file/fileSpec.pl
```

A part of the output of running this program on an Macintosh machine with OS X Server is given below.

```
The Operating System is rhapsody
The root directory is /
The current directory is .
The current absolutized directory is /Local/Users/kalita/perl/file
The up directory is ..
The PATH environment variable contains
        /Local/Users/kalita/bin/powerpc-apple-rhapsody
        /Local/Users/kalita/bin
        /usr/local/bin
        /usr/bin
        /bin
        /usr/sbin
        /sbin
The directory is /home/kalita/perl
The directory is kalita/perl
The file is kalita/perl/mkdir.pl

Original Name       Absolute            Relative
-------------------------------------------------------------
FileR.pm            FileR.pm            /Local/Users/kalita/perl/file/FileR.pm
basename.pl         basename.pl         /Local/Users/kalita/perl/file/basename
.pl                                     .pl
```

6.12   Archiving Directories and Files: Archive::Tar **Module**

Unix provides a tool called tar to make so-called "tape archives" of directories and contained files. It is available on all other operating systems too. The name "tape archive" is now somewhat outdated because most people do not use magnetic or other type of tapes any more, and obviously most do not use tar for making only tape archives. Usually, a tar archive is made when it is necessary to transfer a set of directories and contained files that constitute a reasonably sized software project, from one machine to another. A complex software project may consist of tens of files, or even hundreds, organized neatly into one or more directories. It is usually cumbersome to transfer the files and directories one by one from a source machine to a destination machine. Although there are FTP programs that can transfer directories recursively, it still is time consuming to do so.

When one transfers a complex academic or commercial project between two machines, one should do it as neatly and efficiently as possible. The programmers of a complex academic project may want to place the project's code on the Internet so interested individuals can download it easily for free. A company may want to place the software constituting a product at a secure Internet site so that those who have paid can download the software using a given password or by other secure means. In such situations, it is convenient to produce one file out of all the relevant directories and files that constitute the project. Such a comprehensive file is called a *tar file* if we use the tar facility to produce it. In common parlance, it is often called a *tar ball*. Unix's `tar` tool takes various arguments to produce the archive, extract files from the archive, or view files contained in the tar ball. `tarring` and `untarring` tools are available on other platforms as well, quite frequently with graphical user interface. There are *tar* tools with graphical user interfaces on Windows machines and Macintoshes.

First, we present a program that `tars` files of a simple project. All the project files are under one single top level directory. In the top level directory, there are several files of interest. In addition, below the top level directory, the project has two useful sub-directories; there may be other sub-directories that are ignored when archived. The two relevant sub-directories are `HTML` and `perl`. The `perl` directory contains three sub-directories: `cgi-bin`, `code` and `modules`. In each sub-directory, there are files that are either Perl programs or HTML files. There may be other types of files also. When one works on a project, it is quite likely that one produces temporary files, saves duplicate copies of important files, or creates incremental versions of files for testing purposes. Many text editors also automatically keep copies of older versions of files. For example, the *Emacs* editor, quite popular in the Unix and related platforms and also available for the PC and the Macintosh, usually keeps previous versions by appending ~ at the end of the file's name. Thus, the source directories of a project may be cluttered. So, when the project is archived, we want a `tarring` program that is a bit smart in that it archives only selected directories and files.

In the project under discussion, cgi-bin and Perl code files have the extension `.plx`. These are Perl programs. Perl programs are not required to have any specific extensions. The usual extension used is `.pl`, but the authors of this project decided to use `.plx` instead. It is somewhat unconventional. The HTML files have either `.html` or `.htm` extension. The Perl modules have extension `.pm`. Only the specified sub-directories under the top level directory and files with specific extensions are `tarred`.

The Perl `tar` package is called `Archive::Tar`. First, a new empty archive file or `tar` file is produced by making a call to the `new` class method. Then, one adds files to the `tar` file by calling the `add_files` method on the `tar` file object. The list of files to add to the tar file are given as argument to the `add_files` method. If the added files are in directories and sub-directories, the path to these files have to be provided. In this program, the paths are provided in relative form. The program called `archive.pl` is given below. The program also uses what is called POD (Plain Old Documentation) to provide comments. POD comments can be multi-line, and they can be extracted from the program's text file to produce HTML or textual documentation. POD documentation is discussed in Section 1.15.

Program 6.27

```
#!/usr/bin/perl
=head1 NAME
script archive.pl

=head1 SYNOPSIS

Makes a tar ball of the top level files and specified sub-directories
associated with the APTracker project. The default tar ball name is
APTracker.tar.

=head1 UPDATE HISTORY

07/24/2000: Written, Jugal Kalita, recurses from first principles
03/09/2001: Updated, Jugal Kalita, added loop
03/24/2001: Updated, Jugal Kalita, uses File::Find

=head1 DIRECTORIES TARRED

=over 4
```

```perl
=item the top-level directory of the distribution

=item html directory

=item perl/cgi-bin directory

=item perl/code directory

=item perl/modules directory

=back

=cut

use strict;
use File::Find;
use Archive::Tar;
use Cwd;

$" = "\n";   #Separator for printing lists in double-quoted strings
my @ALL_FILES_TO_TAR = ();

my $tar;
my ($cgibinSrcDir, $cgibinExtensions, $htmlSrcDir, $htmlExtensions);
my ($perlCodeSrcDir, $perlCodeExtensions);
my ($perlModuleSrcDir, $perlModuleExtensions);
my ($tarFileName, $sourceTopDir, $excludeExtensions);

$cgibinSrcDir = "perl/cgi-bin";
$cgibinExtensions = "plx";
$htmlSrcDir = "HTML";
$htmlExtensions = "html|htm";
$perlCodeSrcDir = "perl/code";
$perlCodeExtensions = "plx";
$perlModuleSrcDir = "perl/modules";
$perlModuleExtensions = "pm";
$excludeExtensions = "(.*~)";
$sourceTopDir = "/home/kalita/perl/tar/ap.dev";

my @allSrcDirs = ($htmlSrcDir, $perlCodeSrcDir, $cgibinSrcDir,
        $perlModuleSrcDir);
my @allExtensions = ($htmlExtensions, $perlCodeExtensions,
                $cgibinExtensions, $perlModuleExtensions);
if ($#allExtensions != $#allSrcDirs){
    print "Please provide extensions for files in all source directories\n";
    exit 1;
    }

print "\nWhat is the name of the tar file you want to create\n";
print "(Use \"APTracker.tar\" as default)?";
```

```perl
$tarFileName = <STDIN>;
chomp ($tarFileName);
if (!($tarFileName)){
    $tarFileName = "APTracker.tar";
}

print "tar file name = $tarFileName\n";
if (-e $tarFileName){
    unlink $tarFileName or
            die "Cannot reinitialize by deleting existing tar file: $!"
    }

#Start tarring
$tar = Archive::Tar->new();
print "Tarring files into $tarFileName...\n\n";

#Tar files at the top level
my $oldDir = cwd ();
chdir ($sourceTopDir) or die "Cannot chdir to $sourceTopDir: $!";
my $currDir = cwd();
opendir (DIR, $currDir) or die "Cannot open $currDir: $!";
my @files = readdir DIR or die "cannot read $currDir: $!";
@files = grep !/^[.]{1,2}$/, @files;
@files = grep !/[.]$excludeExtensions$/, @files;
@files = grep {if (-d $_) {0} else {1}} @files;

print "\nTarring top-level files...\n@files\n\n";
$tar -> add_files (@files);

#tar all the sub-directories directories
my $i;
for ($i = 0; $i <= $#allSrcDirs; $i++){
        &tarDir ($tar, $allSrcDirs[$i], $allExtensions[$i]);
      }

print "Current working directory is: " . cwd () . "\n";
$tar -> write ("$oldDir/$tarFileName");

####subroutine to tar a directory's contents
sub tarDir{
        my ($tarArchive, $sourceDir, $extensionRegex) = @_;
        @ALL_FILES_TO_TAR = ();
        File::Find::find (\&listAllFilesToTar, $sourceDir);
        print "+++++ALL_FILES_TO_TAR = @ALL_FILES_TO_TAR\n";
        my @sourceFiles;
        @sourceFiles = (grep /\.$extensionRegex/, @ALL_FILES_TO_TAR);
        @sourceFiles = grep !/[.]$excludeExtensions$/, @sourceFiles;
        print "Tarring source files...\n@sourceFiles\n\n";
        $tarArchive -> add_files (@sourceFiles);

}
```

```
sub listAllFilesToTar{
    @ALL_FILES_TO_TAR = (@ALL_FILES_TO_TAR, $File::Find::name);
}
```

The program starts with POD comments and then declares a number of variables. Values are assigned to variables to specify the location of relevant files. The HTML files are stored in the HTML sub-directory below the top level directory. The Perl files are stored in the directory perl. These files have been saved under three sub-directories: cgi-bin, code and modules. This is because usually when a Perl project is installed, cgi-bin, module and regular code files have to be stored in different locations. Usually, cgi-bin files need to be stored in one or more specific directories dependent on the operating system and the Web server. Perl modules written by users for general use, need also to be stored in certain system-specified directories, usually called *site lib* directories so that all Perl programs can find them when needed. Regular Perl code can be stored in any directory. In practice, each one of these sub-directories can have embedded directories down to several levels of containment. The program also requires specification of acceptable extensions for files in all sub-directories below the top level. It also specifies extensions to exclude. The extensions are specified in terms of regular expressions.

The program asks for the name of the tar file to create. If a name is not given, the default name used is APTracker.tar for the project. If the tar file already exists, the file is deleted or unlinked. If this is not done, later when the tar file is written using the add_files and write object methods, the new contents will be added to what is already there in the tar file.

The program creates a new tar file and calls a reference to it $tar by calling new.

```
$tar = Archive::Tar->new();
```

The program then chdirs to the top-level directory where the files to be archived exist. At the top-level, the program obtains the list of all files and directories that are not . or ... . is the current directory and .. is the parent directory. These two dotfile entries show up in the listing of a directory in Unix. They are not added to the list of files to be archived. The program also removes names of files with unacceptable extensions. In this program, the only unacceptable extension is a name that ends with ~. These are older versions of files being edited using the editor called *Emacs*. At this time, the program removes all directories at the top level from the list of files and directories. As a result, the program does not archive any directories that are not specifically added later in the program to the tar archive. The simple file names at the top level are then added to the tar archive by the following command.

```
$tar -> add_files (@files);
```

In the rest of the program, those sub-directories under the top level that are to be archived are specified.

The list of all sub-directories to archive below the top level directory, is available in the variable called @allSrcDirs. The corresponding list of acceptable extensions is available in the variable @allExtensions. The program loops over all sub-directories in @allSrcDirs and calls subroutine tarDir on each. This loop is shown below.

```
for ($i = 0; $i <= $#allSrcDirs; $i++){
    &tarDir ($tar, $allSrcDirs[$i], $allExtensions[$i]);
  }
```

Finally, all files added to the tar archive referenced by $tar are actually written to the archive by the following statement.

```
$tar -> write ($tarFileName);
```

At this point, all the files added to be `tarred` are put together using the `tar` syntax and are available in the single archive file specified by the scalar variable `$tarFileName` in the directory where the archiving program `archive.pl` is situated. A `tar` file is a text file, but with its own syntax to denote file boundaries and locations of files in the archive file hierarchy. It is customary to use the `.tar` extension for a tar file.

The `tarDir` subroutine takes three arguments: a `tar` archive object, a source directory, and a regular expression specifying acceptable extensions. It opens the directory, obtains a list of its files by making the following call.

```
File::Find::find (\&listAllFilesToTar, $sourceDir);
```

It uses an auxiliary function `listAllFilesToTar` to obtain a recursive listing of all files. The program picks out files with acceptable extensions, and removes files with useless extensions. Finally, the list of files is added to the `tar` object using the statement given below.

```
        $tarArchive -> add_files (@sourceFiles);
```

This subroutine does not `write` the files to the archive. `writeing` to the archive is done in the main program.

A recursive listing of the top level directory before the program is run is given below.

```
. :
HTML/  NewSense.tar  archive.pl   archive.plx~  perl/
LOGFILE  README        archive.plx  install.plx

./HTML:
WS_FTP.LOG  basic_config.html  databaseServer.html  operatingSystem.html
XML.html    configure.html     newsSource.html

./perl:
cgi-bin/  code/  modules/

./perl/cgi-bin:
WS_FTP.LOG  basic_configure.plx  configure.plx

./perl/code:
apget.plx  cookies1.txt  cookies2.txt  cookies3.txt

./perl/modules:
AP_DB.pm  AP_Time.pm  AP_XML.pm  AP_globals.pm
```

This listing is given in a Linux generated format. It shows the name of every directory in the project on a line, and the files contained in each directory following the name of the directory.

After the program is run, we can examine the contents of the tar archive. In Unix, `tar tvf` does this. In other systems, this may be done using a graphical user interface. When we examine the content of the tar archive by typing

```
%tar tvf APTracker.tar
```

we see the following.

```
README
archive.plx
install.plx
```

```
perl/cgi-bin/basic_configure.plx
perl/cgi-bin/configure.plx
HTML/configure.html
HTML/newsSource.html
HTML/databaseServer.html
HTML/operatingSystem.html
HTML/XML.html
HTML/basic_config.html
perl/code/apget.plx
perl/modules/AP_DB.pm
perl/modules/AP_globals.pm
perl/modules/AP_Time.pm
perl/modules/AP_XML.pm
```

The names of files are given with addresses relative to the top level directory. The listing clearly shows that the program produces a "clean" tar archive with only the files that we specifically required it to contain and files that we excluded.

Once we have a tar archive, the archive can be put on the Internet for downloading, FTPed to the destination, sent in an e-mail message, or transferred to the destination on a floppy, zip disk, CD or tape. To extract the files and directories from the tar file at the destination and get the directory structure again, we can either use the command tar xvf in Unix or we may use a GUI-based tar tool. Untarring can also be done using a Perl program. If we write an untar program in Perl, we can make the program store files in appropriate locations as directed either by the operating system, by the Web server, or by the Perl system. Although there are other alternatives to do so, this is acceptable unless we need to compile programs using a language like C before distributing files to appropriate places. Having some of the programs of a project written in a language like C is not uncommon though.

The following program install.pl takes the tar archive produced earlier and extracts all the files and places them in the right locations in the target system. The recipient edits the module called AP_Conf.pm to specify the target locations and then runs install.pl to install the programs. The content of the configuration file AP_Conf.pm is given below.

Program 6.28

```
package AP_Conf;

use strict;
our qw($webServerAbsPath $cgiAbsPath $htmlAbsPath );
our qw($perlSourceInstallAbsPath $perlSiteModuleAbsPath);
our qw($distributionTarFileName $tmpDir);

$webServerAbsPath = "/home/kalita/www/Apache";
$cgiAbsPath = "/home/kalita/www/Apache/cgi-bin/aptracker";
$htmlAbsPath = "/home/kalita/www/Apache/htdocs/newsense";
$perlSourceInstallAbsPath = "/home/kalita/www/data/ap";
$perlSiteModuleAbsPath = "/home/kalita/www/bin/Perl/site/lib";
$distributionTarFileName = "APTracker.tar";
$tmpDir = "/home/kalita/.tmp";

1;
```

The values of the variables in this file need to be edited by hand to suit the current operating system and the current system configuration. The paths given above are arbitrarily made up for purposes of illustration only. For example, on a machine with Red Hat Linux, files related to the Web server are usually in the directory /home/httpd. The cgi-bin files are usually at /home/httpd/cgi-bin/, the html files are at /home/httpd/html, the perl site modules are usually at a location such as /usr/lib/perl5/site_perl/5.6.0 or /usr/local/lib/perl5/site_perl/5.6.0/. It must be noted that this program needs to be run by the *root* on a Unix machine if we want the files to be written to these system required locations in a Unix based machine. On a Windows machine or Mac OS (pre- OS X), anyone usually can run this program even with sensitive system required paths because the security infra-structure is lax in such systems. This program also writes a log file about whatever it was able to do. The log file is quite detailed. Information is also printed to the screen as the untarring proceeds.

First, the variables are declared and values assigned to them. The log file is opened. The main program gets several pieces of information from the configuration module. The program follows.

Program 6.29

```
#!/usr/bin/perl

=head1 NAME
script install.pl


=head1 SYNOPSIS

Untars the  tar ball of a Perl project called the APTracker project.
The tar file's name comes from the configuration module AP_Config.pm.

=head1 UPDATE HISTORY

=for text

07/24/2000: Written, Jugal Kalita
03/09/2001: Updated, Jugal Kalita

=cut

use strict;
use Archive::Tar;
use File::NCopy;
use File::Path;
use Cwd;

use AP_Conf;

$" = "\n";   #Separator for printing lists in double-quoted strings

sub printlog;

#######Main program###########
my ($webServerRoot);
my $tar;
```

```perl
my ($cgibinSrcDir, $cgibinDestDir, $htmlSrcDir, $htmlDestDir);
my ($perlCodeSrcDir, $perlCodeDestDir);
my ($perlModuleSrcDir, $perlModuleDestDir);
my ($tarFileName);
my ($tmpDir, $logFile, $logHandle);
my $filePermissions;

$filePermissions = "0777";
$cgibinSrcDir = "perl/cgi-bin";
$htmlSrcDir = "HTML";
$perlCodeSrcDir = "perl/code";
$perlModuleSrcDir = "perl/modules";
$logFile = "LOGFILE";


open (LOG, ">$logFile") or warn "Cannot write log file $logFile: $!";
$logHandle = *LOG;

$webServerRoot = "$AP_Conf::webServerAbsPath";
printlog $logHandle, "Using $webServerRoot as Web server root directory\n";
$cgibinDestDir = "$AP_Conf::cgiAbsPath";
printlog $logHandle, "Using $cgibinDestDir as cgi-bin path\n";
$htmlDestDir = "$AP_Conf::htmlAbsPath";
printlog $logHandle, "Using $htmlDestDir as HTML document path\n";
$perlCodeDestDir = "$AP_Conf::perlSourceInstallAbsPath";
printlog $logHandle, "Using $perlCodeDestDir as path to Perl installation\n";
$perlModuleDestDir = "$AP_Conf::perlSiteModuleAbsPath";
printlog $logHandle, "Using $perlModuleDestDir as path to site Perl modules\n";
$tmpDir = $AP_Conf::tmpDir;
printlog $logHandle, "Using $tmpDir as path to temporary directory\n";
$tarFileName = "$AP_Conf::distributionTarFileName";

my $oldDir = cwd ();
#Testing; Need to take care of permission for newly created directory in Unix
if (!(-e $tmpDir)){
    File::Path::mkpath ($tmpDir, $filePermissions)
            or die "Cannot create directory $tmpDir: $!";
    printlog $logHandle,
            "Created directory $tmpDir with permissions $filePermissions\n";
}

#my $oldDir = cwd ();
chdir $tmpDir or die "Cannot change directory to $tmpDir: $!";
printlog $logHandle, "Untarring $tarFileName...\n";

#Start untarring
$tar = Archive::Tar->new();
$tar-> read ("$oldDir/$tarFileName")
        or die "Cannot read tar file $tarFileName: $!";

my @files = $tar->list_files();
```

```perl
$tar -> extract (@files);

chdir ($oldDir);
my @allSrcDirs = ($htmlSrcDir, $cgibinSrcDir, $perlModuleSrcDir,
                  $perlCodeSrcDir);
my @allDestDirs = ($htmlDestDir, $cgibinDestDir, $perlModuleDestDir,
                   $perlCodeDestDir);
my $i;
for ($i = 0; $i <= $#allSrcDirs; $i++){
    &copyDir ($logHandle, $allSrcDirs[$i],
             $allDestDirs[$i], $filePermissions, $tmpDir);
}
##NEED to CLEAN UP TMP FILE, i.e., delete everything in it and itself
File::Path::rmtree ($tmpDir);
close LOG;

##########subroutine to copy a sourceDir to a dest recursively
sub copyDir{
    my ($logHandle, $srcSubDir, $dest, $filePermissions, $tmpDir ) = @_;
    my $copyAgent;
    my $src = "$tmpDir/$srcSubDir";

    printlog $logHandle,
        "Trying to copy directory $src to directory $dest...\n";
    return () unless ($src);
    die "There is no $src directory from which to copy file: $!"
               unless (-e $src);
    if (-e $dest){
       printlog ($logHandle, "$dest exists\n");
    }else{
       printlog ($logHandle, "$dest doesn't exist. Creating it...\n");
       File::Path::mkpath ($dest, $filePermissions)
           or die "Cannot create $dest: $!";
    }

    #recursive copying
    $copyAgent = File::NCopy->new(recursive=>1);
    $copyAgent->copy ("$src", "$dest");
}

#subroutine for printing to STDOUT and a log handle
sub printlog{
    my ($logHandle, $message) = @_;
    print STDOUT $message;
    print $logHandle $message;
}
```

The program gets several pieces of information from the configuration module. It prints information on the screen and to the log file about these locations. The program also needs a temporary directory which is created if it does not exist already.

First, a new `Archive::Tar` object is created. Then, the tar archive is read into this object by executing the following statements.

```
$tar -> extract (@files);
$tar-> read ("$oldDir/$tarFileName") or
          die "Cannot read tar file $tarFileName: $!";
```

The list of archived files and directories is obtained by issuing the following command.

```
my @files = $tar->list_files();
```

The list of files is extracted. The extraction takes place into the temporary directory `$tmpDir` to which the program had `chdir`ed earlier. The extraction process recreates the directory structure and obtains the contained files in their individual form.

The program goes through all the source directories and copies them to the appropriate destination directories. The destination directories are obtained from the `AP_Conf` module discussed earlier. To copy a directory recursively, the program uses the `copyDir` subroutine. After the directories have been copied to their rightful locations, the program deletes the temporary directory `$tmpDir` recursively by calling the `File::Path::rmtree` function.

The `copyDir` subroutine creates the destination directory by calling `File::Path::mkpath` if necessary. It creates a new `File::NCopy` object called `$copyAgent` that copies directories recursively. The `copy` method is used by `$copyAgent` to copy directories recursively.

6.13 Conclusions

This chapter has discussed how directory structures—small or large—can be processed using recursive subroutines. Dealing with file and directory structures is important in many applications and this chapter shows how a variety of useful tasks can be performed with ease. There are quite a few pre-defined modules beyond the ones discussed in this chapter. One can search the Comprehensive Perl Archive Network (`www.cpan.org`) for the latest modules available.

6.14 Exercises

1. *(Easy: Documentation Reading)*
   Read Perl documentation on file tests by running

   ```
   %perldoc perlfun
   ```

   There is quite a bit of additional material in this section of the Perl on-line documentation. Therefore, you will have to search a little to find information on the filetest operators.

2. *(Medium to Hard: Removing Comments, Recursive Directory Processing, Text Processing, Long)*
   Write a program that removes all comments from Perl programs. Given a directory containing sub-directories and program files dispersed among the sub-directories, it creates a modified mirror of the top-level directory. Let it create a new top-level directory with the suffix `.new` attached to it. It creates any contained directories with the same names as the original, and stores program files after modifying them by taking out the comments. It checks to see if the first line of a program file has a comment starting at column 1. It does not remove this comment. A comment starts with #. In general, a comment can start at any column. A comment starting with # continues till the end of the current

line. The program name is given as a command-line argument. The modified program has the same name as the original, but is written to a different directory.

Assume the name of a Perl script file ends in .pl or .pm. The program modifies only Perl scripts. The modified program have the same name as the original, and are written to a different directory that has been created earlier. It copies non-Perl files as they are, to the right location in the mirror.

3. *(Medium: Recursive Directory Processing, Text Processing, Long)*
Write a program that takes a command-line argument that is the name of a directory containing embedded directories and program files. The program creates a mirror of the top-level directory. It asks for the location of the Perl interpreter on your computer. It then looks at the directory and traverses it recursively, and if the name of a file ends in .pl, checks to see if the first line is a comment specifying the location of the Perl interpreter. If not, it adds the comment as seen in programs in this book. The first comment line is not needed on PCs and older Macintosh operating systems. However, it is not a bad idea to place them if we want the programs to be portable across systems. Remember paths on PCs and older Macintoshes are written differently than on a Unix machine. Files that are not Perl programs are copied as they are.

4. *(Medium: Recursive Directory Processing)*
Write a program that prints the name of every file in a directory and the number of lines in it. It prints the result to a file. The directory has embedded directories in it. Print the results in the form a horizontal histogram. Scale the numbers so that the histogram lines fit the screen. Use repetition of an alphabetic character, say x, to draw the lines.

5. *(Medium: Recursive Directory Processing, File Tests)*
Write a program that prints out the names of all text files in a directory recursively. The directory name is given as command-line argument. It prints the results in a manner so that containment of directories and files is clear.

6. *(Medium: Recursive Directory Processing, Text Processing, Letter Frequency Counting)*
Write a program that counts the frequency of letters in English (irrespective of case). Ignore all non-alphabetic characters. Process as much text as you can obtain, from any source. For example, process all the text files that you have under a certain large directory. Let the directory contain sub-directories. As you encounter a word, you will have to increment the number of times it has occurred so far. Use a hash to store frequency of occurrence. A word is a key and its frequency of occurrence is its value.

Study what are called Huffman codes that can be used to represent letters. Generate Huffman codes for the letters based on their frequency count.

7. *(Medium: Recursive Directory Processing, Text Processing)*
Write a program that reads a directory recursively and creates a mirror. It looks at text files and breaks long lines into smaller lines. It takes a command-line argument that is an integer n and checks to make sure that it is an integer. It breaks lines after the last non-blank character that occurs before the nth column of input. It removes the original files and directories once the mirroring is over.

8. *(Medium: Recursive Directory Processing, Text Processing)*
Write a program to remove trailing blanks and tabs from every file in a directory, recursively. Also, delete more than one consecutive blank line. Make a mirror first and once the mirroring is complete, remove the original directories and files.

9. *(Medium: Recursive Directory Processing, Text Processing)*
Write a program that reads a directory recursively. It reads the text files in it a paragraph at a time. It reports the lengths of the longest and the smallest paragraphs in the whole directory structure, in terms of numbers of words. It also reports the file names where they occur. The program also reports the lengths of the shortest and the longest sentences, in numbers of words along with the file names. Make any simple assumptions you need regarding when a sentence starts.

10. *(Medium: Recursive Directory Processing, Text Processing, Program File Dependencies)*
    In Perl you can include one file in another by writing either use *file* to include a module in your program. Write a program that takes a set of directories as command line argument and prints out the names of all the modules that have been used in the Perl programs in the contained directories, recursively. It prints the modules only once. It then checks to see if the modules are available in a library directory given to the program as the first command line argument.

11. *(Medium: Recursive Directory Processing, Text Processing, Text Substitution)*
    Write a subroutine `replace` that examines a file given to it and replaces the occurrence of $old by $new everywhere in the file. The function takes three arguments as specified in the example given below.

```
$old =   "MCI, Inc.";
$new = "MCI WorldComm, Inc.";
$file = "index.html";
replace ($old, $new, $file);
```

    Assume that $old can have several words that can occur in one or more consecutive lines of the file. For example, MCI, can occur in one line, and Inc. can occur in the next line. There can be other whitespaces between two words.

    Now write a subroutine `replaceR` that is like `replace`, but performs the substitution recursively in all directories. That is, the substitution is performed in every file of every directory given as argument. A generic call to this function is given below.

```
replaceR ($old, $new, @FDList);
```

    Here @FDList is a list of files and directories. You can call `replace` from `replaceR` if you want.

12. *(Medium: Recursive Directory Processing, Soft Links)*
    In all the programs we have seen in this Chapter and the Exercises, we consider a directory structure to be a tree. However, it can be a little more complicated. There can be links from a name to a directory or file. For example, in Unix, we can make soft links using the `ln` command with the -s option. Thus, we can actually have a graph or a network instead of a tree. A tree has no loops whereas a graph or a network does. Modify all the programs in these Exercises so that they work with network of files.

13. *(Easy: File Processing, Directory Processing)*
    Redo all the directory and file processing exercises so far using the file and directory modules discussed. Compare the amount of time taken using the two approaches, especially if the data being handled, i.e., the file structures are large.

14. *(Medium: Tar and Untar, Software Installation, Research)*
    Being able to archive a set of directories and files is useful for writing software for a complex project. Suppose you can archive the relevant files for a project in the *tar* format. The *tar*red archive can be transferred to a machine where the project is to be installed. Study how the installation process for a project can be automated as much as possible. Describe how this can be done so that a Perl-based complex project can be installed on a Linux, a Macintosh, and a Windows machine. The same project tar ball is to be installed in the three different platforms. Remember a complex project normally would have many files that need to be housed at different locations in the target machine.

Chapter 7

On Communicating

The most obvious manner in which a program can communicate with the environment is by reading and writing. We are already familiar with how we can write a Perl program that reads from the standard input or from a file, and write out to the standard output or to a file. In this chapter, we learn more about other ways in which a Perl program can have more complex and fruitful interactions with the environment.

When we talk about the environment, we mean dealing with the local environment as well as the non-local environment. Speaking locally, a Perl program may have to communicate requests and get responses back from the operating system on the machine in which the Perl program resides. A Perl program may also want to communicate with other processes that are running on the machine in which the program is running. However interesting such local communication may be, in this era of the Internet and the World Wide Web, Perl programs may need to communicate with a program running on a distant machine, maybe, in the same building or half-way around the world. We will learn how Perl programs can speak the language that a distant computer understands and communicate back and forth.

This chapter looks briefly at how one calls system functions, and how pipes work as a means for inter-process communication. A substantial part of the chapter discusses how new processes can be created and how processes running on the same computer can communicate. We see that there can be only very limited communication among related processes created using the well-known `fork` command. Another substantial part of the chapter discusses the concept of sockets, and how processes running on the same or different machines can interact via the use of sockets.

7.1 Calling System Functions: `system` and **backticks**

We can call a system function by including the name of the system command to run as a string argument to the `system` command.

Program 7.1
_____

```perl
#!/usr/bin/perl
#lssystem.pl
use strict;

my $result;
$result = system ("ls");
print "result = $result\n";
```
_____

The call to `system` runs the Unix `ls` command. `ls` is a new process or program. The `system` command does not capture the STDOUT output of the new process or program that is run. For example,

```perl
system ("ls");
```

causes the `ls` command in Unix to run, but does not capture the listing of files that `ls` produces. When `system` is used to call a new program from within a program, the original program's execution is suspended till the new program is finished running. In this case, although the `ls` command's STDOUT output is not captured by Perl, the file listing shows up on the screen because `ls` produces the listing and directs it to STDOUT. The `system` command returns the so-called exit status of the new program. Usually a system program returns with an exit status of 0 if it succeeds and a non-zero value, say 1, if it does not. What is returned as failure exit status depends on the program. In this case, the listing caused by `ls` is printed on STDOUT first, and then the exit code of 0 returned by `ls` is printed by the original program. The output of the program for one particular run is given below.

```
%lssystem.pl
lsRFind1.pl     lsbacktick1.pl lssystem.pl     system.pl
lsbacktick.pl   lsbacktick1.pl~ lssystem.pl~
result = 0
```

It is possible to use the `system` call to run other Perl programs if the file name is given as the argument. For example, if in the current directory we have a Perl program called `hello1.pl` in addition to the program we want to run, we can run the program `hello1.pl` from inside the current program.

Program 7.2
_____

```perl
#!/usr/bin/perl

#Running previously written scripts using "system"
print "Running the script hello1.pl\n";
system ("hello1.pl");
```

System commands can also be executed using the backtick method. The following program runs the system command ls using backticks.

Program 7.3

```
#!/usr/bin/perl
#lsbacktick.pl

use strict;
my $listing;

$listing = `ls`;
```

The program calls the system command ls to get a listing of files in the current directory. When a system command is run using backticks, the results returned by the command are returned by the backtick operator as a string. Thus, the variable $listing contains the string that would have been sent to STDOUT by ls. As a result, the ls command does not send its output to STDOUT in this case. This program prints nothing. The following program prints the listing produced by ls.

Program 7.4

```
#!/usr/bin/perl
#lsbacktick.pl

use strict;
my $listing;

$listing = `ls`;
print $listing, "\n";
```

The printing to STDOUT is not done by the ls command, but by the Perl script.

7.2   Pipes

In Perl, a filehandle can be associated with a file, a device, pipe or a socket. A pipe is essentially a Unix concept where the output of one program or process can be fed to another program or process. The idea of sockets has origin in the Unix operating system although it has been ported to many other platforms. If a program or a process on a machine wants to send or receive information from another program or process on another (or, the same) machine, the two programs or processes can create sockets on their respective machines and then communicate via the sockets. We will see how sockets work later in this chapter.

7.2.1   Printing Typed Lines

The following program shows another simple use of pipes.

Program 7.5

```perl
#!/usr/bin/perl
#more.pl

#prints the two lines on the laser printer
open (LPR, "|more | lpr ");
print LPR "This is the first line.\n";
print LPR "This is the second line.\n";

close (LPR);
```

The program opens a pipe handle called LPR. Two lines of text are printed to the pipe handle. These two lines are piped to the more command and then piped again to a printer using the lpr command. The more command in Unix shows a long text document page by page on the terminal. It is useless here, but used to show that there can be several pipes in the pipe handle's string argument. The two lines of text are sent to the printer once the LPR pipe handle is closed. One can easily see that this program can be modified so that it can read input from a keyboard, a file or a database and send the output directly to a printer, or any other device or program.

A pipe has a source process and a destination process. The following program uses a pipe whose source process is the Unix system's

```
ls -R
```

command, and whose destination process is the Perl script.

Program 7.6

```perl
#!/usr/bin/perl
#lsRFind1.pl

use strict;
use Cwd;

my ($filename, @lines, $lines, $word);
$word = $ARGV[0];
open LSR, "ls -R|";
while ($filename = <LSR>){
    chomp $filename;
    next if (!(-T $filename));
    open TEXTFILE, $filename;
    @lines = <TEXTFILE>;
    $lines = join "", @lines;
    if ($lines =~ /$word/){
        print "Found word $word in file ", cwd(). "/$filename\n";
    }
}
```

This program takes a command line argument that is a word. The program searches for the presence of this word in any file recursively under the current directory. The pipe handle is called LSR.

```
open LSR, "ls -R|";
```

ls -R gives a recursive listing of files under the current directory. The LSR pipe handle returns one file name at a time when read using the read operator <...>. Thus, $filename used in the conditional of the while loop gets one file at a time. If this file is a text file, the program opens it for reading using the filehandle TEXTFILE. The file is read in list context, and hence @lines is a list containing all the lines in the file in sequence. The lines are joined together into a single string $lines. If the word given as command line argument occurs in the file, the file's fully qualified name is printed. The Cwd module's cwd() command is used to print the full name of the current working directory. The output of the program for one particular run is given below.

```
%lsRFind1.pl open
Found word open in file /home/kalita/cikm.pdf
Found word open in file /home/kalita/cikm1.pdf
Found word open in file /home/kalita/counter.pl
Found word open in file /home/kalita/lsRFind1.pl
ls: ./Math-Cephes-0.25/blib: Permission denied
Found word open in file /home/kalita/lsRFind1.pl
Found word open in file /home/kalita/lsRFind1.pl
```

Perl also provides a mechanism where the two ends of a pipe can be assigned names—one a producer process and the other a consumer process. It is called a *named pipe*. We not do discuss named pipes in this book.

7.2.2 Determining Who is Logged On

Let us assume that we are running Unix under *C-shell* or *csh*. In a workstation, a person may have several windows open, each window running a copy of the C-shell program. In addition, a person may be logged in several workstations. If we want to count the number of times a person is logged in or is running C-shell, we can run a program like the one that follows.

Program 7.7

```
#!/usr/bin/perl

#prints out the people who are logged in
use strict;

open (PROCESSES, "ps -aux |");

#Assuming csh is the shell used, it shows all who are logged in.
#We can do more stuff such as log out those who have been idle for
#a long time, if we have the privilege to do so.
while (<PROCESSES>){
    if (/csh/) {print STDOUT;}
}
close (PROCESSES);
```

The output of this program for one run is given blow.

```
% csh.pl
kalita   10693  0.0  0.4  2656 1252 pts/9    S    15:39   0:00 perl csh.pl
```

7.2.3   Using a Filehandle and a Pipe to Send Email

In this section, we have seen an example of a pipe used to produce an electronic mail message. There is an example of using a pipe to produce an automatic e-mail message from a CGI program in Section 8.3.11.

In Perl, we can create filehandles that are associated not with files but with processes. System (e.g., Unix) processes can accept inputs or send outputs to Perl programs by using filehandles that are associated with the processes. A system process here means a system command. A command takes time, however small, to execute and hence is called a *process* in computer terminology. For example, if we want to write some text in our Perl program and use the text to compose a mail message that we want to send out using the Unix `mail` program, we can open a filehandle that sends output to this filehandle. We write out to this filehandle before closing it. Closing of the filehandle sends out the mail message.

Let us look at a program that generates the letter somewhat like the one that we saw in the beginning of the chapter and actually e-mails it. The program is given below.

Program 7.8

```
#!/usr/bin/perl

$you = $ARGV[0]; $me =  $ARGV[1];
$high = $ARGV[2]; $low = $ARGV[3];

$space = " ";
$date = `date`;

open (MAIL,
'| /usr/ucb/mail -s "Today\'s and Tomorrow\'s Weather" larsen\@pikespeak.uccs.edu');

print MAIL "\t" x 5, $date, "\n";
print MAIL "Dearest \u$you,\n\n";
print MAIL $space x 5;
print MAIL "How are you doing? ";
print MAIL "Today's high and low temperatures here in Colorado Springs were";
print MAIL " $high and $low degrees F. ";
print MAIL "Tomorrow will be hotter!\n";
print MAIL "\n\u$me\n";

close (MAIL);
```

This program expects to get four command line arguments: the person receiving the message, the person sending it, the high temperature and the low temperature. It reads the four arguments from the `@ARGV` list and stores them in four scalars. Then, it calls the system's `date` command to obtain the current date and time. This date is printed on top of the message that is created and e-mailed automatically. Next, it opens a filehandle called `MAIL`. This filehandle is not associated with a file, but with a process. The process is `/usr/ucb/mail` which is where the Unix mail program is normally stored. This mail program takes an argument that is given by preceding it with `-s`. In this case, this argument gives us the subject of the mail message to be sent. The last argument to the mail program is the address of the person to whom the mail message is sent. The `@` in the e-mail address has to be escaped with a backslash.

As we can see, when we `open` the filehandle `MAIL`, we need to state the second argument to it in string format. This string is single-quoted. The first character in the string is the vertical line (`|`). The vertical line is called a *pipe* in Unix terminology. This vertical line states that the contents of the filehandle will be used as input to (or, piped into) the following process, the `mail` command in this case. So, when we write to the filehandle, the stuff that we write will be kept in the filehandle, and when the filehandle is closed, this stuff will be sent to (or, piped into) the mail process as its input. In this case, we write a brief letter to the MAIL filehandle. Once the complete text of the letter is written, we close the filehandle.

Closing the MAIL filehandle has the effect of sending all the contents of the filehandle (i.e., the letter we have composed) to the mail process. The mail process will create a subject based on the value of the first argument given to it. The mail program then sends the electronic message to the address given as its second argument.

As an example, the program is invoked as

```
%mailpipe mia jugal 80 40
```

The output of the program for this invocation is that it sends a mail message out to larsen@pikespeak.uccs.edu. The mail message sent out is given below.

```
Date: Tue, 17 Jun 1997 15:29:49 -0600
From: "J. Kalita" <kalita@pikespeak.uccs.edu>
To: larsen@pikespeak.uccs.edu
Subject: Today's and Tomorrow's Weather

                                    Tue Jun 17 15:29:48 MDT 1997


Dearest Mia,

How are you doing? Today's high and low temperatures here in Colorado Springs
were 80 and 40 degrees F. Tomorrow will be hotter!

Jugal
```

7.3 Forks

Any command or program that runs (in the Unix environment) is considered a *process*. Thus, a process can be a simple Unix command such as ls that gives a listing of files and takes very little time to execute, or a program that we have written ourselves that takes a considerable amount of time to execute.

7.3.1 Starting A Child Process

A process, whether long-lived or short-lived, takes a certain amount of time. A process runs, does some computation, possibly changes the environment and usually returns, i.e., it finishes. Once the process is finished, it no longer exists. A process that is running can create one or more clones of itself. In the Unix environment, the only way to create a new process is by using the fork command. All Unix shells provide a fork command. Perl provides a counterpart with the same name. fork is usually called with no arguments. It creates a process that is exactly similar to the one that created it.

The original process is called the *parent* process. The new process that is a clone is called a *child* process. Usually, a program is only one process that runs alone. However, after forking, the program is no longer one single process, but two processes running. In other words, the code following the fork is two processes running in parallel. These two processes need not be synchronized. They run at their own speed, and are independent of each other.

Thus, we need to distinguish between a *program* (or, a *script*) and a *process*. A program can have several processes running its code. A process, is in some sense, a thread of execution.

The following program forks a child process.

Program 7.9

```
#!/usr/bin/perl

#fork a child process
fork ();

#Two processes running
print "After forking a child\n";
```

The program simply makes a call to `fork`. There is no argument given to `fork`. After `fork()` has been executed there are two processes running at the same time. Both processes execute the statements that follow the fork. Therefore, the statement

```
print "After forking a child\n";
```

is run two times, once by each independent process. The output of this program is given below.

```
After forking a child
After forking a child
```

To verify that there is only one process before the execution of `fork()`, and two afterwards, let us modify the program slightly and run it again. The modified program is given below.

Program 7.10

```
#!/usr/bin/perl

print "Before forking a child\n";

fork ();

print "After forking a child\n";
```

The output of the program is given below.

```
Before forking a child
After forking a child
After forking a child
```

The print statement before the call to `fork()` is executed once, whereas the print statement afterwards is executed twice.

Of course, we can have more complex statements before and after the `fork()`. The following is another program that illustrates `forking` further.

Program 7.11

```
#!/usr/bin/perl

my ($i, $j);
```

```
#Before forking
for ($i=0; $i <= 5; $i++){
    print "\$i = $i\n";
}

fork ();

#After forking
for ($j=0; $j <= 4; $j++){
    print "\$j = $j\n";
}
```

The output of the program is given below.

```
$i = 0
$i = 1
$i = 2
$i = 3
$i = 4
$i = 5
$j = 0
$j = 1
$j = 2
$j = 0
$j = 1
$j = 3
$j = 4
$j = 2
$j = 3
$j = 4
```

Here we see that the lines with the index $i are printed only once because before forking, there is only one process in the program. However, after forking, there are two processes: a parent process and a child process. The child process executes the for loop with index $j once, and the parent process executes the loop another time. The two processes share the variable name $j, but keep two separate copies of it. Also, the two processes run in parallel without any synchronization. Therefore, the lines printed by the two processes can occur in any sequence.

We can fork as many processes as we want although it may not be a great idea if the processes are not doing anything useful. But, for the purpose of illustration, let us look at the next program.

Program 7.12

```
#!/usr/bin/perl

my ($i, $j);

#fork 7 child processes
for ($i=0; $i <= 2; $i++){
    fork ();
```

```
}

#The for loop is executed four times by four  different processes
for ($j=0; $j <= 2; $j++){
    print "\$j = $j\n";
}
```

Here, the first `for` loop `forks` seven processes leading to a total of eight processes when the loop is fully executed. This happens in the following manner.

Before the loop starts, there is only one process in the program. The execution of the first run of the loop for $i = 0$, forks a child process. Therefore, before the second run of the loop, we have two processes. Now, the second run of the loop causes each one of the two processes to produce two new children, leading to 4 processes overall. The third and the final run of the loop produces four more children, causing a total of eight processes to exist at the same time. That is why the second loop is executed 8 times. Each process executes the second `for` loop independently. The eight processes run independently without any synchronization. The parent for each child process is the original process that existed in the beginning of the program.

A sample output of this program is given below.

```
$j = 0
$j = 0
$j = 0
$j = 0
$j = 0
$j = 0
$j = 1
$j = 2
$j = 1
$j = 2
$j = 1
$j = 2
$j = 0
$j = 1
$j = 2
$j = 1
$j = 2
$j = 0
$j = 1
$j = 2
$j = 1
$j = 2
$j = 1
$j = 2
```

The output is quite likely to vary from one run to another.

Finally, we write a small program that has several `fork` statements, one after the other. These statements are not included in a loop like in the previous program.

Program 7.13

```
#!/usr/bin/perl

print "Before forking\n";
fork (); #1st forking
print "After first forking\n";
fork (); #2nd forking
print "After second forking\n";
fork();   #3rd forking
print "After third forking\n";
sleep 1;
```

The program has only one process to start with. Then, it forks a process. Therefore, after the first fork, we have two processes—the original process and a child process. Therefore, the line

```
After first forking
```

is printed twice. Next, we call fork() a second time. Each of the two processes creates two children. Therefore, the line

```
After second forking
```

is printed four times. The last line is printed eight times. A sample output from running the program is given below.

```
Before forking
After first forking
After second forking
After third forking
After first forking
After second forking
After second forking
After third forking
After second forking
After third forking
After third forking
After third forking
After third forking
After third forking
After third forking
```

We see that the lines can be printed in an arbitrary order depending on how the processes run. The output will vary from one run to another. We put the sleep command at the end to make the output printed look nice. Otherwise, the Unix prompt may be printed after any one of the processes has finished printing the last line. This statement causes each of the eight processes to wait a second after the last line is printed. During this time, all the other processes also print their output.

7.3.2 Forking and Variables

We know forked processes execute the same code. In other words, forked processes share the same code. This also means that forked processes have the same programming environment. However, on fork(), the parent process is cloned. A program's code (or, the *instruction segment*) is usually read-only and therefore is not usually copied by the cloned process. Both execute or share the same code. The variables that a process deals with are stored in a separate part of the memory called *data segment*. A copy of the data segment for the parent process is made for the child process. Therefore, although the child process uses the same variable names, it has a separate copy of each variable.

Let us look at the program that follows and see how the variables are updated by the two processes after a fork().

Program 7.14

```
#!/usr/bin/perl
use strict;

my $i = 0;

fork ();

#Each process increments its copy of $i
$i++;
print "\$i = $i\n";
```

Here, the variable name $i is available to both processes after the fork() command is executed. However, there are two separate copies of $i in the two data segments of the two processes. Therefore, each updates its copy of $i and prints the updated value separately. The output of the program is given below.

```
$i = 1
$i = 1
```

From what we have seen so far, it is not possible to know which process printed which line of output. But, we will soon know how to distinguish the two processes from each other.

By this time, one should realize that forking is expensive on system resources. Copies have to be made of the data for each process. Depending on how much data is involved and depending on how many processes are spawned or forked, it can become quite resource intensive. So, forking should be done with caution.

7.3.3   Forking and Files

When we fork() a child process, separate copies are created for the data handled by the processes. This is true for filehandles also. That is, a child process gets a copy of a filehandle. In other words, there are two filehandles with the same names (in two separate data segments). However, it is the same file with which the two filehandles are associated. Let us make this clear again. There are two filehandles (each with the same name), but only one file. So, if we write to the same filehandle, the same file is written to. If we read from the same filehandle, the pointer moves ahead in the same file.

We will first look at a program that opens a file and then creates two processes. The two processes write to the same file.

Program 7.15

```
#!/usr/bin/perl
use strict;
```

```perl
open (OUT, ">out.txt");

fork ();

#two processes writing to the same file
print OUT "After forking\n";
close OUT;
```

This program does not write to the file before forking. The two processes: parent and child, write to the file. They have two copies of the filehandle OUT. However, each copy is associated with the same file out.txt that is open for output. Therefore, the same line gets written two times to the file. Here is the output of this program.

```
After forking
After forking
```

Next, we modify this program a little bit so that the program writes to the file before forking. Here is the program.

Program 7.16

```perl
#!/usr/bin/perl
use strict;

open (OUT, ">out.txt");
#one process writing
print OUT "Before forking\n";

fork ();

#two processes writing
print OUT "After forking\n";
close OUT;
```

When we examine the contents of the file out.txt, we see the following.

```
Before forking
After forking
Before forking
After forking
```

This is not what we expected. It seems wrong that the string Before forking gets printed twice. Only one process is running before the fork and this should not have happened. However, understanding how a computer performs input-output functions readily explains the anomaly. When Perl writes to a filehandle (i.e., the associated file), it usually buffers the output. This means that a statement that prints to a file does not really write to the file right away, i.e., after every print statement. In reality, a print statement writes to a buffer and the buffer is written out to the physical file from time to time, or when the filehandle is closed. In this case, the parent process writes to the buffer associated with the filehandle OUT. Then, before the buffer is written out to the file, the parent process forks creating a child process. Now, the parent process continues to have its OUT filehandle associated with the file. The child process creates a copy of the OUT filehandle; this filehandle is also associated with the same file. At the time of forking, a copy is made of the buffer associated with the OUT filehandle for the child. The child gets whatever was present in its own copy of the buffer. Thus, the copy of the buffer the child gets also has the line Before forking just as the original copy of the buffer that the parent's filehandle has. After forking, both filehandles write to their individual buffers. At a certain point before the filehandle is closed (or when the filehandle is closed) the two buffers are written out to the physical file. This explains the contents of the output file.

To avoid this situation, we can write code that flushes the parent's filehandle just before forking. Flushing means we force the filehandle to be emptied and written out to the physical file. There are several ways we can flush a buffer, and from the moment of flushing, make the file handle unbuffered. In the program that follows, we use a module called IO::Handle that has a function that helps us flush a buffer. The function is called autoflush.

Program 7.17

```perl
#!/usr/bin/perl
use IO::Handle;
use strict;

open (OUT, ">out.txt");
print OUT "Before forking\n";
#flush the buffer associated with the parent process
autoflush OUT 1; #flush the output, i.e., print to file immediately

fork ();

#Both processes print this line
print OUT "After forking\n";
close OUT;
```

The statement that flushes the buffer is given below.

```
autoflush OUT 1;
```

autoflush takes two arguments: the filehandle, and an integer. 1 means unbuffer the output, that is flush what's already in the buffer and from now on, print it right away to the file instead of putting it in a buffer to be written to the file later. Therefore, in this program, the parent process's buffer is written out before the fork. After the fork both processes have copies of the filehandle OUT and both are unbuffered. Therefore, the output printed to the file is what we expect.

```
Before forking
After forking
After forking
```

We must note that unbuffering is quite likely to slow the program down. This is because the actual process of writing out to file on the disk is time consuming. The buffers are RAM and writing to RAM is much faster than writing to disk.

Discussing how files can be shared for reading becomes a little complex and is discussed later in the chapter. In Perl, it is difficult to read a line of text in an unbuffered mode.

7.3.4 Distinguishing Between Parent and Child Processes

In addition to creating a child process, `fork` returns an ID to the parent and the child. The child process that is created gets a value of 0 from `fork`. The parent process that created the child gets a non-zero value from `fork`. This is the identification number for the child that is created. If `fork` fails, it returns `undef` to the parent process. If `forking` fails, there is no child process. `forking` can fail because of reasons such as too many processes in the system, whether running or not.

The following program tests the idea that `fork` returns a separate value to each of the processes.

Program 7.18

```
#!/usr/bin/perl
use strict;

my $processID;

print "Before forking\n";
#fork returns a process ID number to the parent and another to the child
$processID = fork ();
print "My process ID number = $processID\n";
```

After `fork` we have two processes running. So, the `print` statement at the end of the program is executed by each of these two processes. But, because `fork` returns a different number to each of the two processes, the two processes print two different numbers. The output of a run of the program is given below.

```
Before forking
My process ID number = 32350
My process ID number = 0
```

The fact that `fork` returns a different number to the parent and the child processes can be used to distinguish one from the other. That is, the program code can have a conditional that checks for the returned value to tell one process from the other. The following is a simple program that performs such a conditional test.

Program 7.19

```
#!/usr/bin/perl
use strict;
my ($childProcessID);

print "I AM THE ONLY PROCESS.\n";

$childProcessID = fork ();

if ($childProcessID){
    print "I am the parent process.\n";
    }
else{
    print "I am the child process.\n";
}
```

Before the call to `fork`, there is only one process. It the prints

```
I  AM  THE  ONLY  PROCESS.
```

to announce itself to the world. Next, we have the call that creates a child process.

```
$childProcessID = fork ();
```

Following this line of code, we have an `if-else` statement. We have two processes running at this time. Both processes execute the `if-else` statement. The `$childProcessID` variable is available to both processes. However, `$childProcessID` has a non-zero value when examined by the parent process, and is zero when examined by the child process. Although the variable name is shared, each process has its own separate copy of the variable. In particular, there are two copies of `$childProcessID` for the two processes. For one process (the child), the associated value is 0, whereas it is non-zero for the other (the parent). For the parent, the value stored is the process ID of the child process. Because each process is associated with an ID, processes are able to communicate with one another, as we see later.

In this program, both processes are printing to STDOUT. These two processes run in parallel. Therefore, when we run the program, in some cases,

```
I  am  the  child  process.
```

is printed before the string

```
I  am  the  parent  process.
```

is printed.

In this program, the two processes are not very long-lived. After printing

```
I  am  the  parent  process.
```

the parent process has nothing more to do as there is no line of code following the `if-else` statement. Therefore, after printing the, the parent process is finished or dies naturally. Similarly, the child process is also finished after it prints its own string:

```
I  am  the  child  process.
```

After this string is printed, the child process has no additional lines of code to execute because it also reaches the end of the program.

In this program, there is no way to tell which process prints first and which process prints second. In addition, there is no way to tell which process ends first and which process ends next. The two processes have independent lives after the child process has been forked. They perform their actions independently although the instructions they follow are the same. They do so without communicating with each other. Since the amount of code in our program after the call to `fork()` is very small, everything happens fast. Therefore, it is most likely that the parent process does its printing before the child process.

The next program we discuss is a slight variation of the previous program. The only difference is that once a child process has been forked, each of the two existing processes runs a little longer than before and produces more output. It is because we have a small `for` loop inside the `if` block as well as inside the `else` block.

Program 7.20

```perl
#!/usr/bin/perl

use strict;
my ($childProcessID, $i);

print "I AM THE ONLY PROCESS.\n";

$childProcessID = fork ();

if ($childProcessID){
    for ($i = 0; $i <= 10; $i++){
        print "I am the parent process: Counting $i\n";
    }
}
else{
    for ($i = 0; $i <= 10; $i++){
        print "I am the child process: Counting $i\n";
    }
}
```

Because the two processes run in parallel, have independent existence, and do not synchronize their actions, the output of the program is intermixed between what the two processes print to STDOUT. Each process counts sequentially, but the two counts are interwoven. A possible output of the program to STDOUT is given below.

```
I AM THE ONLY PROCESS.
I am the parent process: Counting 0
I am the parent process: Counting 1
I am the child process: Counting 0
I am the child process: Counting 1
I am the child process: Counting 2
I am the child process: Counting 3
I am the child process: Counting 4
I am the child process: Counting 5
I am the child process: Counting 6
I am the child process: Counting 7
I am the parent process: Counting 2
I am the parent process: Counting 3
I am the parent process: Counting 4
I am the parent process: Counting 5
I am the parent process: Counting 6
I am the parent process: Counting 7
I am the parent process: Counting 8
I am the parent process: Counting 9
I am the parent process: Counting 10
I am the child process: Counting 8
I am the child process: Counting 9
I am the child process: Counting 10
```

7.3.5   forking and files again: Using process IDs

Let us look again at the programs we looked at a short while ago. In this section, we clearly determine which process is writing into a specific file in what order. We also discuss reading from files in this section. First, we look at a program that forks a process and each process prints one line to the same shared filehandle. This time, a process indicates that it is writing to the file.

Program 7.21

```perl
#!/usr/bin/perl
use IO::Handle;
use strict;

open (OUT, ">out.txt");
print OUT "Before forking\n";
#flush the buffer associated with the parent process
autoflush OUT 1; #flush the output, i.e., print to file immediately

my $pID = fork ();

#Both processes print this line
if ($pID){ #parent process
    print OUT "Parent: After forking\n";
}
else{
    print OUT "Child: After forking\n";
}

close OUT;
```

The output of this program redirected to the file out.txt is given below.

```
Before forking
Parent: After forking
Child: After forking
```

As we know, after forking, one line is written to the file by the parent process and the other by the child. Both processes close the filehandle.

In the next program, we fork a process right in the beginning. These two processes each open the same file in.txt for reading. The two processes print out what they read to the standard output. The file has the numbers 1 through 10, one number per line.

Program 7.22

```perl
#!/usr/bin/perl
use strict;

my $pID = fork ();

#Both processes read lines from IN
```

```
if ($pID){ #parent process
    print "File opened by Parent\n";
    open (IN, "in.txt");
    while (<IN>){
        print "Parent: $_";
        sleep 1;
    }
    close IN;
    print "File closed by Parent\n";
}
else{ #child process
    print "File opened by Child\n";
    open (IN, "in.txt");
    while (<IN>){
        print "Child: $_";
        sleep 2;
    }
    close IN;
    print "File closed by Child\n";
}
```

We have used two different amount of sleep time in the two processes to stagger the printing each one does. The output of the program printed to STDOUT is given below.

```
File opened by Parent
Parent: 1
File opened by Child
Child: 1
Parent: 2
Child: 2
Parent: 3
Parent: 4
Child: 3
Parent: 5
Parent: 6
Child: 4
Parent: 7
Parent: 8
Child: 5
Parent: 9
Parent: 10
Child: 6
File closed by Parent
Child: 7
Child: 8
Child: 9
Child: 10
File closed by Child
```

The output clearly shows that each of the two processes opens the same file separately. Each process keeps a copy of the filehandle IN. Each process has a pointer that points to, possibly a different part of the same file. Each process closes its access to the file using its filehandle. When one process closes the file, the other process still has the file open.

The following program shows a more complex situation in reading from a shared file. In the previous program, there were two filehandles and two file pointers to begin with. That is not the case in this program. Here, the parent process opens a file before forking. Therefore, there is only one filehandle to begin with. But, then, the parent process forks. This causes a copy of the filehandle to be made and given to the child process. In this case, we are performing unbuffered read and write operations. In Perl, a file can be opened for unbuffered reading using sysopen instead of open. In addition, to read in an unbuffered mode from a file, we need to use the sysread command instead of the angle bracket operator we have used most frequently so far. To print in unbuffered mode, the command used is syswrite instead of print.

Program 7.23

```perl
#!/usr/bin/perl
use Fcntl;
use strict;
my ($childPID);

sysopen (IN, "in1.txt", O_RDONLY);

$childPID = fork ();

while (1){
#Both processes read lines
    if ($childPID){ #parent
        sysread (IN, $_, 1);
        if (!$_){last;}
        syswrite  STDOUT, "Parent: $_", 9;
        syswrite  STDOUT, "\n", 1;
    }
    else { #child
        sysread (IN, $_, 1);
        if (!$_){last;}
        syswrite  STDOUT, "Child: $_", 8;
        syswrite  STDOUT, "\n", 1;
    }
}

close IN;
```

Assume the file in1.txt has the following content.

```
1234567891011121314151617181920
```

The output of the program is given below. Each process in the program reads one character in unbuffered mode. Each process also prints in unbuffered mode. As a result, the printing operations performed by the two processes is mixed up.

```
Parent: 1
Child: 2
Child: 3
Child: 4
```

```
Child: 5
Child: 6
Child: 7
Child: 8
Child: 9
Child: 1

Parent: 1
Parent: 1
Parent: 1
Parent: 2
Parent: 1
Parent: 3
Parent: 1
Parent: 4
Parent: 1
Parent: 5
Parent: 1
Parent: 6
Parent: 1
Parent: 7
Parent: 1
Parent: 8
Parent: 1
Parent: 9
Parent: 2
```

This program uses the Fcntl module to use certain constants such as O_RDONLY with the sysopen command. The program opens a file by the name in1.txt for reading. It uses sysopen so that it can read byte by byte. The O_RDONLY argument to sysopen indicates that the file is opened for reading only. The program forks next creating a process whose process ID is $childPID, as known by the parent process. Next, the program goes into a while loop that runs for ever, i.e., till exited explicitly from within the loop.

As we know well by now, after the fork, there are two processes executing the code in the program. As usual, we have an if-else statement inside the while loop so that the two processes can execute some part of the code independently of each other. The parent process uses sysread to read one byte from the filehandle IN. The second argument to sysread contains the variable to which the value is being read. If the byte read is 0 or the empty string, the parent process finishes the loop by executing the last command. If the byte read is non-zero or non-empty, the parent process prints it using syswrite. The last argument to syswrite is the number of bytes written.

The child process executes the code in the else block. The child process also reads a byte and prints it if it is non-zero or non-empty. If it is zero or the empty string, the child process exits the loop.

7.3.6 waitpid (), A Parent Waiting for a Child

It is quite possible that sometimes we want a parent process and a child process to communicate. Only very limited communication is possible between a parent and a child. In fact, the parent can usually just wait for a child to die and nothing more. In the human context, usually a parent dies before a child. However, in the context of Unix processes, quite commonly it is the opposite. Usually, a parent process creates a child and engages it in doing something useful. Once the child process finishes the designated task, the child dies. If later another child is needed for performing another task, the parent creates a second child. Thus, usually, the parent is long-lived whereas the children are more ephemeral. A parent process can wait to be informed when a child dies. There are two waiting functions: wait and waitpid.

A parent process can execute waitpid after forking a child. waitpid takes the child's process ID as argument. waitpid causes the parent process to suspend itself and wait till the child executes its given task and dies. Thus, the parent process just waits, doing nothing, till the child with the process ID expires. At this point, the system informs the parent process and it wakes up and starts executing from where it was suspended. The following program illustrates this.

Program 7.24

```
#!/usr/bin/perl
use strict;
my ($childProcessID, $i);

print "I AM THE ONLY PROCESS.\n";

$childProcessID = fork ();

if ($childProcessID){
        print "I am the parent process.\n";
        print "I spawned a new process with ID $childProcessID\n";
        waitpid ($childProcessID, 0);
        print "The child process is terminated with status $?\n";
    }
else{
    for ($i = 0; $i <= 10; $i++){
        print "I am the child process: Counting $i\n";
    }
}
```

The output may look like the following. It is possible that the "I spawned" line is printed after the child process finishes printing at count 10

```
I AM THE ONLY PROCESS.
I am the parent process.
I spawned a new process with ID 7610
I am the child process: Counting 0
I am the child process: Counting 1
I am the child process: Counting 2
I am the child process: Counting 3
I am the child process: Counting 4
I am the child process: Counting 5
I am the child process: Counting 6
I am the child process: Counting 7
I am the child process: Counting 8
I am the child process: Counting 9
I am the child process: Counting 10
The child process is terminated with status 0
```

It shows that the parent creates a child process and then it waits doing nothing, specifically waiting morbidly for the recently created child to die. The child process prints a sequence of lines using the for loop and dies. Once the child dies, the operating system informs the parent process of the death of the child. This causes the parent to get active again and print the line informing the child has been terminated.

To be precise, `waitpid` suspends execution of the current process until the child process specified by the process ID argument has died, or until a signal has been delivered whose action is to terminate the current process or call a signal handling function. We do not discuss signals much in this book. If a child as requested by the process ID has already exited by the time of the call, the function returns immediately.

The second argument to `waitpid` is called the *options* argument. The meaning of this argument is complicated and we do not discuss it here. The value of zero suffices for our purpose. To understand the value of the argument, the reader is instructed to consult the Unix man page on `waitpid` or `wait`. There are discussions on processes in *Unix for Programmers and Users* [GA99] and *Unix System Administration Handbook* [NSSH01].

The special variable `$?` stores the status returned by the `waitpid` function. The value can vary from system to system, situation to situation.

The `wait` function is similar to the `waitpid` function except that `wait` waits for any child and *not* a specific numbered child to die.

7.4 Sockets

The Unix operating system uses *sockets* as one means for allowing two computer programs to communicate. The two programs can reside on the same machine, but it is more interesting if the programs are on two different computers on a network, possibly the Internet. In such a case, it is possible for two programs running on two different computers, whether across the hall or across the world, to communicate. Such programs work using the *client-server* model of computing. The *server* is a program that runs continuously on a computer. It usually does not do anything on its own except wait for some request to come to it. The *client* program does not run all the time. It runs only when the user activates it.

A client usually sends a request to a server program running on the same or another machine in the network. When a server program gets a request from a client program, it performs the requested operation, and sends the result back to the client. This is how all modern service-based programs run. Some of the most prominent and useful client server programs are Web servers and clients (browsers), electronic mail servers and clients (e-mail readers), and ftp servers and clients for transferring files between two machines on a network.

Sockets are a tool that can be used to build such client-server programs. As we already know, there are two counterparts in such programs—the client runs on one machine, and the server runs on (possibly) another machine. For the two programs to communicate, each program must create a socket. When a client program sends a request to the server, the client sends the information to a certain port on the server. The server has a socket attached to this port. The port is simply a specialized memory location that the server program checks frequently to see if there is a request or some data sitting at it. Once the server finds something on the port, it performs the operations requested with the data given, obtains any results and sends the results to the socket associated with its port. The socket is smart enough to send the information back through the network to the client program's machine at the specified port used by the client. The client program has a socket associated with the local port on its machine. It reads the information that has arrived at the socket and does whatever it deems appropriate.

A specific example pair is a Web server and a Web client. The Web server runs a *daemon* process on a machine connected to the Internet. A daemon is the Unix name for a process that runs all the time. On a Unix machine, the Web server is called the *httpd* daemon. The httpd daemon process listens to a certain port. The default port is 80 although someone setting up a Web server can specify another port such as 1080 or 8080.

The Web client is a browser program that runs on a user's machine. Examples of Web browsers are Netscape Communicator, Microsoft Internet Explorer, NCSA Mosaic, Opera, Lynx, etc. The user uses a browser program to get on the Web. When a user specifies a URL such as http://www.shillong.com and wants to read a Web page, the browser creates a socket associated with a specific port on the local machine. This socket is authorized to talk to a socket on port 80 of the machine serving the Web pages for www.shillong.com. When the request for a page arrives at port 80 of www.shillong.com, the HTTP server works on the request. It retrieves the page requested by the browser and sends it to the socket on the specific port on the machine running the client program. Once the browser gets the requested HTML file, it displays the file and its contents.

The socket is an interface so that programmers can develop their own distributed applications. The socket interface has not been standardized by any institution although they are a *de facto* standard. This is because sockets work very easily with the Unix environment. Sockets are seamlessly integrated with the Unix operating system. An implementation of the socket programmer interface is available for the Windows operating systems also. It is called WinSock and has become the standard in the IBM-compatible PC world. There are sockets that work with Macintosh computers also, whether the older Mac OS (up to OS 9), or Unix-based OS X and later.

The socket interface is very symmetrical in server programs and client programs. With minor differences, the same sequence of systems calls is executed to set up connections by the client program, and to accept a connection by a server program.

Sockets work with two lower-level network protocols. A protocol defines a precise sequence of steps for communication. Thus, a protocol is very constrained language for communication. The two lower-level protocols that sockets work with are the Transmission Control Protocol (TCP) and the User Datagram Protocol (UDP). We do not need to know many details about these protocols to write socket programs. One is advised to read a book such as *Computer Networks and Internets* [Com99], or *Data and Computer Communications* [Sta97] for details regarding how networks work and the differences between TCP and UDP.

In very simple terms TCP is a connection-oriented protocol. Thus, the TCP protocol can be likened to the way telephones work. When two people talk on the phone, there is a clear physical line of communication established between the two parties. The voice data goes back and forth between the two individuals on this line. Similarly, for TCP to work, a line or channel of communication must be established between the client and the server. Well-known applications such as the World Wide Web that use the higher level (application layer) protocol called HTTP use TCP as the protocol at a lower level. TELNET used for remotely logging on to a computer, and FTP used for transferring files between two computers use TCP as a lower level protocol.

The UDP is also a lower level protocol at the same level as TCP in network operations. UDP is connectionless. In other words, it is like the postal system. When we mail a letter at the post office for a specific destination, no direct physical line of communication is established between the source and the destination. The mailed letter moves from postal station to postal station, and finally is delivered to the destination address by a mailman. The UDP protocol is similar. When data is sent by UDP, there is no physical line of communication established between the source and the destination. The data is sent from computer to computer on the route till it arrives at the destination. Remote Procedure Calls (RPC) available on Unix and other systems use UDP as a lower-level protocol.

There are other significant differences between TCP and UDP, but we do not discuss them in this book.

7.4.1   Perl's Built-in Sockets

Perl provides us with a set of built-in functions for dealing with sockets. The names of Perl functions that deal with sockets are the same as the names of the corresponding system calls one sees in the Unix environment. The number and the names of the arguments, however, vary.

In Unix, all devices have a file-like interface. Sockets are treated like devices and therefore, have a file-like interface. Perl also takes this approach to files, pipes, sockets and other so-called devices.

The concept of a socket provides an abstraction that is file-like, but deals with communication. When a program creates a socket, Perl creates a handle just like a filehandle or stream. This filehandle is used in all further socket-related commands and can be used to read and write just like filehandles. Writing to a socket causes the written information to be sent to the corresponding peer or companion socket on the same or another machine. Reading from a socket lets a process get the information sent to it by another process. Of course, the line of communication has to be open for the information to be transferred. That is, if we are talking about two separate machines, they have to be linked by a network.

Perl's built-in socket functions are quite low-level. They provide enormous flexibility, but at the same time require significant effort to understand and hence, use. In this book, we refrain from discussing them, since for almost all practical purposes, the contributed modules discussed next suffice.

7.4.2 `Sockets::IO` and `Sockets::IO::INET` Packages

It is possible to write socket programs using the built-in functions that Perl provides. However, it is cumbersome to do so, since a lot of details need to be specified and dealt with. An easier way to write socket programs in Perl is to use a module called `IO::Socket` or `IO::Socket::INET`, if we are dealing with the Internet. These modules provide the functionality to write socket programs easily. In this section, we discuss how these modules work.

7.4.2.1 A Simple Client-Server Set-up

Let us start with two simple programs that creates two sockets: a server socket and a client socket. The two programs can run either on the same machine or on two different machines. If they run on the same machine, say, in two different terminals, the communication that takes place between the two processes, takes place in the same machine. However, if the two processes are on two different machines, whether in the same laboratory, or across the globe, the communication travels through either the local network, or the Internet, as the need be.

In the following, there are two programs. Each program creates a process. One process is a sending process and the other is a receiving process. The sending process is the *client*, and the receiving process the *server*. The receiving process or the server responds in some way to the information or request it gets from a sending process or client.

The first program we present is the receiving program, named `simpleReceive.pl`. It runs on a machine called `pikespeak.uccs.edu`. It uses the module `IO::Socket::INET`. This module provides for socket communication for so-called Internet-type communication.

Program 7.25
_____

```perl
#!/usr/bin/perl
#simpleReceive.pl

use IO::Socket::INET;
$sock = new IO::Socket::INET (LocalHost => 'pikespeak.uccs.edu',
      LocalPort => 1200,
      Proto => 'tcp',
      Listen => 5,
      Reuse => 1);
die "Couldn't connect: $!" unless $sock;

while ($newSock = $sock->accept()) {
    while (defined ($buf = <$newSock>)) {
          print $buf;
```

```
    }
    close ($newSock);
}

close ($sock);
```

The program starts by creating a socket called $sock. The socket is created by calling the constructor new of the IO::Socket::INET module, with a set of arguments. The arguments are given in terms of key-value pairs. The LocalHost argument specifies the machine on which the socket is running. The address can be given as a name or in terms of an IP address. Unless we need the program to run on a specific machine, it is not necessary to give the value of LocalHost. If LocalHost is not specified, the program can run on any host.

The second argument, given above, is called LocalPort, and it specifies the port which the program will use on the local machine. It is necessary to specify this port number for a server program, and publish it so that clients know where to find it. For a user-written program, it is advisable to use a port number above 1024 such that it does not conflict with any existing service or program.

The third argument specifies the protocol to use for communication. Any communication across a network has to follow a specific rule for construction of messages. Transmission Control Protocol (TCP) is a protocol that can be used to send messages back and forth among machines. In the Internet, TCP is the dominant protocol. This argument also does not need to provided. TCP is assumed if no protocol is specified.

The argument Listen provides the size of the wait queue for listening. When a socket is operative, it listens at a certain port number for input coming to it. A port's listening queue has a certain default size. If the number of incoming connections is less than the limit, the next connection request is blocked. This means that the request is not rejected, but the request is put in the queue to be processed. Usually, a blocked process does not get any reply and hangs till it is unblocked. In general, unblocking happens when it moves to the front of the listening queue at the server end of the communication line. Only one request can be processed at any time. However, if the queue size is at its maximum, when an additional request comes to the server later, the request is outright rejected. The program sending the request gets a response saying the request cannot be serviced.

The argument Reuse says that we are able to restart our server manually without waiting a little while to allow system buffers to clear out. It is optional.

The server program's call to new performs all the lower level preparation needed to establish a socket that listens at port 1200. It then does nothing but listen at that port or memory location. In other words, it samples that port every once in a while to see if there is a message for it. If there is no message, it does not do anything, but blocks.

If the socket could not be established for whatever reason, such as TCP not working, the call to new returns false. The program dies if a socket could not be established. If the program could create a socket successfully, the program then goes into the while loop. In the conditional of this loop, the program makes a call to the accept method of the socket.

The accept method returns a new object which is in the same class as the listening object. In other words, it returns a new socket. It is this new socket that is then used to communicate with the client that was trying to make a contact by sending information. In a scalar context, as it is being used here, accept returns the new socket if it is successfully created. In this program, as long as a new socket for the current communication can be created, the conditional of the while loop returns true. If there are situations in the system that do not allow socket creation after a request has come from a client, accept returns undef. The connection created by accept is bidirectional, although in this program, only one directional communication is used.

Inside the first while loop, there is a second while loop. The second loop's conditional reads from the socket. Once a socket has been created successfully, it can be read from or written to as if it were a filehandle. The conditional of the second while loop reads a line from the socket if there is a line to be read. If there are no lines to be read, it returns `undef` which evaluates to false. Inside the second `while` loop, the program simply prints the line read from the socket to the standard output.

Thus, in summary, the server program creates a socket, listens for incoming requests creating a new socket for each new request, and then reads the input coming to it from a communicating party, and prints the information it receives on the standard output at its terminal.

The second program also uses the `IO::Socket::INET` module. It runs on any machine, including `pikespeak.uccs.edu` on which the listening program is running. It sends some information to the `simpleReceive.pl` program and terminates. This is the *client* program.

Program 7.26

```perl
#!/usr/bin/perl
#simpleSend.pl
#works with simpleReceive.pl

use IO::Socket::INET;
$sock = new IO::Socket::INET (PeerAddr => 'pikespeak.uccs.edu',
                              PeerPort => 1200,
                              Proto => 'tcp');

die "Couldn't connect: $!" unless $sock;

foreach (1..10){
        print $sock "Repeating $_ time(s): How are you?\n";
}

close ($sock);
```

This program is written to work with the previous program `simpleReceive.pl` that creates a listener or server on the machine `pikespeak.uccs.edu`. Like the listening program, the sending program also creates a socket by calling the new method of the `IO::Socket::INET` package. This time, the arguments given are different.

The first argument is called `PeerAddr`. In socket communication, two sockets talking to each other, are considered equals or peers. This argument specifies the peer machine to which this socket is going to talk. This is the machine on which our listening program or server is running. If the listening program was running somewhere else, this line will have to be edited to reflect the machine on which the listening program is running. In this case, `PeerAddr` gives the address of the server machine. Next, the `PeerPort` argument gives the number of the port on which the listener is listening. This port was earlier published by the author of the server program to facilitate communication from clients. The `Proto` argument says that the communication is going to be taking place using the communication language of TCP.

Like the listening program, this program `dies` if the socket could not be created successfully. For the socket creation to be successful, the program has to be able to create a new socket on the machine on which it is running, and also establish connection to the socket that is waiting to listen on the other machine. If any of these two steps are not successful, the socket creation step fails.

In the rest of the program, the client simply goes into a loop and in every iteration of the loop, prints a simple sentence to the socket. Writing to a socket is done using the same syntax as writing to a file. Because we are writing to a socket, the socket delivers the strings written to it directly to the destination socket on the listening machine. This transfer of the information between two programs on the same machine (if the programs are running on the same machine) or across the world transported via the Internet, happens almost magically as far this program in concerned. However, all the details of communication are being taken care of by lower-level implementations that we do not see. Thus, the socket provides a high-level abstraction for communicating programs to work with.

To run this pair of programs, we place the program `simpleReceive.pl` on the `pikespeak.uccs.edu` machine, start a terminal, and start it on the command line. It does nothing but wait. This is how a server program essentially behaves. We then place the other program `simpleSend.pl` on the same machine, or on another machine, say `cs.uccs.edu`, and start it. This is the client program. If the client program is successful in creating the socket link, it starts to write to its own socket next, and the lines of text the client writes on the socket start to appear at the other end of the socket, at the server. In this case, the server does not do anything with the lines, but simply prints them on the standard output at its end.

Once the client finishes writing the lines onto its end of the communication line, it automatically finishes as it has nothing to do. However, the server program does not die. It goes back to its waiting mode, waiting for more information to come to it. We can kill the server program by typing in Control-C or a similar command on the terminal it is running.

The output of the program on the server side is given below. Remember, in this case, the server runs on the machine `pikespeak.uccs.edu`, but could run on any machine.

```
Repeating 1 time(s): How are you?
Repeating 2 time(s): How are you?
Repeating 3 time(s): How are you?
Repeating 4 time(s): How are you?
Repeating 5 time(s): How are you?
Repeating 6 time(s): How are you?
Repeating 7 time(s): How are you?
Repeating 8 time(s): How are you?
Repeating 9 time(s): How are you?
Repeating 10 time(s): How are you?
```

At this point, the server program is killed by typing control-C. However, it is not necessary to kill the server program. We can run the client program a second or a third time on the client machine. Every time we do so, the client writes lines of text into its socket which show up at the server end. So, if we keep the server alive and run the client three times, we will see the following output at the server end.

```
Repeating 1 time(s): How are you?
Repeating 2 time(s): How are you?
Repeating 3 time(s): How are you?
Repeating 4 time(s): How are you?
Repeating 5 time(s): How are you?
Repeating 6 time(s): How are you?
Repeating 7 time(s): How are you?
Repeating 8 time(s): How are you?
Repeating 9 time(s): How are you?
Repeating 10 time(s): How are you?
Repeating 1 time(s): How are you?
Repeating 2 time(s): How are you?
Repeating 3 time(s): How are you?
Repeating 4 time(s): How are you?
Repeating 5 time(s): How are you?
Repeating 6 time(s): How are you?
Repeating 7 time(s): How are you?
Repeating 8 time(s): How are you?
```

```
Repeating 9 time(s): How are you?
Repeating 10 time(s): How are you?
Repeating 1 time(s): How are you?
Repeating 2 time(s): How are you?
Repeating 3 time(s): How are you?
Repeating 4 time(s): How are you?
Repeating 5 time(s): How are you?
Repeating 6 time(s): How are you?
Repeating 7 time(s): How are you?
Repeating 8 time(s): How are you?
Repeating 9 time(s): How are you?
Repeating 10 time(s): How are you?
```

It is the same output, but now repeated three times. Note that it is not necessary to run the client program several times on the same machine; we can run it on different machines across the Internet. The effect at the server end will be the same nonetheless.

Most arguments to the new method are not necessary when running the server and client programs. The following minimum are necessary in the server program.

```
$sock = new IO::Socket::INET (
    LocalPort => 1200,
    Listen => 5, #Without Listen, get error
    );
```

At the client end, the following shows the minimum number of arguments needed.

```
$sock = new IO::Socket::INET (PeerAddr => 'pikespeak.uccs.edu',
                              PeerPort => 1200
    );
```

We can replace the name of a machine by its IP address.

```
$sock = new IO::Socket::INET (PeerAddr => '128.198.162.231',
                              PeerPort => 1200
    );
```

If only one argument is given to new, it is assumed to be a specification of peer address followed by a peer port, the two being separated by a colon. So, the following specifications work in the client program.

```
$sock = new IO::Socket::INET ('pikespeak.uccs.edu:1200'
    );
$sock = new IO::Socket::INET ('128.198.162.231:1200'
    );
```

These two programs—server and client—work equally well if the package used is IO::Socket and not IO::Socket::INET. That is, we can use the new method in IO::Socket instead of IO::Socket::INET. These two packages provide the same functionality as far as Internet-based sockets go.

7.4.2.2 Fetching a Web Page

In this section, we discuss a program that acts as a simple HTTP client, fetching a Web Page from a specified Web server. Here, we write the client program only. The companion server program already exists and is one of the standard servers such as Apache Web server that the site we want to communicate with employs. A Web browser like Netscape or Microsoft Internet Explorer is a very sophisticated HTTP client. Fetching textual Web pages from servers is a very small part of all that a sophisticated browser can do. A simple textual browser like Lynx is more close to what we do below in that it can deal with only textual image pages.

The program given below has a main section toward the end. There it calls a subroutine called getURL that parses an absolute URL and if it is of the right syntax, fetches the file denoted by the URL, by contacting the Web server specified in the URL. The program is given next with discussions following it.

Program 7.27

```perl
#!/usr/bin/perl -w
#file fetchURL1.pl
use strict;
use IO::Socket;

#Open a TCP connection and get the URL as specified in the
#input list: (server-name, port-number, file-address)
sub openTCPConnection{
    my ($server, $port, $fileAddr) = @_;
    my $socket = new IO::Socket::INET (
                        PeerAddr => $server,
                        PeerPort => $port,
                        Proto => 'tcp');
    die "Couldn't connect: $!" unless $socket;
    print "Created a TCP socket with $server\n";
    print $socket "GET $fileAddr  HTTP/1.1\n\n";

    #Read all the lines of the remote file to @remoteFile
    my @remoteFile = <$socket>;
    close ($socket);
    return @remoteFile;
}


#parse the URL and return a list: (server-name, port-number, file-address)
sub parseURL{
    my ($url) = @_;
    my ($server, $port, $file);

    $url =~ m#http://([^/:]+)(:(\d+))?(/.+)#i;
    $server = $1;
        #If port is not provided, default to 80
    ($port = $3) || ($port = 80);
        #$4 is the file name;  if $4 is empty, "/" is the file name
    ($file = $4) || ($file = "/");
    return ($server, $port, $file);
}


#Given a URL, get the file. Assume HTTP protocol
sub getURL{
    my ($url) = @_;
```

```
    my ($server, $port, $file) = parseURL ($url);
      #open the TCP connection and return the fetched file
    openTCPConnection ($server,  $port, $file);
}


#main
my $url = "http://www.uccs.edu/";
print getURL ($url);
```

The program has three subroutines: openTCPConnection, parseURL and getURL. The main program calls getURL with a URL as argument. We make the assumption that the URL is absolute, i.e., starts with http://, and is well-formed.

The getURL subroutine calls parseURL on the URL passed to it. parseURL returns three components of the URL: the HTTP server name, the port number, and the file. Once these three components are obtained, getURL calls openTCPConnection with these components as argument. openTCPConnection returns a list containing the textual lines of the file on the server corresponding to the requested URL. getURL simply returns what openTCPConnection returns.

The parseURL subroutine gets a well-formed URL as argument. It performs pattern matching to extract the server name, the port number if specified, and the file name that follows. If the port number is not provided, it defaults to 80. If the file name is empty after parsing, the file name is returned as / by default.

The openTCPConnection subroutine takes three arguments: server name, port number and file address. It opens a TCP socket at port 1200 on the local machine. The other end of the socket is at the HTTP server at the port obtained from the URL. If the creation of the socket is successful, the subroutine prints the HTTP GET method on the socket with the required arguments: the file name on the server, and the HTTP protocol version. HTTP is the protocol or language used by a Web server and a Web client to talk to each other. There are several methods or commands that the HTTP protocol allows, one of them being GET.

The GET method must be followed by two newlines—\n\n, because the HTTP protocol requires a blank line following the method call for the server to work on it. The GET method instructs the HTTP server to fetch a file. The HTTP server simply tries to obtain this file from its file structure, and if the file can be found, returns it using the socket to the requesting client. At the other end of the socket, that is, in openTCPConnection, the program reads what arrives at its end. This reading is done using the following line of the program.

```
my @remoteFile = <$socket>;
```

This is a read operation in list or array context. Such a read operation reads all the lines available at the socket and stores them as elements of the list @remoteFile. For the socket reading operation to happen correctly, the socket must be unbuffered, i.e., it must be read as input comes to it, instead of the reading taking place only after there is a certain amount of material to read. In the current version of Perl, sockets are automatically unbuffered. In older versions of Perl, this had to be done explicitly using select or autoflush. openTCPConnection simply returns the list containing all the lines in the file corresponding to the URL.

The main part of the program simply fetches a URL, and prints the fetched file on the terminal window. Of course, it prints it as text, and it is not formatted using the HTML tags in the text, as one would expect in a regular Web client or browser.

7.4.2.3   A Simple Web Crawler

In this section, we discuss a simple attempt at writing a program that crawls the World Wide Web. The program starts from a specified URL, fetches it, parses it, culls the URLs that are in this file, and then traverses these URLs in turn. It traverses text URLs only. We have broken the program into three packages or modules: URLConf.pm, Tcp.pm, Crawl.pm, and the main program findURLs.pl. We start by presenting the main program.

Program 7.28

```
#!/usr/bin/perl -w
#file findURLs.pl
use strict;
use diagnostics -verbose;
use Crawl;

my ($server, $file, $port);
my $url = "http://www.cs.uccs.edu/~kalita";

Crawl::getURLsRecursively ($url);
```

The main program uses a package called Crawl that we discuss a little later. In Perl, a package is stored in a file with .pm extension. A package can be stored in the same directory as where the script that uses it, or in an operating system-specific location (or, *site* location) so that all programs by all users can access it. Here, we assume the file Crawl.pm is in the same directory as the main file findURLs.pl. The statement

```
use Crawl;
```

loads the package for us, and makes all its identifiers, i.e., variables, subroutines, and objects, available without qualification. In the main program, we specify a URL where we start crawling. Then, we make the call

```
Crawl::getURLsRecursively ($url);
```

to start the crawling process. getURLsRecursively is a subroutine defined in the Crawl package. The package name qualification Crawl:: is not necessary. We use the qualifier to make explicit where the subroutine is defined. Even if we use a fully qualified name, we must use the use directive so that the package's names are available.

Before we discuss the contents of the Crawl package, we discuss two simple packages that Crawl uses: URLConf, and Tcp.

The URLConf package defines a few global variables. These variables are declared only once and used by all the other packages. It is a simple package where we do not make any attempts at exporting variable names.

Program 7.29

```
#!/usr/bin/perl
#file URLConf.pm
package URLConf;

#number of URLs  we want to collect
```

```perl
$FILE_NO_LIMIT = 10000;

#The file where we store the URLs collected
$TRAVERSED_URL_FILE = "traversedURLs.txt";

#Specify patterns whose presence in a URL will disqualify it,
#as regular expressions
$EXCLUDEPATTERNS = "(cgi-bin|mailto:|cgi\?|#.*)";

#Specify all MIME extensions whose presence at the end of a file name
#causes the file to be considered a simple file and not a directory
$MIMEEXTS = "(html?|xml|gif|jpg|jpeg|css|xsl|asp)";

#Specify the MIME extensions of files that we want to fetch and analyze
$INCLUDEDEXTS = "(html?|xml)";

#The domains in which we are collecting URLs
#Write multiple domains separated by | as in
#If you want to cover all domains, put ".*" as the domain name.
$DOMAINS_COVERED = "uccs.edu|colorado.edu|cudenver.edu|uchsc.edu|cusys.edu";

#We need to escape the . in a name like uccs.edu
if ($DOMAINS_COVERED ne ".*"){
    $DOMAINS_COVERED =~ tr/./\./;
}

1;
```

$FILE_NO_LIMIT specifies the maximum number of URLs the crawler will fetch. It may fetch a fewer number if it cannot find the maximum number of URLs requested. $TRAVERSED_URL_FILE specifies the name of the file where the fetched URLs will be stored, one per line. $DOMAINS_COVERED specifies the domains which will be explored. In other words, when the program finds a URL outside these domains, it will silently reject the URL. The variable $EXCLUDEDPATTERNS gives a regular expression that specifies the URLs that should be rejected. For example, in this case, URLs that should be rejected are ones that have the substring cgi-bin, cgi?, mailto:, etc., in them. Such URLs will not be explored. Also, URLs containing # will not crawled. Some of the URLs that the program will access are directories and others are simple files. The variable $MIMEEXTENSIONS specifies a regular expression listing a set of file extensions. File names ending with these extensions are considered by the program as simple files. Others are considered directories.

The second package that Crawl.pm uses is Tcp.pm. The package's contents are a minor variation of the program defined in section 7.4.2.2. There are two subroutines: openTCPandFetch and parseURL. If openTCPandFetch cannot create a socket to a certain server, it does not die, but simply warns and carries on with the next URL. It sends the GET method to the HTTP server as usual. It sends a couple more headers, saying it accepts all kinds of file **MIME** (Multi-purpose Internet Mail Extensions) types. The program also identifies itself to the server as an agent, or the so-called user agent, called *UCCSAgent*, version 1.0. If the reply that comes back from the sever does not contain the string

```
200 OK
```

on line 1, saying the GET request was successful, the subroutine returns empty handed. Otherwise, it returns the contents of the file fetched. The parseURL subroutine is exactly like the one discussed in

Section 7.4.2.2.

Finally, we discuss the package `Crawl.pm`. It contains two fairly long subroutines: `findURLs` and `getURLsRecursively`. `getURLsRecursively` is the one called from the main program `findURLs.pl`.

Program 7.30

```perl
#!/usr/bin/perl -w
#file Crawl.pm
package Crawl;

use strict;
use diagnostics -verbose;
use Tcp;
use URLConf;

#Given a URL, fetch the document and find all text URLs in it.
sub findURLs{
    my ($pushedURL, $fileNew);
    my ($href);
    my (%thisFileURLHash);
    my ($directoryNew);

    my ($url) = @_;
    my ($server, $port, $completeFilePath) = Tcp::parseURL ($url);

    $completeFilePath =~ m@(.*/)(.*)@;
    my ($directory, $file) = ($1, $2);
    #We were getting files or directory names with spaces in them.
    #This was trouble.
    if ($directory =~ /\s+/ or $file =~ /\s+/){return;}

    my @HTMLText = Tcp::openTCPandFetch ($server, $port, $completeFilePath);
    chomp @HTMLText;
    my $text = join " ", @HTMLText;
    my @hrefs = ($text =~ /<A\s+href\s*=\s*"([^"]+)"/ig);
    @hrefs = grep !/$URLConf::EXCLUDEPATTERNS/, @hrefs;

    my ($serverNew, $portNew, $completeFilePathNew);

 FIND_TEXT_URLS:
   foreach $href (@hrefs){
      #Absolute URL: $href starts with http://
      if ($href =~ m@http://@){
          my ($serverNew, undef, undef)  = Tcp::parseURL ($href);
          next FIND_TEXT_URLS if ($serverNew !~ m@$URLConf::DOMAINS_COVERED@);
          $thisFileURLHash{$href}++;
          next FIND_TEXT_URLS;
        }

      #Relative URL; Need to take care of situations where
      #the embedded URL starts with ., ../, or ../.., or just a file name.
      #We ignore a URL if it has more than two sequences of ../
      if ($href =~ m@^/@){
              ($fileNew) = $href =~ m@^/(.*)@;
```

```perl
                $directoryNew = $directory;
        }
        elsif ($href =~ m@^([.]{2}/){3,}@){
                next FIND_TEXT_URLS;
        }
        elsif ($href =~ m@^[.]{2}/[.]{2}/@){
                ($directoryNew) = ($directory =~m@(.*/)[~\w]+/\w+/@);
                if (!$directoryNew){ $directoryNew = "/";}
                ($fileNew) = $href =~ m@^[.]{2}/[.]{2}/(.*)@;
        }
        elsif ($href =~ m@^\.\./@){
                ($directoryNew) = ($directory =~ m@(.*/)[~\w]+/@);
                if (!$directoryNew){ $directoryNew = "/";}
                ($fileNew) = $href =~ m@^[.]{2}/(.*)@;
        }
        elsif ($href =~ m@^\./@){
                ($directoryNew) = $directory;
                ($fileNew) = $href =~ m@^\./(.*)@;
        }
        else {   #Takes care of URLs  in the same directory.
                $fileNew = $href;
                $directoryNew = $directory;
        }

        #Place the relative URLs in the hash %thisFileURLHash
        if ( (!$fileNew) or ($fileNew =~ m@(/$)|(.+\.$URLConf::INCLUDEDEXTS$)@)){
                $pushedURL = "http://$server:$port$directoryNew$fileNew";
                $thisFileURLHash{$pushedURL}++;
                }
    }#foreach href

    my @allUniqueURLs = keys %thisFileURLHash;
    return @allUniqueURLs;
}#sub findURLs


#We will now write  a subroutine  that will  take a URL as its
#only argument and find all the hyperlinks to text (i.e., HTML) files
#to which the initial URL is linked. This finding of URLs is
#done recursively up to a limit specified in the global
#variable $FILE_NO_LIMIT.
#List of obtained URLs are stored in the file $URLConf::TRAVERSED_URL_FILE.

sub getURLsRecursively{
    my ($startURL) = @_;
    my ($noURLsTraversed, $aURL, @thisURLsSons);
    my (%traversedURLs, %openURLs,  $key);
    $openURLs{$startURL} = 1;

    #If file $URLConf::TRAVERSED_URL_FILE exists, delete it, start fresh
    if (-e $URLConf::TRAVERSED_URL_FILE){
        unlink ($URLConf::TRAVERSED_URL_FILE) or
            die "Cannot unlink $URLConf::TRAVERSED_URL_FILE: $!";
    }
```

```
open (TRAVERSED_URLS, ">$URLConf::TRAVERSED_URL_FILE");

RECURSIVE_LOOP:
  while (my @openURLKeys = keys %openURLs){
      $aURL = shift (@openURLKeys);
      if (exists ($traversedURLs{$aURL})) { next RECURSIVE_LOOP;}
      $traversedURLs {$aURL}++;
      delete $openURLs {$aURL};
      print TRAVERSED_URLS "$aURL\n";
      $noURLsTraversed++;
      print "Just traversed URL No $noURLsTraversed: $aURL\n\n";
      if ($noURLsTraversed >= $URLConf::FILE_NO_LIMIT){
          last RECURSIVE_LOOP;
  }

      @thisURLsSons = findURLs ($aURL);
      foreach $key (@thisURLsSons){
          if (exists ($openURLs{$key}) or exists ($traversedURLs{$key})){
          next;}
          $openURLs{$key}++;
      }
  }#end RECURSIVE_LOOP
  close (TRAVERSED_URLS);

  print "\n\n*******Statistics********\n";
  print "Number of URLs recorded = $noURLsTraversed\n";
}

1;
```

The subroutine findURLs is given a URL to traverse to. It parses the URL by calling Tcp::parseURL, i.e., the parseURL subroutine in the Tcp package. Given the URL, the parser subroutine returns a server name, a port, and a file name with complete path. The file path is then split into a directory name and a file name. Some people use blank spaces in file or directory names, and such names are summarily disqualified from further consideration. The next few lines obtains all the URLs specified in an <A tag using the href attribute.

```
my @HTMLText = Tcp::openTCPandFetch ($server, $port, $completeFilePath);
chomp @HTMLText;
my $text = join " ", @HTMLText;
my @hrefs = ($text =~ /<A\s+href\s*=\s*"([^"]+)"/ig);
@hrefs = grep !/$URLConf::EXCLUDEPATTERNS/, @hrefs;
```

After obtaining the URLs by calling Tcp::openTCPandFetch, the subroutine discards URLs with any offending patterns as specified in the variable $EXCLUDEDPATTERNS in the URLConf package.

Next, the subroutine goes into a foreach loop where it examines every URL that is specified in the file. A URL can be absolute or relative. It handles absolute URLs that start with http:// first and then later the relative URLs. For an absolute URL, it parses the URL by calling Tcp::parseURL, and continues with a URL only if it is one of the domains expressly indicated. If it is in one of the indicated domains, it enters the URL as a key in the hash %thisFileURLHash that contains all the URLs that have been obtained as useful from the file under consideration.

If it is a relative URL, it can take several forms: it can start with no . or / (e.g., abc.html, /abc/def.html), it can start with a single dot followed by a slash (./, e.g. ./abc.html), or it can start with ../

(e.g., `../abc/def/ghi.html`), `../..`, etc. We take care of these possibilities using an `if` statement with several `elseif` clauses. Our goal is not be exhaustive, but take care of the most common cases. In each case, we parse the URL, obtain its components, and then make the URL absolute based on the URL of the page where it occurs and what form the URL takes. The newly composed absolute URL is then entered as a key in the hash `%thisFileURLHash`. Finally, below the `foreach` loop, the subroutine returns all the keys of this hash to the program that called it.

The second subroutine in the `Crawl.pm` package is called `getURLsRecursively`. It starts with a starting URL given to it, fetches URLs recursively from this starting URL till the number of URLs specified by the variable `$URLConf::NO_FILES_TRAVERSED` have been fetched and recorded in the file specified by `$URLConf::TRAVERSED_URL_FILE`.

`getURLsRecursively` uses two main data structures: `%traversedURLs` and `%openURLs`. The keys of the hash `%traversedURLs` are the unique URLs that have been traversed to by the subroutine and then recorded. The reason we use a hash to store traversed URLs is to ensure that only unique URLs are traveled to and recorded in the file. The hash `%traversedURLs` has the URL key, and the number of times the URL has been opened. In reality, we are not interested in the number of times a URL has been traversed, just the list of unique URLs traversed.

The subroutine also uses the hash table `%openURLs`. This hash stores the URLs that are being considered for visiting at a certain time. To start with, `%openURLs` contains just the starting URL `$startURL`. Once again, we are using a hash and not a list to store the "open" URLs because we are not interested in having any duplicate entries in the open data structure at any time. Since hash keys are unique, using a hash ensures that the entries in the open data structure, here, the hash `%openURLs`, are all unique. The value stored corresponding to a URL in `%openURLs` is not really used anywhere for any purpose.

The subroutine looks to see if the file specified by `$URLConf::TRAVERSED_URL_FILE` exists. If the file exists, it is deleted so that we can start recording traversed URLs fresh in every run of `getURLsRecursively`.

Next, the subroutine gets into a `while` loop labeled as `RECURSIVE_LOOP`. It is not really a recursive subroutine; it is iterative. In the conditional of this `while` loop, we obtain the keys in `%openURLs` and store them in `@openURLKeys`. It gets the first URL in `@openURLKeys` and records it as traversed in `%traversedURLs` by increasing its traversal count. It then deletes this URL from the `%openURLs` hash because it is no longer "open" or yet to-be-traversed. Then, the line

```
@thisURLsSons = findURLs ($aURL);
```

obtains all the URLs specified in the HTML text of this URL.

There is now a `foreach` loop where we go through every URL in the current file. If a relevant URL does not exist as a key in `%openURLs` or in `%traversedURLs`, it is entered as a key in `%openURLs` so that it will be traversed later. This is in a sense, the agenda of URLs to travel to in the future.

The number of URLs traversed is next incremented. If the number of URLs traversed crosses the limit specified by the variable `$URLCOnf::FILE_NO_LIMIT`, the subroutine's work is done and it gets out of the `while` loop labeled `RECURSIVE_LOOP`.

After the `while` loop is executed, the keys of `%traversedURLs` are printed to the file specified in the variable `$URLConf::TRAVERSED_URL_FILE`.

Note, since the `open` and `traversed` data structures are hashes, the URLs are not being traversed in any specific order. The order depends on the way hashes are ordered.

7.4.2.4   An Interactive Client-Server Set-up

Now, we discuss a client program and an associated server program that are interactive and run either on the same machine or two different machines. The user sits at the client and types in one of several commands the client understands. The client sends the command over to the server which responds appropriately. We assume that the server is running on a Unix machine. The server returns the results of running system commands for certain queries, and for certain other commands, it returns files on the server. The program is given below.

Program 7.31

```perl
#!/usr/bin/perl
#interactiveServer.pl

use IO::Socket::INET;
use Net::hostent;
use strict;

sub readFile {
    my ($fileName) = @_;
    open (IN, $fileName);
    my @contents = <IN>;
    return @contents;
}

my $PORT = 2000;   #Pick something not used
my %socketDescription = (Proto => 'tcp',
                         LocalPort => $PORT,
                         Listen => SOMAXCONN,
                         Reuse => 1);

my $server = IO::Socket::INET -> new (%socketDescription);
die "Cannot set up server" unless $server;
print "[Interactive server $0 accepting clients]\n";

my $client;
while ($client = $server -> accept()){
    print $client "Welcome to server $0 on $ENV{'HOST'}\n";
    print $client " type ? for command list\n";
    my $hostInfo = gethostbyaddr ($client -> peeraddr);
    print "[Connect from ", $hostInfo -> name, "]\n";

    while (my $clientCommand = <$client>){
        if ($clientCommand =~ /localtime/){
            print $client scalar ('date'), "\n";
        }
        elsif ($clientCommand =~ /passwd/){
            print $client  readFile ('/etc/passwd');
        }
        elsif ($clientCommand =~ /services/){
            print $client  readFile ('/etc/services');
        }
        elsif ($clientCommand =~ /who/){
            print $client  scalar ('/usr/bin/who'), "\n";
        }
        elsif ($clientCommand =~ /quit|q/){
            print "[Disconnect with ", $hostInfo -> name, "]\n";
```

```
            last;
        }
        else {
            print $client
                "Commands are:  passwd localtime services who quit\n";
        }
    }
    close $client;
}
```

The server program uses two Perl modules: IO::Socket::INET and Net::hostent. As we know from before, the IO::Socket::INET package allows us to build sockets for Internet communication. The Net::hostent package allows us to obtain certain details about a computer or host on the Internet.

The server program has a subroutine called readFile that returns the contents of a file whose full name is given to it. The server program establishes a TCP socket connection at a certain port on the local machine. The maximum number of connections to this server socket is SOMAXCONN whose value is obtained from Perl's Socket package which actually obtains it from some C language files available on the machine. The IO::Socket or IO::Socket::INET package inherits this value from the Socket package. The value of SOMAXCONN on the Linux machine the author uses is 128.

If the server socket $socket cannot be established, the program dies. Otherwise, the server prints its name on its terminal and says it is accepting connections.

In the conditional of the main while loop, the program calls accept () method on the server socket. accept () accepts an incoming connection and creates a new socket called $client. $client is automatically unbuffered. The program prints a welcome message on the $client socket. This welcome message actually shows up at the other end of the communication line from the server: the actual client program, if a line of communication has been successfully set up with a client program. $0 gives the name of the script running, i.e., the server program name.

The $client socket obtains the name of the machine it is connected to at the other end by calling peeraddr on it: $client->peeraddr(). It then calls gethostbyaddr of the Net::hostent package to obtain details of this machine. The gethostbyaddr method takes as input an IP address, and returns what is called a Net::hostent or hostent (host entity) object in networking terminology. This object contains certain fields: name, aliases, addrtype, length and addr_list. We use only the name field in our program.

```
    my $hostInfo = gethostbyaddr ($client -> peeraddr);
    print "[Connect from ", $hostInfo -> name, "]\n";
```

First, the argument sent to gethostbyaddr is given below.

```
$client -> peeraddr
```

$client is a socket created by

```
$server -> accept().
```

This socket is an IO::Socket::INET type object. An object of this type understands several methods, one of them being peeraddr(). peeraddr () returns the address component of the socket on the peer host. $client is a socket on the server. Therefore, its peer or counterpart is the socket on the client program. As a result,

```
$client -> peeraddr
```

returns the IP address of the client program that is attempting to talk to the server program. In Perl, when a method is called on an object, it is not necessary to use ( ) following the method name, if no arguments are being passed to the method.

Thus, `gethostbyaddr` gets as its argument the IP address of the machine on which the client program is running. The call to `gethostbyaddr` returns the `Net::hostent` or `hostent` object containing details about this machine. The reference to the object containing these details is stored in `$hostInfo`.

```
$hostInfo -> name
```

is a call to obtain the name associated with the IP address of the machine on which the client program is running. Thus, the statement

```
    print "[Connect from ", $hostInfo -> name, "]\n";
```

prints the name, not the IP address, of the client. The details that `gethostbyaddr` gathers about a host comes either by reading the file `/etc/hosts` on a Unix machine, or by consulting a Domain Name Server (DNS) database.

Next, we have another `while` loop inside the first `while` loop. In the conditional of the inner `while` loop, the program reads a command that comes to it from the user sitting at the client program. Depending on what the command is, it returns the appropriate answer. For the command `localtime` typed on the client, the server runs the `date` system command on the server machine and returns the string that `date` returns. `scalar` is a unary operator that takes an expression and forces it to be interpreted in the scalar context. In this case, the `date` system command, run by enclosing `date` in backticks, returns a string containing the result of running `date` at the operating system level. The use of `scalar` here is actually useless. But, if the result returned by running a system command is a list of lines, `scalar` will make a string out of it.

If the command is `passwd` or `services`, the server returns the files `/etc/passwd` and `/etc/services` respectively, on the server, to the client. On a Unix machine, `/etc/passwd` contains brief details of accounts that users have on the system. In earlier days, this file used to contain an encrypted version of the login passwords for users on the system, but no more. `/etc/passwd` is a file readable by everyone on a Unix system, and now-a-days, the place where the encrypted password used to be contains one or more meaningless characters such as `*`. The encrypted passwords are now stored in the file `/etc/shadow`, a file that is readable only by the root user of a Unix system. The `/etc/services` file on a Unix system is readable by everyone. It contains a list of network facilities or services provided by a system, and the port number at which the service is available.

If the command typed in at the client and arriving at the server is `who`, the server runs `/usr/bin/who` and returns the server's response to the client, giving the list of users logged in at the server at the time. If the client sends `quit` or `q`, the server's control goes to the end of the inner loop which also ends the outer `while` loop. If a user sitting at the client types in something that the server does not understand, the server prints the list of acceptable commands on the client's terminal. The server hangs if there are no requests arriving at it from client(s).

Let us now look at the client program that talks to the server program discussed above. The client program assumes that the server program is running on the machine `www.cs.uccs.edu`. This is where the server program must be running for this client-server pair to work correctly. The client program times out after 30 seconds if it does not get a response from the server.

Program 7.32

```
#!/usr/bin/perl
#interactiveClient.pl
#Creates a socket, keeps it interactive so that a user types
#commands and gets replies
```

```perl
use strict;
use IO::Socket::INET;
use Net::hostent;
my ($interactiveSocket, $childProcessID);

$interactiveSocket = new IO::Socket::INET (
        PeerAddr => 'www.cs.uccs.edu',
        PeerPort => 2000,
        Proto => 'tcp',
                                        Timeout => 30
);

die "Couldn't connect: $!" unless $interactiveSocket;
my $hostInfo = gethostbyaddr ($interactiveSocket -> peeraddr);
my $hostName = $hostInfo->name();

print "[Created a TCP socket with $hostName]\n";

$childProcessID = fork ();
die "Fork failed: $!" unless defined ($childProcessID);

if ($childProcessID > 0){
    #parent
    #copy the socket to standard output. This lets us see what
    #comes back to the socket from the server
    while (defined (my $responseLine = <$interactiveSocket>)){
            print STDOUT $responseLine;
    }

    #When the remote server closes its connection, send a TERM  signal
    #to the child process and kill it.
    kill ("TERM", $childProcessID);
    #Eliminates the child as as soon as the server closes its end.
    #Shut the socket down for input as well as output
    shutdown ($interactiveSocket, 2);
    #exit the program normally
    exit 0;
}
else{
    #child process reads from STDIN
    #copy standard input to the socket. This lets us type a command
    #on the screen and have it written to the socket, i.e., sent to the server
    while (defined (my $command = <STDIN>)){
        chomp $command;
        print $interactiveSocket "$command\r\n"; #\r\n is needed
    }
}
close ($interactiveSocket);
```

The client program, after creating the socket, calls fork(). fork() works only on a Unix system. Following this call, the lines of code in the program are executed by two processes—the child and the parent. fork() returns 0 to the child process and the positive process ID of the child to the parent process. Thus, the if part is executed by the parent, and the else part is run by the child.

The socket $interactiveSocket was created before fork(). Therefore, there is only one socket that is accessed by the parent as well as the child process. The parent process reads the socket represented by $interactiveSocket. The child process writes to the same socket. In other words, the socket is read as well as written into. However, the action of reading and the action of writing are divided between the two processes—the parent and the child, respectively.

The parent is the reader process. The parent executes a while loop. In the while loop, it continuously reads the socket, i.e., it reads what comes back from the server end of the socket. This is the result that the server sends back for a command typed in at the client at an earlier time. The parent process reads all the lines of response that comes back from the server.

The child process in the client program is the writer process. The child process executes another while loop inside the else block. The conditional of this while loop reads the standard input STDIN. If there is an input that can be read, i.e., if a user has typed in a command at the client's terminal window, this command is written onto the socket $interactiveSocket. In other words, this command is sent to the server. The server responds to this command by executing its code. What comes back from the server is read by the client in the parent process discussed earlier.

In reality, the server program does not do anything on its own unless asked by a client. Thus, although the reader (the parent) and the writer (the child) processes seem to be reading from and writing the socket in parallel, the effect of the reader-writer pair's actions is that the user's input at the client terminal is read first, and then the server's results are printed next, and this continues giving a sense of synchronized sequential input and output at the client's terminal window.

In the code that the parent process runs, we see the following statements at the very end.

```
#When the remote server closes its connection, send a TERM signal
#to the child process and kill it.
kill ("TERM", $childProcessID);
#Eliminates the child as as soon as the server closes its end.
#Shut the socket down for input as well as output
shutdown ($interactiveSocket, 2);
#exit the program normally
exit 0;
```

When processes are running on a Unix system, various signals can be sent back and forth among the processes. kill is a function that sends such a signal to a process. Although the name of the function is kill, it can send several types of signals such as TERM and KILL. Note that the kill function and the KILL signal are different things. The signals can be given in terms of numbers or strings. The TERM signal kills a process that does not do any specialized processing of signals. It is possible for a process to have code that catches the TERM signal and does something with it. A good way to kill a process, in general, is to send a TERM signal first and then a KILL signal. The KILL signal is the 9 signal in terms of numbers. Thus,

```
kill (9, $childProcessID);
```

is also acceptable. The KILL signal cannot be intercepted by the process receiving it. That is the KILL signal is final. Here, we send a TERM signal only because we know what the process exactly does because we wrote it ourselves.

In the parent process, we first kill the child process by sending the TERM signal. Next, we shut the socket down using the shutdown socket method. shutdown takes the socket as the first argument, and either 0, or 1, or 2, as the second argument. 0 closes a socket for reading, 1 closes a socket for writing, and 2 closes a socket for both reading and writing.

Finally, we exit the parent process with a 0 argument. This means that the parent process ends normally. Before exiting, the parent process killed the child process. As a result, both parent and child are dead, and the program's execution is completely finished.

It is possible that sometimes when the client is still alive, we kill the server process, by say, typing an interrupt signal such as CONTROL-C. In such a case, the client also dies because the server is not sending anything to the client and as a result, the client has nothing defined to read from its end of the socket. In the client program, the parent process's (or, the reader's) while loop has nothing to read in such a case. The execution of the while loop of the parent is finished. This causes the KILL signal to be sent, the socked shut down, and the parent exited.

The following discusses a simple interaction between the server program and the client program. The server is running on the machine www.cs.uccs.edu. The client can run on any machine. In this particular case, it is run once on the machine pikepeak.uccs.edu and then on the machine blanca.uccs.edu.

When the server starts, the output on its terminal looks like the following.

```
[Interactive server interactiveServer.pl accepting clients]
```

At this point, the server is waiting for input from one or more clients. Next, we start a terminal on pikespeak.uccs.edu and start the client program. The output on the client's terminal looks like the following.

```
[Created a TCP socket with cs.uccs.edu]
Welcome to server interactiveServer.pl on cs.uccs.edu
 type ? for command list
```

At this time, the output at the server terminal looks like the following.

```
[Interactive server interactiveServer.pl accepting clients]
[Connect from pikespeak.uccs.edu]
```

At the client, the user types in commands for the server to respond. While the first client is running on pikespeak.uccs.edu, we start a second client (i.e., the same program) on blanca.uccs.edu. The client on the second machine prints the following on the terminal at blanca.uccs.edu.

```
[Created a TCP socket with cs.uccs.edu]
Welcome to server interactiveServer.pl on cs.uccs.edu
 type ? for command list
```

But, then the second client blocks because our server can handle only one client at a time. Next, we do a few things on the client, and finally type quit at the client on pikespeak.uccs.edu. At this time, the output at the first client's terminal looks like the following.

```
[Created a TCP socket with cs.uccs.edu]
Welcome to server interactiveServer.pl on cs.uccs.edu
 type ? for command list
?
Commands are:  passwd localtime services who quit
who
lli       pts/0     Jan 30 16:29
kalita    pts/1     Jan 29 11:08
lohmann   :0        Jan 30 09:18
lohmann   pts/2     Jan 30 09:19
lli       pts/4     Jan 30 16:34
```

```
Commands are:   passwd localtime services who quit
localtime
Tue Jan 30 17:00:00 MST 2001

Commands are:   passwd localtime services who quit
quit
```

When the user types in `quit` at the client on `pikespeak.uccs.edu`, the client on this machine dies. The output on the terminal above shows this. At this time, the output on the server at `www.cs.uccs.edu` looks like the following.

```
[Interactive server interactiveServer.pl accepting clients]
[Connect from pikespeak.uccs.edu]
[Disconnect with pikespeak.uccs.edu]
```

As soon as the first client dies, the server program can attend to the second client, the only interacting client. The output on the server changes to the following.

```
[Interactive server interactiveServer.pl accepting clients]
[Connect from pikespeak.uccs.edu]
[Disconnect with pikespeak.uccs.edu]
[Connect from blanca.uccs.edu]
```

This indicates that the client from `blanca.uccs.edu` is being serviced at this time. This second client can ask questions of the server and then finally `quit`. The output on the server end changes to the following.

```
[Interactive server interactiveServer.pl accepting clients]
[Connect from pikespeak.uccs.edu]
[Disconnect with pikespeak.uccs.edu]
[Connect from blanca.uccs.edu]
[Disconnect with blanca.uccs.edu]
```

The server is hanging at this point. We can either kill it by typing in an interrupt signal like CONTROL-C, or keep it hanging, waiting to hear from a third client, and so on.

7.4.2.5   Forking A Simple Server

In the previous section, we `forked` the client so that it can handle reading and writing of the same socket. One `forked` process reads from the socket and the other writes to it. This makes for a versatile client.

However, there are problems with the servers we have seen so far. One major problem is that the server can respond to only one client at a time. Several clients can try to connect to the server at the same time. These clients are able to make TCP connections as we have seen in the earlier example. But, after making the TCP connection, all but one client hangs. Several clients can wait in a queue to be serviced. The size of the waiting queue is given by the `Listen` parameter when a socket is created. As a client finishes being serviced, the next client in the queue moves to the front, and gets serviced. If more than the maximum number of clients try to connect, they are refused right away.

Definitely, this is a problem. For real-world servers, we want the server to be able to handle several clients at the same time. For example, we want a Web server such as the Apache Web server to handle multiple clients. If only one client takes 100% of the server's time, in reality it is no good. Therefore, it is necessary that we find ways in which it is possible for the server to handle many clients. It is because, quite frequently, servers just wait doing nothing. When most time is, thus, wasted by a server, it may as well service additional clients.

In this section, we will discuss how we can `fork` a server such that the parent works like the main receptionist at an organization. As soon as new request from a client comes, the parent process `forks` a child process and hands over the responsibilities of handling the requirements of the child to this process. The parent process immediately goes back to waiting for new client requests.

Thus, the arrangement is pretty simple. To service n clients, there will be $n + 1$ processes in the system. One process is the parent process and each one of the rest of the processes handles one client each. When a client's requests are handled completely and the client closes the connection, the corresponding child process is finished; it dies and is ultimately removed from the list of processes that the operating system maintains. There are some details associated with removing dead child processes. We have discussed some of this before in the section on `forking`. We will discuss it again a little later.

First, here is the client program. The client program is a slight modification of the `simpleSend.pl` program discussed earlier. It is called `simpleSend1.pl` and is given below.

Program 7.33

```perl
#!/usr/bin/perl
#simpleSend1.pl
#works with simpleReceive.pl or simpleForkedReceive.pl

use IO::Socket::INET;
$sock = new IO::Socket::INET (PeerAddr => 'pikespeak',
     PeerPort => 1200,
     Proto => 'tcp');

die "Couldn't connect: $!" unless $sock;

foreach (1..10){
    print $sock "Repeating $_ time(s): How are you?\n";
    sleep 1;
}

close ($sock);
```

It is the exact same program as before except that, inside the `foreach` loop, the following instruction has been inserted to make the program go a little slow.

```perl
    sleep 1;
```

It makes the client program sleep one second between iterations of the loop. This is done so that the client's interaction with the server takes a while to be easily viewable on the terminal of the server.

The server program is given below. It is also a modification the server program `simpleReceive.pl` we have seen before. It is now called `simpleForkedReceive.pl`.

Program 7.34

```perl
#!/usr/bin/perl
#simpleForkedReceive.pl
use IO::Socket;

$SIG{CHLD} = sub {wait ();};
```

```perl
$sock = new IO::Socket::INET (LocalHost => 'pikespeak.uccs.edu',
      LocalPort => 1200,
      Proto => 'tcp',
      Listen => 5,
      Reuse => 1);
die "Couldn't connect: $!" unless $sock;

while ($newSock = $sock->accept()) {
    $processID = fork ();
    next if ($processID > 0);

    #child process
    while (defined ($buf = <$newSock>)) {
          print $buf;
    }
    close ($newSock);
}
close ($sock);
```

There are two aspects to `forking` the server. The first is how the parent and the child coordinate their tasks. The second is how the child is disposed of once the child has finished its task.

First, let us look at the main `while` loop in the server program. The conditional of the `while` loop is a call to `accept ()`. `accept` blocks till there is a client to respond to. When a client requests service, a new socket called $newSock is created to serve the request.

Immediately inside the main `while` loop, a call is made to `fork ()`. Thus, a child process is produced at this line if `forking` is successful. So, the lines of code following the `forking` is run by two processes: the parent and the child. As we know from before, `fork` returns the positive process ID of the child to the parent, and 0 to the child itself.

Immediately after `forking`, we have the following statement.

```perl
    next if ($processID > 0);
```

This causes the server process to go to the next iteration of the main `while` loop. In other words, the server process does not do anything at all except look at the conditional of the main `while` loop and `fork` when needed.

The child processes are the workhorse of the program. A child process is dedicated to servicing a client. The child process simply reads the socket and prints its contents onto the standard output.

We can start the server on a certain machine, say, `cs.uccs.edu` and then start two clients on two machines. Because there are two child processes to handle two clients, the output printed on the server terminal is mixed, unlike the previous attempt at writing the client-server pair, when one client owned the services of the server completely till it was fully serviced. The output at the server terminal is shown below.

```
Repeating 1 time(s): How are you?
Repeating 2 time(s): How are you?
Repeating 3 time(s): How are you?
Repeating 4 time(s): How are you?
Repeating 5 time(s): How are you?
Repeating 1 time(s): How are you?
Repeating 6 time(s): How are you?
```

```
Repeating 2 time(s): How are you?
Repeating 7 time(s): How are you?
Repeating 3 time(s): How are you?
Repeating 8 time(s): How are you?
Repeating 4 time(s): How are you?
Repeating 9 time(s): How are you?
Repeating 5 time(s): How are you?
Repeating 10 time(s): How are you?
Repeating 6 time(s): How are you?
Repeating 7 time(s): How are you?
Repeating 8 time(s): How are you?
Repeating 9 time(s): How are you?
Repeating 10 time(s): How are you?
```

Now, there is still the issue of disposing of child processes properly. We know every child process dies off after the corresponding client is serviced. This is because the child process is created inside the main while loop of the simple forked server, and as such, it does not execute the main while loop in its entirety. It executes only the portion of the code inside the main while loop after its creation. Thus, it executes the second or included while loop, and once this included while loop is completely executed, the child is finished and dies automatically.

A child process usually dies before the parent that creates it. The operating system maintains a list of live—stopped, sleeping, or running—processes in the system at any time. In case a child process dies before a parent, the ID of the child process remains in the process table maintained by the operating system even after death. Normally, parents or the kernel takes care of removing dead processes from the process table maintained by the operating system. If the process table is not cleaned up, it is possible that the number of dead processes whose parents are alive, called *zombie* processes, in the process table could become significantly large. This is because servers on a Unix machine, such as Web servers, sometimes run for months creating, possibly millions of child processes. In the case of a server, the parent usually lives as the children die. If the number of recorded processes, including zombies, becomes large, the operating system may prohibit the creation of new child processes. Even if the creation of new processes is not hampered, having too many zombie processes in the process table is a nuisance. This is of no concern in our simple example, but it real life, it could happen with a complex and reliable server program.

Thus, there is a potential problem with deaths of child processes created by long-running server processes. The solution to use the fact that, in Unix, the operating system allows a process that creates a child to inquire of the child's health, in particular of its death. This is one of the very few ways a parent can relate to children it creates. Otherwise, the relationship between a parent and a child is quite tenuous. There are two functions or methods, wait and waitpid, that a parent process can use to wait till a child dies. wait or waitpid blocks the parent till a child (a child with a specific process ID in case of waitpid) dies and then it cleans up the process table for the system, and returns control to the parent.

Therefore, wait or waitpid suspends execution of the current process until a child (a specific child for waitpid) has exited, or a signal has been delivered to it whose action is to terminate the current process or call a signal handling function. If a child has already exited by the time of the call, the function returns immediately. In the case of waitpid, if the specific child requested has already exited by the time of the call, the function returns immediately. In both case, resources used by the child are freed. This is called *reaping* a child. The parent reaps a child by using wait or waitpid.

To handle the problem of zombified children processes, we use *signals*. A process can send and receive signals. A signal can be generated intentionally by a user from a keyboard sequence like CONTROL-C and sent to a process, can be sent to a process by another process, or can be automatically sent by the kernel when special events take place, such as a process running out of activation stack space, or file hitting its size limit. One signal a process can receive is called the CHLD signal. The signal is sent by the kernel of the operating system to a parent process when a child process dies or is stopped.

To *trap* a signal that comes to a process, the process has to set up a *handler*. The handler should be small in size and do as little as possible so that the handler is efficient, and does not cause problems itself. Handlers run very close to the functioning of the operating system and should be written with caution. If a process does not trap a certain signal coming to it, the process has no control over what the signal does.

To trap or handle a signal coming to a process, the process must maintain an associative array or hash called %SIG and store various values for specific signals. The signal names are the keys in the hash table. The values are usually subroutines or references to subroutines. The values represent the handlers. The operating system monitors signals coming to a process, and if the signal has an entry in %SIG in a process, the signal is redirected to the process for handling. The process calls the corresponding handler routine to take care of it.

In our program, we do not want our parent process to block and wait for the death of its children because this could mess up a server that is supposed to handle many clients over time. However, we want the parent process to help clean up the process table maintained by the operating system. In our program, the handler for the CHLD signal, in the parent process (before the children are forked), is set with the following line of code,

```
$SIG{CHLD} = sub {wait ();};
```

toward the beginning of the program. The subroutine simply contains a call to wait. When a child process dies, the kernel sends the parent a CHLD signal. The handler for the CHLD signal calls wait to clean up the process table. Because wait is called only after a child has died, there is no real waiting on the part of the parent for a child to die. Thus, the effect of wait is to clear up the process table after a child does. The delay due to use of wait is minimal.

However, there is a subtle and potential problem in using wait in the handler for the CHLD signal because wait waits for any child process to exit, not a specific child. If several children processes die simultaneously, the Unix operating system combines two CHLD signals into one and gives it to the parent process. This is because Unix can handle only one signal of a particular type at any one time. So, even if two children are dead, only one CHLD signal may be sent, and only one dead child reaped. This is sometimes called a *zombie leak*. Thus, it is possible that we have many dead or zombie processes in the process table after a server has lived and worked for a while. A subsequent call to wait simply looks to see if there is one, any one dead process. If it finds such a dead process, it cleans up after it, and then returns. If there are many zombie processes at a certain time, wait cleans up after only one, leaving the other dead or zombie processes in the process table.

Problems also arise when a child is stopped or restarted using a signal. Stopping of a child causes the operating system to send a CHLD signal to the parent although no child has actually died or exited. This can cause a process to hang, making the whole server wait for nothing.

There are ways to solve these problems, but we do not discuss them here.

In summary, there is a whole list of signals that can be created and received in a Unix system. In this chapter, we have already seen the kill command that sends a signal to a process. The name kill is, in some sense, a misnomer, because kill can send other signals as well. We have also seen how specific signals such as CHLD can be trapped and handled by a process.

7.4.2.6   Forking An Interactive Server

We will now modify the interactive server discussed in section 7.4.2.4 so that the server is forked, and as a result, it can service multiple clients at the same time. The program discussed in that section could service only one client at a time. If more clients attempt to connect, it put all but the first client, the one currently being serviced on hold, in the listen queue. When the current client is finished talking, only then the second client is serviced. This is not a desirable state of affairs since a more robust server should be more efficient and should be able to handle several interactive clients at the same time.

Below, we present a modified version of the `interactiveServer.pl` program discussed in section 7.4.2.4. It is now called `forkedServer.pl`. The code is given below.

Program 7.35

```perl
#!/usr/bin/perl
#forkedServer.pl
use IO::Socket;
use Net::hostent;
use strict;

$SIG{CHLD} = sub {wait ();};

my $PORT = 2000;   #Pick something not used
my %socketDescription = (Proto => 'tcp',
                         LocalPort => $PORT,
                         Listen => SOMAXCONN,
                         Reuse => 1);

my $server = IO::Socket::INET -> new (%socketDescription);
die "Cannot set up server" unless $server;
print "[Interactive server $0 accepting clients]\n";

my ($client, $processID);;
while ($client = $server -> accept ()){
    $processID = fork ();
    die "Cannot fork: $!" unless defined ($processID);
    next if ($processID > 0);

    #In the child process
    serviceAClient ($client);
    close $client;
}

#########################################
#Subroutines
#Read a file and return its contents
sub readFile {
    my ($fileName) = @_;
    open (IN, $fileName);
    my @contents = <IN>;
    return @contents;
}


#Service a client connection
sub serviceAClient{
    my ($socket) = @_;

    print $socket "Welcome to server $0 on $ENV{'HOST'}\n";
    print $socket " type ? for command list\n";
```

```perl
    my $hostInfo = gethostbyaddr ($socket -> peeraddr());
    print "[Connect from ", $hostInfo -> name, "]\n";

    while (my $socketCommand = <$socket>){
        if ($socketCommand =~ /localtime/){
            print $socket scalar ('date'), "\n";
        }
        elsif ($socketCommand =~ /passwd/){
            print $socket  readFile ('/etc/passwd');
        }
        elsif ($socketCommand =~ /services/){
            print $socket  readFile ('/etc/services');
        }
        elsif ($socketCommand =~ /who/){
            print $socket  scalar ('/usr/bin/who'), "\n";
        }
        elsif ($socketCommand =~ /quit|q/){
            print "[Disconnect with ", $hostInfo -> name, "]\n";
            last;
        }
        else {
            print $socket "Commands are:  passwd localtime services who quit\n";
            }
    }

}
```

It is essentially the same program as the previous one, except that we fork the server, and that we have broken up the client servicing code into a subroutine called serviceAClient. We will not discuss the details of this subroutine because it has been discussed at length in section 7.4.2.4.

Let us look at the main program and focus on the while loop that is executed after a listening socket has been successfully set up. This while loop is repeated below.

```perl
while ($client = $server -> accept()){
    $processID = fork ();
    die "Cannot fork: $!" unless defined ($processID);
    next if ($processID > 0);

    #In the child process
    serviceAClient ($client);
    close $client;
}
```

In the conditional of the while loop, the server waits to accept a client that requests its attention. When a client requests to talk, a dedicated socket $client is set up to communicate with it. The new socket $client is exactly like the listening socket $server. Inside the while loop, the server process immediately forks to produce a child process with ID $processID. After the fork, both the parent and the child processes run the same code. Both processes die if the forking was unsuccessful.

The two processes have a copy of the variable $processID each. The child sees a value of 0, and the parent sees a positive integer value corresponding to the process ID of the child. Next, the statement

```
        next if ($processID > 0);
```

is executed. This statement causes the parent process to go to the top of the while loop for the next iteration, and wait to accept additional incoming connections. Thus, the child process is the only one that calls the subroutine serviceAClient with the new dedicated socket $client as the argument. Once the client is serviced, the child process dies automatically.

The corresponding client program is a slight modification of the program interactiveClient.pl discussed in section 7.4.2.4. The new client program is given below.

Program 7.36
_____

```perl
#!/usr/bin/perl
#interactiveClient1.pl
#Creates a socket, keeps it interactive so that a
#user types commands and get replies
use strict;
use IO::Socket::INET;
use Net::hostent;
my ($interactiveSocket, $childProcessID);
my $peerAddr = "cs.uccs.edu";

$interactiveSocket = new IO::Socket::INET (
     PeerAddr => $peerAddr,
     PeerPort => 2000,
     Proto => 'tcp',
                              Timeout => 30
);

print "Established socket connection to $peerAddr\n";

die "Couldn't connect: $!" unless $interactiveSocket;
my $hostInfo = gethostbyaddr ($interactiveSocket -> peeraddr);
my $hostName = $hostInfo->name();

print "[Created a TCP socket with $hostName]\n";

$childProcessID = fork ();
die "Fork failed: $!" unless defined ($childProcessID);

if ($childProcessID > 0){
    #parent
    #copy the socket to standard output. This lets us see what
    #comes back to the socket from the server

    while (defined (my $responseLine = <$interactiveSocket>)){
         print STDOUT $responseLine;
    }

    #When the remote server closes its connection, send a TERM signal
    #to the child process and kill it.
    kill ("TERM", $childProcessID);
```

```
        #Eliminate the socket as as soon as the server closes its end.
        #Also, exit the process.
        callItQuits ($interactiveSocket);
}
else{
        #child process reads from STDIN
        #copy standard input to the socket. This lets us type a command
        #on the screen and have it written to the socket, i.e., sent to the server
        while (defined (my $command = <STDIN>)){
                chomp $command;
                print $interactiveSocket "$command\r\n"; #\r\n is needed on Internet
                        if ($command =~ /quit/){
                                callItQuits ($interactiveSocket);
                        }
                }
        }
    }


##########subroutines
sub callItQuits{
        #Shutdown the specified socket and kill the process
        my ($socket) = @_;
        #Shut the socket down for input as well as output
        shutdown ($socket, 2);
        exit 0;
}
```

This program is essentially the same as the program interactiveClient.pl. The only difference is that we now have a subroutine called callItQuits that takes a socket as an argument, shuts it down for reading as well as writing, and exits the current process with a 0 indicator or in good health. This subroutine is called both by the parent and the child processes after forking. We know from our discussions in section 7.4.2.4 that the parent reads the socket $interactiveSocket for responses coming back from the server and displays them on the terminal in which the client program is running. We also know that the child reads what the user types in at the terminal and sends it to the distant server.

In the new version, the subroutine callItQuits is called by the parent process if the server is killed to shut down the socket and to exit the parent process. This is done after killing the child process. This was done in the previous version of the program as well. In this new version of the program, the child process also calls callItQuits if the child reads quit at the client terminal.

We can start the server on a particular machine, say cs.uccs.edu. It waits to hear from clients. When the first client calls, the server forks, and the newly minted child process services the client call. The parent process goes back and listen for additional connection requests from clients. If a second client calls as the first one is being serviced, the parent process forks again. The second child services the second connection request, and so on and so forth. Thus, the parent process acts like a receptionist at a company or organization, taking the initial call and transferring it to the person the call is intended for, so that there is a direct line of communication between the external caller and the intended recipient within the company or the organization. This allows the receptionist to take additional calls even as the first call proceeds using its "dedicated" line of communication.

7.5 Conclusions

This chapter has discussed inter-process communication using pipes and sockets. Sockets are explained in great detail although we do not discuss Perl's built-in sockets. We discuss Perl modules that make socket programming a lot easier. In this chapter, we also discuss how processes can be created on a Unix system using `fork` and how `forking` can help us write more powerful and more useful socket programs. Sockets work on Windows and pre-OS X Macintosh systems as well although the details may vary from what is discussed in this book.

7.6 Exercises

1. *(Easy to Medium: System Commands)*
   Use the `system` command or the backquote method to compress a file. Use a command such as the ones commonly available on a Unix platform: `compress`, `zip`, or `gzip`, etc. Extend the program to compress every file in a certain directory. Leave sub-directories as they are.

   Finally, extend the program further to compress sub-directories recursively. Use the system command `cd` to go into a directory. Use system commands wherever you can. Avoid using Perl functions such as `chdir`.

2. *(Easy: Pipe)*
   Study documentation on the Unix `find` command. The `find` command generates the names of files recursively below a certain directory. Now, use this command in a pipe to search every file in a directory recursively. The program's first command-line argument is the directory to be searched recursively. The arguments that follow are one or more words to be searched in the files. Report full paths for every file where all the words occur.

3. *(Easy: E-mail, Pipe)*
   You are given one or more files each of which contains a number of valid e-mail addresses, one per line. Use a pipe to create a simple mailing list of your own. Your program takes the names of a message file, and one or more mailing list files as command-line argument. It sends a mail message to every individual in the mailing list files, one by one. The message file contains a well-demarcated subject on top, say indicated by the keyword `Subject:`. This keyword is followed by the subject of the mail message. The keyword and the text of the subject are in one line. There are one or more blank lines following the subject line, and then the actual text of the mail message.

4. *(Medium: E-mail, Pipe, Fork)*
   Write a program that modifies the mailing list program in the previous problem. Its purpose is exactly the same as the program in the previous problem. However, it `forks` a new process for each mailing list file. In other words, if the program is given several mailing list files containing e-mail addresses, it `forks` a separate process to send the message to the e-mail addresses in one file. The main process does not send any e-mail, only the child processes do. As the program's processes send e-mail, each process logs who the e-mail has been sent to in a log file. Each process logs to the same log file, not to separate files. The log file's name is given as a command-line argument as well.

5. *(Medium to Hard: Web Site Mirroring)*
   Write a program that mirrors a Web site. It takes a URL as a command-line argument. It also takes a destination mirror directory name on the machine where it is run. It fetches every file under the top-level URL and creates appropriate sub-directories. Every file is copied to the right location in the mirror. Use sockets and do not use any other more powerful packages that you may be able to find. There may be a large number of problems you can face in writing such a program. Document your problems, discuss and implement the solutions that you can find.

6. *(Medium: Web Site Traversal, Stale Links)*
As a Web site usually gets older, it starts to contain dead or stale links, if not kept up-to-date. Write a program that takes a Web site's URL, recursively looks at the Web pages at the Web site, and reports any dead or stale links along with the URLs of the file where it occurs. Define a stale link as one that cannot be fetched within a certain timeout period. Write the URLs of all stale links to a file whose name is also given as a command-line argument. Discuss any problems you face and how you solve them. Use TCP-based sockets.

7. *(Medium to Hard: Traversing Web Site, System Commands)*
Given a URL as argument, recursively obtain the files in the Web site indicated by the URL. The goal here is to find out how many graphic files with .jpg, .jpeg, or .gif extensions are there in the site, and the individual and cumulative sizes of these files. Report these data by printing a table to a file whose name is given as command-line argument.

Now, extend the program in the following way. Give the program an additional command-line argument. It is a number, say 100,000. As the user if he or she wants to view the "large" graphic files once all the graphic URLs have been fetched, and written to a file. If the user says so, let the program use a system command to display the files bigger than the given size, one by one in graphic viewer, say, *Electric Eyes (ee)* on a Unix machine, or a Web browser such as *Netscape*. Show the files one by one, in decreasing order of size. Discuss any problems you face, and how you solve them. Use TCP-based socket connections for communication.

8. *(Medium to Hard: Text Processing, Traversing Web Site, Research)*
Write a search engine for a "small" Web site. The program takes a URL as a command-line argument. It fetches every text file in the site. For each file fetched, it removes all HTML tags. It also removes commonly occurring words such as "is", "the", "it", etc. Make a good list of such words. Such words are called *stop words*. We will take a simplistic approach to creating our search engine. For each file, compute the frequencies of the words that occur in it. Consider the words with the top five frequency counts as *keywords*. For each keyword, store in a file (one would normally use a database, but we have not learned how to use one) where it occurs. The organization of this file should be such that it is easy to search.

The search program is a separate program. Normally, it is a CGI program that is invoked by an HTML form, but CGI is not discussed till later in this book. The search program, for now, is invoked on the command-line. It takes one or more keywords, and returns a list containing the URLs where all the keywords occur.

This is a very simple start to writing a search engine. Discuss any problems you face and how you solve them. Discuss what bigger problems arise that you cannot solve, or solve well. Research into the problems, possible solutions, and write a research report.

9. *(Medium to Hard: Text Processing, Traversing Web Site, Research, Can be a long-term project)*
Write a program that takes a URL as a command-line argument. Use TCP-based sockets for communication. It finds the most commonly used words, bigrams and trigrams in each file of the site. A bigram is a a pair of consecutive words. A trigram is a sequence of three words. The program removes all HTML tags found in the Web pages. The program has a stop list of words. The program removes all such words from consideration. The program also removes bigrams and trigrams that begin or end with such words.

Extend the search program in the previous problem so that it can search for bigrams and trigrams as well.

Examine the bigrams and trigrams you collect. There are a huge number of them. Many of these are sequences for which no one would ever search. How can we reduce the number of bigrams and trigrams to those for which a Web server may conceiveably search. Write your thoughts out in a report.

10. *(Medium to Hard: Text Processing, Traversing a Web Site, Research, Can be a long-term project)*
    Write a program that takes a URL as command-line argument. It removes all HTML tags from the Web pages that it recursively fetches. The goal of this program is to parse the pages and try our best to obtain all proper names used in these pages. Use heuristics such as that all proper names in English start with an uppercase letter. Use any other heuristics you can come up with. Use bigrams and trigrams as well. List all the "proper names" you gather. Examine them to see what percentage of the collected words and phrases are actually proper names. Discuss how this percentage can be improved.

11. *(Medium: FTP, File Transfer, Client-Server)*
    Write a program which is similar to the interactive client-server programs discussed in this Chapter. Here, we assume you preferably have accounts on two machines, although one also will work. The program is like a simple FTP (File Transfer Protocol) client-server pair.

    A client can request the server with a file name to send. When the client gets the file, it stores the file on the client's machine with the same file name.

    A client can also tell the server that it is sending the server a file with a specific name. If the server agrees, the client sends the file. Once the server gets the whole file, it stores it on the server with the same file name.

    First, think of the details of how the communication should proceed between the client and the server. Once you have it clear in your mind, write it down, and then write the code. Discuss any problems you face, and how you solve them. Use TCP-based sockets for communication.

    Note that in a real FTP program, a remote user has to log in to the server's computer. We do not bother about this issue here. Do not `fork` your client or server.

12. *(Medium: FTP, Client-Server, Forking)*
    Modify the program you write for the previous program so that the client and server are both `forked`.

13. *(Hard: FTP, File Transfer, Client-Server, Forking)*
    In a real FTP program, the client and the server actually use two ports for communication. One pair of ports is used for the communicating the commands for sending a file, receiving a file, and for reporting status such as a command has been carried out successfully. Another pair of ports is used to actually transfer the contents of the files or the data between the client and the server. Extend your program to follow this model of communication. Continue using TCP-based sockets for communication.

    Draw a nice diagram showing the communication steps first. Write out the algorithms on paper before you start implementing them. Once again, we are not worried about the user logging in and being authenticated.

14. *(Hard: FTP, Recursive File Transfer, Client-Server, Forking)*
    Extend the program in the previous problem by adding two more commands.

    - A command that a client can use to send all files in a directory, recursively to the server.
    - A command that a client can use to request all files in a directory recursively from a server.

15. *(Hard: FTP, File Transfer, Client-Server, Can be a long-term project)*
    The File Transfer Protocol (**FTP**) is a commonly used protocol on the Internet, used for transferring files between two machines. It works using the client-server model of computing, above TCP/IP.

    Familiarize yourself with the FTP client. Learn the commands. FTP works across different hosts and file structures. However, let us focus on how it works on the Linux machines in our labs.

    Summarize the FTP client commands on a single page.

    Study the RFC from 1985 that describes the initial FTP protocol. Summarize the RFC on a page or two.

Write code for an FTP client and an FTP server. Implement the following FTP client commands: open, user login and password, cd, lcd, ls, mkdir, get, put and close. You do not have to implement it faithfully following the RFC, but make the program functional.

Use TCP-based sockets.

16. *(Medium to Hard: E-Commerce, SET, Research, Can be a long-term project)*
    The Secure Electronic Transaction (**SET**) is an encryption and security specification designed to protect credit card transaction on the Internet.

    SET is quite complicated. It provides for secure secure communication channels among all parties involved in a transaction. The specification of SET came out in 1997 and is 971 pages long.

    The participants in SET are:

    (a) the card holder,

    (b) the merchant,

    (c) the card issuer,

    (d) the acquirer,

    (e) the payment gateway, and

    (f) the certification authority.

    SET is discussed in somewhat detail in chapter 14 of a text such as Stalling [Sta99]. Study the description of SET in this text, or any other book, or on the Web.

    Write code that allows you to set up the entities involved in a transaction and allow communication among them, two at a time. Note that not all parties have to communicate with every other party.

    Describe the code you write in one or two typed pages.

17. *(Hard: Instant Messaging, Research, Can be a long-term project)*
    Write a program that is an *instant messenger* (**IM**). Instant messenger programs are not new. A program called `talk` or variants of it have been available on Unix machines for decades. These days, instant messengers have graphical user interface (GUI), and can handle graphic images, audio, and video files. However, to start, let us focus on text exchange only. Write a program that allows two individuals to exchange text messages like one of the currently popular instant messenger programs. Do not worry about the beauty of the display to begin with. Just make it functional.

    Once you have a working IM program, now write down a list of all the ways you can improve it. Also, write how you can implement the improvements. Of course, one way for improvement is to use a graphical user interface. It is not difficult to build graphical user interfaces in Perl although we have not discussed how to do so in this book.

    Extend the program so that you can exchange images and audio files. Invoke a display program for invoked images. Similarly, invoke an audio program for fetched audio files.

18. *(Hard: Peer-to-peer File Exchange, Research, Can be a long-term project)*
    Write a program that allows *peer-to-peer* exchange of files between two individual computers over the Internet. This program can be an extension of the file transfer programs that some of the earlier problems have asked you to write. List the problems you need to address in writing such a program. Peer-to-peer file exchange programs can be used to transfer text, music or video files among users, dispersed around the world.

    Extend the program to invoke programs on your computer to display or play the exchanged files.

19. *(Medium to Hard: Network Services, Research)*
    Perl has a large number of modules that deal with network services such as TELNET, FTP, Netnews, Mail, etc. Find out what these modules are. Learn how to telnet to a remote machine and run commands on it from your Perl program. Learn how to FTP files and directories automatically from a Perl program. Such a program can be used to back up your files to another machine from time to time. Learn how to read and post messages to to Internet newsgroups from a Perl program. Finally, learn how to read POP or IMAP mail from your Perl program.

20. *(Medium to Hard: Remote Procedure Calls, Research)*
    Find how remote procedure calls (RPC) can be made from Perl. Where can you use RPCs?

21. *(Medium to Hard: Domain Name Server, Research)*
    Perl has modules to interface with a DNS (Domain Name Server). Find out what these modules are and learn how to use them. Use them to rewrite your network programming problems in Chapter 7.

Chapter 8

On CGI Programming

In This Chapter

The Internet is a product of the US military's efforts dating back to the late 1960s. For a long time, the use of the Internet was restricted to the military and selected academic and research institutions in the US. In the 1980s, the number of academic and research institutions connected to the Internet proliferated rapidly. However, the Internet was still restricted to non-commercial use. The situation changed dramatically when in the early 1990s, the US Government opened the Internet for potential commercial use. A very lucid book on the Internet that discusses its history, the technologies that have made the Internet feasible, and the applications of the Internet is the *Internet Book* [Com00].

The expansion of the Internet to public and commercial domains accelerated at a rapid pace due to a simple but earth-shattering invention called the **World Wide Web** in 1989 by the physicist Tim Berners-Lee working in a European nuclear research institution in Switzerland. He proposed a client and server set-up to serve documents dispersed across Europe as a connected and coherent network so that scientists could easily share experiences and results of their experiments. The first Web client and server were written and demonstrated by Berners-Lee in 1990. The first implementation dealt exclusively with text documents with links to other documents or *hyperlinks*.

The first Web client or browser with a graphical user interface was written in the US at the National Center for Supercomputing Applications (NCSA) at the University of Illinois in Champaign-Urbana in 1993. It was called **Mosaic** and was available for free downloading on the Internet. Millions of copies were quickly downloaded and in a sense, the Internet revolution really started. Mosaic could display graphic images and was easy and pleasant to use with a point-and-click interface. Soon afterwards, Marc Andressen, one of the undergraduate student project leaders on the Mosaic project moved to California and started the company called Netscape. The Web client or browser called the **Netscape Navigator** was soon released. Microsoft Inc., although a late starter in Internet software production, re-engineered itself in the mid-1990s and released its Internet browser, the **Internet Explorer** in 1996. These are the two main Web clients at this time.

The Web has changed society in general. It is available across the globe, from the richest countries to the poorest. It has revolutionized human communication. It has rapidly become a medium for commercial communication, among far-flung divisions or departments of companies. It also has changed how governments at all levels communicate with the public and the ruled. It has also already become the marketplace of the world where anything conceivable from anywhere is available for buying and selling with the click of a mouse. The Web has also become a hotbed of entertainment possibilities with music, video and other data files being transmitted easily across the globe. Hundreds of TV and radio stations are available on the Web at this time.

Perl has been an important language in the development of the Web, with Perl-based CGI programs leading the way in delivering dynamic Web pages by collecting and collating information from disparate sources. Perl works easily with a Web server such as the leading Apache server. With its strong networking capabilities, powerful string handling, and a large number of enthusiastic followers who write and distribute free quality software, it is easy to develop sophisticated CGI programs and Web clients in Perl. Perl plays a major role on the Web and will continue to do so for the foreseeable future.

8.1   The Nature of Web Pages

The World Wide Web's architecture is simple. It has a large number of Web servers and a much larger number of Web clients. The Web clients most users use are the Web browsers although it is possible to develop simpler Web clients for very specific purposes. A Web client and a Web server communicate using HTTP—the HyperText Transfer Protocol. HTTP is a protocol or language for communication between a Web server and a Web client. The HTTP communication between a Web server and a Web client is translated into lower level communication to go over the network lines, but this translation is of no relevance to us here. There are a lot of books, primarily on computer networks that discuss the HTTP protocol in great depth. Two such books are *Computer Networks and Internets* [Com99] and *Data and Computer Communication* [Sta97]. An easy and readable discussion of the HTTP protocol is found in *Webmaster in a Nutshell* [SQ96].

Web documents are of three types although the general perception is that a Web page is a simple textual file served by a Web server to a requesting Web client. They are the following.

- *Static*: A static Web page is a textual file that resides on a Web server. It is composed by a Web developer. Every time a such a page is requested by a Web client, the same unvarying page is sent to it by the Web server.

- *Dynamic*: A dynamic Web page is not composed a-priori and stored in a file. A dynamic Web page is created by a Web server, with the assistance of an additional program when a client requests it. When a request for such a page arrives at a Web server, the server hands over the responsibility of creating the page to an auxiliary application program. Usually, the application program produces an HTML or XML page, gives it to the Web server that in turn, returns it to the requesting Web client. The client does neither know nor care whether it is a static page or a dynamic page. Since a new document is created to respond to each request from a client, the page served for the same request can vary from time to time. Quite often, the dynamically created Web page is based on a template where data values are inserted for each request.

- *Active*: An active Web page is a program that resides on the server. A Web server sends this program to the Web browser in response to a request. The program runs on the browser, communicates with the Web server and/or other programs, and displays the results on the browser.

A static Web page is easy to create. It is usually created using HTML, but more frequently using XML as well. One does not need to know HTML to produce HTML-based Web pages. One can use GUI-based tools sold by various companies for this purpose. An example of such a tool is **Dreamweaver** by Macromedia, Inc. Such a tool produces HTML automatically. There are a few XML-based GUI tools as well, but in general, producing an XML page requires more work. A static Web page can be served quickly and reliably by a Web server without any fuss or delay. A static Web page can be placed in its cache for a short period of time by a Web browser for future display without contacting the server. The main disadvantage of a static Web page is that its contents are fixed. A static Web page cannot contain data that is dynamic.

A dynamic Web page can present time-varying data, or data that is dynamic in some other fashion such as being dependent on a browser's characteristics. Time-varying information includes current time, current temperature and other weather-related information, price of plane tickets, and stock market quotes, etc. When a browser makes a request for a dynamic Web page, the server contacts an application program that creates the Web page by inserting the current values of the dynamic data. The server sends this page to the client. The main disadvantage of a dynamic document is that it places additional burden on the Web server compared to returning a static Web page. A dynamic document needs a programmer to create it. A dynamic document requires more extensive testing than a static document, because the data can come from various sources. One very common source of data is HTML forms.

A dynamic document has another problem. It places the computational responsibility solely on the Web server. It does not place any additional burden on the Web client or the machine on which the Web client runs. Now-a-days, most users have reasonably fast computers, and therefore, some of the computing burden can be easily shifted to the client or the client's computer. This is exactly what happens in the case of an active Web page. The server sends a program to the Web client that runs on the client's computer. Such an active Web page can perform animation, display time-varying graphs, produce sound, among other things. This is useful for displaying data that changes very quickly, such as stock quotes or weather information in the middle of a fierce storm. If we depend on dynamic pages for such situations, the server will be over-burdened. In addition, the updates on the client will be slow. An active Web page must be able to communicate with the Web server or other server programs to continuously retrieve data and update the presentation. The main disadvantage of an active Web page is that it requires programming, and thus, cannot be produced by a person without programming skills. An active Web page is difficult to test because it can be requested by any computer on the Internet, and computers on the Internet vary widely in terms of computing power, operating system used, and applications that reside on them. Finally, an active Web page can be a security risk. For example, an active Web page may contain a computer virus that can run on the client machine unless checked and deterred. An active Web page may also be able to export data from the client's computer to other machines. If mischievous, such a program may be able to scan the client machine's hard drive and report on the preferences of the user such as what programs reside on it, the presence or absence of specific kinds of files such as bootlegged programs or music files, or pornographic images or video files. Thus, an active Web page is not always the boon it is made out to be by its advocates. It can be a bane as well, compromising security and privacy.

In this chapter, we discuss how to create dynamic Web documents. We focus on one type of dynamic documents—ones that are produced by CGI programs. A Web server that serves only static Web pages must be modified in the following ways to be able to serve dynamic Web pages.

- The server program must be extended so that it can execute another application that creates the dynamic Web page for each client request. This application program may, in turn, communicate with other programs such as a Web server.

- A separate application program must be written for each dynamic document. These programs normally reside on the same machine as the Web server.

- The Web server must be configured so that it knows which URL corresponds to a static Web page and which to a dynamic Web page. For each dynamic Web page, the URL itself specifies the application program to run.

8.2   The Apache Web Server

To understand how a Web server serves static HTML or XML pages, or dynamic pages created by CGI programs, we need to be somewhat familiar with Web servers. There are several Web servers in common use. Of these, the **Apache Web Server** is the most popular. The Apache project has a home page at www.apache.org from where one can download it for free. The Apache Web server works on machines with Unix or Unix-like operating systems such as Linux, Sun Solaris, and BSD. It also works on Macintosh machines with OS X built on top of BSD Unix. The Apache Web server is also available for various flavors of the Windows operating system from Microsoft, Inc. To understand how the Apache Web server works, one should look at documentation at www.apache.org or a book such *Apache Desktop Reference* [Eng01].

The following discussion pertains primarily to the Apache installation on Red Hat Linux, a variation of standard Unix. Details may be different on other operating systems. A Web server other than Apache may allow one to configure it using a GUI, but the basic ideas are the same. There are many decisions an administrator or a webmaster needs to make when setting up a Web server. The Apache Web server comes as a part of the standard distribution in all Linux distributions including Red Hat Linux. It is also available as a standard tool in Mac OS X.

Modern operating systems are very security conscious. In the latest versions of Red Hat Linux, for example, most every network service comes shut off by default. So, the Apache Web server daemon httpd needs to be explicitly started by the systems administrator. If we want the Web server to start at boot time, this needs to be assured by the systems administrator by changing the boot script. This can be done by running a program such as ntsysv on a Red Hat Linux machine and indicating that httpd is one of the services to be started when the machine boots.

In Red Hat Linux, the Apache Web server is configured by editing the configuration file which is usually located at /etc/httpd/conf/httpd.conf. On Mac OS X Server, the configuration file for the Apache Web server is located at
/Library/WebServer/Configuration/apache.conf. This file can be edited using a text editor. The information contained is very crucial and thus, utmost caution should be exercised in editing the file. Only the root or super-user has permission to edit it. Editing this file without a clear understanding of what is being changed is an invitation to trouble.

The configuration file has many well-defined lines or sections that are described reasonably well with explanatory text or comment. A few of the lines relevant to our present discussion are shown below. These lines are called *directives* to the server. The directives are shown in the order in which they appear.

The first directive in the file from the Red Hat Linux Apache configuration file is the following.

```
ServerType standalone
```

This line specifies that the server runs as a stand-alone *daemon* process. A daemon process is a Unix server program. A server is a program that runs all the time doing nothing, but waiting for client requests. When a client makes a request, it responds appropriately. There is another possibility for running the Web server on a Unix machine, but the second option is not advised at this time since it is inefficient. The next directive in the file is the following.

```
ServerRoot "/etc/httpd"
```

This line specifies the root directory in which the administrative files related to the server resides. Typically, it contains sub-directories conf/ and logs/. The conf/ directory stores configuration files including the `httpd.conf` file under discussion. The `logs/` directory contains details of Web page accesses as well as errors encountered in Web page accesses. A directive that follows a little later in the `httpd.conf` file specifies a listening port.

`Port 80`

This directive specifies the port number on the system at which the Web server receives requests from clients. The standard HTTP server port number is 80 although other port numbers can be used. Acceptable port numbers range from 0 to $65,535 (= 2^{16} - 1)$ although numbers below 1024 are usually reserved. Another directive that follows shortly is the following.

`DocumentRoot "/var/www/html"`

This directive sets the directory from which the Apache Web server serves documents. In this case, Web pages reside on the system at `/var/www/html`. One can create sub-directories under this directory, as needed. The server usually attaches this path in front of the path obtained from a requested URL to create the fully qualified path to a requested Web page on the sever. For the Apache Web server program to work, one should avoid trailing slashes in specifying a directory in the configuration file, unless instructed to do so. The next directive of interest is the following.

`UserDir public_html`

The `UserDir` directive is the name of the directory that is appended to a user's home directory if a `~user` request in received. Thus, if `kalita` is a user on the machine `pikespeak.uccs.edu`, the URL `http://pikespeak.uccs.edu/~kalita/jk1.jpg` is translated to the directory `public_html` in `kalita`'s home directory on `pikespeak.uccs.edu`. So, if the user `kalita`'s home directory is `/home/kalita`, the URL is translated to the path `/home/kalita/public_html/jk1.jpg`. The next directive we discuss specifies the name of the default file that works as directory index.

`DirectoryIndex index.html index.htm index.shtml index.php index.php4 index.php3 index.cgi`

This is the name of the file to use when a client requests a directory by specifying a slash at the end of a URL. When several files are listed, the server looks for these files in sequence. Thus, if one types the URL `http://pikespeak.uccs.edu/` in a browser's `Location` box, the request is sent to `pikespeak.uccs.edu` where a Web server is running. The Web server looks in the directory `/var/www/html` and then looks for one of the files listed above. It looks for an index file in the sequence given above. As a second example, the URL `http://pikespeak.uccs.edu/~kalita/` looks for an index file in the directory `/home/kalita` on the server `pikespeak.uccs.edu`. Another directive that is relevant to our discussion is the following.

`ScriptAlias /cgi-bin/ "/var/www/cgi-bin/"`

The `ScriptAlias` directory specifies the directory where server scripts are found. A document found in an `ScriptAliased` directory is automatically treated as an application by the server. Thus, whenever a path such as `http://pikespeak.uccs.edu/cgi-bin/` is found, the `/cgi-bin/` portion of the URL makes the server program aware that it is a script and thus, an application program must be run. In addition, the `/cgi-bin/` portion of the URL is replaced by the server to its `ScriptAlias`. In this case, it becomes the path `/var/www/cgi-bin/` on the `pikespeak.uccs.edu` machine. The path given as `ScriptAlias` to the string `/cgi-bin/` is the system CGI directory. Usually, the Apache Web server is set up such that in addition to the CGI files in the system directory (here, `/var/www/cgi-bin`), an individual user has his or her CGI programs in his or her own home directory. This can be achieved on a Unix machine by creating a *soft link* from the system CGI directory to a sub-directory in the user's home directory. A soft link is a software based pointer from a name to a file or a directory that exists. A user needs to consult one's systems administrator to be able to create soft links so that the user's CGI programs can be placed in the user's home directory instead of the system CGI directory.

There is one more change that needs to be made to the `httpd.conf` file so that CGI programs actually work. The `httpd.conf` file, as it comes from the manufacturer, does not allow the execution of CGI programs. The section of `httpd.conf` that deals with CGI programs looks like the following to begin with.

```
<Directory "/var/www/cgi-bin">
    AllowOverride None
    Options None
    Order allow,deny
    Allow from all
</Directory>
```

This section needs to be changed so that the `ExecCGI` is an option. We also may allow `FollowSysmLinks` as an option so that users can have their CGI programs in their home directories, as briefly alluded to a little earlier. This allows the Web server to follow symbolic or soft links when starting a CGI program. For more details, the reader is requested to consult one's systems administrator. The change is incorporated in the directive section as shown below.

```
<Directory "/var/www/cgi-bin">
    AllowOverride None
    Options ExecCGI FollowSymLinks
    Order allow,deny
    Allow from all
</Directory>
```

There are many other directives in the configuration file. We have discussed just a few of the directives to make the basics of setting up a server clear. In summary, the configuration file specifies a host of details essential for the functioning of the Web server such as the port at which the server listens, the directory where log and configuration files are, the directory where static Web pages are, and the directory in which CGI script files are situated.

8.3 Writing CGI Programs

In the simplest mode of operation, a Web server simply returns a Web page corresponding to the URL requested by the browser. For example, when one types in `http://pikespeak.uccs.edu` on a Web browser, the request is sent by the browser to the server at `pikespeak.uccs.edu`. The server at `pikespeak.uccs.edu` returns the default initial page for the site which, depending on the server, may be called `index.html`, `index.htm` or some other name based on the configuration of the Web server.

However, quite frequently, a Web server needs to return a dynamic page, a page that is created by a program on the fly. A CGI program allows a Web server to contact other programs that can produce dynamic content. They can be simple programs producing simple dynamic content, or could be complex programs that query databases or map producing program and such. The term *CGI* stands for the Common Gateway Interface. It was originally developed by the National Center for Supercomputing Applications (NCSA) for use with the NCSA Web server. The CGI standard specifies how a server interacts with an application program that creates a dynamic document. CGI provides general guidelines. It does not specify a particular programming language. Perl is a language that is very commonly used for implementing CGI programs.

In addition, languages such as FORTRAN, C, C++, TCL, Unix shells, LISP, and AppleScript has been used by authors of CGI programs.

The output of a CGI program is most frequently an HTML document. However, the output can, in general, be in any arbitrary document format. Many CGI programs generate documents in XML—the Extensible Markup Language. Since most CGI programs discussed in this chapter generate HTML code, a basic knowledge of HTML is assumed.

8.3.1   A Very Simple CGI Program: Counting

We start with a CGI program that can be called directly from the `Location` field of a browser, or from an `HREF` link on a Web page. It is not called from an HTML form as is usually the case with most CGI programs. For a CGI program to work, it has to be placed in one or more pre-determined places in the computer that contains the Web server. One must ask one's system administrator what such a location is. The locations can be obtained by looking at the Web server configuration file as well. Assuming we know the location, it is possible to call a CGI program directly by typing in its URL in the browser.

Assume the server is `pikespeak.uccs.edu`. `pikespeak.uccs.edu` is a Red Hat Linux machine whose system CGI directory is `/var/www/cgi-bin` as discussed in Section 8.2. In this directory, we can create soft link to a designated directory in user `kalita`'s home directory. The home directory for the user `kalita`, viz., `/home/kalita` is also, called `~kalita` in abbreviated form in Unix. In the home directory, we create a sub-directory, say `public_html/cgi-bin` if it does not already exist. On a Unix machine, we can now create a soft link using the `ln` command with the `-s` option.

```
%ln -s /var/www/cgi-bin/kalita ~kalita/public_html/cgi-bin
```

The first argument is the name of the new link we create, and the second argument is the existing file or directory to which the link refers. The `ln` command links the `kalita` name in the system CGI directory (`/var/www/cgi-bin`) to the sub-directory `public_html/cgi-bin` in `kalita`'s home directory. Now, when we use a URL such as
`http://pikespeak.uccs.edu/cgi-bin/kalita/perlbook/countdown.pl` on a Web browser, the server knows right away it is a CGI program due to the presence of the sub-string `cgi-bin` in the URL, and the URL is translated by the `pikespeak.uccs.edu` server to the path
`/home/kalita/public_html/cgi-bin/countdown.pl` in order to execute the CGI program.

Let us assume that we invoke a simple CGI program by typing
`http://pikespeak.uccs.edu/cgi-bin/kalita/perlbook/countdown.pl`. The output this program produces on a browser is given in Figure 8.1.

Program 8.1

```perl
#!/usr/bin/perl
#countdown.pl

print "Content-type: text/html", "\n\n";

print "<HTML>", "\n";
print "<HEAD><TITLE>Simply counting...</TITLE></HEAD>", "\n";
print "<BODY><H1>Simply counting...</H1>";

print "<P>", "\n";

$countdown = 10;
while ($countdown != 0) {
```

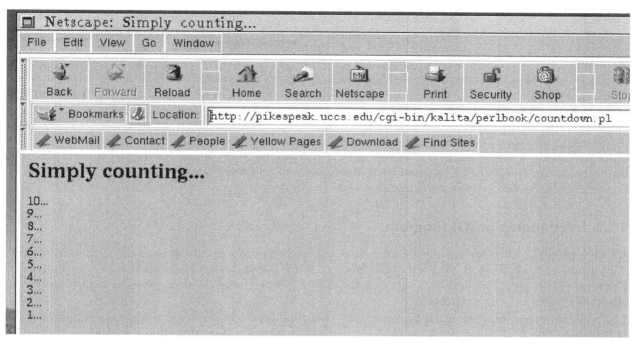

Figure 8.1: Counting in a CGI Program

```
    print "$countdown...\n";
    print "<BR>", "\n";
    --$countdown;
}

print "</BODY></HTML>", "\n";
```

Usually, a CGI program must have the location of the Perl interpreter as a comment on the first line starting from the first column. The Apache Web server requires such a line whether it is being used in the Unix or Windows environment.

Whatever a CGI program prints to the standard output is sent over by the Web server to the browser. When a Web page comes to a Web browser, the first one or more lines must be *HTTP headers* so that the Web browser knows how to display the page. This is the standard way an HTTP server communicates with an HTTP browser. This is not something special about a Web document produced by a CGI program. There could be quite a bit of header information that the Web server sends to the browser. Each header is one single line by itself and contains the name of a header field and its value. At a minimum, the server must tell the Web browser the kind of content being returned so that the browser knows how to display the information appropriately. In this program, we have only one header being returned.

```
Content-type: text/html
```

This line says that the content being sent is text and it follows HTML syntax. It is important to know that the headers returned must follow the header syntax in the HTTP protocol. The last header line must be followed by a blank line. This blank line separates the headers from the actual content of the page. Here, there is only one line of header and this line is followed by two newline characters or a single blank line.

Next, a CGI program must produce the contents of the document to be displayed. In this case, the CGI program produces simple HTML content, but it is conceivable that a CGI program produces XML content, or even graphic content. The CGI program creates HTML content by printing to the standard output HTML tags and text. An HTML document is enclosed within <HTML> and </HTML> tags. The tags are case-insensitive. An HTML page is composed of a head section enclosed within <HEAD> and </HEAD> tags, and a body enclosed within <BODY> and </BODY> tags. The head part usually contains a title to be displayed on the title bar of the browser. In the document produced by this program, the body repeats the title within <H1> and </H1> tags, creating a first-level header. The body of the Web page is produced inside the while loop. <P> is a paragraph break, and <BR> is a newline. In the HTML, we must use the HTML tag <BR> or <P> to break a line. The Perl newline character \n does not produce a line break in HTML because the browser considers it as space in HTML and ignores it. Once the body is produced, the program produces the terminating tags. Thus, a CGI program is like any other Perl program except that it must produce HTTP headers before it does any other writing to standard output.

8.3.2   Debugging a CGI Program

A CGI program is usually difficult to debug because errors printed on the browser are frequently cryptic. A CGI program can produce an error in many ways. Some situations are discussed below. The books *Perl Debugged* [SW01] and *Writing CGI Applications with Perl* [MM01] have more suggestions regarding how to effectively debug a Perl CGI program.

The Web browser complains if the CGI program cannot be found in the place where is is supposed to be (see Figure 8.2). The Web browser complains if the CGI program does not have the location of the Perl interpreter as the first line. In such a case, the Web server can find the CGI program, but does not know how to execute it. The Web browser complains if the first thing the Perl script writes to standard output is not one or more HTTP headers. In addition, the Web browser complains if the headers are not followed by an empty line. The Web browser also complains if there is any syntactic or run-time error in the Perl program.

Let us go through some usual steps in debugging an errant CGI program. A working CGI program must be syntactically correct. Therefore, it makes sense to check the Perl program for syntactic correctness in a terminal window before calling it from a browser. One can simply use the -c flag to do so as shown below.

```
%perl -c countdown.pl
countdown.pl syntax OK
```

In additon to the c option, one can use the w flag as well to get more detailed warnings about errors and possible errors of all kinds.

```
%perl -cw countdown.pl
```

If the syntax of the CGI program is incorrect, it produces an Internal Server Error when called from a Web browser (see Figure 8.3). A working CGI program must produce no run-time error. We can run the program from the command-line to make sure there are no run-time errors. This CGI program requires no input, and hence can be run easily from the command-line. When we run the current program from the command-line, it produces the following output. We can examine this output to determine if it is the expected output to be displayed on a Web browser.

```
%countdown.pl
Content-type: text/html

<HTML>
<HEAD><TITLE>Simply counting...</TITLE></HEAD>
<BODY><H1>Simply counting...</H1><P>
10...
```

```
<BR>
9...
<BR>
8...
<BR>
7...
<BR>
6...
<BR>
5...
<BR>
4...
<BR>
3...
<BR>
2...
<BR>
1...
<BR>
</BODY></HTML>
```

In this case, the HTML produced seems acceptable. Also, there is the required HTTP header line(s) on top followed by a blank line. If a CGI program produces a run-time error, the browser reports an Internal Server Error (see Figure 8.3).

Suppose our CGI program is syntactically correct and produces no run-time error, but we still get an error message when we run it from a browser. Obviously, there are other problems with the CGI program in such a case. The HTTP server's logs are very helpful in such a situation. If an error of any kind is reported on the browser, a corresponding error which is usually more informative, is logged on the server. The errors are logged in the directory specified in the ServerRoot directive in the configuration file discussed in Section 8.2. In the case of the Apache Web server on a Red Hat Linux machine, the logs are in the directory /etc/httpd. One should go to this directory and then look at the logs/ sub-directory in a Red Hat Linux machine. This directory may have a different name if we are using a Web server other than Apache. Usually there are one or more error log files. In the case of the Apache Web server, the files are named with the substring error_log somewhere in the name. One should look at the end of the latest error log file if there are several error log files. Usually, the error log files are huge. Therefore, bringing up an error log file in an editor or looking at this file in the terminal may be tedious. In Unix, one can use the tail command to look at the last few lines of the file. If one checks the error log on the server machine immediately after finding an error in a CGI program being tested on a Web browser, it is most likely to that the error is at the bottom of the log file. Note that the browser can be anywhere on the Internet. The errors are always logged on the server.

Suppose we intend to look at the URL
http://pikespeak.uccs.edu/cgi-bin/kalita/perlbook/countdown.pl, but type
http://pikespeak.uccs.edu/cgi-bin/kalita/perlbook/mycountdown.pl
by mistake on the browser's Location box. Therefore, we get an error on the browser screen. The error on the screen looks like that in Figure 8.2. In addition, as mentioned earlier, the Perl script must be in one of the acceptable places on the server. Otherwise, the browser gets an error message saying the CGI program cannot be found. Now, if we look at the bottom of the HTTP error log file on the Web server pikespeak.uccs.edu more or less immediately after the occurrence of the error, we see the following entry. The line has been broken into two since it is very long.

```
[Tue Jun 19 09:04:40 2001] [error] [client 128.198.162.231]
  script not found or unable to stat: /var/www/cgi-bin/kalita/perlbook/mycountdown.pl
```

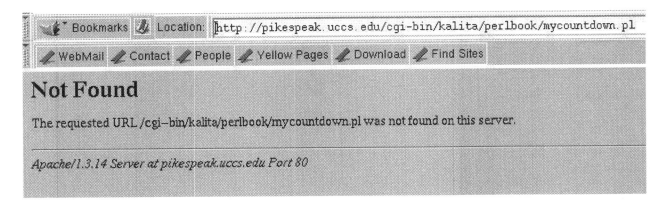

Figure 8.2: Not Found Error in a CGI Program

It gives us the time at which the error occurred, the machine on which the browser is running, and a brief description of the error. It says that the CGI script could not be found or crucial system-level details about the file could not obtained by the server. The `stat` command in Unix gives information on a file.

To simulate another error, let us rewrite the same CGI program, but leave out the line that prints the HTTP header. The revised program is given below.

Program 8.2

```
#!/usr/bin/perl
#countdownError1.pl

print "<HTML>", "\n";
print "<HEAD><TITLE>Simply counting...</TITLE></HEAD>", "\n";
print "<BODY><H1>Simply counting...</H1>";

print "<P>", "\n";

$countdown = 10;
while ($countdown != 0) {
        print "$countdown...\n";
        print "<BR>", "\n";
        --$countdown;
}

print "</BODY></HTML>", "\n";
```

The modified CGI program is stored in the file in the same directory as the original `countdown.pl` file. It is called `cuntdownError1.pl`. Now, if we type
`http://pikespeak.uccs.edu/cgi-bin/kalita/perlbook/countdownError1.pl` on the
`Location` box on a browser, we see an error as shown in Figure 8.3. When we look toward the end of the error log file on the server, we see the following. It has been broken into several lines because it is long.

```
[Tue Jun 19 09:12:15 2001] [error] [client 128.198.162.231]
```

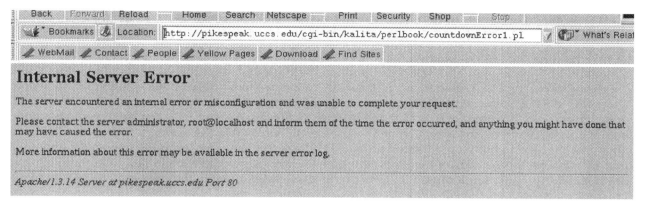

Figure 8.3: Internal Server Error in a CGI Program

Figure 8.4: Forbidden Error in a CGI Program

```
malformed header from script. Bad header=<HTML>:
        /var/www/cgi-bin/kalita/perlbook/countdownError1.pl
```

It says that the string <HTML> is not a valid HTTP header. The browser does not get an acceptable HTTP header and therefore chokes. As noted earlier, the first thing the CGI program must write to the standard output is one or more HTTP header lines followed by a blank line. This requirement is not satisfied by the modified CGI program.

If we change the permission on the CGI file countdown.pl so that it is not readable by everyone, we see the error as shown in Figure 8.4 on the browser. The Perl CGI script must have read and executable permission by everyone, and any directories it is contained in must be accessible to everyone. In a Unix system, this means that the directories must be readable and executable by everyone. Note that if a CGI program is in a user's directory, accessible by a soft link, the user's home directory must be readable and executable by everyone. The Web browser complains if this is not the case. The Forbidden Error is caused by insufficient permission. On a PC or a Macintosh (pre-OS X), permissions are usually not a major source of problem. In a Unix machine, we can change the permission by using the chmod command. An entry is written in the log file as well.

It is possible that there are two, even more, entries in the error log for a single Perl error, as shown below.

```
syntax error at /users/server/students/www/cgi-bin/smarndt/register.pl line 18, near "'email';"
Execution of /users/server/students/www/cgi-bin/smarndt/register.pl aborted
    due to compilation errors.
[Sat Mar 16 15:11:51 2002] [error] [client 128.198.60.23] Premature end of script headers:
                /users/server/students/www/cgi-bin/smarndt/register.pl
```

Here, there is a syntax error in the program register.pl. The error causes the program to be aborted due to compilation errors. This error string is sent out to the browser before the CGI program can send out an HTTP header. This results in a complaint by the server about premature end of script headers.

8.3.2.1   The `CGI::Carp.pm` Module

The error reported by a CGI program on the browser is quite frequently very cryptic (see Figure 8.3). It does not convey much. It sometimes seems to say that the error is really serious when it is not. In the case shown in the figure, there is nothing wrong with the manner in which the server has been configured, assuming there is a competent systems administrator. The problem here is that the server is not prepared to send out an HTML file to a browser without a proper HTTP header. The error log, quite frequently, has much more informative specification of the error. But, even the error log can sometimes lack time-stamping and may not identify which script caused it. The error that is normally sent to the error log, can be sent to the browser as well by using the `CGI::Carp.pm` module discussed below.

The `CGI::Carp.pm` module causes functions such as `warn` and `die` that we frequently use in Perl programs to produce time-stamped error messages so that they are useful. Most HTTP servers send STDERR, the default stream to which error messages are written, to the server's error log. Thus, when we use `CGI::Carp.pm`, an error is always nicely time-stamped and always identified by the script that causes it. In addition, `CGI::Carp.pm` can ask the server to send out fatal errors such as those caused by `die` or other errors that terminate the program, to the Web browser. For this to happen, we must explicitly import the `fatalsToBrowser` subroutine.

Below is a rewrite of the program `countdown.pl`, now called `countdownError2.pl`, that uses the `CGI::Carp.pm` module and imports `fatalToBrowser`. It is exactly the same program as `countdown.pl` except that a syntactic error has been introduced.

Program 8.3

```perl
#!/usr/bin/perl
#countdownError2.pl
use CGI::Carp qw(fatalsToBrowser);

print "Content-type: text/html", "\n\n";

print "<HTML>", "\n;
print "<HEAD><TITLE>Simply counting...</TITLE></HEAD>", "\n";
print "<BODY><H1>Simply counting...</H1>";

print "<P>", "\n";

$countdown = 10;
while ($countdown != 0) {
        print "$countdown...\n";
        print "<BR>", "\n";
        --$countdown;
        }

print "</BODY></HTML>", "\n";
```

Note that in the line

```perl
print "<HTML>", "\n;
```

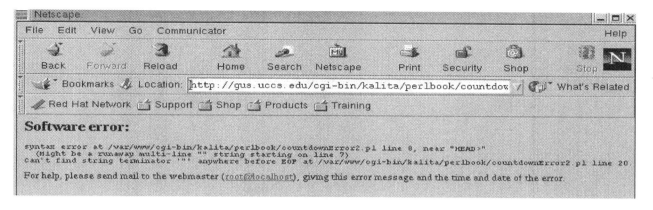

Figure 8.5: Error Sent to Browser by a CGI Program

the string containing \n is not closed with a double quote. This causes a syntactic error. Without `fatalsToBrowser`, this would have resulted in an "Internal Server Error" message displayed on the browser. But, with `fatalsToBrowser`, the error is displayed on the browser as in Figure 8.5.

Note that it may not be appropriate to use `fatalsToBrowser` in a production or working system since it may give out more details to the whole world than we want. Thus, it is advisable to use it only during development, and comment out the `use` line when the program starts to work.

8.3.3   The Environment Hash: `%ENV`

On any system, Perl has available to it a hash by the name `%ENV`. This hash has details of the environment in which Perl is working. Any operating system, whether Unix, Macintosh or Windows-based, has a number of variables called *environment variables*. Usually, the operating system needs them to be set so that so that various programs run on the system correctly. These refer to details such as the operating system used, the name of the machine, the user who is logged in, the nature of the display terminal used, etc. There are a host of other system-specific and session-specific details as well. The number, the names and the values of the environment variables are different on different machines.

The names of the environment variables and their corresponding values are acquired by Perl from the operating system as well as the Apache Web server. The Perl software may create some environment variables as well. Since the environment variables are inherited by Perl from the operating system and stored as key-value pairs, the keys and their corresponding values vary from machine to machine. Even on the same machine, the keys and values are different depending on whether a Perl script is run from the command line or from the Web as a CGI program.

The following program is run on the command line and prints the keys and corresponding values in the environment variable `%ENV`. It is *not* run as a CGI program.

Program 8.4

```perl
#!/usr/bin/perl
#environCommand.pl

use strict;

my $key;
foreach $key (sort (keys %ENV)){
```

```
    print "The value of the ", $key, " field is ", $ENV{$key}, "\n";
}
```

The program iterates over every key-value pair in %ENV hash and prints the pair. The output this program prints on the screen when run from the command-line is shown below. Some lines have been broken up because they are too long.

```
The value of the AUTOBOOT field is YES
The value of the BOOT_FILE field is /boot/vmlinuz-2.2.19-7.0.1
The value of the BOOT_IMAGE field is linux
The value of the COLORTERM field is gnome-terminal
The value of the CONSOLE field is /dev/console
The value of the DISPLAY field is :0
The value of the EDITOR field is /usr/ucb/vi
The value of the GDMSESSION field is Default
The value of the GDM_LANG field is en_US
The value of the GROUP field is kalita
The value of the HOME field is /home/kalita
The value of the HOST field is pikespeak.uccs.edu
The value of the HOSTNAME field is pikespeak.uccs.edu
The value of the HOSTTYPE field is i386-linux
The value of the INIT_VERSION field is sysvinit-2.78
The value of the KDEDIR field is /usr
The value of the LANG field is en_US
The value of the LESSOPEN field is |/usr/bin/lesspipe.sh %s
The value of the LOGNAME field is kalita
The value of the LS_COLORS field is no=00:fi=00:di=01;34:ln=01;36:pi=40;
        33:so=01;35:bd=40;33;01:cd=40;33;
        01:or=01;05;37;41:mi=01;05;37;41:ex=01;32:*.cmd=01;32:*.exe=01;32:*.com=01;
        32:*.btm=01;32:*.bat=01;32:*.sh=01;32:*.csh=01;32:*.tar=01;31:*.tgz=01;31:*.arj=01;
        31:*.taz=01;31:*.lzh=01;31:*.zip=01;31:*.z=01;31:*.Z=01;31:*.gz=01;31:*.bz2=01;
        31:*.bz=01;31:*.tz=01;31:*.rpm=01;31:*.cpio=01;31:*.jpg=01;35:*.gif=01;
        35:*.bmp=01;35:*.xbm=01;35:*.xpm=01;35:*.png=01;35:*.tif=01;35:
The value of the MACHTYPE field is i386
The value of the MANPATH field is /usr/man:/usr/local/man:/usr/users/kalita/man:/usr/share/man
The value of the OSTYPE field is linux
The value of the PATH field is
.:/home/kalita/bin:/bin:/usr/bin:/usr/local/bin:/usr/sbin:/usr/bin/X11:/usr/bin/mh
The value of the PREVLEVEL field is N
The value of the PWD field is /home/kalita/perl/cgi-bin
The value of the QTDIR field is /usr/lib/qt-2.2.0
The value of the RUNLEVEL field is 5
The value of the SESSION_MANAGER field is local/pikespeak.uccs.edu:/tmp/.ICE-unix/1179
The value of the SHELL field is /bin/csh
The value of the SHLVL field is 2
The value of the SSH_ASKPASS field is /usr/libexec/openssh/gnome-ssh-askpass
The value of the TERM field is xterm
The value of the USER field is kalita
The value of the USERNAME field is kalita
The value of the VENDOR field is intel
The value of the VISUAL field is /usr/bin/emacs
The value of the WINDOWID field is 92274812
The value of the WWW_HOME field is http://www.cs.uccs.edu/~kalita
The value of the XAUTHORITY field is /home/kalita/.Xauthority
The value of the _ field is /usr/bin/gnome-terminal
```

We do not have to understand every key and its value. The purpose of showing the output is to make the reader aware of the variety of environment variables and their values that an operating system maintains. We clearly see that many of the environment variables represent information that is static or permanent. An example is the VENDOR field whose value is intel, indicating it is an Intel machine on which the Perl script is running. However, the field WINDOWID is very specific and temporary giving an integer with the ID number of a window where the script just ran.

8.3.4   Printing CGI Environment Variables

The CGI standard allows a CGI program to be parameterized. In other words, a server can pass parameters to a CGI program that it invokes. Values of some of these parameters are supplied by the browser. When a browser sends a request for a page to a server, it sends additional information such as its identity, the machine on which it is running, etc. Such information is passed over to the CGI program so that if necessary the CGI program can use it. Among other things, the information can be used to customize the output for a specific browser. For example, if the program is being invoked from a personal digital assistant (PDA) such as palm top computer or a cellular phone, the CGI program can produce smaller pages that can fit the PDA's screen and that reduce the amount of information transmitted.

A Web server can parameterize a CGI program in two ways.

- The Web server directly sends the parameters and their values sent by the browser to the CGI program. These are usually names of HTML form fields and their values. These are sent following the same simple syntax that the browser uses to send them to the server. We see a discussion of this syntax in Section 8.3.5.

- The Web server sends additional parameters to the CGI program using environment variables. The use of environment variables is an unusual convention for passing arguments. The Web server places certain parameter values in Unix or operating system environment variables and then invokes the CGI program. The CGI program inherits a copy of these environment variables. A CGI program can extract these values and use them.

In this section, we convert the program that prints the environments variables on the command line, first discussed in Section 8.3.3, into a CGI program. We do so by printing one or more HTTP headers to the standard output, followed by a page that follows HTML syntax. The meat of the program is still the `while` loop that prints the key-value pairs from the environment hash `%ENV`. The variable values are printed in the body of the page. This program prints the values of environment variables as seen by a CGI program. The environment variables define the context in which the CGI program runs.

Whether a Perl program runs from the command-line or as a CGI program, the environment variables are available to it in the `%ENV` hash. However, the contents of `%ENV` are different in the two cases. When a Web server is started, it runs its own environment. That is, it knows quite a bit of information about its identity, the machine it is running on, the programs it can count on to call for various purposes, etc. These variables are available to a CGI program.

The environment variables that a Web server maintains may be long-term information. For example the IP address and the name of the machine on which the Web server is running usually never change. Another environment variable that does not change is the type of Web server software, say an Apache server. However, there are other environment variables such as the name and the IP address of the machine on which the browser is running change from one interacting browser session to another. A variable that records the name of the current CGI script obviously changes with every CGI program that is started by either clicking on an HTML link or by giving the name of the CGI program as a URL on the location box of a browser.

Program 8.5

```perl
#!/usr/bin/perl
#file environ.pl
use strict;

print "Content-type: text/html", "\n";
print "Pragma: no-cache", "\n\n";

print "<HTML>", "\n";
print "<HEAD><TITLE>Printing Environment Variables...</TITLE></HEAD>", "\n";
print "<BODY><H1>Printing Environment Variables...</H1>";
```

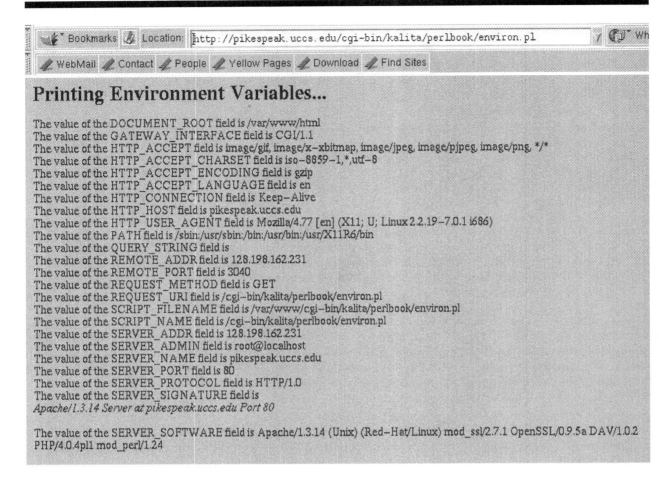

Figure 8.6: Printing Environment Variables in a CGI Program

```
my $key;
foreach $key (sort (keys %ENV)){
    print "The value of the ", $key, " field is ", $ENV{$key}, "<br>\n";
}

print "</BODY></HTML>", "\n";
```

We can run this CGI program from a browser using a URL such as the following assuming the script has been saved in the appropriate location on the server.

```
http://pikespeak.uccs.edu/cgi-bin/kalita/perlbook/environ.pl
```

In a Web page using HTML, the CGI program can be invoked by using a construct such as the following.

```
<a href="http://pikespeak.uccs.edu/cgi-bin/kalita/perlbook/environ.pl">
    Click for environment variables</a>
```

The output produced by the CGI program on a Web browser is shown in Figure 8.6. A cursory glance at Figure 8.6 and the output shown in Section 8.3.3 show that the contents of the %ENV hash in the two cases are entirely different. In the case of the CGI program, the `%ENV` hash stores information about the current state of the HTTP interaction, the participants in the interaction, and attributes of the participants as well as the interaction itself. We discuss some of these environment variables below. The reader is advised to look at a book such as *Webmaster in a Nutshell* [SQ96], *CGI Programming on the World Wide Web* [Gun00], or *Writing CGI Applications with Perl* [MM01] for more details on these and other CGI environment variables.

CGI environment variables can be classified into several categories.

- **Server:** Information such as the server name, the port used by the server, the version of the server protocol, etc.

- **Client:** Information such as the identity of the remote host on which the client is running, the port used by the client, etc.

- **HTTP Protocol:** Information about the protocol such as the protocol version, languages acceptable, character set used, etc.

- **CGI:** Information about the CGI interaction such as its version, method used, name of the script, the query string, location of the script, etc.

- **Redirection:** It may also contain information about redirection if the original HTTP request is redirected by the original server after modifying the query string to a new server at a new port with a new URL. Such redirection is not uncommon, especially in commercial sites such as a Web-based bookstore.

First, we specify some of the server environment variables.

- `SERVER_NAME`, `SERVER_ADDR`, and `SERVER_PORT` give the name of the machine on which the server is running, its IP address, and the listening port used by the server, respectively.

- `SERVER_PROTOCOL` specifies the version of the HTTP protocol used by the Web server.

- `SERVER_SOFTWARE` gives a somewhat detailed specification of the Web server.

The client information includes fields such as `REMOTE_ADDR` and `REMOTE_PORT`. Usually, a Web client is automatically given an unused port by the machine on which it is running. The HTTP protocol information includes the following and a few additional fields.

- `HTTP_HOST`: It contains the name of the server or one of its aliases that the client says it wants to contact when it sends out the HTTP request.

- `HTTP_CONNECTION`: This specifies if the network link between the server and the browser is for transmitting one document or for several documents. In the early days of the Web, the HTTP protocol transmitted only one document from a server to a client per transmission. If several documents needed to be sent from a server to the same client, the communication channel between the client and the server was opened and closed several times, once for each document. Therefore, if a Web page had several images that had to be loaded from the same Web server, each was obtained separately, and each involved elaborate opening and closing of the channel of communication between the same pair of computers. This inefficiency can be gotten rid of in the currrent version of the HTTP protocol by using the `Keep-Alive` facility. If several files need to be transferred from the same server to the same client, `Keep-Alive` states that the server keep the line open till all required files have been transmitted.

- `HTTP_ACCEPT_LANGUAGE`: It specifies the languages the browser can accept. The list of languages and their abbreviations are specified in terms of a document called *Request For Comments (RFC) 1766*. A list is found in a book such as *Web Design in a Nutshell* [Nie99]. A few language codes are given in Table 8.1.

as	Assamese
el	Greek
en	English
es	Spanish
fi	Finnish
no	Norwegian
pt	Portuguese
ru	Russian
sv	Swedish

Table 8.1: RFC 1766 Language Codes Used by the HTTP Protocol

8859-1	Europe, Latin America, Caribbean, Canada, Africa
8859-2	Eastern Europe
8859-3	SE Europe/miscellaneous (Esperanto, Maltese, etc.)
8859-4	Scandinavia/Baltic (mostly covered by 8859-1 also)
8859-5	Cyrillic
8859-6	Arabic
8859-7	Greek
8859-8	Hebrew
8859-9	Latin5, same as 8859-1 except for Turkish instead of Icelandic
8859-10	Latin6, for Lappish/Nordic/Eskimo languages

Table 8.2: Some Non-Western European Language Standards

- `HTTP_ACCEPT_CHARSET`: It specifies the default character set or sets that the browser can display. This environment variable specifies one or more encodings for character sets. A character set is encoded in terms of a sequence of numbers. The HTML specification uses the ISO-8859-1 (Latin 1) character set for encoding documents. If we want to create an HTML document that is universally viewable, it must use this character set. It uses 8 bits for each character. ISO-8859-1 is an internationally standardized character set to used type accented characters. This character set contains all characters necessary for all major languages of Western Europe. Table 8.2 gives a list of other ISO-8859 character sets that are internationally accepted for languages outside Western Europe. ISO-8859-1 is only one of the ISO-8859 standards. There are additional standards for Asian and other regions of the world. The Unicode specification, a universal character encoding scheme, is a superset of all these standards.

  It is hoped the Unicode will replace ASCII and Latin-1 in a few years everywhere. The Unicode handles practically any script and any language in the world, and also provides a comprehensive set of mathematical and technical symbols. The UTF-8 encoding allows Unicode to be used in a convenient and backward-compatible way in environments that, like Unix, were designed entirely around ASCII. UTF-8 is the way in which Unicode is going to be used under Unix, Linux and similar systems.

  The asterisk (*) says that the browser accepts any character encoding other than the two explicitly specified. However, the browser may not know how to display the text that uses other character encoding schemes.

- `HTTP_ACCEPT`: It is a list of Internet media types in which the client prefers to receive data. The browser decides how to display the information based on the media type. For example, a data item of type `image/gif` is a GIF graphic file and needs to be rendered by the browser. Certain content, say of type `application/pdf`, requires the browser to run an auxiliary application of plug-in. In this case, a PDF viewer such as the Adobe Acrobat Reader needs to be run. Internet media types used by HTTP closely resemble Multipurpose Internet Mail Extension (MIME) types originally designed as a method for sending attachments in mail over the Internet. Like MIME, media types follow the type/subtype format. Asterisks (*) represent a wild card. `*/*` means accept all formats. Although it nominally accepts all formats, the browser brings up a dialog box for a format it does not know how to deal with, asking the user what to do. See a book such as *Webmaster in a Nutshell* [SQ96] for a list of Internet media types.

- `HTTP_USER_AGENT`: It is the browser or the client that issued the request.

- `HTTP_ACCEPT_ENCODING`: It specifies the if the browser can accept compressed data and automatically uncompress it. Browsers such as Netscape, Internet Explorer and Lynx can all accept data that is compressed using the `gzip` technique. What additional compression methods are a acceptable depends entirely on the browser. Compressing textual data can reduce the amount of transmission by 70% or more.

The CGI information in the environment variables includes the following.

- `GATEWAY_INTERFACE`: It specifies the version of the CGI standard that the Web server implements.

- `REQUEST_METHOD` gives the method used for transmitting data. It is GET or PUT. A regular Web page is accessed using GET. An HTML form can be submitted using GET or POST. The Web browser uses a simple encoding scheme to send data to the server. The GET method sends the requested URL and additional data specific to the request in one HTTP transmission. The POST method uses two transmissions: one for the URL, and the other for any accompanying data.

- `SCRIPT_NAME`, and `SCRIPT_FILENAME`: These are two ways of specifying the script being executed.

- `QUERY_STRING` provides the query that the client sends to the server. The query is essentially the data sent by the client to the server when it makes a CGI request. It is clearly seen only in the case of a GET request. It is what follows the question mark (?) after the URL when a GET form sends data to the server.

Document information and redirection information may also appear among the environment variables. There is no redirection information in Figure 8.6.

8.3.5   HTML Forms

A lot of CGI programs work with HTML forms. Such a CGI program accepts form information sent to it by a browser, and processes the information to produce results that are sent back to the browser for display as response. Usually, the CGI program takes other requested actions such as enrolling a person in a mailing list, starting the process needed to accept credit card payment and ship a book to the customer, etc. Therefore, is is necessary to understand the syntax of forms well. The reader is advised to consult a book such as *HTML and XHML: The Definitive Guide* [MK00], *XHMTL By Example* [Nav00] or *Web Design in a Nutshell* [Nie99].

There is a very powerful Perl module called `CGI.pm` that makes many aspects of CGI programming much easier than starting from scratch [Ste98]. In this book, we examine only a few of the capabilities of the `CGI.pm` module. In particular, we use `CGI.pm` to obtain the parameters that have been passed to the CGI program. Many of the functions that `CGI.pm` provides allows one to produce HTML tags in the correct manner. However, the author of this book does not find much use for most such constructs. If one produces HTML using a CGI program, the author feels that he or she should know HTML syntax. There is no need to learn another language that produces HTML code, albeit at a slightly higher level. There are too many programming languages to learn and use, and the author prefers one less! And, HTML is extremely simple.

There are two types of HTML forms on the Web: GET forms and POST forms. The two names are associated with the type of method for data submission used by the form. When an HTML form is filled with data by a viewer, the data needs to be sent to the server. Action is taken by the server based on the form data by delegating the task to a helper program such as a CGI program. This program is accessible on the Web using a URL, and this URL is available as the value of the ACTION attribute of the HTML form. Each data field in the form has a name and each of the fields in the form that is filled has a value. A form field that remains unfilled has no associated value. The name-value pairs are sent to the Web server by the browser using a specific format. The form data is encoded using a standard and simple encoding process. Some character transformations are performed by the browser before the name-value pairs are constructed. For a name-value pair, the name is followed by an equal sign, and then the value. There are no spaces in-between. Name-value pairs are separated from each other with the ampersand character. Thus, the form data may look like the following assuming we have three fields in the form.

> *name1=value1&name2=value2&name3=value3*

The difference between a GET form and a POST form lies in the manner in which data is sent to the server by the browser. In a GET form, the browser sends the ACTION URL and the form data to the browser in one transmission with a question mark character between the two.

> *URL?name-value-pairs*

URL is the full URL of the program that is found in the ACTION attribute of the form. *name-value-pairs* follow the format given earlier. In a POST form, data is sent by the browser to the server in two transmissions unlike the single transmission in the case of a GET form. In the case of a POST form, the URL is sent alone first. Next, in a separate transmission, the name-values pairs constructed in the manner discussed earlier are sent.

Since the data are sent in two different ways, a general servicing CGI program has to capture the data in two different ways. The encoding process is the same in the two cases, and hence, the decoding process is the same as well. The CGI.pm module makes the capturing of data easy. If we use the CGI.pm module, we do not have to worry about whether it uses the GET or the POST method. We do not have to know the encoding process so we can undo it to be able to decode. One of the functionalities that is most useful in the CGI.pm module is the param method that captures a piece of field data based on the name of the form's field. It is also possible to write a form-handling CGI program without using the CGI.pm module [Gun00] although we do not discuss it here.

For a CGI program that responds to a user-filled HTML form, there are usually two things that have to work together. First, we must have an HTML file. A CGI program is usually called by the server when a browser submits an HTML form. An HTML form has an ACTION attribute whose value must be a URL that corresponds to a program that can take the form input and process it and return a result. For several years in the early years of the Web, CGI programs were the only way to handle forms, although now there are other mechanisms such as *Microsoft ASPs* and *Java servlets*. Thus, the second requirement to handle form data is a program. The CGI program must examine the form data, see if they are acceptable (although JavaScript and other scripting languages can help by doing some filtering on the browser itself), and if they are appropriate produce the appropriate output in HTML format and send it back to the browser for display. The CGI program may be able to produce the output directly by performing some computation, but frequently a CGI program contacts a data source like a database and gets data from it before producing the HTML page it returns. The output of the CGI program is automatically sent to the browser that made the request to the CGI program by filling in the form.

8.3.6   Capturing and Echoing HTML Form Data

We now discuss a CGI program that receives data from an HTML form that is filled by a user and echoes the field names and field values back to the browser. This can be a part of a more complex program where the echoing is used to give the user feedback. We use the CGI.pm module to capture data.

We have an HTML file that shows a Web-based subscription form for an electronic mailing list. We show the code for only the HTML form here. The mailing list is called the *Assam* mailing list that the author of this book has managed for many years. It is a mailing list that allows individuals to subscribe by filling in a form on the Web. Individuals can also unsubscribe by filling up a related form. The HTML code is given below.

```html
<FORM METHOD="POST"
   ACTION="http://pikespeak.uccs.edu/cgi-bin/kalita/assamListFormEcho.pl">
  <TABLE BORDER="0" WIDTH="75%">
    <TR>
      <TD HEIGHT="18" WIDTH="30%">Your Email:</TD>
      <TD HEIGHT="18" width="70%">
        <INPUT TYPE="TEXT" NAME="email">
      </TD>
    </TR>
    <TR>
      <TD WIDTH="30%">First Name:</TD>
      <TD WIDTH="70%">
        <INPUT TYPE="TEXT" NAME="firstName">
      </TD>
    </TR>
    <TR>
      <TD WIDTH="30%">Last Name:</TD>
      <TD WIDTH="70%">
        <INPUT TYPE="TEXT" NAME="lastName">
      </TD>
    </TR>
    <TR>
      <TD WIDTH="30%">Surface Mailing Address</TD>
      <TD WIDTH="70%">
        <INPUT TYPE="TEXT" NAME="surfaceAddress" MAXLENGTH="80" SIZE="80">
      </TD>
    </TR>
    <TR>
      <TD WIDTH="30%">Occupation</TD>
      <TD WIDTH="70%">
        <INPUT TYPE="TEXT" NAME="occupation">
      </TD>
    </TR>
          <TR>
      <TD WIDTH="30%">Telephone Number</TD>
      <TD WIDTH="70%">
        <INPUT TYPE="TEXT" NAME="telephoneNumber">
      </TD>
    </TR>
  </TABLE>

  <P><FONT COLOR="#DE190F">To be able to unsubscribe from the list on
     a later date by coming to this site on the World Wide Web, please provide
```

```
        answers to the following two questions. You can remove
        yourself from the mailing list by filling in the form for
        <A
        HREF="http://pikespeak.uccs.edu/~kalita/unsubscribe.html">unsubscribing
        from the Assam List </A> </FONT> <FONT COLOR="blue"> <BR><B>
        Please remember: If you don't
        fill proper values for answers to
        the two questions and enter inappropriate
        values, you will be removed from the mailing list by
        its administrator(s).</B>  </FONT> </P>

    <TABLE WIDTH="75%">
      <TR>
        <TD WIDTH="46%">What is your mother's maiden name (her last name
           before marriage):</TD>
        <TD WIDTH="54%">
           <INPUT TYPE="TEXT" NAME="motherMaidenName">
        </TD>
      </TR>
      <TR>
        <TD WIDTH="46%">What is your village, town or city of birth?</TD>
        <TD WIDTH="54%">
           <INPUT TYPE="TEXT" NAME="homeTown">
        </TD>
      </TR>
    </TABLE>
    <P>
      <INPUT TYPE="submit" NAME="submit" value="Become a Subscriber">
     <INPUT TYPE="reset" NAME="rest" value="Clear Form">
    </P>
</FORM>
```

The form has several fields or input boxes. Each field has a name. The names of the fields are: email, firstName, lastName, surfaceAddress, occupation, telephoneNumber, motherMaidenName, and homeTown. The form's input boxes are organized into two tables for a pleasant display. All but the last two form fields are in one table. The last two fields are in a table by themselves. It is a common practice to use HTML tables to format form data. HTML allows almost all tags inside the <FORM> and </FORM> tags so that the form can be made nice to look at.

The Web page as it looks on a Web browser is shown in Figure 8.7. This figure shows the form with all the input boxes filled with values. Note that the ACTION attribute of the form is given as a URL on the machine pikespeak.uccs.edu. It also uses the POST method for submitting the form data.

```
<FORM METHOD="POST"
    ACTION="http://pikespeak.uccs.edu/cgi-bin/kalita/assamListFormEcho.pl"   >
```

On the Red Hat Linux machine pikespeak.uccs.edu discussed in Section 8.2, this program is located at /home/kalita/public_html/cgi-bin/assamListFormEcho.pl.

The CGI program that services this HTML form is given below. The program uses the CGI.pm module. It captures the data from the form fields and simply echoes the data to the browser.

Program 8.6

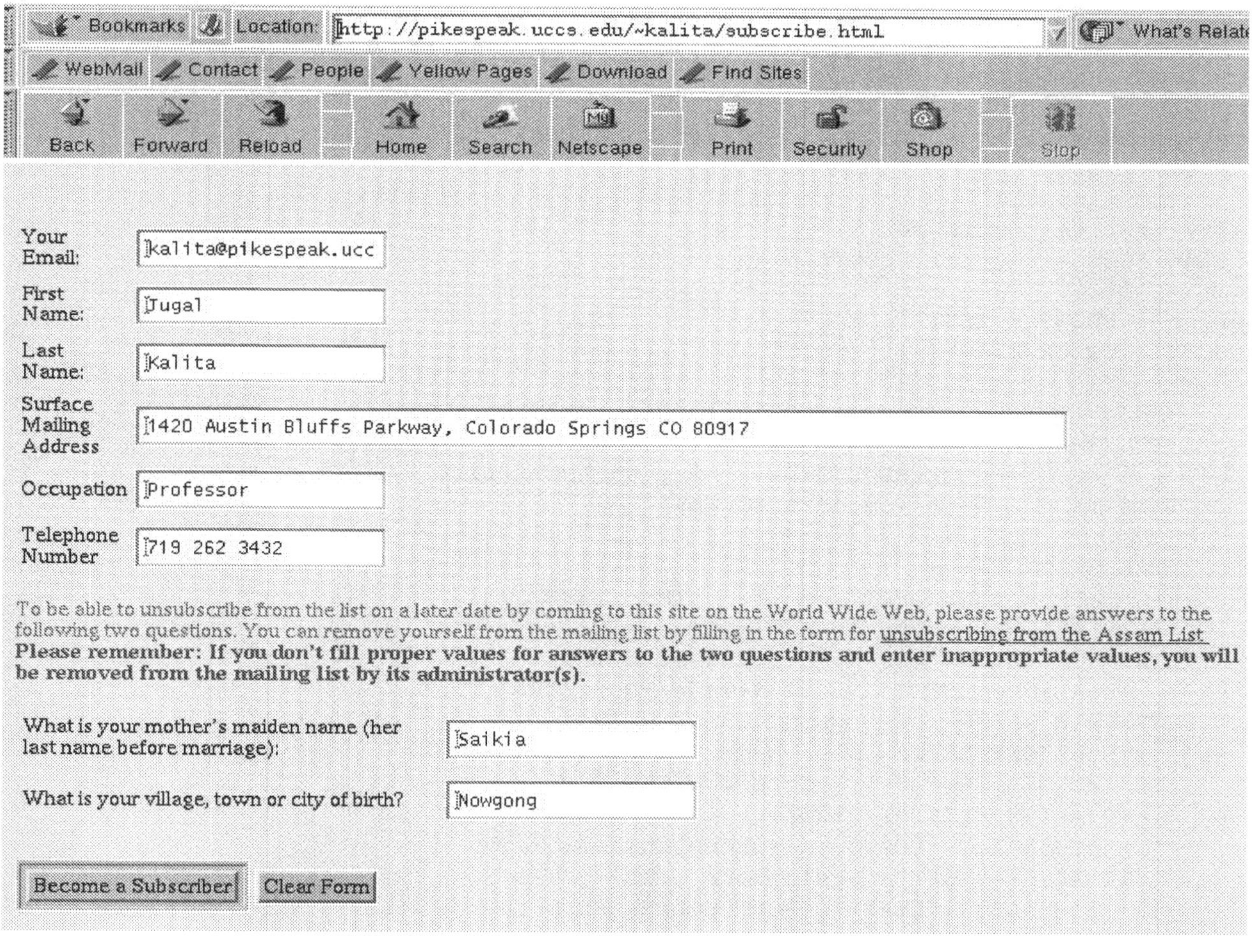

Figure 8.7: HTML Form whose Contents are Echoed by a CGI Program

```perl
#!/usr/bin/perl
#assamListFormEcho.pl

use CGI qw(:standard);
use strict;

#########################
my $email = param ("email");
my $firstName = param ("firstName");
my $lastName = param ("lastName");
my $address = param ("surfaceAddress");
my $telephone = param ("telephoneNumber");
my $motherName = param ("motherMaidenName");
my $homeTown = param ("homeTown");

#######Write to browser
print "Content-type: text/html\n\n";

print <<BROWSER_TEXT
<BODY BGCOLOR=BISQUE>
<HTML>
    <HEAD><TITLE>Subscribe to Assam List</TITLE></HEAD>
    <BODY><H1>
        <FONT COLOR=BLUE>Subscribing to Assam List </FONT></H1>
    This is the data you entered.<p>

    <TABLE BORDER=0>
    <TR> <TH ALIGN="LEFT">Email: </TH>
      <TD ALIGN="LEFT"> $email </TD> </TR>
    <TR> <TH ALIGN="LEFT">First Name: </TH>
      <TD ALIGN="LEFT"> $firstName </TD> </TR>
    <TR> <TH ALIGN="LEFT">Last Name: </TH>
      <TD ALIGN="LEFT"> $lastName </TD> </TR>
    <TR> <TH ALIGN="LEFT">Address:</TH>
      <TD ALIGN="LEFT"> $address </TD> </TR>
    <TR> <TH ALIGN="LEFT">Telephone Number: </TH>
      <TD ALIGN="LEFT"> $telephone </TD> </TR>
    <TR> <TH ALIGN="LEFT"> <FONT COLOR=RED>Mother's Maiden Name: </FONT> </TH>
      <TD ALIGN="LEFT"> <FONT COLOR=RED>$motherName </FONT> </TD> </TR>
     <TR> <TH ALIGN="LEFT"><FONT COLOR=RED>Home Village/Town/City:</FONT></TH>
      <TD ALIGN="LEFT"> <FONT COLOR=RED>$homeTown </FONT> </TD> </TR>
  </TABLE>

  This is just a test form handling program that echoes what you entered
  and does nothing else.
  <p>

Thank you!
<p>
Assam List Administrators<p>
```

```
</BODY>
</HTML>
BROWSER_TEXT
```

Like many Perl modules, the `CGI.pm` module has two interfaces: object-oriented and functional. In the object-oriented interface, a new `CGI` object is constructed and then method calls are made. In the functional interface, no object is created. The `CGI.pm` module exports many functions and these functions can be called from within the Perl using function calls. The `CGI.pm` module has a large number of functions that deal with creating HTML tags, generating HTML forms that can be sent back to the browser in response to a submit action of a prior HTML form, and in dealing with specifics of a CGI query request. These can be imported by using the `:standard` keyword.

```
use CGI (:standard);
```

We also use `CGI::Carp.pm` and import the `fatalsToBrowser` function explicitly so that fatal script errors are reported to the browser, at least during the development phase of a program.

The program starts by capturing the values filled in by the user of the form. Let us look at one statement that captures a form value.

```
my $email = param ("email");
```

The `param` function of the CGI module takes the name of a form's field and obtains the value sent for it by the browser. It returns a string. If we look at the HTML corresponding to the form at hand, we see the `email` field right at the top. The value of the field is called `$email` after it is captured. If no value is supplied by the user for the field, the value of `$email` is simply empty.

As usual, the Perl script must write to the standard output. Whatever it writes to the standard output is sent to the browser. If the CGI program writes nothing to the standard output, the browser gives an error. Therefore, just performing a task in the background is not enough for a CGI program. It must produce an output that a browser can display as well. The first thing the CGI program must write to the standard output is one or more HTTP header lines. If it prints anything else to the standard output, the browser gives an error. If there is some code before the printing of the HTTP headers to standard output, and if any of this code produces an error and if the error message is printed to standard output, the browser produces an `Internal Server Error`. For example, such an error can occur if one wants to open a file for reading or writing at the outset of the CGI program and the program cannot do so for whatever reasons. A CGI program can be run by any individual in the world. Therefore, in general, CGI programs run with very little authority on a system such as Unix machine for security reasons.

The CGI program under consideration produces an HTML table. The values that the user enters in the HTML form are captured by the CGI program and are entered in this table. The table is returned as a part of the response to the Web browser.

A CGI program usually prints a lot of HTML code. It can use a sequence of `print` statements to do so. In this program, we use a variant of the `print` statement as a short cut. The text that is printed by the CGI program to the standard output is printed using only one `print` statement. The beginning of this `print` statement is repeated below.

```
print <<BROWSER_TEXT
```

Anything that follows this line is printed till the string `BROWSER_TEXT` is detected starting on the first column of the program. This is informally called *print to here* or a *here document*. The string `BROWSER_TEXT` occurs in the first column at the very end of the program. The response of the CGI program on the browser is shown in Figure 8.8.

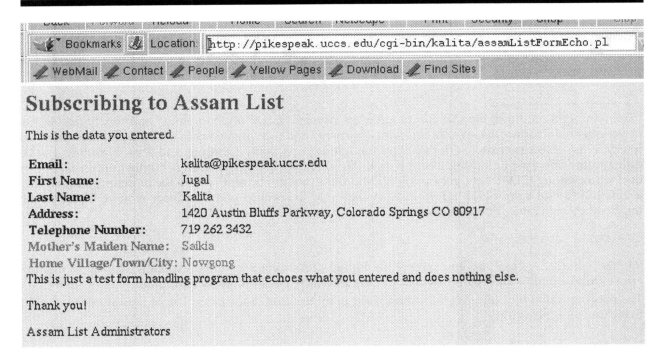

Figure 8.8: HTML Form whose Contents are Echoed by a CGI Program

The CGI.pm module has a large number of functions that deal with the production of HTML output. In the current program, we have used CGI.pm to just to obtain values of parameters. This is the extent to which the author of the book normally uses the CGI.pm module. However, there are many additional functions that others may find useful.

8.3.7   Security Issues in CGI Programs: Untaint.pm

CGI programs are usually accessed through either links on Web pages, including from *submit buttons* (i.e., the ACTION attribute of a form). There are two primary issues one needs to be concerned about when dealing with a CGI program.

1. A CGI program, especially when called in the context of an HTML form, gets input from outside the CGI program. The data entered by an individual into the input and other boxes in an HTML form are sent to the CGI program on the server, across the network. Now-a-days, a browser can perform validation of the data entered using scripts in a language such as JavaScript. However, a CGI program should not make any such assumption, and therefore, do its part to validate the data.

2. The data sent by a CGI program to the server can potentially be very large in size, especially, if file uploading from a CGI program is allowed. If the data size is extremely large, not only can it slow down the server because it needs to allocate space, it may bring the server down causing a *Denial of Service (DOS)* attack. Even worse, the computer hosting the Web server may be brought to a state by the buffer overflow when it is possible to attack it using other means.

Both these issues are discussed below.

In Perl, any data that comes to a program from outside is considered *tainted*. Thus, any input to any program, not just a CGI program, can be considered tainted. However, it is crucial that we consider data input to a CGI program as tainted. There have been instances in the past when tainted data have caused damage to a Web server and the machine hosting the Web server.

The process of examining a tainted piece of information and validating it is called *untainting* or *laundering*. A programmer can do so fairly easily by passing the parameter data that arrives at a CGI program through a regular expression to see if the parameter's value is what it expects. For example, in the program discussed in Section 8.3.6, the program can untaint the first name submitted from the form as follows.

```
$firstName = param ("firstName");
($firstName) = ($firstName =~ /^[a-zA-Z]+$/;
```

This piece of code captures the value of the CGI query parameter `firstName`, checks if it contains only one more alphabetic characters. It should ideally be able to check that it is a string whose length is bounded by a small integer, say 15 or 20. We are not doing this here.

There is a Perl module `Untaint.pm` that works in conjunction with the module `Taint.pm` that allows a Perl program, whether CGI or not, to untaint input that comes to the program from outside. For a Perl program to untaint inputs, whether from CGI queries, or from file input, or other outside sources, the program must run in *taint mode*. This can be done by running the Perl interpreter with `-T` option or switch. Thus, the first line in the CGI program that provides the location of the Perl interpreter must have the `-T` option. It can have other options or switches as well.

A Perl program in the taint mode is very cautious. It does not trust any data or value that is not generated within the program. It does not allow the program to do much with such tainted or possibly corrupt or harmful data till the data have been untainted or laundered or validated.

Note that, ideally speaking, every CGI program, even the program that prints the value of CGI environment variables, discussed in Section 8.3.4 should untaint the values of the environment variables. The values come from outside the program and hence, cannot be trusted in the strictest sense till they are validated. It is possible that someone who has access to the computer where the Web server is located has put invalid, even harmful data (say, containing Unix shell special characters such as > or < or & with calls to harmful programs) as values of environment variables. The following program is a rewrite of the program in Section 8.3.6 that echoes back values of CGI query parameters to the browser. This program works with the same HTML form shown in Figure 8.8. Of course, the value of the `ACTION` attribute must be changed to reflect the new CGI program.

Program 8.7

```
#!/usr/bin/perl -Tw
#assamListFormEcho1.pl

use CGI qw(:standard -nodebug);
use CGI::Carp qw(fatalsToBrowser);
use Untaint;
use strict;

#######Set CGI size limit; disable file upload
$CGI::POST_MAX = 1024; #max 1024 bytes posts
$CGI::DISABLE_UPLOADS = 1;

#########################
my $email = param ("email");
#$email = untaint (qr/^\w+@\w+$/, $email);
$email = untaint (qr/^[\w.]+@[\w.]+$/, $email);
my $firstName = param ("firstName");
```

```perl
$firstName = untaint (qr/^[a-z]+$/i, $firstName);
my $lastName = param ("lastName");
$lastName = untaint (qr/^[a-zA-Z]+$/, $lastName);
my $address = param ("surfaceAddress");
$address = untaint (qr/^[\d\w\s]+$/, $address);
my $telephone = param ("telephoneNumber");
$telephone = untaint (qr/^\d+$/, $telephone);
my $motherName = param ("motherMaidenName");
$motherName = untaint (qr/^[a-zA-Z]+$/, $motherName);
my $homeTown = param ("homeTown");
$homeTown = untaint (qr/^[a-zA-Z]+$/, $homeTown);

#######Write to browser
print "Content-type: text/html\n\n";

print <<BROWSER_TEXT
<BODY BGCOLOR=BISQUE>
<HTML>
    <HEAD><TITLE>Subscribe to Assam List</TITLE></HEAD>
    <BODY><H1>
        <FONT COLOR=BLUE>Subscribing to Assam List </FONT></H1>
    This is the data you entered.<p>

    <TABLE BORDER=0>
    <TR> <TH ALIGN="LEFT">Email: </TH>
      <TD ALIGN="LEFT"> $email </TD> </TR>
    <TR> <TH ALIGN="LEFT">First Name: </TH>
      <TD ALIGN="LEFT"> $firstName </TD> </TR>
    <TR> <TH ALIGN="LEFT">Last Name: </TH>
      <TD ALIGN="LEFT"> $lastName </TD> </TR>
    <TR> <TH ALIGN="LEFT">Address:</TH>
      <TD ALIGN="LEFT"> $address </TD> </TR>
    <TR> <TH ALIGN="LEFT">Telephone Number: </TH>
      <TD ALIGN="LEFT"> $telephone </TD> </TR>
    <TR> <TH ALIGN="LEFT"> <FONT COLOR=RED>Mother's Maiden Name: </FONT> </TH>
      <TD ALIGN="LEFT"> <FONT COLOR=RED>$motherName </FONT> </TD> </TR>
    <TR> <TH ALIGN="LEFT"><FONT COLOR=RED>Home Village/Town/City:</FONT></TH>
      <TD ALIGN="LEFT"> <FONT COLOR=RED>$homeTown </FONT> </TD> </TR>
  </TABLE>

  This is just a test form handling program that echoes what you entered
  and does nothing else.
  <p>

Thank you!
<p>
Assam List Administrators<p>

</BODY>
</HTML>
BROWSER_TEXT
```

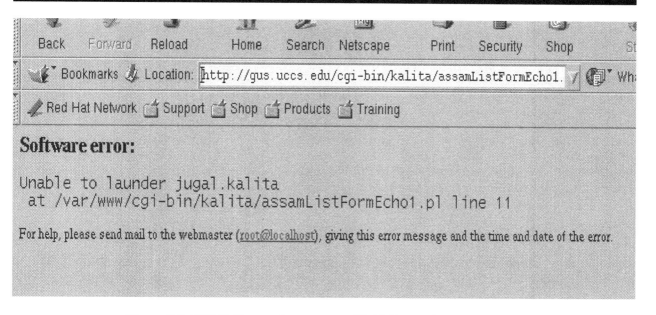

Figure 8.9: HTML Form whose `email` Field Cannot be `untainted`

The program uses the `CGI.pm` module and imports the standard set of functions that is extensive and is sufficient for most needs. We use the functional interface to the `CGI.pm` module. It uses the `-nodebug` pragma to indicate that we do not provide input from the command-line for testing purposes. We can change it to `-debug` if needed. We can then provide inputs from the command-line for testing purposes. We use the `CGI::Carp.pm` module and export the `fatalsToBrowser` function so that CGI errors are reported to the browser. We use `Untaint.pm` module to validate, untaint or launder the input from the CGI query. We should untaint the input as soon as they are obtained so that do not get any chance to corrupt other data by taking part in computation. In fact, in the taint mode, Perl chokes and dies if we try to use tainted data in most computations.

Let us look at one untainting episode.

```
my $email = param ("email");
$email = untaint (qr/^[\w.]+@[\w.]+$/, $email);
```

The `email` CGI query parameter's value is read and is assigned to the scalar `$email`. The value is next validated using the `untaint` function of the `Untaint.pm` module. `untaint` takes two arguments: a regular expression compiled with the `qr` operator, and a value to untaint. The regular expression is used to perform the validation. The regular expression must match the value for `untaint` to succeed. If `untaint` succeeds, it returns the value; if it fails, it `croaks`. `croak` is a function made available by the `CGI::Carp.pm` module, or the `Carp.pm` module. It is similar to `die`, except that it reports where the error is in the code that called it. For example, if a certain function or method in a module called `X.pm` is called and this function or method `dies`, `croak` reports not where the death occurred inside the `X.pm` module, but where it occurred in the code that called the method or function defined in `X.pm`. For example, if we entered a value that is unacceptable by the corresponding regular expression, for the `email` field, say `jugal.kalita`, the CGI program the message shown in Figure 8.9 to the browser. To be doubly secure, beyond `untainting`, we should see that the value is within a reasonable length.

In this program, we have `untainted` scalars. Arrays can be `untainted` as well. Elements of a hash can be validated using `untaint`, using different regular expressions for values corresponding to different keys, if necessary. One is requested to consult documentation on `Untaint.pm` to learn more details about how tainted values can propagate through a program, what operations are not allowed on untainted variables, and how data structures other than scalars can be untainted.

It is easy to note that `untainting` a scalar requires writing a regular expression that matches the expected value. This may not always be straigthforward. For example, if we want to validate a URL that has been input from a CGI program, it may require writing a complex regular expression that covers all possible ways in which a URL can be specified, e.g., with our without a port number, with or without the `http://` in front, absolute or relative, or with or without a trailing /, etc. If we want to validate a credit card number, one may require complex regular expressions as well. Validating a date in all possible formats is not easy either. Therefore, there are a few modules that have been specifically written to launder different kinds of inputs. Some examples include `CGI::Untaint::creditcard.pm`, `CGI::Untaing::date.pm`, `CGI::Untaint::email.pm`, and `CGI::Untaint::url.pm`.

Before finishing up the discussion of the program, it must be noted that it takes more precautions in addition to `untainting` the values of the CGI parameters. This is done right in the beginning of the program before any CGI parameter values have been captured using the `param` function.

```
$CGI::POST_MAX = 1024; #max 1024 bytes posts
$CGI::DISABLE_UPLOADS = 1;
```

The first line says that the maximum amout of data that the form can send to the CGI program is 1024 bytes. This includes all the input boxes and file uploads if any. The HTML form that calls the current CGI program does not have a file upload box. If there were one or more file upload boxes, the total size of all files and other input strings is within the byte limit specified by `$CGI::POSTMAX`. Thus, it should be set to a value that is reasonable for the purpose at hand. There are ways in which a CGI program can be coaxed to accept file uploads even though the corresponding HTML form does not have any upload box. Being extremely security conscious, file uploading is disallowed by setting `$CGI::DISABLE_UPLOADS` to a value other than zero. If file uploads are desired, this variable should be set to 0.

It is extremely important that a CGI program is safe. Therefore, it is recommended that the two lines of code given above be placed on top of any CGI program. These two lines should be placed before any CGI related processing starts. If the functional interface to `CGI.pm` is used, the values should be set before any `param` or similar `CGI.pm` functions are called. If the object-oriented interface to `CGI.pm` is used, the values should be set before any call to the `new` constructor of the `CGI.pm` module. Quite frequently, even cautious programmers forget to write these lines of code in their CGI programs. Thus, there is a module called `CGI::Safe.pm` that can be used to set these two values automatically. The default value allowd by `CGI::Safe.pm` for the `$CGI::POSTMAX` scalar is $512 * 1024$ or 512 kilobytes. The default value for `$CGI::DISABLE_UPLOADS` is 1. The default values can be easily overriden. The `CGI::Safe.pm` module takes a few other safety precautions as well. The interested reader is requested to consult documentation on `CGI.pm` and `CGI::Safe.pm`.

8.3.8   More on The `CGI.pm` Module

We have seen the use of the `CGI.pm` module in programs discussed earlier. However, our use has been very minimal; we have used it only for capturing parameters coming to a Web server from a CGI program, for limiting the size of CGI data sent by a form, and for disabling file uploads. The `CGI.pm` module is quite a bit more powerful than what we have seen. The `CGI.pm` module is large and has a very large number of functions that help construction of dynamic Web pages. For example, it provides us with functions for the following:

- Creating HTML tags of all kinds. For example, the function `h1` produces the first-level HTML header `<H1>`. The module provides boilerplate HTML that may reduce typing and coding, and consequently, errors associated with typing and coding. The module also has a function called `table` that can be used to produce HTML tables. In fact, the module claims to have a function corresponding to every

HTML tag. The name of a function or method is the same as the name of the corresponding HTML tag. Case does not matter for names of CGI.pm functions, methods and other symbols the module exports.

- Not only can the CGI.pm module capture what has been sent by a server, it can manipulate them in various ways. For example, it can *delete* one or more parameters and make them unavailable. It can read the parameters into a hash instead of into an array.

- It is especially useful in writing CGI programs that send out HTML forms in response. These forms can contain information sent out by the original CGI program. This allows session continuity from form to form when several forms are used in sequence.

- The CGI.pm module also provides ability to deal with file uploads in HTML forms.

- The CGI.pm module allows the creation of cookies that can be sent back to the browser from which the CGI program was originally invoked.

- The CGI.pm module also provides facilities to deal with cascading style sheets, and frames among other things.

- In addition, there is a large number of modules which are subclasses of the CGI class of modules. These modules perform a wide variety of tasks such as caching of the results of time-intensive CGI scripts, for debugging CGI programs, for using encryption to send form data, for dealing with XML forms, for dealing with cookies, for buffering output when building output, for dealing with the Apache Web server sessions, for validating credit card information sent through a form, for dealing with HTML image maps, for handling database access, etc.

We do not have room in this book to discuss everything that the CGI.pm module and other CGI:: modules can do. We discuss just a small fraction of the possibilities in this Chapter. Those who are interested in finding more about the modules should go to the *Comprehensive Perl Archive Network* (www.cpan.org) and use one of the search engines to find the relevant modules, read the documentation, download and install and run some simple programs to determine if the module is suitable for the purpose at hand.

The following program is a rewrite of of the program that echoes values of CGI parameters that is discussed in Section 8.3.7. The program uses the functional interface to construct the HTML code that is returned by the the the the the CGI program.

Program 8.8

```
#!/usr/bin/perl -Tw
#assamListFormEcho2.pl

use CGI qw(:standard -nodebug);
use CGI::Carp qw(fatalsToBrowser);
use Untaint;
use strict;

#######Set CGI size limit; disable file upload
$CGI::POST_MAX = 1024; #max 1024 bytes posts
$CGI::DISABLE_UPLOADS = 1;

#########################
my $email = param ("email");
$email = untaint (qr/^\w+@\w+$/, $email);
```

```perl
my $firstName = param ("firstName");
$firstName = untaint (qr/^[a-z]+$/i, $firstName);
my $lastName = param ("lastName");
$lastName = untaint (qr/^[a-zA-Z]+$/, $lastName);
my $address = param ("surfaceAddress");
$address = untaint (qr/^[\d\w\s]+$/, $address);
my $telephone = param ("telephoneNumber");
$telephone = untaint (qr/^\d+$/, $telephone);
my $motherName = param ("motherMaidenName");
$motherName = untaint (qr/^[a-zA-Z]+$/, $motherName);
my $homeTown = param ("homeTown");
$homeTown = untaint (qr/^[a-zA-Z]+$/, $homeTown);

#######Write to browser
print header ("text/html");
print start_html (-title => "Subscribe to Assam List",
                  -BGCOLOR => "BISQUE");
print qq{<FONT COLOR="BLUE">}, h1 ("Subscribing to Assam List"),
    qq{</FONT>};

print table ({-border => 0},
             caption ("Details You Supplied"),
             Tr( th({-align => "LEFT"},  ["Email:"]), td ($email)),
             Tr( th({-align => "LEFT"},  "First Name:"), td ($firstName)),
             Tr( th({-align => "LEFT"},  "Last Name:"), td ($lastName)),
             Tr( th({-align => "LEFT"},  "Address:"), td ($address)),
             Tr( th({-align => "LEFT"},  "Telephone Number:"), td ($telephone))
             Tr( th({-align => "LEFT"},
                      font({-color => "red"}), "Mother's Maiden Name:"),
                 td ($motherName)),
             Tr(  th({-align => "LEFT"},
                      font({-color => "red"}),  "Home Village/Town/City:"),
                 td($homeTown))
            );

print qq{
  This is just a test form handling program that echoes what you entered
  and does nothing else},
  p,
  qq{Thank you!},
  p,
  qq{Assam List Administrators},
  p;

print end_html;
```

The initial part of the program is exactly the same as the program in Section 8.3.7. It uses the CGI.pm module's functional interface, and the CGI::Carp.pm module to send details of fatal error to the browser. It also sets the maximum length of data entered to be 1024 bytes. It explicitly disallows file uploads.

The program reads the values of the CGI parameters and launders them using the `untaint` method of the `Untaint.pm` module. Once the parameter values have been `untainted`, it creates the HTML page to be returned to the browser. It, more or less exclusively, uses HTML creating functions provided by the `CGI.pm` module to do so.

The first thing a CGI program needs to do is create one or more valid HTTP headers.

```
print header ("text/html");
```

At a minimum, it needs to tell the browser the type of content that it is sending. This is done by sending the `content-type` HTTP header. There can be other HTTP headers as well. The last HTTP header line must be followed by a blank line. The `header` function provided by the `CGI.pm` module produces one or more HTTP header lines. Only one call must be made to `header` even if several HTTP headers are produced. The `header` function can be called with one argument, the MIME type of the information returned by the CGI program. If it is called with no arguments, `text/html` is assumed to be the default content type. The `header` function can set values of other HTTP headers such as `content-length`, `cookies`, and `status`, etc. In such a case, the arguments should be provided in name-value pairs. How name-value pairs can be specified in a function call is discussed later.

Next, the program generates `<HTML>` and `<BODY>` HTML tags. These tags are produced by the `start_html` `CGI.pm` function. All parameters to the `start_html` function are optional. Thus, one can make the call

```
print start_html ();
```

to produce just the `<HTML>` and `<BODY>` tags in sequence, and nothing else. Just like most other `CGI.pm` functions, arguments can be given to the `start_html` function as name-value pairs.

```
print start_html (-title => "Subscribe to Assam List",
                  -BGCOLOR => "BISQUE");
```

If name-value pairs are provided to a `CGI.pm` function, the name and the value of a pair are separated by `=>`. Various pairs are separated by the comma. The name of a parameter is the name of the corresponding HTML tag to be produced, preceded by the dash. The `start_html` function understands `-title`, `-author`, `-base`, and a few other parameters. These produce corresponding HTML tags within the HTML head, i.e., within `<HEAD>` and `</HEAD>`. Any "unrecognized" parameters can be provided to the `start_html` function as well. For example, the `-BGCOLOR` parameter is such a parameter. Unrecognized parameters are added as attributes to the `<BODY>` HTML tag. The call to `start_html` given above produces the following HTML code.

```
<head><title>Subscribe to Assam List</title></head><body bgcolor="BISQUE">
```

Note that the HTML tags and attributes produced by the `CGI.pm` module are in lower-case although they are case-insensitive. Next, the program produces a first-level header in blue color.

```
print qq{<FONT COLOR="BLUE">}, h1 ("Subscribing to Assam List"),
     qq{</FONT>};
```

`h1` is the function that produces the `<H1>` and `</H1>` tags with the actual text of the header included in between. This line shows that printing of strings and calls to `CGI.pm` functions can be mixed. `qq` is the quoting function that allows variable interpolation. Using `qq` is the same as including the string within double quotes.

Next, the program produces an HTML table, and then prints some strings interspersed with the printing of some `<P>` tags. The `CGI.pm` function `p ()` produces a `<P>` tag. As noted earlier, the name of a `CGI.pm` function is usually the same as the name of the corresponding HTML tag. Also, the case used in calling a `CGI.pm` function does not matter. Finally, the program makes a call to `end_html`.

```
print end_html;
```

This produces

```
</body></html>
```

in HTML.

Let us now look back at the creation of the HTML table.

```
print table ({-border => 0},
             caption ("Details You Supplied"),
             Tr( th({-align => "LEFT"},  ["Email:"]), td ($email)),
             Tr( th({-align => "LEFT"},  "First Name:"), td ($firstName)),
             Tr( th({-align => "LEFT"},  "Last Name:"), td ($lastName)),
             Tr( th({-align => "LEFT"},  "Address:"), td ($address)),
             Tr( th({-align => "LEFT"},  "Telephone Number:"), td ($telephone))
             Tr( th({-align => "LEFT"},
                     font({-color => "red"}), "Mother's Maiden Name:"),
                 td ($motherName)),
             Tr(  th({-align => "LEFT"},
                     font({-color => "red"}),  "Home Village/Town/City:"),
                 td($homeTown))
            );
```

The `table` function produces the HTML table. We know that an HTML tag such as `<TABLE>` can take one or more attributes with corresponding values. For example, an attribute that the `<TABLE>` tag can take is BORDER. If attribute-value pairs are provided to a CGI.pm HTML-producing function, the pairs are included inside curly braces. For example, the code given above produces

```
<table border="0">
```

on top of the HTML table. TABLE is the HTML tag, and BORDER is the attribute with a value of 0. If several attributes are provided, they are all included inside curly braces. The pairs are separated from one another using the comma. An HTML tag such as TABLE takes attributes that are placed inside the `<TABLE>` tag. A table also has *content* that is included inside the `<TABLE>` and `</TABLE>` tags. The content is provided to the `table` CGI.pm function as arguments that are separated from each other using the comma. The first content argument provided to the `table` function is `caption` that takes a string giving the value of the caption. A table has rows and a row has one or more elements or cells in it. In HTML, the contents of a row are included inside `<TR>` and `</TR>` tags. A cell can be of two types: a *table head* element included inside `<TH>` and `</TH>`, and a *table data* element included inside `<TD>` and `</TD>` tags. In CGI.pm, a table row is specified using the `tr` function, and a table head element by using the `th` function, and a table data element using the `td` function. Calls to `tr` are included as arguments to the `table` function; calls to `th` and `td` are included as arguments to the `tr` function. As mentioned earlier, the names of CGI.pm functions are case-insensitive, although Perl, in general, is case-sensitive. There is a function in Perl called `tr` that performs text substitution or text transliteration. The CGI.pm function `tr` clashes with the text transliteration function `tr`. Therefore, the CGI.pm documentation advises using `Tr`, with T in upper case, for the function that creates a table row. The `Tr`, `td`, `th` and many other functions take arguments that correspond to HTML tag attributes. In the program given above, each call to `th` takes two arguments. The first argument to `th` is included inside curly braces indicating it corresponds to an attribute for the tag `<TH>`. There can be several attribute name-value pairs although we have only one pair in each call to `th` in the program. The name of the attribute is the same as the name of the HTML attribute, but it is preceded by a dash. For example,

```
th({-align => "LEFT"},   ["Email:"])
```

translates to

```
<th align="LEFT">Email:</th>
```

It is instructive to compare the Perl code and the corresponding HTML to figure out clearly how the CGI.pm functions work. The complete HTML table produced is quite similar to the table seen in Section 8.3.7.

In general, CGI.pm is a module with a large number of functions, a substantial subset of which is used for producing HTML fragments. Some of the functions are quite versatile taking unnamed or named arguments. The functions can also take attribute arguments. The names of attributes are the same as the names of corresponding HTML tag attributes, but are preceded by a dash. Attribute arguments are included inside curly braces. If a list is given as an argument, it is usually included in square brackets to create an anonymous array. There are several other details that one needs to know to be able to program well using the CGI.pm module. Sometimes, the syntax of CGI.pm function calls can become quite confusing with all the variations that are allowed. Also, it seems to the author that it may sometimes be more straightforward to produce the HTML code directly rather than using CGI.pm functions as intermediary in the process. In addition, it is possible to use a module such as HTML::Template to use an HTML template, stored in a file, with variable interpolation. However, whether one produces HTML directly, or uses CGI.pm functions, depends on an individual's choice. The author uses the HTML producing functions of the CGI.pm module sparingly. That is why, in the programs that follow there are not many CGI.pm function calls.

8.3.9   Creating a Mailing List

A simple electronic mailing list can be implemented with the assistance of a text file that contains a number of e-mail addresses, one per line. The file is associated with a *system mail alias*. An alias is a(n alternate) name or a short-cut. The mailing list file is tied to an alias that is recognized by the mail program used by the operating system. It is also possible to create mail aliases that are known locally within the context of an individual user's account. The purpose of creating a system mail alias is that it can be treated just like the name of a user on the system. Assume, we do not have a user with the name assam on our system, say, pikespeak.uccs.edu. Now, we create a system mail alias assam. After this, we can send an e-mail to the newly created alias as assam@pikespeak.uccs.edu. When anyone sends an e-mail to assam@pikespeak.uccs.edu, the e-mail is automatically forwarded to every e-mail in the mailing list file.

Our discussion is with respect to a machine running Red Hat Linux. The creation of a system alias for mailing purposes is quite similar in other Unix and Unix-like machines including Mac OS X, although the file names may be different. On the Red Hat Linux machine, system aliases are created by placing an entry in the file /etc/aliases. On a Mac OS X machine, the system alias file is also located at the same place. One must have root or super-user access to edit this file. The discussions here do not apply to a Windows machine.

If we have a mailing list that is private and contains only a few email addresses, we can maintain it manually. However, if it is a public list, with say, several hundred or more e-mail addresses, maintaining it becomes a time-consuming chore. In such a case, it makes sense to automate the process of adding and removing addresses from the list. We allow any interested individual to add his or her e-mail address to the mailing list by going to a site on the Web and after providing a little information. We call this *subscribing* to the mailing list. We also allow an individual to automatically *unsubscribe* from the mailing list provided the individual can answer a few simple personal questions whose answers were provided by the individual at the time of subscription. A real mailing list manager must be a lot more complex. The example we discuss here is fairly simple.

We now discuss a modification of the program from the previous sections so that we allow subscription to a mailing list. The program in the previous section simply echoed the information the potential subscriber entered in the form. The form remains the same as before except that we now have an ACTION URL that does additional work. The steps performed for creating a subscription program are discussed below.

- We create a global mail alias called assam by editing the /etc/aliases file.

- We present the user with an HTML form. The HTML page is called subscribe.html and looks exactly like the one seen in Figure 8.8 except that the ACTION URL for the form is different. Specifically, the HTML file is located at
  /home/kalita/public_html/subscribe.html and is accessible on the Web with the URL http://pikespeak.uccs.edu/cgi-bin/kalita/subscribe.html.

- The form data is captured by the CGI program just like we see in the previous section. The CGI program is called assamListSubscribe.pl. The URL for the CGI program is http://pikespeak.uccs.edu/~kalita/assamListSubscribe.pl. The CGI program stores the captured form data in a text file called assamList.txt using a very simple format where the data fields are separated from each other by a pre-specified field separator string. The text file is located in the same directory as where the CGI program is located.

- There is a companion program called updateAssamList.pl that updates the actual mailing list file containing the e-mail addresses, one per line. The companion program is located in the same directory as the CGI program. This program reads the file assamList.txt and parses out the e-mail addresses from among all the other details, and creates the actual mailing list file that contains only the e-mail addresses. The mailing list file is located at
  /home/kalita/mailing-lists/assam.dis.

- We use Unix crontab to run updateAssamList.pl the file once every 24 hours. As a result, the mailing list is updated every day. There is an associated Web page for unsubscribing as well. The CGI program for unsubscribing removes any entry from the intermediate data file assamList.txt. Thus, the new additions and deletions are carried out once a day. The crontab facility allows one to periodically run a specified program at certain specific instances of time. For example, one can run a program every minute, or every hour, or every day, or every week, or every Monday, etc.

In a sophisticated mailing list program, it is likely that one would use a database to store details about a subscriber, and not a text file like assamList.txt. We discuss how databases can be accessed from within a Perl program, whether CGI or not, in Chapter 10. In addition, there must be a way to automatically remove addresses from which e-mails sent bounce and hence, are wrong.

We now go through each step in detail. The discussion is in the context of a Linux machine running Red Hat Linux, and may have to be adjusted for other systems. The first step is to edit the file /etc/aliases and enter a line for the assam alias. The contents of the file after entering this line may look like the following.

```
#
# @(#)aliases 8.2 (Berkeley) 3/5/94
#
#  Aliases in this file will NOT be expanded in the header from
#  Mail, but WILL be visible over networks or from /bin/mail.
#
# >>>>>>>>>>The program "newaliases" must be run after
# >> NOTE >>this file is updated for any changes to
# >>>>>>>>>>show through to sendmail.
#
```

```
# Basic system aliases -- these MUST be present.
MAILER-DAEMON:  postmaster
postmaster:  root
# General redirections for pseudo accounts.
bin:  root
daemon:  root
games:  root
ingres:  root
nobody:  root
system:  root
toor:  root
uucp:  root
# Well-known aliases.
manager:  root
dumper:  root
operator:  root
# trap decode to catch security attacks
decode:  root
# Person who should get root's mail
#mailing lists; run 'newaliases' every time something is changed below
cs-faculty:  :include:/home/kalita/mailing-lists/cs-faculty.dis
aol:  :include:/home/kalita/mailing-lists/aol.dis
assam:  :include:/home/kalita/mailing-lists/assam-list.dis
```

The file comes with a few pre-defined aliases for useful or well-known system aliases. The line added for a user-defined alias has the syntax

     alias: :include:*mailing-list-file*

The e-mail addresses for the assam alias are in the file /home/kalita/mailing-lists/assam-list.dis. The next step is to create an HTML file visible on the Web for potential subscribers to the mailing list. This HTML file looks exactly like the one in Figure 8.8. The only difference is that the form's ACTION URL has been changed. The new FORM tag looks like the following.

```
<FORM METHOD="POST"
    ACTION="http://pikespeak.uccs.edu/cgi-bin/kalita/assamListSubscribe.pl"
    >
```

Note that the actual HTML file contains several JavaScript scripts to examine the validity of the data entered. JavaScript runs on the client and thus allows data validation code to be executed on the client itself, obviating the need for data transmission across the Internet. The reader is advised to read a book such as *QuickStart to JavaScript* [Lin99], *JavaScript for the World Wide Web* [NS98], and *JavaScript : The Definitive Guide* [Fla00]. The next step is writing the CGI program referenced in the form's ACTION URL. The CGI program is given below.

Program 8.9

```
#!/usr/bin/perl -Tw
#assamListSubscribe.pl

use CGI qw(:standard);
```

```perl
use CGI::Carp qw(fatalsToBrowser);
use Untaint;
use strict;

##########
$CGI::POST_MAX = 1024; #max 1024 bytes posts
$CGI::DISABLE_UPLOADS = 1;

#############global declarations
my $assamListDetailsFile = "assamList.txt";
my $separator = ":::";

#print header ();

#########################
my $email = param ("email");
$email = untaint (qr/^[\w.]+@[\w.]+$/, $email);
my $firstName = param ("firstName");
$firstName = untaint (qr/^[a-z]+$/i, $firstName);
my $lastName = param ("lastName");
$lastName = untaint (qr/^[a-zA-Z]+$/, $lastName);
my $address = param ("surfaceAddress");
$address = untaint (qr/^[\d\w\s,.]+$/, $address);
my $telephone = param ("telephoneNumber");
$telephone = untaint (qr/^\d{3} ?\d{3} ?\d{4}$/, $telephone);
my $motherName = param ("motherMaidenName");
$motherName = untaint (qr/^[a-zA-Z]+$/, $motherName);
my $homeTown = param ("homeTown");
$homeTown = untaint (qr/^[a-zA-Z]+$/, $homeTown);

########################
###Read the data file. This is not the mail alias file where the
#email addresses are stored for the mailer.
open (IN, "$assamListDetailsFile") or
    warn "Cannot open $assamListDetailsFile: $!";
#   my @allLines = <IN>;
my @allLines = ();
while (<IN>){
#    print "line= ", $_, "<br>";
    $_ = untaint (qr/^.{1,200}$/, $_);
    @allLines = (@allLines, $_);
}

close IN;

my ($selectedLine) = grep /^$email$separator/, @allLines;
#print "selected line = $selectedLine<br>\n";

#######Write to browser

print "Content-type: text/html\n\n";
```

```perl
print q{
<BODY BGCOLOR=BISQUE>
<HTML>
  <HEAD><TITLE>Subscribe to Assam List</TITLE></HEAD>
  <BODY><H1>
        <FONT COLOR=BLUE>Subscribing to Assam List </FONT>    </H1>
};

#If the email already exists in the database
if ($selectedLine){
print q{
    <H3>
        <FONT COLOR=RED>Unable to Subscribe to Assam List </FONT></H3>
        The e-mail address you have specified is already subscribed to
        to the Assam mailing list. You have thre options available.
        <UL>
        <LI>If the email address is yours,
                remove the email address first and resubscribe.
                Go to the Web page for <B>Unsubscribing</B> and
                remove the email address first using the form available.
        <LI>Use another email address. Click on the <B>Back</B> button
                of the browser and change the email address in the form.
        <LI>If you do not know what to do, please write to
            please write to <A HREF="mailto:kalita\@pikespeak.uccs.edu">
            Jugal Kalita.</A>
        </UL>

};
    }
else{ #If the email doesn't exist in the database

  #Process the input data, write it into a file, append to the file
  my $newLine =  "$email" . $separator;
  $newLine .=  "$firstName$separator$lastName$separator";
  $newLine .= "$address$separator$telephone$separator";
  $newLine .= "$motherName$separator$homeTown\n";
#   print "newline = $newLine <br>";

  open (OUT, ">$assamListDetailsFile")
        or warn "Cannot open $assamListDetailsFile: $!";
#   print OUT sort (@allLines, $newLine);
   @allLines = sort (@allLines, $newLine);
  print OUT join "\n", @allLines;
  close OUT;
  chmod 0666, $assamListDetailsFile;


  print qq{
  This is the data you entered.<p>
```

```
<TABLE BORDER=0>
<TR> <TH ALIGN="LEFT">Email: </TH>
  <TD ALIGN="LEFT"> $email </TD> </TR>
<TR> <TH ALIGN="LEFT">First Name: </TH>
  <TD ALIGN="LEFT"> $firstName </TD> </TR>
<TR> <TH ALIGN="LEFT">Last Name: </TH>
  <TD ALIGN="LEFT"> $lastName </TD> </TR>
<TR> <TH ALIGN="LEFT">Address:</TH>
  <TD ALIGN="LEFT"> $address </TD> </TR>
<TR> <TH ALIGN="LEFT">Telephone Number: </TH>
  <TD ALIGN="LEFT"> $telephone </TD> </TR>
<TR> <TH ALIGN="LEFT"> <FONT COLOR=RED>Mother's Maiden Name: </FONT> </TH>
   <TD ALIGN="LEFT"> <FONT COLOR=RED>$motherName </FONT> </TD> </TR>
<TR> <TH ALIGN="LEFT"><FONT COLOR=RED>Home Village/Town/City:</FONT></TH>
   <TD ALIGN="LEFT"> <FONT COLOR=RED>$homeTown </FONT> </TD> </TR>

</table>

It will take a day or so for you to start receiving mail messages. Please
be patient. If you do not get mail messages from the list within this
time, please write to <A HREF="mailto:kalita\@pikespeak.uccs.edu">
Jugal Kalita.</A>
<p>
};
}


print q{
Thank you!
<p>
Assam List Administrators<p>
</BODY>
</HTML>
};
```

The program's purpose is to create a file called assamList.txt. It uses the separator ::: to concatenate subscriber data before writing a line per user in the file. The $assamListDetailsFile variable is set to the name assamList.txt. We make the assumption that the file was already created with nothing in it to begin with. All data provided by the subscriber are captured. The file is opened, and any lines of data in it are read into the variable @allLines. Note that in a more sophisticated program, one should use a relational database, instead of a flat text file. If the e-mail address provided by the potential subscriber already exists, the program does not add the line, but writes a message on the returned Web document. This document is shown in Figure 8.10.

If the e-mail address does not exist in the file, the $newLine variable is assigned the string obtained by concatenating the data provided by the user. The $newLine string is added to all the lines that were obtained from the data file. THe $assamListDetailsFile is re-written after the lines are sorted alphabetically. The data fields entered by the potential subscriber are echoed back to the browser, just like the way we saw it in the previous section. At this point, the assamList.txt file has been updated to reflect the new subscriber. Note that we have used the q and qq operators to quote long strings of multiple-line HTML code instead of using "here documents." q and qq each takes one argument. q does not interpolate scalar and list variable names within the string whereas qq does. In this respect, they are like single-quoted and

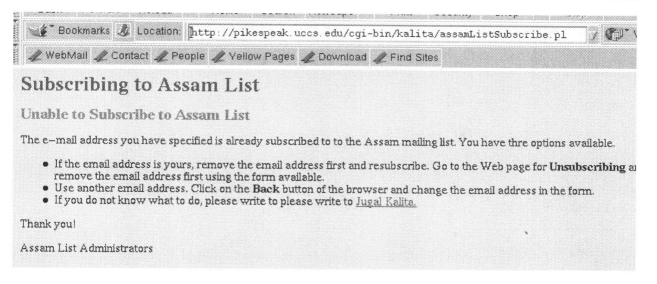

Figure 8.10: Subscription Error Response

double-quoted strings.

However, the assamList.txt file is the data file or the "database". One line in the file assamList.txt looks like the following. It has been broken into two lines here.

```
kalita@pikespeak.uccs.edu:::Jugal:::Kalita:::5050 Copernicus Way,
        Colorado Springs CO 80917:::719 574 3656:::Saikia:::Nowgong
```

It is not the mailing list file. The updateAssamList.pl script reads the data file and updates the mailing list file located at
/home/kalita/mailing-lists/assam-list.dis. The script is simple and is given below.

Program 8.10

```perl
#!/usr/bin/perl
#updateAssamList.txt

use strict;

my $separator = ":::";

my $webCreatedFile = "/home/kalita/public_html/cgi-bin/assamList.txt";
my $mailingListFile = "/home/kalita/mailing-lists/assam-list.dis";

open (IN, "$webCreatedFile") or warn "Cannot open file, $webCreatedFile: $!";;
my @allLines = <IN>;
close IN;

my @allEmails = map {/^(.+?)$separator/} @allLines;
@allEmails = join "\n", (sort @allEmails);

#print "allEmails = @allEmails\n";
```

```
open OUT, ">$mailingListFile" or warn "Cannot open file $mailingListFile: $!";
print OUT @allEmails;
close OUT;

chmod 0644, $mailingListFile;

system ("/usr/bin/newaliases");
```

The program culls out only the e-mail addresses from the `assamList.txt` file and writes them out to the mailing list file. Thus, the mailing list file `/home/kalita/mailing-lists/assam-list.dis` looks like the following

```
9amit@mica.ac.in
KJDEKA@aol.com
NBa5252203@cs.com
anuz10@usa.net
assamlive@yahoo.com
bora03@aol.com
colorsofdawind@yahoo.com
crazynem@yahoo.com
dkalita123@rediff.com
dmedhi@aazoli.cstp.umkc.edu
gcbora@rocketmail.com
gmedhi@aol.com
howtodo@rediffmail.com
ices77@yahoo.com
inmanas@gw1.dot.net.in
kalita@pikespeak.uccs.edu
```

After the new mailing list file is created, the `/usr/bin/newaliases` system command must be run so that the changes made to the global alias takes effect.

The final detail in this long saga involves adding a command to the `crontab` command for the user `kalita`. On the Linux machine, we can run

```
%crontab -e
```

to edit the `crontab` file for an individual user. The line added to the `crontab` file is the following.

```
0 0 * * * perl /home/kalita/public_html/cgi-bin/updateAssamList.pl
```

It runs the `updateAssamList.pl` program once every day at the 0th hour and the 0th minute. Thus, the mailing list gets rejuvenated once a day with the new subscriptions and removals. To know how `crontab` or `newalises` work, the reader is advised to read the Unix manual pages on his or her system, or a book such as *Unix for Programmers and Users* [GA99] or *Unix Systems Administration Handbook* [NSSH01].

8.3.10   Creating a Perl Module From a CGI Program

It is possible for a program to create another program. This is not an unusual behavior when we deal with artificial intelligence (AI) type programs. Computational learning is one of the cornerstones of AI. Some approaches to computational learning create programs or functions on the fly. We are not so ambitious here. We discuss a Perl CGI program that creates a Perl module that consists of only variable declarations and assignments. A CGI program such as this can be used to install a complex product that works on platforms such as Unix or Windows. An HTML form can ask a limited number of configuration-related questions and then assign values to variables based on the answers. Filling up the form with values correct for a particular computer system is one of the steps in the installation.

The HTML page discussed here configures a program called *NewSense*. It is a sophisticated program that collects news reports from various on-line sources, automatically classifies items into categories such as political, entertainment and sports, removes duplicates or very similar stories, and presents a personalized newspaper to every individual reader of a Web site. Newsense is a trademark of Personalogy, Inc., of Colorado Springs, Colorado. What we present here is a Web page and its associated CGI program that help install NewSense at a specific site such as an on-line newspaper. The personalization process in the actual program involves AI-based computational learning built after an analysis of the content of stories read by an individual. There is no need for the individual to provide any details of his or her likes or dislikes in terms of a questionnaire. We do not intend to discuss the details of the NewSense program. The program discussed here is similar to one initially used when NewSense was being tested, before its first release. Aspects of the real program have been removed or simplified for purposes of presentation in a book.

The person who is about to install the program on a certain computer system is shown the HTML from shown in Figure 8.11. The questions need to be answered by filling in text in input boxes. Default answers are provided for some of the questions.

The actual HTML code for the form contains JavaScript scripts for data validation that can be performed on the browser, before the from data is transported to the server. The use of a Web page, if accompanied with proper precautionary measures, can make remote installation and update of the program over the Web possible. The FORM tag used in the HTML code is the following.

```
<FORM METHOD="GET"
  ACTION=
    "http://pikespeak.uccs.edu/cgi-bin/kalita/personalogy/basic_configure.pl">
```

It can also be written as the following if we intend to fill the form on the same machine on which the NewSense system is to be installed.

```
<FORM METHOD="GET"
      ACTION="http://localhost/cgi-bin/kalita/personalogy/basic_configure.pl">
```

The form has several fields. It is not important to know what the fields are. The CGI program that handles the form is at
`http://pikespeak.uccs.edu/cgi-bin/kalita/personalogy/basic_configure.pl`. The Web page shown in Figure 8.11 is located at
`http://pikespeak.uccs.edu/~kalita/personalogy/basic_configure.pl`.
The program is fairly simple.

Program 8.11

```
#!/usr/bin/perl -Tw
#basic_config.pl

use CGI qw(:standard);
use CGI::Carp qw(fatalsToBrowser);
use Untaint;
use strict;
```

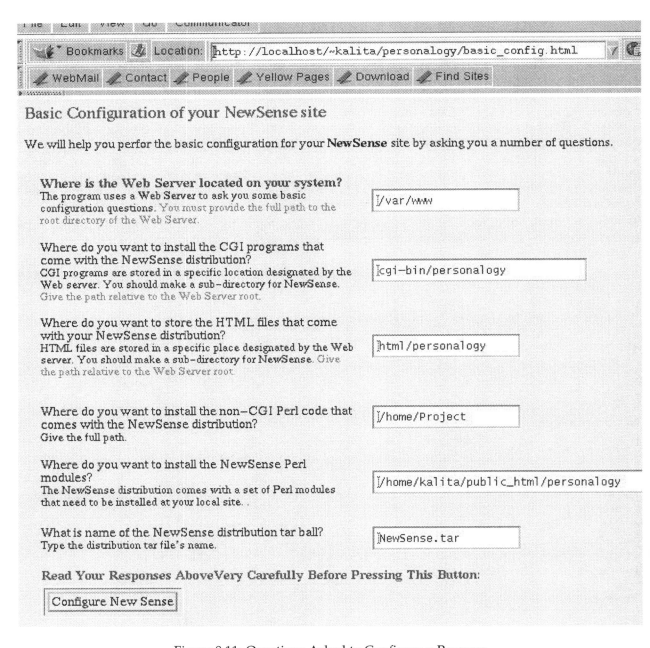

Figure 8.11: Questions Asked to Configure a Program

```perl
##########
$CGI::POST_MAX = 1024; #max 1024 bytes posts
$CGI::DISABLE_UPLOADS = 1;

my $configFileName = "AP_basic_config.pm";

print "Content-type: text/html\n\n";

my $webServerAbsPath = param ("WebServerLocation");
$webServerAbsPath = untaint (qr{^[a-zA-Z_0-9.-/]+$}, $webServerAbsPath);
my $cgiRoot = param ("CGIRoot");
$cgiRoot =  untaint (qr{^[\w\d/.-]+$}, $cgiRoot);
my $htmlRoot = param ("HTMLRoot");
$htmlRoot = untaint (qr{^[\w\d.-/]+$}, $htmlRoot);
my $perlSourceInstallAbsPath = param ("PerlSourceInstallDirectory");
$perlSourceInstallAbsPath = untaint (qr{^[\w\d.-/]+$}, $perlSourceInstallAbsPath);
my $perlSiteModuleAbsPath = param ("PerlSiteModuleDirectory");
$perlSiteModuleAbsPath = untaint (qr{^[\w\d-/.]+$}, $perlSiteModuleAbsPath);
my $distributionTarFileName = param ("DistributionTarFileName");
$distributionTarFileName = untaint (qr{^[\w\d-/.]+$}, $distributionTarFileName);

my $cgiAbsPath = "$webServerAbsPath/$cgiRoot";
$cgiAbsPath = untaint (qr{^[\w\d-/.]+$}, $cgiAbsPath);
my $htmlAbsPath = "$webServerAbsPath/$htmlRoot";
$htmlAbsPath = untaint (qr{^[\w\d-/]+$}, $htmlAbsPath);

print "<HTML>\n<TITLE>Preliminary Configuration of Newsense complete!</TITLE>\n";
print "<BODY BGCOLOR=#FAF0E6>\n";
print "<H3>Configuration of Newsense: Step 1 successful!</H3>";

print <<ALL;

<P STYLE="BACKGROUND-COLOR: RED; TEXT-ALIGN=CENTER; COLOR=WHITE">
This is what you entered. If any of it is not what you want, click
on the Back button of the browser, make the correction,
and submit the form again.</P>
<P>
ALL


print <<ALL;
<TABLE BORDER=1 BORDERCOLOR=DARKBLUE ALIGN=CENTER>
<TR> <TH STYLE="COLOR: BLUE"> Question Asked </TH>
        <TH STYLE="color: blue">Your answer </TH></TR>
<TR> <TD> Web Server Location  </TD><TD> $webServerAbsPath </TD> </TR>
<TR><TD>  CGI Root </TD><TD> $cgiAbsPath</TD></TR>
<TR><TD>   HTML Root </TD><TD>  $htmlAbsPath </TD></TR>
<TR><TD>   Perl Source Install Directory </TD><TD>
                $perlSourceInstallAbsPath </TD></TR>
<TR><TD>   Perl Site Module Directory </TD><TD>
                $perlSiteModuleAbsPath </TD></TR>
<TR><TD>   Distribution Tar File Name </TD><TD>
                $distributionTarFileName </TD></TR>
</table>
ALL
```

```
print <<ALL;
<P STYLE="BACKGROUND-COLOR: RED; COLOR=WHITE; TEXT-ALIGN=CENTER">
Recheck your responses
before proceeding! </P>
ALL

print q{
<B>Proceed to Step 2: Bring up
    <A HREF="http://localhost/~kalita/personalogy/configure.html
">
the configure.html </A> file on your
localhost in NewSense HTML directory and answer the questions </B>
</BODY>
</HTML>;
};
#NO MORE PRINTING TO THE WEB BROWSER

open OUT, ">$perlSiteModuleAbsPath/$configFileName" or
        warn "Cannot open file $perlSiteModuleAbsPath/$configFileName : $!";

my $time = localtime ();

print OUT q{
package AP_basic_config;

#Created by:} .  "$0\n" .
q{#Creation date:} .  "$time\n" .
q{#Define all basic site-specific global variables to make preparation to install
#This file is created by a CGI program

use strict;
use vars qw($webServerAbsPath $cgiAbsPath $htmlAbsPath );
use vars qw($perlSourceInstallAbsPath $perlSiteModuleAbsPath);
use vars qw($distributionTarFileName);
};

#This needs to be changed if the HTML file is changed to allow more choices
print OUT q{$webServerAbsPath = "} . $webServerAbsPath . q{"} . ";\n";
print OUT q{$cgiAbsPath = "} . $cgiAbsPath . q{"} . ";\n";
print OUT q{$htmlAbsPath = "} . $htmlAbsPath . q{"} . ";\n";
print OUT q{$perlSourceInstallAbsPath = "}
            . $perlSourceInstallAbsPath . q{"} . ";\n";
print OUT q{$perlSiteModuleAbsPath = "} . $perlSiteModuleAbsPath . q{"} . ";\n";
print OUT q{$distributionTarFileName = "}
            . $distributionTarFileName . q{"} . ";\n";

print OUT "\n\n1;";
close OUT;
```

The initial part of the program captures the parameters that the HTML form sends to the Web server. It is quite likely that the browser and the server are running on the same machine unless remote installation is being attempted.

Next, the program creates an HTML page in the form of a table that echoes the values that the individual performing the installation is able to see for purposes of verification. As usual, one or more HTTP headers

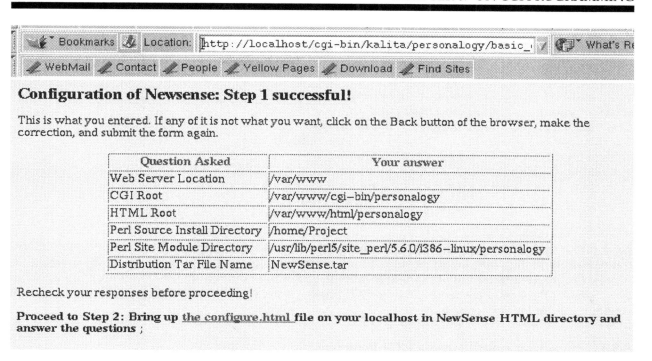

Figure 8.12: Response to Questions Asked to Configure a Program

are first printed to standard output, and then, the actual HTML page. Anything printed to standard output after the HTTP headers is displayed by the browser. The response Web page for the interaction is shown in Figure 8.12.

After this, the program writes to a file the details provided by the user. The program creates a simple Perl module with the values filled by the individual performing the installation. The variables created by the program have names that have been selected by the programmer. The module created is called `AP_basic_config` and is stored in a file called `AP_basic_config.pm`.

The module contains declarations of variables that can be seen by other programs. A variable declared with my is visible only within the current program. A variable declared with use vars can be seen by programs that are contained in other files as well. There are some limitations to what var use can do as regards to making the variable completely available outside the file, but it is acceptable in most situations. Such declarations are usually made in writing Perl modules. The module created also contains statements where the variables declared earlier are assigned values based on the answers provided on the Web page. The module written out by the program to the file `AP_basic_config.pm` is given below.

Program 8.12

```
package AP_basic_config;

#Created by:/var/www/cgi-bin/kalita/personalogy/basic_config.pl
#Creation date:Mon Jun 25 16:26:11 2001
#Define all basic site-specific global variables to make preparation to insta
ll
#This file is created by a CGI program

use strict;
```

```
use vars qw($webServerAbsPath $cgiAbsPath $htmlAbsPath );
use vars qw($perlSourceInstallAbsPath $perlSiteModuleAbsPath);
use vars qw($distributionTarFileName);
$webServerAbsPath = "/var/www";
$cgiAbsPath = "/var/www/cgi-bin/personalogy";
$htmlAbsPath = "/var/www/html/personalogy";
$perlSourceInstallAbsPath = "/home/Project";
$perlSiteModuleAbsPath = "/home/kalita/public_html/personalogy";
$distributionTarFileName = "NewSense.tar";


1;
```

Note that it is a very simple module and contains only variable declarations and assignments. It does not contain any other statements or subroutines. This module AP_basic_config can be used by the NewSense program to be installed. The NewSense program is written as a large number of Perl modules. Some of these modules use the module AP_basic_config. A Perl module has to have a statement containing 1; at the very end.

8.3.11   Sending Email from a CGI Program

In this section, we discuss a CGI program which is very much like the others we have discussed earlier, except that the CGI program sends electronic mail from within the code after a form has been filled. A user is presented a form. After the user fills the form and submits it, the form data is sent to the server where a CGI program takes control of the processing. First, the CGI program obtains the values of the form fields. The form contains details necessary for membership of a cultural organization called ASA. A portion of the form is shown in Figure 8.13. Next, the program creates an electronic mail message regarding the details of the new member and sends the message to those who keep records. Once the e-mail has been sent, the program creates an HTML page that it sends back to the browser.

Program 8.13

```
#!/usr/bin/perl -Tw
#file asa_membership_form.pl

use CGI qw(:standard);
use CGI::Carp qw(fatalsToBrowser);
use Untaint;
use strict;

##########
$CGI::POST_MAX = 1024; #max 1024 bytes posts
$CGI::DISABLE_UPLOADS = 1;

#print header information
print "Content-type: text/html\n\n";

my $year = param ("year");
my $membership_type = param ("membership_type");
my $general_donation = param ("general_donation");
```

```perl
my $endowment_donation = param ("endowment_donation");
my $donation_target = param ("donation_target");
my $other_donation = param ("other_donation");
my $name = param ("name");
my $spouse_name = param ("spouse_name");
my $children_name = param ("children_name");
my $address = param ("address");
my $phone_no = param ("phone_no");
my $mail_address = param ("mail_address");
my $WWW_Home_Page = param ("WWW_Home_Page");

($membership_type, $donation_target, $name, $spouse_name, $children_name)
    = untaint (qr{^[\w\s]+},
               $membership_type, $donation_target, $name, $spouse_name,
                 $children_name);
($year, $general_donation, $endowment_donation, $other_donation)
    = untaint (qr{^\d+(.\d\d)?$},
               $year, $general_donation, $endowment_donation, $other_donation);
$address    = untaint (qr{^[\d\w\s]+$}, $address);
$mail_address = untaint (qr{^[\w.]+@[\w.]+$}, $mail_address);
$phone_no = untaint (qr/^\d{3} ?\d{3} ?\d{4}$/, $phone_no);
$WWW_Home_Page = untaint (qr{^[\w\d.-/]+$}, $WWW_Home_Page);

my $asaexecs = "asaexecs\@pikespeak.uccs.edu";

$ENV{PATH} = "";
open (MAIL, "|/bin/mail  $asaexecs");
print MAIL "ASA Membership Form\n";
print MAIL qq{
year: $year
membership_type: $membership_type
general_donation:  $general_donation
endowment_donation: $endowment_donation
donation_target: $donation_target
other_donation: $other_donation
name: $name
spouse_name: $spouse_name
children_name: $children_name
address: $address
phone_no: $phone_no
mail_address: $mail_address
WWW_Home_Page: $WWW_Home_Page

};

close (MAIL);
my $date = `date`;

print qq{
<HTML>
<HEAD><TITLE>ASA Membership For The Year $year!</TITLE></HEAD>
```

```
<BODY BGCOLOR="BISQUE">
 <H3> <FONT  COLOR=BLUE>ASA Membership!</FONT></H3>
Dear <strong> $name,</strong><P>
Thank you for becoming a member of ASA. We
appreciate your interest in the activities of the ASA.
Please make plans to attend our next annual convention.

<STRONG>
<FONT COLOR=RED>
Please do not forget to send in your contribution check soon.
</FONT></STRONG>

<P>

Sincerely,
<P> <STRONG>K. Bhuyan</strong>,
President, Mays Landing,  New Jersey, USA
<br>
<P>

$date<p>
</BODY>
</HTML>
};
```

The program first creates an HTTP header to send out with the HTML response page to the browser. Next, it captures the values of all the form fields. After this, the program creates a mail message to be sent to the global mail alias asaexecs@pikepeak.uccs.edu. The mail message is created using a Unix pipe, first discussed in Section 7.2.3. A pipe can be used in Unix to communicate among processes. For example, the input of one command can be sent to another for further processing. Here, our Perl program is a process and the system mail program /bin/mail is another process. It should be noted that the system mail program may be at different locations on different machines such as /bin/mail or /usr/ucb/mail. On Mac OS X server, it is at /usr/bin/mail. Therefore, for this program to work, we should be on a Unix machine and know where the mail program is located. The communication between the current program and the mail program is established by the open command.

```
open (MAIL, "|/bin/mail  $asaexecs");
```

After this statement is executed, an outgoing line of communication is established between the Perl script and the mail program. The | in front says that the current process, i.e., the current Perl script, pipes data out to the /bin/mail process. The pipe that communicates between the two programs is called MAIL. The MAIL pipe accumulates information from the current program and delivers them to the mail program only after the current program closes the pipe. Thus, when the program executes the following statement,

```
print MAIL "ASA Membership Form\n";
```

the string ASA Membership Form is printed to the pipe, but not sent to mail program yet. So, it is buffered. Till it has to be sent out. Similarly, any other writing to the pipe is buffered. All the values captured from the HTML form are written to the mail message using a simple format. Finally, the pipe is closed.

```
close (MAIL);
```

At this point the information in the buffer is piped into the mail program and the mail message sent. The mail message sent looks like the following.

```
Return-Path: apache@pikespeak.uccs.edu
Delivery-Date: Tue Jun 26 10:08:18 2001
Delivery-Date: Tue, 26 Jun 2001 10:08:18 -0600
Received: (from apache@localhost)
by pikespeak.uccs.edu (8.11.0/8.11.0) id f5QG8I301548
for asaexecs@pikespeak.uccs.edu; Tue, 26 Jun 2001 10:08:18 -0600
Date: Tue, 26 Jun 2001 10:08:18 -0600
From: Apache <apache@pikespeak.uccs.edu>
Message-Id: <200106261608.f5QG8I301548@pikespeak.uccs.edu>
To: asaexecs@pikespeak.uccs.edu

ASA Membership Form

year: 01
membership_type:
general_donation:  100
endowment_donation: 100
donation_target:
other_donation: 100
name: Jugal Kalita
spouse_name:
children_name:
address:   1420 Austin Bluffs Parkway
 Colorado Springs CO 80917

phone_no: 719 262 3432
mail_address:
WWW_Home_Page: http://www.cs.uccs.edu/~kalita
```

The program creates the HTML page it sends to the browser The Web page displayed on the browser looks like that in Figure 8.14.

The CGI program given in this Section is security-conscious. It limits the size of the CGI parameter data to 1024 bytes. It disables file uploads. It untaints all inputs from the associated HTML form. untaint, as used here, uses a compiled regular expression to launder a list of values. The purpose of data laundering by a Perl program is to make sure that it will not allow data from outside a program be propagated through it to influence something else outside the program, at least by accident. This is simply being a good citizen. In the taint mode, Perl is paranoid and will die even at a hint of such influence i.e., unless the outside data has been validated. Perl is a large binary, hard to test and audit, so the language designers assume that it contains security holes. The taint system is another layer of protection.

A final point to note about the security strategies used by the program is that it sets the value of $ENV{PATH} environment variable to the empty string before it uses a Perl pipe to send email using /bin/mail.

```
$ENV{PATH} = "";
open (MAIL, "|/bin/mail  $asaexecs");
```

This is important because we do not want the CGI program, that can be run in response to anyone in the world clicking on a submit button in an HTML form to have access to the original PATH information on the server. The PATH information is used by system calls inside the program, including pipe calls, to find the

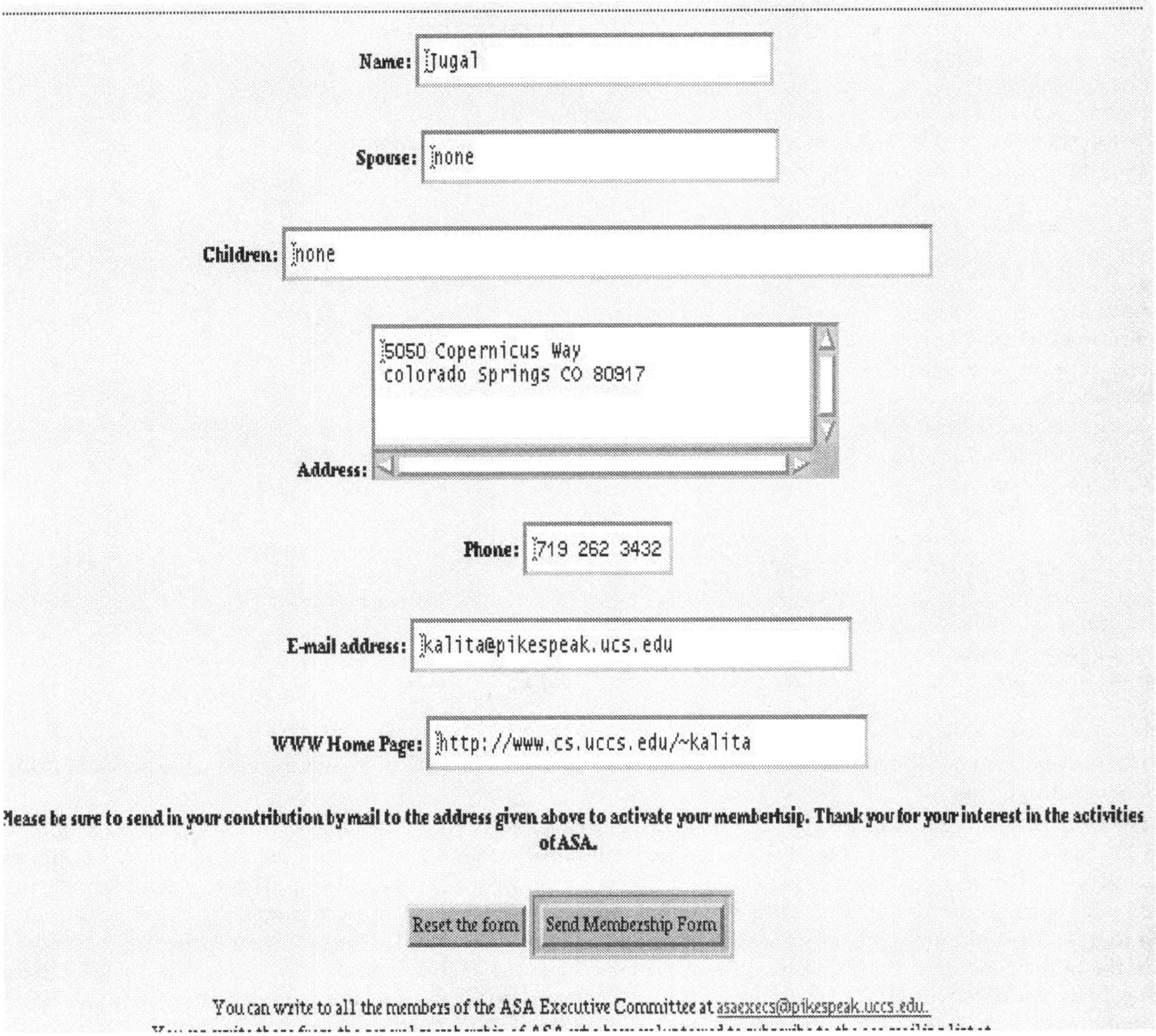

Name: |Jugal

Spouse: |none

Children: |none

```
|5050 Copernicus Way
 colorado Springs CO 80917
```
Address:

Phone: |719 262 3432

E-mail address: |kalita@pikespeak.ucs.edu

WWW Home Page: |http://www.cs.uccs.edu/~kalita

Please be sure to send in your contribution by mail to the address given above to activate your membership. Thank you for your interest in the activities of ASA.

Reset the form   Send Membership Form

You can write to all the members of the ASA Executive Committee at asaexecs@pikespeak.uccs.edu.

Figure 8.13: Filling up a Membership Form for an Organization

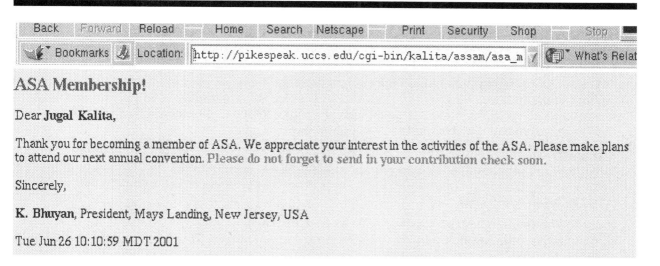

Figure 8.14: Filling up a Membership Form for an Organization

location of system commands that do not use absolute address. In the above, we have used /bin/mail as the command and it is in absolute format, and therefore, the PATH information does not matter. However, the *taint* mode of Perl, requires a CGI program to set the value of $ENV{PATH} inside the program so that only safe and well-known directories can be searched to find commands for which relative locations are given. In our case, setting it to the empty string suffices. Thus, one must know the absolute address of a program so that it can be run from within Perl. Setting of PATH inside program is mandatory in taint mode because Perl cannot guarantee that the executable in question (here, /bin/mail isn't itself going to turn around and execute some other program that is dependent on the PATH. Therefore, it makes sure the programmer consciously set the PATH. Although we set the value to the empty string, a more usual assignment is the following.

$$\$ENV\{\,'PATH'\,\} \ = \ '/bin:/usr/bin:/usr/local/bin';$$

One can add other safe and well-known directories if needed. One should *not* add "." or one's own directory to the list in this statement. This assignment only allows programs from the directories /bin, /usr/bin/, and /usr/local/bin to run. These are system directories, and presumably are safe.

One might ask "What is unsafe about the path?". Historically, paths have been considered unsafe because if there are multiple versions of an executable, it is difficult to tell which one is actually being executed. If there is a bug in one of the versions, then this can pose a security hazard.

8.4   Conclusions

This chapter has discussed many aspects of CGI program. The chapter discusses the nature of Web pages, introduces Web servers, and gives examples of CGI programs. Data entering a CGI program should be dealt with caution and should be untained or laundered before use. A CGI program can be used to create a mailing list, create a simple Perl module, and send out email messages. A CGI program can do many more things such as allowing file uploads, creating cookies, creating graphics or graphs, creating XML output, interacting with a DBM file or a relational database, etc. Creating graphics using GD.pm, and using DBM files and relational databases are discussed in Chapter 10.

8.5 Exercises

1. *(Easy: Environment Variables)*
Write a CGI program that returns the values of the environment variables. Run this program from a browser running on a Unix, a Windows, and a Macintosh machine. Compare the value of the environment variables. Make a table showing the values for the three systems. Understand the names of the environment variables and the values they have.

2. *(Easy: Web Graphic Creation)*
Write a CGI program that returns a graphic image that it creates on the fly. The image is in JPEG format. Use a module such as GD.pm to do so. Let the CGI program return a random, but somewhat appealing image every time.

3. *(Easy: Web Graphic Creation, Access Counter, Multiple Counters)*
Write a CGI program that returns a graphic image of an integer. This CGI program reads from a simple text file where the current value of the integer is stored. The text file contains only one integer. Every time the CGI program is called, the integer is incremented by the program and a graphic image corresponding to the new value of the integer is sent to the Web browser. Link this CGI program from a Web page, with appropriate arguments if any, using the *GET* syntax to show the image. Use this link as a counter in the bottom of a Web page, possibly, your personal Web page.

    Learn how a file can be locked. Lock the counter file so that two or more browsers invoking the CGI program at the same time does not override each other's update of the counter value.

    Extend the program further so that several counters can be kept in the same file on the server. Give each counter a name. Identify the counters in the text file with the name assigned. Use the same CGI program but with different counter names to update the appropriate counters. Place links to the CGI program with appropriate arguments on various Web pages.

4. *(Easy: Environment Variables, Browser)*
Write a CGI program that keeps a log file with statistics on browsers that access the Web site. Assume there are at least two main browser brands and their various versions. Keep track of version numbers as well.

    The program should run discreetly. For example, a program that maintains a graphic counter on the top Web page for a site can keep the browser statistics as well.

5. *(Easy: Web Log Analysis)*
Write a CGI program that keeps statistics on the type of domains that access a Web site. The domain types can be edu, org, com and gov for the United States. The program also keeps track of which country the visitors have come from, for those domains for which it can figure out the country of origin. The program does so discreetly. For example, the program can do the statistics gathering along with the CGI-based counter program discussed earlier.

6. *(Medium to Hard: Web-based E-mail, Can be a long-term project)*
Write a CGI program that can interface with a Unix mail server and allow one to read mail over the Web. This can be potentially hard. Research into how Unix mail servers work and how one can read the mail from the server. Write an algorithm and then implement it. List all problems you face and how you solve them.

7. *(Medium: Cookies, Research)*
A CGI program can send cookies to a browser. Due to lack of space, cookies are not discussed in this Chapter although they are briefly discussed in the next Chapter. Read documentation on cookies on the Web at a site such as *www.cookiecentral.com*. Perl has modules that can help a program generate cookies with the correct syntax. Look at *www.cpan.org* for relevant modules. Now, enhance the CGI programs discussed in this book so that they can set cookies.

8. *(Hard: Chat Program, Reseach, Can be a long-term project)*
Write a program that allows individuals to chat on the Web. Such a program can be potentially hard to write, depending on how much sophistication you want to incorporate. Concepts and tools from CGI programming as well as network programming are needed to write such a program. Start very simply. Once you have a simple working version, document the improvements that can be made to such a program. Discuss how improvements can be implemented, and implement some. Go through several cycles of improvement.

9. *(Hard: Chat Program, Cryptography, Research, Can be a long-term project)*
Extend the chat program in the previous problem so that chatting can be done securely using encryption techniques.

10. *(Simple to Medium: Amortization)*
Write a CGI program that calculates loan repayment schedules on the Web. Suppose someone types in a principal amount, the rate of interest, whether it is simple or compound, and the length of the loan period, on an HTML form on the Web. The program prints the length of time that will be needed to repay the loan, and also an amortization schedule.

11. *(Simple to Medium: Amortization, Web Graphics)*
Learn how you can draw a graph using a Perl module. Write a CGI program that returns a bar graph or any other kind of graph, showing how the principal decreases after every year of a loan's life. This problem extends the previous problem.

12. *(Medium to Hard: Text Processing, Artificial Intelligence, Can be a long-term project)*
Write a program that can chat with a user like the simple version of the Eliza program discussed in Section 4.12.2. The program allows a user to type in a statement, reads it, and responds to it in an "intelligent" manner. Document the problems you see in the implementation. Discuss how you can solve them. Implement some of your solutions.

13. *(Medium to Hard: XML, Research)*
A CGI program can return XML documents. However, you will have to know how to use XML, its syntax, DTDs, XSL stylesheets, etc. All these are outside the scope of this book. We assume you will learn all these on your own. Now, once you have done that, rewrite all the CGI programs in the text that produce HTML pages to produce XML pages instead.

14. *Medium to Hard: Search Engine, Text Processing, Can be a long-term project)*
In the exercises for Chapter 7, you were asked to write a search engine for a "small domain." Re-read the description of these problems. Now, write a CGI program that allows users to interface to the underlying search engine using an HTML form. The form allows users to search for keywords using logical *and* and logical *or*. The CGI program returns a nice-looking HTML document with the search results.

15. *(Medium: Research, Module Installation, May need root permission)*
Learn how the Apache web server works. The Web server usually has to `fork` a process for each CGI interaction with a browser. This is expensive in terms of resource requirements and time. It is now possible to make the process faster so that a new process does not have to be created every time. This is done by embedding Perl in the Apache web server. Research into how this can be done. Install any modules that you can find to do this that is free or costs just a little.

16. *(Hard: Many interactive components, Long-term project)*
A Virtual Bookstore
You are going to write a program that supports the operation of a virtual bookstore called the *Garden of the Gods Booksellers*.

You need to have a large textual bibliographic file in the *bibtex* format for the project. An example bibliographic file is at
`http://www.cs.uccs.edu/~kalita/work/bookstore/all-books.html`. An entry in this file looks like the following.

```
@Book{edward-gait-1906,
  author =        "Gait~b1863, Edward Albert",
  title =         "A History of Assam",
  publisher =     "Thacker, Spink \& Co.",
  year =          "1906",
  editor =        "",
  volume =        "",
  series =        "",
  address =       "Calcutta",
  topic =   "History; Assam",
  edition =       "",
  price  =   "$20",
  month =         "",
  note =          "PATG"
}
```

It tells us that it is a book entry. All our entries are for books in this file. It has an internal index called 'edward-gait-1906.'[1] Then, it gives us some details about the entry.

Please note that some fields may not be specified. Also, you cannot assume that the fields are in the same order all the time. You also should anticipate that some fields may be added or removed later. There can be blank spaces or lines anywhere inside an entry.

Note that in a real project, one would use a database and not a text file. The database will have tables, and one of the tables will correspond to the text file we talk about here.

Things to Do

Make a directory called *bookstore* and put all your files and sub-directories under it. Divide the work you do into an ample number of subroutines so that later modification to the program is easy. The sub-tasks are listed below. These assume you know HTML fairly well. If you do not, pick up a book in a bookstore and learn on your own. HTML is a very easy language.

(a) Let the user search this file in three possible ways: by title, by topic, and by author. Searching is done by presenting a form to the user. You need to link the Perl search program to the home page for the bookstore.

(b) Provide a clickable help file for users who want to do complex searches. You should not allow them to use all possible regular expressions Pearl allows. It could be very complex and confusing for a lay person surfing the Web.

(c) Process the selected entries to produce a presentable HTML document that contains the bibliographic entries. This HTML document should look nice and be easily readable. Present only the author and title now. But, make the information that you supply for each book clickable for more information. When the user clicks on a book, show all the details about the book from the database entry.

(d) Give the customer a way to choose any of the search results and put it in a *shopping cart*. Any time the user puts anything in a shopping cart, let the customer see the whole shopping cart at

---

[1]This can be later replaced by a unique, globally-recognized identifier, such as the book's ISBN number.

that point in time if he/she wishes. Tell the user that he/she can pop books out of the shopping cart now or any time later. For the shopping cart, use a temporary file in the /tmp directory. This tmp file should be unique to each order.

(e) Let the user search as many times as he or she wants to. This you can do by having a little form that shows up somewhere on the screen: A form that asks the user whether he or she wants to search again, or whether he or she is done with searches.

(f) Once the user is done with all his or her searches, allow him or her to look at the shopping cart. Use a form to present the selected entries. Compute the total price. Let the user deselect books at this time if he or she wants. Let the user go back to the search mode also.

(g) Select some books as *specials of the week* and sell them at 25% discount. Gently show one special of the week at a time as the user performs search. The special of the week should be selectable for buying. The specials of the week are stored in a file called specials.html using the bibtex format. Create this file on your own.

(h) Give a discount of 10% if the user buys more than three books, and a discount of 20% if the user buys more than 6 books. Add shipping and handling cost.

(i) Once the user has selected a set of books, ask the user to enter (in a form), a name, an e-mail address, a surface address, a phone number (use it as an internal index or key; make up a unique key if the phone number is not provided), a credit card number with its type (let the user select among popular credit cards) and expiration date. Keep all the customer information in a textual database that you add to as you get new customers. Note that the program at this time is not secure.

(j) Send a confirmation of the order with the list of books and prices to the user. This confirmation is sent by an e-mail message that the system generates automatically.

(k) Let the user the choice of joining one of several mailing lists whose names appear in a pop-up menu. Get the names of the mailing lists by looking at the *topic* entries of the books the user has bought. You create a mailing list by keeping e-mail addresses in a file with an appropriate name. If the customer decides to join a mailing list, append his or her e-mail address to the end of the file that contains the e-mail addresses for the appropriate list. Keep all the mailing list files in a specific sub-directory named mailing-lists.

(l) Keep all the orders from all users in a file that store employees can access later for shipping purposes. Each entry in the order information database should contain the customer identifier (phone number), the book identifier (the book's internal index), the date of purchase, the date of shipping, and the price of the book. Keep this information in a textual file.

For The Employees

We want to allow the employees of the bookstore to be able to look at customer data. You need to write the Perl routines which the employees of the bookstore can use to search the customer information.

(a) Make available a password protected link on the WWW page for employees so that they can look at the customer and order databases. Store your passwords in a file called passwords, which can be a text file. Before they are given access to the customer and order information, the employees first must be given a way to enter a username, a social security number, and then a password. Once they have registered with a password, they may change their password any time if they can provide their username and the old password. Note that here are simulating a very simple authentication mechanism that is not really secure.

(b) Make an HTML table to allow employees to view a list of customers in descending order of money they have spent. The owner and employees should be able to do this from the browser, but by using the password.

(c) We will allow empolyees to enter new books into our book database. New books are entered by the employee by typing in a file name that contains a list of new books. The list of new books is in a file called `newItems.txt`. This file also uses the same format given earlier. Create this file on your own. As each new book is added, make the system send e-mail to the users who have shown interest in books of that kind and have joined the appropriate mailing list. Use the *topic* field in the new book's entry to select for appropriateness. You send details about a book in a mail message. You loop through every e-mail address in the mailing list file.

17. *(Hard: Many interactive components, Long-term project)*
A Virtual Grocery Store

Assume there is a grocery store called *Kalita's* and you have been employed to develop Web presence for it.

All the machine specific instructions pertain to a Unix or Linux machine. Create a directory called `public_html` as a subdirectory in your home directory. The directory must be readable and executable by everyone, and the file must be readable by everyone.

Now, we are going to make an initial effort at writing our grocery store program. Make a directory called `GroceryStore` in your `public_html` directory and store all your files for the effort under this directory.

We are going to make up a syntax for entering our grocery store items. This may not be the best syntax, but this works. It gives us the flexibility that we need for our purposes. In real life, such a program would use a database with one or more tables.

Let us assume that we have grocery items belonging to the following categories `Produce, Deli, Dairy, Meat, Beverages, Snack Foods, Paper Products, Books and Magazines, Spices and Condiment,` and `Frozen Foods`.

Write up a file for the grocery items that we have in the store. Let this file have 15 items belonging to any five categories given above. Have 3 items per category.

An entry in this file looks like the following.

```
@Item{
   ID =                   "20-130-5000",
   name =                 "Philadelphia Cream Cheese",
   category =             "Dairy",
   manufacturer =         "General Foods, Inc.",
   price =                "0.99",
   unit=                  "ounce",
   unitsPerItem =         "16",
   packaging =            "plastic container",
   inventory =            "1000",
   description =          "Low calorie; No fat"
}
```

It tells us that it is a grocery item. It has an internal ID. Then, it gives us details about the entry. Note that some fields may not be specified. Also, a field may be specified over several lines.

Our goal now is to make up a Web page from the item file. By processing this file, we want to make an HTML page where the item categories are shown as clickable links. Show the items in a sorted manner. When a user clicks on a link for a certain category, show all the products in that category with detailed information that you deem important. You should sort the items.

Things to Do

The sub-tasks are given below. Divide the work you do into an ample number of subroutines so that later modification to the program is easy.

(a) We will let a customer look at items in virtual aisles. When a customer wants to search items belonging to a certain category (say, `Dairy`), produce (a) neat-looking aisle(s) where clickable names of the items belonging to the category are shown. When a customer clicks on a name, more details about that item are shown in a pleasing format.

(b) Let the customer also search the database by the name of an item. Allow for partial specification of the item's name. The result of the search should be a clickable list of items that the customer can click for more detailed information.

(c) Give the customer a way to choose any of the search results and put it in a *shopping cart*. Any time the user puts anything in a shopping cart, let the customer see the whole shopping cart at that point in time if she wishes. Tell the customer that she can remove items out of the shopping cart now or any time later. For the shopping cart, use a temporary file in a *temporary* directory. This *temporary* file should be **unique** to each order.

(d) Let the customer search as many times as she wants to. This you can do by having a little form that shows up somewhere on the screen: A form that asks the user whether she wants to search again, or whether she is done with searches.

(e) Once the user is done with all her searches, allow her to look at the shopping cart. Use a form to present the selected entries. Let the user deselect items at this time if she wants. Let the user go back to the search mode also.

(f) Once the user has selected a set of items, ask the user to enter (in a form), a name, an e-mail address, a surface address, a phone number (use it as an internal index or key; make up a unique key if the phone number is not provided), a credit card number with its type (let the user select among popular credit cards) and expiration date. Keep all the customer information in a textual database that you add to as you get new customers.

(g) Send a confirmation of the order with the list of items and prices to the customer. This confirmation is sent by an e-mail message that the system generates automatically.

(h) Keep all the orders from all users in a file that store employees can access later for shipping purposes. Each entry in the order information database should contain the customer identifier (phone number), the item identifier (the item's internal index), the date of purchase, the date of shipping, and the price of the item. Keep this information in a textual file.

For The Employees

We want to allow the employees of the grocery store to be able to look at customer data. You need to write the Perl routines which the employees of the store can use to search the customer information.

(a) Make available a password protected link on the WWW page for employees so that they can look at the databases. Store your passwords in a file called `passwords`, which can be a text file. Before she is given access to the customer and order information, the employee first must be given a way to enter a username, a social security number, and then a password. Once an employee has registered with a password, she may change their password any time if she can provide their username and the old password. Note that the passwords are insecure.

(b) We will allow employees to enter new grocery items into our items database. New items are entered by the employee by typing in a file name that contains a list of new items. The list of new items is at `newItems.txt` using the format given earlier. Create this file on your own.

18. *(Hard: Many interactive components, Long-term project)*
    A Virtual Auction Site

Assume there is an auction house called *priceIsRight.com* and you have been employed to develop Web presence for it. You can develop the pages on any machine of your choice, but ultimately, you must transfer the files to a Web server. The machine-specific instructions below are about a Unix machine.

Create a directory called `public_html` as a subdirectory in your home directory. The directory must be readable and executable by everyone, and the file must be readable by everyone. Create the top page for the auction site under this directory.

We will now enhance the auction Web site to make it dynamic in nature. To make things dynamic, we need to have our data in files and create HTML or XML pages from these files using Perl programs, which may or may not be CGI programs. Note that the project requires you to learn HTML and XML on your own.

Organizing the Files

In your `public_html` directory, Make subdirectories `html`, `xml`, `data` and `cgi_bin` to store your files. Organize them neatly under each sub-directory. You can make additional subdirectories or sub-subdirectories if you find the need for it.

Data Files

We will keep all the data that are needed in text files. There will be at least four data files. Let's call them `sellers.txt`, `bidders.txt`, `auctionCategories.txt` and `auctionItems.txt`. In the `sellers.txt` file you will save details about persons putting items on the auction block. In the `bidders.txt` you will store information about persons bidding on items. Both sellers and bidders will provide the data to you by filling in forms on the Web site.

In the file `auctionCategories.txt` store details about categories of items to be sold. In the file `auctionItems.txt`, store details of all items being auctioned. Of course, you will have to store the category of an item being sold in the `auctionItems.txt` file. Therefore, there should be some correspondence between what you store in the `auctionCategories.txt` file and the `auctionItems.txt` file.

Decide on a reasonable syntax for all four files. In a real company, such files will be stored in databases, but we will have to make do with text files where you can store various "fields" for an entry separated by some predefined text separator.

Programs to Generate HTML and XML files (non-CGI) for Categories and Items

You will now write programs that will generate HTML files for the site. These files should automatically create the files that are going to be displayed on the Web. Do as little as possible by hand. For example, when you create any files or directories, change their permission modes within your program. These programs will not be linked to the Web, but you will run these programs by hand from time to time. Create files or sub-directories within the program. Don't move files by hand if you can help it.

These new files that you generate are going to be form the core of your auction site. Link the new files to the main page of the auction site. Indicate that they were program-created when you link them. Of course, you may need a few hand-created files to make the site complete.

Extra Credit

Write Perl programs to create XML files corresponding to categories of items and individual items.

CGI programs for Sellers and Bidders

You will now write additional Perl scripts that are going to be linked to forms on the Web site. You will have a CGI program linked to the page where the seller registers to put an item on the auction block. This CGI program will take the seller data entered in the form and add the new details to the `sellers.txt` file. On the page where a seller enters personal information, provide a link to those who have already registered. When someone registers, ask her or him to choose a seller ID and a password. You are going to store the seller ID and password in the `sellers.txt` file. Do not worry about security issues. Normally passwords would be stored in an encrypted form. If a person is already registered, let him or her be able to put items on the auction block without having to enter personal data again. If a person has not registered earlier, allow the person to enter personal data and register.

Once a person is registered, take him to the page where he or she can put items on the auction block. Once again, here you need a form where the person enters all the data about the item he or she wants to auction. You need to write a CGI program that is going to take all this data and put it in the file `auctionItems.txt`. If the item's category doesn't exist already, you need to modify the `auctionCategories.txt` file also.

You need to write CGI programs for bidding also. The bidder side is similar to the seller side also. You need to ask bidders to create an ID and a password in addition to entering other details. If a person is a registered bidder, he or she should be able to enter the ID and password, and go to a page where he or she can bid on an item. If he or she is not already registered, he or she should be asked to enter personal details.

Programs to Work with Additional Data Files

Corresponding to every item in the auction block, we should also have a file that contains details of how the auction is proceeding. It should have details such as when the auction started and when it is going to end, the minimum price accepted, and the current maximum price, etc. You can keep this information on top of the file. Then, you should keep details of who have bid and what price he or she is willing to pay. For this assignment, you can make the assumption that each item is on the auction block for 48 hours. Once 48 hours are over, declare a winner, and the winning price. You need to do this by a Perl program that is not going to be connected to the Web, but run by you, say every once in a while.

A Search Engine for Your Auction Site

You will now create a search engine for the auction Web site that you have created. You will perform searches over HTML pages only. You must have all your HTML pages in the directory called `html` under your `public_html` directory. You may have subdirectories in the `html` directory. If you have not placed all your HTML files in the `html` directory, please do so now.

You will make an analysis of all your HTML pages related to the auction house including those in the sub-directories.

The following is the bare minimum idea. Search engines are much more sophisticated than this. When you analyze an HTML file, keep track of all the words that occur in the title, in the `meta` tag with `content` attribute, at various heading levels, and in regular paragraph text. You will have to strip all unneeded HTML tags. You will use what is called a *stop list* of the most common words such as *of, the, a, an,* etc., to take out such words. You should then build a "database" of the remaining words and keep information such as the URL of the file where the word occurs.

You will create a form for searching your Web site. Give it a heading such as `Search the Auction House` or something similar. You will link the `submit` button of the form to search the "database" you have created and present in a nice format the results of the search. The user should be able to go to the URL by clicking on the generated page. Allow for search by more than one word. Allow the user to use *and* and *or* with the keywords when searching.

19. (*Hard: Many interactive components, Long-term project*)
    A Sports Site

Assume there is a site called *CollegeSports.com* (or, *HighSchoolSports.com*; choose one) and you have been employed to develop Web presence for it. This site is going to have news and scores.

You can develop the pages on any machine of your choice, but ultimately, you must transfer the files to a Web server. The machine-specific details correspond to a Linux machine. Create the top page for the Web site by hand.

Next, we will enhance the Web site to make it dynamic in nature.

Our goal is to have a sports site that is viewed either as XML or HTML. Learn HTML or XML on your own if you do not know them. The sports site will be essentially all dynamic except, maybe, for the top page that will be designed to look nice and appealing. For the rest of the pages that are dynamic, functionality matters more than looks, although they should not be ugly. The sports site will carry information about schools or universities, teams a certain school or university has, statistics on individual players, and statistics on individual teams.

Some initial data may be provided by you in the form of text files. However, most data is expected to be entered by volunteers (or, if you make money, by "paid volunteers") who register to enter data for specific schools.

Organizing the Files

In your `public_html` directory, make subdirectories `html`, `xml`, `data` and `cgi_bin` to store your files. Organize them neatly under each sub-directory. You can make additional subdirectories or sub-subdirectories if you find the need for it.

Data Files

We will keep all the data that are needed in text files. In a real application, we will use a database. There will be at least five data files. Let's call them `schools.txt`, `schoolTeams.txt`, `teamStatistics.txt`, `player.txt` and `personnel.txt`.

The file `schools.txt`, there is data about specific schools. These include data such as school name, a unique abbreviation or ID, a name for the teams, and any additional information you deem important. Keep the information in a clearly and consistently formatted manner. You should create the data file with data about one or two schools to start with. Later, a registered volunteer should be able to enter data from the Web. You can think of storing data for a school, one per line, or one per paragraph. Clearly separate the parts of an individual record using a pre-specified textual separator.

The file `schoolTeams.txt` is a text file that contains information about specific teams. The data for a team contains fields such as the unique abbreviation for the school, a unique abbreviation or ID for the sport, names of coach(es), etc. Again, create the file with some initial information. Allow that information will be entered by registered volunteers later from the Web.

File `teamStatistics.txt` includes fields such as the unique school abbreviation, the sports abbreviation, win-loss statistics for the season, and any other additional information you need. Enter some initial data when you create the file. Additional data will be entered from the Web or calculated automatically.

File `players.txt` includes fields such as the name of a player, his or her unique ID or abbreviation (unique within the team for a specific school), unique school abbreviation, unique sports abbreviation, his or her summary statistics for the season in some acceptable fashion. Create the file with some initial data. Allow data to be entered from the Web or to be automatically created later.

The `personnel.txt` file contains fields such as the name of an individual, an email addressed that is used as a login ID, a unique school abbreviation, a password, and any other pertinent information. There is no initial data in this file. All data is entered from the Web.

Programs to Generate HTML and XML files (non-CGI)

Write individual Perl functions that will scan the contents of each of the files individually (you may have to consult more than one file) and produce XML data files. The XML data files will have accompanying DTD files that are non-dynamic. You have to pre-write these DTD files. In addition, there are accompanying non-dynamic XSL files that transform the XML data files to HTML for the browsers. The XSL files are pre-written also.

Write a function called `createpages.pl` that calls all the functions for individual files and does anything else needed to create a whole new Web site (except for the top page) every time you run. Store the program-created XML data files in non-changing file names so that they can be linked easily from the top page.

There are many details to be considered in generating these pages. Make your own decisions regarding the complexity of the pages and do the best you can.

CGI programs

You will now write CGI programs so that data can be entered from the Web. First create a form such that an individual, volunteer or paid, can register to enter data for a specific school. This will populate the file `personnel.txt` from the Web.

Next, create a form to allow someone registered to enter data. There is an email address and a password that need to be entered. This is checked against the file `personnel.txt`. If the login is successful, allow the person to choose what type of data he/she wants to enter: basic school or team data, team statistics, player data, etc. Different types of data update different data files. Based on the choice, bring up appropriate forms. Each form is linked to a CGI program that performs appropriate checks and updates corresponding files.

Once again, all this is a lot of work, and make the best decisions you can.

A Search Engine for The Sports Site

You will now create a search engine for the sports-based Web site that you have created. You will perform searches over HTML and XML pages. You must have all your HTML pages in the directory called `html` under your `public_html` directory. You may have subdirectories in the `html` directory. If you have not placed all your HTML files in the `html` directory, please do so now. You will place all your XML files, similarly, in an directory called `xml` under the `public_html` directory. Once again, you can create subdirectoriess if you want to.

You will make an analysis of all your HTML and XML pages including those in the sub-directories.

The following is the bare minimum idea. Search engines are much more sophisticated than this. When you analyze an HTML or XML file, keep track of all the words that occur in the title, in the `meta` tag with `content` attribute, at various heading levels, and in regular paragraph texts. You will have to strip all unneeded HTML tags. You will strip your XML tags although, in reality, the XML tags contain semantic information and should not be summarily dismissed. You will use what is called a *stop list* of the most common words such as *of, the, a, an,* etc., to take out such words. You should then build a "database" of the remaining words and keep information such as the URL of the file where the word occurs. In our case, the "database" is just one or more text files.

You will create a form for searching your Web site. Give it a heading such as `Search My Sports Site` or something similar. You will link the `submit` button of the form to search the "database" you have created and present in a nice format the results of the search. The user should be able to go to the URL by clicking on the generated page. Allow for search by more than one word. Allow the user to use and and or with the keywords when searching.

Chapter 9

On Web Client Programming

In This Chapter

In this chapter, we discuss at length how to write programs that work as Web clients. The World Wide Web is a ubiquitous application that sits atop the Internet which is a diffused network of networks encompassing the globe. It came into existence in 1990 with the first Web server and Web client developed by Berners-Lee. The first client was textual whereas the dominant browsers or clients at this time, viz., Netscape Navigator and Microsoft Internet Explorer are GUI-based.

As we are well-aware, the World Wide Web employs the client-server model of computing. We discuss client-server computing at length in Chapter 7. The dominant servers at this time are the Apache Server, and Microsoft's IIS Server. Other severs include AppleShare IP that runs on Macintosh computers. Web servers are extremely complex programs that serve Web pages to Web clients. Commercial Web clients are extremely complex programs as well. As a result, we do not venture into writing of complex clients, but simple ones that can fetch Web pages and perform useful computation on these Web pages. By definition, a Web client communicates with Web servers. A Web server usually listens on port 80 on the machine that hosts it. Web clients and servers communicate using the HTTP protocol. A protocol defines a language's syntax as well as imposes constraints on what can be said when. Web pages are written mostly using the HTML language although increasingly the language called XML is finding wider acceptance. In addition, when dynamic Web pages are served by a Web server, the Web server does not respond directly to a request from a client, but obtains responses by talking to an intermediary. This intermediary can take various forms such as a CGI program, an ASP program, a PHP program, or a JSP program.

In this section, we discuss how to write programs that can send a request to a Web server, get a response back, and perform useful computation with the page that is returned. Unlike a commercial Web browser, we do not format the page returned to make it pretty, or deal with graphics, audio or video. However, we write programs that can be immediately useful. For example, a comparison-shopping program that presents a table of prices for a specific product from competing on-line stores performs Web client programming. A program that monitors various on-line auction sites performs Web client programming. A program that obtains news stories from several Web sites and presents the stories best suited to an individual's tastes performs Web client programming.

The communication takes place between a Web server and a Web client uses the HTTP protocol that sits atop the TCP protocol we discuss in Chapter 7. The TCP protocol sits on top of the IP protocol which is discussed at length in any book on computer networking. Thus, Web clients and servers must understand TCP and IP. A Web client such as a program that fetches a single Web page, or crawls the Web fetching many relevant pages, can be written employing sockets that use the TCP protocol. We wrote such programs in Chapter 7. However, Perl makes writing Web clients much easier than starting from scratch using TCP-based sockets. It has a set of related modules for developing fairly sophisticated Web clients. We discuss the most important such modules in this section.

9.1 Fetching a Web Page: Module `LWP::Simple`

There is a large set of Perl modules that are bundled together and are called the **Library for (World Wide) Web Programming** or **LIBWWW** or **LWP**. It is also sometimes called **libnet**.

One of the simplest modules is `LWP::Simple`. As the name suggests, it is a subclass of the module `LWP`. If the goal at hand is to fetch a Web page and do something with it, this package is all that we need. The following program fetches a Web page, and saves it to a local file. It also prints all the URLs that are in the page and were used as a hyperlink using the `<A href=...>` construct in HTML.

Program 9.1

```perl
#!/usr/bin/perl
#file fetchHeadURL.pl
use LWP::Simple;
use strict;

#URL to fetch
my $url = "http://www.assam.org";
my $localFile = "assamorg.html";

my @head = LWP::Simple::head ($url);
exit 0 unless (@head);
my ($contentType, $documentLength,
        $modificationTime, $expires, $server) = @head;
print "$url is a file of type $contentType\n";
print "$url is $documentLength bytes long\n";

print "$url was last modified on ", scalar (localtime($modificationTime)), "\n";
print "$url expires on $expires\n" if ($expires);
print "$url is served by $server\n";

#get gets the URL as a string
my $content= LWP::Simple::get ($url);
my @hrefs = ($content =~ /<A\s+href\s*=\s*"([^"]+)"/ig);
print "All hrefs in the page = \n\t@hrefs\n";
```

```
open FILE, ">$localFile";
print FILE $content;
close FILE;
```

The program is given a URL to fetch and a local file where to save the fetched URL. First, it fetches the head of the page. The LWP::Simple::head function returns a list with five elements. The elements are extracted out of the list and printed. The first element gives the MIME type for the content of the Web page. The content type is sent by the Web server to a client or a browser in the header so that the client can decide how to display it. In this example, the content type is text/html signifying that it is a text file written using the syntax of the HTML language. The second element gives the length of the page in bytes. The third element gives the time when the page was last modified in terms of number of seconds after the so-called *epoch*. The epoch is system-specific. For Unix, it is January 1, 1970. In other words, it is the age of the page. The *expiry date* can be empty for a Web page. The server gives details of the server software and hardware. Next, the program gets the actual content of the URL by using the LWP::Simple::get function. While head obtains the header from the Web server, get obtains the actual Web page. Each takes a URL as an argument. These two functions automatically set up TCP-based socket connections to the designated Web servers, send the HTTP-based commands as needed, capture the data that come back to the client, and then save it in appropriate data structures. Because connections need to be set up and communications need to take place, these functions usually take some time in coming back with responses.

The program culls out all hrefed URLs from the page. This part of the program is based on the discussion in Section 4.8.3.2.3. It also prints out the contents of the URL to a file. Such a program can be the basis for a sophisticated crawler or a search engine program.

A partial output of one run of the program is given below.

```
http://www.assam.org is a file of type text/html
http://www.assam.org is 25141 bytes long
http://www.assam.org was last modified on Thu Jan 25 02:07:54 2001
http://www.assam.org is served by Apache/1.3.14 (Unix)
            (Red-Hat/Linux) ApacheJServ/1.1.2 mod_ssl/2.7.1
            OpenSSL/0.9.6 PHP/4.0.2 mod_perl/1.21
All hrefs in the page =
        http://www.assamcompany.com
        mailto:kalita@pikespeak.uccs.edu,webmaster@assam.org
        http://assamcompany.com/netourism/start.html
        http://mail.bigmailbox.com/users/assamorg/signup.cgi
        http://mail.bigmailbox.com/users/assamorg/forgotpassword.cgi
        chat/livechat.htm
        http://assam.org/assam/AssamBulletinBoard/
        http://www.assam.org/assam/individuals/
        http://www.wunderground.com/global/stations/42314.html
        http://www.wunderground.com/global/stations/42410.html
```

The output continues with more such URLs.

9.1.1   Fetching Documents from the Web: Simple "Web Crawling"

There are many sites on the Web where useful documents are stored so that interested individuals can download them. For example, the site
http://www.cis.upenn.edu/~techreports/abstracts01.html at the University of Pennsylvania contains abstracts of all technical reports published by the Computer Science Department in the year

2001. Most of these abstracts have links to PostScript or PDF files that are downloadable from the Web. The following program fetches the HTML page corresponding to the URL given above, obtains the links to the technical reports, and then downloads the technical reports to local files.

Program 9.2

```perl
#!/usr/bin/perl
#file getFiles.pl
use LWP::Simple;

my ($ftpURL, $ftpContents, $ftpFile);
my ($htmlURL, $ftpHrefs, $includedExts);
$includedExts = "ps[.]gz|pdf|ps";
$htmlURL = "http://www.cis.upenn.edu/~techreports/abstracts01.html";

$htmlContents = LWP::Simple::get ($htmlURL) or
        die "Couldn't fetch $htmlURL using LWP::Simple::get: $!";
@ftpHrefs = ($htmlContents =~ /<A\s+href\s*=\s*"([^"]+)"/ig);
@ftpHrefs = grep /[.]$includedExts$/, @ftpHrefs;
#print "ftp hrefs = @ftpHrefs\n";

foreach $ftpURL (@ftpHrefs){
    print "Fetching URL: $ftpURL\n";
    ($ftpFile) = ($ftpURL =~ m@.+/(.+)$@);
    print "Saving to local file:  $ftpFile\n";
    $ftpContents = LWP::Simple::get ($ftpURL);
    warn "Couldn't fetch $ftpURL: $!"  unless $ftpContents;
    open FTPFILE, ">$ftpFile";
    print FTPFILE $ftpContents;
    close FTPFILE;
}
```

The program does not really use the FTP protocol although the names of identifiers has the term FTP in them. The HTML file corresponding to abstracts is first fetched using `LWP::Simple::get`. The `href`ed URLs are next culled from the HTML file. From the URLs, only those that end with the required extension are kept. The required extensions in this program are `ps`, `pdf`, or `ps.gz`. In other words, these are files in the Adobe PostScript format or PDF format. The PostScript files may have been compressed using the Gnu `zip` command (i.e., `gzip`). Such compressed files have the `gz` extension. We know that these are the relevant extensions by examining the HTML page. Our goal is to download all technical reports to our local machine so that we can peruse them either on the computer screen or after printing them.

The program goes into a `foreach` loop where it obtains the name of the actual file from the URL. The name of the file is the component in the URL after the last `/`. Then, it obtains the contents of the file by making the following call.

```perl
$ftpContents = LWP::Simple::get ($ftpURL);
```

The contents of the downloaded file are written into the local file. The downloading is performed by issuing the `GET` command to the HTTP server. That is what the `get` function does. A part of what is printed by this program on the screen for a sample run is given below.

```
Fetching URL: http://www.cis.upenn.edu/~rtg/papers/MS-CIS-01-01.ps.gz
```

```
Saving to local file:  MS-CIS-01-01.ps.gz
Fetching URL: http://www.cis.upenn.edu/~lwzhao/papers/cognitive.pdf
Saving to local file:  cognitive.pdf
Fetching URL: http://www.cis.upenn.edu/~sotiris/papers/strongman.ps
Saving to local file:  strongman.ps
Fetching URL: http://www.cis.upenn.edu/~sotiris/papers/subos.ps
Saving to local file:  subos.ps
Fetching URL: http://www.cis.upenn.edu/~rtg/papers/MS-CIS-01-07.ps.gz
Saving to local file:  MS-CIS-01-07.ps.gz
Fetching URL: http://www.seas.upenn.edu/~sachinc/report.ps
Saving to local file:  report.ps
Fetching URL: http://www.cis.upenn.edu/~pengs/publications/fc_tech_report.ps.gz
Saving to local file:  fc_tech_report.ps.gz
Fetching URL: http://db.cis.upenn.edu/DL/ubql.pdf
Saving to local file:  ubql.pdf
```

In this sample run, the program downloads eight technical reports to the local machine. The downloading is done not using the FTP protocol, but by using the HTTP protocol. This could have been done using the FTP protocol also, but we do not discuss that here. In this specific case, it so happens that all the URLs referring to downloaded files are absolute URLs. Therefore, we do not have to massage the URL to make it absolute before we start the downloading process. If the URLs were relative, it would be necessary to make them absolute first before starting to download.

A variation of the program given above can be used to download Perl modules from the http://www.cpan.org site. The following program looks at the Web page that lists the recently contributed Perl modules and downloads those that satisfy a certain regular expression.

Program 9.3
<hr>

```perl
#!/usr/bin/perl
#file PerlModules.pl
use LWP::Simple;

my ($ftpURL, $ftpContents, $ftpFile);
my ($htmlURL, $ftpHrefs, $includedExts, $baseURL);
my ($searchPattern) = @ARGV;

$includedExts = "tar[.]gz";
$htmlURL = "http://www.cpan.org/RECENT.html";
$baseURL = "http://www.cpan.org";

$htmlContents = LWP::Simple::get ($htmlURL) or
        die "Couldn't fetch $htmlURL using LWP::Simple::get: $!";
@ftpHrefs = ($htmlContents =~ /<A\s+href\s*=\s*"([^"]+)"/ig);
@ftpHrefs = grep /[.]$includedExts$/, @ftpHrefs;
@ftpHrefs = grep /$searchPattern/, @ftpHrefs;
@ftpHrefs = map {"$baseURL/$_"} @ftpHrefs;

foreach $ftpURL (@ftpHrefs){
    print "Fetching URL: $ftpURL\n";
    ($ftpFile) = ($ftpURL =~ m@.+/(.+)$@);
    print "Saving to local file:  $ftpFile\n";
```

```
    $ftpContents = LWP::Simple::get ($ftpURL);
    warn "Couldn't fetch $ftpURL: $!"  unless $ftpContents;
    open FTPFILE, ">$ftpFile";
    print FTPFILE $ftpContents;
    close FTPFILE;
}
```

The program is called with a command-line argument that acts as a regular expression. This program obtains the Web page at http::://www.cpan.org/RECENT.html, parses the page to obtain all URLs that end with the tar.gz extension. Then, it obtains those URLs that satisfy the regular expression given as command line argument. Finally, it downloads all the tarred sources of recent Perl modules that satisfy the search criterion. An interaction with this program is given below.

```
%getPerlModules.pl "XML"
Fetching URL: http://www.cpan.org/authors/id/A/AN/ANDREIN/DBIx-XMLMessage-0.04.t
ar.gz
Saving to local file:  DBIx-XMLMessage-0.04.tar.gz
Fetching URL: http://www.cpan.org/authors/id/K/KR/KRAEHE/XML-Handler-YAWriter-0.
18.tar.gz
Saving to local file:  XML-Handler-YAWriter-0.18.tar.gz
Fetching URL: http://www.cpan.org/authors/id/K/KR/KRAEHE/XML-Handler-YAWriter-0.
19.tar.gz
Saving to local file:  XML-Handler-YAWriter-0.19.tar.gz
Fetching URL: http://www.cpan.org/modules/by-category/07_Database_Interfaces/DBI
x/DBIx-XMLMessage-0.04.tar.gz
Saving to local file:  DBIx-XMLMessage-0.04.tar.gz
Fetching URL: http://www.cpan.org/modules/by-category/11_String_Lang_Text_Proc/X
ML/XML-Handler-YAWriter-0.19.tar.gz
Saving to local file:  XML-Handler-YAWriter-0.19.tar.gz
Fetching URL: http://www.cpan.org/modules/by-module/DBIx/DBIx-XMLMessage-0.04.ta
r.gz
Saving to local file:  DBIx-XMLMessage-0.04.tar.gz
Fetching URL: http://www.cpan.org/modules/by-module/XML/XML-Handler-YAWriter-0.1
9.tar.gz
Saving to local file:  XML-Handler-YAWriter-0.19.tar.gz
pikespeak[98]: ls
```

The program is called with "XML" as the command line argument. Hence, the program finds those Perl modules that have been recently contributed to the http://www.cpan.org site and have the character string XML in them, and then downloads them to the local machine. These are compressed tar files corresponding to the source programs for these modules. One can then go about installing these modules on the local computer if so desired.

9.1.2   Filling a GET form on the Web: Automatically Finding Book Prices

Web pages are full of forms. A form is a way to interact with a Web server and get a response back. For example, we fill in a form to become a member of a mailing list, or to search for items using a search engine or an electronic store. A simple form can have only one or two elements in them whereas a complex form can have many elements to fill.

There are two ways that a filled form can be submitted to a Web server requesting an action on its part and a subsequent response. The two methods are called GET and PUT. The GET method sends all the form's filled contents to the server in one network transmission whereas the PUT method needs an additional transmission, one to send the form's URL and headers, and another to send the form's data. The form's

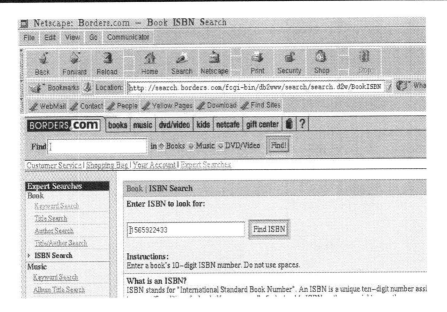

Figure 9.1: A Search Form at www.borders.com

data are accepted by the server and then processed by a program such as a CGI program and the response is sent back to the user either via the Web server or directly.

The designer of a form decides what method between the two to use. For simple forms, GET is sufficient. The differences between the two methods can be found in any book that discusses HTML and the HTTP protocol. Mimicking a form submitted with PUT is a little difficult to handle. However, GET-submitted forms can be treated as a regular URL as we see below.

The following program fills in a form at the Web site for the electronic book and music store called http::://www.borders.com. The site has a simple form that allows a visitor to search for books using an ISBN number. This form is at the location

http://search.borders.com/fcgi-bin/db2www/search/search.d2w/BookISBN.

Before discussing the program, it must be noted that Web sites change frequently, and therefore, the form being discussed in the book may not exist at a future date. The form, as it looks on the Web site at the time of writing, is shown in Figure 9.1.

On the top left, we see a form that allows a visitor to search for book, music or video/DVD titles. There is a second form that allows search using a ten-digit ISBN number. If we look at the HTML for the second form, we see a form that looks like the following.

```
<TD BGCOLOR="#ffffcc"><FORM NAME="ISBNUPC_form" METHOD="get" action="Details">
        <B>Enter ISBN to look for:</B><SMALL><BR> <BR></SMALL>
        <INPUT TYPE="text" name="code" SIZE="30" MAXLENGTH="100">
        <INPUT TYPE="submit" VALUE="Find ISBN">
        <INPUT TYPE="hidden" NAME="mediaType" VALUE="Book">
        <INPUT TYPE="hidden" NAME="searchType" VALUE="ISBNUPC">
        <INPUT TYPE="hidden" NAME="prodID" VALUE="">
        <P><B>Instructions:</B><BR>
        Enter a book's 10-digit ISBN number. Do not use spaces.</P>
    </TD>
</FORM>
```

Finding the correct form in the source of the Web page may take a little time. The form is inside an HTML table's cell represented by the tag TD. This form's ACTION attribute refers to the URL Details. The form's METHOD attribute has the value get. Note that HTML is case-insensitive in the way we specify tags such as FORM, and their attributes such as ACTION. Thus, the form submission takes place using the GET method of the HTTP protocol. The form has several hidden arguments: code, mediaType, searchType and prodID. They all have values specified in HTML. These values are sent to the server when the form is submitted by clicking on the button labeled Find ISBN. The code text field is the one we see in the form in the Web browser. In the program that follows, we automatically fill in this form and submit it to the Web server. The Web server performs the search and returns an HTML-formatted page with the result of the search. We examine this page carefully and see that the price of the book is always preceded by certain keywords. We key in on this repeated occurrence and parse the returned page to obtain the price of the book, and print it on the screen.

Program 9.4

```
#!/usr/bin/perl
#file bordersISBN1.pl

use strict;
use LWP::Simple;

my ($url, $content);
my $ISBN = "1565922433";
print "ISBN = $ISBN\n";

#Make up the URL to search for the book's ISBN
$url = "http://search.borders.com/fcgi-bin/db2www/search/search.d2w/Details?";
$url .= "code=$ISBN&mediaType=Book&searchType=ISBNUPC";

$content = LWP::Simple::get ($url);
my ($price) =  ($content =~ m#Our Price:.+?\$(.+?)<#si);
print "price = $price\n";
```

The program uses the module LWP::Simple. It is given an ISBN number that happens to be 1565922433. Of course, this ISBN number could have been given as a command-line argument or read from the terminal after an appropriate prompt. The program creates a URL to request the server to initiate a search. To perform a search using a GET-submitted form, the server is sent the URL followed by a question mark, and then by one or more form field name, form field value pairs. The name and the value are separated by an equal sign. Different pairs are separated by the ampersand (&). Note that values must be supplied to hidden form elements with the correct values as found in the Web page for the form. This is the manner in which GET submitted forms are sent by a browser to a server. In this case, the URL sent to the server is the following. We have broken it into two lines whereas it is sent as a single line to the server.

```
http://search.borders.com/fcgi-bin/db2www/search/search.d2w/Details?
          code=$ISBN&mediaType=Book&searchType=ISBNUPC
```

There are no intervening spaces. The search URL seems to work without a prodID value.

This program simply mimics what a Web browser does. When the form is received by the Web server, it does the needful to get the search performed, and then returns the results of the search. If we were actually doing this search using a Web browser, we see the result page that looks like the one given in Figure 9.2. We carefully look at the HTML of this result page and result pages of several additional searches, and find that

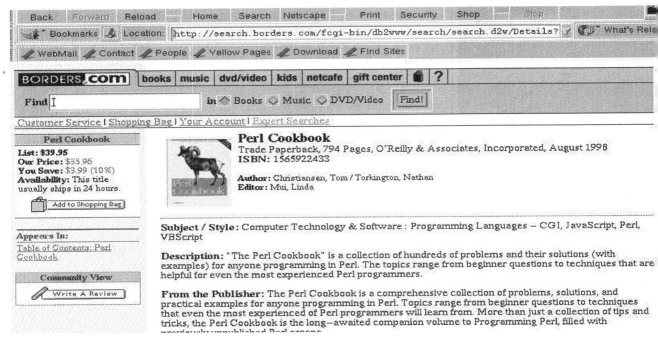

Figure 9.2: A Search Form at www.borders.com

every time we perform an ISBN search, the price of the book charged by the store follows the keywords Our Price. We obtain the price by simply parsing the Web page's HTML. Note that if we wanted to find additional information such as the title of the book, author, shipping information, etc., we will have to do additional search of the Web page's HTML. The output of running this program is given below.

```
%bordersISBN1.pl
ISBN = 1565922433
price = 35.96
```

This printout says that the books with ISBN number 1565922433 is sold by www.borders.com at a price of $35.96. This program can be easily extended to read a sequence of ISBN numbers from a file or a database, and obtain prices for each one of the ISBN numbers. If prices can be fetched from several bookstores, we can very easily compare prices of books.

9.2   The LWP Bundle:: Writing Sophisticated Web Clients

The LWP::Simple module discussed in the previous section provides a simple functional interface for simple Web-client related tasks. However, to write sophisticated Web clients, we need more muscle. The set of modules that constitute the bundle called LWP provides additional facilities.

To write powerful Web clients, we need to be familiar with the HTTP protocol or the Hypertext Transfer Protocol. It is the language that Web clients and servers use to communicate with each other. A request from a client to a server and a subsequent response from the server to the client constitute an HTTP transaction. A client request and a server response follow the same syntax. There is a request or response line followed by a header section and then the entire body.

A client always initiates a transaction by using the following steps.

1. The client contacts the server at the port number used by the Web server. The default port number is 80.

   Once the connection has been established, the client sends a request to the server. The request is framed in terms of an HTTP command, usually called a *method*. The method is given arguments such as the address of the document to be fetched, and an HTTP version number.

   The number of HTTP requests or methods is limited and they are discussed in books on networking, or in a site such as www.w3.org, the **World Wide Web Consortium**. The commonly used HTTP methods are GET, HEAD, POST and PUT. The GET method is used by a client to request a server to send a document found at a specific location. It can be used to fill forms that use the GET action attribute. The HEAD method is similar to GET, but it requests only some information on a file or a resource, and not the actual document. The POST method allows data to be sent to the server in a client request. For example, it can be used to provide data to a server for a newsgroup posting, or for a database operation. The POST method is frequently used by forms instead of the GET method. The PUT method is normally used to publish a document on a Web site.

2. Next, the client may send some header information to the server. The header information tells the server of the client's configuration and document types that the client can accept. The header information is a sequence of lines, each line containing a header name followed by a header value. The header information is optional.

3. Finally, the client may optionally send additional data. This additional data is usually meant for POST forms. It may also contain the content of a file to be published by the server.

The server gets the client's request at the specified port and performs the needed action and then responds in the following manner.

1. The first line is the status line containing the HTTP version, the status code, and a description of the status such as the word OK.

2. The next several lines are header information sent by the server to the client. The header information usually contains information about the server itself and information about the requested document. The header lines are terminated by a blank line.

3. If the server is successful in fulfilling the client's request, the requested data is sent next.

When a client sends an HTTP request to a server, if the server is alive and can respond to the request, it does so. As far as client programming goes, we do not have to worry about what the server does and how. The client however needs to capture the response that comes back from the server and deal with it. If the client requests a header, a header comes back and Perl captures it. If a file is requested, Perl gets a header back as well as the contents of the file.

Perl provides two object-oriented modules: HTTP::Request and HTTP::Response to model an HTTP interaction at the client's end. These are used to create a request to send and capture the response that comes back. A program creates an HTTP::Request object, and sends it. The response is captured automatically as an HTTP::Response object. To send out an HTTP::Request and to receive the response, Perl provides a class called LWP::UserAgent. The user agent is a software entity that actively pursues Web client related activities on behalf of a user or an application. It is a conduit between an application and a Web server. In simple and informal terms, it is an incarnation of the Web client. It takes an HTTP request, say to fetch a Web page, and then waits for the response to arrive from the server. Once the response is received, the user agent makes it available to the rest of the program.

In the simple use situation, an application creates a LWP::UserAgent object, and creates an HTTP::Request object for the request that needs to be performed. The request is then given to the request method of the UserAgent object. The request method opens up a communication channel with the server and sends the request out. When the response comes back, the response is captured by Perl in the form of a HTTP::Response object. Figure 9.3 describes the process diagrammatically.

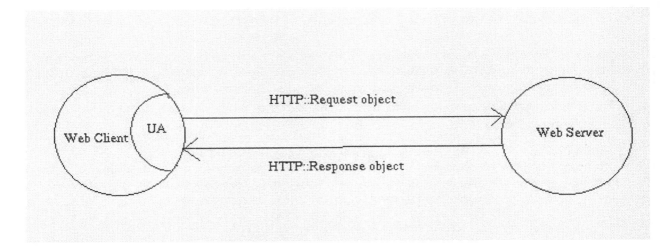

Figure 9.3: The LWP::UserAgent object on the client sends an HTTP::Request object to the server. The UserAgent object receives the reply as an HTTP::Response object.

The request() method of the UserAgent object can make arrangements to get the response in one of three ways: as a scalar available for direct manipulation, to be saved in a file, or handed over to a *callback* routine for processing. The first alternative is useful if the returned content is small and needs additional processing such as parsing to cull out relevant data. The second alternative is suitable for large objects such as a graphic or audio file. The last alternative can be used to process data in chunks as it comes in.

9.2.1 Requesting URL Header From a Web Server

We start with a program that communicates with a Web server requesting the header information for a file.

Program 9.5

```perl
#!/usr/bin/perl
#file fetchHead1.pl

use LWP::UserAgent;
use HTTP::Request;
use URI;
use strict;
$" = "\n\t";

my ($url, $uri, $ua);
my ($headerRequest, $headerResponse, $headers);

#URL to fetch
$url = "http://www.cs.uccs.edu/~kalita";
$uri = URI->new($url);

#Creating a user agent and sending a request, and getting response
$ua = LWP::UserAgent->new();
$headerRequest = HTTP::Request->new(HEAD=>$uri);
```

```perl
$headerResponse = $ua->request ($headerRequest);
if ($headerResponse->is_success){
    $headers = $headerResponse->headers;
}
else{
    print $headerResponse->error_as_HTML;
    exit 0;
}

print  "-" x 60, "\n";
print "THE HEADER RESPONSE IS...\n",
      $headerResponse->as_string, "\n";
print  "-" x 60, "\n";
print "status line: ", $headerResponse->status_line, "  status\n";
print  "-" x 60, "\n";

print "HEADERS AS STRING IS...\n", $headers->as_string, "\n";
print  "-" x 60, "\n";
print "content type: ", $headers->content_type, "\n";
print "date: ", $headers->date, "\n";
print "server: ", $headers->server, "\n";

printf "%-15s %-30s\n", "Header Name", "Header Value";
print  "-" x 60, "\n";
$headers->scan (\&headerScanner);
print  "-" x 60, "\n";

#callback subroutine to process header entries
sub headerScanner{
    my ($headerName, $headerValue) = @_;
    printf "%-15s %-30s\n", $headerName, $headerValue;
}
```

The program uses the LWP::UserAgent and HTTP::Request modules. It also uses a module called URI to create a *Uniform Resource Identifier* for the URL to fetch. It is not really necessary to create a URI out of a URL to use it. We do so for illustration purposes only.

The program is given a value for a URL it fetches. A URL is given in the form of a string. The program converts the URL to an URI object. A URI is a more generalized abstraction of an address than a URL. However, the differences are not important to us at this time.

```perl
$url = "http://www.cs.uccs.edu/~kalita";
$uri = URI->new($url);
```

As mentioned earlier, it is not necessary to convert the URL to a URI, a more generalized address, for the purpose of this program. Next, the program creates a user agent object using the following line.

```perl
$ua = LWP::UserAgent->new();
```

The program also creates an HTTP request and passes this request to the user agent.

```perl
$headerRequest = HTTP::Request->new(HEAD=>$uri);
```

The request is for header information, and takes the URI created earlier as an argument. The argument could have been a URL in string form as well. Next, the request is given to the user agent's `request` method.

```
$headerResponse = $ua->request ($headerRequest);
```

The user agent's `request` method opens a TCP-based communication socket with the server. If successful, the user agent converts the request to the proper HTTP format and sends it to the server over the socket. We discussed sockets in detail in Chapter 7. The LWP bundle of modules makes it unnecessary to perform low-level tasks such as creating sockets for Web client programming, making things simple for the programmer. The user agent waits for the response to come back from the server. When the response comes, the user agent composes an `HTTP::Response` object out of it automatically. Thus, `$headerResponse` is an instance of the `HTTP::Response` class, whether the request was successful in fetching the header or not. The `HTTP::Response` class has two methods `is_success` and `headers`. If the HTTP request is successful in obtaining the HEAD information for the URI, the `is_success` returns true. If the request fails, the program prints the error sent to it by the server in HTML format and exits. The `error_as_HTML` method of the `HTTP::Response` class does so.

The `HTTP::Response` object has an internal format for storage in the program. To print the content of the object in string form, we can use the `as_string` method provided by the `HTTP::Response` object. If we look at the output printed below, we see that the statement below

```
print "THE HEADER RESPONSE IS...\n",
     $headerResponse->as_string, "\n";
```

prints the complete response that comes back from the server. The information printed by the statement is given later in this discussion. The first line is the *HTTP response* line we discussed earlier. It says the protocol used is HTTP/1.1. The request was successful and came back with a 200 status code. The status is given as OK in text form. Following this, there is a list of HTTP header and value pairs. The headers listed here are Connection, Date, Server, Content-Length, etc. The value of `$headerResponse` when printed as a string contains one or more blank lines at the end although the HTTP specification says there should be only one blank line. Thus, the `HTTP::Response` class has several useful methods such as `is_success`, `is_error`, `as_string`, `error_as_HTML`, etc. Another method that we use in this program is `status_line` that prints just the status line or the first line of the response. Two other useful methods that the `HTTP::Response` object has are called `headers` and `content`. Every HTTP request comes back with a response that contains headers. However, for the HEAD HTTP request, no content comes back. Thus, we capture only the headers in the response if the request is successful. The capturing is done in the program inside the `if-else` statement.

```
    $headers = $headerResponse->headers;
```

The `headers` method of the `HTTP::Response` class returns an object of yet another class called the `HTTP::Headers` class that is also available as a part of the LWP bundle of packages. When sending out an HTTP Request, one can optionally create headers to be sent out with the request. On the flip side, when a response has come back, the headers that have come back can be captured for examination.

The `HTTP::Headers` class also has several methods that are quite useful in examining the contents of the headers. Examples of these methods are `content_type`, `date`, and `server` used in this program. One interesting method that `HTTP::Headers` class has is called `scan`. A call to `scan` is given below.

```
$headers->scan (\&headerScanner);
```

The argument taken by `scan` is a reference to a function. The function must take two arguments, the name of a header and the value of a header. The definition of such a function used in the program is given below.

```
sub headerScanner{
    my ($headerName, $headerValue) = @_;
    printf "%-15s %-30s\n", $headerName, $headerValue;
}
```

A function such as this is called a *callback* function. A callback function is applied to every header in turn. It is called with a header name and a single value. It can do whatever it pleases with the arguments. In this case, it simply prints them in the form of a formatted string. Note that if a header has several values, the function is called once for each value. The output of this program is given below.

```
------------------------------------------------------------
THE HEADER RESPONSE IS...
HTTP/1.1 200 OK
Connection: close
Date: Wed, 04 Apr 2001 20:01:12 GMT
Accept-Ranges: bytes
Server: Apache/1.3.14 (Unix)   (Red-Hat/Linux) PHP/3.0.18 mod_perl/1.23
Content-Length: 4225
Content-Type: text/html
ETag: "650328-1081-3ab64734"
Last-Modified: Mon, 19 Mar 2001 17:51:48 GMT
Client-Date: Wed, 04 Apr 2001 13:04:48 GMT
Client-Peer: 128.198.162.68:80


------------------------------------------------------------
status line: 200 OK   status
------------------------------------------------------------
HEADERS AS STRING IS...
Connection: close
Date: Wed, 04 Apr 2001 20:01:12 GMT
Accept-Ranges: bytes
Server: Apache/1.3.14 (Unix)   (Red-Hat/Linux) PHP/3.0.18 mod_perl/1.23
Content-Length: 4225
Content-Type: text/html
ETag: "650328-1081-3ab64734"
Last-Modified: Mon, 19 Mar 2001 17:51:48 GMT
Client-Date: Wed, 04 Apr 2001 13:04:48 GMT
Client-Peer: 128.198.162.68:80


------------------------------------------------------------
content type: text/html
date: 986414472
server: Apache/1.3.14 (Unix)   (Red-Hat/Linux) PHP/3.0.18 mod_perl/1.23
Header Name     Header Value
------------------------------------------------------------
Connection      close
Date            Wed, 04 Apr 2001 20:01:12 GMT
Accept-Ranges   bytes
Server          Apache/1.3.14 (Unix)   (Red-Hat/Linux) PHP/3.0.18 mod_perl/1.23
```

```
Content-Length   4225
Content-Type     text/html
ETag             "650328-1081-3ab64734"
Last-Modified    Mon, 19 Mar 2001 17:51:48 GMT
Client-Date      Wed, 04 Apr 2001 13:04:48 GMT
Client-Peer      128.198.162.68:80
------------------------------------------------------------
```

9.2.2 Obtaining a URL From a Web Server

The next program makes a call to the HTTP method HEAD to obtain information on a URL. If the call to HEAD returns successfully, only then the program obtains the actual file. The program follows.

Program 9.6

```perl
#!/usr/bin/perl
#file fetchHeadURL1.pl

use LWP::UserAgent;
use URI;
use strict;
$" = "\n\t";

my ($url, $uri, $ua);
my ($localFile);
my ($headerRequest, $headerResponse);
my ($contentRequest, $contentResponse, $headers, $content, @hrefs);

$url = "http://www.cs.uccs.edu/~kalita";
$uri = URI->new($url);
$ua = LWP::UserAgent->new();

$localFile = "assamorg.html";

$headerRequest = HTTP::Request->new(HEAD=>$uri);
$headerResponse = $ua->request ($headerRequest);
unless ($headerResponse->is_success){
    print $headerResponse->error_as_HTML;
    exit 0;
}

$contentRequest = HTTP::Request->new(GET=>$uri);
$contentResponse = $ua->request ($contentRequest);
$headers = $contentResponse->headers;
$content = $contentResponse->content;

printf "%-15s %-30s\n", "Header Name", "Header Value";
print   "-" x 60, "\n";
$headers->scan (\&headerScanner);
print   "-" x 60, "\n";
```

```
#get gets the URL as a string
@hrefs = ($content =~ /<A\s+href\s*=\s*"([^"]+)"/ig);
print "All hrefs in the page = \n\t@hrefs\n";

open FILE, ">$localFile";
print FILE $content;
close FILE;

#callback subroutine to process header entries
sub headerScanner{
    my ($headerName, $headerValue) = @_;
    printf "%-15s %-30s\n", $headerName, $headerValue;
}
```

Like the previous program, this program also is given a URL which it converts to a URI object. It creates a LWP::UserAgent object and sends out an HTTP request for the HEAD of a URI using the request method of the LWP::UserAgent object. If the HEAD request is unsuccessful, the program prints the error and exits. If the HEAD request is successful, it makes up a GET request, sends it over and then captures the response. The following lines of code do that.

```
$contentRequest = HTTP::Request->new(GET=>$uri);
$contentResponse = $ua->request ($contentRequest);
$headers = $contentResponse->headers;
$content = $contentResponse->content;
```

The GET method requests a URI on the server. As usual, the request is sent to the server by using the request method of the LWP::UserAgent object. The response that comes back from the server is called is $contentResponse. The response captured by the user agent is automatically an HTTP::Response object. We call the headers method to capture the header part of the response. Unlike the previous program, this time we also call the content method to capture the content in the variable $content. In the previous program, we fetched only the HEAD from a Web server and hence, the content part of the response was empty. But, this time, the content part contains the actual text of the file requested. The headers method returns an object of type HTTP::Headers whereas the content returns the actual content of the requested URL. The content can be textual or binary.

Before we look at the requested URI's contents, we look at the HTTP headers that came back with the file. HTTP headers always accompany a response from a server. We make a call to the scan method of the HTTP::Headers class to print the contents of the header lines one by one. Next, we look at the actual content of the file. Since the file requested is small in size, we handle it directly. This program uses a regular expression to cull all URLs used in the file fetched and print them on the screen. The program also prints the contents of the file fetched into a local file, thus mirroring the Web page locally.

The output of the program is given below.

```
Header Name      Header Value
-------------------------------------------------------------
Connection       close
Date             Wed, 04 Apr 2001 20:03:52 GMT
Accept-Ranges    bytes
Server           Apache/1.3.14 (Unix)  (Red-Hat/Linux) PHP/3.0.18 mod_perl/1.23
Content-Length   4225
Content-Type     text/html
```

```
ETag                "650328-1081-3ab64734"
Last-Modified       Mon, 19 Mar 2001 17:51:48 GMT
Client-Date         Wed, 04 Apr 2001 13:07:28 GMT
Client-Peer         128.198.162.68:80
Link                <default.css>; rel="stylesheet"; type="text/css"
Title               Jugal Kalita
-----------------------------------------------------------
All hrefs in the page =
xml/index.xml
teaching-philosophy.pdf
schedule.html
research.html
http://www.shillong.com
http://www.autoindia.com
http://www.indiashipping.com
http://www.assam.org
http://www.assamcompany.com
cultural.html
http://www.upenn.edu/index.html
http://www.usask.ca
http://www.rahul.net/kgpnet/iit/iit.html
http://www.uccs.edu
http://www.cs.uccs.edu/~kalita/accesswatch/accesswatch-1.32/index.html
```

It is not really necessary to issue the HEAD request to gather information about a page before issuing the GET command to fetch the page. One can simply use the GET command bypassing the HEAD command. The HEAD command is used only if our goal is to find out certain information about the file such as its last modification date before deciding whether to fetch the file or not. This could be useful if one is trying to create a local mirror of a large Web site. Only files modified after the last time mirroring was done need to be fetched, possibly reducing the amount of fetching to be done to a great extent. Fetching the head or the whole file both need one transmission over the network. But, the head is a lot less information than the whole file, and thus, the amount of transmission as well computation, both at the server end and the client end is reduced quite a bit.

The following program fetches a URL without fetching the head information first. The program also culls out all the hrefed URLs specified in the file, just like the previous program.

Program 9.7

```
#!/usr/bin/perl
#file fetchURL3.pl

use LWP::UserAgent;
use URI;
use strict;
$" = "\n\t";

my ($url, $uri, $ua);
my ($localFile);
my ($contentRequest, $contentResponse, $headers, $content, @hrefs);

$localFile = "assamorg.html";
```

```perl
$url = "http://www.cs.uccs.edu/~kalita";
$uri = URI->new($url);
$ua = LWP::UserAgent->new();

$contentRequest = HTTP::Request->new(GET=>$uri);
$contentResponse = $ua->request ($contentRequest);
if ($contentResponse->is_success){
    $content = $contentResponse->content;
}
else{
    print $contentResponse->error_as_HTML;
    exit 0;
}

#get gets the URL as a string
@hrefs = ($content =~ /<A\s+href\s*=\s*"([^"]+)"/ig);
print "All hrefs in the page = \n\t@hrefs\n";

open FILE, ">$localFile";
print FILE $content;
close FILE;
```

The program sends out at GET method using the `request` method of the user agent. When the response comes back, it uses the `is_success` method of the `HTTP::Response` object to see if the request was successfully processed by the server. If the response contained an error, the program exits. Otherwise, it fetches the content from the response, culls out all the `hrefed` URLs, like before. It also prints the fetched file to a local mirror file.

9.2.3 Automatically Filling a *GET* Form Using `HTTP::Request`

In section 9.1.2, we see how a form that uses the GET method can be automatically filled using the `LWP::Simple` module. We see in that section that filling a GET form and obtaining response is very simple. Of course, the same can be done with the more complex LWP modules such as `LWP::UserAgent`, `HTTP::Request`, `HTTP::Response` and others.

A GET form request is sent to the Web server in a single transmission as a URL. That is why processing GET forms is easy. The following program is similar in objective and functionality to the program described in 9.1.2.

Program 9.8

```perl
#!/usr/bin/perl
#file bordersISBN2.pl

use strict;
use HTTP::Request;
use LWP::UserAgent;

my ($url, $content);
my ($ua, $contentRequest, $contentResponse, $price);
my $ISBN = "1565922433";
```

```perl
print "ISBN = $ISBN\n";

#Make up the URL to search for the book's ISBN
$url = "http://search.borders.com/fcgi-bin/db2www/search/search.d2w/Details?";
$url .= "code=$ISBN&mediaType=Book&searchType=ISBNUPC";

$ua = LWP::UserAgent->new();
$contentRequest = HTTP::Request->new(GET=>$url);
$contentResponse = $ua->request($contentRequest);
if ($contentResponse->is_success){
    $content = $contentResponse->content;
}
else{
    print $contentResponse->error_as_HTML;
    exit 0;
}
($price) =  ($content =~ m#Our Price:.+?\$(.+?)<#si);
print "price = $price\n";
```

The program is almost exactly like the programs we see in Section 9.2. The program uses the `LWP::UserAgent` module to create a new user agent called $ua. The request is formed in terms of a URL where the form parameters follow the ? mark following the URL. Although we have a statement

```perl
use HTTP::Request;
```

on the top of the program, it is not necessary to use the `HTTP::Request` module. The form is automatically submitted by creating an `HTTP::Request` object with the URL as the argument. Note that, in general, it is not necessary to convert the URL to a URI before sending it to a Web server, as we have done in examples in previous sections.

The response that comes back from the server is captured by the user agent $ua. The response is automatically an `HTTP::Response` object. If the response has a successful status code, the HTML content of the content is saved in the variable $content. This variable is later parsed to obtain the price of the book with the ISBN number given in the variable $ISBN.

There is another module called `HTTP::Request::Common` that makes it slightly more convenient to write common HTTP requests. For GET forms, we need to simply set up a user agent and then issue a GET request as given below.

```perl
$contentRequest = GET $url;
```

Thus, it is as simple as the `LWP::Simple` module to use. The GET $url call automatically sets up the appropriate `HTTP::Request` object. It also captures the response coming back from the Web server automatically. A program given earlier in this section can be rewritten as shown below.

Program 9.9

```perl
#!/usr/bin/perl
#file bordersISBN4.pl

use strict;
use HTTP::Request::Common;
use LWP::UserAgent;
```

```perl
my ($url, $content);
my ($ua, $contentRequest, $contentResponse, $price);
my $ISBN = "1565922433";
print "ISBN = $ISBN\n";

#Make up the URL to search for the book's ISBN
$url = "http://search.borders.com/fcgi-bin/db2www/search/search.d2w/Details?";
$url .= "code=$ISBN&mediaType=Book&searchType=ISBNUPC";

$ua = LWP::UserAgent->new();
$contentRequest = GET $url;
$contentResponse = $ua->request ($contentRequest);
if ($contentResponse->is_success){
    $content = $contentResponse->content;
}
else{
    print $contentResponse->error_as_HTML;
    exit 0;
}
($price) =  ($content =~ m#Our Price:.+?\$(.+?)<#si);
print "price = $price\n";
```

9.2.4   Automatically Filling a *POST* Form

We have seen how forms that use the GET method can be submitted automatically. We can do so with forms submitted using the POST method as well, although it takes a little more work to do so. The following program finds the price of a book given the ISBN number at an Internet bookstore called powells.com.

Program 9.10

```perl
#!/usr/bin/perl
#file powellISBN1.pl

use strict;
#use LWP::Debug qw(+);
use HTTP::Response;
use HTTP::Request;
use LWP::UserAgent;

my ($ua, $response, $url);
my ($content, $req);
my $searchFor = "1565922433";
my $searchType = "ISBN";
print "ISBN = $searchFor\n";

$ua = LWP::UserAgent->new();
$ua->agent ("Mozilla/6.0; compatible");
$ua->timeout(200);
```

```
$url = "http://www.powells.com/search/DTSearch/search";
$req = HTTP::Request->new(POST=>$url);
$req->content(qq{isbn=$searchFor});

$response = $ua->request($req);
$content = $response->content();


###########################****************************************
###NEEDS MORE WORK.   IT'S PICKING UP THE FIRST PRICE
#ONLY, BUT POWELLS.COM MAY RETURN SEVERAL ENTRIES FOR THE SAME BOOK.
###########################*******************
my ($price) =  ($content =~ m#RESULT ITEM START.+?\$(.+?)<#si);
print "price = $price\n";
```

The program creates a user agent $ua and gives the user agent a couple of attributes. Using the agent method, it identifies itself as compatible to Mozilla/6.0 type browsers. It also sets a timeout of 200 seconds to get the result back. It then specifies the URL of the form's action attribute in terms of the variable $url. This URL has to be found by examining the source of the appropriate Web page where the form for searching book prices at *powells.com* is situated. We determine that the HTML source of the form specifies that it is using the POST method. The GET method is default if nothing is specified. An HTTP::Request object is created using the URL as the argument for a POST form. The HTTP::Request object's new method takes one or more arguments in the form of hash fields. One such hash field's name is POST and the corresponding value is the URL. The HTTP::Request object $req uses the content method to specify the form element names and their values. In this case, there is only one relevant form attribute and it is called isbn. Its value is given as the value of the variable $searchFor. qq is the quoting function that allows interpolation of variable values. It is like using double quotes to delimit a string. If there were several fields, each field's name and value are written separated from the next pair by a comma.

The user agent uses the request method of the LWP::UserAgent object to send the HTTP request to the Web server. The Web server responds and the response is the result of the request method. The content method of the HTTP::Response object gives the content of the response, as opposed to the header. The response is very simply parsed to obtain the price of the book with the given ISBN number. Once again, to find out where the price occurs in the returned Web page, we need to fill in the form manually several times and see if we can determine a simple way to figure out where the price occurs in the returned result. In this specific case, the price always occurs after the phrase RESULT ITEM START. However, in this particular store *powells.com*, the search for a single book can return several prices. Here, only the first one is captured.

We have seen in section 9.2.3 how the HTTP::Request::Common module can be used to process GET forms. The HTTP::Request::Common module can be used to submit POST forms as well. The following program is a rewrite of the program given earlier in this section.

Program 9.11

```
#!/usr/bin/perl
#file powellISBN2.pl

use strict;
#use LWP::Debug qw(+);
use HTTP::Response;
use LWP::UserAgent;
use HTTP::Request::Common;
```

```
my ($ua, $response, $url);
my ($content, $req);
my $searchFor = "1565922433";
my $searchType = "ISBN";
print "ISBN = $searchFor\n";

$ua = LWP::UserAgent->new();
$ua->agent ("Mozilla/5.0");
$ua->timeout(600);

$url = "http://www.powells.com/search/DTSearch/search";
$req =    POST "$url", ["isbn" => $searchFor];
$response = $ua->request($req);
$content = $response->content();

my ($price) =    ($content =~ m#RESULT ITEM START.+?\$(.+?)<#si);
print "price = $price\n";
```

In this program, the statement that sends out the POST form is given below.

```
$req =    POST "$url", ["isbn" => $searchFor];
```

There is only one relevant field in the form. If there were several fields, the field name, value pairs are separated from each other by commas. Of course, instead of having the URL defined earlier, we could have specified the URL with the POST call directly, as given below.

```
$req = POST "http://www.powells.com/search/DTSearch/search",
    ["isbn" => $searchFor];
```

9.3   Using Cookies

Cookies are mechanism by which a Web server can store information on a Web client. This information can be later retrieved by the Web server. Cookies are used frequently by many Web servers to keep track of who comes and visits the sites. The first time someone comes to a site, the server can send one or more cookies to the client. The client stores the cookies in a local file, if the client is enabled to do so. Many Web servers do not allow a client to visit the site unless cookies are enabled. Some sites allow only partial access if the client is not enabled to accept cookies.

The following program is somewhat complex. It is a small part of a much bigger program, written by the author and others, that fetches news items from various on-line sources, puts them together, removes duplicates, classifies them automatically, and then presents the news items to every individual that visits the Web site as a personalized newspaper. The details are fairly involved using sophisticated techniques based on artificial intelligence based learning.

The program presented here logs onto the site apnewstracker.com using a login name and a password. The top page of the site at a certain instant of time is shown in Figure 9.4. If the login is unsuccessful, it attempts to login several times, waiting a specified number of seconds after each attempt. The number of times is obtained from a separate file that we call a configuration file. The site sends back cookies to the browser and the browser needs to save them locally to be able to proceed further with retrieving the news items posted on the site. If the login is successful, the site automatically returns a page containing an index

Figure 9.4: The Top Page at `www.apnewstracker.com`

of news items with a headline for each item and a link to a URL containing the text of the item. The index page for a particular instant of time is shown in Figure 9.5. The program parses the index page sent to it, and culls the URLs of the individual news item. There are several parts to the index page and the program picks out the news items in the first part only. The first part is indicated by the presence of certain specific syntactical items in the HTML of the index Web page. Next, the program fetches each one of the news items. A partial Web page for a specific news item is shown in Figure 9.6.

To fetch each news item URL, it has to present cookies to the Web server along with the request to fetch the page. In the more sophisticated program not discussed here, the program parses each news item's text, saves it in some form in a database, classifies it into pre-determined categories, and performs much additional computation to be useful. We do not present these other processing steps in this simplified version of the program since these are irrelevant to our current discussion.

The program's text is given below, followed by more explanation.

Program 9.12

```perl
#!/usr/bin/perl
#file apget1.pl

use strict;
#use LWP::Debug qw (+);
use HTTP::Response;
use LWP::UserAgent;
use HTTP::Cookies;
use HTTP::Request::Common;
use Time::Local;
use AP_config;

###Main Program ###############################
##########Global declarations. These are declared in  a configuration file####

my ($cookie_jar, $ua, $loginResponse, $newsItemIndex);
my (%newsIndexHash);
my ($itemURL, $itemText);

#Create cookie_jar to be stored in file $AP_config::cookieFile
$cookie_jar = HTTP::Cookies -> new (file => $AP_config::cookieFile,
                    ignore_discard => 1);

#define the user agent
```

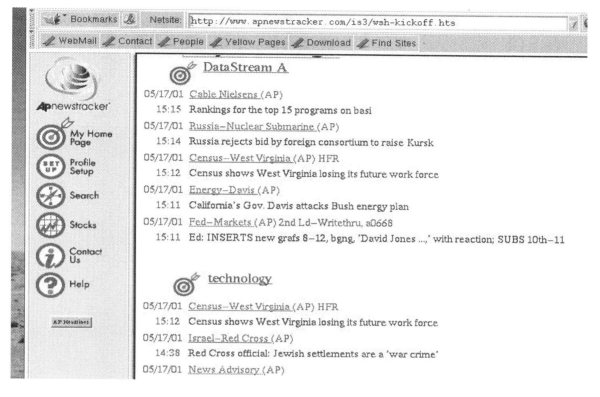

Figure 9.5: The News Index Page at www.apnewstracker.com

Figure 9.6: A News Item at www.apnewstracker.com

```perl
$ua = LWP::UserAgent -> new ();
$ua -> agent ($AP_config::userAgentDescription);
$ua -> timeout ($AP_config::userAgentTimeout); #default is 180 seconds

#Do for ever. Login+fetch news items every
#$$AP_config::waitTimeBetweenFetches seconds
while (1){
    my $noLoginTriesThisTime = $AP_config::noLoginTries;

  LOGIN:{
        print "\nTrying to login to $AP_config::loginURL...\n\n";
        #log into the AP site and Fetch the news item index
        $loginResponse = &login($ua, $cookie_jar);
        print "After login\n";

        if (!$loginResponse){
            print "Couldn't login\n";
            $noLoginTriesThisTime--;
                  #Reduce the number of times login will be tried sequentially
            if ($noLoginTriesThisTime){
                print "SLEEPING $AP_config::waitTimeBetweenFailedLogins seconds...\n";
                sleep ($AP_config::waitTimeBetweenFailedLogins);
                goto LOGIN;  #Try to login again
            }else{
                print "Tried logging in $AP_config::noLoginTries, didn't succeed, exiting...\n";
                exit 1;
            }
        }
    } #LOGIN block ends

    print "Just logged onto the http://www.apnewstracker.com site...\n";

    for (my $i = 1; $i <= $AP_config::repeatFetchTimesBetweenLogins; $i++){
        #logged in at this point
        $newsItemIndex = &fetchIndexPage ($ua, $cookie_jar);

        #Parse the news index page that comes back; if there is an HTTP error,
        #$newsItemIndex is the number 0
        %newsIndexHash = ();
        if (!$newsItemIndex){
            print "Couldn't fetch news items index page...\n";
            print "SLEEPING $AP_config::waitTimeBetweenFailedLogins";
            print "seconds before retrying login...\n";
            sleep ($AP_config::waitTimeBetweenFailedLogins);
            goto LOGIN;  #Try to login again
        }
    }

    &parseIndexPage ($newsItemIndex); #This puts values in %newsIndexHash

    #Next, need to fetch the URLs specified in the index page
    #But, need to fetch only those URLs that are not already there in  cache
    foreach $itemURL (reverse (sort (keys %newsIndexHash))){
        $itemText = &fetchNewsItemURL ($ua, $cookie_jar, $itemURL);
        if (!$itemText){
                    print "Could not fetch url: $itemURL\n";
        }
    } #foreach ends

    #sleep for a while
    print "\nSLEEPING FOR $AP_config::waitTimeBetweenFetches SECONDS...\n\n";
    sleep ($AP_config::waitTimeBetweenFetches);
        } #for my $i ends, fetched news indices
           #$AP_config::repeatFetchTimesBetweenLogin times

} #while (1) ends

##########SUBROUTINES###############################
###############sub login#######################
#login to the AP newstracker page. This page is at
#$AP_config::baseURL = http://www.newstracker.com.
#The form to fill in to login is at $AP_config::loginURL
sub login{
    my ($ua, $cookie_jar) = @_;

    my ($request, $response);
    my ($indexContents);
```

```
        #add cookie information to the request
        #the request logs one the apnewstracker.com site
        $request = POST $AP_config::loginURL,
                [username => $AP_config::loginName, password => $AP_config::loginPassword];
        print $request->as_string . "\n";
        $cookie_jar -> add_cookie_header ($request);

        #Get the response to the request and extract cookies from what comes back
        $response = $ua -> request ($request);
        $cookie_jar -> extract_cookies ($response);

        #print HTTP error message if the user couldn't login or there was an HTTP error
        if ($response -> is_success){
            return $response;
        } else {
            print "Could not login to the http://www.apnewstracker.com site\n";
            print $response -> error_as_HTML;
            return 0;    #If it couldn't login or there was an HTTP error, it returns the number 0
        }
} #sub login ends


###############sub fetchIndexPage###############################
#Fetch the index page of news items
sub fetchIndexPage{

    my ($ua, $cookie_jar) = @_;
    #print "Inside fetchIndexPage subroutine\n";

    my ($request, $response);
    my ($indexContents);

    #Now, get the actual page where the news index is.
    #This page http://www.apnewstracker.com/is3/runprofile.hts is updated
    #every minute or two.
    $request = GET $AP_config::newsIndexURL;
    $cookie_jar -> add_cookie_header ($request);
    $response = $ua -> request ($request);
    $cookie_jar -> extract_cookies ($response);

    #Parse the news index page if it comes back. If there
    #is HTTP error, print an error page
    if ($response -> is_success){
        print "Obtained $AP_config::newsIndexURL\n";
        $indexContents = $response -> content;
        return $indexContents;
    } else {
        print $response -> error_as_HTML;
        return 0;    #return 0 if there is a HTTP error
    }
} #sub fetchIndexPage   ends

###############sub parseIndexPage###################################
#A subroutine that parses the AP News index page:
#               http://www.apnewstracker.com/is3/runprofile.hts
#The page is passed to the subroutine as a string

sub parseIndexPage{
    my ($fileContents) = @_;
    my (@tables, @items);
    my ($item, $month, $day, $year, $url, $title, $hour, $minute, $headline);

    my ($relevantPart)  =
        ($fileContents =~ m#DataStream A</FONT>(.+?)technology<#s);

    @items = ($relevantPart =~ m#(<TABLE.+?</TABLE>)#gsi);

    foreach $item (@items){
        #The sequencing of the substitutions and pattern matches matter
        ($month, $day, $year) = ($item =~ m#(\d{2})/(\d{2})/(\d{2})#);

        ($url, $title) = ($item =~ m#<a href="([^"]+).+?>(.+?)</a>#);
        $item =~ s#<a.+?</a>##gsi; #obtained the URL, now remove <a...>...</a>

        #Removing all the things below to clean things up.
```

```
        #Otherwise, difficult to parse
        $item =~ s#<!--.+?-->##gs;   #remove comments
        $item =~ s#[\s]+# #gs;        #remove multiple spaces
        $item =~ s#</?table.+?>##gsi;
        $item =~ s#</?tr.+?>##gsi;
        $item =~ s#</?td.+?>##gsi;
        $item =~ s/ / /gs;       #substitute an   by white space
        $item =~ s#<font.+?>##gsi;
        $item =~ s#</font>##gi;

        ($hour, $minute)  = ($item =~ /(\d{2}):(\d{2})/);
        ($headline) = ($item =~ /$hour:$minute(.+)/sg);
        ($headline) = ($headline =~ /^\s*(.+)\s*/sg);  #remove spaces from front and end
        #Sometimes there are HTML tags in headline, remove them
        $headline =~ s#<.+?>##gs;

        print "Parsing index item...\n";
        $year = "21$year";
        print "time = $month/$day/$year $hour:$minute\n";
        print "title = $title\n";
        print "headline = $headline\n\n";

        my $itemData = join ":::",
                ($year, $month, $day, $hour, $minute, $title, $headline);
        $newsIndexHash{$AP_config::baseURL.$url} = $itemData;
    } #foreach ends
} #sub parseIndexPage ends

###############sub fetchNewsItemURL #########################
###A subroutine that fetches a news item URL ############
sub fetchNewsItemURL{
    my ($ua, $cookie_jar, $url) = @_;
    my $request = GET $url;
    $cookie_jar -> add_cookie_header ($request);
    my $response = $ua -> request ($request);

    $cookie_jar -> extract_cookies ($response);

    if ($response -> is_success){
        my $newsItemText = $response -> content;
        return $newsItemText;
    }else{
        print $response -> error_as_HTML;
        print "Couldn't fetch news item URL: $url\n";
        return 0;
    }
}
```

The program uses several modules we have seen earlier: HTTP::Response, LWP::UserAgent, HTTP::Cookies and HTTP::Request::Common. These are pre-defined well-regarded modules that can be downloaded from the Internet. We also have a module called AP_config that declares and gives values to certain variables used in the program. The module is shown below. The login name and the password have been replaced by a sequence of Xs.

Program 9.13

```
package AP_config;
#Define all site-specific global variables
use strict;
use vars qw($baseURL $loginURL $newsIndexURL);
use vars qw($loginName $loginPassword);  #To login to apnewstracker.com
use vars qw($waitTimeBetweenFetches $waitTimeBetweenFailedLogins);
use vars qw($repeatFetchTimesBetweenLogins $noLoginTries);
use vars qw($userAgent $userAgentTimeout);

$baseURL = "http://www.apnewstracker.com";
```

```
$loginURL = "$baseURL" . "/is3/wsh-kickoff.hts";
$newsIndexURL = "$baseURL" . "/is3/runprofile.hts";
$loginName = "XXXXXXX";
$loginPassword = "XXXXXX";

#Global variables for database access
$waitTimeBetweenFetches = 180;
$waitTimeBetweenFailedLogins = 180;
$noLoginTries = 10;
$repeatFetchTimesBetweenLogins = 20;
$userAgent = "Mozilla/4.7 (Compatible; MSIE 5.0; Windows2000)";
$userAgentTimeout =400;

1;
```

One of the first things that the main program does is to specify a file to store cookies sent by a Web server.

```
#Create cookie_jar to be stored in file $AP_config::cookieFile
$cookie_jar = HTTP::Cookies -> new (file => $AP_config::cookieFile,
                     ignore_discard => 1);
```

This is done by creating a new HTTP::Cookies object. The call to the new object constructor method takes one or more parameters, given in the form of a hash. The file argument gives the name of the file where cookies are stored when they are sent to the browser by the Web server. The second argument is boolean. It is not necessary that we use it like we do here. This parameter instructs that the program save even cookies that are requested to be destroyed by the server. Initially, the cookie file is empty.

Next, the program creates a user agent $ua, gives a description to the agent using the agent method and specifies a time after which the user agent should give up by using the timeout method. Once the setup is over, the program goes into a while loop where it attempts to log in the the www.apnewstracker.com site. The logging is done using the login subroutine that takes the user agent and the cookie file, called $cookie_jar, as arguments. If the login is not successful, the program sleeps for a pre-determined amount of time and retries. It attempts to login only a pre-specified number of times, say 10. If even after all attempts, the program does not succeed, it dies. This can happen because of reasons such as that the server is down or is overloaded, or the server is unreachable.

Once the program has logged in to the site, it fetches the index page a specified number of times after which it logs in again. This makes the program robust because it was found that the site logged the program out after a certain amount of time. The way the program is written now, it can go for many days fetching news items without any problems. The fetching of the news index page is done using the following statement.

```
        #logged in at this point
        $newsItemIndex = &fetchIndexPage ($ua, $cookie_jar);
```

If the news item index page cannot be fetched, it generally means that the program has been logged out. Therefore, in such a case, the program tries to log in again. The cookie file, which is a component of the cookie jar being passed as argument to fetchIndexPage may look like the following after the program has logged in.

```
#LWP-Cookies-1.0
Set-Cookie3: entitlements="dsa{?tag"; path="/";
domain="www.apnewstracker.com"; path_spec;
     discard; ; version=0
Set-Cookie3: numhits=12; path="/"; domain="www.apnewstracker.com";
```

```
path_spec;
     discard; ; version=0
Set-Cookie3: sessionid=470092; path="/"; domain="www.apnewstracker.com"; path_spec;
     discard; ; version=0
Set-Cookie3: sortval=1; path="/"; domain="www.apnewstracker.com";
path_spec;
     discard; ; version=0
Set-Cookie3: userid=6001210; path="/"; domain="www.apnewstracker.com";
path_spec;
     discard; ; version=0
Set-Cookie3: usertype=A; path="/"; domain="www.apnewstracker.com";
path_spec;
     discard; ; version=0
```

Each individual line has been broken into two for the purpose of this example since the lines are too long to be printed.

We do not discuss the syntax of the cookies here. In the cookie file displayed above, each row stands for a cookie.

After fetching an index page, the program parses the index page using the following call.

```
&parseIndexPage ($newsItemIndex); #This puts values in %newsIndexHash
```

Parsing places the news items in the hash %newsIndexHash. Finally, the program goes through each item in this hash and fetches the text of each news item by following the URL for the news item.

```
foreach $itemURL (reverse (sort (keys %newsIndexHash))){
    $itemText = &fetchNewsItemURL ($ua, $cookie_jar, $itemURL);
    if (!$itemText){
            print "Could not fetch url: $itemURL\n";
    }
} #foreach ends
```

In the call to fetchNewsItemURL that fetches individual URLs corresponding to individual news items, the cookies in the stored cookie file are sent to the Web server. This sending of cookies needs to be done every time when we attempt to retrieve pages from the Web server. This is important. If the appropriate cookies are not sent with the request, the server rejects the request. In this particular case, since we obtain the cookies to be sent from the cookie file that got the cookies from the previous page fetched, everything should be in proper order.

The program has several subroutines: login, fetchIndexPage, parseIndexPage and fetchNewsItemURL. We briefly look at each one next.

The subroutine login takes a user agent and a cookie jar as the arguments. It makes a POST request using the following statement.

```
$request = POST $AP_config::loginURL,
    [username => $AP_config::loginName, password => $AP_config::loginPassword];
```

The request is printed on the screen as a string for verification purposes. The HTTP::Request object needs to have appropriate cookie headers set. This is done using the following statement.

```
$cookie_jar -> add_cookie_header ($request);
```

The contents of the cookies as well as all HTTP interactions taking place between the server and the client can be seen if we use the LWP::Debug module and import the + symbol. In the current program, the line that imports this module has been commented out. The line looks like the following and occurs on the top of the program.

```
#use LWP::Debug qw (+);
```

If we want to see the HTTP interactions, this line needs to be uncommented. Seeing what is going back and forth between the Web server and the Web client is instructive as well as useful for debugging.

The `HTTP::Request` object `$request` must have a valid URL attribute before the `add_cookie_headers` method can be called. A response is obtained whether the request is successful or not. The cookies are extracted from the response and the cookie file, the so-called cookie jar, is updated using the following statement.

```
$cookie_jar -> extract_cookies ($response);
```

The subroutine then looks to see if the status code associated with the response indicates success. If so, it returns the response to the calling program. Otherwise, it prints an error message and returns 0 to the calling program. Of course, the extracting of cookies can be done after checking the status code.

The `fetchIndexPage` subroutine also takes the user agent and the cookie jar as arguments. It obtains the index page for news items using the GET function call of the `HTTP::Request::Common` module. Cookie headers are added to the request. From the response, the cookies are extracted and the cookie file is updated if any of the cookie value is new. If successful, `fetchIndexPage` returns the content of the page fetched to the calling program.

The `parseIndexPage` subroutine parses the contents of the index page fetched earlier. We examine the HTML of the index page carefully and determine where the individual news items are. Thus, the HTML-level parsing that takes place in this subroutine is very much dependent on the syntax of the HTML page under consideration. Web sites are known to change the format of their Web pages frequently, and hence, the parsing performed here will have to be changed if the structure of the Web page is found to change. The components obtained for a news item are: `$year`, `$month`, `$day`, `$hour`, `$minute`, `$file` and `$headline`. Once the items of news have been obtained, they are `joined` to form a single string called `$itemData`. This string is stored in the global variable `%newsIndexHash` with the URL of the news item as its key.

The `fetchNewsItemURL` subroutine is simple. It gets the user agent, the cookie file, and the URL to fetch as argument. It creates a GET request, adds the cookie headers to it, and fetches the file.

As indicated earlier, the program described above is the shell of a much more complex program written by the author and others. The program shows that cookies play an important role in Web programming. A lot of Web servers use such cookies, which are small pieces of data, to keep track of information about the clients fetching pages from them. Some cookies are short-lived whereas others are valid for longer periods, such as days or months. Some cookies are to be discarded by the client whereas others are to be saved for a certain duration of time. In the cookie file shown earlier, all cookies are to be discarded after the current session is over.

During a single session, as a Web client goes from page to page within a certain Web site, the server checks the names and contents of the cookies for various informational bits about the client. Without the appropriate cookie names and the appropriate values, the Web server may refuse to send the Web page requested to the client. A cookie may indicate if the user is logged in during this session, when the user logged in the last time, the type of machine and browser being used, etc. Therefore, when we program a Web client to interact with such a Web server, cookie headers need to be appropriately filled in for each Web page request. The cookies are saved in a cookie file and usually this file is updated after each interaction with the Web server. The program discussed above uses cookies fairly extensively and illustrates how they can be manipulated. More detailed discussion on cookies can found on a Web site such as www.netscape.com and www.cookiecentral.com.

Figure 9.7: A Search Form at www.fatbrain.com

9.4 Handling Redirected Web Pages

A problem that a Web client program sometimes faces is that when it requests a page from a Web server, the server responds saying that the page has moved, or something similar. It is possible for Web servers to redirect requests to pages. To find out if such a situation occurs in a specific case, one has to look at the result that comes back from the Web server when a program attempts to fill in a form and get response from a server. Let us take one specific example. Our goal is to find the price of a book at the www.fatbrain.com site given the ISBN number of a book. We start by going to the www.fatbrain.com site and follow the links to a form that allows advanced search for books. The form can be found in the page with the URL http://www1.fatbrain.com/search/AdvancedSearch.asp. The form is shown in Figure 9.7.

We look at the HTML source for this page and see that the ACTION attribute for the form specifies the URL for the program that handles the form data as
http://www1.fatbrain.com/asp/Search/SearchResults.asp.
Also, the form uses the POST method for transmission of data from the client to the server. Based on this knowledge, we write the following program.

Program 9.14

```perl
#!/usr/bin/perl
#file fatISBN.notwork.pl
use strict;
use HTTP::Response;
use HTTP::Request;
use LWP::UserAgent;
use HTTP::Cookies;
use HTTP::Request::Common;
use LWP::Debug qw(+);
```

```
my ($cookie_jar, $ua, $response,$url);
my ($content, $req);
my $searchFor = "0534934056";
$cookie_jar = HTTP::Cookies->new(file=>"cookies.dat");
$ua = LWP::UserAgent->new();
$ua->agent ("Mozilla/5.0");
$ua->timeout(600);

$req = POST "http://www1.fatbrain.com/asp/Search/SearchResults.asp",
     [SearchFunction => "reg",
      VM => "c",
      RegAction => "t",
      ISBN => $searchFor];
$cookie_jar->add_cookie_header($req);
$response = $ua->request($req);
$cookie_jar->extract_cookies($response);
$content = $response->content();
print "****content = $content\n";
```

This program seems adequate for the purpose at hand. Please note that we are using the LWP::Debug module and imported the + symbol to see on the screen the HTTP interactions taking place. When we run this program, we find an unexpected error saying that the page has moved permanently. The HTTP interactions when this program is run and the program's output to the screen are given below. Some lines have been broken into two so that they can be printed without crossing into the margin of the paper.

```
LWP::UserAgent::new: ()
HTTP::Cookies::add_cookie_header: Checking www1.fatbrain.com for cookies
HTTP::Cookies::add_cookie_header: Checking .fatbrain.com for cookies
LWP::UserAgent::request: ()
LWP::UserAgent::simple_request:
                    POST http://www1.fatbrain.com/asp/Search/SearchResults.asp
LWP::UserAgent::_need_proxy: Not proxied
LWP::Protocol::http::request: ()
LWP::Protocol::http::request: POST /asp/Search/SearchResults.asp HTTP/1.0
Host: www1.fatbrain.com
User-Agent: Mozilla/5.0
Content-Length: 51
Content-Type: application/x-www-form-urlencoded

LWP::Protocol::http::request: POST /asp/Search/SearchResults.asp HTTP/1.0
Host: www1.fatbrain.com
User-Agent: Mozilla/5.0
Content-Length: 51
Content-Type: application/x-www-form-urlencoded

LWP::Protocol::http::request: reading response
LWP::Protocol::http::request: HTTP/1.1 301 Moved
Server: Microsoft-IIS/4.0
Date: Thu, 17 May 2001 22:21:18 GMT
Location: http://www1.fatbrain.com/search/SearchResults.asp?
Connection: Keep-Alive
Content-Length: 0
Content-Type: text/html
```

```
Cache-control: private

LWP::Protocol::http::request: HTTP/1.1 301 Moved
LWP::UserAgent::request: Simple response: Moved Permanently
****content =
```

If we carefully look at toward the bottom of this HTTP interaction, we see that it says that the page that we have requested, i.e., the program that is supposed to service the form request has Moved Permanently. In other words, it is possible that the Web server has redirected the request to another URL. To find out where the redirection is taking us, we need to go the Web browser and perform an ISBN search. Assume we fill in the ISBN number box with the valid ISBN number 0534934056 and then click on the Search Now submit button. When the response comes back from the server, we look at the Location box of the browser and see that the URL that is visible is not
http://www1.fatbrain.com/asp/Search/SearchResults.asp, but is
http://www1.fatbrain.com/asp/bookinfo/bookinfo.asp?theisbn=0534934056&vm=. Thus, we see that the form request has been redirected to the second URL from the first. The second URL has a question mark following it, indicating that the submission of the form at the second URL uses the GET method for form submission. In addition, there is one attribute isbn with the ISBN number as its value. The second attribute vm does not have an associated value and thus, seems not useful to the current endeavor. Therefore, we try to write a program that mimics the behavior of the client and the server and thus, sends a GET request to second URL. This new request is given the ISBN as an argument. In addition, this request is given the cookies that came as response to the POST request made to the first URL. Finally, when the response comes back from the second HTTP request, we parse the page and obtain the price of the book. The complete program where we take care of redirection is given below.

Program 9.15

```perl
#!/usr/bin/perl
#file fatISBN.pl
use strict;
use HTTP::Response;
use HTTP::Request;
use LWP::UserAgent;
use HTTP::Cookies;
use HTTP::Request::Common;

#############fatbrain.com starts#######################
my ($cookie_jar, $ua, $response, $sessid,$url);

my ($content, $req);
my $searchFor = "0534934056";
$cookie_jar = HTTP::Cookies->new(file=>"cookies.dat");
$ua = LWP::UserAgent->new();
$ua->agent ("Mozilla/5.0");
$ua->timeout(600);

$req = POST "http://www1.fatbrain.com/asp/Search/SearchResults.asp",
    [SearchFunction => "reg",
    VM => "c",
    RegAction => "t",
    ISBN => $searchFor];
$cookie_jar->add_cookie_header($req);
```

```
$response = $ua->request($req);
$cookie_jar->extract_cookies($response);
$content = $response->content();
$url =
"http://www1.fatbrain.com/asp/bookinfo/bookinfo.asp?theisbn=$searchFor";

$req = HTTP::Request->new(GET=>$url);
$cookie_jar->add_cookie_header($req);
$response = $ua->request($req);
$cookie_jar->extract_cookies($response);
$content = $response->content();
#print $content;

#Make the assumption that name, author, etc., are known for the book
my ($price) =  ($content =~ m#Online Price:.+?\$(.+?)<#si);
print $price;
```

If we use the LWP::Debug module and import the + symbol, we see HTTP communication beyond what we presented earlier. The additional communication is given below. We have broken some lines so that they can be printed on the available space.

```
TTP::Cookies::add_cookie_header: Checking www1.fatbrain.com for cookies
HTTP::Cookies::add_cookie_header: Checking .fatbrain.com for cookies
LWP::UserAgent::request: ()
LWP::UserAgent::simple_request:
    GET http://www1.fatbrain.com/asp/bookinfo/bookinfo.asp?theisbn=0534934056
LWP::UserAgent::_need_proxy: Not proxied
LWP::Protocol::http::request: ()
LWP::Protocol::http::request:
    GET /asp/bookinfo/bookinfo.asp?theisbn=0534934056 HTTP/1.0
Host: www1.fatbrain.com
User-Agent: Mozilla/5.0

LWP::Protocol::http::request: reading response
LWP::Protocol::http::request: HTTP/1.1 200 OK
Server: Microsoft-IIS/4.0
Date: Thu, 17 May 2001 23:06:05 GMT
Content-Type: text/html
Set-Cookie: Jar=BID=0478B379EF7D2A06;
        expires=Mon, 01-Jan-2024 05:00:00 GMT; domain=.fatbrain.com; path=/
Cache-control: private

LWP::Protocol::http::request: HTTP/1.1 200 OK
LWP::Protocol::collect: read 1460 bytes
LWP::Protocol::collect: read 411 bytes
LWP::Protocol::collect: read 1460 bytes
LWP::Protocol::collect: read 1460 bytes
LWP::Protocol::collect: read 1460 bytes
LWP::Protocol::collect: read 1460 bytes
LWP::Protocol::collect: read 1460 bytes
LWP::Protocol::collect: read 1105 bytes
```

```
LWP::Protocol::collect: read 1459 bytes
LWP::Protocol::collect: read 1502 bytes
LWP::Protocol::collect: read 1460 bytes
LWP::Protocol::collect: read 1199 bytes
LWP::Protocol::collect: read 1504 bytes
LWP::Protocol::collect: read 1460 bytes
LWP::Protocol::collect: read 95 bytes
LWP::UserAgent::request: Simple response: OK
HTTP::Cookies::extract_cookies: Set cookie Jar => BID=0478B379EF7D2A06
```

This interaction shows that the second HTTP request is successful and comes back with a response code of 200 and a response string of OK. The program prints the price of the book we are looking at as 127.95 dollars. Commenting out the use LWP::Debug line on the top of the program causes the program to suppress the HTTP interaction strings to be printed on the screen, but just print the price.

This program shows that to write successful Web client programs, it is sometimes necessary to peform careful detective activities, cautiously monitor the HTTP interactions, and then find ways to solve the problems that arise in a straight-forward program by mimicing the behavior of a real browser and its counterpart Web server in such situations. Determining what a Web browser and a Web server do in such problematic situations is crucial in writing a successful Web client program. The manner in which a client such as Netscape Communicator works in various situations is publicly available. But, finding the appropriate action for the situation at hand is usually difficult from among mountains of information available at sites such as www.netscape.com and www.mozilla.com. There is a mailing list to discuss problems that arise when programming with the LWP modules. One can subscribe to this mailing list by writing to the address libwww-subscribe@perl.org. One can post a problem, a response or an experience by writing to libwww@perl.org. This mailing list is read by many experienced LWP programmers, including the authors of the various modules. This is the best place to get information and have one's vexing questions answered.

9.5   Extracting Links from Web Pages Using HTML::LinkExtor

We have seen in Section 7.4.2.2 how we can extract links from a Web page fetched over the network by parsing the page. Extracting links and fetching the Web pages pointed to by the links either recursively or in some other fashion is useful for purposes such as creating indices for a Web site with the purpose of facilitating searching. Hyperlinks that appear on a Web page point to resources of various kinds: HTML pages, XML pages, graphic files, audio or video clips, CGI programs, etc. To be able to extract links of a type we are interested in, or extracting all links from the various HTML attributes they can appear in, is, in general, time consuming. There is a Perl module HTML::LinkExtor that can be used for this purpose.

The HTML::LinkExtor module can be used to parse HTML pages fairly easily for extracting links. Below, we present a program that finds the so-called dead or stale links in a Web site. It starts with a URL given to it and traverses the site recursively, and examines each traversed page in order to collect stale or dead URLs.

Program 9.16

```
#!/usr/bin/perl
#linkExtract5.pl

use strict;
use LWP::UserAgent;
use HTML::LinkExtor;
```

```perl
use URI;  #Needed to absolutize a URL, if necessary

$" = "\n";
my $MAXURLCOUNT = 100;   #The max no of unique URLs to look at
my $COUNT = 0;
my $ua;
my %TRAVERSED; #Keeps track of all traversed URLs
#Note the / at the end is needed
my $STARTURL = "http://www.cs.uccs.edu/~kalita/";
#Used to see if a link is inside the domain represented by $BASEURL or outside.
my $BASEURL = "http://www.cs.uccs.edu/";
my $MIMEEXTS = "(s?html?|xml|asp|pl|css}jpg|gif|pdf)";
my ($domain) = ($BASEURL =~ m#http://(.+?)/?$#);
my $RECORDFILE = "ERRORS.$domain.txt";

#Need a UserAgent to be the client
$ua = new LWP::UserAgent;
open OUT, ">$RECORDFILE";
extractLinks ($STARTURL, $BASEURL);
close OUT;

####################
sub  extractLinks{
    my ($url, $containingURL)  = @_;
    exit if $TRAVERSED{$url};
    $TRAVERSED{$url}++;
    $COUNT = $COUNT + 1;
    if ($COUNT > $MAXURLCOUNT){
        exit 0;
    }
    print "Looking at an in-domain URL #$COUNT: $url\n";

    #Make the parser. Can give 0, 1 or 2 args. The first is  an optional sub to
    #process the urls. the second is used to absolutize any relative URLs
    #that may occur.
    #Not giving any args here. Absolutization is done separately.
    my $p = HTML::LinkExtor -> new ();
    #Request document using HTTP
    my $res = $ua->request(HTTP::Request->new(GET => $url));
    if (!($res -> is_success)){
     print OUT
     "Stale URL:  $url\nContaining URL:  $containingURL\nHTTP Message: ",
             $res->message, "\n\n";
     return;
    }
    #We have the contents of the file now
    my $file = $res -> content;
    #This produces an anonymous array with the links
    $p -> parse ($file);
    my @links = $p->links();
    my ($aLinkRef,  %linkHash, @linkArray);
```

```perl
    foreach $aLinkRef (@links){
        my ($tag, $attr, $theUrl) = @$aLinkRef;
        #Absolutizing done below doesn't work if a directory-level
        #URL doesn't have a / at the end.
        if ($url !~ /[.]$MIMEEXTS$/ and  $url !~ m@/$@)
                {$url = $url . "/"};
        my $theURI = new URI ($theUrl);

        $theURI = $theURI->abs($url);
        $linkHash{$theURI}++;
    }
    @linkArray = sort (keys %linkHash);
    my $newURL;
    foreach $newURL (@linkArray){
        next if $TRAVERSED{$newURL};
        if ($newURL =~ m/^$BASEURL/){
            extractLinks ($newURL, $url);
}

        else {
    checkLink ($newURL, $url);
        }
    }
}


##################
sub checkLink{
    my ($url, $containingURL) = @_;
    exit if $TRAVERSED{$url};
    $TRAVERSED{$url}++;
    $COUNT = $COUNT + 1;
    if ($COUNT > $MAXURLCOUNT){
        exit 0;
    }
    print "Looking at an out-of-domain URL #$COUNT: $url\n";
    #Request document using HTTP
    my $res = $ua->request(HTTP::Request->new(GET => $url));

    #$res-> code gives the response code
    #$res-> is_success is a boolean
    #$res -> message returns the error message
    if (!($res -> is_success)){
        print OUT
            "Stale URL:  $url\nContaining URL:  $containingURL\nHTTP Message: "
            $res->message,  "\n\n";
        return;
    }
}
```

The program uses the LWP::UserAgent, HTML::LinkExtor and URI modules. The value of $MAXURLCOUNT specifies the maximum number of unique URLs the program examines. The program has two URLs, $STARTURL and $BASEURL. $STARTURL specifies the URL where the recursive examination of URLs start. $BASEURL is the base URL for the $STARTURL. Clearly, the base URL can be easily obtained by parsing the $STARTURL and keeping the portion of the URL from the beginning till the end of the server name. The program culls out the domain name from $BASEURL The program looks for stale URLs and records the ones it finds in the file $RECORDFILE. We define a stale URL as one that cannot be retrieved from a Web server during the default timeout period of the user agent. Most frequently, a stale URL corresponds to a page that no longer exists. The recursive extraction of links is done by making a call to the first extractLinks subroutine. The call is given below.

```
extractLinks ($STARTURL, $BASEURL);
```

The subroutine extractLinks takes two arguments: the URL to start searching from, and the base URL of the starting page. The subroutine is recursive and exits when the count of unique URLs examined exceeds $MAXURLCOUNT, a global variable. The subroutine starts by examining if the URL $url, to be fetched and analyzed, has already been examined and hence occurs in the global hash %TRAVERSED. Using a hash to keep track of examined URLs, we can easily ensure that the URLs examined by the program are unique. If the URL is not a key in %TRAVERSED, our program enters it in %TRAVERSED before analyzing it. We examine at most $MAXURLCOUNT URLs.

The subroutine associates a parser with the scalar variable $p. The parse is associated with the following statement of code.

```
my $p = HTML::LinkExtor -> new ();
```

The constructor new for HTML::LinkExtor can take zero, one or two arguments; The first argument, if given, is reference to a so-called *callback* subroutine. If a callback subroutine is provided, it is called once automatically for each link found. If a callback subroutine is not provided, as is the case here, the links are collected internally and can be retrieved by calling the links method of the parser. The second argument, if given, is used to absolutize any relative URLs that are obtained from the analyzed Web pages. We do not specify either of the two arguments in our call. When necessary, we absolutize relative URLs on our own, as discussed later.

A GET request is created for the Web page addressed by $url and the request sent to the Web server. The response from the Web server is called $res. If the success code associated with $res indicates that the GET request is successful, the subroutine stores the content of the response in the variable $file. If the GET request is unsuccessful, the URL is recorded as stale or dead. Next, the subroutine calls the parse method of the Link::Extor class on the parser object $p using the argument $file.

```
$p -> parse ($file);
```

parse is a method of the HTML::Parse class that we do not discuss here. The class HTML::LinkExtor is a subclass of HTML::Parse and hence, inherits the parse method from HTML::Parse. The URLs specified in the HTML file are extracted by the following call.

```
my @links = $p->links();
```

The HTML::LinkExtor parse $p stores the links internally in the program. The links() method returns these links in a list. Here, the list is called @links. @links contains a list of references to links.

The first foreach loop that follows gets each reference to a link and then processes it. A link stored by the HTML::LinkExtor parser contains three parts: a tag, an attribute, and the URL. For example, if in the HTML file, the tag is

```
<A HREF="http://www.cs.uccs.edu/~kalita">
```

the tag is A, the attribute is HREF and the URL is http://www.cs.uccs.edu/~kalita. If the HTML file contains

```
<IMG SRC="http://www.cs.uccs.edu/~kalita/jk1.jpg">
```

the tag is IMG, the attribute is SRC and the URL is
http://www.cs.uccs.edu/~kalita/jk1.jpg.

Before we collect the URLs specified in a page, we need to absolutize any relative URLs that may occur in the page. A relative URL is one that does not start with the protocol string such as http or ftp. Thus, if we have a relative URL garden-of-the-gods.jpg, and it occurs in the page with absolute URL http://www.cs.uccs.edu/~kalita, it is absolutized as http://www.cs.uccs.edu/~kalita/garden-of-the-gods.jpg. To absolutize a URL, we use the abs method in the URI module. The absolutization steps are given below.

```
#Absolutizing done below doesn't work if a directory-level
#URL doesn't have a / at the end.
if ($url !~ /[.]$MIMEEXTS$/ and  $url !~ m@/$@)
        {$url = $url . "/"};
my $theURI = new URI ($theUrl);
$theURI = $theURI->abs($url);
```

The abs() method of the URI class does not return the correct absolute URL for an argument if the URL with respect to which absolutization is performed does not end with a /. To take care of this anomalous situation, we use the global variable $MIMEEXTS that gives a non-exhaustive list of extensions used by non-directory files, in the form of a regular expression. If the URL $url being analyzed does not end with one of the file extensions listed in $MIMEEXTS, we assume that $url refers to a directory. If it is a directory, and does not have a trailing /, we append a / at the end. The next step in absolutization is to take the current individual URL $theURL found in the page with address $url, and create a URI object out of it. To finish the absolutization process, the abs method of the URI class is called on $theURI with the containing URL $url as an argument. If a URL is already an absolute form, it does not change. Otherwise, it is transformed syntactically to make it absolute.

The first foreach loop goes over every element of @links and takes the URL out of the current link data structure and stores it in %linkHash. We use a hash so that there is o duplication of the URLs collected. That is, if a URL occurs several times in a Web page, we register it only once. A new array called @linkArray is created containing the unique URLs that are collected, i.e., the keys of %linkHash.

The extractLinks subroutine has a second foreach loop. In this loop that iterates over every unique and unexamined URL collected, the subroutine extractLinks is recursively called if the URL happens to be in the domain we are exploring. Such in-domain link sare examined for staleness in extractLinks. If the URL is from another domain, the subroutine checkLink is called to see if the URL is stale or dead. URLs pointing to locations outside the focussed site are not explored recursively.

The checkLink subroutine is called with two arguments: $url, the link to check for staleness and the URL in which the first URL was mentioned. The subroutine makes a GET request to retrieve $url. If this request is not successful, the subroutine prints a message saying which URL timed out, and is thus, stale. The subroutine also prints the URL of the page that contains a reference to the stale URL. The program prints the URLs it examines on the screen. A partial printout of the screen is given below. Lines have been broken to fit the printed page.

```
Looking at an in-domain URL #1: http://www.cs.uccs.edu/~kalita/
Looking at an out-of-domain URL #2: http://www.assam.org
Looking at an out-of-domain URL #3: http://www.assamcompany.com
Looking at an out-of-domain URL #4: http://www.autoindia.com
Looking at an in-domain URL #5:
     http://www.cs.uccs.edu/cgi-bin/jkkalita/counter.pl?counter=kalita-index-page
Looking at an in-domain URL #6:
     http://www.cs.uccs.edu/~kalita/accesswatch/accesswatch-1.32/index.html
Looking at an in-domain URL #7: http://www.cs.uccs.edu/cgi-bin/jkkalita/counter.pl
```

```
Looking at an in-domain URL #8: http://www.cs.uccs.edu/~kalita
Looking at an in-domain URL #9: http://www.cs.uccs.edu/~kalita/college.gif
Looking at an in-domain URL #10: http://www.cs.uccs.edu/~kalita/cultural.html
Looking at an out-of-domain URL #11: http://www.amnesty.org
```

The program stores the list of stale URLs in the file ERRORS.$domain.txt. In this specific case, $domain has the value www.cs.uccs.edu. Therefore, the record file is called ERRORS.www.cs.uccs.edu. A partial content of this file after the program is run is given below.

```
Stale URL:   http://www.acsu.buffalo.edu/~talukdar/assam/humanrightsassam.html
Containing URL:   http://www.cs.uccs.edu/~kalita/assam/human-rights-violations.html
HTTP Message: Not Found

Stale URL:
   http://www.cs.uccs.edu/cgi-bin/jkkalita/access_counter.pl.old?counter=human-rights
Containing URL:   http://www.cs.uccs.edu/~kalita/assam/human-rights-violations.html
HTTP Message: Not Found

Stale URL:
   http://193.135.156.15/tbs/doc.nsf/c12561460043cb8a4125611e00445ea9/
   f2261dd9e000fbe4802565090051a509?OpenDocument
Containing URL:   http://www.cs.uccs.edu/~kalita/assam/human-rights/ajit-bhuyan.html
HTTP Message: Can't connect to 193.135.156.15:80 (Timeout)

Stale URL:   http://www.hri.ca/partners/sahrdc/armed/toc.shtml
Containing URL:   http://www.cs.uccs.edu/~kalita/assam/human-rights/ajit-bhuyan.html#soe/
HTTP Message: Object Not Found

Stale URL:   http://www.hri.ca/partners/sahrdc/india/detention.shtml
Containing URL:   http://www.cs.uccs.edu/~kalita/assam/human-rights/ajit-bhuyan.html#soe/
HTTP Message: Object Not Found

Stale URL:   http://vag.vrml.org/
Containing URL:   http://www.cs.uccs.edu/~kalita/2000-CS301-roster.html
HTTP Message: Can't connect to vag.vrml.org:80 (Bad hostname 'vag.vrml.org')
```

We note that, some of the URLs are recorded as stale because the URL cannot be accessed within the default timeout period of the user agent $ua. It is possible to increase the timeout period by using the timeout method of the LWP::UserAgent class.

9.6   Exercises

1. *(Medium to Hard: E-Commerce)*
   Write a program that compares the prices of books from five different Web bookstores. First, present an HTML page where a visitor can search for books by *title words*, *author name* or *ISBN number*. Your program should search the five stores, collate the results, and present them in an easily readable format. What are some of the problems you face? How do you solve them? How can you make your program more efficient, more user-friendly and more robust? Discuss ideas regarding these issues.

2. *(Hard: E-Commerce, Can be a long-term project)*
   Write a program that compares prices of electronic goods such as cameras from three to five different e-commerce sites.

3. *(Hard: E-Commerce, Long-term project)*

Write a program that compares the prices of airlines tickets. This program is going to be harder to write than the previous programs. This is mainly because an itinerary may consist of several legs.

4. *(Hard: E-Commerce, Long-term project)*
   Write a program that compares the prices of automobiles from a few dealers. This is going to be difficult in general because of the plethora of options that manufacturers usually provide for cars.

5. *(Hard: Meta-Search Engine, Long-term project)*
   This problem instructs you to write a meta-search engine. You have a Web page where a user can search for keywords, just like a commercial search engine such as **Google** or **Lycos**. Your CGI program connects to three or four commercial search engines, performs searches on their sites, collates the results, and prints the results to the browser. At a minimum, remove duplicates, and present the information consistently. Different search engines usually return the search results using different formats. What are some of the problems you face?

6. *(Easy: Fetching Web Page, Research)*
   Write a program that fetches a Web page, given its URL, only if it has been modified from the last time it was fetched. Run the program from time to time.

7. *(Easy to Medium: Monitoring Web Site)*
   Write a program that detects changes in certain Web page of interest to you. It monitors the page every few hours. If it detects changes, it alerts you with a mail message. Such a program can be of value to the programs you are asked to write in the previous problems. This is because you may spend a lot of time writing your code to perform searches on Web sites to make your programs work. However, the format in which Web sites return search results can change frequently. Such changes can reduce the usefulness of your program at any time. Therefore, a program that monitors to see if the format in which results are entered has changed at a certain Web site can alert you so that you can make the appropriate changes in your own program.

8. *(Medium: Web-site Mirroring)*
   Write a program that mirrors a Web site locally on your machine. This program copies every directory recursively to your machine. However, it does not copy everything. It runs from time to time, and copies only those files and directories that have changed. It copies new files and directories as well. What are some problems in writing such a program so that it is efficient? Implement some of your ideas.

9. *(Medium: HTML Forms, Research)*
   There is a Perl module called `HTML::Forms` that can parse out a Web page and capture the forms in it. Install this module if you do not have it already. Use this module to capture a form, fill it, and submit it. Rewrite the programs discussed in the text of this Chapter and the problems here, so that they use `HTML::Forms`.

10. *(Medium to Hard: Authentication, Cryptography, Research)*
    Many Web sites require a client to *authenticate* with a name and a password. Perl provides modules for doing such authentication. Research into these modules. Write a program that fetches a Web page that requires authentication.

11. *(Easy: Secure Web Sites, Research)*
    There are Web sites which are secure. Their URLs start with `https://` instead of `http://`. These sites use encryption to ensure that the data transferred back and forth between the client and the server is encoded so that interceptors cannot read them. Research how a Perl program can obtain a Web page from such a secure server. Write a program that obtains such a page.

12. *(Hard: Movie Database, Can be a long-term project)*

    Write a program that searches for a movie's review from a site such as *www.imdb.com* (The International Movie Database). Write code for an HTML form that allows one to search for a movie with a keyword. The CGI program associated with this form actually performs searches at the IMDB or a similar site. It then obtains the names of the movies that the site returns. Your program further obtains reviews of these movies from the site, if necessary by performing traversal of additional hyperlinks. The CGI program you write presents the name of each movie followed by its review.

13. *(Medium to Hard: Text Processing, Vector Computation, Can be a long-term research project)*

    Write a program that is given a URL as command-line argument. It fetches the URL. Assume it is a text file. Remove all the HTML tags from the page. Remove commonly used words such as *it, is, some,* etc. Count the frequencies of occurrence of the words in the file.

    Now, you are given the URL of another Web page. Repeat the above steps for the second file as well. Make a single sorted list of the words in the two files. Assign a numeric ID to each word. Form a frequency vector, one per URL. You will create two frequency vectors. The vector for a file should contain the frequencies of the words in the file, in order of the word number. Words that do not occur in a file have the frequncy of zero for that file. Find a way to normalize this vector so that the values do not grow unbounded, i.e., become large. In addition, it is easier to do computation with normalized numbers.

    Given these two vectors, we can perform a computation called the *cosine* computation to find how similar the two files are. The cosine computation treats the finds the cosine of the angle between the two vectors. Although the dimension of the two vectors is large, we can still find the angle between the two vectors by computing its cosine. Find out the cosine of the angle between the two vectors for the two URLs. It will tell us how similar are the two Web pages that we started with. A small value of the cosine means that the angle between the two vectors is small.

    Now, we will extend the program. We are still given the first URL to start with. It is the base page with which we will compare all the other pages. The program is also given another URL. It traverses the Web site represented by the second URL recursively. It finds the similarity of each page with the base page. It prints the similarity numbers in a table. It also sorts the pages by the similarity values in ascending order.

    A program such as this can be used to traverse the Web and automatically classify pages according to whether they are similar to a base page or not. The base page's vector does not have to correspond to a real page, but could be the representation of a class of pages. For example, a vector can represent the characteristic word frequencies for a class such as *news*. A program like the one you have written can then crawl the Web and automatically find Web sites that are news related.

Chapter 10

On Persistent Data

In This Chapter

A well-regarded book written in the 1970s by one of the pioneers of Computer Science, Niklaus Wirth was aptly titled *Algorithms + Data Structures = Programs* [Wir75]. The title of the book explicitly reflects the fundamental essence of Computer Science: that a program's *raison d'etre* is efficient manipulation of data using well-motivated algorithms. A program takes explicit or implicit data as input, performs computations while employing internal structures to store and manipulate data, and possibly carries out actions whose effects are seen by the outside world. In order to effectively manipulate data, it is necessary to use structures that can store and access data efficiently. In certain programs, the structure of the internal data used by the program can become fairly complex, requiring use of techniques found in books on data structures such as [Knu78, CCELS01]. Additionally though, there are applications where the data is not structurally overly complex, but there is an overabundance of it. For example, a program may deal with tens of thousands of employees of a corporation, a few million customers of a telephone company, or hundreds of millions of records kept on citizens for administrative purposes such as assignment of social security benefits.

In this book, we deal with both aspects of data mentioned above, albeit to a limited extent. In chapter 3, we discuss the basic data types that Perl provides: scalars, arrays, hashes and references. We also discuss how references can be used to develop complex data structures. A data structure, whether simple or complex, may need to be stored in a file, so the same program or another program can use it later. For complex data structures, the components need to be unraveled or unrolled in some fashion, so that they can be stored in a file for faithful re-assembly later and subsequent use. This process is called *serialization*. We discuss this issue in this chapter. This chapter primarily deals with techniques that we can use to make data, whether simple or complex, small amounts or large, persistent. That is, how the data can be stored in files in disk so that related or unrelated programs can access or manipulate the same data, simultaneously or at different times.

When the amount of data is large, it may not be possible to keep all the data in the program's resident memory. In such a case, it is necessary to write data into files. In simple application programs, if we need access to data, we can store the data in text files for purposes of reading, writing and other manipulations such as deleting or inserting information, finding information that satisfies certain query criteria, and sorting the data. If the amount of data is small, and speed of access is not critical, we can use text files that we format ourselves in certain ways. Using text files is extremely simple. Every programming language provides facilities for reading and writing text files. Usually, a record is written one per line with \n being the record delimiter although other record delimiters are possible. The fields are usually separated with a pre-specified delimiter, say one or more commas or colons or tabs. The obvious drawback of using text files is that it is inefficient. Disk access is slow. If we need to sort records or keep them in sorted order in a text file, it becomes a slow process. A flat text file has no additional structure, so insertion and deletion of data becomes time-consuming, possibly requiring a pass through all the records. This may work for a simple application with a small amount of data. However, if the amount of data becomes large, there are several possibilities for the program author. Some of these are given below.

- We can use a data structure more complex than a straight file although the data can still be stored in files. For example, we can use a binary tree, a binary search tree, a red-black tree, a regular heap, a Fibonacci heap, or a B-tree. These structures are discussed in detail in most books on data structures and algorithms, such as [CLR97, CCELS01]. Writing one's own code becomes complex, but depending on the task at hand, it may be the only option open to a programmer. There are also off-the-shelf commercial, freeware, or shareware software one may be able to find.

- If the information is not very complex in structure, but the amount of data is somewhat large, we can use a built-in facility called DBM files or databases. DBMs are not really as powerful as relational databases, but for many purposes, they are enough. DBMs have been historically used in Unix machines although they are available in other platforms as well.

  The DBM library provides a simple database management facility. The structure of the record allowed is simple, just key-value pairs. They are stored in disk, not in the form of a flat file, but using complex hashing algorithms. DBMs have been in use in the Unix environment since the 1970s [Sel91]. A DBM file can be used to add new values, update existing values, or delete old values. The DBM library is fairly simple, but is readily available and frequently used.

  Perl provides access to the DBM files using a clever mechanism whereby a hash can be associated with a DBM database through a process similar to opening a file. Creating a new element in the array modifies the DBM database immediately. Deleting an element deletes the value from the DBM database. The size, number and kind of keys and values in a DBM database are restricted. In general, one is advised to keep both the keys and values down to about 1000 characters or less.

- Another option is using a full-fledged database. This is absolutely necessary if the amount of data is large and the data has complex structure. A complex structure can be represented using several related tables that are simple in themselves individually. Databases store huge amounts of data, and structure them using complex mechanisms for easy access and manipulation. Although there are different kinds of databases, relational databases are the most prevalent ones. A freely available relational database is MySQL. Another is Postgresql. Commercially available relational databases include ones from Oracle, Microsoft, and IBM.

A relational database is usually a complex software system. To be able to install and use a relational database needs considerable expertise, including learning a language called SQL or a variant of it. Quite frequently, it is necessary to employ an individual called a database administrator to help perform all the activities needed to keep a database system functioning well.

10.1   DBM Files

DBMs have been available in Unix systems for a long time. DBMs were first introduced as a mechanism for disk-oriented hashing in the form of a small library written by Ken Thompson in the Seventh Edition Unix system [AT79]. DBMs and their derivatives provide access to data in disks using keys. An extended version of the DBM library, NDBM, was later introduced. A public-domain clone of NDBM, called SDBM was later developed as well. Another version called GDBM which is compatible in terms of interfaces was made available by the Free Software Foundation.

The DBM and NDBM library implementations are based on the same algorithm by Ken Thompson. DBMs allowed only one database to be open at a time whereas NDBMs added support for multiple databases to be open concurrently. The SDBM library is a public-domain clone of the NDBM library, developed by Ozan Yigit to provide NDBM's functionality under some versions of UNIX that exclude NDBM for licensing reasons. The basic structure of SDBM is identical to NDBM, but internal details of the access function, such as address calculation and different hashing functions used make the two databases incompatible.

DBMs have several shortcomings. Since data is disk-resident, each access requires a system call, and a disk operation. Caching may be able to reduce the number of disk operations to achieve efficiency. A DBM cannot store data items whose total key and data size exceeds the page size of the hash table. Similarly, if two or more keys produce the same hash value, the table cannot store colliding keys.

10.1.1   Using DBM Files: `dbmopen` and `dbmclose`

The simplest way to use a DBM file is to use the `dbmopen` and `dbmclose` functions. To associate a DBM database with a hash, we use `dbmopen`. The syntax is given below.

```
dbmopen (%hash, dbmfilename, permissionmask)
```

Here, `%hash` is a Perl hash. `dbmfilename` is the name of a DBM file or database to which the hash is linked. The DBM file(s) may exist from before. If not, they are created by the call to `dbmopen` with the permission mask specified. The permission mask is a number given following the standard Unix directives. Using `undef` as the permission mask prevents Perl from creating the file if it does not exist. The following program illustrates the use of a DBM file.

Program 10.1

```perl
#!/usr/bin/perl
#Stores keys and values for customers in  a DBM  database
#file dbm1.pl

        #Open the 'customers' file and let the entries
        #be available in the %CUSTOMERS hash table.
        #If the file is not there, create
dbmopen (%CUSTOMERS, "customers", 0644);
print "Hash %CUSTOMERS linked to DBM file customers\n";
%CUSTOMERS = (
            "719-262-3432-1" =>
```

```
                    "Larsen::719-262-3432::larsen\@brain.uccs.edu"
                    );

$CUSTOMERS {"719-574-3656-1"}  =
    "Kalita::719-574-3656::kalita\@pikespeak.uccs.edu";

while (($key, $value) = each %CUSTOMERS){
    print "Customer ID = $key; Value = $value\n";
}


dbmclose(%CUSTOMERS);
print "Hash %CUSTOMERS de-linked from DBM file customers\n";

#********************
print "Printing contents of DBM file customers\n";
dbmopen (%CUSTOMERS, "customers",0644)
       || die "Cannot open customers database.\n";
while (($key, $value) = each %CUSTOMERS){
    print "Customer ID = $key; Value = $value\n";
}
dbmclose(%CUSTOMERS);
```

In this program, we have a hash table or associative array called %CUSTOMERS. The program starts by linking %CUSTOMERS to the DBM database file called customers. If the customers DBM file does not exist, it is created with permission mask of 0644.

Initially, the hash has only one element. This element has the key 719-262-3432 and the corresponding value is Larsen::719-262-3432::larsen@brain.uccs.edu. The value is information about an individual. When the hash has been assigned a value, the value is immediately written out to the DBM file. We add a second element to the hash. Following this, the link between the hash and the DBM files are severed by making the call

```
dbmclose(%CUSTOMERS);
```

Any updates to the hash after the connection has been cut off are not reflected in the disk-based DBM file. However, there is nothing wrong in adding to, deleting from or otherwise updating the contents of the hash when it is no longer attached to a file.

To check that the hash has been written to a file, we link a hash to the same file again. Although the name of the hash, %CUSTOMERS, is the same as the one used previously, the new name could have been different. After the hash has been linked to the DBM file, once again, its contents become available to the program. In this part of the program, we simply print the contents to the terminal. The output of the program is given below. Lines have been broken where necessary to fit the printed page.

```
Hash %CUSTOMERS linked to DBM file customers
Customer ID = 719-262-3432-1;
    Value = Larsen::719-262-3432::larsen@brain.uccs.edu
Customer ID = 719-574-3656-1;
    Value = Kalita::719-574-3656::kalita@pikespeak.uccs.edu
Hash %CUSTOMERS de-linked from DBM file customers
Printing contents of DBM file customers
Customer ID = 719-262-3432-1;
    Value = Larsen::719-262-3432::larsen@brain.uccs.edu
```

Digit Value	Permission mode
4	read
2	write
1	execute

Table 10.1: Permission Modes for Files and Directories

```
Customer ID = 719-574-3656-1;
    Value = Kalita::719-574-3656::kalita@pikespeak.uccs.edu
```

The output clearly shows that the program links to the hash two times; the first time it connects, it sets a couple of key-value pairs, and disconnects. When it links to the hash a second time, it simply prints out the contents of the hash.

10.1.1.1   The Permission Mask

In the program discussed in Section 10.1.1, there was no DBM file to begin with. Although the file name given in the program is customers, the extension .db is added to it automatically in some implementations. Note that depending on the system, the .db extension may or many not be added. The program created a file called customers.db to store the contents of the hash. The program was run on a Linux machine running Red Hat Linux. A Unix call

```
%file customers.db
```

gives the following information on the file.

```
customers.db: Berkeley DB 2.X Hash/Little Endian
(Version 5, Logical sequence number: file - 0, offset - 0, Bucket Size 4096, Overflow Point 1,
Last Freed 0, Max Bucket 1, High Mask 0x1, Low Mask 0x0, Fill Factor 40, Number of Keys 0)
```

It is not really important to understand all the details about the format of the file. It is not a text file and cannot be read directly on the terminal.

If the program does not have write access to the DBM file, or write and execute access to the directory containing the DBM file, the program can read the contents of the hash variable, but not update its contents. To test whether one can write to the hash, one can use the file test operators in Perl, if necessary. In addition, one can try setting a dummy hash entry inside an eval. eval is the usual mechanism to trap errors in Perl.

The permission mask parameter used in dbmopen needs additional explanation. On a Unix machine, every file or directory has a permission mode associated with it. The permission mask can be considered a three-digit octal number. There are three types of users: a) the owner of the file or directory, b) the group of users to which the owner belongs, and c) everyone else. Every user in Unix belongs to a group. The group a user belongs to is established when the user's account is created, although it can be changed later. Anyone not in the user's group is considered everyone else. Each number in the permission mask can be considered as specifying permission modes for three types of users. We can abbreviate the three digits as U, G and O, standing for the owner, the group and others, respectively. The three digits occur in the order UGO.

For example, a permission mode of 0444 gives read permission to each of the owner, everyone in the owner's group, and to everyone else as well. In other words, everyone who has a user account on the system can read a file that has permission mode 0444. The 0 in front says it is an octal number. The permission mode for a single type of user (i.e., U, G or O) can be obtained by adding the three permission values of 4, 2 and 1. Table 10.1 specifies the value of the individual digit values for file or directory permission. For example, a permission value of 7=4+2+1 gives read, write and execute permission to a specific type of user. Thus, if the permission associated with a file is 754, the file is readable, writable and executable by individuals in the owner's group, and only readable by everyone else. Thus, the use of the three digits allows one to specify somewhat fine-grained access modes for a file or a directory.

This is not the whole story though. The dbmopen function does not directly specify a permission mode for a DBM file it creates if the DBM file does not exist already. What it specifies is a called a *mask* that can be used to obtain the permission mode using simple arithmetic computation.

Suppose the DBM file under consideration does not exist. Assume the program is running on a Unix machine or a Unix-like machine, say Linux or Macintosh OS X. On such a machine, every user is associated with a global variable called umask, the user mask for file creation. umask takes an integer value and is used to specify the default permission mode associated with newly created files and directories. In the case of dbmopen, the value of the global umask is subtracted from the permission mask specified in dbmopen. In other words, the permissions in the umask are turned off from the mode argument given to a command like dbmopen.

Assume the value of umask is 22 and the permission mask provided in dbmopen is 0666. In such a case, the permission mode associated with the created DBM file is $0666-22=0644$. We assume all numbers are in octal. Thus, the DBM file created is readable, writable and executable by the owner; and is readable and writable by everyone else. If the mask given in dbmopen were 0777, the DBM file created will have permission mode of $0777-22=0755$. In other words, the owner has all permissions while everyone else has read and execute permissions. In the specific case of a DBM file, execute permission is not really useful in practice. It is used here for illustration only.

10.2   Tied Variables

Every substantive program uses many variables. In Perl, variables are scalars, arrays or lists, hashes and references. We also frequently use filehandles. Usually a variable or a filehandle is assigned values during a program; the values may be updated from time to time; and finally it is quite likely that we stop using the variable or it goes out of scope, or the program ends. Thus, usually, a variable is implemented directly, in the program, in terms of assignment and other statements.

However, we can think of variables in a more complex way. We can implement variables in terms of external modules or packages. The implementation can be as simple or as complex as the programmer wants. The package can implement anything it wants. In particular, the package can mimic the implementation of dbmopen and dbmclose, and perform more complex computation as well. Thus, in Perl, we can write a program that ties or links a variable name to a package that provides its implementation. A variable, whether a scalar, an array or a hash, can be tied to a package. In this section, we get a feel for it by looking at how hashes are tied. We do not delve into the details of writing a package that implements a tie. We see how packages that implement the tie of a hash variable to a DBM file.

There are several types of DBM files such as the following.

- NDBM

- BSD DB

- GDBM

- SDBM

- ODBM

Each type of file can be tied. However, not every type of DBM file may be available on every machine. Even if a DBM file type is available, the corresponding Perl module that performs a tie may not be available on the system. If simply the module is not available, it may be downloadable from a site such as www.cpan.org, The Comprehensive Perl Archive Network.

The first program we see below links an NDBM file to a hash. In order to be able to do so, we need to use a package called `NDBM_File.pm` that provides the implementation of the associated hash variable. It is possible to link the hash with other kinds of DBM files as well, using the appropriate package and if the other kinds of DBM files are available in the system being used.

In the program, we also use another package called `Fcntl.pm`. This package is called the File Control package. `Fcntl.pm` imports a set of names to the user program's namespace. Examples of imported names are `O_APPEND`, `O_CREAT`, and `O_RDWR`. These are constants that are usually defined in a so-called header file in the C language. The imported constants can be used inside our own program.

Program 10.2

```
#!/usr/bin/perl
#file dbm2.pl
#Stores keys and values for customers in a a so-called NDBM  database

use NDBM_File;  #Uses a package that lets us us create what
                #are called NDBM database files.
use Fcntl;
tie %CUSTOMERS, "NDBM_File", "customers1", O_RDWR|O_CREAT, 0644;
print "Hash %CUSTOMERS linked to NDBM file customers1\n";
%CUSTOMERS = (
                "719-262-3432-1" =>
                "Larsen::719-262-3432::larsen\@brain.uccs.edu"
                );
$CUSTOMERS {"719-574-3656-1"}  =
    "Kalita::719-574-3656::kalita\@pikespeak.uccs.edu";

while (($key, $value) = each %CUSTOMERS){
    print "Customer ID = $key; Value = $value\n";
}

untie(%CUSTOMERS);
print "Hash %CUSTOMERS de-linked from NDBM file customers1\n";
#********************

print "Linking again  to and Printing contents of NDBM file customers1\n";
tie %CUSTOMERS, "NDBM_File", "customers1", O_RDWR|O_CREAT, 0644;
while (($key, $value) = each %CUSTOMERS){
    print "Customer ID = $key; Value = $value\n";
}
untie(%CUSTOMERS);
```

The program `dbm2.pl` is similar to the program `dbm1.pl` discussed in Section 10.1.1. Instead of `dbmopen` to link a hash to a file, it uses the `tie` command.

```
tie %CUSTOMERS, "NDBM_File", "customers1", O_RDWR|O_CREAT, 0644;
```

The hash variable `%CUSTOMERS` is being `tied`. The class that provides an implementation for it is `NDBM_File.pm`. There are additional arguments provided to `tie` in the form of a list. Of course, in Perl, the elements of a list do not have to be enclosed within parentheses. The first element of the list of additional arguments is `O_RDWR|O_CREAT`. These two are constants the are defined within the `Fcntl.pm` module. In this specific case, they simply say that the NDBM file should be created if it does not exist. If it is created, it is should be readable and writeable. As usual `0644` gives the permission mode if a file is created. This permission mode is used with umask, as discussed in the Section 10.1.1.1, to obtain the actual permission for the NDBM file created.

The rest of the program is similar to dbm1.pl, discussed in Section 10.1.1. The hash %CUSTOMERS is initialized with one key-value pair. As soon as the hash is initialized, its contents are written out to the associated NDBM file. Next, another key-value pair is entered into the hash. Once again, this pair is also immediately written out to the file. In this illustration program, the tie between the hash variable %CUSTOMERS and the associated NDBM file are severed after this by using the untie command.

```
untie(%CUSTOMERS);
```

If the hash %CUSTOMERS is updated beyond this statement, it is not reflected in the NDBM file.

To test that the hash's contents are written out to the file as intended, we tie a hash again to the same NDBM file. This new hash is also called %CUSTOMERS although it does not have to be. The file name, of course, is the file written out earlier, customers1. Once the hash and the file are tied, we print the contents of the hash. We see that the contents of the hash are exactly what were written out earlier. The output of the program is given below. Lines have been broken where necessary to fit the printed page.

```
Hash %CUSTOMERS linked to NDBM file customers1
Customer ID = 719-262-3432-1;
    Value = Larsen::719-262-3432::larsen@brain.uccs.edu
Customer ID = 719-574-3656-1;
    Value = Kalita::719-574-3656::kalita@pikespeak.uccs.edu
Hash %CUSTOMERS de-linked from NDBM file customers1
Linking again  to and Printing contents of NDBM file customers1
Customer ID = 719-262-3432-1;
   Value = Larsen::719-262-3432::larsen@brain.uccs.edu
Customer ID = 719-574-3656-1;
   Value = Kalita::719-574-3656::kalita@pikespeak.uccs.edu
```

Thus, using tie is a more generalized approach to linking a variable to a file. With dbmopen and dbmclose, only a hash can be linked to a file. With tie, any type of variable can be linked to any external module. In particular, if the variable implements how the contents of a hash can be written to a specific kind of file, and how the file can be accessed and updated, we get a module that implements the functionality of dbmopen and dbmclose. Of course, using tie, we can attach any type of variable to any module that does anything its implementor wants to do.

10.2.1   Using a tied Hash to Store Word Frequencies

Now, we discuss a program that reads all files in a certain directory, splits the contents of the files into "words", and obtains frequencies of words across all files read. We assume that the files have .tex extension indicating they are text files written in the TeX/LaTeX format. Once again, we use an NDBM file in this example. The word frequencies are kept in a hash that is tied to an NDBM file. Thus, the contents of the hash are actually written out to the NDBM file.

Program 10.3

```
#!/usr/bin/perl5.6.0
#file makeWordFreq.pl
#Takes the diamond input, splits the files into words
#and computes the frequency of each word and stores
#the frequencies in a DBM file. We assume that the words
```

```
#are not hyphenated.

use NDBM_File;   #Uses a package that lets us us create what
                 #are called NDBM database files.
use Fcntl;

tie %WORDS, "NDBM_File", "words", O_RDWR|O_CREAT, 0644;

@ARGV = grep /[.]tex/, @ARGV;
while (my $line = <>){
    $line =~ s/^\s+//;
    $line =~ s/\s+$//;
    foreach my $word (split /\W*\s+\W*/, $line){
        $WORDS{$word}++;
    }
}
untie(%WORDS);
```

The program is called with * as the sole argument indicating all files in the current directory. The files with .tex extension are the only ones considered. Each line of such files are read, initial and terminal spaces removed, and broken up into individual words. The hash %WORDS is used to store the number of times a word recurs.

Once the word frequencies have been written out to the hash, we untie the hash variable and sever the link. For testing purposes, we have a second program where we tie a hash to the same NDBM file words. We print the contents of the hash, i.e., the contents of the NDBM file to see the word frequencies. The second program is given below.

Program 10.4

```
#!/usr/bin/perl5.6.0
#file readWordFreq.pl

use NDBM_File;   #Uses a package that lets us us create what
                 #are called NDBM database files.
use Fcntl;

#The program reads the words from the
#DBM file and prints them out such that the frequency counts
#are sorted.

tie %WORDS, "NDBM_File", "words", O_RDWR, 0644;
foreach $word (sort {$WORDS{$b} <=> $WORDS{$a}} keys %WORDS)
{
    printf "%20s\t%3d\n", $word, $WORDS{$word};
}
untie (%WORDS);
```

The program ties to the NDBM_File words using the hash %WORDS. In the hash, the words are keys and the number of occurrences are the values. The program sorts the keys of the hash %WORDS in descending order of frequency of occurrence and prints a two-column output to the standard output or screen.

A small part of the output is given below.

```
        the      426
         to      246
         of      246
        and      150
          a      144
       cell      108
         we       96
         in       90
      amino       84
         is       84
       acid       84
         be       72
      model       60
        The       54
         We       54
         as       48
         bf       48
       need       48
       that       42
      \item       42
```

10.2.2   `tie` in General

The `tie()` function binds a variable to a class that provides the implementation of various methods for that variable. These are methods that construct objects of the class and provide access methods for the `tied` variable. Once the `tie` function performs the association, accessing a `tied` variable automatically triggers method calls in the proper class. The complexity of the implementation is all hidden from the user.

In `tie()`, the first argument is the variable that is to be associated with the class. The second argument is the name of the class that implements objects of the correct type. The additional arguments are considered to be in a list and are passed into the constructor method for the class. For example, there is a method called `TIEHASH()` in any module that implements the `tie` link such as `NDBM_File.pm`. However, it is not necessary for us to know the details of how such a function works.

The variables that can be `tied` are

- scalars,

- arrays,

- hashes, and

- file handles.

We do not discuss much details of a class that implements a `tie`; interested readers are instructed to consult the `perltie` manual page in Perl documentation. In most computers, this should be accessible by typing

```
%perldoc perltie
```

The documentation is also available at the site `www.cpan.org`, The Comprehensive Perl Archive Network.

A module such as `NDBM_File.pm` that implements a `tie` to a hash is required to implement at least the following methods in its definition.

- `TIEHASH` is the constructor method that returns reference to a new object. This method is automatically called when we make a call to `tie` in Perl.

- `FETCH` is the access method. This method is automatically called when an element of the `tied` hash is accessed, i.e., read.

- `STORE` is the method for writing. This method is automatically called when an element in the `tied` hash is set.

- `DELETE` is the method that is triggered when we remove an element from the `tied` hash, e.g., by using the `delete()` function.

- `CLEAR` is the method that is triggered when the whole hash is cleared. This is usually done by assigning the empty list.

- `EXISTS` is the method triggered when in a Perl program, we use the `exists()` function on a `tied` hash.

- `FIRSTKEY` and `NEXTKEY` are two methods that are triggered when a Perl program iterates through a `tied` hash using `keys()` or `each()`.

- `UNTIE` is the method that is called when the Perl program calls `untie()`.

- `DESTROY` is the method that is called when a `tied` hash is about to go out of scope.

Any class or package that implements `tie()` to a hash must implement these methods. However, there is a module called `Tie::Hash` that provides an implementation of each of these methods. Therefore, anyone writing a class that `ties` a hash to a class needs to write only those methods that need to modified from those available in `Tie::Hash`.

The `DB_File`, `NDBM_File`, `GDBM_File`, `ODBM_File` and `SDBM_File` modules provide implementation of the `tie` of a hash to a class. Therefore, each one of these classes needs to provide an implementation of the methods named earlier. An interested reader can examine the source code of these modules to see the definitions of these methods.

10.2.3 Using Tied Variables in CGI Programs

Variables tied to modules that help store values in files can be used with a CGI program, if the need arises. We have seen in Section 10.2 that any type of variable can be tied to a module that implements how it behaves. In particular, as associative array or hash can be linked to a module such as `NDBM_File` or `GDBM_File` that ties the variable to a file.

The following program creates an access counter for use on a Web page. Such a counter is not an uncommon sight on many Web pages. The CGI program `counter.pl` that follows is invoked with the name of a counter. The same program can keep track of many counter values. A counter's name and its value are stored in a DBM database. In this program, it is a GDBM database although we can use another type of DBM file if we want. The name of the counter is used as a key. The program follows.

Program 10.5

```perl
#!/usr/bin/perl -T
#counter.pl

use GD;
use CGI qw(:standard);;
```

```perl
use CGI::Carp qw(fatalsToBrowser);
use Untaint;
use GDBM_File;

#######Set CGI size limit; disable file upload
$CGI::POST_MAX = 1024; #max 1024 bytes posts
$CGI::DISABLE_UPLOADS = 1;

$query = new CGI;
$name_counter = $query->param(counter);
$name_counter = untaint(qr{^[\d\w.-]+$}, $name_counter);
tie %access, 'GDBM_File', "gdbmcounterdb", GDBM_WRCREAT, 0777;

$freq = $access{$name_counter};
$freq = untaint(qr{^\d+$}, $freq);
$freq++;
$access{$name_counter} = $freq;
$counter = sprintf("%06d", $freq);

untie %access;

#Find the number of digits in the counter
@digits = split(//, $counter);
$length = length($counter);

#Create a new GD image
$im = new GD::Image($length*14-2,20);
#Create colors by allocating RGB
$black = $im->colorAllocate(0, 0, 0);
$white = $im->colorAllocate(255, 255, 255);
$blue = $im->colorAllocate(0,0,255);
#Create the GD image containing the counter's value
srand();
for ($i=0; $i < $length; $i++)
{ $im->string(gdLargeFont, 2+$i*14, 1+int(rand(3)), $digits[$i], $white);
  if($i < $length-1)
  { $im->filledRectangle(12+$i*14, 0, 13+$i*14, 20, $blue);
  }
}

# print the image to STDOUT, i.e., send to browser
print header("image/jpeg");
binmode STDOUT;
print $im->jpeg;
exit;
```

The program uses several modules: GD.pm to draw an image; CGI.pm to perform CGI-related tasks; CGI::Carp.pm to handle errors that may arise during execution of a CGI program; and GDBM_File.pm to tie a hash to a GDBM database file. The CGI.pm module exports a set of functions and constants for performing the usual CGI-related tasks using the :standard keyword. A CGI program can produce many errors, such as syntax errors, run-time errors in the program's execution, not printing the proper HTTP headers as the initial strings to STDOUT, etc. In particular, if the CGI program has some run-time error before the HTTP headers are printed to STDOUT, the associated error strings are printed to STDOUT before the HTTP headers, causing trouble at the browser end. To ameliorate such situations, we use the line

```
use CGI::Carp qw(fatalsToBrowser);
```

so that fatal errors in the CGI program are printed to the browser. Without such help, a CGI program may become difficult to debug. One may need to look at the error log entries on the machine where the Web server is running as well. On a Linux machine, the usual location of the error log file is /var/log/httpd/error_log for the Apache Web server. On a Macintosh OS X machine, the usual location of the error log file is /private/var/log/httpd/error_log. On a Windows machine, the location of the error log file is dependent on where the Web server is installed.

The program starts by creating a new CGI object. It obtains the only argument sent to it called counter using the following line of code.

```
$name_counter = $query->param(counter);
```

The value is laundered or untainted. The argument is called $name_counter inside the program. Next, the program ties a GDBM file gdbmcounterdb to a hash called %access. The reader is requested to consult documentation on GDBM_File.pm to find out what arguments need to be passed to the tie command in the case of a GDBM file. In particular, GDBM_WRCREAT is an additional argument that specifies that the file should be readable and writeable, and should be created if it does not exist. The last argument provides the permission mode if the file is created.

The gdbmcounterdb file contains key-value pairs of a hash. If there is a value corresponding to $name_counter, it is accessed. The value is $freq. The value is incremented to indicate that the corresponding Web page has been accessed one more time, because the CGI program has been called. The new value is recorded in the hash, i.e., the newly incremented value placed in the GDBM file as well. The new value of the counter is written into a string $counter using sprintf. We assume the maximum length of the counter is six digits.

We use the GD.pm module to create a graphic image on the fly. In this case, the graphic image is in JPEG format although it can be several other formats such as GIF, or PNG. The image contains the value of the appropriate counter in an attractive graphical format. The value of the counter has already been read from the GDBM file using the name as the key. Each digit of the number read is depicted in a small rectangle whose background is blue. The digit itself is an image in white. The numeric calculations in the for loop are needed to position the individual rectangles corresponding to each digit. The GD.pm module and a program that is very similar to the one discussed here is explained in Section 5.7. Once the program has created an image corresponding to all the decimal digits in the value of the counter, the program creates an HTTP header using the following call.

```
print header("image/jpeg");
```

This header is printed on the STDOUT, and hence sent to the browser. Images are binary objects and the binary mode is ensured by using the following command.

```
binmode STDOUT;
```

The image is printed in a straightforward manner.

There are several things to note when a DBM file is used in the context of a CGI program. A CGI program is invoked from a Web page, i.e., the CGI program is run by a Web server. Usually a Web server does not have permission to do much. As a result, for the CGI program to run, it must be executable by everyone. The DBM file must be readable and writeable by everyone so that a CGI program can read the value and update it. When `tie` creates a DBM file, the permission specified is reduced by the `umask`, the file created may not be readable and writeable by everyone. Hence, the person installing the CGI program has to manually check to see that the DBM file created has the appropriate permissions. If not, the file may have to be created and its permission mode changed by hand. In particular, one should make sure of the following.

- The CGI program must be executable by everyone. All directories above it must be readable and executable by everyone. This is especially true on Unix or Unix-like machines such as Linux or Macintosh OS X.

- The DBM file must be readable and writeable by everyone. If necessary, one should create the DBM file by hand. The file may need an extension like `.db`. One needs to find out if the extension is needed by either reading documentation or by experimentation. If necessary, one also needs to change the permission modes on the DBM file by hand so that it is readable and writeable by everyone.

- The HTTP header must be produced right. There cannot be any run-time errors generated by the program before the HTTP header is produced because the errors are normally printed to `STDOUT` as well. Thus, it makes sense to print the header generation line right on top of the program, at least during development. Also, one should make sure that the errors are printed to the browser. One should also run the CGI program by hand on the command-line to see if it has syntax or run-time errors. When run by hand, CGI parameters can be passed on the terminal as `name=value` pairs. If there are several pairs, one can enter a pair on a line and use Control-C (Control-Z in Windows) to indicate that all pairs have been entered. One can also use the `-c` flag to get just a syntax check of the program without execution, and use the `-w` to get as much warning as possible. Thus, the top line of the program can be changed to

```
#!/usr/bin/perl -cw
```

for purposes of testing. If the program checks out for syntax and also runs without error from the command-line, but still gives an error when used as a CGI program, one should check the error log kept by the HTTP server. If using an Apache server,the error log is usually stored in the file such as `/var/log/httpd/error_log` on a Red Hat Linux machine, `/private/var/log/httpd/error_log` on a Macintosh OS X machine running BSD Unix.

A call to the CGI program, discussed earlier in this section, on a Web page may look like the following.

```
<tr> <td>
Number of visitors (<em>since March 18. 1997</em>):
<IMG
SRC="http://pikespeak.uccs.edu/cgi-bin/kalita/counter/counter.pl?counter=kalita-index-page">
<p>
```

Here, `kalita-index-page` is the name of the counter. On another Web page, a call may be the following.

```
Number of visitors (<em>since February 22, 2002</em>):
<IMG
SRC="http://pikespeak.uccs.edu/cgi-bin/kalita/counter/counter.pl?counter=testcounter1">
```

Here, `testcounter1` is the name of the second counter. Thus, the same CGI program may be used in as many Web pages as we want; each counter may have a different name. Figure 10.1 shows a portion of the first Web page with the counter value in the form of a JPEG image. It is an in-line image. Thus, we see that the decimal counter value read from the DBM file is automatically converted into an image by the CGI program, and this image sent to `STDOUT` in binary mode by the CGI program, is displayed on the browser as an attractive image. The CGI program discussed above reads a GDBM file, obtains the value of a certain named counter, updates the values, and creates an image with the counter's value. The CGI program is run from a Web page. Thus, the CGI program is actually being run by a Web server.

We have a DBM file that contains the values of one or more counters indexed by the names of the counters. Below, we discuss three very simple programs that can be run by the administrator of a Web site to work

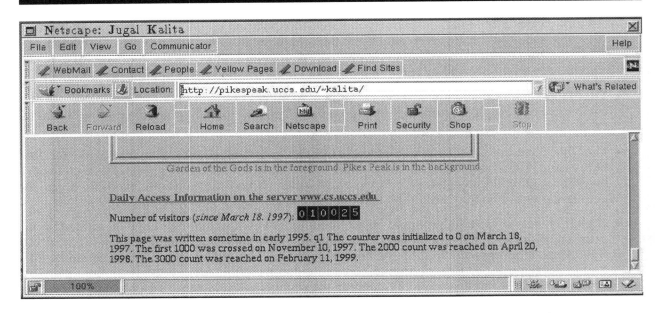

Figure 10.1: A Counter Image Produced by a CGI Program Using GD.pm in a Web Page

with the counter database. The program read_counter.pl allows one to see the current values stored in the GDBM file. The program follows.

Program 10.6

```perl
#!/usr/bin/perl
#read_counters.pl

use GDBM_File;

tie %access, 'GDBM_File', "gdbmcounterdb", GDBM_WRCREAT, 0777;
foreach $key(keys %access){
    print "counter $key has the value $access{$key}\n";
}

untie (%access);
```

An example run of the read_counters.pl program is given below.

```
counter kalita-index-page has the value 10024
counter testcounter1 has the value 4
```

When for some reason, a counter is no longer used, the remove_counter.pl program can be used to remove it from the DBM file. The program is given below.

Program 10.7

```perl
#!/usr/bin/perl
#remove_counter.pl
```

```
use GDBM_File;

$counter_name = $ARGV[0];
tie %access, 'GDBM_File', "gdbmcounterdb", GDBM_WRCREAT, 0777;
delete $access{$counter_name};
print "Deleted $counter_name\n";
untie (%access);
```

An example run is given below.

```
%remove_counter.pl testcounter1
Deleted testcounter1
```

Here, % is the Unix system prompt. After `remove_counter.pl` is run, we can run `read_counters.pl` again, and see the following.

```
%read_counters.pl
counter kalita-index-page has the value 10024
```

There is also a program called `init_counter.pl` that can be used to initialize a new counter or change its value. A counter's value may need to be initialized for reasons such as several counters on several Web pages being merged into one Web page and hence, several counters being added up to make the value of the new counter; the CGI program being moved to a new server so that the DBM file needs to be created anew on the new server, but the old counter values need to retained; for testing purposes, etc.

10.3   Serializing Data

We discuss in Section 10.1, in detail, how data that can be represented as key-value pairs can be stored in a file. This gives persistence to such data so that the data can be retrieved and manipulated by many independent, but possibly related, programs. However, if the structure of the data is more complex, associative arrays or hashes do not provide adequate representation. For example, if the data item is an anonymous array of arrays, or a hash of hashes, or an object belonging to a certain class, it is not enough to be able to tie a file to a hash in order to be able to save the data to a file. We need to perform *serialization* in such cases. Serialization involves converting the contents of any complex data structure into a string following a certain well-designed algorithm. The string produced by the serialization algorithm can then be *deserialized* later in the program when and if necessary. The serialized data structure can be sent over socket connections or used in remote procedure calls as long as the receiving end deserializes it using an appropriate algorithm. The serialized string can be stored to a text file, or a DBM file if it can be somehow associated with a key, or can be stored in a database. The only requirement that before using again, the string should be deserialized. There are several Perl modules that provide for serialization and deserialization facilities.   These include `FreezeThaw.pm`, `Storable.pm`, `Data::Dumper.pm`, `Data::Denter.pm`, etc. A module called `Data::Serializer.pm` provides a common interface to some of the serialization modules. The default module used by `Data::Serializer.pm` is `Data::Dumper.pm` although several additional options are available. In this section, we discuss only the `Data::Serializer.pm` module, and only its default behavior. Additionally, we do not discuss how objects and classes can be deserialized. References to codes can also cause complications. Interested readers are referred to Perl documentation for more details.

10.3.1   Serializing and Deserializing using `Data::Serializer.pm`

The following program shows how the `Data::Serializer.pm` module is used. The
`Data::Serializer.pm` provides a consistent interface to the following modules: `Storable.pm`,
`FreezeThaw.pm`, `Data::Denter.pm` and `Data::Dumper.pm`. It uses `Data::Dumper.pm` as the default
serialization and deserialization module. It is possible to specify that any one of the other modules be used
for serialization and deserialization as well. The following program serializes or deserializes a scalar, a list
or an array, a hash, and an array of arrays.

Program 10.8

```perl
#!/usr/bin/perl
#serialize.pl

use Data::Serializer;
use strict;

my $dumper = Data::Serializer -> new ();

#serialize a scalar; not of much use
my $friend = "Justin O'Malley";
my $serializedFriend = $dumper->serialize (\$friend);
my $friendAgain = $dumper -> deserialize ($serializedFriend);
print "friendAgain = $$friendAgain \n";


#serialize a list or array
my @friends = ("Justin O'Malley", "Christopher Paul", "Shane Jahnke",
               "Seth Gross", "Seth Musselman", "Greg Eisenbeis");
my $serializedFriends = $dumper->serialize (\@friends);
#print "serializedFriends = $serializedFriends\n";
my $friendsAgain = $dumper->deserialize ($serializedFriends);
print "friendsAgain = ", join ("\n\t ", @$friendsAgain), "\n";

#serialize a hash
my %hobbies = ("Chris Paul" => "Skiing/Working out",
               "Justin O'Malley" => "Singing/Acting", ,
               "Shane Jahnke" => "Soccer",
               "Seth Gross" => "Soccer/School",
               "Seth Musselman" => "Sailing",
               "Greg Eisenbeis" => "Girls");
my $serializedHobbies = $dumper->serialize(\%hobbies);
#print "serializedHobbies = $serializedHobbies\n";
my $hobbiesAgain = $dumper-> deserialize ($serializedHobbies);
my $person;
print "\nFriends and their hobbies:\n";
foreach $person (keys %$hobbiesAgain){
    print $person, "\t\t", $$hobbiesAgain{$person}, "\n";
}

#serialize an array of arrays
```

```perl
my $friendsStats = [ ['Chris Paul', 'Colorado Springs', 23, 76, 180],
                     ['Shane Jahnke', 'Colorado Springs', 19, 73, 150],
                     ['Seth Gross', 'Colorado Springs', 20, 70, 160],
                     ['Seth Musselman', 'Colorado Springs', 22, 74, 170],
                     ['Greg Eisenbeis', 'Colorado Springs', 22, 76, 165]
                   ];
my $serializedStats = $dumper->serialize ($friendsStats);
my $statsAgain = $dumper->deserialize ($serializedStats);
my $i;
print "\nFriends and their stats:\n";
for ($i=0; $i <= 4; $i++){
    printf "%-15s %-15s  %3d  %3d  %3d\n",
        $statsAgain -> [$i] -> [0], $statsAgain -> [$i] -> [1],
        $statsAgain -> [$i] -> [2], $statsAgain -> [$i] -> [3],
        $statsAgain -> [$i] -> [4];
}
```

The program uses the `Data::Serializer.pm` module. An instance of a `Data::Serializer` object is needed for serialization and deserialization. The instance is called `$dumper`.

```perl
my $dumper = Data::Serializer -> new ();
```

For purposes of illustration, the program starts by serializing a scalar. The `serialize` method of the `Data::Serializer` object takes a reference to a data structure, here that of a scalar, as argument.

```perl
my $serializedFriend = $dumper->serialize (\$friend);
```

This is an illustrative program, and hence, not particularly useful. The `serialize` method returns a reference to a string that results from the serialization algorithm. The program deserializes this string immediately and prints the output. `deserialize` takes a reference to a serialized string and produces a reference to the deserialized data structure.

```perl
my $friendAgain = $dumper -> deserialize ($serializedFriend);
```

We can clearly see, in the output that follows the program that deserialization obtains the original scalar value back.

Next, the program serializes an array `@friends`. Once again `serialize` takes a reference to the array. The `serialize` method produces a string that is `deserialized` again, immediately. Once again, this program is for illustration purposes only. By looking at the output that follows the program, we see that deserialization reproduces the original list.

The program follows by assigning values to a hash `%hobbies` that relates the name of a person and his hobbies. Following the assignment, the hash is serialized. The serialization process produces a string. This string is `deserialized` immediately. The `foreach` loop prints the key-value pairs in the deserialzed hash. Examination of the output that follows the program confirms that serialization and subsequent deserialization reproduces the original set of key-value pairs.

Finally, the program assigns value to an anonymous array of arrays that contains names of friends and some information about each friend. `$friendStats` stores a reference to the array of arrays. This reference is passed as an argument to `serialize` to obtain a string. The string is immediately deserialized.

```perl
my $serializedStats = $dumper->serialize ($friendsStats);
my $statsAgain = $dumper->deserialize ($serializedStats);
```

The rest of the program traverses the contents of the deserialized data structure and prints the information in a readable manner. The printing confirms that the array of arrays is reproduced without any glitch. The output of the program follows.

```
friendAgain = Justin O'Malley
friendsAgain = Justin O'Malley
          Christopher Paul
          Shane Jahnke
          Seth Gross
          Seth Musselman
          Greg Eisenbeis


Friends and their hobbies:
Justin O'Malley          Singing/Acting
Greg Eisenbeis           Girls
Seth Gross               Soccer/School
Seth Musselman           Sailing
Chris Paul               Skiing/Working out
Shane Jahnke             Soccer


Friends and their stats:
Chris Paul        Colorado Springs    23    76    180
Shane Jahnke      Colorado Springs    19    73    150
Seth Gross        Colorado Springs    20    70    160
Seth Musselman    Colorado Springs    22    74    170
Greg Eisenbeis    Colorado Springs    22    76    165
```

10.3.2   Using a File to Store Serialized Data Structures with `Data::Serialize.pm`

The program in Section 10.3.1 serializes four data structures into strings and deserializes them again, obtaining the original contents. The program illustrates that serialization and deserialization are useful tools whether we are dealing with simple or complex data structures. In this Section, we rewrite the program of Section 10.3.1. In the current program, we write each of the serialized data structures to a file `data.txt`. Each serialized string is printed to the file as a line by itself. In the second part of the program, the file `data.txt` is opened for reading. Each of the serialized or frozen data structures is deserialized or thawed, and the output written to the standard output or screen. The program follows.

Program 10.9

```perl
#!/usr/bin/perl
#serializeFile.pl

use Data::Serializer;
use strict;

#create a new serializer
my $dumper = Data::Serializer -> new ();

#serialize a scalar
my $friend = "Justin O'Malley";
my $serializedFriend = $dumper->serialize (\$friend);
```

```perl
#write the serialized object into file data.txt; follow by "\n";
open OUT,  ">data.txt";
print OUT $serializedFriend, "\n";

#serialize a list or array; print into data.txt, follow by "\n"
my @friends = ("Justin O'Malley", "Christopher Paul", "Shane Jahnke",
               "Seth Gross", "Seth Musselman", "Greg Eisenbeis");
my $serializedFriends = $dumper->serialize (\@friends);
print OUT $serializedFriends, "\n";

#serialize a hash, write to data.txt, follow by |'n";
my %hobbies = ("Chris Paul" => "Skiing/Working out",
               "Justin O'Malley" => "Singing/Acting", ,
               "Shane Jahnke" => "Soccer",
               "Seth Gross" => "Soccer/School",
               "Seth Musselman" => "Sailing",
               "Greg Eisenbeis" => "Girls");
my $serializedHobbies = $dumper->serialize(\%hobbies);
print OUT $serializedHobbies, "\n";

#serialize an array of arrays; write into OUT, follow by "\n"
my $friendsStats = [ ['Chris Paul', 'Colorado Springs', 23, 76, 180],
                ['Shane Jahnke', 'Colorado Springs', 19, 73, 150],
                ['Seth Gross', 'Colorado Springs', 20, 70, 160],
                ['Seth Musselman', 'Colorado Springs', 22, 74, 170],
                ['Greg Eisenbeis', 'Colorado Springs', 22, 76, 165]
                ];
my $serializedStats = $dumper->serialize ($friendsStats);
print OUT $serializedStats, "\n";

#Close the file handle; reading the serialized data in the same
#program will not work if not closed; at the end of a program
#a file handle is closed automatically.
close OUT;

#######################
#READ BACK FROM THE FILE
open IN, "data.txt";

#Read the serialized scalar back, remove "\n" from end, deserialize it
my $serializedFriend = <IN>;
chomp ($serializedFriend);
my $friendAgain = $dumper -> deserialize ($serializedFriend);
print "friendAgain = $$friendAgain \n";

#Read the serialized array back, remove "\n", deserialize it
$serializedFriends = <IN>;
chomp ($serializedFriends);
my $friendsAgain = $dumper->deserialize ($serializedFriends);
print "friendsAgain = ", join ("\n\t", @$friendsAgain), "\n";
```

```
#Read the serialized hash back, remove "\n", deserialize it
$serializedHobbies = <IN>;
chomp ($serializedHobbies);
my $hobbiesAgain = $dumper-> deserialize ($serializedHobbies);
my $person;
print "\nFriends and their hobbies:\n";
foreach $person (keys %$hobbiesAgain){
    print $person, "\t\t", $$hobbiesAgain{$person}, "\n";
}

#Read the serialized array of arrays back, remove "\n", deserialize it
$serializedStats = <IN>;
chomp ($serializedStats);
my $statsAgain = $dumper->deserialize ($serializedStats);
my $i;
print "\nFriends and their stats:\n";
for ($i=0; $i <= 4; $i++){
    printf "%-15s %-15s   %3d   %3d   %3d\n",
        $statsAgain -> [$i] -> [0], $statsAgain -> [$i] -> [1],
        $statsAgain -> [$i] -> [2], $statsAgain -> [$i] -> [3],
        $statsAgain -> [$i] -> [4];
}

close IN;
```

The program starts by creating a new Data::Serializer object called $dumper. $dumper is used for all serialization and deserialization. First, the scalar $friend is serialized into $serializedFriend which is written into the file data.txt followed by a newline character.

```
open OUT,   ">data.txt";
print OUT $serializedFriend, "\n";
```

Next, the list @friends is assigned a value, serialized, and the serialized string written out to the file data.txt, followed by a newline character.

```
print OUT $serializedFriends, "\n";
```

Similarly, the hash %hobbies, and the array of arrays referenced by $friendsStats, are serialized and written out to the same file data.txt. Finally, an anonymous array of arrays is serialized and stored to the file. The OUT filehandle is closed so that everything is written out to the file correctly.

The second part of the program opens the same file data.txt for reading, reads the four lines in the file one by one, and deserializes the strings to obtain the original data structures. The contents of the original data structures are printed out to the standard output or screen. For example, the following lines of code read the fourth string from the file, and obtain the original contents of the array of arrays.

```
$serializedStats = <IN>;
chomp ($serializedStats);
my $statsAgain = $dumper->deserialize ($serializedStats);
```

Note that when the program writes into the file in the first half, the serialized string is followed by a \n as it is printed into the file. Therefore, at the unrolling end, after the line containing the serialized string has been read, it is chomped to remove the \n inserted at the end.

When several serialized strings are stored in the same file, they must be read back in the exact same order. In addition, if any additional characters, such as \n are inserted into the same file, they must be read back in the exact same order, in the exact same place. If the order is not followed exactly, the deserialization process complains about extraneous or non-understood characters and fails.

The contents of the file `data.txt` after the program has been run are given below for the perusal of the curious-minded. The strings that are produced by serialization are a sequence of hexa-decimal digits. Some of the lines are long and hence are broken into pieces. Each data structure starts with the string `^Data::Dumper|||hex|^`.

```
^Data::Dumper|||hex|^5c274a757374696e6204f5c274d616c6c657927
^Data::Dumper|||hex|^5b274a757374696e6204f5c274d616c6c6579272c274368726973746f7068657220
5061756c272c275368616e65204a61686e6b65272c27536574682047726f7373272c2753657468204d5737
3656c6d616e272c27477265657220456973656e62656973275d
^Data::Dumper|||hex|^7b2747726565720456973656e6265697327203d3e20274769726c63732272c274a7573
74696e204f5c274d616c6c657927203d3e202753696e67696e672f416374696e67272c2753657468204d757
3736e6c616e27203d3e20275361696c696e67272c27536574682047726f7373272c27536f636365
722f5363686f6f6c272c275368616e65204a61686e6b6527203d3e2027536f63636572272c2743687269932
05061756c27203d3e2027536b69696e672f576f726b696e67206f7574277d
^Data::Dumper|||hex|^5b5b274368726973205061756c272c27436f6c6f7261646f20537072696e6773273
2c32332c37362c3138305d2c5b275368616e65206b65272c27436f6c6f7261646f20537072696e6696
e6773272c31392c37332c3135305d2c5b27536574682047726f7373272c27436f6c6f7261646f2053707269
6e6773272c32302c37302c3136305d2c5b2753657468204d757373656c6d616e272c27436f6c6f7261646f2
0537072696e6773272c32322c37342c3137305d2c5b2747726565720456973656e62656973272c27436f6c6f
7261646f20537072696e6e6773272c32322c37362c3136355d5d
```

10.4   Connecting to Databases

When a program deals with a small amount of data or deals with data whose structure is simple, but the program needs a persistent existence for the data, a text file or a DBM database works well. We already know from our discussion in Section 10.1 that a DBM database is essentially very simple. A DBM database contains a set of key-value pairs, and can be associated easily with a Perl hash. In Perl, a key for a hash is a scalar. A value in a hash is a scalar as well. Thus, we can compare a DBM database to a simple data table containing two columns: a *key* column and a *value* column. The content of each column is a scalar, in particular, a string. No other data types can be used. For example, if we want the key or the value to correspond to a date in a specific format (say, *yyyymmdd*) or a number in a specific format (say, floating point number with 10 digits including 4 after the point), we cannot really enforce the requirement unless we write the data validation code ourselves. If we want the data table to contain five columns for an individual, say, a last name, a first name, a social security number, a phone number and an address, we cannot do so in a straight-forward manner. If we want the data to contain several related tables (say, a table containing identifying information for individual customers, and another table containing orders customers have placed at a store), we cannot do so straight-forwardly either. In addition, a DBM database becomes inefficient beyond a few tens of thousands of key-value pairs. Additionally, a DBM database can be queried in only one way: given a key, find the value. Sometimes, we may prefer to have more flexibility in querying the database. For example, we may want to find all individuals that have an associated value larger than a certain threshold.

When we are interested in storing a large amount of data with rich structure, and also want to be able to query the data in a flexible and efficient manner, we need to use a database. There are several *models* that can be used to build a database. Building a database system is very complex, expensive and time-consuming, and only a large organization or a dedicated group of individuals can do so in practice. The *relational model* is the dominant model at this time. The relational model was introduced by Codd [Cod70] and is based on the *Entity-Relationship (ER) Model* of data representation, introduced by Chen [Che76]. Simply speaking, the relational model looks at data as one or more tables of data. Each piece of data in a table in a *row* or a *record*. A record or row has several *fields* or *columns*. One field is required to be unique across all records in a particular table. This field is called the *key* for the table. The key can be a combination of several fields as well. If there are several tables, they are not all independent; they are usually related using so-called *foreign keys*. However, this text book is not the place if one is not familiar with databases. One is referred to a book such as [NE02] for a tutorial introduction to databases.

There are many database servers available in the market for use by a programmer. The prices vary from being free to hundreds of thousands of dollars depending on the sophistication of the system, and the philosophy of the manufacturers. Freely available database systems include the widely-used **MySQL** system, and also the **Postgresql** system. There are many commercial database systems. These include **Access** and **SQLServer** from Microsoft, Inc., various versions of Oracle databases from Oracle, Inc., **FileMaker Pro**, originally from Apple Computers, Inc., and now from FileMaker, Inc., etc.

A database consists of the data and the engine that accesses and manipulates the data based on user or administrator requests, usually called *queries*, sometimes called *statements*. All relational databases use a language called the *Structured Query Language (SQL)* to query the actual storehouse of data. The database stores all the tables and for a program to be able to use the knowledge stored, the program has to be able to access and manipulate the contents of the database. All databases provide user interfaces in which a query can be typed and the response obtained from the database. SQL queries can be embedded in programs in other languages as well. SQL is supposed to be a standardized language, but every database manufacturer seems to add a little extra to it, making it somewhat incompatible from system to system. Thus, in practice there are many dialects of SQL. In this chapter, we primarily look at the MySQL database and the version of SQL that it uses.

First, to work with a database, the database server must be running and must be accessible to the program. The database does not have to run on the same machine as the program that tries to access it. The database server may run on another machine across the Internet. However, wherever the database program may run, the Perl program must be able to make a connection to it, send it SQL queries, and receive responses in return from it. Usually, any database that is properly set up, specifies a set of authorized users, the machines they can login from, a password for each user-machine combination, and the type of access allowed for each user-machine combination. It is possible for a database to have very fine-grained authentication and access mechanisms. This is especially necessary if the database is accessible over the Internet with many different types of users having access to it, or if the database contains sensitive information crucial to an organization's functioning.

To access a specific database from a Perl program, we need two modules: `DBI.pm` and a driver module. The `DBI.pm` module is a database access module. It defines a consistent database access interface irrespective of the actual database used behind the scene. By a consistent interface, we mean a set of methods, variables and conventions that all program have access to and use.

An actual database has a database engine or a database server. We need a driver specific to the actual database to be able to communicate with the actual database. Thus, we need to install the appropriate driver modules. The programming interface provided by the `DBI.pm` module actually talks to low-level driver modules that do most of the work.

The `DBI.pm` module sends the method calls from the Perl program to the appropriate database-specific driver, if necessary. The `DBI.pm` module also loads the appropriate drivers. The drivers have private interface functions that implement certain specific functions the specific database server or engine. For example, for connecting to a MySQL database server, we need to install the `mysql.pm` driver module. It is a DBD module. One way to install the `mysql.pm` module is to download and install the `Msql-Mysql-modules`. If one wants to install just the `mysql.pm` module, one should indicate during the installation process that the MSQL-specific module `msql.pm` is not needed.

Two terms are frequently used in programs that use the `DBI.pm` module.

- *A database handle:* A database handle is used to open a connection with an actual database. Later, it is used in all steps required in query processing. We will discuss the steps in detail later.

- *A statement handle:* To execute an SQL statement from within a Perl program, several steps are necessary. As a result, it helps to have an SQL statement. We discuss the steps later.

We see how these two handles are used in detail in the rest of the section. There are other handles that can be created and used within the Perl program as well.

10.4.1 Creating a MySQL Table in a Perl Program

In MySQL or any other database server, a database needs to be first created. A database can be created using an SQL command. This can be done by opening a MySQL client on the command line. One is advised to consult appropriate documentation on MySQL. Once a database has been created, one can use the database, and can create tables within the used database. Database servers other than MySQL also provide similar functionality, but the commands used may be different. To create a table, we need to use an SQL command. This SQL command can be run on the MySQL client using a command-line interface. The same SQL command used for creating a table can be embedded in a Perl program as well. This is precisely what the following program illustrates.

Program 10.10

```perl
#!/usr/bin/perl
#creatDB.pl
#Create a table

use DBI;
use strict;

my $databaseDriver = "mysql";
my $databaseName = "test";
my $databaseDSN = "DBI:$databaseDriver:$databaseName";
my $databaseUserName = "Project";
#this is for illustration only; a better idea is to prompt for the password
#and not hardcode it in the program
my $databasePassword = "Project";

#connect to DB and make a handle
my $dbh = DBI -> connect ($databaseDSN, $databaseUserName, $databasePassword)
    or die $DBI::errstr;
#issue a query to create a table
my $sth = $dbh -> prepare(
                qq{create TABLE friends
                    (STUDENT_ID INT (6) UNSIGNED AUTO_INCREMENT PRIMARY KEY NOT NULL,
                        SSNUM INT (9) UNSIGNED NOT NULL UNIQUE,
                        NAME CHAR (50) NOT NULL,
                        AGE INT(3) NOT NULL,
                        HOMETOWN CHAR (100) NOT NULL,
                        SCHOOL CHAR (150) NOT NULL,
                        NOTES CHAR (255)
                    )});
$sth -> execute () or warn $dbh->errstr();
$sth -> finish();

$dbh -> disconnect();
```

The program uses the DBI.pm module that provides general connectivity to databases. The driver used in mysql.pm. In other words, the functionality provided by the MySQL-dependent mysql.pm driver. However, we do not have to use the mysql.pm driver. The DBI.pm method connect installs the appropriate driver when needed. There may be other ways to install drivers, but let us just use `connect` to do so implicitly. A database with the name `test` has already been created by the database administrator prior to executing the current program. Usually, the database is created using the `MySQL` command-line interface or by running a script containing SQL commands. The database administrator also has created a user `Project` on the machine on which the Perl program and the `mysqld`, i.e., the MySQL server are running. For the user `Project` on the local host or machine, the administrator has given the password `Project`.

To use the database from within the Perl program, the program must establish a connection to the database. One must note that the database server a program connects to, does not have have to run on the same machine where the Perl program is running. The database server can be running on any other machine that is accessible over the network, as long as the network connectivity exists and the proper user-password-machine combination has been established by a database administrator. The proper access privileges need to be granted by a database administrator even if the Perl program is running on the same machine as the database server `mysqld`. The connection to the database from within the program is established using the `connect` method of the `DBI.pm` module. It is a class method.

```
my $dbh = DBI -> connect ($databaseDSN, $databaseUserName, $databasePassword)
        or die $DBI::errstr;
```

`$dbh` is a database handle. The database handle is used to communicate with the database. If `connect` succeeds, a database handle has been created. If `connect` fails, it returns `undef` and the program `dies` with a message. `connect` can be called with various numbers of arguments. One is advised to consult MySQL documentation for the alternatives. The form we use here requires three arguments: a database source name or DSN argument, called `$databaseDSN` here, the name of the database user and the associated password. The DSN argument is formed by concatenating the string `DBI` and the database driver name and the database name, and gluing them with the colon (`:`). The Perl program and the database server are running on the same machine.

If a connection can be established to the named database source `$databaseName` with the `$databaseDriver` using the user name and password specified, we have the handle `$dbh` to work with later in the program. In the current program, we simply `create` a table within the database `$databaseName` in MySQL running on the local machine. The database administrator has given the user `Project` privilege to create tables within the `test` database and access the tables within `test`. To create a table called `friends`, the MySQL query or request that needs to be issued is given below.

```
create TABLE friends
                (STUDENT_ID INT (6) UNSIGNED AUTO_INCREMENT PRIMARY KEY NOT NULL,
                        SSNUM INT (9) UNSIGNED NOT NULL UNIQUE,
                        NAME CHAR (50) NOT NULL,
                        AGE INT(3) NOT NULL,
                        HOMETOWN CHAR (100) NOT NULL,
                        SCHOOL CHAR (150) NOT NULL,
                        NOTES CHAR (255)
                )
```

This query or statement can be issued directly using a MySQL client, usually on a the command-line, but possibly using a graphical user interface as well. However, when the command is issued from inside a Perl program, there are two steps: *preparation* and its *execution*. This is why, we create a statement handle `$sth` by `prepareing` the query. `qq` simply double quotes the SQL query like a string. The query uses SQL although the SQL used is specific to MySQL. It may be a little different with other database servers such as Oracle or FileMaker Pro or Microsoft SQL server. There is no other way but to consult the appropriate server-specific documentation to be able to formulate the SQL query correctly. In general, the data types allowed, and the options that can be used are different in different versions of SQL. In the MySQL version of SQL, the `create` command takes the keyword `TABLE` followed by the name of the table being created. Here, we are creating a table called `friends`. Following the name of the table, the fields or column names are specified separated by the comma (,). The fields to be created are STUDENT_ID, SSNUM, AGE, HOMETOWN, SCHOOL and NOTES. Every SQL table needs a key or a *primary key*. Here, STUDENT_ID field represents the primary key. It is an unsigned number with up to six digits in it. It is specified using the attribute or option PRIMARY KEY. A primary key must also have the NOT NULL attribute. In other words, when we enter data, the field must always have a value. The field STUDENT_ID also has the AUTO_INCREMENT attribute. That is, the value of the key is an integer that is automatically incremented by one for every row or record entered into the table. The second field is SSNUM representing a Social Security Number. It is an unsigned integer with up to 9 decimal digits. The field is required in every row or record of data. The third field is AGE, a 3-digit integer, and is required as well. HOMETOWN and SCHOOL are character or text data and are required. HOMETOWN can contain up to 100 characters and SCHOOL can contain up to 150 characters. The CHAR data type is fixed length. In other words, the specified amount of space is allocated in each record or row, whether it is used or not. Unused length is padded automatically by MySQL using its own padding character, which is the empty string. The last field is NOTES that is a 255-byte character string. This field need not be field in each record.

Once a statement has been prepared, we have a statement handle. Some database drivers convert the statement into an internal format during preparation while others do not do anything at all. Here, the statement handle is $sth. The statement is executed by calling the execute method on the statement handle. execute sends the statement to the database server using the $dbh database handle. If there are problems during execution, the error string is available using the errstr method of the database handle. If the execution of the statement takes place without any problem, the program wraps up the handling of the statement using the finish method on the statement handle $sth.

When this program is run on the command prompt, assuming everything is flawless, nothing is seen on the terminal. To verify that the program has run and done what it is supposed to, we can run the MySQL client mysql on the command-line. An extended interaction is given below.

```
pikespeak[139]: mysql -u Project -p
Enter password:
Welcome to the MySQL monitor.  Commands end with ; or \g.
Your MySQL connection id is 152 to server version: 3.23.22-beta

Type 'help' for help.

mysql> show databases;
+-----------------+
| Database        |
+-----------------+
| AP_news_archive |
| cprfproj        |
| kalita          |
| kasireddy       |
| movies          |
| mysql           |
| prohilla        |
| reuters         |
| test            |
+-----------------+
9 rows in set (0.00 sec)

mysql> use test;
Reading table information for completion of table and column names
You can turn off this feature to get a quicker startup with -A

Database changed
mysql> show tables;
+----------------+
| Tables_in_test |
+----------------+
| SITES          |
| friends        |
| testac         |
| testad         |
| testae         |
| trainingSet    |
+----------------+
```

```
6 rows in set (0.00 sec)

mysql> select * from friends;
Empty set (0.00 sec)

mysql> describe friends;
+------------+------------------+------+-----+---------+----------------+------------------------------------+
| Field      | Type             | Null | Key | Default | Extra          | Privileges                         |
+------------+------------------+------+-----+---------+----------------+------------------------------------+
| STUDENT_ID | int(6) unsigned  |      | PRI | NULL    | auto_increment | select,insert,update,references    |
| SSNUM      | int(9) unsigned  |      | UNI | 0       |                | select,insert,update,references    |
| NAME       | char(50)         |      |     |         |                | select,insert,update,references    |
| AGE        | int(3)           |      |     | 0       |                | select,insert,update,references    |
| HOMETOWN   | char(100)        |      |     |         |                | select,insert,update,references    |
| SCHOOL     | char(150)        |      |     |         |                | select,insert,update,references    |
| NOTES      | char(255)        | YES  |     | NULL    |                | select,insert,update,references    |
+------------+------------------+------+-----+---------+----------------+------------------------------------+
7 rows in set (0.00 sec)
```

The user is Project. The -p command-line option prompts for a password. Entering the correct password puts us in an interaction with the MySQL server. We can run the

```
show databases;
```

command to see all the databases that are known by the MySQL server. Here, there are nine databases: AP_news_archive, cprfproj, kalita, kasireddy, movies , mysql, prohilla, reuters and test . Our program works with the last database called test. We then run the

```
use test;
```

MySQL command to start working with the database test. We use the

```
show tables;
```

MySQL command to look at the tables in the test database. There are 6 tables: SITES, friends, testac, testad, testae, trainingSet . The table friends is the one the Perl program created. We use the SQL command

```
select * from friends;
```

to look at the rows or records in this newly created table. Obviously, there are no records since we have entered no data into the table. We use the MySQL command

```
describe friends;
```

to look at the fields or columns in the table created. The information about the fields is printed in columnar form in a table. The fields are the ones we have declared in the Perl program. The information showed confirms that the Perl program is able to communicate with the MySQL database server, and that the MySQL database server has executed the SQL statement that is passed to it by the Perl program.

If we run the program another time, we get the following message.

```
DBD::mysql::st execute failed: Table 'friends' already exists at createDB.pl line 29.
Table 'friends' already exists at createDB.pl line 29.
```

10.4.2   Working with an Existing MySQL Table

In Section 10.4.1, we discuss a program that creates a table in MySQL from within a Perl program. Usually, a table is created using an interface—using either command-line or GUI-based—without the need of writing a program. A table can also be created using pure SQL commands stored in a file, without using Perl as an intermediary. The program in Section 10.4.1 is an exercise illustrating that a program can create a table if necessary.

Once a table has been created, we can populate it. A program can populate a table from data using various sources, such as from a terminal, a graphical user interface, a text file, another database table—either of the same kind of database or another. For example, it is possible to read from a table in an Oracle database and write to a table in a MySQL database. The program that follows populates a database by inserting data hard-coded within the program as well by reading from a text file. The program also runs a few SELECT queries. SELECT statements in SQL ask the database to select certain rows from within a table within it that satisfy specified constraints. SELECT is a very commonly used SQL query or statement.

Program 10.11

```perl
#!/usr/bin/perl
#insertFetch.pl
use strict;
use DBI;

my ($driver, $database,  $user, $password);
my ($dsn, $dbh, @databases, @tables, $table,  $sth, $query);
my ($numRows, $numFields, $fieldNames);
$driver = "mysql";
$database = "test";
$dsn = "DBI:$driver:$database";
$user = "Project";
$password = "Project";

##need to start the connection
$dbh = DBI->connect ($dsn, $user, $password) or
    die "Cannot connect to $dsn: $DBI::errstr";

#List all the tables; private driver functions
@tables = $dbh->func ('_ListTables');
print "Tables in database $database are ...\n",
        join "\n",  @tables, "\n\n";

#prepare a query;
$table = "friends";
$query = "select * from $table";
$sth = $dbh -> prepare ($query);
$sth -> execute;
$numFields = $sth ->{'NUM_OF_FIELDS'};
print "Number of fields in table $table = $numFields\n";
$numRows = $sth -> rows;
print "Found $numRows rows in $dsn\n";
$fieldNames = $sth -> {'NAME'};
print "The fields in table $table = \n ",
    join ("  ", @$fieldNames), "\n\n";

#Create a query with
$query = qq{
```

```perl
                INSERT INTO $table (SSNUM, NAME, AGE, HOMETOWN, SCHOOL)
                      VALUES (?, ?, ?, ?, ?)};
$sth = $dbh -> prepare ($query);
$sth -> execute (198640756,"Joe White", 18, "Colorado Springs", "PPCC")
    or warn $dbh -> errstr;

open IN, "friends.txt";
while (<IN>){
    chomp;
    my ($ssnum, $name, $age, $hometown, $school) = split /::/, $_;
    print "$ssnum $name $age $hometown $school\n";
    $sth -> execute ($ssnum, $name, $age, $hometown, $school)
        or warn $dbh -> errstr;
}
$sth -> finish ();

#all entries
print "\n\nAll entries in TABLE $table\n\n";
$query = qq{select STUDENT_ID, SSNUM, NAME,
                AGE, HOMETOWN, SCHOOL from $table};
fetchPrintRows ($dbh, $sth, $query);

#Find entries from Springs
print "\n\nAll entries in TABLE $table sorted by AGE and SSNUM\n\n";
$query = qq{select STUDENT_ID, SSNUM, NAME,
                AGE, HOMETOWN, SCHOOL from $table
                WHERE HOMETOWN like "%Springs%"
                ORDER BY AGE, STUDENT_ID, SSNUM};
fetchPrintRows ($dbh, $sth, $query);

#perform an update
$query = qq{update friends set SSNUM = 222334444 where
                name="Christopher Paul"};
$sth = $dbh -> prepare ($query);
$sth -> execute () or warn $dbh -> errstr;
print "\n\nAll Colorado Springs entries in TABLE $table";
print " sorted by AGE, STUDENT_ID and SSNUM\n\n";
$query = qq{select STUDENT_ID, SSNUM, NAME,
                AGE, HOMETOWN, SCHOOL from $table
                WHERE AGE > 20
                ORDER BY AGE, STUDENT_ID, SSNUM};
fetchPrintRows ($dbh, $sth, $query);

#disconnect from the database
$dbh -> disconnect ();

############################
#subroutine to fetch the rows
sub fetchPrintRows{
    my ($dbhandle, $sthandle,  $aQuery) = @_;
    $sthandle = $dbhandle -> prepare ($aQuery);
```

```
    $sthandle -> execute () or warn $dbhandle -> errstr;
    while (my $row = $sthandle -> fetchrow_hashref()){
        printf "%5d   %9d   %-20s %3d %-20s %-5s\n",
        $row -> {'STUDENT_ID'},
        $row -> {'SSNUM'},
        $row -> {'NAME'},
        $row -> {'AGE'},
        $row -> {'HOMETOWN'},
        $row -> {'SCHOOL'};
    }
} #sub ends
```

The program starts by declaring to use the DBI.pm module and hence, imports all variables, functions and methods in the DBI.pm module. As discussed earlier, depending on the underlying database, the appropriate driver needs to be loaded on the system. Here, the database is MySQL. Therefore, the driver used is mysql. The DBI.pm is the high, database-independent level interface from the side of the Perl program; the mysql.pm module provides the low-level MySQL-specific interface. The program connects to a database using the login name Project and the password Project. If it cannot connect, the program dies.

Using the DBI.pm method func, one can call *private* methods that are non-standard and non-portable and that are implemented by a specific driver, here the MySQL driver. func takes a function name as argument, here _ListTables.

```
@tables = $dbh->func ('_ListTables');
```

A function argument sent to func takes arguments, the arguments come first, and the function name comes last. One must consult driver-specific documentation to determine what is appropriate. In this specific case, the MySQL server returns the number of tables in the test database. The list is printed by the program. We can look at the output given later in the section to confirm.

Next, the program takes an SQL query and prepares it.

```
$query = "select * from $table";
$sth = $dbh -> prepare ($query);
```

prepare takes as its argument an SQL statement for later execution. Some database driver modules put the statement into an internal compiled form so that it runs faster with execute. At this time, MySQL does not really do anything to prepare a statement and merely stores the statement. prepare returns a handle that can be used to get attributes of the statement as well as to execute the statement. Some drives can give useful information only after the statement has been executed. In general, DBI drivers do not parse; the contents of the statement are passed directly to the database driver and subsequently to the database engine. The query prepared and executed is given below.

```
$query = "select * from $table";
```

The select SQL statement asks the database to obtain one or more rows of data from a specified table to satisfy specified conditions, if any. This select statement does not have any associated conditions. As a result, every row of the table is returned by the database. A select statement can request the database to return a set of explicitly listed fields for each row returned. In this select statement, no explicit list of fields has been given. Instead, * has been specified as the field list. * indicates that all fields of the chosen rows be returned.

Once the select statement is executed, we can query to find the number of fields in the table.

```
$numFields = $sth ->{'NUM_OF_FIELDS'};
```

We can find the number of rows returned by a query. Here, assuming that the table `friend` has been constructed recently with no rows of data, the number of rows returned by the `select` statement is given above is zero. The `rows` method returns the number of rows affected by the last row-affecting command or -1 if the number of rows is not known or not available. The reader is advised to consult the output of the program given later in the section.

The names of the fields in the table are found by using the `NAME` attribute of the statement handle `$sth`.

```
$fieldNames = $sth -> {'NAME'};
```

The attribute returns a reference to a list of field names. The field names are printed by the program.

Next, the program creates a string that represents a query for inserting rows of data into the table. The SQL query for insertion is given below.

```
INSERT INTO $table (SSNUM, NAME, AGE, HOMETOWN, SCHOOL)
                VALUES (?, ?, ?, ?, ?)
```

The query or statement asks the database to insert five fields when it inserts a row into the table `friends`. The fields are `SSNUM`, `NAME`, `AGE`. `HOMETOWN`, and `SCHOOL`. Note that the table can have six columns in each row. Here, the column `NOTES` remains unspecified. The fields to be inserted are specified within parentheses. The SQL keyword `VALUES` is used to specify the values to be inserted into the table. The values are given in a list. The values can be given directly, or one or more values can be left empty with placeholders. A placeholder is represented by `?`. In the current SQL statement, five field values need to be specified. Each of the five fields is left unspecified at this time. The values are specified later in the program. The query is `prepared` and the statement `executed`.

```
$sth = $dbh -> prepare ($query);
$sth -> execute (198640756,"Joe White", 18, "Colorado Springs", "PPCC")
    or warn $dbh -> errstr;
```

We have seen the `execute` method of the statement handle earlier. It has been called so far with no arguments. However, in the current invocation of `execute`, we provide five argument values. These five values correspond to the five unspecified fields in the SQL query. Thus, an SQL query may have one or more unspecified fields in the query string that is `prepared`. Any unspecified field values must be specified in the `execute` method call. Thus, the SQL query must be fully specified by the time it is `executed`. The unspecified fields in the original SQL query do not have to be in sequence. Also, a few fields may be specified in the `prepared` query and the rest specified in the `execute` method call. The values unspecified in the `prepared` query must be specified in the same sequence in the `execute` method call. In the current `INSERT` SQL statement, the values of all the fields are specified directly in terms of the program code.

The sequence of statements that follow are used to read a text file line by line. Each line represents a row of data. The fields in a row are separated from each other by two colons. This is a made-up separator for our data file. The program separates the fields using the `split` statement. The values obtained by `splitting` are given the names `$ssnum`, `$name`, `$age`, `$hometown`, and `$school`, respectively. The call to the `execute` method that follows are passed these five variables in the same order as argument.

```
$sth -> execute ($ssnum, $name, $age, $hometown, $school)
    or warn $dbh -> errstr;
```

The point to note here is that there is time expended in `prepareing` a query. Thus, if many similar queries are prepared individually, one at a time, time is wasted. Some such waste of time can be obviated by `prepareing` the query with one or more missing values, and specifying the missing values during execution. In the current program, we could have `prepared` the query inside the `while` statement. However, in such a case, the query would have been `prepared` for every iteration of the loop, i.e., for every line of data in the text file `friends.txt`. We save some time by `prepareing` the query once, before the `while` loop is entered. It results in saving of time which may not be noticeable only if a few lines of data are inserted inside the `while` loop, but would be substantial if tens or hundreds of thousands of line are inserted. The contents of the file `data.txt` are printed to the screen as the data are entered into the table.

Next, the program prints every row of data that has been entered into the table onto the standard output. This requires the program to `prepare` the following query.

```
select STUDENT_ID, SSNUM, NAME,
               AGE, HOMETOWN, SCHOOL from $table
```

Note that this `select` query has no conditions associated with it. As a result, execution of this query results in selection of all rows in the database. Only the specified fields are selected from each row. The `prepareing` of the query, its execution and the printing of every row's data takes place in the subroutine `fetchPrintRows`. This subroutine, seen at the bottom of the program, takes three arguments: a database handle, a statement handle, and a query. The query is `prepared` and `executed`. There is a `while` loop in the subroutine. The conditional of the `while` loop is given below.

```
my $row = $sthandle -> fetchrow_hashref()
```

The right hand side of the assignment has a call to the `fetchrow_hashref` method of the statement handle object `$sth`. `fetchrow_hashref` returns a reference for the next row of data returned by the database. The row of data is represented within Perl as a hash. That is, as soon as row of data is returned by the database driver, Perl converts it into a hash automatically before making it available to the program. The program sees the row of data as a hash table where each field name is used as a key and the corresponding content of the field as value. The program prints the field values nicely using `printf` and an associated format specification. The `while` loop in the subroutine is executed as many times as there are rows in the result returned by the database driver.

Next, the main program executes another SQL query. The query is given below.

```
select STUDENT_ID, SSNUM, NAME,
               AGE, HOMETOWN, SCHOOL from $table
               WHERE HOMETOWN like "%Springs%"
               ORDER BY AGE, STUDENT_ID, SSNUM
```

This query has one condition. The condition requires that the value of the HOMETOWN field is

```
like "%Springs%"
```

The `like` keyword allows pattern matching. The `%` sign inside the string to be matched stands for any sequence of characters. Thus, the HOMETOWN field's value needs to contain the word `Springs`. It can be preceded or followed by any number of other characters. The query also has an ORDER clause. The ORDER clause asks the database to sort the returned rows by using the fields specified. Here, sorting is performed using the fields AGE, STUDENT_ID and SSNUM, in this specific order. The default sort order is ascending. By looking at the output that follows the program, we an see the results of sorting.

The next SQL query executed is an `update` statement. When giving an SQL keyword, it can be specified in any case. Thus, keywords such as `update`, `select`, `where`, `order by` can be specified in upper case or lower case. However, the names of tables and fields are case-sensitive in Unix machines including Mac OS X. On Windows machines, case does not matter for names. However, it is advisable that case be observed so that the program is portable. The `update` query is given below.

```
update friends set SSNUM = 222334444 where
               name="Christopher Paul"
```

It changes Christopher Paul's social security number.

This is followed by the execution of an SQL query that prints the names of all rows in the updated table for which the value of the AGE field is more than 20. The rows are printed sorted by AGE, STUDENT_ID and SSNUM, in this specific order.

This program has quite a bit of output. The reader is advised to look at the output carefully and compare it with the text of the program. It will aid in understanding the code. Once all the SQL statements have been executed, the program disconnects from the database source. An output run is shown below.

```
Tables in database test are ...
SITES
friends
testac
testad
testae
trainingSet


Number of fields in table friends = 7
Found 0 rows in DBI:mysql:test
The fields in table friends =
 STUDENT_ID  SSNUM  NAME  AGE  HOMETOWN  SCHOOL  NOTES

198640757 Shane Jahnke 19 Colorado Springs UCCS
198640758 Seth Gross 20 Colorado Springs UCCS
198640759 Matt Gustafson 21 Colorado Springs UCCS
198640760 Christopher Paul 23 Colorado Springs CTU
198640761 Justin O'Malley 19 Colorado Springs NULL
198640762 Nick Freeman 19 Colorado Springs NULL
198640763 Clint Trebesh 18 Glenwood Springs UCCS
198640764 Griffin Heath 20 Evergreeen UCCS
198640765 Qin Jiang 22 Trinidad UCCS
198640766 Brooke Peterson 22 Denver UCD


All entries in TABLE friends

      1    198640756    Joe White           18 Colorado Springs    PPCC
      2    198640757    Shane Jahnke        19 Colorado Springs    UCCS
      3    198640758    Seth Gross          20 Colorado Springs    UCCS
      4    198640759    Matt Gustafson      21 Colorado Springs    UCCS
      5    198640760    Christopher Paul    23 Colorado Springs    CTU
      6    198640761    Justin O'Malley     19 Colorado Springs    NULL
      7    198640762    Nick Freeman        19 Colorado Springs    NULL
      8    198640763    Clint Trebesh       18 Glenwood Springs    UCCS
      9    198640764    Griffin Heath       20 Evergreeen          UCCS
     10    198640765    Qin Jiang           22 Trinidad            UCCS
     11    198640766    Brooke Peterson     22 Denver              UCD


All entries in TABLE friends sorted by AGE and SSNUM
```

```
   1  198640756   Joe White           18 Colorado Springs      PPCC
   8  198640763   Clint Trebesh       18 Glenwood Springs      UCCS
   2  198640757   Shane Jahnke        19 Colorado Springs      UCCS
   6  198640761   Justin O'Malley     19 Colorado Springs      NULL
   7  198640762   Nick Freeman        19 Colorado Springs      NULL
   3  198640758   Seth Gross          20 Colorado Springs      UCCS
   4  198640759   Matt Gustafson      21 Colorado Springs      UCCS
   5  198640760   Christopher Paul    23 Colorado Springs      CTU


All Colorado Springs entries in TABLE friends sorted by AGE,
                STUDENT_ID and SSNUM

   4  198640759   Matt Gustafson      21 Colorado Springs      UCCS
  10  198640765   Qin Jiang           22 Trinidad             UCCS
  11  198640766   Brooke Peterson     22 Denver               UCD
   5  222334444   Christopher Paul    23 Colorado Springs      CTU
```

10.4.3   Using a MySQL Database Across the Internet

MySQL is a network database. In other words, a MySQL database is easily accessible through the Internet using TCP/IP. It is possible to write socket programs to access a MySQL database running on a machine that is accessible using TCP/IP. However, it is not necessary since MySQL provides us a simple way to do so, by simply providing the machine name and the port number at which the MySQL database is published. The standard port at which MySQL publishes by default is 3306. Although the example that follows uses MySQL, the same should be possible on all modern databases as long as the database has been configured to publish on the Internet at a certain pre-specified port number. In addition, the user specified in the program must have access to the database.

The following program runs on the machine cs.uccs.edu. The MySQL database server is running on the machine pikespeak.uccs.edu. The port at which the database server listens is 3306.

Program 10.12

```perl
#!/usr/bin/perl
#fetchFromCS.pl
use strict;
use DBI;

my ($driver, $database,  $user, $password);
my ($dsn, $dbh,, $table,  $sth, $query);
$driver = "mysql";
$database = q{database=test;host=pikespeak.uccs.edu;port=3306};
$dsn = "DBI:$driver:$database";
$user = "Project";
$password = "Project";

##need to start the connection
$dbh = DBI->connect ($dsn, $user, $password) or
    die "Cannot connect to $dsn: $DBI::errstr";

#prepare a query;
```

```
$table = "friends";

#Find entries NOT from Springs
print "\n\nAll entries in TABLE $table sorted by AGE and SSNUM\n\n";
$query = qq{select STUDENT_ID, SSNUM, NAME,
                AGE, HOMETOWN, SCHOOL from $table
                WHERE HOMETOWN not like "%Springs%"
                order by AGE, STUDENT_ID, SSNUM};
fetchPrintRows ($dbh, $sth, $query);


print
  "\n\nAll Colorado Springs entries in TABLE $table 20 years old or younger";
print " sorted by AGE, STUDENT_ID and SSNUM\n\n";
$query = qq{select STUDENT_ID, SSNUM, NAME,
                AGE, HOMETOWN, SCHOOL from $table
                WHERE AGE <= 20
                order by AGE, STUDENT_ID, SSNUM};
fetchPrintRows ($dbh, $sth, $query);

#disconnect from the database
$dbh -> disconnect ();

#############################
#subroutine to fetch the rows
sub fetchPrintRows{
    my ($dbhandle, $sthandle,  $aQuery) = @_;
    $sthandle = $dbhandle -> prepare ($aQuery);
    $sthandle -> execute () or warn $dbhandle -> errstr;
    while (my $row = $sthandle -> fetchrow_hashref()){
        printf "%5d  %9d  %-20s %3d %-20s %-5s\n",
        $row -> {'STUDENT_ID'},
        $row -> {'SSNUM'},
        $row -> {'NAME'},
        $row -> {'AGE'},
        $row -> {'HOMETOWN'},
        $row -> {'SCHOOL'};
    }
} #sub ends
```

As usual, the program uses `mysql.pm` driver since it connects to a MySQL database. The database is specified using the following statement.

```
$database = q{database=test;host=pikespeak.uccs.edu;port=3306};
```

This clearly specifies that the database name is `test`. It is listening at port 3306 of the machine `pikespeak.uccs.edu`. This program can run anywhere on the Internet and can connect to the MySQL database if the machine name, user name, and password combination is correct. The user name and password are usually given for a specific machine from which the MySQL client, and hence, the Perl program can connect. It is also possible to specify, by the database administrator, that the machine from which a user connects to the database does not really matter when creating authentication of grant tables.

The program connects to the database in the usual manner. In fact, for a Perl program running on one machine and connecting to another machine, the only thing that needs to be changed is the specification of the database source. Everything else in the code is the same as the program running on the machine where the MySQL database is running.

This program executes two SQL queries. The first query finds entries where the HOMETOWN field does not contain the word Springs. The second SQL query obtains the rows of data for which the age field is 20 or less. The program uses a subroutine called fetchPrintRows to prepare an SQL query, execute the query, and obtain and print each of the rows that are returned by the database. The output of running this program on the machine cs.uccs.edu is given below. Note, once again, that the database server is running on the machine pikespeak.uccs.edu.

```
All entries in TABLE friends sorted by AGE and SSNUM

    9   198640764   Griffin Heath        20 Evergreeen          UCCS
   10   198640765   Qin Jiang            22 Trinidad            UCCS
   11   198640766   Brooke Peterson      22 Denver              UCD


All Colorado Springs entries in TABLE friends 20 years old or
younger sorted by AGE, STUDENT_ID and SSNUM

    1   198640756   Joe White            18 Colorado Springs    PPCC
    8   198640763   Clint Trebesh        18 Glenwood Springs    UCCS
    2   198640757   Shane Jahnke         19 Colorado Springs    UCCS
    6   198640761   Justin O'Malley      19 Colorado Springs    NULL
    7   198640762   Nick Freeman         19 Colorado Springs    NULL
    3   198640758   Seth Gross           20 Colorado Springs    UCCS
    9   198640764   Griffin Heath        20 Evergreeen          UCCS
```

10.4.4 Using Databases In CGI Programs

Of course, a CGI program can query a database server, either running on the same machine or on a machine across the Internet. There is nothing complicated in connecting to a database from a CGI program. In fact, it is CGI programming as usual. In the following, we discuss two CGI programs: a program that queries a database to obtain the value of a Web page access counter, and a program that allows a user to search a database by submitting a filled HTML form.

10.4.4.1 Web Page Counters Using a MySQL Database

In Section 10.2.3, we discuss how Web page counters can be kept in a DBM file. A DBM file stores a set of key-value pairs. A key corresponds to the name of a counter and the value corresponds to the current value of the counter. A counter is referenced by name in a Web page. Actually, the counter's name is passed as an argument to a CGI program. The CGI program accesses the DBM file, obtains the current value of the named counter, creates a graphic image using the GD.pm module, sends it as an in-line image to the Web page that is displayed by the Web browser in the appropriate location on the Web page. Of course, a database table can be used to store counter names and their corresponding values. A very simple two or three-column table that uses the unique counter name or a unique numeric counter ID as the primary key can accomplish this requirement. In the context of databases, the representational and storage needs are very simple. However, if a company, an organization or an individual, wants to provide a service that allows any individual creating a Web page anywhere in the world maintain counter values for free or for a cost, such as thecounter.com, using a database is very appropriate. The single table used in the example given below can be used together with other related tables in a database to store information about the Web pages, the subscribers of the counter service's facilities, the access statistics for a page, etc. Thus, the table discussed below can be a component of a much more complex and sophisticated system.

The following interaction with a MySQL database gives the definition of the table used. It also shows that the initial value of the counter DBBasedCounter1 is zero. This is an illustrative example, and we assume that there is only one counter in the table called COUNTERS. In a sophisticated, possibly commercial system, such a table may contain millions of entries. We create a MySQL table using the following SQL statement typed in from the command-line at a MySQL client. The database user is Project.

```
mysql> create table COUNTERS (
    COUNTER_ID INT (6) UNSIGNED AUTO_INCREMENT PRIMARY KEY NOT NULL,
    COUNTER_NAME CHAR (50) NOT NULL UNIQUE,
    COUNTER_VALUE INT(10) UNSIGNED NOT NULL);
Query OK, 0 rows affected (0.00 sec)
mysql> describe COUNTERS;
```

Field	Type	Null	Key	Default	Extra	Privileges
COUNTER_ID	int(6) unsigned		PRI	NULL	auto_increment	select,insert,update,references
COUNTER_NAME	char(50)		UNI			select,insert,update,references
COUNTER_VALUE	int(10) unsigned			0		select,insert,update,references

```
3 rows in set (0.00 sec)

mysql> select * from COUNTERS;
```

COUNTER_ID	COUNTER_NAME	COUNTER_VALUE
1	DBBasedCounter1	0

```
1 row in set (0.00 sec)
```

The table COUNTER is created by typing the appropriate SQL in a MySQL client. In a Linux machine, the MySQL client usually has a command-line interface and is invoked by typing mysql as a command. The table has three columns: COUNTER_ID, COUNTER_NAME, and COUNTER_VALUE. COUNTER_ID is an integer that can be up to six decimal digits in length. It cannot be empty in any row. It is the primary key, and hence unique across all the rows of the table. The value of COUNTER_ID is automatically incremented by 1 for every new row (or counter) entered in the table. COUNTER_NAME is a character string of length up to 60. A counter must have a name; thus, COUNTER_NAME cannot be empty. In addition, COUNTER_NAME is unique across all rows in the table. The third column is COUNTER_VALUE. It is an unsigned integer up to 10 digits in length. Its value cannot be empty. The default initial value of this field is zero. A counter called DBBasedCounter1 is created an an appropriate row entered into the table. This is an illustrative situation, and the table contains only one row.

Once we have the COUNTER table, and the counter named DBBasedCounter1, we can use it in a Web page to produce a GD-based graphical access counter. The program that follows is similar to the one that we discuss in Section 10.2.3 except that it uses a database to store counter values instead of a DBM file.

Program 10.13

```perl
#!/usr/bin/perl -T
#counterDB.pl

use GD;
use CGI qw(:standard);
use CGI::Carp qw(fatalsToBrowser);
use Untaint;
```

```perl
use DBI;

#######Set CGI size limit; disable file upload
$CGI::POST_MAX = 1024; #max 1024 bytes posts
$CGI::DISABLE_UPLOADS = 1;

#database details
my ($driver, $database,  $user, $password);
my ($dsn, $dbh,, $table,  $sth, $DBQuery);
my ($CGIQuery, $name_counter, $counter,  @digits, $length, $im);
my ($black, $white, $blue, $i, $counter_value);
$driver = "mysql";
$database = "test";
$dsn = "DBI:$driver:$database";
$user = "Project";
$password = "Project";

#CGI details
$CGIQuery = new CGI;
$name_counter = $CGIQuery->param(counter);
$name_counter = untaint(qr{^[\d\w.-]+$}, $name_counter);

##need to start the connection
$dbh = DBI->connect ($dsn, $user, $password) or
    die "Cannot connect to $dsn: $DBI::errstr";

#prepare a query;
$table = "COUNTERS";
$DBQuery = qq{select COUNTER_VALUE from $table
              WHERE COUNTER_NAME = "$name_counter"};
$sth = $dbh -> prepare ($DBQuery);
$sth -> execute () or warn $dbh -> errstr;
my $row = $sth -> fetchrow_hashref();
$counter_value = $row -> {'COUNTER_VALUE'};
$sth -> finish();

$counter_value  = untaint(qr{^\d+$}, $counter_value);
#Increment the retrieved counter value and write it back to the database
$counter_value++;
$DBQuery = qq{update COUNTERS set COUNTER_VALUE = $counter_value
                  where COUNTER_NAME = "$name_counter"};
$sth = $dbh -> prepare ($DBQuery);
$sth -> execute () or warn $dbh -> errstr;
$sth -> finish ();
$dbh -> disconnect ();

#Find the number of digits in the counter
@digits = split(//, $counter_value);
$length = length($counter_value);
#Create a new GD image
$im = new GD::Image($length*14-2,20);
```

```
#Create colors by allocating RGB
$black = $im->colorAllocate(0, 0, 0);
$white = $im->colorAllocate(255, 255, 255);
$blue = $im->colorAllocate(0,0,255);
#Create the GD image containing the counter's value
srand();
for ($i=0; $i < $length; $i++)
{ $im->string(gdLargeFont, 2+$i*14, 1+int(rand(3)), $digits[$i], $white);
  if($i < $length-1)
  { $im->filledRectangle(12+$i*14, 0, 13+$i*14, 20, $blue);
  }
}


# print the image to STDOUT, i.e., send to browser
print header("image/jpeg");
binmode STDOUT;
print $im->jpeg;

exit;
```

The program uses the GD.pm module to create a graphic image of a counter, the CGI.pm module to handle CGI queries, and the DBI.pm module to interact with a database. The CGI::Carp.pm module is used to get notification of CGI errors. The CGI errors are printed to the browser for purposes of easy debugging. The program used a MySQL database server. Therefore, the DBD driver module used is mysql.pm.

The program connects to the MySQL database running on the same machine as the CGI program. The database used is test. The database requires a valid user name and password combination. The program creates a new CGI object called $CGIQuery to handle the current query or request coming from a Web browser. It obtains the parameter named counter and calls the value of this parameter $name_counter. We have used an object-oriented interface to CGI.pm in this program.

```
$CGIQuery = new CGI;
$name_counter = $CGIQuery->param(counter);
```

The value is untainted or laundered. The program follows by attempting to make a connection to the specified database source using the user name-password combination given.

```
$dbh = DBI->connect ($dsn, $user, $password) or
    die "Cannot connect to $dsn: $DBI::errstr";
```

The program next writes up a database query and quotes it appropriately using qq. qq allows variable interpolation, and the string inside can span more than one line. The SQL query is given below.

```
select COUNTER_VALUE from $table
                WHERE COUNTER_NAME = "$name_counter"
```

As usual, the query is prepared before execution. The prepare method of the database handle object $dbh takes the database query string as argument and returns a statement handle $sth which is used later to execute the query and fetch the result of execution of the query.

```
$sth = $dbh -> prepare ($DBQuery);
$sth -> execute () or warn $dbh -> errstr;
```

Once a database query has been successfully executed by the database, the results are returned by the database server to the Perl program. The returned results can be accessed in several ways from within the Perl program. This program shows one way, using `fetchrow_hashref`. The name of a counter is unique in the database table COUNTER, and therefore, only one row is returned as a response to the successful execution of the database query. The row can be accessed within the Perl program as an array, or as a hash, or as a reference to an array or a hash. `fetchrow_hashref` returns a reference to this row where the contents of the row itself is a hash. In such a hash, a field or column name is a key, and the content of the field is the value. `fetchrow_arrayref`, which is not used in this program, would have returned a reference to the contents of the row, where the row itself is considered to be returned in the from of an array. Similarly, `fetchrow_array` returns the contents of the row as a regular array. Any one of these three methods can be used to obtain the contents of one row, and which one is used depends on the programmer's preference. Obtaining a reference, and dereferencing takes time. However, if the contents of a row are fairly voluminous, it makes sense to use references instead of dealing with the contents directly. Using a hash requires additional time compared to obtaining a row directly as an array. When a row is accessed as an array, one needs to know the sequence of field names as they are returned. However, when a row is accessed as a hash, the fields are accessible using the field names as keys. Thus, there are certain decisions to be made regarding how the data in a row is accessed.

If a database query returns several rows, `fetchrow_array`, `fetchrow_arrayref` or `fetchrow_hashref` returns information about the next row of results. If there is no row left, each one of these methods returns `undef`. Thus, when more than one row is returned, the fetching of all rows of results requires the use of a `while` loop with the fetching method as a conditional. The program discussed in Section 10.4.4.2 illustrates the use of such a loop. In the current program, we know that the result contains only one row, and hence, performing `fetchrow_hashref` once is enough. The value of the counter is obtained from the hash.

```
my $row = $sth -> fetchrow_hashref();
$counter_value = $row -> {'COUNTER_VALUE'};
$sth -> finish();
```

When the results associated with a successfully executed database query or statement are extensive, and they are read sequentially, it makes sense to use the `finish` method to clean things up at the end before the next query is issued. In the current program, it is not really necessary to use the `finish` method.

Next, the value of the counter obtained from the database is incremented. This reflects the fact that our program is a CGI program that records accessed to a Web page. Every time the CGI program is executed, there is an additional access to the associated page. The database also needs to reflect the incremented value of the counter. The appropriate database query is given below.

```
update COUNTERS set COUNTER_VALUE = $counter_value
               where COUNTER_NAME = "$name_counter"
```

The query is `prepared` using the database handle $dbh and a statement handle $sth obtained. The statement is executed. If it is executed successfully, the new value of the counter is available in the database. The statement is `finished`, and the connection to the database killed.

At this point in the program, it has the value of the access counter it needs to display graphically on the Web page as an in-line image. The value is converted into a JPEG image that is sent back to the browser with an appropriate HTTP header. The manner in which the image is created has been discussed in Section 10.2.3 and Section 5.7. A Web page where the CGI program discussed above is used is shown in Figure 10.2. The HTML that produces the counter image on the Web page is given below.

```
<html>
<head>
<title> Jugal Kalita </title>
</head>
<body>
```

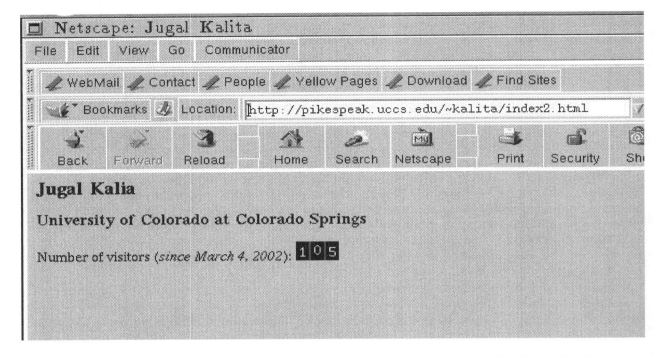

Figure 10.2: A Counter Image Produced by a CGI Program Using `GD.pm` in a Web Page; The Counter is Stored in a Database Table

```
<h2> Jugal Kalita </h2>
<h3> University of Colorado at Colorado Springs </h3>
Number of visitors (<em>since March 4, 2002</em>):
 <IMG SRC=
  "http://pikespeak.uccs.edu/cgi-bin/kalita/counter/counterDB.pl?counter=DBBasedCo
unter1">
   <p>
</body>
 </html>
```

10.4.4.2 Querying a Database From a CGI Program

In Section 10.4.4.1 , we see how a database can be used to maintain values of named access counters for Web pages. The database can potentially contain tens or hundreds of thousands, or even millions of counters. However, in the SELECT query used to find the current value of a counter returns with only one value because names of counters are unique in the table. In most programs that use a database, a SELECT query produces not one, but many rows of response. The program that follows deals with such a situation. This program is invoked by the *Submit Query* button of the HTML form shown in Figure 10.3. The form allows a user to search a database of friends based on certain criteria. It is an illustrative program and hence the form's search criteria are simple. The database queried also contains only a handful of entries. The program searches the database discussed in Section 10.4.1. The database is called test. The table of interest is friends. It has the following fields: STUDENT_ID, SSNUM, NAME, AGE, HOMETOWN and SCHOOL. The STUDENT_ID, SSNUM and AGE fields are integers. The CGI program is invoked by the following form, shown below in HTML.

```
<form method="post" action=
 "http://pikespeak.uccs.edu/cgi-bin/kalita/webQueryDB.pl" name="CGIDBTest">
  <div align="center"><b>Find friends who satisfy the following search criteria:
```

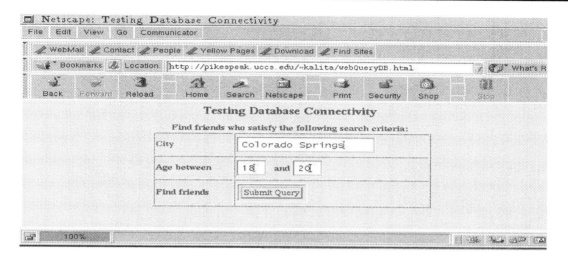

Figure 10.3: A HTML From in a Web Page; Querying a Database

```
    </b>
    <table width="53%" border="1">
      <tr>
        <td><font color="#4865F3"><b>City</b></font></td>
        <td>
          <input type="text" name="city">
        </td>
      </tr>
      <tr>
        <td><b>Age between</b></td>
        <td>
          <input type="text" name="start_age" size="3">
          <b>   and</b>
          <input type="text" name="end_age" size="3">
        </td>
      </tr>
      <tr>
        <td><b>Find friends</b></td>
        <td>
          <input type="submit" name="submit">
        </td>
      </tr>
    </table>
  </div>
</form>
```

The HTML page looks like Figure 10.3 when seen on the Web browser. The CGI program is given below.

Program 10.14

```
#!/usr/bin/perl -T
#webQueryDB.pl
#use strict;
use DBI;
use CGI qw(:standard);
use CGI::Carp  qw(fatalsToBrowser);
use Untaint;
use Data::Table;

my ($driver, $database,  $user, $password);
my ($dsn, $dbh,, $table,  $sth, $DBQuery);
```

```perl
$driver = "mysql";
#$database = q{database=test;host=pikespeak.uccs.edu;port=3306};
$database = "test";
$dsn = "DBI:$driver:$database";
$user = "Project";
$password = "Project";

my ($CGIQuery, $startAge, $endAge, $city);

#get the parameters from the HTML form
$CGIQuery = new CGI;
$startAge = $CGIQuery -> param (start_age);
$endAge = $CGIQuery -> param (end_age);
$city = $CGIQuery -> param (city);

#untaint the parameters obtained from the Web
$startAge = untaint (qr(^\d{1,3}$), $startAge);
$endAge = untaint (qr(^\d{1,3}$), $endAge);
$city = untaint (qr(^[\s\w]{1,50}$), $city);

print header ("text/html");
print start_html ("Results of Database Search");
print h2("Results of MySQL Database Search");

##need to start the connection
$dbh = DBI->connect ($dsn, $user, $password) or
    die "Cannot connect to $dsn: $DBI::errstr";

#prepare a query;
$table = "friends";

#Find entries NOT from Springs
print "\n\nAll $city entries in TABLE $table";
print " between $startAge and $endAge years old<br>";
print " sorted by AGE, STUDENT_ID and SSNUM\n\n";
$DBQuery = qq{select STUDENT_ID, SSNUM, NAME,
            AGE, HOMETOWN, SCHOOL from $table  where HOMETOWN like}
        . " \"%" . $city . "%\" " .
        qq{and AGE >= $startAge and AGE <= $endAge
            order by AGE, STUDENT_ID, SSNUM};
fetchPrintTable ($dbh, $sth, $DBQuery);

#disconnect from the database
$dbh -> disconnect ();

print end_html;

############################
#subroutine to fetch the rows and print a table
sub fetchPrintTable{
    my ($dbh, $sth, $query) = @_;
```

```
    my @data = ();
    $header = ["ID", "SSNUM", "NAME", "AGE", "HOME TOWN", "COLLEGE"];
    $sth = $dbh -> prepare ($query);
    $sth -> execute () or warn $dbh -> errstr();
    while (my $rowRef = $sth -> fetchrow_arrayref()){
        @data = (@data, [@$rowRef]);
    }
    my $dataRef = \@data;
    my $table = new Data::Table ($dataRef, $header, 0);
    print $table -> html;
}
```

The program uses the DBI.pm module to talk to a database, the CGI.pm module to deal with the CGI query coming from the Web browser, and the CGI::Carp.pm module to request that fatal CGI errors be displayed on the Web browser. It uses the Untaint.pm module to cleanse any data that have come from outside the program; here, obviously such data come from the HTML form displayed on the Web and filled by the user. The Untaint.pm module provides facilities to check such data so that they conform to pre-specified requirements. To be able to use the Untaint.pm module, Perl has to be run with the -T option as shown below.

```
#!/usr/bin/perl -T
```

The program also uses the Data::Table.pm module to produce a nice-looking HTML table from the data obtained as search results from the database.

The program interacts with a MySQL database called test using the user name Project. The database server is running on the same machine as the CGI program although it does not have to be the case.

The program obtains the values of the three parameters entered in the Web browser by the user before initiating the search. We use an object-oriented interface to the CGI.pm module.

```
$CGIQuery = new CGI;
$startAge = $CGIQuery -> param (start_age);
$endAge = $CGIQuery -> param (end_age);
$city = $CGIQuery -> param (city);
```

The program untaints the parameter values by calling the untaint function of the Untaint.pm module. The untaint method takes a pattern as the first argument and the variable (here, a scalar) to untaint. If the variable's value passes the test, the value is returned which can then be used in an assignment statement. The program untaints all three variables. qr is an operator that is used to quote a pattern in Perl. This operator quotes (and possibly compiles) its string argument as a regular expression. The string argument is interpolated the same way as PATTERN in m/PATTERN/. If "" is used as the delimiter, no interpolation is done. qr returns a Perl value which may be used instead of the corresponding /STRING/modifiers expression. For example,

```
$regularExp = qr/STRING/im;
s/$regularExp/abc/;
```

is the same as

```
s/STRING/abc/im;
```

The program prints some HTML header information using some of CGI.pm module's functions. Then, the program connects to the database server; it dies if it cannot. The goal of the CGI program is to obtain names of friends for a specified city who are between the two ages given in the form. For example, in Figure 10.3, the query requires the program to search the database and find all friends who are from Colorado Springs and are between 18 and 20 years of age. The corresponding SQL query is given below.

```
select STUDENT_ID, SSNUM, NAME,
             AGE, HOMETOWN, SCHOOL from $table  where HOMETOWN like}
      . " \"%" . $city . "%\" " .
         qq{and AGE >= $startAge and AGE <= $endAge
             order by AGE, STUDENT_ID, SSNUM
```

The query is constructed by concatenating a few strings. The part that deals with the hometown is given below.

```
HOMETOWN like "%$city%"
```

The SQL operator like allows patterns to be used. % stands for one or more characters. Thus, the city name provided can be preceded and followed by additional characters. For example, if the query provides the word Springs, any city that contains the word Springs will satisfy the query's city requirements.

The program calls a subroutine fetchPrintTable that sends the query to the server, obtains the rows of the response, makes the rows into a nice HTML table, and sends the table back to the browser for display. A sample result table is shown in Figure 10.4. The HTML table constructed has the headers given in the anonymous array given below.

```
$header = ["ID", "SSNUM", "NAME", "AGE", "HOME TOWN", "COLLEGE"];
```

$header is a reference to an anonymous list of strings that are to become the headers of the HTML table's columns. This reference is passed as an argument to the Data::Table.pm module's new constructor later. The portion of the program that prepares and executes the query, and fetches the rows of result is given below.

```
$sth = $dbh -> prepare ($query);
$sth -> execute () or warn $dbh -> errstr();
while (my $rowRef = $sth -> fetchrow_arrayref()){
    @data = (@data, [@$rowRef]);
}
```

The SQL query passed to the subroutine is prepared and executed. The database returns a number of rows that satisfy the query. The conditional of the while loop is a call to the following method on the statement handle.

```
$sth -> fetchrow_arrayref()
```

The fetchrow_arrayref method of a statement handle object returns a reference to the next row of data returned by the database server. Perl makes sure that the reference returned is a reference to an array that contains the row's data. When there is no more selected row left, fetchrow_arrayref returns undef. Inside the body of the while loop, an array of references is constructed. Each element of the array @data is an anonymous array containing all the elements of a row. Thus, @data is an array of anonymous rows.

The HTML table can be easily constructed by printing out the appropriate HTML tags along with the data. However, we take a short cut by using the Data::Table.pm module that can perform sophisticated table construction and manipulation. It is powerful although we use it only for constructing a simple HTML table.

```
my $table = new Data::Table ($dataRef, $header, 0);
print $table -> html;
```

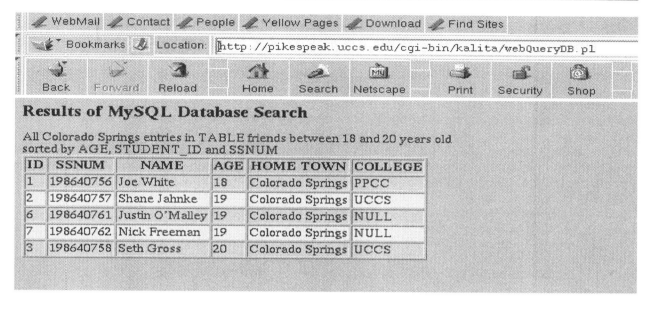

Figure 10.4: An HTML Table Produced by a CGI Program

The new constructor for the Data::Table.pm class takes three arguments, the first being a reference to an anonymous array of anonymous arrays. The inside arrays must have the same number of elements as the number of elements in the anonymous array containing the header strings discussed earlier. The second argument is the reference to this list of header strings. The third argument is a zero saying that the data is an array of table rows. An one means that the data is an array of table columns. The table is sent by the CGI program to the Web browser. The actual HTML produced for the table is shown below.

```
<TABLE  BORDER=1>
<TR BGCOLOR="#CCCC99"><TH>ID</TH><TH>SSNUM</TH><TH>NAME</TH><TH>
        AGE</TH><TH>HOME TOWN</TH><TH>COLLEGE</TH></TR>
        <TR BGCOLOR="#D4D4BF"><TD>1</TD><TD>198640756</TD>
        <TD>Joe White</TD><TD>18</TD><TD>Colorado Springs</TD><TD>PPCC</TD></TR>
<TR BGCOLOR="#ECECE4"><TD>2</TD><TD>198640757</TD>
        <TD>Shane Jahnke</TD><TD>19</TD><TD>Colorado Springs</TD>
        <TD>UCCS</TD></TR>
<TR BGCOLOR="#D4D4BF"><TD>6</TD><TD>198640761</TD>
        <TD>Justin O'Malley</TD><TD>19</TD>
        <TD>Colorado Springs</TD><TD>NULL</TD></TR>
<TR BGCOLOR="#ECECE4"><TD>7</TD><TD>198640762</TD>
        <TD>Nick Freeman</TD><TD>19</TD><TD>Colorado Springs</TD>
        <TD>NULL</TD></TR>
<TR BGCOLOR="#D4D4BF"><TD>3</TD><TD>198640758</TD>
        <TD>Seth Gross</TD><TD>20</TD><TD>Colorado Springs</TD><TD>UCCS</TD></TR>
</TABLE>
</body></html>
```

10.5 Conclusions

This Chapter has dealt with techniques that can be used to make data used within Perl programs persistent. Persistent data can be used by different runs of the same program, or by related or unrelated programs independently. We discuss three approaches for making data live even after a program that creates or manipulates them dies: DBM databases, serialization of contents of data structures, and using relational databases. Serialization produces a string from the contents of a simple or complex data structure, or an object instance. The serialized string can be stored in a file, or even in a DBM or relational database if needed. A DBM database is a simply structured two-columned database. DBM databases have been used in Unix for a long time, and are available on Windows machines and Macintoshes as well. There are various formats for DBM databases. DBM databases can be easily associated with a Perl hash. Finally, currently available relational databases are extremely powerful and can store millions of records in tens or even hundreds of tables. Relational databases use specialized algorithms for efficient storage of and access to complex data. Perl provides an intuitive and simple two-layered interface to relational databases using the DBI.pm database-independent module and database-dependent driver modules that talk to the database directly. The DBI.pm module talks to the appropriate database driver module to communicate with the underlying database engine. Our examples have used only simple databases where one table is sufficient to store the relevant data. In realistic databases, there are usually several tables that are related using so-called foreign keys. Since a Perl program simply passes SQL queries to the appropriate database driver module, there are no complications as far as programming goes to interact with more complex databases with many tables as long as we know how to phrase the appropriate SQL query. Whether there is one underlying table or there are many is of no concern to the Perl program. In writing programs that communicate with databases, one must remember that every vendor of databases modifies the SQL language a little bit to suit their technical or marketing objectives. This sadly means that programs may not be portable across databases since teh SQL dialects vary from database to database, sometimes in subtle manners.

10.6 Exercises

1. *(Easy: Documentation Reading)*
   Use perldoc to learn more about how to write modules that tie a variable to a module. Run

   ```
   %perldoc perltie
   ```

   to bring up the write-up on ties.

2. *(Easy: Documentation Reading)*
   Read Perl documentation on the DBI.pm module. The documentation is fairly extensive and is about 50 pages long. In particular, learn about all the methods that database handles support. Also, learn about all the methods that statement handles support. In particular, learn the various ways in which results from execution of an SQL query can fetched from a statement handle.

3. *(Easy: DBI Alternatives)*
   Rewrite the programs in Section 10.4 so that they use the various approaches to fetching selected rows. Compare the pros and cons of using fetchrow_arryref, fetchrow_array, fetchrow_hashref, fetchall_arrayref and fetchall_hashref. Please note that not all these methods may be available in all versions of the DBI.pm module.

4. *(Easy to Medium: Documentation Reading, Research)*
   In this Chapter, we have discussed how to use only MySQL databases. If you have access to any other databases, learn how to access them from Perl programs. Rewrite all the programs of this Chapter to work with the new databases. What changes to you have to make to the programs?

5. *(Easy: DBM, Search, HTML Forms)*
   Suppose we need to record the following pieces of information for an individual: last name, first name, middle initial, social security number, street address, city, state and zip code. Find a representation for such data in terms of key-value pairs. Save the records in a DBM file for persistence. Populate your DBM file with at least 20 records.

   Write subroutines that do the following.

   (a) Search for individuals from a specific city and return individuals sorted by last name, first name, and middle initial.

   (b) Write an HTML form and link a CGI program to the *submit* button to perform the search above. Return the results in a nicely structured HTML table.

   One idea is to use the social security number as the key. Concatenate the rest of the fields using a pre-specified separator and store the resulting string as value.

6. *(Easy: Database Search, HTML Forms)*
   Solve the previous problem using a database. Create the table with appropriate fields. Use any database to which you have access and is available on your machine or across the network.

7. *(Medium: Recursive Structure, DBM)*
   Suppose we want to keep information about authors of books in a DBM file. For each author, we have the following pieces of information.

   (a) Author ID: a positive integer,

   (b) Author Name consisting of three parts: last name, first name, and middle initial,

   (c) A list of books authored: For each book, there is a title, a publication year, and publisher information. Publisher information includes publisher's name and the name of the city where the publisher is located.

   Informally, the information about an author has the following information.

```
[authorID, [lastName, firstName],
        [bookTitle1, publicationYear1, [publisherName1, publisherCity1]]
        [bookTitle2, publicationYear2, [publisherName2, publisherCity2]]
        [bookTitle3, publicationYear3, [publisherName3, publisherCity3]]
        . . . .
    ]
```

   Thus, there can be one or more books an individual has authored. Can you represent the information as outlined above in terms of key-value pairs so that it can be stored in a DBM file? Think of serializing the data associated with an author.

   Using a DBM file may not be the best approach in this case. However, you are encouraged to implement a program for this problem to gain valuable experience and insight.

8. *(Medium: Database, Research)*
   Solve the previous problem using a database. It would be appropriate to define several related tables so that there is no redundancy is data storage. If you do not know how to do this, consult a tutorial book on databases. One such book is *Fundamentals of Database Systems with E-Book (With CD-ROM)* by Navathe and Elmasri [NE02].

9. *(Medium: DBM, Encryption, Research)*
   Consider a record structure where we have a unique person ID, a last name and a first name, and his or her salary. We want to keep the salary information encrypted using DES or some similar private key encryption scheme. Thus, only those who can supply the proper secret key can read the information. Implement a program that prompts for a key and encodes the salary information using the encryption scheme before saving it to a hash. Store the hash's contents in a DBM file.

   Write another program that returns the salary for individuals with a certain last name, or a last name-first name combination. The program prompts for the key and provides the salary in unencrypted form only if the correct encryption/decryption key is provided.

   Read Chapter 11 to review how encryption algorithms such as DES are used. Assume that the private key is distributed securely, say by hand, to parties who need to know it.

10. *(Medium: Database, Encryption, Research)*
    Redo the previous problem by using a database. Use any database of choice.

11. *(Medium to Hard: Database, CGI Programming, Search, Research)*
    Write a program to organize your music CDs. A record consists of the following information: Song title, Artist name, Album from which the song is taken, Genre, Time the song takes, Year it was published. Create an appropriate database table. Enter at least twenty rows of data in the table. Use any database of choice.

    Create an HTML form that allows one to search for a song by one or more of the following criteria: artist name, song title, album, and genre. Note that only any one field needs to be specified. When the submit button is clicked, a CGI program returns the chosen songs in a nice HTML table.

    Can you extend your program so that when a user clicks on a song's title, the song is actually played on a audio player on the computer?

12. *(Medium to Hard: Guest Book, CGI Programming, Search, Can be a long-term project)*
    Consider adding a guest book to a Web page that belongs to you. A guest book allows individuals visiting the Web page to leave comments. Include an HTML form on the page that allows an interested individual to enter the following information: a name, an email address, a text area where the individual can leave textual comments, geographic location of the individual leaving a comment, the date and time of the posting. Create a database table with appropriate fields. Write the CGI program so that a visitor can add his or her comments.

    Sort the entries in the table by date and time. For each entry in the database table, enclose it within appropriate HTML tags to make it look nice on the Web page. Let the Web page clearly show the date and time of posting, the poster's name, and his or her email. Create this page and provide a link to this page from your Web page. You can create this page by running a Perl program off-line.

    Also, develop a simple form that allows a visitor to search for comments based on one or more of the following criteria: name of the poster, and the date of posting. Sort the entries by date. Write the CGI program to do so.

13. *(Medium: tie, Research)*
    Write a Perl program that implements storing of an array in a text file. In particular, assume that the array contains the following elements that can be interpreted as fields of a record: VIN number of a vehicle, its make, model, color and approximate resale value. Write a `tie` module so that one can enter new vehicles into the text file, and that it can return a record given a VIN number. Assume that the VIN number is a 20 digit alphanumeric value. Keep the fields of a record in a single line of the text file. Separate the fields of the record using a pre-specified separator, say, one or more tabs, colons or commas.

14. *(Medium: tie, Database, Research)*
    Redo the implementation of the `tie` in the previous problem so that the records are stored in a database table instead of a text file.

15. *(Hard: Virtual Bookstore, Contains many components, Long-term project)*
    Redo the problem titled *A Virtual Bookstore* at the end of Chapter 8 on CGI programming. Store all your data in terms of database tables.

16. *(Hard: Virtual Grocery Store, Contains many components, Long-term project)*
    Redo the problem titled *A Virtual Grocery Store* at the end of Chapter 8 on CGI programming. Store all your data in terms of database tables.

17. *(Hard: Virtual Auction Site, Contains many components, Long-term project)*
    Redo the problem titled *A Virtual Auction Site* at the end of Chapter 8 on CGI programming. Store all your data in terms of database tables.

18. *(Hard: Web-based Sports Site, Contains many components, Long-term project)*
    Redo the problem titled *A Sports Site* at the end of Chapter 8 on CGI programming. Store all your data in terms of database tables.

Chapter 11

On Data and Communication Security

In This Chapter

In Chapter 7, we discussed at length, how two programs, more correctly, two processes can communicate using the interface of sockets. It does not matter whether the two communicating programs are situated on the same machine, on two different machines in the same room or in different continents. We assume that all computers involved are on the Internet.

Computers on the Internet communicate through a framework called the *TCP/IP Architecture*. In the TCP/IP architecture, the communication takes place in four layers. They are

- the application layer,
- the transport layer,
- the Internet layer, and
- the network interface layer.

When we write socket-based programs, we deal with the application layer. Most programs, whether simple like the programs in Chapter 7 or complex such as a Web browser, use sockets behind the scene for communication. A socket, in abstract terms, is a five-tuple containing the following components: the source machine's name or IP address, the source machine's port, the destination machine's name or IP address, the destination port and the protocol used. The protocol is usually TCP, but can be UDP as well.

Although we program using sockets, the actual communication between programs takes place at lower levels, below what the application program thinks it is. The commands and data that are transmitted by an application program, are translated into what the transport layer, the layer immediately below the application layer, understands. This is where the protocol specified in a socket description helps. If the protocol specified in the socket is TCP, the application level information is converted into information that uses the TCP specifications. If the socket uses UDP, the translation takes place into the UDP specification. These are complex protocols and we need not worry about their details. Information at this level is broken into small chunks called *packets*. The TCP or UDP packets are the ones that are sent across the Internet.

The Internet layer, the layer immediately below the transport layer, primarily uses a language and a set of communication rules called the Internet Protocol (IP). The TCP or UDP-based information is not really sent across the Internet. It is translated to IP-based information. The information is once again in small chunks called IP packets. IP packets are also known by the term *datagrams*.

Finally, the IP datagrams are converted into what is acceptable to the lowest layer, the network interface layer. The network interface layer deals with the actual physical network, and converts the information into a form that the network hardware can understand. An example of an actual physical layer is the Ethernet. Thus, the commands and data that the application program sends through sockets are actually transmitted as pieces of information at the lowest layer.

The Internet is a network of many networks. These networks use different underlying technologies. Network hardware and software on the Internet route the information at the network interface layer from network to network. There are specialized computers called *routers* that help guide the information along toward the destination. To go from the source to the destination, the information may have to go through many such routers. A router forwards a packet from one network to the next, on the way from the source to the destination.

Finally, the information arrives at the destination. The lowest level information is translated back into the Internet layer, i.e., into IP packets. The IP packets that arrive are converted back to transport layer (TCP or UDP) information. The packets are put together into a whole by the software at the transport level. The composed information is translated back to the application layer, and the socket at the application layer at the destination is given the commands and the data that were sent to it by the application at the source. The application program at the destination deals with the data appropriately, and possibly sends a response back to the source.

Thus, information moves from the source to the destination in small chunks called packets. There may be tens of thousands of packets at various layers involved in one communication in the application layer. There are copies of packets all along the way from the source computer to the destination computer. There are ways using which the packets can be viewed and captured in transit. When a captured message is read, the privacy of the message is violated. The captured packets can then potentially be used maliciously. An eavesdropper may want to change the commands or the accompanying data in part or whole. The eavesdropper may try to destroy the original information, make something up, and send the fake information. These are some of the security issues with Internet-based communication.

The main information security objectives that a cryptographic algorithm or tool provides are the following [MvOV96, Nic99, Sta99]:

Data Confidentiality: The content of information should be secret, except for those who are authorized to see it.

Data Integrity: It should be impossible to forge or tamper with the data in storage or during transmission. Thus, one must be able to detect data manipulation by unauthorized programs or individuals. Tampering includes operations such as insertion, deletion and substitution.

Authentication: Authentication involves identifying an entity or the data itself. Two parties entering into a communication may be required to identify each other. It should be possible to authenticate data delivered over a communication network in regards to the origin, the date of origin, the time sent, etc.

Non-repudiation: An entity should not be able to deny actions it has performed. For example, the receiver of a message should be able to prove that the message was sent by the purported sender. The sender should also be able to prove that the message was received by the purported receiver. When there is a dispute, there must be a means to resolve and find out who performed what action.

In this chapter, we deal with issues in data and communication security. This chapter discusses the concepts of *message digests* and the functionality Perl provides for creating message digests. A message digest is a short fingerprint or footprint of the message that is more or less unique for all practical purposes. However short or large the data or the message is, the digest is the same size for the same digesting algorithm. The message digest can be computed by the sender and sent together with the message or separately to the recipient. The receiver can compute the digest again on the received message. If the digest sent by the sender and the one computed by the receiver are the same, the message can be considered untampered.

Cryptographic algorithms are classified into two broad categories:

- Conventional or symmetric or private-key cryptographic algorithms,

- Asymmetric or public-key cryptographic algorithms.

Conventional cryptographic algorithms have been used from pre-historic times, primarily in diplomacy and at times of war, to send and receive sensitive information. In addition to the data to encode, conventional cryptographic algorithms use an additional piece of information called the *key* to scramble or encode data. The key can be a number, a string, or a sequence of bits. For conventional cryptography, the key is usually small in size. Latest conventional cryptographic techniques usually use keys that are 8 or more bytes long. Conventional cryptographic algorithms use only one key, and hence, are called *symmetric*. The key is sent by the sender to the receiver using a secure channel, e.g., during times of war, using heavily armed guards. The key is used to encipher or encode the data. The encoded data is sent over an unsecured channel to the receiving party. The receiving party decodes the data using the copy of the key he or she has. With the advent of computers, conventional cryptographic methods have become very complex. A symmetric method called the Data Encryption Standard (DES) was used widely by the government and commercial enterprises for securing data for more than two decades. Recently, the strength of security provided by DES has been questioned and found inadequate. In 2001, a new conventional cryptographic algorithm called Rijndael was adopted as the Advanced Encryption System (AES) by the US to become the future encryption workhorse. In this chapter, we primarily discuss Perl's implementation of DES although we briefly note other conventional cryptographic algorithms.

This chapter also discusses a very well-known public-key cryptographic algorithm or information scrambling algorithm called the *RSA algorithm.* This algorithm is based on some very interesting and salient properties of large prime numbers. There are other public-key cryptographic algorithms, but the RSA algorithm is the most celebrated and most widely known. In the RSA algorithm, every individual is in possession of two large related numbers called *keys*: a public key and a private key. The need for two large keys for each individual instead of one relatively small key for each pair of participants distinguishes public-key cryptography from conventional cryptography. Suppose there are two parties A and B that communicate. A has two keys, A's public key and A's private key. B has two keys as well, a public key and a private key. The sender A encrypts a message or scrambles a message the receiving party's i.e., B's *public key*. By previous agreement B has made B's public key publicly available to B or any other potential sender of encoded data to B. Thus, B's public key is potentially known to the whole world. However, an individual keeps his or her private key secure. Scrambling involves performing mathematical computation with large numbers. The scrambled or encoded message is sent by A over normal unsecured channel or line of communication to the receiver B. The receiver B is in possession of a second key called B's *private key*. B performs a mathematical computation on the received message using B's private key and obtains the original message.

In cryptographic terms, the original message is called the *plaintext* or the *cleartext*, and the encoded message is called the *ciphertext*. The two keys in the RSA algorithm are extremely large numbers, say 1024 bits in length each. They are related to each other based on certain properties of hugely large prime numbers. The sender A knows the relation between the two. In fact, A thinks of two large prime numbers first, and then obtains A's public and private keys later. However, A does not let others know what the prime numbers are. A also guards A's private key with his life. Although A's public key is known to B and whole world, it is mathematically impossible to compute A's private key from it, using any computer that exists today, or even hundreds and thousands of computers, or even millions of computers, if the keys are sufficiently large in bit size. This is because of some surprising, seemingly simple properties of large prime numbers. This algorithm was invented by three individuals: Rivest, Shamir and Adelman, three professors at MIT in the late 1970s. The algorithm bears their name. It was a discovery of geniuses. It changed the manner in which data is encrypted or encoded. For a while, an algorithm such as the RSA algorithm was of primary importance mostly to the government, particularly, the military, and possibly, large financial institutions. The government used algorithms like this for secure communication, military or otherwise. The banking and the financial industry used it too. However, with the invention of the World Wide Web in the late 1980s and its enormous and increasing popularity, encryption has become important to the common man so that private data can be securely communicated between a Web browser and a Web server. This can contain data such as bank records, credit card information used during electronic shopping, and medical records, among others.

11.1   Ensuring Integrity of Transmitted Information

Here is the problem. A source socket sends information to a destination socket on the Internet. The information is broken into packets at various levels. The packets at the lowest level are the ones transmitted across the Internet. There can be thousands or even millions of packets involved. The packets travel through many computers where they are forwarded toward the destination. At the destination, the packets are captured and reconstituted into higher levels and finally given to the destination socket at the application level. How do we ensure that the information arrived at the destination without being modified? In other words, how can the destination process be sure of the integrity of the information? For the time being, we do not care if someone views the information along the way. At this time, we just want to make sure that the information arrived without being modified by an interceptor.

One of the techniques used for ensuring information integrity in transmission is by using cryptographic *hash functions*. A hash function H is a transformation that takes an input m and returns a fixed-size string called the hash value h. That is, $h = H(m)$. Hash functions have many computational uses. A hash function, when used in cryptography is required to have the following properties.

- The input can be of any length,

- the output has a fixed length,

- the value $H(m)$ is easy to compute for any value of m.

- $H(m)$ is an one-way function, and

- $H(m)$ is a collision-free function.

A hash function H is called one-way if it is hard to invert, i.e., given a hash value h, it is computationally infeasible to find the input message m that produced it such that $H(m) = h$.

The main use of cryptographic hash functions are in ensuring data integrity checks and in digital signatures. This is how a hash function is used for ensuring communication integrity. At the source, the program uses a hash function to compute what is called a *message digest* of the original message m. Let the digest be called d. The digest is small in size and is fixed in length no matter how long the original information is. The hash value represents concisely the larger message from which it was computed. One can think of the message digest as a *digital fingerprint* of the original message. There are various digest producing hash algorithms and the size of the digest depends on the hash algorithm used. In the simplest use for ensuring integrity, the message digest d is attached to the message m at the source. The sender sends the message along with the digest to the receiver.

At the destination, the receiving program looks at the message m that it receives. It recomputes the digest on the message using the same hashing algorithm that the sender used. Let the new digest be called d'. The receiver compares the new digest d' with the original digest d that came from the sender. If the two are exactly the same, the receiver can be assured that the information was not changed during transmission, and that the integrity of the information can be guaranteed.

Since hash functions are generally faster than encryption or digital signature algorithms, typically the digital signature is not computed on the whole message, but on the message's hash value which is small compared to the original message itself. Additionally, a digest can be made public without revealing the contents of the document it came from. This fact can be used to get a message timestamped digitally without revealing the message to a timestamping service.

11.1.1   Hashing Algorithms and Perl's Hashing Packages

There are several hashing algorithms that are widely used. Among them are the following.

- MD5,

- MD4,

- MD2,

- SHA-1,

- RIPEMD-160, and

- Tiger.

Although they are very different algorithms, using them is very easy. Perl provides us with modules for each one of the hash algorithms given above. They work more or less the same way at the programmer level. Actually, the hash algorithms are implemented mostly in C. The Perl modules provide a friendly and consistent interface to the algorithms.

The `Digest::` modules provide implementation of several algorithms for creating hashes of data. The `Digest::` modules corresponding to the hash algorithms MD2, MD4, MD5, SHA-1, and Tiger, are called `Digest::MD2`, `Digest::MD4`, `Digest::MD5`, `Digest::SHA1` and `Digest::Tiger` respectively. RIPEMD-160 is implemented in the module `Crypt::RIPEMD160`. We will talk about the `Digest` modules now and discuss `Crypt::RIPEMD160` later. All `Digest` modules have the same programming interface. Each one provides a function-based interface for simple use. The functional interface is called on a string. Each one also has an object-oriented interface. The object-oriented interface is used with strings or with files directly. The digest can be produced in three formats shown below.

- **Binary:** The binary digest is the most compact one. However, it cannot be printed easily. Also, it cannot be used in places where binary data cannot be used.

- **Hexadecimal:** It produces a string of lowercase hexadecimal digits. It is twice as long as the binary digest produced.

- **Base 64:** The Base 64 digest is a sequence of printable characters. It is based on the Base 64 representation. Base 64 representation is used primarily for Internet mail using the MIME (Multipurpose Internet Mail Extensions) standard.

In the example programs that follow, we primarily use binary digests.

Next, we will start with the description of the `Digest::MD5` module. All of the rest are similar and will be discussed briefly.

11.1.2　The MD5 Digest: Package `Digest::MD5`

The MD5 message digest algorithm was developed by Rivest at MIT. MD5 takes as input a message of arbitrary length and produces as output an 128-bit message digest. The input can be a string of arbitrary length, or it can be the contents of a whole file. It can be a text file or a binary file such as an image. The input is processed in 512-bit blocks at a time. There is no limit to the size of the message. Irrespective of how large the message is, whether a single bit or tens of millions of bits, the digest produced is always of the same length. If the input is large in size, it is broken into smaller blocks that are processed one at a time. The digest obtained from the previous blocks cumulatively affects the digest obtained in the next round of computation, i.e., when the next block of the message is processed.

The MD5 algorithm has the property that every bit of the hash code is a function of every bit in the input. Whether it is a single bit, a small string or a large file, the message is considered in terms of blocks of bits for the hash computation. Various computations are done on the blocks of bits. Because of the design of the underlying mathematical functions, it is unlikely that two messages chosen at random, even if they exhibit similar regularities, will have the same hash code. According to Rivest, MD5 is as strong as an 128-bit hash code can be.

MD5 was one of the most widely used hash algorithms till recently. Researchers are always trying to find weaknesses of hash algorithms in order to break them. There are two approaches researchers use to break the code: *brute-force* technique and more intelligent techniques called *cryptanalytic* techniques. In a brute-force technique, one tries all possibilities. In cryptanalytic techniques, one uses mathematically based techniques to break the code. The usage of MD5 has gone down in the last few years because it has been shown that brute-force and cryptanalytic attacks can possibly be successful against it. MD5 is now considered breakable. Therefore, the research community has come up with several newer hash functions to replace MD5. Some of the new techniques are SHA-1, RIPEMD-160, and Tiger. However, before discussing any of these newer techniques, we will discuss two older techniques, MD4 and MD2.

We will now present a few programs that use MD5 digest. If we want to use one of the other digest algorithms, the programming are quite similar.

11.1.2.1　Creating Digests for Strings

The first program goes into a loop where it asks the user to type in two messages in each iteration. The program computes the message digests for the two messages using the MD5 algorithm. It prints a message saying if the user typed in the same message twice, or if the user typed two different messages. The user can type in q to get out of the loop and exit the program.

Program 11.1

```perl
#!/usr/bin/perl
#file md5Terminal.pl

use Digest::MD5;
use strict;
```

```perl
my ($context, $message1, $digest1, $message2, $digest2);
my  $round;

$context = Digest::MD5->new ();

while (1) {
    $round++;
    print "Round $round\n";
    print "_" x 50, "\n";
    print "Please type a message, q to quit: ";
    $message1 = <STDIN>;
    chomp ($message1);
    if ($message1 =~ /^q$/){ exit;}

    $context -> add($message1);
    $digest1 = $context -> digest();

    print "Please type a second message: ";
    $message2 = <STDIN>;
    chomp ($message2);
    $context -> reset();
    $context -> add ($message2);
    $digest2 = $context -> digest();

    if ($digest1 eq $digest2){
        print "You typed the same message twice\n";
    }
    else{
        print "You typed two different messages\n";
      }

    printf "%s\t%s\n", "Message", "Digest";
    printf "%s\t%s\n", $message1, unpack ("H*", $digest1);
    printf "%s\t%s\n", $message2, unpack ("H*", $digest2);;
    print "\n";
}
```

The program creates a new context for the digesting to take place. This is done using the following line of code.

```perl
$context = Digest::MD5->new ();
```

We can now use this context to create digests. In this example, the program asks the user to enter a message. The message is read and chomped, and then added to the digest's context. The addition is done using the line given below.

```perl
$context -> add($message1);
```

We can add more data to the context if we like. Once we have added all the data, we can ask that an MD5 digest be computed on the data currently in the context. We compute the digest by issuing the following command.

```
$digest1 = $context -> digest();
```

The digest produced is a binary digest and is stored in the variable `$digest1`.

Next, the program asks the user to type in another message. The program computes the MD5 digest for this message as well. It uses the same context for computing the digest. In order to do so, the program resets the context by using the following line of code.

```
$context -> reset();
```

Of course, we could have used two contexts if we wanted.

The program compares the two digests and lets the user know if he or she typed the same string or two different strings. The program prints the two strings the user typed in along with the corresponding digests. The digests are binary data. Therefore, they are converted to hexadecimal so they can be printed on the terminal. One of the `print` statements is shown below.

```
printf "%s\t%s\n", $message1, unpack ("H*", $digest1);
```

Thus, digest is unpacked before printing. The `H*` argument to `unpack` asks that the resulting bytes be in hexadecimal and thus, printable form. The `unpack` command takes a format template and a string, and converts the string into the form asked by the template.

A terminal interaction with this program is given below.

Round 1

```
Please type a message, q to quit: abcdefghijklmnopqrst
Please type a second message: abcdefghijklmnopqrst
You typed the same message twice
Message Digest
abcdefghijklmnopqrst 6aa8de45918023095f6e831efe48d00b
abcdefghijklmnopqrst 6aa8de45918023095f6e831efe48d00b
```

Round 2

```
Please type a message, q to quit: I love Lucy
Please type a second message: I love Lucy
You typed the same message twice
Message Digest
I love Lucy fd3d476fcddf1d1218afc0b1c77039c7
I love Lucy fd3d476fcddf1d1218afc0b1c77039c7
```

Round 3

```
Please type a message, q to quit: I love Lucy
Please type a second message: I like Lucy
You typed two different messages
Message Digest
I love Lucy fd3d476fcddf1d1218afc0b1c77039c7
I like Lucy 7bc1d963c4aa3af575dfa6d3239df403
```

Round 4

```
Please type a message, q to quit: q
pikespeak[96]:
```

11.1.2.2   Creating Digests for Files

We can obtain the message digest for a file. Sometimes this is the preferred thing to do where we store the message to be sent in a file and then process it. Otherwise, there are situations where we want to ensure that an important file is not tampered with from the time we create it to the time we use it.

The following program reads a text file line by line and then adds the lines to the context of an MD5 hash. Finally, it creates a message digest for the whole file's content. It prints the digest in hexadecimal format for our benefit. It also stores the digest in binary form in a file that has the `.digest` extension. If the file we are digesting is called `processes.tex`, the digest file is called `processes.tex.digest`. The reason for storing the digest file is that later, if we try to use the same original file, we can check to see whether the file has been tampered with from its original condition. We can also give the file to someone else, and that person can verify whether the file is still in its unadulterated original form. For this to be successful, the digest has to be given to the second party as well. Also, the second party has to be told what digest algorithm was used. The program is given below.

Program 11.2

```perl
#!/usr/bin/perl
#file md5File.pl

use strict;
use Digest::MD5;

my ($file, $context, $digest, $lineCount);

print "Give the name of a file to digest: ";
$file = <STDIN>;
chomp $file;

$context = Digest::MD5 -> new ();

open IN, $file;
while (<IN>){
    $context -> add ($_);
    $lineCount++;
  }

print "Added $lineCount lines to the digest context\n";
$digest = $context -> digest ();
printf "The  digest is %s\n", unpack ("H*", $digest);

open OUT, ">$file.digest";
print OUT $digest;
close OUT;
```

The program starts a new MD5 context called `$context`. It reads the file line by line in a while loop. As each line is read, it is added to `$context`. We also print a line count just to see how many lines are there in the file being processed. The digest is written to a new file at the very bottom of the program. An interaction with this program is shown below.

```
Give the name of a file to digest: processes.tex
```

```
Added 3264 lines to the digest context
The   digest is 48a38bf059676b9f7644e64b25de08e9
```

Thus, the digest printed above in hexadecimal format corresponds to all of the 3264 lines of text in the file processes.tex.

The Digest::Message module provides us with a shortcut to produce the digest of the content of a whole file. There is an MD5 context method called addfile that does so. The following program is a rewrite of the previous program.

Program 11.3

```perl
#!/usr/bin/perl
#file md5File1.pl

use strict;
use Digest::MD5;

my ($file, $context, $digest, $lineCount);

print "Give the name of a file to digest: ";
$file = <STDIN>;
chomp $file;

$context = Digest::MD5 -> new ();

open FILE, $file;
$context -> addfile (*FILE);
close FILE;

$digest = $context -> digest ();
printf "The   digest is %s\n", unpack ("H*", $digest);

open OUT, ">$file.digest";
print OUT $digest;
close OUT;
```

This program can produce an MD5 digest of any file, whether text or binary. In Perl, when a filehandle is passed as an argument to a function call, one way to do so is by placing a * in front of it and making it a so-called *typeglob*. Output of two runs of the program is given below.

```
Give the name of a file to digest: processes.tex
The   digest is 48a38bf059676b9f7644e64b25de08e9

Give the name of a file to digest: jk1.jpg
The   digest is 1178ebfe124542afcc586e766d96c1a5
```

Here, processes.tex is a text file whereas jk1.jpg is a binary graphic file. Notice that the digest for the file processes.tex was produced by the program in the previous section as well, and the digest comes out as the same, whether we add the file to the context line by line, or use the addfile construct.

Please note that for the digest to have any value, we must write another program that looks at the digest and verifies it when the digested file is about to be used. Another point to note is that the digest can be stored in the same file as the original, instead of a separate file.

Below, we present a program that is given a file name as a command-line argument. It computes a new MD5 digest of the content of the file and compares it with the MD5 digest previously computed to see if the two digests are the same. If the two are the same, it concludes that the file has not been tampered with and is the original.

Program 11.4

```perl
#!/usr/bin/perl
#file: md5FileVerify.pl
#usage: %md5FileVerify.pl originalFileName
use strict;
use Digest::MD5;

my ($file, $context, $oldDigest, $newDigest);

$file = $ARGV[0];
if (!(-e "$file.digest")){
    print "There is no digest file: $file.digest\n";
    print "Conclusion: The file is not original\n";
    exit;
}

$context = Digest::MD5->new();
open FILE, $file;
$context -> addfile (*FILE);
close FILE;
$newDigest = $context -> digest ();
print "The new digest is " , unpack ("H*", $newDigest), "\n";

open DIGEST, "$file.digest";
$oldDigest = <DIGEST>;
close DIGEST;
print "The old digest is " , unpack ("H*", $oldDigest), "\n";

if ($newDigest eq $oldDigest){
    print "Conclusion: The file is original\n";
  }
  else{
    print "Conclusion: The file is NOT original\n";
  }
```

The program obtains the name of the file to verify from the command line. It checks to see if a corresponding file with the extension .digest exists. If such a file does not exist, it concludes that the file cannot be verified as original and exits.

If the digest file exists, the program opens the file to verify and computes a new digest for the content called $newDigest. It reads the digest file and reads the old digest into the variable $oldDigest. If $oldDigest and $newDigest are equal, the program concludes that the file given as command-line argument is the original.

Here is the output the program runs when it is called with the argument `jk1.jpg`.

```
%md5FileVerify.pl jk1.jpg
The new digest is 1178ebfe124542afcc586e766d96c1a5
The old digest is 1178ebfe124542afcc586e766d96c1a5
Conclusion: The file is original
```

Even if one character is changed in the original file, the program will not verify the file as the original.

If we alter one character of the file `processes.tex` using a text editor, and then we verify it, we get the following printout on the terminal.

```
%md5FileVerify.pl processes.tex
The new digest is 9a969870291ec7368a767acfb93fcd05
The old digest is 48a38bf059676b9f7644e64b25de08e9
Conclusion: The file is NOT original
```

The two digests are quite different after one character was changed in a file with more than 3000 lines of text.

However, the fact that two files are different, is something that can be easily done by a command such as `diff` in Unix. Of course, we need two files, the original and the new to see if the files are the same or different. Quite often, two such files are not available. `diff` uses an efficient string comparison algorithm to find the differences among two files.

11.1.2.3   Secure Message Digests or Message Authentication Codes

A message digest, by itself, does not give us a very high level of security. In the examples in section 11.1.2.2, we can determine if a file has been corrupted because the content of the file will not produce the same message digest that was produced earlier. But, there is no way to prevent someone from changing both the "secured" file and the accompanying digest file so that the new digest file reflects the altered content of the new "secured" file.

There are several ways in which a message digest can be made into a *message authentication code* (MAC). Below, we discuss a technique that uses a *passphrase* with the message digest to calculate a *secure message digest*. A passphrase is a "password" that can have several words in it. We call this a MAC. For the MAC approach to work, it is necessary that both the sender and the receiver of the secured file or data, have a *shared* passphrase. The two communicating parties have to agree on a way to create the passphrase, exchange it securely, and then keep it secret as long as they use it.

Program 11.5

```perl
#!/usr/bin/perl
#file md5SecureFile.pl
use strict;
use Digest::MD5;

######
#subroutine to create .mac file
######
sub computeSecureMd5Digest{
   my ($file) = @_;
   my ($context, $digest, $passphrase, $mac);
```

```perl
    #Read passphrase from the terminal
    print "What is your passphrase?: ";
    $passphrase = <STDIN>;
    chomp ($passphrase);

    #Create hash context and add the file content
    $context = Digest::MD5 -> new();
    open (FILE, $file) or die "$file doesn't exist: $!";
    $context -> addfile (*FILE);
    close $file;

    #add the passphrase to the hash context
    $context -> add ($passphrase);
    #compute the digest of file content + passphrase
    $digest = $context -> digest ();

    $context -> reset ();
    #Again, calculate digest or MAC, of the passphrase and first digest
    $context -> add ($passphrase);
    $context -> add ($digest);
    $mac = $context -> digest ();
    print "MAC saved in file $file.mac = ", unpack ("H*",  $mac), "\n";

    #Write MAC into a file with extension .mac
    open MAC, ">$file.mac";
    print MAC $mac;
    close MAC;
}

#main
my ($file) = $ARGV[0];
&computeSecureMd5Digest ($file);
```

The name of the file to secure is given as a command-line argument to the program md5SecureFile.pl. Here, corresponding to a secured file, we create a new file with the .mac extension appended to its end.

The main program calls the subroutine computeSecureMd5Digest with the name of the file as an argument. The subroutine prompts the user for a passphrase, and then, creates an MD5 digest called $digest that is a fingerprint of the content of the file to be secured and the passphrase. Note that this first digest computed is not stored in the accompanying .mac file. What we have done is computed a "secure" digest which, in a sense, takes the passphrase as key; and then, secured this "secure" digest again by computing a new digest, which we call the MAC. The computation of the MAC uses the passphrase a second time. In other words, we are "doubly secure." The MAC or the second digest is stored in the .mac file.

For this technique for securing the integrity of a file to work, the passphrase cannot be transmitted along with the original file and the accompanying .mac file. Both the original file and the .mac file need to be given by the sender to the receiver. The transmission can take place by various means such as e-mail attachments, *ftp*ing of the files, through the use of a floppy disk, CD, or a zip disk, etc. The passphrase must be transmitted using another channel, preferably secure, such as telephone, secure e-mail, hand exchange, certified surface mail, etc. Note that a telephone conversation is not really secure.

A sample interaction with the program is given below.

```
%md5SecureFile.pl jk1.jpg
What is your passphrase?: It was the best of times, it was the worst of times.
MAC saved in file jk1.jpg.mac = 69f5a2c1dc6834a6c32d9d414c19da4d
```

The program asks for a passphrase which the user gives as It was the best of times, it was the worst of times. including the period. The program computes the secure message digest or the MAC and stores it in the accompanying .mac file.

For verification of the integrity of the "secured" file, the reverse process has to be performed at the receiver's end. The following program accomplishes this for us.

Program 11.6

```perl
#!/usr/bin/perl
#file md5SecureFileVerify.pl
use strict;
use Digest::MD5;

##subroutine to verify a secured MD5 file digest
sub verifySecureMd5Digest{
   my ($file) = @_;
   my ($passphrase, $context, $digest, $mac, $macInFile);

   if (!(-e "$file.mac")){
      print "There is no MAC file: $file.mac\n";
      print "Conclusion: The file $file is not original\n";
      exit;
    }

   #Read passphrase from the terminal
   print "What is your passphrase?: ";
   $passphrase = <STDIN>;
   chomp ($passphrase);

   #Create hash context and add the file content
   $context = Digest::MD5 -> new();
   open (FILE, $file) or die "$file doesn't exist: $!";
   $context -> addfile (*FILE);
   close $file;

   #add the passphrase to the hash context
   $context -> add ($passphrase);
   #compute the digest of file content + passphrase
   $digest = $context -> digest ();

   $context -> reset ();
   #Again, calculate digest or MAC, of the passphrase and first digest
   $context -> add ($passphrase);
   $context -> add ($digest);
   $mac = $context -> digest ();
   print "MAC computed on file $file = ", unpack ("H*",  $mac), "\n";
```

```perl
   #Read the MAC saved in the .mac file
   open MAC, "$file.mac";
   $macInFile = <MAC>;
   chomp ($macInFile);
   close MAC;

   #Compare $mac and $macInFile
   if ($mac eq $macInFile){
      print "Conclusion: File $file is original\n";
    }
   else{
      print "Conclusion: File $file is NOT original\n";
    }
}

#main
my ($file) = $ARGV[0];
&verifySecureMd5Digest ($file);
```

The program takes a file to verify for integrity as command-line argument. The main program calls the subroutine verifySecureMD5Digest that does all the work. If a corresponding .mac file does not exist, the program declares that the file has been tampered with and exits. Otherwise, it asks for a passphrase. The same passphrase that was used for creating the hash has to be entered by the verifying user. It computes the two digests as it did in the MAC creation program discussed earlier. It compares the MAC read from the .mac file and the newly computed MAC on the contents of the "secured" file. If the two MACs are equal, it declares that the file being verified is original.

A couple of interactions with this program are given below.

```
%md5SecureFileVerify.pl jk1.jpg
What is your passphrase?: It was the best of times, it was the worst of times.
MAC computed on file jk1.jpg = 69f5a2c1dc6834a6c32d9d414c19da4d
Conclusion: File jk1.jpg is original


%md5SecureFileVerify.pl jk1.jpg
What is your passphrase?: It was the best of times it was the worst of times
MAC computed on file jk1.jpg = 2795116abd77d3af586e5fff64f8e5f2
Conclusion: File jk1.jpg is NOT original
```

In the second run, the passphrase given was devoid of punctuation and hence it was not acceptable.

11.1.3   The MD4 Digest: Package Digest::MD4

MD4 is a precursor to MD5 designed by the same designer, Rivest. It was originally published in 1990. MD5 shares the design goals of MD4. It addition, several other algorithms are based on the design goals of MD4.

One of the design goals of a hash code is that it should be computationally infeasible to find two messages that have the same message digest. At the time of its publication, MD4 was secure against brute-force attacks. It was also secure against more sophisticated cryptanalytic attacks according to Rivest. MD4 is simple because simple algorithms are easier to implement without errors and can be scrutinized by the research community more thoroughly. MD4 is a little faster to compute than MD5. The Perl module for MD4 is similar to the Perl module for MD5, and hence, used similarly. The module is called `Crypt::MD4`.

11.1.4   The Secure Hash Algorithm: Package `Digest::SHA1`

The Secure Hash Algorithm (SHA) was developed by the National Institute of Standards and Technology (NIST) in 1993, and was revised in 1995. It is now generally know as SHA-1. SHA is based on the MD4 algorithm.

The algorithm takes as input a message of length less than 2^{64} bits and produces as output an 160-bit message digest. The input is processed in 512-bit blocks.

The SHA digest is 32 bits longer than the MD5 digest and hence is much more difficult to break using a brute-force technique, on the order of 2^{128} for MD5 and 2^{160} for SHA-1. MD5 has been shown to be possibly breakable using cryptanlaysis techniques. However, such vulnerabilities have not been discovered for SHA-1. SHA-1 involves more steps (80 instead of 64) and must process an 160-bit buffer compared to MD5's 128-bit buffer. Hence, SHA-1 executes a bit more slowly than MD5 on the same machine. The Perl module `Digest::SHA1` is used in the same manner as the module `Digest::MD5`.

11.1.5   RIPEMD-160: Package `Crypt::RIPEMD160`

The RIPEMD-160 message digest algorithm was developed by a group of European researchers. RIPEMD takes as input a message of arbitrary length and produces as output an 160-bit message digest. The input is processed in 512-bit blocks. The overall processing is similar to that of MD5.

All three algorithms, MD5, SHA-1 and RIPEMD-160, are similar because they are all inspired by the design of MD4. MD5 has been shown to be vulnerable to cryptanalytic attacks, but SHA-1 and RIPEMD-160 are not known to be vulnerable at this time. RIPEMD-160 is also a little slower than MD5, just as SHA-1 is. The Perl module `Crypt::RIPEMD160` is very similar to `Digest::MD5` and hence, used the same way.

11.1.6   Problems with Digests

Although there are many hash algorithms, only a few are popularly used. If the eavesdropper knows one or more original messages, and the corresponding hash codes, the eavesdropper may try a few such algorithms and may be able to discover the name of the hash algorithm used. The eavesdropper may be able to find the hash algorithm used by employing other means as well. If this happens, the eavesdropper may be able to replace the original information with some fake information, and then compute a digest for this fake message with the appropriate hash algorithm and transmit the fake information and the accompanying digest to the receiver. The receiver computes the digest on the fake information, and compares this digest with the digest that came from the eavesdropper. The two are equal because the eavesdropper and the receiver use the same hash algorithm. The receiver thus, concludes that the integrity of the data was not tampered with along the way. However, as we know this conclusion is wrong. Thus, one must find ways to safeguard against such replacement of data and accompanying digest.

11.2   Cryptographic Algorithms

Cryptography is a way to scramble data by the possessor or sender A so that those not intended by A cannot read the data. Cryptography involves complex mathematical computation. When we talk about cryptography, we have at least two individuals or parties to the discussion: the possessor or sender A, and the reader or receiver B. A sends B sensitive data. A does not want anyone else but B to see the data. Therefore, A scrambles or encodes or encrypts or enciphers the data before sending. A wants it to be mathematically impossible for the smartest interceptor (who is not B) in the world with a large bank of the world's fastest computers to be able to unscramble or decode or decrypt or decipher the data. This requires some genius on the part of A to maintain such tremendously high level of protection over the data during transit between A's computer and B's computer over an unsecured channel such as the Internet. The trip the data makes between A's and B's computers involves going over the Internet, and hence, a large number of computers en route. It is quite likely that one or more of these computers is unfriendly, or has unfriendly users with the intent to see the data, capture and decipher it and use it for monetary or other benefits.

Protection over the data during transmission is now readily available by using encryption that is mathematically almost impossible to break. A cryptographic algorithm or tool is evaluated with respect to criteria such as the following [MvOV96].

Level of Security: How secure is the algorithm? That is, how difficult is it to break the algorithm? This may involve trying to obtain the cleartext from captured ciphertext with or without any (partial) knowledge of the keys, and with or without one or more captured cleartext–ciphertext pairs. Usually, the level of security is defined as an upper bound on the amount of work necessary to break the algorithm. Breaking attempts may be straight-forward brute-force techniques where one tries all possible value of the key, or more intelligent approaches where it is not essential to examine the complete key space. Examples of intelligent techniques include differential and linear cryptanalysis, and other mathematics-based attacks.

Performance: How efficient are the encryption and decryption processes? For example, one can judge an encryption algorithm by the number of bits per second that it can encrypt.

Ease of Implementation: How easy or difficult is the algorithm to implement in hardware or software?

Functionality: In what ways various cryptographic algorithms can be used to achieve an information security goal at hand? For example, when should conventional cryptography be applied? When should public-key cryptography be applied? To what effect and why?

Methods of Operation: Cryptographic algorithms when applied in various ways with various inputs may provide different effects such as different levels of security. What are these modes of operation? How should they be used and assessed?

There are essentially two types of cryptographic algorithms:

- conventional or symmetric cryptographic algorithms, and

- public-private key or asymmetric cryptographic algorithms.

We discuss these in the sections that follow in very brief.

11.3 Conventional Cryptographic Algorithms

Conventional cryptographic algorithms have been there for a long long time, dating back thousands of years of human history. They have been used since pre-historic times to the present day. As technology has become sophisticated, as automatic computers were invented, as computers have become stupendously fast, conventional cryptographic algorithms have become increasingly complex to keep up with the times. Conventional cryptographic algorithms are very widely used at this time, and will be for the foreseeable future.

Conventional cryptographic algorithms are fast, and can be performed using specialized hardware as well. Conventional computer-based cryptographic algorithms use a large number of simple bit-based computation. These include permuting a number of bits, performing bit shifts, performing XOR computation between two sequences of bits, and performing table-based bit conversion. The tables that guide table-based conversion, usually called *boxes*, are very carefully constructed. Several such tables are used. A table has a small number of input bits and has some output bits. In table-based conversion, a large input bit string is divided into several small groups of bits. For each small group in the input, it is replaced by the corresponding output of the table. The carefully constructed tables, among other computations, make it difficult to break conventional cryptographic algorithms. Perl provides implementation for several conventional cryptographic algorithms. These include Crypt::DES—the Data Encryption Standard (DES), Crypt::IDEA—the International Data Encryption Algorithm (IDEA), Crypt::Blowfish—Blowfish, and Crypt::Rijndael—the Advanced Encryption Standard. DES was adopted as the national non-military standard for encryption by the US Government in 1977. It was used very widely in industry—banks, financial companies, credit-card companies, as well Web browsers and servers. Over the years, DES has aged and has even been broken in the 1990s. Hence, a new national standard has been adopted in 2001. It is called the Advanced Encryption Standard or AES. Before its acceptance as the new national standard, it was known as the Rijndael encryption algorithm based on a stylish combination of the last names of its inventors. Perl's implementation of AES is called Crypt::Rijndael.

A conventional cryptographic algorithm uses a single key K_A. The sender A encrypts his or her message with this key and sends it to the receiver B over unsecured lines that are open to wiretapping. The key K_A has to be given to B by A before data is transferred. B uses this key to decipher the data. A must generate the key K_A and **safeguard** it. A must deliver it **securely** to B. B must **safeguard** the key as well. Therefore, there are many possibilities for breach. Moreover, every pair (A,B) of sender and receiver must have a separate secure key. In the context of the Web where there are millions of individual companies and hundreds of millions of individual users, the number of keys required to allow any two arbitrary parties to communicate becomes enormous. Hence, conventional cryptographic algorithms are difficult to implement and put in practice. However, they are fast to compute and widely used at this time, with some help from public-private key algorithms.

In this section, we discuss several conventional cryptographic algorithms although our focus is on the Data Encryption Standard (DES). The other algorithms briefly discussed are: IDEA, Blowfish and AES.

11.3.1   The Data Encryption Standard: DES

The Data Encryption Standard (DES) was used as the encryption standard by the National Bureau of Standards from 1977 to 2001. DES works on a block of 64 input plaintext bits and converts it after a series of steps into a 64-bit ciphertext. The key size is 56 bits. If the plaintext data size is more than 64 bits, it has to be broken into blocks of size 64 bits each. That is why, it and similar algorithms are also called *block ciphers*. The last block may have to be padded with some known, but redundant bits so that it is 64 bits long as well. The decryption process uses the same key, and the same steps as the encryption process, but in the reverse order.

DES was criticized right from the time of adoption. There were two main reasons why DES was subjected to relentless criticism during its tenure.

- The key size for DES is 56 bits. A lot of practitioners and researchers in cryptography thought that 56 bits is too short for providing adequate security for sensitive data. Such individuals thought that DES could be broken by trying all possibilities for the key, i.e., by brute-force cryptanalysis. Such fears were confirmed in the 1990s. One such attempt that succeeded was carried out co-operatively on the Internet by many thousands of individuals.

- DES performs a large number of bit operations repeatedly on the input data. A repetition, called a *round*, involves performing computations such as permutations of bits, XORs of the intermediate data bits with bits of the key, and table-based bit transformation. The tables take a few input bits and produce a few output bits. The input bits are used to address a particular column and a particular row of the table to obtain the output. The output bits reside in the addressed cell of the table. The tables play a very crucial role in making a conventional cryptographic algorithm secure.

After DES was designed, the design was submitted to the National Security Agency (NSA) for approval. Not only the NSA reduced the key size from the proposed 128 bits to 56, it also changed all the eight tables used by DES. Also, the design criteria for the tables were classified. As a result, independent researchers cold not perform experiments to verify the claimed strength of DES. These reasons caused consternation in the cryptographic community, some of who believed that there could be weaknesses in DES that may allow DES to be broken so that ciphertext messages could be deciphered without the benefit of the key.

In spite of the potential problems, DES was widely used from 1977 to 2001, when it ruled as the national standard in the US. In 2001, DES was replaced by a cryptographic algorithm called Rijndael as the Advanced Encryption Standard (AES).

The DES algorithm encrypts in blocks of 64 bits. It also takes a key that is 56 bits in size. The input and the key go through 16 rounds of complex bit-based computation. At the end, comes 64 bits of ciphertext. The computation, though complex, is fairly fast. The following program shows how DES can be used.

Program 11.7

```perl
#!/usr/bin/perl
#des1.pl

use Crypt::DES;
use strict;


print "The block size is " . Crypt::DES->blocksize () . "bytes\n";
print "The key size is " . Crypt::DES->keysize () . "bytes\n";

my $key = pack ("H*", "0123456789ABCDEF");
my $cipher = Crypt::DES -> new ($key);
#Will give error if the input is not exactly 8 bytes long
my $plaintext = "J Kalita";
print "plaintext = $plaintext\n";
my $ciphertext = $cipher -> encrypt ($plaintext);
print unpack ("H*", $ciphertext), "\n";
my $decryptedPlaintext = $cipher->decrypt ($ciphertext);
print "decrypted plaintext = $decryptedPlaintext\n";
```

The program prints the plaintext block size and the key size using the methods blocksize and keysize, respectively. The key is normally kept very securely. Here, its value is given in a line of code. The key is simply given as 0123456789ABCDEF. There are 16 hexadecimal digits in the key. Each hexadecimal digit is 4 bits. Thus, the key size given is 64 bits. Of these 64 bits, 8 bits are used as parity bits, leaving 56 bits for the actual key. The Crypt::DES module gives us an error if the input is not exactly 64 bits or 8 bytes. The plaintext in this case is simply J Kalita. It is 8 characters or 64 bits long.

To be able to encrypt or decrypt, we need to first create a new instance of the class Crypt::DES. This is usually called a *cipher*. The new method takes the DES key as argument. Encryption is performed by calling the encrypt method with the plaintext as argument to the cipher. Encryption is performed using the DES algorithm. Encryption produces the ciphertext.

In communicating programs, the ciphertext would be transmitted over unsecured communication lines such as the Internet by the sender to the receiver, possibly using a program that uses sockets. In the program under discussion, we do not have two communicating programs since we simply want to illustrate how encryption and decryption work. In two real communicating programs, each would know the key before communicating and keep them securely. The key is generated, transmitted, and stored with utmost security. In the illustration program under discussion, the same key is used for both encryption and decryption. Decryption is performed using the `decrypt` method.

The program prints several messages with various values just to illustrate how the encryption and decryption processes work. The output of the program is given below.

```
The block size is 8bytes
The key size is 8bytes
plaintext = J Kalita
6b51338ca68d303d
decrypted plaintext = J Kalita
```

We clearly see that the decryption of the encrypted plaintext produces the original plaintext.

As we know by now, DES works on a block of plaintext data. The block size is 64 bits or 8 bytes. If the plaintext data to be encrypted is longer than 8 bytes, we have to break into sequential blocks, each of size 8 bytes. The last block may be smaller than 64 bits, and hence a few additional known bits may have to be appended at the end to make it exactly 64 bits long. This is called *padding*. Once we have a sequence of plaintext blocks, the basic DES algorithm can encrypt each block individually. The blocks of ciphertext can be concatenated to obtain the whole ciphertext. The concatenation can be performed either at the sender's end or at the receiver after transmission. Usually, simple encoding of each individual plaintext block and subsequent concatenation of ciphertext blocks is avoided to endow the resulting ciphertext with additional security against cryptanalytic (or, breaking) attempts. There are several techniques for cryptographic algorithms to work on large data, that have been proposed by researchers and practitioners of cryptography as *modes of cipher operation*. Among them, the following four are popular.

1. Electronic Codebook (ECB) mode

2. Cipher Block Chaining (CBC) mode

3. Cipher Feedback (CFB) mode

4. Output Feedback (OFB) mode

We discuss the first two only. There are Perl modules for them. These work with DES and other conventional cryptographic algorithms.

11.3.2   Electronic Codebook (ECB) Mode

In this mode of cipher operation, each of the 64 plaintext bits is encoded independently using the same key. Assume there are n blocks in the plaintext P. Let the blocks be $p_1, p_2, \cdots, p_n$. Each block is encoded separately and directly as given below.

$$
\begin{aligned}
c_1 &= e_k(p_1) \\
c_2 &= e_k(p_2) \\
&\vdots \\
c_n &= e_k(p_n)
\end{aligned}
\tag{11.1}
$$

Here, e_k is the DES encryption function. k is the securely kept and transmitted DES key. Each cipher-text block is sent out over the network lines independently. This approach is usually used for the secure transmission of single values such as a key used for public-key cryptography.

Since ciphertext blocks are independent of each other, substitution of a ciphertext block (say, a frequently occurring one) by another by an interceptor during transmission, does not affect the decryption of adjacent blocks. The ECB mode is unable to hide the presence of patterns in data. Identical plaintext blocks are encoded in terms of identical ciphertext blocks. This may help smart eavesdroppers to get insight into what is being transmitted, and they may try to break the code partially or completely. That is why the ECB mode is not recommended for messages longer than one block.

The following program uses the ECB mode to encode a piece of plaintext that is longer than 64 bits. It uses the Perl module `Crypt::ECB` that provides an object-oriented interface for programmers. It can be used with several conventional encryption algorithms whose implementations are available in Perl: Blowfish, IDEA and Rijndael, in particular. `Crypt::ECB` provides several methods that a programmer can use for encrypting and decrypting. We discuss the ones needed to explain our program.

Program 11.8

```perl
#!/usr/bin/perl
#desEcb.pl
use Crypt::ECB;
use strict;

my $cipher = Crypt::ECB -> new ();
$cipher -> padding (PADDING_AUTO);
print "padding is " . $cipher -> padding () . "\n";
$cipher -> cipher ("DES");
my $key = pack ("H*", "0123456789ABCDEF");
$cipher -> key ($key);

my ($plaintext, $ciphertext);

$plaintext = "My name is Jugal Kalita of Colorado Springs, Colorado.\n";
$plaintext .= "I am an associate professor in the Department of";
$plaintext .= "Computer Science\n at the  University of Colorado\n";
$ciphertext = $cipher -> encrypt ($plaintext);

print $cipher -> decrypt ($ciphertext);
```

The program creates a new instance of the `Crypt::ECB` class and calls it `$cipher`. It is usual to call such an object a cipher. The module provides a built-in manner to pad the last block, if necessary. The `PADDING_AUTO` argument to the `padding` method does so. It is possible to provide `PADDING_NONE` as a value also. However, in such a case, the `Crypt::ECB` module would require the program to perform the padding itself. The program does not encrypt if the program does not perform padding and dies.

To the `Crypt::ECB` object, we specify the encryption algorithm used as an argument to the `cipher` method. Various encryption algorithms that have been implemented and installed on the system can be passed as argument. Some possible argument values are `DES`, `Blowfish`, `IDEA`, `Rijndael`, and `TripleDES`. The program specifies the key using the `key` method of `Crypt::ECB`. The key is a hexadecimal number, 64 bits long. The plaintext is constructed by concatenating several strings. The plaintext is larger than 8 bytes. The plaintext is encoded by calling the `encrypt` method of the `Crypt::ECB` object.

In real communicating programs, the key would be created earlier, and kept safe by the sender. It would also be transmitted securely to the receiver. All this would be done prior to the beginning of the communication. The sender would encrypt with the key and send the ciphertext to the receiver. The receiver would then decrypt using his or her secure copy of the key. In this program, we simply decrypt using the `decrypt` method and print the resulting plaintext on the terminal. It is an illustrative program and not a practical one. The output of the program is given below.

```
padding is 1
My name is Jugal Kalita of Colorado Springs, Colorado.
I am an associate professor in the Department ofComputer Science
 at the  University of Colorado
```

Sometimes, it is necessary to encrypt a large amount of data, say the content of a whole file. To facilitate such an encryption endeavor, Crypt::ECB provides a method called `crypt`. `crypt` can be used to encrypt as well as decrypt. The cipher needs to be set to appropriate mode, encryption or decryption, and the process of encryption or decryption started. Once the encryption or decryption is finished, it needs to be explicitly indicated. The following program illustrates this process.

Program 11.9

```perl
#!/usr/bin/perl
#file desEcbEncrypt.pl

use Crypt::ECB;
use strict;

my $cipher = Crypt::ECB -> new ();
$cipher -> padding (PADDING_AUTO);
print "padding is " . $cipher -> padding () . "\n";
$cipher -> cipher ("DES");
my $key = pack ("H*", "0123456789ABCDEF");
$cipher -> key ($key);
$cipher -> caching ();

#set the encrypting mode; check if all required variables like key
#and cipher are set.
$cipher -> start ("encrypt") or $cipher -> errstring ();
print "The cipher mode is ", $cipher -> mode (), "\n";

my $ciphertext;

my $data1 = "My name is Jugal Kalita.\n";
$ciphertext = $cipher -> crypt ($data1);

my $data2 = "I work at the University of Colorado at Colorado Springs.\n";
$ciphertext .= $cipher -> crypt ($data2);

my $data3 = "It is a growing campus.\n";
$ciphertext .= $cipher -> crypt ($data3);
$ciphertext .= $cipher -> finish ();
```

```
open OUT, ">CIPHERTEXT";
print OUT $ciphertext;

#set the encrypting mode
$cipher -> start ("decrypt") or $cipher -> errstring ();
print "The cipher mode is ", $cipher -> mode (), "\n";

my $plaintext = ($cipher ->crypt ($ciphertext));
$plaintext .= $cipher -> finish ();
print "plaintext = $plaintext\n";
```

A new `Crypt::ECB` object or cipher is created. The `DES` encryption algorithm is associated with the cipher. A 64-bit key is associated with the cipher as well. The encryption process is started by the following statement.

```
$cipher -> start ("encrypt") or $cipher -> errstring ();
```

The `start` method takes a string argument. If this starts with an `e`, it places the cipher in an encryption mode. A string argument with a `d` places the cipher in a decryption mode. If there is a problem with the change of mode, the `errstring` method returns what the error is. For example, if an encryption algorithm or a key has not been associated with the cipher, or the previous operation has not been terminated, there is an error.

This simple program takes three scalars representing plaintext: `$data1`, `$data2`, and `$data3`, and encrypts each one sequentially to produce a single ciphertext. Encryption is done using the `crypt` method. As we know, the chaining of data is performed using the *ECB* mode of cipher operation for DES. The last block is padded if needed. The contents of the cipher may not be flushed automatically when the last call to `crypt` is made. The contents are flushed using the `finish` method of `Crypt::ECB`. The `finish` method returns the flushed ciphertext if any.

The ciphertext is written to a file with the name `CIPHERTEXT`. In real communicating programs, the key `$key` would be kept safe by a sending program, sent securely by the sender, and the receiver would safe-keep it as well. The key exchange would take place prior to communicating. A program would transmit the ciphertext to the receiver, possibly using the socket interface. However, exchange of the key is done by hand or by using public-key cryptography discussed earlier.

In our illustration program, we do not use a socket. We do not have communicating programs in this example. The same program performs the encryption as well as the decryption. The program places the cipher in a decryption mode by calling the `start` method with an appropriate argument. The ciphertext is decrypted using the `crypt` method, and the decryption process `finished`. The output of the program is given below.

```
padding is 1
The cipher mode is encrypt
The cipher mode is decrypt
plaintext = My name is Jugal Kalita.
I work at the University of Colorado at Colorado Springs.
It is a growing campus.
```

11.3.3   Cipher Block Chaining (CBC) Mode

In the ECB mode of cipher operation, each plaintext block is independently encrypted. This is not the case any more with the CBC mode of cipher operation.

In the CBC mode, the input to the encryption algorithm at a certain stage is not straightforward. Let the plaintext be P. It is broken into n blocks, say, each 64 bits long. The last block may be padded if it is not exactly 64 bits long. Let the blocks be $p_1, p_2, \cdots, p_n$, respectively.

$$P = (p_1, p_2, \cdots, p_n)$$

The CBC mode requires the use of a quantity called the *initial vector* for the first computation. The encryption steps are given below.

$$
\begin{aligned}
c_1 &= e_k(p_1 \oplus IV) \\
c_2 &= e_k(p_2 \oplus c_1) \\
c_3 &= e_k(p_3 \oplus c_2) \\
&\vdots \\
c_n &= e_k(p_n \oplus c_{n-1})
\end{aligned}
\tag{11.2}
$$

e_k is the DES encryption function with key k. $\oplus$ is the XOR operation performed bit by bit. A plaintext block is not independently encrypted. A plaintext block is XORed with the previous ciphertext block. Thus, there is a loop or feedback in the encryption process. There is no immediately preceding block for the first plaintext block. Therefore, a quantity called the IV is needed. According to [MvOV96], the IV or the initial vector in the CBC mode need not be secret. However, the IV's integrity should be protected. That is, it should be impossible to change the IV by a malicious individual during transmission. This is because, it can be shown that known changes in IV allows a ill-motivated interceptor to make predictable changes to the first block of plaintext recovered. Using a secret IV prevents this possibility.

The ciphertext is

$$C = (c_1, c_2, \cdots, c_n)$$

The ciphertext blocks, $c_1, c_2, \cdots, c_n$ can be transmitted one by one or all together, or in any other fashion. At the receiving end, the decryption process involves the following steps.

$$
\begin{aligned}
p_1' &= d_k(c_1) \oplus IV \\
p_2' &= d_k(c_2) \oplus c_1 \\
p_3' &= d_k(c_3) \oplus c_2 \\
&\vdots \\
p_n' &= d_k(c_n) \oplus c_{n-1}
\end{aligned}
\tag{11.3}
$$

d_k is the DES decryption function with key k. Here, it is the same IV as used at the sender's end. p_i' is the plaintext block obtained after encryption. Thus, to obtain a plaintext block from the corresponding ciphertext block, one decrypts the corresponding ciphertext block and XORs the result of decryption with the previous ciphertext block. That is, in general, for the ith plaintext block, the decryption computation is performed as given below.

$$p_i' = d_k(c_i) \oplus c_{i-1} \tag{11.4}$$

The first step in the decryption process uses the initial vector (IV). The decryption process given above actually works although it may not be obvious why at first glance. We can show it very easily in the following manner. Using the formula for the original encryption of the ith block, we get the following.

$$p_i' = d_k \ e_k(p_i \oplus c_{i-1}) \oplus c_{i-1} \tag{11.5}$$

d_k is DES decryption with key k, and e_k is DES encryption with the same key k. If we encrypt a message and decrypt it right away, we get the original message. Thus,

$$d_k \ e_k(p_i \oplus c_{i-1}) = p_i \oplus c_{i-1} \tag{11.6}$$

Using this identity, we can write the following.

$$p_i' = p_i \oplus c_{i-1} \oplus c_{i-1}$$
$$= p_i \tag{11.7}$$

This is because a quantity XORed with itself produces all zero bits. This shows that the decrypted plaintext is the same as the original plaintext.

We do not discuss CFB and OFB in this book. ECB is easy, but researchers have shown that it can potentially be insecure for lengthy messages. This is why CBC is recommended for plaintext messages longer than 64 bits. Here are some of the salient properties of the CBC mode of operation [MvOV96].

Identical First Plaintext Blocks: If the same first plaintext block is encrypted with the same key using the same IV, the ciphertext block is the same. Thus, an interceptor may capture the first ciphertext blocks from several encoded messages and try to find if the first ciphertext blocks are the same across several messages. Changing the IV, or making the first plaintext block either a counter or random, takes away this possibility.

Chaining Dependencies: The ciphertext block c_i depends on the plaintext block p_i and all preceding plaintext blocks. Therefore, changing the order of the ciphertext blocks messes up decryption. To decrypt a ciphertext block correctly, the previous ciphertext block must be correctly identified. Thus, parallelization of encryption and decryption is not possible.

Propagation of Error: An error in transmission of a single bit in the ciphertext block c_i causes ciphertext block c_i and c_{i+1} to be deciphered incorrectly. This is because the deciphered plaintext block p_i depends on the ciphertext blocks c_i and c_{i+1}.

Recovery from Error: The CBC mode is *self-synchronizing*. In other words, an error in transmission in the ciphertext block c_i causes ciphertext blocks c_i and c_{i+1} to be decrypted incorrectly. Blocks $c_{i+2}, c_{i+3}, \cdots$ are decrypted correctly.

The following program is very similar to the program in Section 11.3.2 discussed earlier, that uses the ECB mode. The mode of cipher operation now is CBC. The program follows.

Program 11.10

```perl
#!/usr/bin/perl
#file desCbcEncrypt.pl

use Crypt::CBC;
use strict;

my $key = pack ("H*", "0123456789ABCDEF");
my $cipher = Crypt::CBC -> new ($key, "DES");

#set the encrypting mode; check if all required variables like key
#and cipher are set.
$cipher -> start ("encrypt");

my $ciphertext;

my $data1 = "My name is Jugal Kalita.\n";
$ciphertext = $cipher -> crypt ($data1);
```

```
my $data2 = "I work at the University of Colorado at Colorado Springs.\n";
$ciphertext .= $cipher -> crypt ($data2);

my $data3 = "Colorado Springs is at the foot of Pikes Peak.\n";
$ciphertext .= $cipher -> crypt ($data3);

$ciphertext .= $cipher -> finish ();
print "ciphertext = ", pack ("H*", $ciphertext), "\n";

open OUT, ">CIPHERTEXT";
print OUT $ciphertext;

#set the encrypting mode
$cipher -> start ("decrypt") or $cipher -> errstring ();

my $decryptedPlaintext = ($cipher ->crypt ($ciphertext));
$decryptedPlaintext .= $cipher -> finish ();
print "decrypted plaintext = $decryptedPlaintext\n";
```

The program encrypts a few strings sequentially to form the ciphertext. The ciphertext is stored in a file and printed on the screen as well. The ciphertext is later deciphered. Note that although the methods in Crypt::CBC and Crypt::ECB are similar, they may not be identical. Consult the current documentation on *www.cpan.org* or on your own system, to find the details. The output of the program is given below.

```
ciphertext = }/dU|BJ
6!Xw(7ymxSp$JBpiO;[y}0UO|[
decrypted plaintext = My name is Jugal Kalita.
I work at the University of Colorado at Colorado Springs.
Colorado Springs is at the foot of Pikes Peak.
```

11.4   Other Conventional Encryption Algorithms

Perl provides implementation of several conventional encryption algorithms in addition to DES. Among them are the International Data Encryption Algorithm (IDEA), Blowfish and Rijndael or the Advanced Encryption Algorithm (AES). The implementations are available in the modules
Crypt::IDEA, Crypt::IDEA,
Crypt::Blowfish and Crypt::Rijndael, respectively.

IDEA is an algorithm that was proposed to replace DES. Its block size is 64 bits like DES. The IDEA key is 128 bits making brute-force breaking or cryptanalysis practically impossible for a long time to come. IDEA uses the XOR operation like DES. It also uses two additional bit based operations: addition of integers modulo 2^{16} (modulo 655536), and multiplication of integers modulo $2^{16} + 1$ (modulo 65537). IDEA goes through 8 rounds of repeated operations or rounds, and a ninth output transformation round. IDEA can be used with Crypt::ECB and Crypt::CBC modes of operation.

Blowfish converts 64 bits of plaintext to 64-bit blocks of ciphertext. It is used widely as well. It uses two primitive operations: XOR, and addition modulo 2^{32}. It was designed as a replacement for DES as well. It uses table-based transformation as well, but the tables are considered much more difficult to break than the DES tables. The key lengths can be variable, up to 448 bits. It uses 18 rounds of repeated computation, but is very fast to execute. Blowfish can be used with `Crypt::ECB` and `Crypt::CBC` modes of cipher operation. The Rijndael cipher is designed for use with keys of length 128, 192 and 256 bits [TW01]. The algorithm has 10 rounds of repeated computation. Each round consists of four basic steps. The block size is 128 bits.

ByteSub Transformation: This is table or box-based transformation.

ShiftRow Transformation: This mixes up bits over many rounds. It mixes up elements within a single row.

MixColumn Transformation: Here the mixing of the elements is performed within a column.

AddRoundKey: This consists of XOR operations with the key and result of a previous step.

The output is a 128-bit ciphertext block. Decryption consists of performing the inverse encryption steps in reverse.

The Rijndael algorithm is different from DES, IDEA and Blowfish in that in Rijndael all bits are moved and changed in each round. In DES, IDEA and Blowfish, in each round, only one half of the bits are changed; the other half of the bits are not changed, but moved to the other side. The design of the tables is explicit and algebraic in contrast to DES where the tables were mysterious. Rijndael has been shown to resist various breaking or cryptanalysis attempts such as differential and linear cryptanalysis that spelled the end of the long reign of DES. The Perl module for Rijndael is `Crypt::Rijndael`. It works with the `Crypt::CBC` module defining the CBC mode of cipher operation. The key size used by `Crypt::Rijndael` can be 16, 24, or 32 bytes although to work with `Crypt::CBC`, only 32 bytes can be used at the time of writing this book. `Crypt::ECB` also works with `Crypt::Rijndael`. The block size is 16 bytes.

11.5   Public-Key Cryptography

There was a revolution, the only true revolution in the field or cryptography according to many, in 1977 when the concept of public-private key cryptography was enunciated by Diffie and Hellman. They did not have an algorithm, but outlined in precise terms the properties it must have. Rivest, Shamir and Adelman came up with an algorithm almost immediately afterwards, an algorithm that has endured through the passage of time. This algorithm is called the RSA algorithm. Perl provides an implementation in terms of a module called `Crypt::RSA`. We do not discuss the RSA algorithm, but discuss its usage.

A public-private key algorithm uses two distinct keys instead of one. Thus, if A is the sender of information and B is its receiver, A possesses two keys: a private key KR_A and a public key KU_B. They are large keys, possibly 1024 bits or more in length. They are related by number theoretic properties. A bases the computation of KR_A and KU_A by starting with two hugely large prime numbers p and q. These two prime numbers must be kept secret by A. They should be thrown away as well after the keys have ben computed. A computes KR_A and KU_A. A safeguards KR_A, but makes KU_A public and gives it away to anyone who asks or even without asking.

When A needs to send a message m securely to B, the following steps are performed.

1. A encrypts m using his or her private key, KR_A. The encryption algorithm is known to everyone. The private key must be securely guarded. Let the encoded message or ciphertext be called c. c is sent by A to B. This communication, in the context of computer programs, is usually in the form of socket-based transmission. For example, Web based programs that use the RSA algorithm use socket-based communication.

2. B receives the encoded message c. B performs decryption using A's public key KU_A. The decryption algorithm is known to everyone. KU_A is also known to everyone since A makes it public after computing it. The decryption computation produces the original message or cleartext m although the encryption and decryption keys are different.

Thus, the process of secure communication is simple. But, the numbers involved are very very big, and hence, every computation step is slow, even on the fastest computers. In practice, large amounts of data are not transmitted between a client and a server using public-private key algorithms such as the RSA. The RSA is usually used to transmit the single key needed for conventional cryptography.

Public-private key cryptography requires every potential participant p in communication to possess two keys: KU_p and KR_p. So, if there are n potential participants, $2n$ keys need to be computed. In contrast, if conventional cryptography is used, n parties need n^2 keys. For even a moderately small number, the difference between $2n$ and n^2 is huge. In public-private key cryptography, KR_p is kept secret by the potential participant p, and KU_p is known to the world. Thus, there is no need to transmit a key between two communicating parties securely, as in the case of conventional cryptography. This reduces the infrastructural burden for secure communication enormously. Both conventional cryptographic techniques and public-private key cryptographic techniques are practically impossible to break, i.e., they provide the same level of security. Thus, public-private key cryptography should be preferable to conventional cryptography in practice. But, in reality, conventional cryptographic techniques are much faster to implement.

Perl has an implementation for the RSA algorithm. The implementation of Crypt::RSA uses a fast mathematical module called Math::Pari to perform number theoretic computation. The following program shows how Crypt::RSA can be used. It does not use any socket-based communication, but one can clearly foresee how Crypt::RSA can be used to send data securely across the Internet.

Program 11.11

```perl
#!/usr/bin/perl
#rsatest.pl

use Crypt::RSA;
use strict;

my ($rsa, $public, $private, $plaintext, $ciphertext);
my ($plaintext1);

$rsa = new Crypt::RSA;

#If keysize is small,  it will not encrypt
($public, $private) = $rsa->keygen (
        Size => 2048,
#        Size => 512,
        Identity => 'Jugal Kalita, kalita@pikespeak.uccs.edu',
        Password => "University of Colorado at Colorado Springs",
        Cipher => "DES",
        Verbosity => 1
) or die "Cannot create key pair: " . $rsa->errstr();
#$public->write (Filename => "test.public");
print "_" x 50 . "\n";
print "public key is:\n$public\n";

foreach (keys %$public){
        print "key = " . $_ . "value = " . $$public{$_} . "\n";
    }

#$private->write (Filename => "test.private");
print "_" x 50 . "\n";
```

```perl
print "private key is:\n$private\n";
foreach (keys %$private){
        print "key = " . $_ . "value = " . $$private{$_} . "\n";
    }

print "_" x 50 . "\n";
$plaintext = q{Deposit $250,000.00, Account No 5295023273, Wells Fargo}.
             q{Bank, ABA Routing No= 10200076};
print "plaintext before encryption is:\n$plaintext\n";
$ciphertext = $rsa->encrypt (
        Message => $plaintext,
        Key    => $public,
        Armour => 1
) or die "Cannot encrypt: " . $rsa->errstr();
print "ciphertext is:\n$ciphertext\n";

print "_" x 50 . "\n";
$plaintext1 = $rsa->decrypt (
        Cyphertext => $ciphertext,
        Key => $private,
        Armour => 1
) or die "Cannot decrypt: " . $rsa->errstr();

print "_" x 50 . "\n";
print "The decrypted plaintext is:\n$plaintext1\n";
print "_" x 50 . "\n";

my ($signature, $verify);

#PKCS#1 v1.5 signature
$signature = $rsa->sign(
        Message => $plaintext,
        Key => $private) or die "Cannot sign: " . $rsa->errstr() . "\n";

$verify = $rsa->verify (
        Message => $plaintext,
        Signature => $signature,
        Key => $public
) or die "Cannot verify: " . $rsa->errstr() . "\n";

print "PKCS#1 v1.5 verify = $verify\n";
#Probabilistic Signature Scheme
my ($pss);
$pss = new Crypt::RSA::SS::PSS;
$signature = $pss->sign(
        Message => $plaintext,
        Key => $private
) or die "Cannot sign: " . $rsa->errstr() . "\n";

$verify = $pss->verify (
        Message => $plaintext,
```

```
           Signature => $signature,
           Key => $public
) or die "Cannot verify: " . $rsa->errstr() . "\n";


print "PSS verify = $verify\n";
```

We create a new object of type Crypt::RSA. It is called $rsa. It is used to compute two keys: $public and $private. The keys are generated by the following statement.

```
($public, $private) = $rsa->keygen (
           Size => 2048,
#          Size => 512,
           Identity => 'Jugal Kalita, kalita@pikespeak.uccs.edu',
           Password => "University of Colorado at Colorado Springs",
           Cipher => "DES",
           Verbosity => 1
) or die "Cannot create key pair: " . $rsa->errstr();
```

The generation process uses the keygen method of the Crypt::RSA object $rsa. keygen returns two keys. The size of the keys is 2048 bits. The Crypt::RSA module does not create the keys if the key size is small. The minimum size allowed is 48 according to the documentation. The size must be an even integer. Key generation is time consuming. 2048 bits or more can be used as key size, but the computation time will be quite slow, in terms of minutes, not seconds. The keygen method is be given an identity of the owner. This value is unused in the creation of the keys. A password needs to provided to keygen. This is the string with which the private key is encrypted so that it remains private. To securely keep the private key, the keygen method is given an algorithm to encipher the private key. A conventional cryptographic algorithm is needed. The DES conventional algorithm given as the value of the Cipher argument is used here for encrypting the private key. The default conventional encryption algorithm is one called *Blowfish* which is implemented in Perl as Crypt::Blowfish. If for some reason, the key pair cannot be produced, the program dies and it prints an error using the errstr method. In this example, the public key is written into the file test.public and later printed for illustrative purposes. Each key is a hash, and the program prints the key-value pairs for the hash just to show what they are.

Next, a plaintext or cleartext message is created and stored in the scalar $plaintext. The message is shown below.

```
$plaintext = q{Deposit $250,000.00, Account No 5295023273, Wells Fargo}.
             q{Bank, ABA Routing No= 10200076};
```

The program encrypts the message using the public key $public. In practice, the public key is known to everyone and someone sending a message encrypts the message with the public key of the recipient. The encoded message is called $ciphertext. The Armour argument, if true, causes encrypt to encode the ciphertext as an ASCII message so it can be printed and read easily. The program dies if it cannot encrypt. It prints the encrypted message as illustration.

In a realistic program, at this point the encrypted message is sent by the program, possibly using a socket as a means of communication. To keep the example simple, we do not use sockets, but simply perform the decryption in the same program. The program decrypts the ciphertext using the decrypt method of the Crypt::RSA object. For decryption, the private key $private is used. In practice, after the recipient has received the encoded message, the recipient decodes the ciphertext using the recipient's closely safeguarded private key. The program then prints the decrypted plaintext which is the same as what we started with.

The Crypt::RSA algorithm allows us to produce *digital signatures* as well. Digital signatures are like message digests that are discussed in Section 11.1. The module follows a standard called the PKCS to generate signatures. PKCS stands for Public Key Cryptographic Standards. This is a standard application programming interface (API) to hold cryptographic information and perform cryptographic functions. Digital signatures are like message digests, but provide an adequate amount of security when the sender and the receiver do not trust each other completely. When there is complete trust, i.e., the receiver or the sender is not guaranteed to cheat the other, message digests can be used. Digital signatures are like hand-written signatures. A message digest provides authentication, but a digital signature is more stringent. A digital signature must have the following properties [Sta99].

- It must be able to verify the author, the date and the time of the signature.

- It must be able to authenticate the contents at the time of the signature.

- The signature must be verifiable by third parties, to resolve disputes.

Thus, a digital signature includes the authentication function performed by a message digest. Stallings formulates the following requirements for a digital signature.

- The signature must depend on the message being signed.

- The signature must depend on some information unique to the sender.

- The signature must be easy to produce.

- The signature must be easy to recognize and verify.

- It must be computationally infeasible to forge a digital signature.

- It must be practical to keep a copy of the digital signature in storage.

The `Crypt::RSA` module provides a method called `sign` to produce digital signatures. It creates the signature based on the private key. In practice, an individual signing the message signs it with his or her private signature. Also, in practice, the signature is verified by not the party that produces the signature, but by someone else, possibly, the receiver or a third-party service. In this program, verification is performed immediately for illustration purposes. Verification is performed on the plaintext using the public key. Here, signing and verification are done on the plaintext without encrypting. In practice, it is possible that a message is encrypted first and the ciphertext is signed, and later verified by someone other than the producer of the signature. The verification status is printed by the program.

There are many methods to produce digital signatures. The default signature scheme used by `Crypt::RSA` is called the Probabilistic Signature Scheme (PSS) that the `Crypt::RSA::SS::PSS` module implements. The module implements a `sign` and `verify` method. The first calls to `sign` and `verify` use the default, whereas the second pair of calls uses the same signing and verifying algorithm, but does so explicitly. As an aside, Perl also provides implementation for other digital signature algorithms such as the Digital Signature Algorithm (DSA) in terms of the module `Crypt::DSA`, and Pretty Good Privacy (PGP) based signature in terms of the module `PGP::Sign`. These two signature algorithms are unrelated to the RSA algorithm.

The output of running the program is given below.

```
..+........+(31).....+..+(54).+..+..........+...........+..+.....+.+.........+.....+.
......+.......................................+.+.+(86)..............+.....+(161)...
...............+.........+.....+..+.+..........+(209).+.......+...........+..+.....+...+.
..+..+....+......................+.............+..+.....+.+.+.......+..........+.....
..............................+(374)....+...+.........+.......+(446).....+.........
......+.......+........+...+.+...................+...+...+.......+.+...+.+.......+..
.........+.................+..+.....+.............+.........+...+..+..+.........
+.........+........+...............+.........+.........+...........+...+..
```

```
....+..+........+...........................+.........+...+.+.+..........
..........+.........+.........+.........+.........+.......+...+.+(821).+.....+...+...+.
............................+.....................................................+..........+..
.....+(1024)
....+.....+(32)............+..+(52)...............+........+........+(78).........
.+(134)........+.................................+.........+.....+.........+.........+...+
...............................+.........+.........+................................+.+.....+...
..+...........................+.........+.........+.......................+.........+......+....
....+...+...+.................+..+.........+...+(177)...........+...........+..+....
+........+.......+....+..+.........+.......+.+...............................+.........+....
.+.........+..+.+.........+.........+.......+.+.....................................+...+....+
.........+...+.........+.....................+.+.+.+.................+.........+.........+....
.....-....+.........+.........+.........+.+.+..+.....+..+....+(214)...+.....+.......+...+..+.+..
....+..+...+..........+.........+.........+.........+.........+.........+...+...+.....+
....+...................................+.........+.........+.........+.........+........+...
...........................+.........+........+.......+.+.........+.........+.......+.+..
......+(396)....+.........+.........+.........+.........+.........+.........+.......
................................+.+.+.......+.........+....+....
.+.........+.........+.........+.+.+.........+.........+........................+...+.+..
........+.........................+.+.+..+..+.........+.......+.+.............+.........+..
...............................+.........+.........+.......................+.........+...+....
.......+.........................+(611)..........................+.....+..+.+
....+...+...+...+...+..+(1024)
```

```
public key is:
Crypt::RSA::Key::Public=HASH(0x8102eb8)
key = evalue = 65537
key = nvalue = 1710491749258611481854305487420465055422850394065677606062205245
3080041613655941236348266214068895462246802964418326449221099816124950180346801
3082354458033423119991145354916088420470537117813109602691426058354344706221758715
311450804828533409622913828439860378683755436222692760349030777690915873610979
77000128326622826662377191295854139017091404864603129187200262229304692181368535523
266263992900322702669210356109729285715606603979890831256911810413781176900231371
54085301971704815794899731721404420991796126319667200728726338609631950570146663
968554962588202440743904116243208328082987212720593916979211407032806190
key = Versionvalue = 1.8
key = Identityvalue = Jugal Kalita, kalita@pikespeak.uccs.edu
```

```
private key is:
Crypt::RSA::Key::Private=HASH(0x8102ef4)
key = privatevalue = Tie::EncryptedHash=HASH(0x828d8f8)
key = Versionvalue = 1.8
key = Identityvalue = Jugal Kalita, kalita@pikespeak.uccs.edu
```

```
plaintext before encryption is:
Deposit $250,000.00, Account No 5295023273, Wells FargoBank,
     ABA Routing No= 10200076
blocksize: 214
ciphertext is:
-----BEGIN COMPRESSED RSA ENCRYPTED MESSAGE-----
Scheme: Crypt::RSA::ES::OAEP
```

Version: 1.21

eJwBEQHu/jEwADI1NgBDeXBoZXJ0ZXh0gqChBq8u6f3Lcsdy8zyGyD0skT1w6m3ZKVnZUSmcOFIt
GjNKCdgiJvClhDKkdV56SxIEBcTb6Etstf7jrYlhC4YhFKKYJ2QwitSAO04gPcC8i57x22ZmGV1Y
aVHWKekWtn1cAnBfjalfxXxiXQlptsjgHL8SOIam6MWwKhH5/whHxxGluRJi1vgGl6PESqyeURdI
8usomlcDm1Chrm7jbb/kAijws0BIuUibNQZBNILRl8pqCJdGmsMNo+lcLrD/EKk6tY2n3D35nNuu
Emvy9IuVeDrBpuSYCPaUhfMYuarQMOY4CtdPc8jp2x02k+pqVg3Wg7QiCQ2pd7DQiZkOHgBdgqU=
=86uLtp34INeMsaLgRaIjwg==
-----END COMPRESSED RSA ENCRYPTED MESSAGE-----

---

blocksize: 256

The decrypted plaintext is:
Deposit $250,000.00, Account No 5295023273, Wells FargoBank,
    ABA Routing No= 10200076

PKCS#1 v1.5 verify = 1
PSS verify = 1

The dots show progress of computation on the screen.

11.6   Conclusion

This chapter discusses Perl's implementation of cryptographic techniques. Perl provides implementation of several hash or message digest algorithms, several conventional cryptographic algorithms, and the public-private key algorithm called the RSA. It also provides implementation of some digital signature algorithms. The topics are fairly involved and our discussion here is brief. An interested reader is advised to read books on cryptography to find more details. Some such books are *Cryptography and Network Security, Principles and Practice* [Sta99], *Handbook of Applied Cryptography* [MvOV96], *ICSA Guide to Cryptography* [Nic99], and *Security in Computing* [Pfl96]

11.7   Exercises

1. *(Easy: Symmetric Cryptography)*
   This problem is based on a protocol for *Key Exchange for Symmetric Cryptography*, discussed on page 47 of *Applied Cryptography* [Sch96]. Here, we have three participants. Alice and Bob are the two programs participating in a transaction. Trent is a trusted program that mediates or facilitates the communication.

   Assume everyone uses DES for encryption and decryption. Each of Bob and Alice has a secret key that each one knows individually, but no one else knows, with the exception of Trent. Trent knows everyone's keys.

   You will have to write code that has three programs named Bob, Alice and Trent. They can be running on the same machine or three different machines.

   In what is given below, a *session key* is simply a DES key.

   Write programs using sockets that simulate the following protocol.

   (a) Alice contacts Trent and requests a session key.

(b) Trent generates a random session key of the appropriate size. Trent encrypts two copies of this session key. The first is encrypted with Alice's key, and the second is encrypted with Bob's key. Trent sends both copies to Alice. He clearly labels them.

(c) Alice decrypts her copy of the session key. She knows her own key, so she can do this.

(d) Alice sends Bob his copy of the session key.

(e) Bob decrypts his copy of the session key.

(f) Alice now sends Bob a message in encrypted form using the session key.

(g) Bob decrypts the message and reads it.

Use sockets for communication among the parties.

2. *(Hard: Symmetric Cryptography, Public-key Cryptography, Long-term project)*

Digital Signatures

Let Alice and Bob be the two participants in the communication. Let us see what happens when Alice sends Bob a message. When Bob receives the message, he wants to be able to verify that the message came from Alice and no one else. In addition, the message should come in confidence. A double use of the public-key scheme can satisfy these two requirements. Let a public key be denoted by KU and a private key by KR. A subscript specifies the owner of the key. Thus KU_{Alice} is Alice's public key.

The following protocol can be used with the RSA encryption and decryption algorithms to obtain the effect of a digital signature.

(a) Let m be the message to be sent. It is the plaintext. Alice encrypt m using her private RSA key to obtain m'.

$$m' = E_{KR_{Alice}}(m)$$

Here, E is the RSA encryption function. KR_{Alice} is the key used for encryption.

(b) Alice encrypts m' by using Bob's public key to obtain the ciphertext c.

$$c = E_{KU_{Bob}}(m')$$

Thus, there are two calls to the encryption function by Alice.

(c) Alice transmits the ciphertext c over an unsecured transmission channel. In the case of the program you have to write, c is sent by Alice to Bob through the socket interface.

(d) Bob receives c at his end. Bob performs two decryption steps. First, Bob decrypts c using Bob's private key. This gives us m''.

$$m'' = D_{KR_{Bob}}(c)$$

Here, D is the RSA decryption function. KR_{Bob} is the key used for decryption.

(e) Bob decrypts a second time using Alice's public key.

$$m''' = D_{KU_{Alice}}(m'')$$

It can be shown that $m''' = m$, i.e., m''' is the original plaintext message m that was sent by Alice.

The problem requires you to write two programs that communicate using sockets using the protocol given above. In other words, in your program, a receiver should be able to receive a message confidentially and can also verify the sender's identity.

3. The Secure Electronic Transaction (**SET**) is an encryption and security specification designed to protect credit card transaction on the Internet.

   SET is quite complicated. It provides for secure secure communication channels among all parties involved in a transaction. The specification of SET came out in 1997 and is 971 pages long.

   The participants in SET are:

   (a) the card holder,

   (b) the merchant,

   (c) the card issuer,

   (d) the acquirer,

   (e) the payment gateway, and

   (f) the certification authority.

   SET is discussed in somewhat detail in Chapter 14 of *Cryptography and Network Security* [Sta99]. Study the description of SET in this book or elsewhere. Detailed descriptions are also available on the Web

   Write code that allows you to set up the entities involved in a transaction and allow communication among them, two at a time.

   We will now deal with the manner in which interaction between any two parties proceeds in SET. Let the two parties be called *Alice* and *Bob*. Alice initiates the communication, and Bob receives it. In other words, Alice *encrypts* her message, and Bob *decrypts* the message he receives from Alice.

   There are several keys involved: one symmetric key (say, DES) for encrypting the actual data, also called *property description*; two pairs of public-private keys (RSA), one pair for *signature* (called *public-private signature keys*), and another pair for exchanging public keys (called *public key-exchange key*). There are also a couple of *certificates* involved: one for Alice and another for Bob. We will not deal with certificate issuance. A certificate is like a paper certificate. It contains information such a participant's ID or name, and other relevant information. In this case, a certificate binds the identity of a certificate holder to is or her public key.

   The Encryption Process:
   The encryption process at Alice's end is shown below.

   E_1 : Alice runs her data or property description through an 1-way algorithm, a hash, to produce a unique value known as the *message digest*. This is a kind of digital fingerprint of the data and will be used to test the integrity of the message.

   The digest modules of interest are: `Digest::MD5`, `Digest::SHA1`. Use one of these two algorithms.

   E_2 : Alice then encrypts the message digest with her private signature key to produce the digital signature.

   E_3 : Next, Alice generates a random symmetric key and uses it to encrypt the property description, her signature and a copy of her certificate. The certificate contains her public signature key. In order to decrypt the property description, Bob will require a secure copy of the random symmetric key.

   E_4 : Bob's certificate, which Alice must have obtained prior to initiating secure communication with him, contains a copy of his public key-exchange key. To ensure secure transmission of the symmetric key, Alice encrypts it using Bob's public key-exchange key. The encrypted key, referred to as the *digital envelope*, is sent to Bob along with the encrypted message itself.

   Assume that the certificates are exchanged securely, say, by hand or by certified surface mail.

E_5 : Finally, Alice sends a message to Bob consisting of the following: the symmetrically encoded data or property, signature and certificate, as well as the asymmetrically encrypted symmetric key.

The Decryption Process:

The decryption process at Bob consists of the following steps.

D_1 : Bob receives the message from Alice and decrypts the digital envelope with his private key-exchange key to retrieve the symmetric key.

D_2 : Bob uses the symmetric key to decrypt the property description, Alice's signature and her certificate.

D_3 : He decrypts Alice's signature with her public signature key, which he acquires from her certificate. This recovers the original message digest of the property description.

D_4 : He runs the property description through the same one-way algorithm used by Alice and produces a new message digest of the decrypted property description.

D_5 : Finally, he compares his message digest to the one obtained from Alice's digital signature. If they are exactly the same, he confirms that the message content has not been altered during transmission and that it was signed using Alice's private signature key.

  If they are not the same, then the message either originated somewhere else or was altered after it was signed. In that case, Bob takes some appropriate message such as notifying Alice of discarding the message.

Implement the encryption and decryption processes as two modules or packages. Instantiate them for each of the participants in SET. Store all code and data for each of the participants in a separate directory.

Describe salient details of your implementation in a write-up between one and two pages long.

Chapter 12

On Functional Programming

A subprogram is a program sub-unit that has usually been given a name. Writing a subprogram reduces the size of our code because otherwise it would lead to repetition of program statements. More importantly, it gives us an abstract feel for the task it performs. Additionally, once we have identified a task, abstracted it away, and have written the subprogram, we can use the task without bothering about how the task is actually implemented. We can also change the implementation of the task that is contained in the subprogram without affecting the rest of the program.

Thus, a subprogram takes a collection of programming language statements and makes them reusable. Usually, the collection is given a name although it is possible to write nameless or anonymous subprograms. Subprograms are usually parameterized so that an invocation of a subprogram may be slightly different from another. This individuation comes by due to the use of parameters or arguments. Certain variables in a subprogram can be considered parameters so that an invocation identifies the real values of these parameters. When a subprogram is defined, the parameters used inside the subprogram definition are called *formal parameters*. When a subprogram is called, the parameters supplied in the call are called *actual parameters*.

There are two usual ways of writing subprograms: *procedures* and *functions*. A *procedure* is a collection of statements that performs the computation needed to perform a task. The computation is performed when the procedure is called. A procedure can have side effects such as printing and setting of variables that are visible to the procedure.

A *function* is similar to a procedure, but is modeled after mathematical functions. For example, the mathematical function $f(x, y)$ has a name f, and two formal parameters x and y. When we invoke the function f with two parameters, say x_1 and y_1, where x_1 and y_1 have been assigned some values, it performs a computation with these two values and gives the result as its output. The input variables x_1 and y_1 are not changed by a call to the function f.

In a programming language that supports ideal functions, a function does not produce any side effects, that is, neither does it change any of the parameters sent to it nor does it change any variables declared outside the function. A function works by returning a value as the result of the computation it performs. A procedure does not have to return a value and can perform all its computation as side effects.

In Perl, every subprogram we write is a function in the sense that the subprogram returns a value from it. The value returned is the value returned by the last expression that is executed before the function terminates or a value that is explicitly returned by using a `return` statement. However, the subprogram can have side effects. So, in reality, a Perl subprogram is both a function and a procedure. A Perl function can alter the values of global variables that can be seen from inside the function, and it can have other side effects such as printing of text and values of variables. Perl functions can even change the values of parameters sent to them, especially if the parameters are sent by reference, as we will see later. We will use the terms function and subprogram interchangeably.

In programming languages such as Lisp and ML, functions are *first-class objects*. This means that functions are just like any other data structures that these languages support. In other words, they are not different from scalars, arrays, and hashes, and can be manipulated as such. In most programming languages, this is not the case. Functions are treated differently in these languages. When functions are treated as first-class objects, it is possible to write programs that are much more sophisticated compared to languages that do not allow first-class functions. Perl functions are not quite first-class objects, but are quite powerful as will soon see.

12.1   Parameters of Functions

Strictly speaking, Perl functions have only one formal parameter. This formal parameter is a special list variable available inside the function text. This formal parameter is available implicitly inside the function without the author of the function having to do anything. The parameters with which a function is called are put in a single list before being passed to the called function. In other words, if we want to interpret strictly, we can say that each function is called with only one actual parameter which is in the form of a list. We will see that this simple mechanism of parameter passing is quite powerful and allows us to simulate writing three types of functions as far as the nature of the formal parameters is concerned:

- Functions with no formal parameter,
- Functions with an arbitrary number of "formal parameters", and
- Functions with a specified number of "formal parameters."

We will look at these three types of functions in the rest of this section with examples. In Chapter 1, we saw examples of the first two types of functions.

12.1.1   Functions With No Parameters

Sometimes we want to write a function that is very simple and has no formal parameter. Such a function can be used to print a message explaining an error that occurs again and again. The program is given below.

Program 12.1

```perl
#!/usr/bin/perl
use strict;

#Defines a function that prints an error message on divide by zero.
sub printError {
    print "You are trying to divide by zero.\n"
    }

####main program
my ($num, $denom, $result);

#first division
$num = 100; $denom = 10;
if ($denom == 0) {printError;}
else {
    $result = $num/$denom;
    print "$num/$denom = $result\n";
};

#second division
$num = 100; $denom = 0;
if ($denom == 0) {printError;}
else {
    $result = $num/$denom;
    print "$num/$denom = $result\n";
};
```

The program contains a function definition. The function is called `printError`. To define a function, we use the keyword `sub` and follow it by the name of the subprogram and then the code of the subprogram in a block. The function takes no parameter. It simply prints a sentence saying that the program is attempting to divide by zero. Division by zero is not possible and results in an error. The program is invoked twice in the main program. Before dividing $num by $denom, the program checks to see that $denom is equal to zero. If it is equal to zero, it prints an error message. Otherwise, it prints the result of the division.

Since we use use strict, the variables used in the main program as well as in the function must be declared prior to their use. The function body does not have any variables. The three variables used in the main program are declared before they are used. The function can be defined anywhere in the program, not at the beginning as we have done. However, it is good practice to define all subprograms before they are used. Also, it is a good practice to put all function definitions together and not intersperse them throughout the main program's text.

12.1.2   Functions With Arbitrary Number of "Formal Parameters"

Although in the strictest sense, a Perl function has only one single implicit formal parameter of type list, it is possible to simulate a function that takes an arbitrary number of individual formal parameters each of which is scalar. We have put double quotes around the term *formal parameters* above to indicate that although strictly speaking, we have a single formal parameter, we can think of the single formal parameter to be made up of an arbitrary number of individual formal parameters. When we talk about such individual parameters, we put double quotes around the term.

Thus, in Perl, it is possible to write functions that take an arbitrary number of "formal parameters." All the parameters are put in a single undifferentiated list and the function is called with this list. This undifferentiated list is a available in a special list variable @_ inside the function. The code inside the function looks at this list variable and retrieves the individual "actual parameters" from this list. Once again, we have put double quotes around the term *actual parameters* to indicate that these act like several individual actual parameters that are scalar although strictly speaking, it is a single actual parameter that is a list. As a result of this, it is difficult to pass more than one list or hash to the function because it is awkward to indicate where one list or hash ends and the other starts unless we send the lengths of the lists or hashes as parameters also. If several parameters are passed to a function, it is convenient to send only one list or hash if we do not want to or cannot send the lengths of several lists or hashes. In such a case, it makes sense to send the list or the hash as the last parameter. The first few parameters in such a case are scalars. The text of the function picks out the requisite number of scalars, but treats the rest as a list or a hash. Of course, we can send references to the lists or hashes if we want. A reference is a scalar.

Here is a rewrite of the immediately preceding function. This time, the function has been rewritten to take two parameters.

Program 12.2

```
use strict;

sub divide {
    my $result;
    my ($num, $denom) = @_;
    if ($denom == 0){
        print "You are trying to divide by zero: $num/$denom.\n";
    }
    else {
        $result = $num/$denom;
        print "$num/$denom = $result\n";
    }
}
```

```
#main program
my ($num, $denom);
#first division
$num = 100; $denom = 10;
divide ($num, $denom);

#second division
divide (100, 0);
```

Here, the function is called `divide`. It is called with two "actual parameters." We see two calls to the subprogram in the bottom of the program. In the main program, we create two my variables: $num and $denom. In the body of the subprogram, we create three my variables, $result, $num and $denom. The two variables (viz., $num and $denom) that are common to both the main program and the subprogram are not the same. For example, the $num variables inside and outside the subprogram actually have different memory spaces allocated to them. They are completely distinct. When we refer to $num inside the subprogram, we get the variable local to the subprogram. When the subprogram execution is finished, this variable is no longer available and the variable outside the subprogram becomes visible.

Let us look at the first call:

```
divide ($num, $denom);
```

This call to the subprogram provides two "actual parameters" to the function: $num and $denom. However, in reality, the function is called with not two individual "actual parameters," but a single list that contains the values of the two scalar variables. The value of the resulting list is passed to the function.

So, the function receives an undifferentiated list at initiation. As mentioned earlier, this undifferentiated list is available inside the subprogram as a special variable @_. The code inside the subprogram must look at this variable and then fish out the two scalars that we passed to it. This is done in the expression

```
my ($num, $denom) = @_;
```

inside the subprogram. This expression declares two scalar variables with the my declaration making them statically scoped inside the subprogram. In addition, it initializes the two variables by taking the @_ list apart. The first element of @_ becomes the value of $num and the second element of @_ becomes the value of $denom inside the subprogram.

The rest of the subprogram looks at the value of $denom. If $denom is zero, it prints an error message, otherwise, it performs the requested division.

12.1.3   Specifying the Number and Type of "Formal Parameters"

As we know by now, Perl does not allow us to write a function with a specified set of "formal parameters" like most other programming languages do. However, through a facility called *prototypes*, Perl allows one to state the number of individual scalar parameters sent to a subprogram and their types.

Suppose we want to rewrite our subprogram `divide` so that we make the types of the two "formal parameters" sent clear. We require that we send two scalars as parameters.

Program 12.3

```
use strict;

#The function divide specifies the types of parameters it needs.
```

```
#The function takes two parameters each of which is a scalar
sub divide ($$) {
    my $result;
    my ($num, $denom) = @_;
    if ($denom == 0){
        print "You are trying to divide by zero: $num/$denom.\n";
    }
    else {
        $result = $num/$denom;
        print "$num/$denom = $result\n";
    }
}

#main program
my ($num, $denom);

$num = 100; $denom = 10;
divide ($num, $denom);
divide ($num, 0);
divide (100, 20);
#divide (100);            #Error because not enough parameters are provided
#divide (100, 20, 3);   #Error because too many parameters are provided
```

That the function `divide` needs two scalar parameters is mandated by the presence of (`$$`) in the first line of the subprogram definition.

```
sub divide ($$)
```

The first $ sign tells us that the first parameter must be a scalar. This is because in Perl, all scalar variable names start with the $ sign. Similarly, the second parameter is also specified to be a scalar. That is, when we call the subprogram `divide`, we must pass two scalars as "formal parameters." We cannot pass fewer than two or more than two "actual parameters." If we do so, we get a compiler error. If we do not have the parameter types specified in the definition of the function, we would have been able to call with zero to any number of "actual parameters." All the parameters would have been passed as an undifferentiated list.

As we know by now, unlike most programming languages, Perl still does not allow us to write subprograms with a list of formal parameters. But, it is quite likely that a future version of Perl will provide this facility. The ability to provide a list of "formal parameter" types is a first step towards doing so.

12.1.4   Optional Parameters

Perl also allows us to write functions that take optional parameters. In Perl, we can state some parameters to be *required* parameters and some more to be to `optional` parameters. This is to some extent like Common LISP that allows us to write functions that take optional parameters. The following program shows this facility.

Program 12.4

```
use strict;

#Both the first parameter and the second parameter must be scalars.
```

```perl
#the second parameter is optional
sub divide ($;$)
{
    my $result;
    my ($num, $denom) = @_;
    unless (defined ($denom)){
            $denom = 1;
    }
    if ($denom == 0){
        print "You are trying to divide by zero: $num/$denom.\n";
    }
    else {
            $result = $num/$denom;
            print "$num/$denom = $result\n";
    }
}

#main program
my ($num, $denom);
$num = 100; $denom = 10;
divide ($num, $denom);
divide ($num, 0);

#The next call defaults the denominator to 1 because it is not provided.
divide $num;
```

In this program, we write a subprogram called divide that requires one scalar "actual parameter," and may have a second scalar "actual parameter" that is optional. This is done by stating so right after the name of the subprogram when we state the types of the parameters for the subprogram. Here, the first line of the subprogram definition looks like the following.

```perl
sub divide ($;$)
```

In specifying the types of the function's "formal parameters," we separate the types of the required "formal parameters" from the types of the optional "formal parameters" by a semicolon. In this specific case, the types of the parameters are specified using $;$. This means that one scalar parameter is necessary and the second scalar parameter is optional.

In the body of the subprogram, there is a conditional unless statement whose condition is given as the following.

```perl
(defined ($denom))
```

This checks to see if in a call to divide, a value has been provided for the second parameter. If a value has not been provided in the call, the value of the parameter inside the subprogram is undefined. If the value is undefined, the defined function returns true. In such a case, the value of $denom is defaulted to 1. Towards the end of the main program, we have a call to divide that looks like the following.

```perl
divide $num;
```

In this call, the value of the second parameter will default to 1.

12.1.5   Passing References to a Subroutine Using Type Specification

In Perl, it is possible to send the reference to a parameter to a function using the parameter type specification. To pass a parameter as a reference and not by value, we need to precede its type specification by a back slash (\). The following is a rewrite of the divide subprogram where the first "formal parameter" is passed by reference and the second "actual parameter" is passed by value. The two parameters are still passed to the subprogram in terms of the special list variable @_, but the first element of this list inside the subprogram is a reference to a scalar variable and the second is a scalar variable.

Program 12.5

```
use strict;

#Here, the first parameter must start with the $ character. The
#second parameter has to be a scalar, either a variable or a constant.
#A reference to the first parameter will be passed. The value of the
#second parameter is passed.
sub divide (\$$) {
    my $result;
    my ($num, $denom) = @_;
    if ($denom == 0){
        print "You are trying to divide by zero: $$num/$denom.\n";
    }
    else {
        $result = $$num/$denom;
        print "$$num/$denom = $result\n";
    }
}


#main program
my ($num, $denom);
#Here, the first parameter to divide must start with the $ character
#first division
$num = 100; $denom = 10;
divide ($num, $denom);
divide ($num, 0);
#divide (100, 10) is an error because the first parameter doesn't start with $
```

We see that use of \ in front of the type specification for an parameter puts a restriction on how the function can be called. Here, since the first "formal parameter's" type is specified as \$, the first "actual parameter" in any call to divide must start with the $ character. In other words, we cannot put a scalar value as the first "actual parameter." The reference to the first parameter is sent to the subprogram. So, inside the body of the subprogram, the first element of the list @_ is a reference to a scalar variable. That is why, when we perform the addition, we need to dereference $num. Dereferencing is done by using $$num. Since $num points to a scalar, to dereference we precede it with another $ character.

12.1.6   Other Type Specifiers

In specifying the type of the parameters, Perl allows us to use the following characters: $ @ % * and &. @ stands for a list variable or list value, % stands for a hash variable or hash value, & stands for an anonymous subprogram and * stands for a reference to a symbol table entry. We can precede the $, @ and % by a \ to send a reference to the variable of the required kind. In such a case, in invocations of the subprogram, the "actual parameter" has to start with the specified character.

As a last example, the following is a function that takes two list variables and optionally four scalar values or variables. The first two scalars are used as the start and end indices for the first list to pick out a substring. If the first scalar is not given, it is assumed to be 0. If the second scalar is not given, it is assumed to be the last index in the first list. Similarly, the third and the fourth scalars are taken to be the start and end indices of the second list so that a relevant substring can be picked out. The function appendSubSeq takes the specified sublist of the first list, and the specified sublist of the second list and appends them together and returns this appended list. If for any list, the start index is given to be bigger than the end index, no subsequence is picked from the list.

Program 12.6

```perl
#Here is a function that takes two lists followed optionally
#by between zero and four numeric scalars.
#The two lists must be provided as list variables.
sub appendSubSeqs (\@\@;$$$$) {
    my ($firstListRef, $secondListRef, $start1, $end1,$start2, $end2) = @_;
    my @firstList  = @$firstListRef;
    my @secondList =  @$secondListRef;

    unless (defined ($start1)) {$start1 = 0;}
    unless (defined ($start2)) {$start2 = 0;}
    unless (defined ($end1)) {$end1 = $#firstList;}
    unless (defined ($end2)) {$end2 = $#secondList;}
    return (@firstList[$start1..$end1], @secondList[$start2..$end2]);
}
```

Having written the subprogram above, we can instantiate @list1 and @list2 in to various values and see how appendSubSeqs works. Here are some possible calls to appendSubSeqs.

```perl
@list1 = (1, 2, 3, 4); @list2= (10, 11, 12, 13, 14);
@result = appendSubSeqs (@list1, @list2);

@list1 = (1, 2, 3, 4); @list2= (10, 11, 12, 13, 14);
@result = appendSubSeqs (@list1, @list2, 2);

@list1 = (1, 2, 3, 4); @list2= (10, 11, 12, 13, 14);
@result = appendSubSeqs (@list1, @list2, 2, 3);

@list1 = (1, 2, 3, 4); @list2= (10, 11, 12, 13, 14);
@result = appendSubSeqs (@list1, @list2, 2, 3, 2);

@list1 = (1, 2, 3, 4); @list2 = (10, 11, 12, 13, 14);
@result = appendSubSeqs (@list1, @list2, 2, 3, 2, 4);

#If a list is empty, no subsequence is picked
#even if the two indices are given.
@list1 = (); @list2 = (10, 11, 12, 13, 14);
```

```
@result = appendSubSeqs (@list1, @list2, 2, 3, 2, 4);

@list1 = (); @list2 = ();
@result = appendSubSeqs (@list1, @list2, 2, 3, 2, 4);

#if start is bigger than end for a list, no subsequence is picked
@list1 = (1, 2, 3, 4); @list2 = (10, 11, 12, 13, 14);
@result = appendSubSeqs (@list1, @list2, 3, 1, 2, 4);
```

12.1.7 Parameter Profile of Perl Functions

The *parameter profile* of a subprogram is the number, order and types of its formal parameters. In the case of Perl, the parameter profile, for regular subprograms, is very simple. A regular Perl subprogram does not have any individual formal parameters; strictly speaking, it has only one formal parameter: @_, which is an undistinguished list of scalars of arbitrary length. This single formal parameter is a list of individual "formal parameters." The body of the subprogram has to fish out the scalars from this homogeneous list and make sure the appropriate number of parameters has been passed. The manner in which it culls elements from the list gives it the "actual parameters" in the proper order. The elements are all scalars. There are good points as well as drawbacks to this scheme.

Some of the good points are given below.

- The model of parameter passing is simple and simplicity has its virtue. Subprograms are easy to write. This adds to the fact that Perl is a language that is good for rapid prototyping.

- Perl allows one to write functions that take an arbitrary number of parameters. This is of great value in certain contexts. Such functions can be quite powerful.

- Perl allows type checking of parameters for those who want it. We will see that this is done using the concept of *prototypes*.

Some of the drawbacks of Perl functions are given below.

- The only formal parameter is an undifferentiated list. The subprogram code has to obtain the specific elements. This adds code to the body of the subprogram. It is not really a major inconvenience because the code required is usually minimal and the programmer who writes the subprogram knows the order of the parameters. But, it may make updating of code difficult unless the programmer says what the "formal parameters" are through good commenting or good coding.

- This makes it difficult to pass several lists or hashes unless there is some way to indicate the lengths of the lists or hashes. However, we can do so by passing parameter references.

- Since simple Perl functions do not check types of "actual parameters," it is possible to make errors, especially by those who are used to strongly-typed languages like Pascal or C. Some simple type checking can be done using *prototypes*.

12.2 Recursive Functions

Like most programming languages, Perl allows one to write recursive subprograms. A recursive subprogram is one that calls itself either directly or indirectly. To call directly means that the subprogram calls itself. To call indirectly means that the subprogram calls some subprogram which calls the original subprogram directly or indirectly. Recursive programs are introduced in Section 2.9. There are examples of recursive functions in Chapter 6. The examples deal exclusively with files and directories, and are fairly simple to follow. Since the discussion on recursion in Chapter 6 is extensive, we do not discuss recursive functions here.

12.3   Functions Passed As Parameters

In Perl, functions cannot be passed as parameters, but references to functions can. So, if we want to send a function as a parameter, we need to reference it before invoking the function and inside the function's body, we need to dereference the appropriate elements of the @_ array and then call the function on appropriate actual parameters. A reference to a subprogram can be created in two ways:

- If mysub is a subprogram, a reference to it can be created by writing

  ```
  $mysubRef = \&mysub;
  ```

- Otherwise, we can write the subprogram without a name and assign this nameless or anonymous subprogram to a scalar that will contain a reference to it.

  ```
  $mysubRef = sub { #subprogram body
                  };
  ```

In the following program, we define a function called find that takes two parameters: a reference to a function and a list of numbers. The first parameter is a reference to a predicate that returns true or false (actually, 1 or 0, in this case). The function find returns those elements of the list that satisfy the predicate whose reference is passed as the first parameter. Here, we have defined two such predicate functions: biggerThan10P which is a named function, and $between10and45P which is actually a reference to a function.

Program 12.7

```
#Find those elements of a list that satisfy the condition stated in a
#function whose reference is passed as the first parameter

#a conditional function or  predicate
sub biggerThan10P{
    if ( $_[0] > 10) {1} else {0}
}

#another conditional function or predicate
$between10and45P = sub {
    if (($_[0] > 10) && ($_[0] < 45)){1} else {0}
};


sub find{
    my ($subRef,@lst) = @_;
    my @result;

    foreach $elmt (@lst){
        if (&$subRef($elmt)){
```

```
                    @result = (@result, $elmt);
                }
    }

    return @result;
}

print join " ", find (\&biggerThan10P, 10, 2, 30, 45, 7), "\n";
print join " ", find ($between10and45P, 10, 2, 30, 45, 7), "\n";
```

Inside the body of the function find, the first element of @_ is assigned to $subRef which stores the reference to the function supplied as parameter. The function is called by invoking it as &$subRef followed by a list of parameters. When a referenced function is called, the name of the reference scalar must be preceded by the ampersand sign (&).

As mentioned earlier, to obtain the reference to a function, we must precede the function's name by & if the function is defined with a name. Here, the function biggerThan10P is a regular named function and as a result, a reference to it is obtained by writing \&biggerThan10P. This reference is passed as the first parameter to find in the first call. If a function is defined as a nameless function, a reference to it is obtained by setting a scalar variable. We see an example with the definition of the anonymous function whose reference is stored in the scalar $between10and45P.

We also need to note here that a function that works very similarly to the function find is available as a Perl built-in function. It is called grep. The two calls to find given above can be simulated using grep as the following.

```
grep ($_ > 10, 10, 2, 30, 45, 7)
grep ($_ > 10 && $_ < 45, 10, 2, 30, 45, 7)
```

12.4   Mapping

Like Common Lisp and similar languages, it is possible to map functions over a list in Perl. Mapping is introduced in Section 2.8. This means that we can take a function and execute the function with each element of the list taken as its actual parameter. For example, we may want to add 10 to every element of a list. The following function achieves that feat.

Program 12.8

```
#This subprogram is called with a list that contains one element
$add10 = sub {
    my $number = $_[0];
    $number + 10;
};

#calls &$add10 with every element of the list
@newlist = map {&$add10 ($_)} (1, 2, 3);
```

Here, we have defined an anonymous function which can be referenced using the scalar $add10. This function simply takes a parameter and adds 10 to it. The mapping of this function onto every element of a list can be performed using a call to the map function which is a built-in function in Perl. This function takes two parameters. The first parameter is a block of statements that operates on the special variable $\_$. The function is applied to each element of the list that is provided as the second parameter. As each element of the list is taken up for consideration, it is available to the mapped block as the value of the special variable $\_$. Here, the block passed as the first parameter to map calls the anonymous function referenced by the scalar $add10. This function is called with the parameter $\_$. This function that operates on $\_$ is mapped on to the list containing three parameters: $(1, 2, 3)$. So, at the end of the call, @newlist contains $11, 12$ and 13.

12.4.1   Writing Mapping Functions

In this section, we write a few more simple functions that map a function to a sequence of parameters. In particular, we write four mapping functions: mapAtoB, map0toN, map1toN and mapF. We start with the code for mapAtoB and use its definition to write map0toN and map1toN. We then write the code for the more general mapF function. Finally, we write code for a function called newmapAtoB which is a version of mapAtoB written using the mapF function.

Before proceeding with writing these functions, let us first write a function called funcalls which takes a reference to a function and calls this function on a scalar parameter. It returns a scalar result.

Program 12.9

```
sub funcalls {
    my ($fn, $arg) = @_;
    &$fn($arg);
}
```

Next, we write the function mapAtoB that takes as parameters a reference to a function, a low numeric value, a high numeric value, and optionally a numeric step. If the step is not provided, it defaults to 1. mapAtoB takes the referenced function and applies it to a sequence of numbers starting with the low value. It increments the number on which the function is applied by step in each iteration. When the number becomes bigger than the high value, it stops the iteration. If the high value is smaller than low value to start with, the function is not applied even once. mapAtoB returns the results of applying the function to the sequence of numbers in a list. The definition for mapAtoB is given below.

Program 12.10

```
sub mapAtoB {
    my ($fn, $A, $B, $step) = @_;
    my ($i, @result);

    unless (defined ($step)) { $step = 1;};

    for ($i = $A; $i <= $B; $i = $i + $step){
        push (@result, funcalls ($fn, $i));
    }
    return @result;
}
```

In the definition of mapAtoB we check to see if a value has been provided from $step in the call. This check is done using the defined function. If a value has not been provided, $step is initialized to 1. In the for loop, we apply the function referenced by $fn to the current value of the loop index variable $i in each iteration. This application is done by calling the funcalls function defined a little earlier.

Now, we define the add1 function that we map on the desired sequence of numbers and then make two calls to mapAtoB that return the results shown.

```
sub add1 {
    $_[0] + 1;
}
```

The call

```
mapAtoB (\&add1, 20, 40, 2)
```

returns

```
21 23 25 27 29 31 33 35 37 39 41
```

and the call

```
mapAtoB (\&add1, 20.1, 40, 2.5)
```

returns

```
21.1 23.6 26.1 28.6 31.1 33.6 36.1 38.6
```

Once again, note that we obtain the reference to a named function such as add1 by preceding it with &.

Having defined the function mapAtoB, we can define the two functions map0toN and map1toN in terms of it. map0toN applies a function to every integer from 0 through N, and map1toN does the same for integers 1 through N.

Program 12.11

```
sub map0toN{
    ($f, $N) = @_;
    mapAtoB ($f, 0, $N);
}

sub map1toN{
    ($f, $N) = @_;
    mapAtoB ($f, 1, $N);
}

#prints 1 2 3 4 5 6 7 8 9 10 11 12 13 14 15 16 17 18 19 20 21
print join " ",  map0toN (\&add1, 20), "\n";

#prints 2 3 4 5 6 7 8 9 10 11 12 13 14 15 16 17 18 19 20 21
print join " ",  map1toN (\&add1, 20), "\n";
```

We now define the function mapF that is more general than the three mapping functions we have written so far. mapF takes four parameters: a reference to the function to be mapped, a starting value for the mapping sequence, a reference to a function that tests to see if the end of the desired sequence has been reached, and a reference to a function that obtains a succeeding number from the current one.

Program 12.12

```
sub mapF {
    my ($f, $start, $testF, $succF) = @_;
    my ($i, @result);

    for ($i = $start; !funcallS ($testF, $i); $i = funcallS ($succF, $i)){
        push @result, funcallS ($f, $i);
    }
    return @result;
}
```

We see that the new value of the index variable $i is obtained by applying $succF on the current value of $i. This is achieved by the expression

```
$i = funcallS ($succF, $i)
```

The operating condition for the loop is given as

```
!funcallS ($testF, $i);
```

That is, as long as the application of the test function on the index variable returns a false value, the iteration continues. In other words, when an application of the test function $testF on $i returns true, the iteration stops. For example, our test function could see if the number under consideration is a prime number and stop iteration if it is so. A definition for such a test function is given below.

Program 12.13

```
sub isPrimeP {
    my $number = $_[0];
    my $i;

    for ($i= 2; $i <= sqrt ($number); $i++){
        if ($number % $i == 0 ) {
            return 0;}
    }
    return 1;
}
```

Now, we can make the following calls to mapF obtain the results given.

```
#prints 21 22 23
print join " ", mapF (\&add1, 20, \&isPrimeP, \&add1), "\n";

#prints 201 202 203 204 205 206 207 208 209 210 211
print join " ", mapF (\&add1, 200, \&isPrimeP, \&add1), "\n";

#prints 2031 2032 2033 2034 2035 2036 2037 2038 2039
print join " ", mapF (\&add1, 2030, \&isPrimeP, \&add1), "\n";
```

We can now write a couple more functions that print prime numbers between any two integers. The definitions of the two functions are given below.

Program 12.14

```perl
sub printIfPrime{
    if (isPrimeP ($_[0])) {print " $_[0] ";}
    else {}
}

sub printPrimes {
    my ($low, $high) = @_;

    mapAtoB (\&printIfPrime, $low, $high);
}
```

Following these two definitions, we can make the following call

```perl
printPrimes (100000, 100999);
```

and obtain the following primes between $100,000$ and $100,999$.

```
100129   100151   100153   100169   100183   100189   100193   100207   100213
100237   100267   100271   100279   100291   100297   100313   100333   100343
100357   100361   100363   100379   100391   100393   100403   100411   100417
100447   100459   100469   100483   100493   100501   100511   100517   100519
100523   100537   100547   100549   100559   100591   100609   100613   100621
100649   100669   100673   100693   100699   100703   100733   100741   100747
100769   100787   100799   100801   100811   100823   100829   100847   100853
100907   100913   100927   100931   100937   100943   100957   100981   100987
100999
```

Please note that the numbers do not come out formatted as we show them above.

Finally, we close this section by rewriting the mapAtoB function in terms of the mapF function. This new definition is given below.

Program 12.15

```perl
sub newmapAtoB {
    my ($fn, $A, $B, $step) = @_;
    unless (defined ($step)) { $step = 1;};

    mapF ($fn, $A,
              sub { my $x = $_[0];
                        $x >  $B;
                  },
              sub { my $x = $_[0];
                        $x + $step;
                  }
         );
}
```

In this definition, we call mapF with four parameters as required. There is nothing unusual about the first two parameters. However, the third and the fourth parameters are unusual in the sense that they are in-line references to functions. We define the two functional parameters inside the call to mapF without any names. These two are anonymous or nameless functions. To reiterate, we write an anonymous function in Perl by writing the keyword sub and following it by a block that contains the definition of the function. Since these are functions, they return the values computed by the last statements inside them.

12.5   Closures

Before we get into the discussion on closures, let us first note that Perl allows us to define functions inside functions. When a function is defined inside a function, the function can be named or anonymous. An anonymous function is one that does not have a name and is referenced with a scalar reference variable. It is possible that an anonymous function, whether inside another function or not, refers to a variable that is not bound inside the anonymous function, but bound outside. In the case of a closure, the system saves copies of the bindings of such externally bound variables at the time the function is defined. Such a combination of an anonymous function and a set of variable bindings is called a *closure*. Closures are useful in a variety of applications.

12.5.1   When Can Closures Occur?

We now see when closures can occur in Perl. We examine two situations: closures in the main program, and closures inside subprograms.

The following is a closure that can occur in the main program.

Program 12.16

```
my $n = 10;

sub addN{
    return $_[0] + $n;
}

#prints 210
print addN (200), "\n";
```

Here, we have a lexical my variable called $n in the main program. We next define a function called addN that takes one parameter and returns this parameter with $n added to it. Note that $n is not a variable that is bound inside addN.

This is a very simple case and not very interesting. The more interesting case occurs when we define functions inside functions and when such a function inside a function is an anonymous function. Let us see a few examples of functions inside functions.

Program 12.17

```
sub fiveAdds{

    my $m = $_[0];
```

```
    sub add1{
        return $_[0] + 1;
    }

    my $add3 = sub{
        return $_[0] + 3;
    };

    $add4 = sub{
        return $_[0] + 4;
    };

    $addM1 = sub{
        return $_[0] + $m;
    };

    my $addM2 = sub{
        return $_[0] + $m;
    };

    return add1($_[0]) * &$add3($_[0]) * &$add4($_[0]) *
              &$addM1($_[0]) * &$addM2($_[0]);

}

print fiveAdds (2), "\n";

#note add1 and add2 have become functions that are available globally
print add1 (21) * add2 (23), "\n";

#note &$add3 is not available outside the subprogram
#note &$add4 is available outside the subprogram
print add1 (2) * add2 (2) * &$add4(2), "\n";
```

We define a subprogram called fiveAdds. Inside fiveAdds, we declare and assign a lexically scoped or my variable called $m. We then define five different functions that perform addition. Let us look at function add1 first. add1 takes a scalar parameter (which is different from the scalar parameter that fiveAdds takes) and adds 1 to it. Even though add1 is defined inside fiveAdds, add1 becomes a globally defined function. It can be seen and called outside fiveAdds.

Next, we define four more functions. These functions are anonymous functions. References to these functions are stored in the scalars $add3, $add4, $addM1 and $addM2 respectively. $add4 is a globally scoped scalar and as a result, the function that is referenced by $add4 is seen and can be called outside the containing subprogram fiveAdds. The function referenced by $addM1 is similar. However, the scalars $add3 and $addM2 are declared using my and hence are lexically scoped inside fiveAdds. They are not seen and therefore, the functions they reference cannot be called outside the textual body of fiveAdds. Of course, all five functions are seen and can be called inside the containing function fiveAdds.

The functions referenced by $add3 and $add4 are not much different from the function add1 except that the last two functions are defined anonymously and hence have to be referenced using scalar references. However, the last function $addM2 is a bit different. It is referenced using a lexically scoped scalar: $addM2. Inside the body of the function, we use a scalar $m that is defined outside and bound to a value outside the definition of the function. The function referenced by $addM2 cannot be called outside the body of the function fiveAdds. But, because it is referenced by a scalar, the scalar reference can be returned by the function fiveAdds if it so chooses. Nothing is done with these two function referencing scalars in the function fiveAdds, but we see next that this function can behave as closure also if their references are returned to the outside world by the containing function. The first three functions cannot behave as closures.

12.5.2   A Simple Example of A Closure

The following example has an anonymous function and a set of bindings associated with it. Therefore, it is an example of a closure. Here is the code.

Program 12.18

```
sub funcallS{
          my ($funRef, $parameter) = @_;
          &$funRef($parameter);
}

sub listAdd1{
    my ($n, @lst) = @_;

    my $addN = sub {
        my $x = $_[0];
        $x + $n;
    };

    map {funcallS ($addN, $_)} @lst;
};

@list = (1,2,3);
@newlist = listAdd1 (10, @list);
```

Let us focus on the function listAdd1. Inside listAdd1, we define a statically or lexically scoped variable $n which gets its value from the first parameter to the call to listAdd1. We also define another variable called @lst.

Next, we define an anonymous function that is referenced by the scalar $addN. Let us concentrate on this function now. The function defines a local, statically scoped variable $x and assigns a value to it. Next, it returns the sum $x + $n. However, $n is a variable that is not bound inside the anonymous function. The binding of $n comes from outside the anonymous function but from within listAdd1. Thus, here, we have an anonymous function and a binding that is external to it. This is an example of a closure.

Once the anonymous function is defined, the last statement in listAdd1 performs a map of the anonymous function on every element of the list variable lst.

12.5.3   Closures That Share A Scalar Variable

Closures defined inside one function can share a variable. We have three such closures defined inside the counter function in the code below. They all share the value of the scalar variable $counter that is defined as a local variable inside counter.

Program 12.19

```
sub counter{
    my $counter = 0;

    sub returnCounter{
        $counter
        }

    sub incrCounter{
        $counter++
        }

    sub resetCounter{
        $counter = 0;
        }
}

counter;

incrCounter;
#prints 1
printf "\$counter = %d\n", returnCounter;

incrCounter; incrCounter; incrCounter;
#prints 4
printf "\$counter = %d\n", returnCounter;

incrCounter; incrCounter; incrCounter;
#prints 7
printf "\$counter = %d\n", returnCounter;

resetCounter; incrCounter; incrCounter;
#prints 2
printf "\$counter = %d\n", returnCounter;
```

Here, inside counter, we first declare $counter to be a local variable and set it to 0. Then, we define three functions returnCounter, incrCounter and resetCounter that return the current value, increment the current value and reset the value of the $counter variable which is local and inaccessible from outside counter. Since the three functions inside counter are defined with names, the names are visible outside the body of counter. So, by calling these three functions we can access and manipulate the value of $counter which is inaccessible outside counter. The calls to the three functions outside counter show what effect these function calls have.

12.5.4   Closures That Share A Non-Scalar Variable

We will now expand the set of closures we just presented so that non-scalar variables such as arrays, hashes or more complex structures can be shared by a set of closures. Once again, the closures are defined inside a subprogram. In the example that follows, the closures share an array variable.

Program 12.20

```perl
sub counters{
    my @counters;

    sub returnCounter{
        my $counterNo = $_[0];
        $counters[$counterNo];
        }

    sub incrCounter{
        my $counterNo = $_[0];
        $counters[$counterNo]++
        }

    sub resetCounter{
        my $counterNo = $_[0];
        $counters[$counterNo] = 0;
    }

    sub resetCounters{
        @counters = ();
    }

    sub returnCounters{
        @counters;
    }

    sub printCounters{
        printf "\@counters = %s\n", (join " ", @counters);
    }
}
```

Here, we have a set of closures that manipulate a variable local to the subprogram counters. The array variable @counters is not directly accessible from outside counters, but through the subprograms that are globally accessible, we have indirect access to the variable counters. The closures returnCounter, incrCounter and resetCounter each takes a number as a parameter and then returns the value, increments the value or resets the value, respectively. The closures resetCounters, returnCounters and printCounters do not take any actual parameter, and work on the whole array counters.

Below, we have some example calls of these closures. Of course, before we can call any of the closures, we need to call counters so that the variable counters and the subprograms that are defined inside counters are defined.

```perl
counters;

incrCounter(0);
printCounters;          #prints 1 0 0 0

incrCounter(1) ; incrCounter (2); incrCounter (3);
printCounters;          #prints 1 1 1 1
```

```
incrCounter (3); incrCounter (0); incrCounter (0);
printCounters;              #prints 3 1 1 2

resetCounter (2); incrCounter(2); incrCounter(0);
printCounters;              #prints 4 1 1 2
```

In summary, what we see here is that closures can be used to abstract data structures access to which is guarded through the use of subprograms specifically defined for the purpose.

12.5.5   A Subroutine that Returns A Reference to A Closure

Now, we go back to a closure we looked at a learlier and make it a little bit more complex. In the closure definitions we have seen so far, the functions that work as closures have been defined with names and hence have been globally accessible. But, sometimes, this may not be a good idea. We may want to define such functions anonymously and return references to them to the outside world. Here, is an extension of the function listAdd1 that we discussed a short while ago.

Program 12.21

```
sub makeAdder{
    my $n = $_[0];
    my $addX = sub {
                my $x = $_[0];
                $x + $n;
                };
    $addX;
}
```

makeAdder has a lexically scoped variable $n that is accessible only inside it. Inside makeAdder, there is another lexically scoped scalar $addX that stores a reference to an anonymous function defined inside makeAdder. This anonymous function takes one parameter and returns the parameter after adding $n to it. Since $n is local to makeAdder and is accessible only inside makeAdder, the anonymous function whose reference is returned by makeAdder must somehow keep a value of $n available to it. The definition of this anonymous function along with the current binding of $n make a closure.

Outside the function makeAdder, we can call makeAdder with a parameter giving it the value of $n. This value of $n then becomes the value the closure returned by the call remembers. So, if we make the following two calls, the binding of $n associated with the first closure is 2 and the second 10.

```
$add2 = makeAdder (2);
$add10 = makeAdder (10);
```

Therefore, the following calls return

```
funcall$ ($add2, 5)
funcall$ ($add10, 3)
```

7 and 13 respectively.

We extend the makeAdder a little more in the next example. In makeAdder, the value of the remembered numerical value is set in the call to makeAdder. Once a value binding has been associated with a closure, there is no way to change that associated value. In the function makeAdderB that we give below, we can associate a new value with a closure once the closure has been defined.

Program 12.22

```
sub makeAdderB {
    my $n = $_[0];
    my $addXNew = sub {
                    my $x = $_[0];
                    my $change = $_[1];
                    if (defined($change)){
                            $n = $x;
                    }
                    else{
                        $x + $n;
                    }; #else ends
                 }; #sub $addXNew ends
    print "makeAdderB ends; returns \$addXNew = $addXNew\n";
    $addXNew;
} # sub makeAdderB ends
```

makeAdderB takes a numerical value as parameter and assigns the local variable $n to the parameter supplied to it. It also declares a scalar $addXNew that stores the reference to an anonymous function. This anonymous function takes two parameters, the second of which is optional. The first parameter supplied in a call to the anonymous function is used to assign a value to a variable $x local to the anonymous function. The second parameter to the anonymous function, if supplied in a call, causes the anonymous function to reset the value associated with the closure initially supplied by $n. The new value associated with the anonymous function becomes the first parameter $x given in the call of the anonymous function.

Let us look at a call to makeAdderB and follow it by calls to the anonymous function that makeAdderB returns.

```
$addX = makeAdderB (1);
```

Now, $addX stores a reference to a closure. If we now make the

```
funcallS ($addX, 3)
```

it returns a value of 4. This is because the numerical value associated with the function referenced by $addX is 1 and the function referenced by $addX adds its parameter 3 to the value associated with it and returns the sum. However, if we now make the following call to the function referenced by $addX, the value associated with this anonymous function changes to 100.

```
#returns 100
&$addX (100, 1)
```

This is because we have provided a value to the second parameter to the call to the anonymous function and this causes the closure to set the value of the associated variable to 100, the first parameter to the call of the anonymous function. The call above returns 100, the new value associated with the anonymous function. Finally, the following call

```
funcallS ($addX, 3)
```

returns 103.

12.5.6 A Subroutine That Returns Several Closures: Simulating a "Database"

In this section, we write a function that returns a set of references to closures that perform several tasks on a data structure. We can use this to simulate the functions of a simple "database".

Program 12.23

```perl
sub funcall{
          my ($funRef, @argument) = @_;
          &$funRef(@argument);
}

sub makeDBMS{
    my %DB = @_;

    my $accessDB = sub{
                     my $key = $_[0];
                     $DB{$key}
                  };
    my $setDB =   sub{
                    my ($key, $val) = @_;
                    $DB{$key} = $val;
                  };
    my $deleteDB = sub{
                     my $key = $_[0];
                     delete $DB{$key};
                     $key
                  };
    return ($accessDB, $setDB, $deleteDB);
}
```

Once we have defined the subprogram makeDBMS and the closures inside it, we can use the closures returned to work on a shared data structure. A shared data structure is built below.

```perl
@citiesDB = makeDBMS ('Boston' => 'US', 'Paris' => 'France',
           'Nagaon' => 'Assam');
```

This call creates citiesDB as a data structure that provides with associated access, assignment and deletion functions. The data structure is hidden from outside and can be accessed only indirectly through calls to the three functions. The three functions are obtained as elements of the citiesDB array. So, now we can make calls such as the following.

```perl
funcall ($citiesDB[0], 'Boston')
funcall ($citiesDB[1], 'London' => 'UK')
funcall ($citiesDB[0], 'London')
```

The first call accesses the element of the database that has Boston as the key. The call returns US. The second call enters a new pair of elements in the database with London the key and UK the value. So, the third call returns UK, the value corresponding to the new key just entered.

It may be a little awkward to make calls such as the above where the function is an element of an array. To make things look a little nicer, we can define new functions such as lookup given below. lookup is the new access function for a database.

Program 12.24

```
sub lookup{
    my ($key, @myDB) = @_;
    funcall ($myDB[0], $key);
}
```

Once we have defined `lookup`, we can create new databases and access elements as given below.

```
%myBestFriends = ('Tommy' => 'Washington DC', 'Chad' => 'San Francisco',
                  'Jeff' => 'Boulder', 'Rick' => 'Montreal',
                  'Sean' => 'Montreal');
@myBestFriendsDB = makeDBMS (%myBestFriends);

printf "Tommy: %s\n", lookup ('Tommy', @myBestFriendsDB);
printf "Rick: %s\n", lookup ('Rick', @myBestFriendsDB);
printf "Jeff: %s\n", lookup ('Jeff', @myBestFriendsDB);
```

12.5.7   Functions As Network Representation

In this section, we will show that functions can be used to represent a network of nodes. We do this by using closures that share binding or refer to one another. Closures allow us to build networks at a higher level of abstraction than usual. Closures have three useful properties: they are active, they have local state, and we can make multiple instances of them. We can use multiple copies of active objects with local state to capture representation of networks. Since a closure can refer to other nodes (i.e., closures), one node can send its output to other nodes or a node can accept outputs of other nodes. In this way, it is possible to "compile" some networks into pure code.

The problem discussed in this section is a toy problem based on Chapter 6 of *On Lisp: Advanced Techniques for Lisp* [Gra94]. The techniques discussed in this section can be extended and used to build substantial real applications. We first discuss a standard way of building the representation for a network. We then show how the network can also be represented by closures. The application we discuss is a program that plays twenty questions. The network is a binary tree. Each internal node of the network contains a yes/no question. The user is asked this question. Depending on the answer that the user gives, the left or right branch of the binary tree is traversed. Ultimately the player arrives at a leaf node. The leaf node simply contains a value. When the player arrives at a leaf node, the value in the leaf node is returned as the answer to the whole game. The following is a short interaction with the program.

```
Is the person a man?
>> yes
Is he living?
>> no
Was he American?
>> yes
Is he on a coin?
>> yes
Is the coin a penny?
>> yes
Lincoln
```

The programs that we write here have bare minimum code to make the example interaction given above work.

12.5.7.1   A Conventional Way to Represent A Network

Each node in the network is a hash with three fields, all of which need not be filled. Each field is a key value pair. The fields are contents, yes and no. The contents field has a value for each node, leaf or internal. The yes and no fields have no value for leaf nodes. We define functions for defining nodes of the network, we then specify the nodes of the network, and we write a function to start the traversal of the network of nodes. The code is given below.

Program 12.25

```perl
my %NETWORK;

sub makeNode{
    my ($contents, $yes, $no) = @_;
    my $node = {'contents' => $contents, 'yes' => $yes, 'no' => $no};
    return $node;
}

sub defNode{
    my ($name, $conts, $yes, $no) = @_;
    $NETWORK {$name} = makeNode ($conts, $yes, $no);
}

defNode ('people', 'Is the person a man?', 'male', 'female');
defNode ('male', 'Is he living?', 'liveman', 'deadman');
defNode ('deadman', 'Was he American?', 'us', 'them');
defNode ('us', 'Is he on a coin?', 'coin', 'cidence');
defNode ('coin', 'Is the coin a penny?', 'penny', 'coins');
defNode ('penny', 'Lincoln');

sub runNode{
    my $name = $_[0];
    my %n = %{$NETWORK{$name}};

    if ($n{'yes'}){
        printf "%s\n>> ", $n{'contents'};
        if (<STDIN> =~ /^y/i){
            runNode ($n{'yes'});
        }
        else{
            runNode ($n{'no'});
        }
    }
    else{
        printf "%s\n", $n{'contents'}
    }
}

runNode ('people');
```

The makeNode function builds a hash with the three fields we mentioned earlier and returns a reference to the hash. The defNode function calls makeNode to make a hash and then it puts the node in the network. The network is stored in a global hash variable %NETWORK. Since the nodes of the network are also hashes, the network representation is a hash of hashes. Since in Perl, the keys and values of a hash must be scalars, when we build a hash of hashes, the values are actually references to hashes. References to hashes are scalars.

The nodes of the network are constructed by making calls to defNode. Here are two calls to defNode.

```
defNode ('people', 'Is the person a man?', 'male', 'female');
defNode ('penny', 'Lincoln');
```

The first call builds a hash with three fields contents, yes and no with values 'Is the person a man?', 'male' and 'female' respectively. Once this hash is built, a reference to it is stored as the value of the key 'people' of the bigger hash %NETWORK. The second call to defNode builds a leaf node of the network. The node has only a contents field.

The runNode subprogram is used to traverse the network starting with a certain node. If the starting node has a filled yes field (for this example, it means that it also has the no field filled), then the program asks the user a question based on the contents field of the node. If the user answers yes, the program calls runNode recursively on the node whose name is given as the value of the yes field. If the user answers no, the program calls runNode recursively on the node whose name is specified in the no field.

If the current node does not have a value for the yes field (in our simple example, it does not have a value for the no field also in such a case), the program prints the contents field of the node and exits.

12.5.7.2   Network Nodes As Closures

We can rewrite the network program with closures to represent the nodes. We rewrite defNode for this purpose.

Program 12.26

```
my %NETWORK;

sub funcall{
          my ($funRef, @argument) = @_;
          &$funRef(@argument);
}

sub defNode{
    my ($name, $conts, $yes, $no) = @_;

    if ($yes){
        $NETWORK{$name} = sub {
                          printf "%s\n>> ", $conts;

                          if (<STDIN> =~ /^y/i){
                              funcall ($NETWORK{$yes});
                          }
                          else{
                              funcall ($NETWORK{$no});
                          }
                }; #sub ends
```

```
    }
    else{
        $NETWORK{$name} = sub{
                            printf "%s\n", $conts;
                            }#sub ends
    }
}

defNode ('people', 'Is the person a man?', 'male', 'female');
defNode ('male', 'Is he living?', 'liveman', 'deadman');
defNode ('deadman', 'Was he American?', 'us', 'them');
defNode ('us', 'Is he on a coin?', 'coin', 'cidence');
defNode ('coin', 'Is the coin a penny?', 'penny', 'coins');
defNode ('penny', 'Lincoln');

funcall ($NETWORK{'people'});
```

Here, the defNode function is called, just like before, for each node we want to build. Depending on whether it is an internal node or a leaf node (i.e., whether the yes field is defined or not), it builds two different anonymous functions for each node. If it is a leaf node, it builds an anonymous function that simply prints the answer. A reference to this anonymous function becomes the value of the node. If it is an internal node, the anonymous function built is a little more elaborate. It prints the text associated with the node, and then waits for the user to type a response to the standard input or the terminal. Depending on whether the response is yes or no, it calls an appropriate function.

The network is traversed by calling the anonymous function stored at the root node. The call is given below.

```
funcall ($NETWORK{'people'});
```

The interactions are exactly the same as in the previous implementation.

12.5.7.3   Eliminating Data Structures Altogether

In the last version of the network program, each node has reference to a function and the appropriate function has to be called after each user response. In this version, it is possible that we redefine the contents of an existing node using the defNode function for the same node. However, if the network is known to be unchangeable once it has been built, it is possible to "compile" the network into a set of functions and get rid of any data structures that we use to build the network. Here is the version of the program that lets us do so.

Program 12.27

```
my %NETWORK;

sub defNode{
    my ($key, @data) = @_;
    $NETWORK {$key} = \@data;
}

sub compileNet{
    my $root = $_[0];
```

```perl
    my @nodeData = @{$NETWORK{$root}};

    if (! @nodeData){return "";}
    else{
        my ($conts, $yes, $no) = @nodeData;
        if ($yes){
            my $yesFn = compileNet ($yes);
            my $noFn = compileNet ($no);

            sub {
                printf "%s\n>> ", $conts;

                if (<STDIN> =~ /^y/i){
                        funcall ($yesFn);
                }
                else{
                    funcall ($noFn);
    }
            }; #sub ends
        }
        else{
          sub{
             printf "%s\n", $conts;
          }#sub ends
        }
    }
}

defNode ('people', 'Is the person a man?', 'male', 'female');
defNode ('male', 'Is he living?', 'liveman', 'deadman');
defNode ('deadman', 'Was he American?', 'us', 'them');
defNode ('us', 'Is he on a coin?', 'coin', 'cidence');
defNode ('coin', 'Is the coin a penny?', 'penny', 'coins');
defNode ('penny', 'Lincoln');

$n = compileNet ('people');

%NETWORK = ();

funcall ($n);
```

Here, initially, we define all the nodes by calling defNode, once for each node. Each node is initialized to be an element of the overall hash %NETWORK. Each node is accessed with a key. The value of the node is an array that contains the contents, and if they are not unspecified, the names of the nodes that correspond to the yes and no user answers. So, the call

```perl
defNode ('people', 'Is the person a man?', 'male', 'female');
```

adds an element to the hash %NETWORK for which the key is 'people and the value is the following list.

```perl
('Is the person a man?', 'male', 'female')
```

Once the initial version of all the nodes are built, we can *"compile"* the network by calling the `compileNet` function with the root node with the hash key `'people'` as the parameter. In the program we do so using the following call.

```
$n = compileNet ('people');
```

The `compileNet` function looks at the initial data structure for the node passed to it as a parameter. If the initial data structure has non-nil values for `yes` and `no` user responses, it calls `compileNet` recursively once for each response. These two calls build the functions corresponding to the `yes` and `no` user responses. Finally, the original call to `compileNet` for the root node `'people'` builds an anonymous subprogram and returns it. This anonymous subprogram for the root node calls the two anonymous subprograms that were built by the two recursive calls to `compileNet` for the `yes` and `no` user responses.

If for a certain node, there are no input values corresponding to `yes` and `no` user nodes, the `compileNet` function returns a reference to a subprogram that simply prints the answer.

Since `compileNet` is called recursively, the single call to `compileNet` with the root node converts the contents of each node in the network into an appropriate subprogram. Since this single call to `compileNet` compiles the whole network into code, once we have made the call to `compileNet` with the root node as the parameter, we no longer need the data structure built by the calls to `defNode` and therefore can set the network hash to nil. This is done by the following call.

```
%NETWORK = ();
```

We can now traverse the network of closures by making the following call.

```
funcall ($n);
```

Once again, the interaction of the user with the program will be exactly the same as before.

12.6   Composing Functions

When we talk about functions in mathematics, we can talk about concepts such as the *complement* of a function and the *composition* of functions. We will now see how we can implement these two ideas in Perl. In mathematics, the complement of a function f is usually written as $\sim f$ or $\overline{f}$. The complement of a function f is a function that returns true whenever f returns false, and vice versa. The composition of two functions is usually denoted by the operator $\circ$. If f and g are two mathematical functions, their composition $f \circ g$ is also a function. The result of obtaining the composed function $f \circ g$ on a parameter x is given as $f \circ g(x) = f(g(x))$. This can be done using the idea of closures that we have discussed earlier.

12.6.1   Complementing A Function

We write a function `complement` that takes a reference to a function and returns a reference to a function that behaves as a mathematical complement of the input function. The definition of this function is given below.

Program 12.28

```
sub complement{
    my $fn = $_[0];
    my $complementFRef = sub {
                             my $res = funcallS $fn, $_[0];
```

```
                        return !$res;
                };
        return $complementFRef;
}
```

This function creates a local my variable called $complementFRef that is assigned the value of an anonymous function created inside the function. This anonymous function remembers the value of the variable $fn that contains the reference to a function passed to the complement function. This remembering is done because of the property of closures. The anonymous function calls the remembered function referenced by $fn on a scalar parameter passed to the anonymous function. The anonymous function returns the negation of this call. Therefore, whenever the function referenced by $fn returns true, the anonymous function returns false, and vice versa. For purposes of our code here, we assume that 1 represents true and 0 represents false.

A call to the complement function is the following.

```
funcallS (complement $between10and45P, 90)
```

This call returns a result of 1. The predicate function referenced by $between10and45P was defined earlier in the chapter. It returns true if the scalar parameter given to it is a number between 10 and 45. The complement of this function is obtained by the following call.

```
complement $between10and45P
```

This call returns a reference to a function that behaves like the mathematical complement of the function referenced by $between10and45P. This complement function is called with the parameter 90 using the funcallS function we have defined earlier. funcallS returns 1 because the function referenced by $between10and45P returns false or 0.

Another call to the complement function is seen below.

```
find (complement (\&biggerThan10P), 10, 2, 30, 45, 7)
```

Here we use the find function defined earlier. The function biggerThan10P has also been defined earlier. \&biggerThan10P returns a reference to the function biggerThan10P and this reference is given as parameter to complement. complement returns a reference to a new function that acts like the mathematical complement of its input. find culls all those elements of the list of numbers given to it that satisfy the function whose reference is given to it as the first parameter. In this case, that means that the call to find returns all those elements that do not satisfy the function biggerThan10P. Consequently, the call to find returns the list containing the numbers 10, 2, and 7.

A final illustrative use of complement is seen below.

```
find (complement ($between10and45P), 10, 2, 30, 45, 7)
```

This call to find returns all those numbers from the list given that satisfy the complement of the function referenced by $between10and45P. As a result, the call returns the list

```
10 2 45 7
```

12.6.2   Composing A Set of Functions

We now write a function composeS that takes a list of function references and returns a reference to a composed function. We use the function funcallS defined earlier to apply a referenced function to a scalar parameter. Here is the composeS function.

Program 12.29

```
sub composeS{
    my $firstFunction = pop @_;
    my @functions = reverse @_;

    my $composedFunction = sub{
                        my $temp = funcallS ($firstFunction, $_[0]);
                        foreach $function (@functions){
                                $temp = funcallS ($function,  $temp);
                        };
                        return $temp;
    };
    return $composedFunction;
}

$add1 = sub {$_[0] + 1;};
$add2 = sub {$_[0] + 2;};
$add3 = sub {$_[0] + 3;};
```

A call to composeS looks like the following.

```
funcallS (composeS ($add1, $add2, $add3), 10)
```

We have defined three simple anonymous functions. These functions are referenced using the scalars $add1, $add2 and $add3. The functions simply add 1, 2 and 3, respectively to a scalar parameter given. The call

```
composeS ($add1, $add2, $add3)
```

composes these three functions and returns a reference to the new function. This newly created function is then called on the parameter 10 using the funcallS function. The result of the call to funcallS returns 16.

Let us now look at the definition of the composeS function. Its parameter list @_ is a list of function references. The first function reference is separated from the rest of the functions and is stored in the scalar $firstFunction. The rest of the function references are stored in @functions.

Following this, we create a local variable $composedFunction that is assigned the reference to the anonymous function composed by applying all the functions to the scalar parameter provided. This anonymous function inside the composeS function first calls $firstFunction on the scalar parameter. Then, it goes through a for loop in which each of the remaining functions referenced in @functions are applied on the result of the first function application. This anonymous function inside our main function returns the value obtained after all the referenced functions have been applied to the scalar parameter.

Finally, the composeS function returns the value of $composedFunction. In other words, composeS returns a reference to an anonymous function that calls all the composed functions on the scalar parameter. Since composeS returns a reference to a function, we have to use funcallS to apply the composed function on the scalar parameter.

12.6.3   Mapping A Composed Function

Now, we will write a composing function composeL that is quite similar to what we have already seen, but one which takes two lists as parameters: the first is a list of function references, and the second is a list of numbers. composeL composes the functions and maps the composed function on every element of the second list.

Program 12.30

```
#funcallL is given a reference to a function and a list of
#parameters in a list.
#It maps the  function on the list elements and returns the result.

sub funcallL{
    my ($funRef, @parameters) = @_;
            map {funcallS ($funRef, $_)} @parameters;
}

sub composeL{
    my $firstFunction = pop @_;
    my @functions = reverse @_;

    my $composedFunction = sub{
                my @temp = map {funcallS ($firstFunction, $_)} @_;
                foreach $function (@functions){
                            @temp = map {funcallS ($function, $_)}  @temp;
                };
                 return @temp;};
    return $composedFunction;
}

$add1 = sub {$_[0] + 1;};
$add2 = sub {$_[0] + 2;};
$add3 = sub {$_[0] + 3;};
```

Here, we define a function funcallL that maps a referenced function onto a list of parameters. It calls the funcallS function we have defined earlier.

Here is a call to composeL.

```
funcallL (composeL ($add1, $add2, $add3), (10, 200, 391))
```

composeL composes the three functions references to which are given in in the list parameter given to it. funcallL then applies the composed function to the list given as the second parameter to it.

Below we see that we can use the combination of funcallL and composeL to apply the composed function to a single parameter, which happens to be 10 here.

```
funcallL (composeL ($add1, $add2, $add3), 10)
```

12.6.4   Another Function Builder: The Functional *if*

It is possible to combine functions in ways other than complementing or composing them. Those who are adept at functional programming, frequently write code that looks like the following.

Program 12.31

```
$add1 = sub {$_[0] + 1;};
$add3 = sub {$_[0] + 3;};

sub oddP {
    if ($_[0] =~ /[13579]$/) {1} else {0}
}

@numbers = (200, 301, 593, 785, 884, 932);

@result = map { if (oddP $_)
                    {funcalls ($add1, $_)} else {funcalls ($add3, $_)}
              } @numbers;
```

Here, we are map a piece of code on every element of a list. The mapped code checks if a list element is odd, and if so, adds 1 to it, otherwise it adds 3. It returns the resulting list.

We want to make the same call to map in a slightly compact manner.

```
@result = map { funcalls (fif (\&oddP, $add1, $add3), $_)} @numbers;
```

This call returns the following.

```
203 302 594 786 887 935
```

We do this by writing a function called fif or the *functional if* function. The code for the fif function is given below.

Program 12.32

```
sub fif {
    my ($ifF, $thenF, $elseF) = @_;
    my $fifF = sub {
                  if (funcalls ($ifF, $_[0])) {funcalls ($thenF, $_[0])}
                  else {funcalls ($elseF, $_[0])}
                  };

    return $fifF;
}
```

fif is sent references to three functions, the test function, the function to be applied if the test function returns to true, and the function to be applied if the test function returns false. fif builds an anonymous function, a reference to which is stored in the scalar $fifF. This anonymous function calls the test function on the parameter given in a call to the anonymous function. Depending on the result of the test, the anonymous function calls the proper function on the parameter sent to the anonymous function. Note that the anonymous function is being built inside fif but not called. fif returns a reference to the code of this anonymous function. So, a call to fif such as

```
fif (\&oddP, $add1, $add3)
```

actually returns a reference to a function. This function is the anonymous function we talked about in the previous paragraph. When we make a call to this anonymous function, as in,

```
funcalls (fif (\&oddP, $add1, $add3), $_)
```

the anonymous function is called with $_ as a parameter. This parameter is available to the anonymous function as the value of its own $_[0]. The anonymous function now calls the appropriate function depending on the test of the if statement. Finally, when we map this anonymous function using the map function, as in,

```
map { funcalls (fif (\&oddP, $add1, $add3), $_)} @numbers;
```

the appropriate function is called on each element of the list numbers.

12.6.5   More Function Constructors: Functional Intersection and Union

Below, we give the code for two more function constructors: functions that build the intersection or the union of one or more function parameters. We call them fint and fun respectively. The fint function takes one or more references to predicate functions and returns an intersection of these functions. In other words, it builds a function that returns true only if each function given as a parameter returns true for a specific input. The definition for the fint function is given below.

Program 12.33

```
sub fint{
    my $firstFunction = pop @_;
    my @restFunctions = @_;

    if ($#restFunctions == -1){
        return $firstFunction}
    else{
        my $chainF = fint (@restFunctions);
        my $fintFunction = sub{
                            my $x = $_[0];
                            return (funcalls ($firstFunction, $x) &&
                                    funcalls ($chainF, $x));
        };
        return $fintFunction;
    }
}
```

Here are some calls to fint. The calls use functions that we have defined earlier in the chapter. Each function passed as an parameter to fint is a predicate function in the sense that it returns true or false as an answer.

```
funcalls (fint (\&oddP), 11)
funcalls (fint (\&isPrimeP), 11)
funcalls (fint (\&oddP, \&isPrimeP))
funcalls (fint (\&oddP, \&isPrimeP, \&biggerThan10P, $between10and45P)
```

We can use fint with the find function we have defined earlier. Here are some calls that use fint as the test predicate with find

```
find (fint (\&oddP), 10..100))
find (fint (\&isPrimeP), 10..100))
find (fint (\&isPrimeP, \&oddP), 10..100))
find (fint (complement (\&isPrimeP), \&oddP), 10..100))
find (fint ($between10and45P), 10..100))
find (fint ($between10and45P, \&oddP), 10..100))
find (fint ($between10and45P, \&oddP, \&isPrimeP), 10..100))
```

Assuming we have defined another function that looks for perfect squares, we can use the following calls to find perfect squares of various kinds in a certain range of integers. First we give the definition of the function that finds perfect squares and then some calls to find that use this function.

```
$perfectSquareP = sub {
                    my $root = sqrt ($_[0]);
                    if ($root =~ /.\d/) {0} else {1};
};
```

We see that we can use any combine calls to the function complementing function complement or the function composition functions: composeS or composeL with fint.

```
find (fint ($perfectSquareP), 10..100))
find (fint ($perfectSquareP, \&oddP), 10..100))
find (fint ($perfectSquareP, \&oddP), 1..1000))
find (fint ($perfectSquareP, \&oddP), 1..10000))
find (fint ($perfectSquareP, (complement \&oddP)), 1..10000))
```

The last two calls return

```
1 9 25 49 81
4 16 36 64
```

respectively.

Finally, we end this section by giving the definition of a function that gives the union of several predicates given to it. The definition is very similar to the definition of the fint function.

Program 12.34

```
sub fun{
    my $firstFunction = pop @_;
    my @restFunctions = @_;

    if ($#restFunctions == -1){
        return $firstFunction}
    else{
        my $chainF = fint (@restFunctions);
        my $fintFunction = sub{
                            my $x = $_[0];
                            return (funcallS ($firstFunction, $x) ||
                                        funcallS ($chainF, $x));
                          };
        return $fintFunction;
    }
}
```

Here are some calls to `fun`.

```
find (fun ($perfectSquareP), 10..100))
find (fun ($perfectSquareP, \&oddP), 10..100))
```

The first call finds all the perfect squares between 10 and 100: $16, 25, 36, 49, 64$ and 81. The second call finds all perfect squares between 10 and 100, and also all odd numbers between 10 and 100:

12.7 Conclusion

The author consulted the following books while writing this chapter. *Concepts of Programming Languages* [Seb99] provides a comparative study of a large number of programming languages, although Perl is not one of the languages studied. *On Lisp, Advanced Techniques for Lisp* [Gra94], is a lucidly written book on aspects of Lisp, the primary language used in Artificial Intelligence. It has many wonderful examples of clever use of functions that show programming with functions can be elegant, powerful and fun.

This chapter illustrates that functions can be far from mundane, boring and simple. Functional programming excites a lot of mathematical and computer science researchers and practitioners. In Perl, we can write functions that are close to the mathematical ideal, and use them to achieve complex tasks. Many of the tasks discussed in this chapter can be achieved by without resorting to first-class functions, but others cannot be. The study of the basic concepts of programming, as discussed in many well-regarded text books such as *Structure and Interpretation of Computer Programs* [ASS99] uses functions generously and as a result uses a functional programming language such as Scheme (a variant of LISP). It is possible that even theoretical purists can be pursuaded to use Perl for an enjoyable and comprehensive discussion of functions, without using an excellent but non-mainstream language like LISP.

12.8 Exercises

1. *(Easy: Documentation Reading)*
   Read the Perl documentation on subroutines in Perl by running the following.

   ```
   %perldoc perlsub
   ```

2. *(Easy: Recursion)*

   How are parameters passed to a Perl subroutine? What are your comments on the mechanism of parameter passing in Perl? How will you pass two arrays to a Perl script? Write a script that takes two arrays as actual parameters, and returns a hash where the elements of the first array are keys and elements of the second array are values. The two arrays that are passed to the function are of the same length although the length can be arbitrary. Use statically scoped variables.

3. *(Easy: List Processing)*
   The operators `++` and `--` increment and decrement a number by one, respectively. Write a recursive function `add` for adding two numbers without using `+` explicitly. Use `++` and `--`.

4. *(Easy: List Processing)*
   Define a function `removeIf` that takes a reference to a list and a reference to a predicate as argument, and returns reference to a list that contains elements of the original list that satisfy the predicate. A predicate is a subroutine that takes a scalar input and returns either true or false.

   Write the function `removeIf` in three ways:

   (a) using iteration,

   (b) using recursion, and

   (c) using map.

5. *(Easy: List Processing)*
   Write a function `filter` that takes a reference to a predicate function and a list as argument. It returns the elements of the list that satisfy the predicate.

```
filter (\&numberP, 1, 2, "a", 3, "b")
```

returns

```
(1, 2, 3)
```

Here, `numberP` is a function that takes a scalar and returns true if it is not.

6. *(Easy: List Processing)*
   Define a function `group` that takes an integer n and reference to a list as argument, and returns a list where the elements have been grouped into sublists of length n. The last sublist may have fewer than n elements. For example, if `@list` contains `qw(a b c d e f g)`, the call

```
group (2, \@list)
```

produces the following list as result.

```
(["a", "b"], ["c", "d"], ["e", "f"], "g")
```

7. *(Easy: List Processing)*
   Define a function `flatten` that takes a predicate and an anonymous list as an argument and returns a list that flattens the internal lists. For example, the call

```
flatten (["a", ["b",   "c"], "[[d","e"], "f"]])
```

returns

```
("a", "b", "c", "d", "e", "f")
```

8. *(Easy: List Processing)*
   Write a function `prune` that takes a reference to a predicate function of one argument and an anonymous list with embedded lists in it, and returns a list after removing all leaf-level elements that satisfy the predicate. It keeps the structure of the list intact.

```
prune (\&evenP, [1, 2, [3, [4, 5], 6], 7, 8, [9]])
```

returns

```
(2, [[4], 6], 8)
```

Here, `evenP` is a function that takes an argument and returns true if it is an even number.

9. *(Easy: List Processing)*

Write a function `before` that takes two elements and a reference to a list and returns true if the first argument occurs before the second argument in the list.

```
before ("b", "d", ["a", "b", "c", "d"])
```

returns true. Modify it to return `("b", "c", "d")`, the part of the list starting from the point where the *before* requirement holds. Write two versions, using iteration and using recursion.

10. *(Easy: List Processing)*

Write a function `duplicate` that returns those elements of a list that are duplicated. For example,

```
duplicate ("a", ["a", "b", "c", "a", "d"])
```

returns

```
("a", "d")
```

In other words, it returns the part of the list starting from where the duplication occurs. Write two versions, using iteration and recursion, respectively.

11. *(Easy: List Processing)*

Define a function `splitIf` that takes a list and splits it if a predicate is satisfied.

```
splitIf (sub { $_[0] > 4}, [1, 2, 3, 4, 5, 6, 7, 8, 9, 10])
```

returns something like

```
([1, 2, 3, 4], [5, 6, 7, 8, 9, 10])
```

12. *(Easy: List Processing)*

Write a function `most` that takes a scoring function and a list and returns the element with the highest score. In case of ties, the element occurring first wins. For example,

```
most (sub{return $#_ + 1},
     [["a", "b"], ["a", "b", "c"], ["a"], ["e", "f", "g"]])
```

returns

```
("a", "b", "c")
```

Here, the scoring function returns the length of a list given as argument.

13. *(Easy: List Processing)*

Write a function `best` that takes a function and a list. The function is a predicate of two arguments. It returns the elements which according to the predicate, beats all others. For example,

```
best (sub{$_[1] > $_[2]}, (1, 2, 3, 4, 5))
```

returns 5.Here, the function compares two elements given to it as argument and returns true if the first element is larger than the second element. This call results in sorting in ascending order.

14. *(Easy: List Processing)*
    Write a function `sqrtL` that takes a list as argument and returns a list containing the squares of all elements that are numeric. It removes any non-numeric elements from the result list. Use `map`.

15. *(Easy: List Processing)*
    Write a function `mapS` that takes an anonymous subroutine as the first argument, and a list of references to lists. It applies the first function to every element of the list.

    ```
    mapS (\$sqrt, $list1, $list2, ...)
    ```

    Here, `$sqrt` is is a reference to a function. `$list1`, `$list2`, etc., are references to lists.

16. *(Medium: List Processing, Recursive)*
    Write a function `rmap` that takes one list as argument. It stands for *recursive map*. For example,

    ```
    rmap (sub{$_[0] + 1}, [1, 2, [3, 4, [5], 6], 7, [8,9]])
    ```

    returns

    ```
    [2, 3, [4, 5, [6], 7], 8, [9 ,10]])
    ```

17. *(Medium: List Processing, Recursive)*
    Write a function `copyTree` that takes a reference to a list that contains embedded lists. A list containing embedded lists can be considered a tree. It makes a new copy of the original tree and returns a reference to it.

18. *(Medium: List Processing, Recursive)*
    Write a function `rFindIf` that generalizes `findIf` for trees, that is, for lists with embedded lists in them. For example,

    ```
    rfindIf (fint (\&numberP, \&oddP), [2. [3, 4], 5])
    ```

    returns 3. Here, `fint` is the function discussed in the Chapter. `numberP` and `oddP` are predicate functions of one argument each.

19. *(Easy: Closure)*
    Write a function `toggle` such that successive calls to it alternately returns 1 and 0, respectively. Use closure. Do not use a global variable. Make the function self-contained.

20. *(Medium: Closure)*
    Write a function `greatest` that takes one argument, a number, and returns the greatest argument passed to it so far in many calls. Use closure. Do not use a global variable or a file.

21. *(Medium: Closure)*
    Write a function `greater` that takes one argument, a number, and returns true if it is greater that the argument passed to the function the last time it was called. The function returns an undefined value the first time it is called. Use closure. Do not use a global variable or a file.

22. *(Medium: Closure)*
    Suppose `factorial` is a function of one argument. It takes an integer between 0 and 100 inclusive, and returns the result $n!$. Define a function `frugalFactorial` that returns the same answer, but only calls *factorial* when the given argument has not been seen before.

    Write two versions of a function that computes the nth Fibonacci number. Do not use a global variable or a file. Use closure.

Chapter 13

On Scientific and Engineering Computation

In This Chapter

Perl is not really known to be a language suitable for complex mathematical computations. The number of built-in mathematical functions it provides is quite small. However, the initial perception is surprisingly wrong. There are many modules contributed by individuals from around the world to facilitate efficient and complex mathematical processing. Some of the modules Perl provides are interfaces to well-known C-based libraries. There are also modules that interface with commercially available packages such as Mathematica. Thus, one can program any conceivable mathematical computation in Perl in an efficient and flexible manner. This ability to write complex mathematical programs is helpful because it complements Perl's strong text-processing and networking capabilities. Some of the complex programs that are written in Perl in the context of the Web, such as learning a Web browser's preferences, and serving targeted advertisements, require efficient text-processing, networking and mathematical computation.

In this chapter, we briefly discuss Perl's built-in mathematical functions and operators. We follow by discussing only one contributed module among the many available. Our discussion gives an overview and a few introductory examples. There are large number of additional useful modules, but we leave it to the interested reader to research, explore and use them.

In particular, there are three useful and powerful modules that stand out: `Math::Cephes`, `PDL` and `Math::Pari`. These three modules are able to assist in a wide variety of mathematical and scientific computation.

`Math::Cephes` provides access to an extensive C-based library of over 150 functions that deal with arithmetic, probabilistic, trigonometric, and hyperbolic functions. `Math::Cephes` also has powerful routines to handle complex numbers, fractions and calculus-based computation. The `PDL` module allows fast matrix-based calculation and is especially useful when the task at hand calls for large data sizes needed in manipulation of images, time series data, and audio and video data. `Math::Pari` provides access to a package that is primarily aimed at number theory-based computation, but can be used by anybody whose primary need is speed. It performs many symbolic computations as well. However, its authors admit that compared to commercially available systems such as Maple, Mathematica or Macsyma, `Math::Pari`'s abilities are limited, but the `Pari` package can be 5 to 100 times faster than such systems on many computations. In this section, we discuss only module: `Math::Cephes`. Even when discussing it, we barely scratch its surface.

13.1   Built-in Numeric Operators and Functions

Perl provides the standard arithmetic operators: `+`, `-`, `*`, `/` and `**` for addition, subtraction, multiplication, division, exponentiation, respectively. It also provides the modulo division operator `%`. `a % b` gives the remainder when `a` is divided by `b`. In addition, Perl provides two operators, `++` and `--`, for auto-incrementing and auto-decrementing. `$a++` and `++$a` both increment the value of the numeric scalar `$a`. However, `$a++` performs the incrementation before the value of `$a` is used, if `$a` happens to appear in any expression or statement. This operation should be carefully used. Otherwise, an expression or statement may become difficult to understand. The auto-decrement operator `--` also works similarly.

For purposes of creating Boolean expressions with numbers or numeric expression, the available operators are

```
==     !=    <   >   <= >=
```

for equality, inequality, less than, greater than, less than or equal to, and greater than or equal to, respectively. Additionally, there is the "ship" operator `<=>`.

```
$a <=> $b
```

returns -1, 0, or 1, depending on whether `$a` is less than, equal to, or greater than `$b`, respectively.

Perl also has a few built-in functions that deal with mathematical calculations. It has functions for the basic trigonometric calculations: `sin`, `cos`, `tan` and `atan2`. The last function `atan2` takes two arguments `Y` and `X`, and returns the *arc tangent* of `Y/X`. There also a few other built-in functions such as `abs`, `int`, `sqrt`, `exp`, `rand` for performing obvious tasks such as obtaining the absolute value of an operand, the integer part of a number, the square root of a positive number, the value of *e* raised to the power of an exponent, and to generate random numbers.

13.2   Binary Arithmetic

We can perform bit-wise operations on integers. The operators available are `&`, `|` and `^` for bit-wise AND, OR, and XOR, respectively. The following simple program illustrates these operations.

Program 13.1

```
#!/usr/bin/perl
#binary .pl

use strict;
my @CONVERSIONS = qw(000 001 010 011 100 101 110 111);
my $a = 0b100111;
print "a = ", conv2bin($a), "\n";
```

```
my $b = 074;
print "b = ", conv2bin($b), "\n";

#This is the only bit-wise and operator. && and "and" are not bit-wise and
my $aAndb = $a & $b;
print "a & b = ", conv2bin($aAndb), "\n";

#This is the only bit-wise or operator. || and "or" are not bit-wise or
my $aOrb = $a | $b;
print "a | b = ", conv2bin($aOrb), "\n";

#Bit-wise XOR operation
my $aXorb = $a ^ $b;
print "a xor b = ", conv2bin($aXorb), "\n";

#convert a decimal integer to a binary printable string
sub conv2bin{
    my $octal = sprintf ("%o", $_[0]);
    my @threeBitSeqs = map {$CONVERSIONS [$_]} (split //, $octal);
    return (join "", @threeBitSeqs);
}
```

The program assigns numeric integer values to two scalars. $a and $b. Integer values can be assigned to a variable in several ways. We see see two such possibilities in the program. $a is assigned the binary value 0b100111. The 0b in the front indicates that it is a binary value. $b is assigned the octal or base 8 value of 070. The zero in the front suggests it is octal. Integer values can be assigned as regular decimal or hexa-decimal as well. Thus, the variable $a can be assigned the same value in the following four ways, each having the same effect.

```
my $a = 0b100111;
my $a = 047;
my $a = 39;
my $a = 0x27;
```

The last two assignments specify the value in decimal and hexa-decimal (base 16), respectively.

Because we want to illustrate the binary operations of AND, OR and XOR, we want to print the numbers in binary format. This requires writing the a small subroutine since the function sprintf (or, printf) does not give us a direct way to do so. It should be noted that sprintf prints a string following a format specification. sprintf allows one to print an integer in octal or hexa-decimal, but unfortunately, not in binary base. The subroutine we write first converts the input number into a string of octal digits. Next, the octal digits are split individually, and each octal digit converted to the appropriate 3-bit string sequence by a simple lookup of the global table @CONVERSIONS. Finally, the subroutine concatenates the 3-bit sequences and returns the binary string.

Perl's &, |, and ^ perform bit-by-bit AND, OR, and XOR operations, respectively, Perl's && and and do not perform bit-wise AND operation. They are logical operations returning true or false. The difference between the two is that and has low precedence so that in complex logical operations, it is not necessary to use many parenthesis pairs. Both are short-circuit operators. In other words, if several values are ANDed, && or and continues going from left to right only if there is a chance of success. If it encounters a value that is deemed false, it stops. && returns the last value evaluated. Similarly, || and or are not bit-wise operations, returning true or false. || returns the last value evaluated. It is short-circuit operation and returns true when it first encounter a non-false value. or is also a short-circuit operation.

13.3   `Math::Cephes`: **Arithmetic and Calculus-Based Computation**

The `Math::Cephes` module provides a Perl interface to the well-known *Cephes* mathematical library of over 150 functions. The `Math::Cephes` module's main strengths lie in its handling of trigonometric, hyperbolic and probabilistic functions; calculus-based *special functions* such as gamma, beta and elliptic and functions and the corresponding integrals; and, complex numbers and fractional arithmetic. Thus, the module is best discussed by separately illustrating its various capabilities. The functions are divided into groups. We discuss a few functions from a few selected groups, and hence, the interested reader must install the package, and read its documentation, to appreciate its full power. No functions are exported by default, but must be exported either individually or as named groups.

13.3.1   Constants

The `Math::Cephes` gives access to a set of frequently used constants in scientific computation such as π, $\frac{\pi}{2}$, $\frac{\pi}{4}$, $\sqrt{2}$, $\sqrt{\frac{2}{\pi}}$, $\frac{2}{\pi}$, $ln\,2$, $\frac{1}{ln\,2}$, etc. The following program simply prints out the values of some such constants. The constants can be either imported individually, or as a group, using the keyword `:constants`.

Program 13.2

```perl
#!/usr/bin/perl
#file const.pl

use Math::Cephes qw(:constants);
print "PI = " . $Math::Cephes::PI . "\n";
print "PI over 2 = " . $Math::Cephes::PIO2 . "\n";
print "PI over 4 = " . $Math::Cephes::PIO4 . "\n";
print "SQRT of 2 = " . $Math::Cephes::SQRT2 . "\n";
print "SQRT of 2 over PI  = " . $Math::Cephes::SQ2OPI . "\n";
print "2 over PI  = " . $Math::Cephes::TWOOPI . "\n";
print "LOG to base E  of 2 = " . $Math::Cephes::LOGE2 . "\n";
print "1 over LOG to base E  of 2 = " . $Math::Cephes::LOG2E . "\n";
print "Machine Roundoff Error = " . $Math::Cephes::MACHEP . "\n";
print "Maximum log on the machine = " . $Math::Cephes::MAXLOG . "\n";
print "Minimum log on the machine  = " . $Math::Cephes::MINLOG . "\n";
print "Maximum number on the machine = " . $Math::Cephes::MAXNUM . "\n";
```

The output of the program is mostly self-explanatory. The bottom of the program prints out certain machine-dependent constants that are useful for performing certain mathematical computation.

```
PI = 3.14159265358979
PI over 2 = 1.5707963267949
PI over 4 = 0.785398163397448
SQRT of 2 = 1.4142135623731
SQRT of 2 over PI  = 0.797884560802865
2 over PI  = 0.636619772367581
LOG to base E  of 2 = 0.693147180559945
1 over LOG to base E  of 2 = 1.44269504088896
Machine Roundoff Error = 1.11022302462516e-16
Maximum log on the machine = 709.782712893384
```

```
Minimum log on the machine  = -745.133219101941
Maximum number on the machine = 1.79769313486232e+308
```

13.3.2   Trigonometric Functions

Although standard Perl provides a few trigonometric functions, the set is limited. Math::Cephes allows us to compute the values of all trigonometric functions and their inverses, using angle measurement in radian or degrees. The following program illustrates some of the functions.

Program 13.3

```perl
#!/usr/bin/perl
#file trig.pl

use Math::Cephes qw(:trigs :constants);
my $angleR = $Math::Cephes::PIO4;
my $angleD = 45;
my $value = 1;

print "cosine (PIO4 rad) = " . Math::Cephes::cos ($angleR) . "\n";
print "sine (PIO4 rad) = " . Math::Cephes::sin ($angleR) . "\n";
print "tangent (PIO4 rad) = " . Math::Cephes::tan ($angleR) . "\n";
print "cotangent (PIO4 rad) = " . Math::Cephes::cot ($angleR) . "\n";

print "cosine (45 deg) = " . Math::Cephes::cosdg ($angleD) . "\n";
print "sine (45 deg) = " . Math::Cephes::sindg ($angleD) . "\n";
print "tangent (45 deg) = " . Math::Cephes::tandg ($angleD) . "\n";
print "cotangent (45 deg) = " . Math::Cephes::cotdg ($angleD) . "\n";

print "acos ($value) = " . Math::Cephes::acos ($value) . " rad \n";
print "asin ($value) = " . Math::Cephes::asin ($value) . " rad \n";
print "atan ($value) = " . Math::Cephes::atan ($value) . " rad \n";
```

Once again, the program is simple and performs only an illustrative purpose. It imports the set of trigonometric functions as a group using the keyword :trigs. It also imports the constants using the :constants keyword discussed earlier. $angleR has the value $\frac{\pi}{4}$ radians, and $angleD is 45 degrees. Both represent the same angle. Each of the sin, cos, tan and cot functions takes an angle in radians, whereas sindg, cosdg, tandg and cotdg each takes an angle argument given in degrees. Each of the inverse trigonometric functions: asin, acos and atan returns its result in radians only. The output of the program is given below.

```
osine (PIO4 rad) = 0.707106781186548
sine (PIO4 rad) = 0.707106781186547
tangent (PIO4 rad) = 1
cotangent (PIO4 rad) = 1
cosine (45 deg) = 0.707106781186548
sine (45 deg) = 0.707106781186548
tangent (45 deg) = 1
cotangent (45 deg) = 1
acos (1) = 0 rad
```

```
asin (1) = 1.5707963267949 rad
atan (1) = 0.785398163397448 rad
```

`Math::Cephes` can obtain values of all trigonometric functions for complex arguments as well.

13.3.3   Hyperbolic Functions

The `Math::Cephes` module provides access to hyperbolic functions with real arguments as well as complex. Hyperbolic functions are certain combinations of the exponentials e^u and e^{-u}. There are two main uses of hyperbolic functions: for solving differential equations and for solving many engineering problems that are specified in terms of differential equations. For example, the tension at any point in a cable suspended by its ends and hanging under its own weight can be computed using hyperbolic functions.

The combinations $\frac{1}{2}(e^u + e^{-u})$ and $\frac{1}{2}(e^u - e^{-u})$ occur so frequently that it has been found convenient to give names to them. They are called *cosh u* and *sinh u*, respectively. Thus, the definitions of the *hyperbolic cosine* and the *hyperbolic sine* are the following.

$$cosh\ u = \frac{1}{2}(e^u + e^{-u}) \tag{13.1}$$

$$sinh\ u = \frac{1}{2}(e^u - e^{-u}) \tag{13.2}$$

The properties the hyperbolic functions exhibit are quite similar to those shown by trigonometric functions. In addition, there is another parallel. When we talk about trigonometric functions, we think of a point (x, y) on the *unit circle* $x^2 + y^2 = 1$. It can be shown that we can describe hyperbolic functions with respect to the coordinates of a point (x, y) on the *unit hyperbola* $x^2 - y^2 = 1$. The hyperbolic function *tanh u* is defined in terms of *sihn u* and *cosh u* as follows.

$$tanh\ u = \frac{sihn\ u}{cosh\ u} = \frac{e^u - e^{-u}}{e^u + e^{-u}} \tag{13.3}$$

The hyperbolic cotagent, secant and cosecant: *coth u*, *sech u* and *csch u* respectively, are defined as inverses of *tanh u*, *sihn u* and *cosh u* respectively.

Computing inverses of hyperbolic functions is also useful for many mathematical and engineering computations. The following program illustrates the use of the functions.

Program 13.4

```perl
#!/usr/bin/perl
#file hyper.pl
use strict;

use Math::Cephes qw(:hypers);

my $angle = $Math::Cephes::SQRT2;
my $coshVal = cosh ($angle);
my $sinhVal = sinh ($angle);
my $tanhVal = tanh ($angle);

print "cosh ($angle) = " . $coshVal . "\n";
print "sinh ($angle) = " . $sinhVal . "\n";
```

```
print "tanh ($angle) = " . $tanhVal . "\n";

print "acosh ($coshVal) = " . acosh ($coshVal) . "\n";
print "asinh ($sinhVal) = " . asinh ($sinhVal) . "\n";
print "atanh ($tanhVal) = " . atanh ($tanhVal) . "\n";
```

In this program, we call the variable passed as argument to the hyperbolic functions $angle simply to illustrate the parallel to trigonometric functions discussed earlier. The argument taken by the hyperbolic functions is not an angle in any sense, and can be any number, real or complex.

The output of the program is given below.

```
cosh (1.4142135623731) = 2.17818355660857
sinh (1.4142135623731) = 1.93506682217436
tanh (1.4142135623731) = 0.888385561585661
acosh (2.17818355660857) = 1.4142135623731
asinh (1.93506682217436) = 1.4142135623731
atanh (0.888385561585661) = 1.4142135623731
```

Math::Cephes provides functions to obtain the value of a hyperbolic function for a complex argument as well. The functions are called ccosh, csihn, ctanh, cacosh, casinhn and catanh, for cosine, sine, tangent and their inverses with complex arguments, respectively.

13.3.4 Special Functions

The Math::Cephes module provides many functions that are based on advanced calculus. Thus, the following discussion assumes that the reader has a good background in calculus. The material discussed is frequently needed by many engineers and scientists. Undergraduate students in engineering disciplines such as mechanical, civil and electrical, and students in physics are familiar with the use of such functions. In earlier days, the values of these functions were computed painstakingly and large tables of values made available in the form of printed books for scientists and engineers to use. Computing the values with desired accuracy requires careful work. These days, the values are computed sufficiently accurately using computers.

Math::Cephes contains definitions of many of the so-called special functions found in standard mathematical or engineering handbooks. The term *special functions* is a common name used for functions that usually arise from solving differential equations of order two or higher. Although they arise mostly in solving differential equations, it is not necessary to talk about differential equations to understand some of the simple special functions. In technical literature, there are often several conflicting definitions of many special functions. Therefore, when one uses a special function from Math::Cephes, one should look at the definition given in the documentation to confirm that it is exactly what one wants. The special functions defined in Math::Cephes take only real arguments.

We start with the discussion of a few useful special functions that are obtained by integrating certain functions within pre-specified limits. The functions we look at are the gamma function, the beta function, the exponential function, the sine and cosine integrals, the hyperbolic sine and cosine integrals, the Fresnel integral and the error function. These are all commonly used in scientific and engineering computation. In each case, we simply illustrate how the values of the functions can be computed. We follow with a more detailed discussion of the Bessel's functions. Interested readers are advised to consult one of the following books or a similar book for detailed discussions on these functions and the corresponding integral: *Advanced Engineering Mathematics* [Kre93], *Advanced Engineering Mathematics* [BMW77], *Advanced Engineering Mathematics with MATLAB* [HDR00].

13.3.4.1   The Gamma Function

The *gamma function* was first introduced by Euler to generalize the factorial function to non-integer values. It has been studied by eminent mathematicians such as Gauss, Legendre, Liouvlle, Hermite and Weirstarss. Some famous mathematical constants such as the *Euler constant* γ are related to the gamma function.

The gamma function is denoted by $\Gamma(n)$ and is defined in terms of a special and useful integral. The definition is given below.

$$\Gamma(n) \;=\; \int_0^\infty x^{n-1} e^{-x} dx \tag{13.4}$$

The integral can be shown to converge for all values $n > 0$. If we integrate by parts and take the limiting values, we can obtain the following recurrence relation for describing the gamma function.

$$\Gamma(n+1) \;=\; n\Gamma(n) \tag{13.5}$$

By evaluating the integral 13.4 for $n = 1$, we can show that $\Gamma(1) = 1$. From Equation 13.5, $\Gamma(n)$ can be determined for all $n > 0$ when the values for the gamma function have been determined for a certain interval of unit length, e.g., $1 \le n < 2$. In particular, it can be shown that if n is a positive integer, the following holds for $n = 1, 2, 3, \cdots$.

$$\Gamma(n+1) \;=\; n! \tag{13.6}$$

For this reason, $\Gamma(n)$ is sometimes called the *factorial function*. It also can be shown that

$$\Gamma\left(\frac{1}{2}\right) \;=\; \sqrt{\pi} \tag{13.7}$$

The recurrence relation 13.5 is a difference equation that has Equation 13.4 as a solution.

The following program simply prints the value of the gamma function for a sequence of arguments.

Program 13.5

```perl
#!/usr/bin/perl
#gamma.pl
use Math::Cephes qw (:gammas);
use strict;
for (my $i = -1; $i <= 100; $i = $i + 3.5 ){
    my $gammaVal = Math::Cephes::gamma ($i);
    print "gamma($i) = $gammaVal\n";
 }
```

The output of the program is given below.

```
gamma domain error
gamma(-1) = nan
gamma(2.5) = 1.32934038817914
gamma(6) = 120
gamma(9.5) = 119292.461994609
gamma(13) = 479001600
gamma(16.5) = 5189998453040.12
gamma(20) = 1.21645100408832e+17
```

```
gamma(23.5)  = 5.36130358754441e+21
gamma(27)    = 4.03291461126606e+26
gamma(30.5)  = 4.82269693349091e+31
gamma(34)    = 8.68331761881189e+36
gamma(37.5)  = 2.25511578410651e+42
gamma(41)    = 8.15915283247898e+47
gamma(44.5)  = 3.99612665510252e+53
gamma(48)    = 2.58623241511168e+59
gamma(51.5)  = 2.16668377073774e+65
gamma(55)    = 2.30843697339241e+71
gamma(58.5)  = 3.07979367469713e+77
gamma(62)    = 5.07580213877225e+83
gamma(65.5)  = 1.02102976358767e+90
gamma(69)    = 2.48003554243683e+96
gamma(72.5)  = 7.20403236376959e+102
gamma(76)    = 2.48091408113954e+109
gamma(79.5)  = 1.00493279593549e+116
gamma(83)    = 4.75364333701284e+122
gamma(86.5)  = 2.60868045964056e+129
gamma(90)    = 1.65079551609085e+136
gamma(93.5)  = 1.19790604809448e+143
gamma(97)    = 9.9167793487095e+149
```

The error statements on top show that the gamma value cannot be computed by the package for negative values. nan seen on the second line stands for *not a number*. Although the gamma function can be defined for negative integers using a process called *analytical continuation*, it has not been implemented in the Math::Cephes module. There are some computations, particularly in number theory, where the logarithm of the gamma function often appears. Math::Cephes provides an implementation of such a function also although we do not discuss it here. Several variations of the gamma function are implemented as well. Of these, the so-called incomplete gamma function and its derivative are commonly used in statistics.

13.3.4.2   The Beta Function

There is a frequently used function called the beta function that is closely related to the gamma function discussed earlier. The *beta function* is denoted by $B(m, n)$ and is defined as the following.

$$B(m, n) \quad = \quad \int_0^1 x^{m-1}(1-x)^{n-1} dx \tag{13.8}$$

$B(m, n)$ can be shown to converge for any $m > 0$ and any $n > 0$.

The beta function is connected to the gamma function according to the relation given below.

$$B(m, n) \quad = \quad \frac{\Gamma(m)\,\Gamma(n)}{\Gamma(m+n)} \tag{13.9}$$

Many integrals can be evaluated in terms of beta and gamma functions. A useful result, frequently used, is the following.

$$\int_0^{\frac{\pi}{2}} sin^{2m-1}\theta \; cos^{2n-1}\theta \; d\theta = \frac{1}{2}B(m, n) = \frac{\Gamma(m)\Gamma(n)}{2\Gamma(m+n)} \tag{13.10}$$

This formula is valid for $m > 0$ and $n > 0$.

Some special values for the beta function are given below.

$$B\left(\frac{1}{2}, \frac{1}{2}\right) = \pi \tag{13.11}$$

$$B\left(\frac{1}{3}, \frac{2}{3}\right) = \frac{2\sqrt{3}}{3}\pi$$

$$B\left(\frac{1}{4}, \frac{3}{4}\right) = \pi\sqrt{2}$$

$$B(x, 1-x) = \frac{\pi}{sin(\pi x)}$$

$$B(x, 1) = \frac{1}{x}$$

The following program computes the value of the beta function for a sequence of pairs of arguments given.

Program 13.6

```perl
#!/usr/bin/perl
#!/usr/bin/perl
#beta.pl
use Math::Cephes qw (:betas);
use strict;

for (my $j = 10, my $k = 20; $j <= 100, $k <= 200;
     $j = $j + 10, $k = $k + 10) {
  my $betaVal = Math::Cephes::beta ($j, $k);
  print "beta($j, $k) = $betaVal\n";
}
```

The output of this function is given below.

```
beta(10,  20)  = 4.99250874063468e-09
beta(20,  30)  = 1.7681885473062e-15
beta(30,  40)  = 1.05394246037965e-21
beta(40,  50)  = 7.51617121185538e-28
beta(50,  60)  = 5.84256439064177e-34
beta(60,  70)  = 4.77068553860886e-40
beta(70,  80)  = 4.01922740820151e-46
beta(80,  90)  = 3.45937739021208e-52
beta(90, 100)  = 3.02385319165625e-58
beta(100, 110) = 2.6740239592764e-64
beta(110, 120) = 2.3860676103157e-70
beta(120, 130) = 2.14445046188729e-76
beta(130, 140) = 1.93857877864822e-82
beta(140, 150) = 1.7609569287595e-88
beta(150, 160) = 1.60611588795791e-94
beta(160, 170) = 1.46996016336776e-100
beta(170, 180) = 1.34935375284916e-106
beta(180, 190) = 1.24184863959569e-112
beta(190, 200) = 1.14550146955917e-118
```

`Math::Cephes` provides implementation of several variations of the beta function as well. Of these, the so-called incomplete beta function and its inverse are commonly used in statistics.

13.3.4.3 Exponential Integral

The *exponential integral* is defined as

$$Ei(n) = \int_{-\infty}^{x} \frac{e^t}{t} \, dt \tag{13.12}$$

The Equation 13.12 is not defined for $x \leq 0$.

There is a second version of the exponential integral known as $E_n(x)$ defined as given below.

$$E_n(x) = \int_{1}^{\infty} \frac{e^{-xt}}{t^n} \, dt \tag{13.13}$$

In Equation 13.13, both n and x must be positive. The `Math::Cephes` module allows us to compute values for both $Ei(n)$ and $E_n(x)$. The integrals are called `Ei` and `Expn`, respectively in `Math::Cephes`.

13.3.4.4 Sine and Cosine Integrals

The *sine integral* is defined as

$$Si(x) = \int_{0}^{x} \frac{sin \, t}{t} \, dt \tag{13.14}$$

The sine integral is the integration of the dampened sine curve. The sine curve has been dampened by dividing $sin \, t$ by t. The *cosine integral* is defined as

$$Ci(x) = \gamma + ln(x) + \int_{0}^{x} \frac{cos \, t - 1}{t} \, dt \tag{13.15}$$

The sine and cosine integrals are used in number theory, quantum field theory, semi-conductor physics among other application areas. The sine and cosine integrals are obtained by calling the `Math::Cephes` function `sici`. For a given argument, the `sici` function returns both the sine and the cosine integrals.

13.3.4.5 Fresnel Integral

The Fresnel integral is quite frequently used in optics studying Fresnel diffraction patterns and similar topics. It is also used in railway and freeway constructions. The *Fresnel integrals* are defined as given below.

$$C(x) = \int_{0}^{x} cos(\frac{\pi}{2} \, t^2) \, dt \tag{13.16}$$

$$S(x) = \int_{0}^{x} sin(\frac{\pi}{2} \, t^2) \, dt \tag{13.17}$$

It can be shown that $C(\infty) = S(\infty) = \frac{1}{2}$ and $C(-\infty) = S(-\infty) = -\frac{1}{2}$. The Fresnel integrals are obtained in `Math::Cephes` using the `fresnl` function that returns a list containing both $C(x)$ and $S(x)$.

13.3.4.6 The Error Function

The error function $erf(x)$ gives the integral of the frequently used Gaussian probability distribution. It calculates the estimate that the probability of an observation falls within x standard deviations of the mean, assuming the observations follow a normal distribution. The error function and its variations are central to many calculations in statistics. The error function is also used in solutions of partial differential equations, probability theory, Monte Carlo simulations, and for calculating electrostatic lattice constants. The *error function erf(x)* is defined as given below.

$$erf(x) = \frac{2}{\sqrt{\pi}} \int_0^x e^{-t^2} \, dt \tag{13.18}$$

It can be shown that

$$erf(x) = \frac{2}{\sqrt{\pi}} \left(x - \frac{x^3}{1! \, 3} + \frac{x^5}{2! \, 5} - \frac{x^7}{3! \, 7} + \cdots \right) = \frac{2}{\sqrt{\pi}} \sum_{k=0}^{\infty} \frac{(-1)^k \, x^{2k+1}}{k! \, (2k+1)} \tag{13.19}$$

The `Math::Cephes` error function $erf(x)$ is called `erf`.

13.3.4.7 Hyperbolic Sine and Cosine Integrals

The hyperbolic sine and cosine integrals are defined in the fashion of regular sine and cosine integrals. The hyperbolic sine integral is traditionally written as $Shi(x)$ and is defined as given below.

$$Shi(x) = \int_0^x \frac{sihn \, t}{t} \, dt \tag{13.20}$$

The cosine hyperbolic function is represented as $Chi(x)$ and is defined using the following formula.

$$Chi(x) = \int_0^x \gamma + log(z) + \frac{cosh \, t - 1}{t} \, dt \tag{13.21}$$

Just like the sine and cosine integrals, the sine and cosine hyperbolic functions are used in number theory, quantum field theory and semi-conductor physics. The `Math::Cephes` function that returns a list containing both $Shi(x)$ and $Chi(x)$ for an given argument is called `shichi`.

13.3.4.8 Differential Equations and Bessel Functions

A differential equation contains one or several derivatives of an unknown function $y(x)$. The goal is to determine the value of $y(x)$ from the equation. The equation may contain $y(x)$ itself as well as known functions of x and constants. Differential equations arise in many engineering and other applications in terms of mathematical models of physical and other systems. The simplest ones can be solved by using concepts from elementary calculus. However, many complicated differential equations frequently occur in mathematical models of systems.

The *order* of a differential equation is the order of the highest derivative that appears in the equation. A differential equation, in general, may have many solutions. This is because we know from calculus that integration introduces arbitrary constants. A solution to a differential equation is a function and if this function contains arbitrary constants, we call it a *general solution*. If the constants in the general solution are replaced by specific values, we obtain a *particular solution* for the differential equation. A differential equation may also have an additional solution that cannot be obtained from the general solution. Such a solution is called the *singular solution*. A singular solution is not generally interesting to scientists and engineers, but mathematicians find them useful for complete characterization of the solutions of a differential equation. A *general* solution to a differential equation can be particularized if some initial values are given to the unknown function and its derivatives to begin with. Together, the differential equation and its initial values constitute an *initial value problem*.

A *first-order differential equation* (more correctly, a first-order ordinary differential equation) involves first derivatives of the unknown function. A first-order linear differential equation is written as

$$y'(x) + p(x) \, y(x) = r(x) \tag{13.22}$$

where $p(x)$ and $r(x)$ are any two arbitrary known functions of x. The function $p(x)$ is called a coefficient of the equation. $y'(x)$ is the first derivative of $y(x) = \frac{dy}{dx}(x)$. If $r(x) = 0$, it is called a *homogeneous first-order linear differential equation*; otherwise, it is *non-homogeneous*. The term *ordinary* as opposed to *partial* indicates that solutions to an ordinary differential equation is a function of one variable, whereas a solution to a partial differential equation is function of two or more variables. Partial differential equations are more complex to solve than ordinary differential equations and require the development of additional techniques.

A *second-order differential equation* involves second derivatives of an unknown function $y(x)$. A second-order differential equation is called linear if if can be written as

$$y''(x) + p(x)\,y'(x) + q(x)\,y(x) = r(x) \tag{13.23}$$

where $p(x)$, $q(x)$ and $r(x)$ are arbitrary known functions of x, and *non-linear* if it cannot be written in this form. Such an equation is linear in the function $y(x)$ and its derivatives because the derivatives and the function are not raised to any power > 1. Linear equations are much simpler to handle than non-linear equations. If $r(x) = 0$, Equation 13.23 becomes

$$y''(x) + p(x)\,y'(x) + q(x)\,y(x) = 0 \tag{13.24}$$

and is called *homogeneous*. If $r(x) \neq 0$, Equation 13.23 is called *non-homogeneous*. The functions $p(x)$ and $q(x)$ are called *coefficients* of the equation. A *solution* of a second order differential equation on some open interval $a < x < b$ is a function $y = h(x)$ that has derivatives $y' = h'(x)$ and $y'' = h''(x)$ and satisfies the differential equation for all x in that interval. In other words, the equation becomes an identity if we replace the unknown function $y(x)$ and its derivative by h and its corresponding derivatives.

Second-order linear differential equations have many applications in mechanics and electrical circuit theory. It makes them more important than higher-order equations from a practical viewpoint. Some second order differential equations are simple; their solutions are familiar functions from calculus. Others are more involved, their solutions being more difficult. For example, if the coefficients of a homogeneous linear differential equation are constants, it can be solved using algebraic methods, and the solutions are elementary functions known from calculus. However, if the coefficients are not constant but depend on x, the situation is more complicated. *Legendre's equations*, the *hypergeometric equations* and *Bessel's equations* are of this type. These and other equations and their solutions play an important role in applied mathematics. We discuss only one such equation: the Bessel's equations although `Math::Cephes` provides implementation of the other two as well.

Bessel's Differential Equations of Order ν is given by the following.

$$x^2\,y''(x) + x\,y'(x) + (x^2 - \nu^2)\,y(x) = 0 \tag{13.25}$$

Here, $y'(x)$ represents the first derivative and $y''(x)$ represents the second derivative of the function $y(x)$. The parameter ν is a given non-negative real number. This equation appears in problems on vibrations, electric fields, heat conduction, and fluid flow, where the problem shows cylindrical symmetry. Although the Bessel's differential equation is a second-order differential equation, its name is based on the parameter ν that appears in Equation 13.25 The equation given above is called *Bessel's Equation of Order ν* based on the parameter ν and not on the second order of the derivative $y''(x)$. Equation 13.25 can be written in the so-called *standard form*, after dividing throughout by x^2. The standard form is shown below.

$$y''(x) + \frac{1}{x}\,y'(x) + \left(1 - \frac{\nu^2}{x^2}\right)y(x) = 0 \tag{13.26}$$

We clearly see that in this equation, the coefficients are $\frac{1}{x}$ and $\left(1 - \frac{\nu^2}{x^2}\right)$ and are dependent on x.

The number ν is usually a positive integer or a positive rational number. Bessel's differential equations of integral or half-integral orders (an integer plus $\frac{1}{2}$) are particularly important in applications. The Bessel's

Fist kind functions	Second kind functions
j0	y0
j1	y1
jn	yn
jv	yv

Table 13.1: Some Bessel's Functions in `Math::Cephes`

.

differential equation must be solved differently depending on the value of ν There are two standard methods of solving such equations: the *power-series method* which obtains solutions in the form of power series, and an extension of it called the *Frobenius method*. We do not discuss these methods here, but want the reader to be aware of them.

There are several solutions to the Bessel's equation and the solutions are complicated. Bessel's equation is a second-order homogeneous ordinary differential equation. It is second-order because it contains $y''(x)$, the second derivative of the unknown function $y(x)$. It is a homogeneous equation because the right-hand side is 0. A second-order homogeneous equation needs two particular solutions if we want to write a general solution for it. The two particular solutions must be independent of each other so that one is not derivable from the other. In the 1700s and 1800s, many mathematicians toiled over solving the Bessel's equation and obtained two widely accepted particular solutions. The particular solutions are complicated, and are in terms of summation of series. Their names are also universally accepted. The two particular solutions are called $J_\nu(x)$ and $Y_\nu(x)$, the subscript ν referring to the order of the Bessel's equation. $J_\nu(x)$ has a well-accepted name: *Bessel's function of the first kind*, or simply, *Bessel's function*. $Y_\nu(x)$ also has a well-accepted name: *Bessel's function of the second kind*. We look at the values of $J_\nu(x)$ and $Y_\nu(x)$ a little later. If we know $J_\nu(x)$ and $Y_\nu(x)$, we can obtain a general solution to the Bessel's equation as given below.

$$y(x) = c_1 \, J_\nu(x) + c_2 Y_\nu(x) \tag{13.27}$$

Here c_1 and c_2 are two arbitrary constants. Thus, the general solution for the $y(x)$ function used in the Bessel's equation is obtained as a linear combination of the two particular solutions: Bessel's function of the first kind, and Bessel's function of the second kind.

`Math::Cephes` gives us functions that return values of $J_\nu(x)$ and $Y_\nu(x)$ for various values of ν and x. `Math::Cephes` has several such functions. The names of these functions are given in Table 13.1.

The names follow standard names used by mathematicians. Mathematicians usually talk about four variations of Bessel's functions of the first kind: $J_0(x)$, $J_1(x)$, $J_n(x)$ and $J_\nu(x)$. $J_0(x)$ is the particular solution of the first kind when the constant ν used in the Bessel's equation is zero. In other words, it is the first particular solution to the differential equation given below.

$$x^2 \, y''(x) + x \, y'(x) + x^2 \, y(x) = 0 \tag{13.28}$$

Its value can be obtained from the solution $J_n(x)$ discussed later. However, because it is used frequently, `Math::Cephes` defines it as a separate function. The value of $J_0(x)$ is given below.

$$J_0(x) = \sum_{m=0}^{\infty} \frac{(-1)^m x^{2m}}{2^{2m} \, (m!)^2} = 1 - \frac{x^2}{2^2 \, (1!)^2} + \frac{x^4}{2^4 \, (2!)^2} - \cdots \tag{13.29}$$

$J_0(x)$ is called the Bessel function (of the first kind) of order 0. In `Math::Cephes`, it is simply called `j0` and is called with an argument x, integer or non-integer.

$J_1(x)$ is the particular solution of the first kind of order 1. In other words, it is the first particular solution when the constant ν in the Bessel's equation is 1. Thus, $J_1(x)$ is the first particular solution of the differential equation given below.

$$x^2\, y''(x) + x\, y'(x) + (x^2 - 1)\, y(x) = 0 \tag{13.30}$$

The value of $J_1(x)$ is given below.

$$J_1(x) = \sum_{m=0}^{\infty} \frac{(-1)^m\, x^{2m+1}}{2^{2m+1}\, m!(m+1)!} = \frac{x}{2} - \frac{x^3}{2^3\, 1!\, 2!} + \frac{x^5}{2^5\, 2!\, 3!} - \frac{x^7}{2^7\, 3!\, 4!} + \cdots \tag{13.31}$$

$J_1(x)$ is called the *Bessel function (of the first kind)) of order 1*. In Math::Cephes, the corresponding function is j1. j1 takes one argument that can take integer or non-integer value.

If the constant ν used in the Bessel's equation is an integer, it is written as n. The particular solutions to the Bessel's equation are different when ν is an integer n, and when it is not. The first particular solution when ν is an integer is written as $J_n(x)$. In Math::Cephes, the corresponding function is jn. It takes two arguments. The first argument is an integer and corresponds to n. The second argument corresponds to x and can be integer or non-integer. The value of $J_n(x)$ is given below.

$$J_n(x) = x^n \sum_{m=0}^{\infty} \frac{(-1)^m\, x^{2m}}{2^{2m+n}\, m!(n+m)!} \tag{13.32}$$

The values of $J_0(x)$ and $J_1(x)$ given earlier can be obtained by instantiating n in the value of $J_n(x)$. $J_n(x)$ is called the *Bessel function (of the first kind) of order n*. It is also called the Bessel function (of the first kind) of integer order.

When ν is not necessarily an integer, the first particular solution is written as $J_\nu(x)$. Its value is given below.

$$J_\nu(x) = x^\nu \sum_{m=0}^{\infty} \frac{(-1)^m\, x^{2m}}{2^{2m+\nu}\, \Gamma(\nu+m+1)} \tag{13.33}$$

$J_\nu(x)$ is called the *Bessel function (of the first kind) of order ν*. It is also called the Bessel function (of the first kind) of non-integer order. We have seen the definition of the gamma (Γ) function already. If $x = n$, an integer, $\Gamma(n+1) = n!$. Thus, the gamma function in the denominator of the formula for $J_\nu(x)$ becomes $(n+k)!$ when ν, a non-integer.

In Math::Cephes, the corresponding function is jv. It takes two arguments. The first argument corresponds ν and the second to x. Both can take integral or non-integral values.

Now, that we have discussed the first particular solution to the Bessel's equation, we discuss the second particular solution. The Bessel's functions corresponding to the second particular solution are called Bessel's functions of the second kind. Before proceeding further, we need to make it very clear that one does not have to be confused by the distinction between the first kind and the second kind Bessel functions. These are two particular solutions to the Bessel's equation and mathematicians, long ago, agreed upon their values and the corresponding names, as either the first kind or the second kind. There is nothing mysterious or baffling about the names and their values, except that they are universally accepted by mathematicians. For our purposes, we do not need to know how the exact values of the two particular solutions are obtained. However, for many applications, we do not need to remember the values. The only thing we need to know is whether a solution of the first or the second kind is needed. We also need to know the value of the constant ν and whether it is an integer or a non-integer. When it is an integer, there are two special cases corresponding to 0 and 1.

The Bessel's functions of the second kind correspond to the second particular solution of the Bessel's equation. Once again, there are four solutions that are usually discussed: $Y_0(x)$, $Y_1(x)$, $Y_n(x)$ and $Y_\nu(x)$. The corresponding functions in Math::Cephes are y0, y1, yn and yv. Each of the first two takes one argument, corresponding to x. The argument can take integer or non-integer values. Each of the last two takes two arguments each, the second argument corresponding to x. The first argument to yn is an integer. The first argument to yv can be an integer or a non-integer. The four solutions are called Bessel's function of the second kind of order 0, Bessel's function of the second kind of order 1, Bessel's function of the second kind of integer order, and Bessel's function of the second kind of non-integer order, respectively. The values of the functions $Y_0(x)$ and $Y_1(x)$ are given below. One can obtain the other two in many advanced mathematics books for engineers and scientists. Some such books have been listed earlier in the section.

$$Y_0(x) = \frac{2}{\pi}\left[J_0(x)\left(\ln\frac{x}{2}+\gamma\right) + \sum_{m=1}^{\infty}\frac{(-1)^{m-1}\,h_m}{2^{2m}\,(m!)^2}\,x^{2m}\right] \tag{13.34}$$

$$Y_n(x) = \frac{2}{\pi}\,J_n(x)\left(\ln\frac{x}{2}+\gamma\right) + \frac{x^n}{\pi}\sum_{m=0}^{\infty}\frac{(-1)^{m-1}\,(h_m+h_{m+n})}{2^{2m+n}\,(m!)\,(m+n)!} \tag{13.35}$$

$$-\frac{x^{-n}}{\pi}\sum_{m=0}^{n-1}\frac{(n-m-1)!}{2^{2m-n}\,m!}\,x^{2m}$$

Here h_m is given as below.

$$h_m = 1 + \frac{1}{2} + \frac{1}{3} + \frac{1}{4} + \cdots + \frac{1}{m} \tag{13.36}$$

It is the so-called *harmonic series*. Once again, the values are very complicated, but it is not necessary to remember them for most purposes. Here, the assumption is that $x > 0$ and $n = 0, 1, \cdots$.

Bessel's functions have been extended to take care of the Bessel's equation when the solutions are complex even when x is real. This extension comes in handy in some practical situations. The complex solutions are called *Bessel's functions of the third kind or order ν* or *Hankel functions*. `Math::Cephes` defines such functions although we do not discuss them here.

The following program simply prints out the values of the Bessel's functions of first and second kind for a sequence of argument values.

Program 13.7

```perl
#!/usr/bin/perl
#bessel.pl
use Math::Cephes qw(:bessels);
use strict;

print "Bessels function of first and second kind of order  0 and 1\n";
print "Using integer and non-integer values of x\n";
print "_" x 65, "\n";
printf "%5s%15s%15s%15s%15s\n", "x", "J0       ", "J1       ",
               "Y0       ", "Y1       ";
for (my $x = 1; $x <= 30; $x = $x + 2.5 ){
    my $j0 = Math::Cephes::j0 ($x);
    my $j1 = Math::Cephes::j1 ($x);
    my $y0 = Math::Cephes::y0 ($x);
    my $y1 = Math::Cephes::y1 ($x);

    printf "%5.0f%15.10f%15.10f%15.10f%15.10f\n",
           "$x", "$j0", "$j1", "$y0", "$y1";
}

print "\nBessels function of first kind of integer order n\n";
print "Using integer and non-integer values of x\n";
print "_" x 30, "\n";
```

```
printf "%6s%6s%15s\n", "x", "n", "Jn (x)        ";

for (my $n = 0; $n <= 10; $n = $n + 1){
  for (my $x = 1; $x <= 5; $x = $x + 2.5){
          my $jn = Math::Cephes::jn ($n, $x);
          printf "%6.0f%6.0f%20.15f\n", $n, $x, $jn;
  }
}


print "\nBessels function of second kind of integer order n\n";
print "Using integer and non-integer values of x\n";
print "_" x 30, "\n";
printf "%6s%6s%15s\n", "x", "n", "Jv (x)        ";

for (my $n = 1000; $n <= 2000; $n = $n + 100){
  for (my $x = 10000; $x <= 50000; $x = $x + 25000){
          my $jv = Math::Cephes::jv ($n, $x);
          printf "%6.0f%6.0f%20.15f\n", $n, $x, $jv;
  }
}


print "\nBessels function of second kind of integer order n\n";
print "Using integer and non-integer values of x\n";
print "_" x 45, "\n";
printf "%6s%6s%30s\n", "x", "n", "Yn (x)        ";

for (my $n = 100; $n <= 200; $n = $n + 10){
  for (my $x = 1000; $x <= 5000; $x = $x + 2500){
          my $yn = Math::Cephes::yn ($n, $x);
          printf "%6.0f%6.0f%35.20f\n", $n, $x, $yn;
  }
}


print "\nBessels function of second kind of non-integer order n\n";
print "Using integer and non-integer values of x\n";
print "_" x 45, "\n";
printf "%6s%6s%30s\n", "x", "n", "Yv (x)        ";

for (my $n = 1000; $n <= 2000; $n = $n + 100){
  for (my $x = 10000; $x <= 50000; $x = $x + 25000){
          my $yv = Math::Cephes::yv ($n, $x);
          printf "%6.0f%6.0f%35.20f\n", $n, $x, $yv;
  }
}
```

The obvious output of the program is given below.

```
Bessels function of first and second kind of order  0 and 1
Using integer and non-integer values of x
```

x	J0	J1	Y0	Y1
1	0.7651976866	0.4400505857	0.0882569642	-0.7812128213
4	-0.3801277400	0.1373775274	0.1890219439	0.4101884179
6	0.1506452573	-0.2766838581	-0.2881946840	-0.1750103443
8	0.0419392518	0.2731219637	0.2702051054	-0.0261686794
11	-0.1711903004	-0.1767852990	-0.1688473239	0.1637055374
14	0.2149891659	0.0380492921	0.0300770090	-0.2140229303
16	-0.1748990740	0.0903971757	0.0958109971	0.1779751689
18	0.0771648214	-0.1666336400	-0.1686563450	-0.0817478585
21	0.0365790710	0.1711202728	0.1702017584	-0.0325392608
24	-0.1239282316	-0.1109461434	-0.1082861177	0.1216532807
26	0.1559993155	0.0150457306	0.0120446259	-0.1557965532
28	-0.1262911314	0.0777013579	0.0799040393	0.1277119251

Bessels function of first kind of integer order n
Using integer and non-integer values of x

x	n	Jn (x)
0	1	0.765197686557967
0	4	-0.380127739987263
1	1	0.440050585744933
1	4	0.137377527362327
2	1	0.114903484931900
2	4	0.458629184194307
3	1	0.019563353982668
3	4	0.386770111716881
4	1	0.002476638964110
4	4	0.204405293034632
5	1	0.000249757730211
5	4	0.080441986647992
6	1	0.000020938338002
6	4	0.025428954531059
7	1	0.000001502325817
7	4	0.006743000315638
8	1	0.000000094223442
8	4	0.001543046731495
9	1	0.000000005249250
9	4	0.000310927599766
10	1	0.000000000263062
10	4	0.000056009495875

Bessels function of second kind of integer order n
Using integer and non-integer values of x

x	n	Jv (x)
1000	10000	-0.006125542627871
1000	35000	-0.003838920559852
1100	10000	0.007383381920807
1100	35000	0.004062560128311
1200	10000	0.006400582471112
1200	35000	-0.003832595491154

```
1300  10000    0.006239599017745
1300  35000    0.002700741714056
1400  10000    0.007667802080306
1400  35000    0.000132422675327
1500  10000   -0.005236691541957
1500  35000   -0.003665604513534
1600  10000    0.004305604218381
1600  35000    0.003118912440980
1700  10000   -0.007962214731132
1700  35000    0.002923690058194
1800  10000   -0.001399594542335
1800  35000   -0.002143915573544
1900  10000    0.000542522692455
1900  35000   -0.004262799481617
2000  10000   -0.005247203319043
2000  35000   -0.003373537212417
```

Bessels function of second kind of integer order n
Using integer and non-integer values of x

x	n	Yn (x)
100	1000	-0.0224386882577327158

pikespeak[98]: bessel.pl
Bessels function of first and second kind of order   0 and 1
Using integer and non-integer values of x

x	J0	J1	Y0	Y1
1	0.7651976866	0.4400505857	0.0882569642	-0.7812128213
4	-0.3801277400	0.1373775274	0.1890219439	0.4101884179
6	0.1506452573	-0.2766838581	-0.2881946840	-0.1750103443
8	0.0419392518	0.2731219637	0.2702051054	-0.0261686794
11	-0.1711903004	-0.1767852990	-0.1688473239	0.1637055374
14	0.2149891659	0.0380492921	0.0300770090	-0.2140229303
16	-0.1748990740	0.0903971757	0.0958109971	0.1779751689
18	0.0771648214	-0.1666336400	-0.1686563450	-0.0817478585
21	0.0365790710	0.1711202728	0.1702017584	-0.0325392608
24	-0.1239282316	-0.1109461434	-0.1082861177	0.1216532807
26	0.1559993155	0.0150457306	0.0120446259	-0.1557965532
28	-0.1262911314	0.0777013579	0.0799040393	0.1277119251

Bessels function of first kind of integer order n
Using integer and non-integer values of x

x	n	Jn (x)
0	1	0.765197686557967
0	4	-0.380127739987263
1	1	0.440050585744933
1	4	0.137377527362327
2	1	0.114903484931900
2	4	0.458629184194307
3	1	0.019563353982668

```
     3        4      0.386770111716881
     4        1      0.002476638964110
     4        4      0.204405293034632
     5        1      0.000249757730211
     5        4      0.080441986647992
     6        1      0.000020938338002
     6        4      0.025428954531059
     7        1      0.000001502325817
     7        4      0.006743000315638
     8        1      0.000000094223442
     8        4      0.001543046731495
     9        1      0.000000005249250
     9        4      0.000310927599766
    10        1      0.000000000263062
    10        4      0.000056009495875
```

Bessels function of second kind of integer order n
Using integer and non-integer values of x

x	n	Jv (x)
1000	10000	-0.006125542627871
1000	35000	-0.003838920559852
1100	10000	0.007383381920807
1100	35000	0.004062560128311
1200	10000	0.006400582471112
1200	35000	-0.003832595491154
1300	10000	0.006239599017745
1300	35000	0.002700741714056
1400	10000	0.007667802080306
1400	35000	0.000132422675327
1500	10000	-0.005236691541957
1500	35000	-0.003665604513534
1600	10000	0.004305604218381
1600	35000	0.003118912440980
1700	10000	-0.007962214731132
1700	35000	0.002923690058194
1800	10000	-0.001399594542335
1800	35000	-0.002143915573544
1900	10000	0.000542522692455
1900	35000	-0.004262799481617
2000	10000	-0.005247203319043
2000	35000	-0.003373537212417

Bessels function of second kind of integer order n
Using integer and non-integer values of x

x	n	Yn (x)
100	1000	-0.0224386882577327158
100	3500	0.0106418522669406260
110	1000	0.0009881101355703 9687
110	3500	-0.0126170356815 3656890

120	1000	0.02272104813302647935
120	3500	0.01348328645714888009
130	1000	-0.01772668382981033158
130	3500	-0.01278890188506738926
140	1000	-0.01388177755258548397
140	3500	0.01023254356937828603
150	1000	0.02269608597029840885
150	3500	-0.00582596306741794707
160	1000	0.01102679107014443299
160	3500	0.00004672403396424286
170	1000	-0.02185319243590612415
170	3500	0.00608917537589039048
180	1000	-0.01685511442008628263
180	3500	-0.01111975680487314010
190	1000	0.01345405131756458733
190	3500	0.01346009756222942347
200	1000	0.02514448829969110830
200	3500	-0.01194863905945314948

Bessels function of second kind of non-integer order n
Using integer and non-integer values of x

x	n	Yv (x)
1000	10000	0.00514396947362373135
1000	35000	-0.00185990697949652830
1100	10000	0.00308809559860151201
1100	35000	0.00130143437095710658
1200	10000	-0.00481226536390960431
1200	35000	-0.00187377916118748188
1300	10000	-0.00502734928731265584
1300	35000	0.00330267926607841211
1400	10000	0.00234520773789003269
1400	35000	-0.00426452451986259265
1500	10000	0.00608009482429516367
1500	35000	0.00218385147320785322
1600	10000	-0.00677898294411331294
1600	35000	0.00291213962045935165
1700	10000	0.00109793493614591432
1700	35000	-0.00310848300465291346
1800	10000	0.00792213316408093768
1800	35000	-0.00369010357454917400
1900	10000	0.00803422823320607687
1900	35000	-0.00021103897370279657
2000	10000	0.00611895339565993873
2000	35000	0.00261498613795894388

Math::Cephes has a large number of additional functions that we do not discuss here. Similarly, the two other packages PDL and Math::Pari that we cursorily mentioned in the beginning of the section are also extremely powerful. There is a large number of additional mathematical modules as well.

13.4 Conclusion

This chapter briefly discusses how Perl can be used for scientific and engineering computation by introducing the `Math::Cephes` module. We simply discuss a few of the many functions available in this module. There are several other rich modules for scientific and engineering computation and those who are seriously interested in such topics should at least read up on the `PDL` and `Math::Pari` modules.

We wrap up our book on Perl with this chapter. Perl is a modern language with roots in Unix that explain a few quirkiness it possesses, e.g., the naming of variables. Perl is an extremely powerful language. Its core is very strong providing a capable foundation for a huge number of contributed modules that make it even more powerful and useful. Perl has a large number of enthusiastic developers, porters and well as users. Perl programs are easy to write and usually are fairly short compared to programs of comparable complexity in other languages. With proper care in coding, Perl programs can be easy to maintain, deploy and upgrade. This books has given a fairly in-depth overview of Perl's varied capabilities although a lot more can be discussed. The interested reader is advised to go to the CPAN site, *www.cpan.org* and start additional journeys into the wonderful world of Perl.

13.5 Exercises (Miscellaneous)

1. *(Easy: Documentation Reading, Research)*
   In a program, it is quite often necessary to deal with date and time, convert from one format to another, and convert one time in one zone to another. Find out what time-related functions are there in Core Perl. Perl has several modules that deal with time. Search *www.cpan.org* to locate some of these modules. Read their documentation, and use them in your programs.

2. *(Hard: C, Perl and C, Research)*
   Quite frequently, parts or whole Perl modules are written in C. Research into how such modules are organized and written. Write some modules in C, but provide Perl interface to them. In addition, take some existing C modules and provide Perl interface for them.

3. *(Medium to Hard: Perl and C, Research)*
   Research into how Perl scripts can be embedded in C code and vice versa. Write programs to illustrate what you learn.

4. *(Easy to Medium: Unicode, Research)*
   The Unicode is a coding scheme for a huge number of alphanumeric and other characters for most major languages of the world. Perl provides modules for dealing with the Unicode. Find out what these modules are. Learn how Perl can be used with characters in the following languages: Greek, Russian, Arabic and Assamese.

5. *(Medium to Hard: Mathematical Computation, Research)*
   Perl has a large number of modules for performing mathematical computation. Learn about the `Math::Pari` module that provides an interface to a large library of number-theoretic functions written in C. Read the documentation on this module. Study the RSA public-key algorithm, briefly discussed in Chapter 11. Implement the algorithm using the `Math::Pari` module.

6. *(Medium to Hard: GUI, Research)*
   Learn how to write an attractive graphical user interface (GUI) in Perl. Rewrite any program that you have written already that can use a GUI. Write the GUI code and integrate it with your existing code.

7. *(Medium to Hard: Mathematical Data Processing, Research)*
   Perl has a module called `PDL` and several related modules that allow one to deal with large matrices. Learn how to use these modules for image and audio processing.

Appendix A

On Acquiring Perl from FTP Sites

Perl is available for free from several sites. The best place to get started is by visiting the following two sites on the World Wide Web: `http://www.perl.org` and `htpp://www.perl.com`.

`http://www.perl.org` is the site for The Perl Institute. It is a non-profit organization whose mission is to support the community of people who use Perl and facilitate the development of Perl as a programming language. It has links to *CPAN* sites. CPAN stands for Comprehensive Perl Archive Network. The URL for CPAN is `http://www.cpan.org`. There are many sites around the world that store Perl core and many well-designed Perl modules that do almost anything anyone wants. Perl and its modules have been ported to many different machines. If you want to obtain Perl for Unix, Macintosh, DOS, and Windows machines, CPAN is one place where you obtain it. You can download Perl to your machine if you are connected on the Internet and have a World Wide Web browser. Otherwise, you will have to obtain a Perl CD that comes with many books on Perl. Perl also comes as pre-loaded software on many Unix machines.

The Perl Institute site also links to the Perl FAQ, i.e., a list of questions that people frequently ask about Perl and the answers to those questions. There are many simple as well as tricky questions answered here.

The `www.perl.com` site is also a very useful site. Anything you want to find about Perl is available on this site or has a link from this site. It is also a CPAN site and has a search facility to find what you want.

If your machine is a Macintosh computer, the version of Perl to download depends on your operating system. For MacOS 9 or lower, there is a version called *MacPerl*. There are links to MacPerl from `perl.org` or `perl.com`. It is available directly from `http://www.macperl.com`. If the Macintosh operating system you are using is Mac OS X or Mac OS X Server, it has FreeBSD underneath the graphical user interface. Perl for Unix will build on such a platform.

If you use a Windows machine, another place to obtain Perl from is `http://www.activestate.com`. The version of Perl available here is called *ActivePerl* and installs easily. ActivePerl is also available for several Unix platforms.

Appendix B

On Portability

Perl and most of its modules are available for free for many different platforms. Whether you want to run Perl on versions of Unix, DOS, versions of Windows, or MacOS, Perl is available. On Unix, Perl is run from the command line. It is usual for a Perl script to have a line such as

```
#!/usr/bin/perl
```

the first line of code on a Unix machine. This is a feature of Unix that allows the programmer to tell the system where to find the Perl interpreter that is going to execute the code. This line is actually a comment and must start on the first column. If on your system, Perl is not at /usr/bin/perl and is somewhere else, you must write the correct address here.

In Unix, before a Perl script can be run, the script must be made executable. It can be done by typing:

```
%chmod u+x progamfile
```

Here programfile is the actual name of the file that contains the Perl script. Once the file containing the script has been made executable, it can be run by typing in the name of the file containing the script. If the file is not made executable, one can still run it by typing

```
%perl scriptfile
```

assuming Perl is available on the operating system *path* variable and scriptfile is the name of the file where the Perl script is stored.

On DOS and Windows systems, Perl also runs from the command line. You simply type in the Perl script file name and it will run. The extension of the Perl program (say, pl) will have to be associated with the Perl executable to be able to do so. Otherwise, something like

```
%perl scriptfile
```

should work.

On Macintosh systems (Mac OS 9 or lower), Perl has a graphical interface. Perl programs can be run on such a system by choosing the appropriate menu item. On Mac OS X or Mac OS X Server, Perl can be run from the command-line like any other Unix system.

Since underlying processes of an operating system vary from platform to platform, the process facilities of Perl may not work the same way on all systems.

Appendix C

On Selected Special Variables

A special variable is a variable that has special meaning to Perl. Below we list a short selected set of special variables. Special variables are mostly scalars, although there are a few list variables and hash variables as well. They are used for various purposes such as during the processing of regular expressions, during subroutine calls, during printing of lists, etc.

- $_: This is the default parameter for a lot of functions. It is also the default result of reading using the diamond operator (< . . . >).

- $.: It holds the current record or line number of the file handle that was last read. It is read-only and is reset to 0 when the file handle is closed. If ARGV is used as a file handle, the numbers increase from one file to another as more files are read.

- $/: It holds the input record separator. The record separator is usually the newline character. However, if $/ is set to an empty string, two or more newlines in the input file are treated as one. If it is undefined, the whole file is read in one operation.

- $,: This is the output separator for the print function. Normally, this variable is an empty string. When we use a comma (,) to give several arguments to print, the comma is replaced by the current value of $,.

- $|: If its value is nonzero, it causes Perl to flush the output buffer after every write or print function call. Normally, it is set to 0. In other words, buffering of the output is the normal procedure.

- $$: Its value is derived from the Unix operating system. It contains the process number of the process running the Perl interpreter.

- $?: It holds the status of the last pipe closed, or the last back-quoted string that calls a system command, or the last call to the system function.

- $&: It holds the string that was matched by the last successful pattern match.

- $`: It holds the string that preceded whatever was matched by the last successful pattern match.

- $?: It holds the string that followed whatever was matched by the last successful pattern match.

- $0: It holds the name of the file containing the Perl script being executed.

- $<number>: A variable such as $1, $2, $3, etc., holds the substring that matches a parenthesized part of a regular expression.

- `$"`: This is the separator used between list elements when an array variable is interpolated into a double-quoted string. Normally, its value is a space character.

- `$!`: When used in a numeric context, it holds the current error number. If used in a string context, it holds the error string associated with the error number.

- `$^T`: It holds the time, in seconds, at which the script begins running.

- `$ARGV`: It holds the name of the current file being read when using the diamond operator (`<...>`).

- `@ARGV`: This array variable holds a list of the command line arguments. `$#ARGV` gives the number of arguments minus one.

- `@INC`: This array variable holds a list of directories where Perl can look for scripts to execute.

- `%ENV`: This hash variable contains entries for the current environment variables. Changing or adding an entry affects only the current process or a child process, never the parent process.

- `%SIG`: This hash variable contains entries for signal handlers.

- `STDERR`: This file handle is used to send output to the standard error file. Normally, this is connected to the terminal, but it can be redirected if needed.

- `STDIN`: This file handle is used to read input from the standard input file. Normally, this is connected to the keyboard, but it can be changed.

- `STDOUT`: This file handle is used to send output to the standard output file. Normally, this is the display, but it can be changed.

Appendix D

On Built-in Functions

Perl has a large number of built-in functions. Descriptions of these functions are readily available in Web site such as *www.cpan.org*. We list only some functions below.

- **Functions for SCALARs or strings**: chomp, chop, crypt, hex, index, lc, lcfirst, length, oct, ord, pack, q/STRING/, qq/STRING/, reverse, rindex, sprintf, substr, tr///, uc, ucfirst, y///

- **Regular expressions and pattern matching**: m//, s///, split

- **Numeric functions**: abs, atan2, cos, exp, hex, int, log, oct, rand, sin, sqrt, srand

- **Functions for real @ARRAYs**: pop, push, shift, splice, unshift

- **Functions for list data**: grep, join, map, qw/STRING/, reverse, sort, unpack

- **Functions for real %HASHes** delete, each, exists, keys, values

- **Input and output functions**: close, closedir, die, print, printf, read, readdir, select, sysread, , warn, write

- **Functions for filehandles, files, or directories**: chdir, chmod, chown, chroot, glob, link, lstat, mkdir, open, opendir, rename, rmdir, unlink

- **Keywords related to the control flow of a perl program**: continue, die, do, eval, exit, goto, last, next, redo, return, sub

- **Keywords related to scoping**: local, my, our, package, use

- **Functions for processes and process groups**: exec, fork, getppid, kill, pipe, qx/STRING/, sleep, system, wait, waitpid

- **Keywords related to perl modules**: do, import, no, package, require, use

- **Keywords related to classes and object-orientedness**: bless, package, ref, tie, tied, untie, use

- **Low-level socket functions**: accept, bind, connect, getpeername, getsockname, getsockopt, listen, recv, send, setsockopt, shutdown, socket, socketpair

- **Fetching network information**: gethostbyaddr, gethostbyname, gethostent, getnetbyaddr, getnetent, getprotobyname, getprotobynumber, getprotoent, getservbyname, getservbyport, getservent, sethostent, setnetent, setprotoent, setservent

- **Time-related functions**: `gmtime`, `localtime`, `time`, `times`

Appendix E

On Selected Modules

Perl has a large number of pre-written modules that can perform a wide variety of tasks. One simply needs to go on the Web, visit the site `http://www.cpan.org`, perform a search, read the documentation, decide which module to download, and then download it and start using it. Finding the right module is not difficult and whether one is using Perl on a Unix machine or a PC or a Macintosh, it is very easy to install packages. Once a package is installed, one has to read its documentation carefully to be able to start using it.

All Perl modules are available for free downloading. There are modules to do almost anything one wants. So, before trying to write Perl code for a project, it makes good sense to see if there are any modules that may be of help.

Perl modules are classified at CPAN into many categories. Some of the categories are listed below. Under each category there are a large number of modules.

- **Archiving and Compression**: This category includes modules archiving, modules for managing Perl modules on various systems, conversion among various formats of data and character sets.

- **Control Flow Utilities**: This category has packages that allow subroutines to have pre- and post-call hooks, tracers for interfaces for function callbacks, etc.

- **Data Type Utilities**: There are modules that implement a large number of mathematical functions and capabilities. There are modules that provide persistent data types. There are modules that create and help access data structures such as trees, graphs and heaps. There are modules that serialize complex data types into strings.

- **Database Interfaces**: It contains modules for interfacing with a large number of databases: MySQL, Postgresql, Sybase, Oracle, etc.

- **Development Support**: There are a large number of modules to help those who develop Perl programs. There are modules to help write Perl modules—in pure Perl or in C. There are modules to help perform version control.

- **File Handle**: Input and output

- **Images, Pixmaps and Bitmaps**: These include modules to create and edit charts, graphs, and drawings. There are modules that play MP3 music, creat VRML, edit images, etc.

- **Internationalization and Locale**: This category includes modules that deal with the Unicode, letter codes for countries of the world and states of the US, codes for the world's languages, sorting strings in various ways, etc.

- **Programming Language Interfaces**

- **Mail and Usenet News**: This contains modules that can be used to handle interaction with the mailer program on a machine. There are modules to read POP3 mail messages, filter mail messages, etc. There are also modules for posting newsgroup articles, scan newsgroups, post articles, etc.

- **Microsoft Windows Modules**

- **Networking Devices and IPC**: A large number of modules to help inter-process communication, and implement various networking tasks such as DNS and Bind, FTP, Remote Procedure Calls (RPC), Remote Method Invocation (RMI), capture network packets, help program with sockets, etc.

- **Operating System Interfaces**: There are a large number of modules for interacting with various operating systems such as Macintoshes, OS2, Unix, SGI machine, MSDOS machines, Windows machines, etc.

- **Optional arguments, parameters and procedures**

- **Perl Core Modules**: These are modules that come with the standard Perl distribution.

- **Security and Encryption**: There are a large number of cryptographic modules. There are also modules for prime number generation and random number generation. There are modules that assist in authentication in various ways such as passwords, message digests, PINs, Kerberos, etc. There are modules for creating a certificate authority.

- **Server and Daemon Utilities**

- **String, Languages and Text Processing**: There are modules that deal with natural language processing such as stemming words in English, deal with fonts, summarizing English text, etc.

- **User Interfaces**: There are modules that help create graphical user interfaces.

- **World Wide Web, HTML, HTTP, CGI**: There are a large number of modules to maintain Web sites, mirror Web sites, parse and create HTML and XML pages, perform HTTP protocol based communication to help write Web clients, and write CGI program.

Bibliography

[AK88]   Alfred V. Aho and Brian Kernighan. *The AWK Programming Language*. Addison-Wesley, Reading, Massachusetts, 1988.

[ASS99]   Harold Abelson, Gerald Jay Sussman, and Julie Sussman. *Structure and Interpretation of Computer Programs*. MIT Press, Cambridge, Massachusetts, 1999.

[AT79]   AT and T. *UNIX Programmer's Manual*. AT and T, 7th edition, 1979.

[AV97]   Doris Appleby and Julius J. VandeKopple. *Programming Languages Paradigm and Practice*. McGraw-Hill, Inc., 2nd edition, 1997.

[BMW77]   A.C. Bajpai, L.R. Mustoe, and D. Walker. *Advanced Engineering Mathematics*. John Wiley & Sons, London, England, 1977.

[Bod87]   Margaret Boden. *Artificial Intelligence and Natural Man*. Basic Books, New York, New York, 2nd edition, 1987.

[CCELS01] Thomas H. Cormen, Ronald L. Rivest Charles E. Leiserson, and Clifford Stein. *Introduction to Algorithms*. McGraw-Hill Book Company, New York, New York, 2nd edition, 2001.

[Che76]   Peter P.S. Chen. The entity-relationship model–toward a unified view of data. *ACM Transactions on Database Systems*, 1(1):9–36, March 1976.

[CLR97]   Thomas H. Cormen, Charles E. Leiserson, and Ronald L. Rivest. *Introduction to Algorithms*. McGraw-Hill Book Company, New York, New York, 1997.

[Cod70]   E.F. Codd. A relational model of data for large shared data banks. *Communications of the ACM*, 13(6):377–387, June 1970.

[Com99]   Douglas E. Comer. *Computer Networks and Internets*. Prentice Hall, Inc., Upper Saddle River, New Jersey, 2nd edition, 1999.

[Com00]   Douglas E. Comer. *The Internet Book*. Prentice Hall, Upper Saddle River, New Jersey, 3rd edition, 2000.

[DR97]   Dale Dougherty and Arnold Robbins. *sed and awk*. O'Reilly & Associates, Sebastopol, California, 2nd edition, 1997.

[Eng01]   Ralf S. Engelschall. *Apache Desktop Reference*. Addison Wesley, Upper Saddle River, New Jersey, 2001.

[Fla00]   David Flanagan. *Javascript : The Definitive Guide*. O'Reilly & Associates, Sebastopol, California, 3rd edition, 2000.

[Fri97]   Jeffrey E.F. Friedl. *Mastering Regular Expressions*. O'Reilly & Associates, Inc., Sebastopol, California, 1997.

[GA99]   Graham Grass and King Ables. *Unix for Programmers and Users*. Prentice Hall, Upper Saddle River, New Jersey, 2nd edition, 1999.

[Gra94]   Paul Graham. *On Lisp, Advanced Techniques for Common Lisp*. Prentice Hall, Englewood Cliffs, New Jersey, 1994.

[Gun00]   Shishir Gundavaram. *CGI Programming on the World Wide Web*. O'Reillly & Associates, Inc., Sebastopol, California, 2nd edition, 2000.

[HDR00]   Thomas L. Harman, James Dabney, and Norman Richert. *Advanced Engineering Mathematics with MATLAB*. Brooks/Cole Thomson Learning, Pacific Grove, California, 2nd edition, 2000.

[Hor84]   Ellis Horowitz. *Fundamentals of Programming Languages*. Computer Science Press, Rockville, Maryland, 1984.

[Knu78]   Donald K. Knuth. *The Art of Computer Programming, Volume 1, Fundamental Algorithsm*. Addison Wesley, Boston, Massachusetts, 3rd edition, 1978.

[KR98]   Brian K. Kernighan and Dennis M. Ritchie. *The C Programming Language*. Prentice-Hall, Englewood Cliffs, New Jersey, 2nd edition, 1998.

[Kre93]   Erwin Kreyszig. *Advanced Engineering Mathematics*. John Wiley & Sons, New York, New York, 1993.

[Lin99]   Forest Lin. *QuickStart to JavaScript*. Scott/Jones, Inc., Publishers, El Granada, California, 1999.

[MK00]   Chuck Musciano and Bill Kennedy. *HTML and XHTML: The Definitive Guide*. O'Reilly & Associates, Sebastopol, California, 2000.

[MM01]   Kevin Meltzer and Brent Michalski. *Writing CGI Applications with Perl*. Addison-Wesley, Upper Saddle River, New Jersey, 2001.

[MvOV96]   Alfred J. Menezes, Paul C. van Oorschot, and Scott A. Vanstone. *Handbook of Applied Cryptography*. CRC Press, Boca Raton, Louisiana, 1996.

[Nav00]   Ann Navarro. *XHTML By Example*. Que, Indianapolis, Indiana, 2000.

[NE02]   Shamkant B. Navathe and Ramez A. Elmasri. *Fundamentals of Database Systems with E-Book (With CD-ROM)*. Addison-Wesley, Upper Saddle River, New Jersey, 2002.

[Nic99]   Randall K. Nichols. *ICSA Guide to Cryptography*. McGraw-Hill, New York, New York, 1999.

[Nie99]   Jennifer Niederst. *Web Design in a Nutshell, A Desktop Quick Reference*. O'Reilly & Associates, Sebastopol, California, 1999.

[NS98]   Tom Negrino and Dori Smith. *JavaScript for the World Wide Web*. Pechpit Press, Berkley, California, 2nd edition, 1998.

[NSSH01]   Evi Nemeth, Garth Snyder, Scott Seebass, and Trent R. Hein. *Unix System Administration Handbook*. Prentice Hall PTR, Upper Saddle River, New Jersey, 3rd edition, 2001.

[Pfl96]   Charles P. Pfleeger. *Security in Computing*. Prentice-Hall PTR, Upper Saddle River, New Jersey, 1996.

[Sch96]   Bruce Schneier. *Applied Cryptography: Protocols, Algorithms and Source Code in C*. Jonh Wiley and Sons, New York, New York, 2nd edition, 1996.

[Seb99]   Robert W. Sebesta. *Programming Languages*. Addison Wesley, Reading, Massachusetts, 4th edition, 1999.

[Sel91]   Margo Seltzer. A new hashing package for unix. In *Proc. of USENIX, Winter*, Dallas, Texas, 1991.

[SQ96]   Stephen Spainhour and Valerie Quercia. *Webmaster in a Nutshell*. O'Reilly & Associates, Sebastopol, California, 1996.

[Sta97]   William Stallings. *Data and Computer Communications*. Prentice Hall, Inc., Upper Saddle River, New Jersey, 5th edition, 1997.

[Sta99]   William Stallings. *Cryptography and Network Security, Principles and Practice*. Prentice Hall, Upper Saddle River, New Jersey, 2nd edition, 1999.

[Ste98]   Lincoln D. Stein. *Official Guide to Programming with CGI.pm*. Wiley Computer Publishing, New York, New York, 1998.

[SW01]   Peter Scott and Ed Wright. *Perl Debugged*. Addison-Wesley, Upper Saddle River, New Jersey, 2001.

[TC03]   Jean Paul Tremblay and Grant A. Cheston. *Data Structures and Software Development in an Object-Oriented Domain*. Prentice Hall, Upper Saddle River, New Jersey, 2003.

[TW01]   Wade Trappe and Lawrence C. Washington. *Introduction to Cryptography with Coding Theory*. Prentice Hall, Upper Saddle River, New Jersey, 2001.

[Wat90]   David A. Watt. *Programming Language Concepts and Paradigms*. Prentice Hall International (UK) Ltd., Hertfordshire England, 1990.

[WCS96]   Larry Wall, Tom Christiansen, and Randall L. Schwartz. *Programming Perl*. O'Reilly & Associates, Inc., Sebastopol, California, 2nd edition, 1996.

[Wir75]   Niklaus Wirth. *Algorithms + Data Structures = Programs*. Prentice Hall, Englewood Cliffs, NJ, 1975.

Index